CB

A LIFE OF
SIR HENRY CAMPBELL-BANNERMAN

JOHN WILSON

CB

A LIFE OF
SIR HENRY CAMPBELL-BANNERMAN

ST. MARTIN'S PRESS
NEW YORK

For Shirley

'All other things, to their destruction draw,
Only our love hath no decay;
This, no to-morrow hath, nor yesterday,
Running it never runs from us away,
But truly keeps his first, last, everlasting day.'

'Sensible men of substantial means are what we wish to
be ruled by.'

Walter Bagehot, *The English Constitution*
Introduction to the Second Edition, 1872

Contents

Contents

Contents

Illustrations

Illustrations

Preface

Interest in the past takes many forms. In 1971 a stuffed great auk was sold in London for £9,000. The great auk is extinct. And the political figures of Victorian and Edwardian times have vanished no less irrevocably. But, like the auk, they remain curious and interesting.

Henry Campbell-Bannerman died only a little more than sixty years ago. He had known the extremes of political failure and success. At one time he was generally execrated as a man who was supposed to sympathize with the enemies of his country. He was denounced day after day in *The Times*, and his company was shunned by his Sovereign. Within four years he led his party to its most overwhelming victory, and overnight became an exceedingly popular Prime Minister, with a unique position in the House of Commons. Today he is almost forgotten. Most people have never heard of him, and those who have tend to class him as a dim and secondary figure.

Yet the truth is that Campbell-Bannerman, or C.B., as he was always called, was a singularly attractive and interesting man. He was moreover an unusual person to emerge as the leader of a great political party in England, or indeed to be a politician at all, for he was easy-going, had little ambition and was inclined to let well alone.

When he died in 1908 his successor, Asquith, praised his courage, idealism, shrewdness and tenacity. Two younger members of his government, Lloyd George and Winston Churchill, also paid tributes to his generosity and to the affection in which he was held by his colleagues. What these three men said was patently sincere.

The Liberal government decided to put up a memorial in Westminster Abbey. The Conservative leaders were compelled by convention to support the proposal, but privately they thought it ridiculous.

Lord Lansdowne told the Dean: 'Personally I hold a very strong view as to the impropriety of erecting a monument to Sir Henry Campbell-Bannerman in the Abbey.'[1] A. J. Balfour argued that 'it is absurd to still further crowd your overcrowded space in favour of this particular candidate for posthumous honours'.[2] The Dean's own secretary, evidently a sound Tory, told his master that the proposal 'plunged me into the depths of despair, misery, horror etc. .... the authorities . . . must die in the last ditch to prevent such a monstrum, horrendum, infandum'.[3]

Where there are such wildly differing contemporary opinions of the worth of a statesman, it seems appropriate to try to form a new estimate. This is what this book sets out to do, and the task is made easier by the quantity of new material which has become available in the last fifty years. I have tried also to describe the kind of life C.B. and his contemporaries led, as it is utterly remote from the kind of life we lead today.

'A real life of anybody', wrote G. K. Chesterton, 'is a very difficult thing to write.' This is true, but I have found the pursuit of Campbell-Bannerman absorbing. I have been greatly struck, too, by the kindness and helpfulness of historians, librarians, scholars, owners of papers and others, in this country, in the United States, Ireland and South Africa, and by the freemasonry which seems to exist among those who seek the truth about the past.

Too many have helped me for me to be able to thank everyone individually but I am deeply grateful to them all.

I must however express my gratitude for the Queen's gracious permission to use material in the Royal Archives at Windsor, to the Royal Librarian, Mr. Robin Mackworth-Young, and to Miss Jane Langton and Mrs. de Bellaigue for the great help they gave my wife and myself, not least in deciphering King Edward VII's handwriting. For permission to consult family archives, I am grateful to the Duke of Devonshire, Viscount Harcourt, Earl Spencer, the Haldane family, Lord Ponsonby of Shulbrede, who kindly allowed two total strangers to borrow a number of boxes of his father's letters, Miss Jennifer Gosse, Mrs. Gell, the Earl of Cromer, the 5th Marquess of Salisbury, Viscount Esher, Mrs. Elizabeth Clay and Mrs. Pauline Dower. For permission to use copyright material and to quote letters I must thank Sir Walter Moberly, the Dean and Chapter of Westminster, the Trustees of the National Library of Scotland, Lady Cecilia Milnes-Coates, Mrs. G. A. Morley, Mr. L. P. Scott, the Earl of Rosebery, Lady Primrose, Mr.

J. R. Colville, Sir William Gladstone, the Warden and Fellows of New College, Oxford, Mr. Mark Bonham Carter, the Trustees of the Beaverbrook Library, the Controller of Her Majesty's Stationery Office, the Trustees of the British Museum, Lord Balfour, Sir Richard Acland, Mrs. Freeman-Thomas, the Earl of Selbourne, the Duke of Atholl, Mr. John Grigg, the London School of Economics and Political Science, the Librarian of the British Library of Political and Economic Science, the Dowager Lady Hardinge of Penshurst, Lady Graves, Brigadier A. W. A. Llewellen Palmer, Mr. Charles Winnifrith, Mr. J. C. Medley, the 6th Marquess of Salisbury and C. and T. Publications. For access to the Lloyd George papers I am grateful to the First Beaverbrook Foundation.

Others who have been particularly helpful are my mother, Mr. D. S. Porter of the Bodleian Library, Mr. A. S. Bell of the National Library of Scotland, Mrs. Charlotte Willson-Pepper, who helped me greatly with research and transcriptions, Mr. Eric Holt, the late Marjorie Lady Pentland, Sir Harry Verney, Mr. Jack Dove of the Hove Public Library, Mrs. Hugh Campbell, Mrs. Joan Devas, Mrs. Patricia Gaffney of Cornell University, Mr. D. W. King of the Ministry of Defence Library, the Rector of the High School, Glasgow, the *Guardian* librarian Mr. F. B. Singleton, Mr. D. M. Hunter, Registrar of the National Register of Archives (Scotland), Mr. Ian P. Watson of the University of Aberdeen, the Royal Commission on Historical Manuscripts, the staffs of the British Museum students' room and of the libraries of the Foreign Office, the House of Lords and the House of Commons, Mr. David Goodall, Miss Patricia Stanbridge, Miss Anne Mulling and Miss Rosemary Butt.

I must thank the Leverhulme Trustees for giving me a research award, which was a very great help to me.

My own family have borne patiently with this enterprise and have given me some valuable help. Above all my thanks are due to my wife, who little thought, when she married a member of the Diplomatic Service, that it would involve ploughing through the chaos of the War Office files at the Public Record Office (discovering such curiosities as that in the 1880s there were four army biscuits to the pound, supplied by Spratts and Spillers), making numerous visits to the newspaper library at Colindale and helping to edit the book in addition to all the other innumerable jobs that a wife has to do. I cannot thank her enough.

Aberedw 1972

Part 1

Go South Young Man

CHAPTER 1

1868

I N the autumn of 1868 a young man left Glasgow for London. Henry
Campbell was thirty-two and newly elected to Parliament as
member for the Stirling Burghs, and with him he brought his
young Scots wife. He was beginning the political career which was,
after many ups and downs, to end, forty years later, with his death
in No. 10 Downing Street.

London in 1868 was a burgeoning city of wealth, splendour, teem-
ing life and squalor. It was still, in parts, a city of great elegance. Lord
Esher wrote in 1920:

> The St. James's Street of today bears no resemblance to St.
> James's Street as I recollect it when I was young. Dizzy in his light
> grey coat and brilliant waistcoat sauntering down to the Carlton
> leaning on the arm of Lord Barrington, everyone in faultless
> clothes, Duchesses in open landaus drawn by beautiful horses with
> ribbons in their ears, a Jack-in-the-Green dancing in the courtyard
> of Nellie's old house in Arlington Street, servants in plush knee-
> breeches and silk stockings clinging on to magnificent coaches,
> milkmaids in short petticoats carrying milk-pails slung on their
> shoulders – all this in a London that has passed into oblivion.[1]

A Yorkshire M.P., Sir Alfred Pease, wrote:

> From 1865 into the seventies . . . all west of Exhibition Road was
> open country or brick fields up to Kensington. Cromwell Road did
> not exist; to the east, towards Knightsbridge . . . were fields, and
> elms with cows grazing under them. . . . Each square had its band,

its turn of Savoyards, with hurdy-gurdies and marmots, its dancing bears, its barrel-organs and monkeys, its morning visits by troops of donkeys which supplied asses' milk for infants, its Punch and Judy shows. . . .[2]

In 1935 Sir Max Beerbohm, describing the London of his youth, spoke of the 'demure poetry about her', and recalled that one could see then 'a constant procession of the best-built vehicles in the world, drawn by very beautifully-bred and beautifully-groomed and beautifully-harnessed horses, and containing very ornate people', whose occupants were 'very visible and were looking their best'. In Mayfair, Westminster and St. James's, he maintained, 'the eighteenth century still beautifully reigned'.[3] Beautifully, perhaps, on the surface, but hardly below it. As late as 1866 in London over five and a half thousand people died of cholera.

In the forty years before the Campbells came south, the population of greater London had doubled. It was to double again in the forty years that they lived there, during the whole of which time he was to be a member of the House of Commons.

In the summer of 1868 the new Foreign Office in Downing Street was finished. Landseer's lions had just been set up in Trafalgar Square. Work was in progress on the Albert Memorial and the Albert Hall. The heart of London had been transformed eight years before by the building of Barry and Pugin's Houses of Parliament, but, as if determined to subvert this magnificent study in vertical lines, the authorities had, in the same year, removed, and sent away to Bristol, Brunel's airy suspension bridge, which crossed the river just downstream from Westminster, and replaced it by the hard, horizontal line of the Charing Cross railway bridge. The *Illustrated London News* for July 25 carried this report:

> The attention of every one passing Hyde Park-corner must be struck by the appearance of a new pile of buildings at the upper end of Grosvenor-place, next to St. George's Hospital. . . . These buildings are some of the superb aristocratic mansions, or rather palaces, which the Marquis of Westminster is erecting in that part of his town estate between Piccadilly and Pimlico . . . with the high steep roofs and other characteristic features of the French hotel, or first-rate town house, of the sixteenth century. . . . Their internal accommodation, and the magnificence both of proportions and

ornament displayed inside, will be no less remarkable than the dignity of their external aspect.

Not long ago this pile was pulled down and replaced by a featureless slab of air-conditioned offices. But the houses of the same type, below Halkin Street, still remain, and one of these, No. 6 Grosvenor Place, was to be the Campbells' town house for over twenty-five years.

It was an exuberant, self-confident era. Georgian architecture was despised as poor-spirited and monotonous. The buildings of 1868, even when put up for mundane purposes, like the Smithfield Market, were remarkable architectural compositions. They were built by men who had no doubts about what they were aiming at, and were lavish with pillars, pinnacles, coloured bricks and marbles.

Inside, houses were equally elaborate and florid. The wheel had turned full circle from the classic elegance of the Georgian interior. A contemporary work, making 'a few suggestions as to the display of art and taste throughout the house', contains this comment:

> Nothing is considered too costly a material upon which to paint or embroider a mantel-valance. . . . White velvet, for example, decorated with a wreath of orange-blooms and leaves in oils, intermingled with fronds of that most exquisite of ferns, the 'maiden-hair' . . . is heavily edged with white and green silk fringe, below which falls a row of balls of white carved wood fastened to the fringe. . . . For mantel decoration above . . . are two vases, four feet high, of 'irridescent amber' glass-ware, over the rainbow-like surface of which trail smilax and white honeysuckle. . . . The central ornament is . . . a large and unusually perfect conch shell, with a lining of pure colour, in which reclines the figure of a nymph, sleeping. Above her is a cupid. . . .[4]

1868 was only just over a hundred years ago, but in spirit it seems unimaginably remote. England was at the summit of wealth, security, and good fortune. London was the financial and commercial capital of the world. Income tax was 6d. in the pound. England's trade was still between three and four times that of the United States. Her industry produced goods of a quality and price that could not be matched by any other country. British business supremacy had been built up by men like Henry Campbell's father. He had started with nothing in 1827, but within five years became a rich man – in those days of low taxation the rewards of enterprise, hard work and imagination were swift and striking – and in due course owner of a great estate, Lord Provost of Glasgow, a knight and, naturally, a Tory. To men like James Campbell the commercial future appeared to have no limits. British ships dominated the seas, and the Suez Canal, then being built, held out the prospect of much faster communication with the East.

Cobden had died in 1865, but the surviving hero of the Anti-Corn Law League, John Bright, was able now to say with some complacency to the House of Commons:

> If now, in all the great centres of our population . . . we do not find ourselves surrounded by hungry and exasperated multitudes – if now more than at any time during the last hundred years it may be said, quoting the beautiful words of Mr. Sheridan, that 'Content sits basking on the cheek of Toil' . . . have I not as much as any living man some claim to partake of the glory?[5]

The troubles of earlier decades – the hungry forties; the miseries of the Crimean War in the early fifties; the Indian Mutiny of 1857; all these had rolled away. It seemed an age since, as John Bright learned to his surprise in 1853, two hundred tons of stones had been piled on the roof of the British Museum 'to hurl on the heads of the people', and provisions laid in for a siege of three days.[6] But in fact these panic measures, provoked by the Chartist agitation of 1848, when the fear of revolution had been real and immediate, had been taken only twenty years before. Now, financially, industrially, at home and overseas, in relations between the different classes of society, all seemed set fair.

It is true that those at the bottom of the heap in town and country often led lives of appalling privation and misery. For those in work wages were still very low and hours long. Skilled workmen often received less than 8d. an hour. The slums and alleys of the cities were still as Dickens described them and the agricultural labourer led a hard, grinding life. Joseph Arch was beginning to organize his Agricultural Labourers' Union and to plan strikes aimed at raising their wages from twelve shillings to fourteen shillings a week. 1868 saw the first meeting of the Trades Union Congress, but the unions represented at it had only 118,000 members. As much as a fifth of the working population was in domestic service, and so protected from actual want, but earning derisory wages, an experienced cook getting perhaps £18 a year. A determination to do something to improve the lot of all these people was at the root of much of the support for the new Liberal Party.

But the sixties were, taken in the round, one of those golden intervals of sunshine and peace that come briefly between the storms which now seem to us to be the natural order of things. In this July day of contentment, life in England drifted blissfully along.

The crinoline had just given way to the bustle. Women wore chignons and enormously elaborate hair pieces under tiny hats. *Punch* for 1868 is full of jokes about the happy moments when these hairpieces came adrift. Though elaborate, dresses were not always expensive. One advertisement offered fancy dresses for 2/11d., best wool serges for 12/6d., black silks, gros-grains and glacés from 25/- and velveteens from 17/11d. The young lady of the time was advised that she might, if necessary, brighten up her dress with 'trails of natural flowers or autumn leaves', and that 'a ramble in a wood will give you fresh adornments for your dress, if you have some fine flower wire with you and an ordinary share of taste'. The cosmetic industry was just beginning. An 1868 advertisement ran:

> TO THE LADIES OF ENGLAND—Miss Talbot, thirty years Lady's Maid in the highest circles of England, Paris, and Spain, will forward, on receipt of 30 stamps, full directions in the new and beautiful art of Getting-up the FACE and EYES in the most brilliant style, with other Recipes for the Toilette, standing unrivalled.

New and wonderful cures were offered to an eager public still innocent of antibiotics. Then, as now, the claims of the advertising man were only limited by his imagination. Another advertisement ran:

> The health of the Holy Father is excellent, especially since, abandoning all other remedies, he has confined himself entirely to DU BARRY'S REVALENTA ARABICA FOOD; and His Holiness cannot praise this excellent food too highly—Rome, *Gazette du Midi*, 25 July, 1866.[7]

For men, Dundreary whiskers were the fashion. Young Henry Campbell had a modest pair of rather restrained black whiskers and was otherwise clean shaven. He had not yet grown a moustache and still wore a monocle.

Those who were alive in 1868 found many ways to amuse themselves. In the country there was croquet and archery on the lawn. The Prince of Wales, improbably, pursued a carted stag with the Royal Buckhounds through Wormwood Scrubs to Paddington Station. In the garden, the Bourbon roses were at the height of their glory, and in 1868 a new, pink, thornless climber was introduced and named Zephirine Drouhin. Next year the first hybrid tea rose was to make its appearance.

In London, there were to be found, at St. James's Hall, 'the only veritable and legitimate Christy Minstrels . . . the largest and best Ethiopian troupe in the world', and one could, as a bonus, see Mr. J. Wallace 'repeat his wonderful Dance and also his great Burlesque Lecture on Anatomy at every performance'. At the Queen's Theatre, Long Acre, the graceful Miss Henrietta Hodson, who was to marry Henry Campbell's radical colleague Henry Labouchere, was appearing in the burlesque *The Stranger – Stranger than Ever*, produced by 'Mr. H. Irving and the author', while at the St. James's, two years before, a production with the unpromising name of *Dulcamara, or the Little Duck and the Great Quack*, had been the first venture of a new name in the theatre, W. S. Gilbert. At the Academy, which reached its hundredth year in 1868, Millais, Leighton, Frith and G. F. Watts were dominant, and a notable picture was Faed's *Worn Out*, showing an exhausted parent watching in the dawn beside a dying child. Sir E. Landseer exhibited *Deerhound in the Snow*.

But it was, above all, a time of words – cascades of words, rich, baroque, elaborate. The use of the written and the spoken word was subject to few restraints or inhibitions. It was a time when a speaker or a writer could revel, unabashed, in purple periods or great verbal set-pieces, like John Bright's perorations, Froude's haunting description of Anne Boleyn's last hours, or Gladstone's magnificent but frequently obscure disquisitions lasting for two hours or more.

Tennyson had been Laureate for eighteen years and was at the height of his fame. He was now at work on the *Idylls of the King*. In Cannes Edward Lear was writing his absurd but memorable nonsense rhymes to amuse the two-and-a-half-year-old daughter of Mr. Arthur Symons. Wilkie Collins had just published *The Moonstone*, the Queen *Leaves from the Journal of our Life in the Highlands*, and Mr. Gladstone *A Chapter of Autobiography*. Dickens, just back from America, was giving farewell readings of his works at the St. James's Hall.

Trollope displayed the phenomenal energy characteristic of so many of the leading men of the time. Apart from his work at the Post Office, he got up every day at 5.30 to do three hours' work on his novels before breakfast – writing at the steady rate, timed by a watch, of 250 words every quarter of an hour. He was moving serenely along the path of his sixty-three books. He had become a sharp observer of the political world, in which Henry Campbell was to spend so many years, and was a frequent spectator in the gallery of the House of Commons. None of this prevented him from hunting three times a week, or from playing whist at the Garrick Club in the afternoons.

Some of those with whom Henry Campbell was to work closely in later years were also starting to write books. Mr. John Morley, for example, had written *Edmund Burke: A Historical Study*. The *Illustrated London News* objected to his attitude to royalty – 'Mr. Morley's contempt for George III is almost outrageous . . . the tone adopted towards him by Mr. Morley would be "offensive to a black beetle".'

In 1868 England was still a deeply religious country. There was, for example, that staunch High Churchman, Mr. Gladstone, of whom Sir Philip Magnus has written that he 'sought to mould himself, his country, and the world to the pattern suggested by his personal religion in which he believed with the pure faith of a child. Political life would have been meaningless to him without that purpose . . .'[8] But not everyone clung to their early beliefs so tenaciously. It was a time of questioning. The ripples of doubt were spreading out from the influence of Darwin and John Stuart Mill. A man like John Morley was a proclaimed agnostic. But most households still knew their bibles and had family prayers, and Sunday was still a serious, rather joyless day devoted to religion, rest and contemplation. The religious census of 1851 had shown that two and a half million regularly attended church and two million chapel. The Church of England itself contained many factions – Liberals, Tractarians, Evangelicals, Ritualists. The dissenters, or nonconformists, comprising, with the Roman Catholics, some forty-eight per cent of active Christians, had now, in the main, gained the liberty to worship as they pleased, and supported the Liberal Party with a strength and enthusiasm which were of the utmost value to it. The revival of the Roman Catholic Church in England had begun.

To the men and women of 1868 it may perhaps have seemed that the long summer afternoon would go on for ever. But the halcyon days were numbered.

For the English countryside, only seven or eight years of prosperity were left. The repeal of the Corn Laws in 1846 had brought free imports, but for nearly thirty years there was little effect on British agriculture, and the railways helped to spread prosperity. Sea transport was still slow and expensive, and, in the early sixties, the Americans were preoccupied with their civil war. But sea freight had now become swift and cheap, and the Americans, their war over, had turned their energies into ploughing up the rich virgin soils of the Middle West.

In July 1873 a country curate, Francis Kilvert, wrote in his diary:

> As I walked along the field path I stopped to listen to the rustle and solemn night whisper of the wheat, so different to its voice by day. . . . Across the great level meads near Chippenham came the martial music of a drum and fife band, and laughing voices of unseen girls were wafted from farms and hayfields out of the wide dusk.[9]

The entry is like the sudden opening of a shutter, a momentary glimpse of rural England before the crash which was to come so soon after. The harvests failed year after year in the seventies. Meanwhile the cheap American corn poured in. The high days of English corn growing were done and the drift to the towns became a flood.

But it was not only farming which was threatened. In Europe, Bismarck's expansionist policy had already produced the Austro-Prussian War and the union of German states under Prussia in 1866. It was to lead in two years' time, helped by the folly of the French Imperial government, to Sedan, the fall of Napoleon III, the defeat of the French, and the spectacle of triumphant German soldiers marching through the Arc de Triomphe. On that occasion, England was able to stay clear of involvement, but the Germans became filled with aggressive optimism and the French with bitterness and a determination to avenge their wrongs. The seeds of 1914 were sown. Moreover, for those with eyes to see, the battles of the American civil war had been a portent. Industry had provided new rifles and guns far more accurate than the weapons of Waterloo or the Crimea. Each time the infantry had attacked in those American battles – at Vicksburg, at Gettysburg, at the Bloody Angle and on many other fields – they had met an accurate fire and had suffered dreadful losses. It only remained for machine guns to be perfected to produce the slaughter of the First World War.

In two particular parts of the world, with which Henry Campbell was to be much concerned, Ireland and South Africa, there were also signs of trouble ahead. A visit to Ireland in April by the Prince and Princess of Wales went without a hitch, but there were Fenian outrages in Manchester and elsewhere, the most spectacular being the wounding by one O'Farrell of another of the Queen's sons, the Duke of Edinburgh, near Port Jackson, New South Wales, at a public picnic in May. In 1868 the last public execution took place at Newgate, that of a Fenian, Michael Barrett.

In politics, Mr. Gladstone was leading the Liberal Party. His 1868 election address recognized the urgency of the Irish question and made clear his own preoccupation with it: 'At this time one question . . . overshadows all the rest. The state of Ireland, and the actual temper of no small portion of its people towards the Throne and Government of the United Kingdom, imperatively demand the care of all public men.'[10] His immediate task, proclaimed in March, was the disestablishment of the episcopal Church of Ireland, the church of Swift, but the church also of a small minority.

The Queen was sceptical. She wrote to Disraeli in March:

> Mr. Gladstone must be aware that the chief difficulty in governing Ireland has always been to restrain the mutual violence of the old Orange Party on the one hand, and of the Roman Catholics on the other, and he might, the Queen thinks, to say the least, have well paused before he made a declaration of which the effect will certainly be to revive and inflame the old sectarian feuds. . . .[11]

In South Africa trouble lay further away in the future. The country was still being opened up. The first news was coming in of the finding of gold, which was to be at the root of the South African troubles of the 1880s and the 1890s. In September, the *Cape Argus* reported that 'the discovery of a rich gold country to the north of the Limpopo river, on the borders of the Transvaal Republic and the Portuguese settlement, is being fully confirmed from all quarters. . . . Each digger is charged a sovereign by the native chief to whom the land belongs.' These gold fields were those in the eastern Transvaal around Pilgrim's Rest and Lydenburg. Another eighteen years were to pass before the immense riches of the Rand were discovered.

So at home, in Europe, in Ireland and South Africa troubles gathered. But, happily, we are spared the knowledge of the cancer working unseen within, and in 1868 none of these troubles, except those in Ireland, were apparent to Englishmen. The vast majority of them pursued their daily lives unconcerned by public affairs.

The second half of 1868 was not, moreover, filled with any particularly dramatic events. Dr. Tait was appointed Archbishop of

Canterbury at the desire of the Queen, despite the objections of the Prime Minister, Disraeli, who vainly pointed out to the Queen that Tait was 'obscure in purpose, fitful and inconsistent in action, and evidently, though earnest and conscientious, a prey to constantly conflicting convictions', and, worst of all, that he had 'a strange fund of enthusiasm, a quality which ought never to be possessed by an Archbishop of Canterbury, or a Prime Minister of England'.[12] But the main interest in England lay in the general election, which took place in November, and which resulted in a decisive Liberal victory, with a majority of over a hundred. Disraeli, who was sixty-four and had been Prime Minister only since February, resigned without waiting to meet Parliament and returned to writing novels. Gladstone formed his first ministry.

In politics, 1868 was a milestone on the way to a full popular democracy. The old order was passing away. Palmerston, who had dominated affairs for so long, had died three years before, in 1865. Two years later, the seventy-five-year-old Lord John Russell retired. Monster meetings and riots in 1866 had made it clear that some step must be taken to appease popular agitation, despite the defeat of Russell's Reform Bill of that year.

In 1867 Disraeli introduced his Reform Bill. The bemused Conservatives found themselves responsible for a measure which went much further than anything the party opposite had dared to introduce. It gave the vote to the working class in the towns and, as such, was regarded as a risky step – as Lord Derby said, a 'leap in the dark' – towards what everyone still regarded as the impossible ideal of a full democracy and one man one vote. Lord Salisbury (then Lord Cranborne) described the bill as 'a political betrayal that has no parallel in our annals'. Carlyle regarded it as the 'suicide of the English nation'.[13] Its first result was a Liberal victory at the polls.

The new Liberal Government included some notable figures. Lord Clarendon, a distinguished but elderly Whig now nearing the end of his life, became Foreign Secretary for the fourth time. The Queen objected strongly to his appointment, referring to 'his temper, his manner, his want of discretion, etc.' but finally consented on the understanding that Mr. Gladstone 'would prevent my being annoyed with him, for that must not be'.[14] Gladstone himself later described Clarendon to John Morley as 'the very easiest and most attractive' of all the sixty-odd colleagues he had sat with in Cabinets. The Quaker radical John Bright, called by Lord Salisbury 'the greatest master of English oratory that this generation has produced', and by Disraeli, more tersely, 'that hysterical old spouter', became President of the Board of Trade. Morley said later: 'In Bright there was an unlimited self-confidence which amounted to corruption of the soul.'[15] Edward Cardwell, the man who had earlier abolished transportation of criminals, became Secretary of State for War.

To the Queen the change from a Conservative government was most unwelcome. Only two months before she had sent Disraeli a portrait of the Prince Consort, Disraeli replying that 'he looks upon his relations with that gifted being as among the most interesting passages of his life, nor can he now ever dwell on his memory without emotion'.[16] Disraeli had, on becoming her Prime Minister, written to the Queen to say:

> He can offer only devotion.
> It will be his delight and duty, to render the transaction of affairs as easy to your Majesty as possible; and in smaller matters he hopes he may succeed in this; but he ventures to trust that, in the great affairs of state, your Majesty will deign not to withhold from him the benefit of your Majesty's guidance.[17]

Mr. Gladstone could never match this tone of theatrical servility, which was, sadly, so acceptable to the Queen.

The 1867 Reform Act shifted the balance of voting power to the industrial towns. The new working-class electorate voted for the first time. But the new members they elected were scarcely intent on turning society upside down. They were more concerned with freeing men from the domination of the landlords and the established church. It is with one of them that we are concerned.

In reporting the results of the 1868 election, the press noted that 'at the Stirling Burghs, Liberal contending against Liberal, Mr. Ramsay, the late member, was beaten by Mr. Campbell'. It was as a consequence of this that Henry Campbell and his wife had arrived in London.

CHAPTER 2

A Boy from Glasgow

HENRY CAMPBELL, like Mr. Gladstone, came from a commercial family. His father was a tough, self-made Glasgow business-man. Henry was born in 1836, the year before the accession of Queen Victoria. He was three when the penny post was introduced, six when Mr. Gladstone reached the Cabinet, and nine when the Corn Laws were repealed. He was born at Kelvinside, an eighteenth-century house in what was then open country on the banks of the river Kelvin, near Glasgow, which his father rented as a summer residence. He grew up at the house his father built at 129 Bath Street, Glasgow, and at the country house of Jordanhill. In 1847 his father bought the estate of Stracathro in Forfarshire, now called Angus.

In 1845 Henry went to Glasgow High School, where he was two years ahead of James Bryce, later a close friend and political colleague, whose father, Paddy Bryce, was the mathematics master. Another future Prime Minister, Bonar Law, followed him at the High School. Henry Campbell early formed the view that one man is as good as another. He went to school with the son of the miller, who was called a mealy boy because he brought a sack of meal with him which was his staple diet for the term. Henry thought the miller's son was as good a person as himself, and thought it wrong that he had no chance, as things were then, of going to a university.

In the summer of 1850 James Campbell sent his two sons and a cousin, David Bannerman, on a trip abroad. It lasted ten months and took them to the capitals of seventeen countries and on a journey of 5,500 miles, including three months in Rome, where Henry was tutored in French and the classics. His elder brother James was twenty-five and looked for markets for the family firm. Henry, who was still a fifth-former at the High School, and was not yet fourteen when they set out, went primarily for his education. He was made to keep a full account of everything, and this he dutifully did in ninety-seven letters to his seventeen-year-old sister Louisa, or, as he called her, 'Weezie'. The copies of these letters which she made in three exercise books survive[1] and are lively reading. Not only do they give a picture of Europe as it was before the car and aeroplane, but they give us a first authentic glimpse of the young Campbell-Bannerman. The letters, for a boy of fourteen, are remarkably urbane, shrewd and entertaining.

The brothers crossed over to France in the same boat as Charles Kean, the actor, and made their way down to Switzerland and thence to the Italian lakes and the towns of Northern Italy and on to Rome, where they spent the winter, taking a flat in the Via della Fontanella for the equivalent of £11 a month. In the spring they went on to Sicily and then back by Venice and Trieste to Vienna, Prague, Dresden, Berlin and home by way of Amsterdam. Loftily, young Henry wrote: 'You may trace our course on the large Hist. & Geog. Atlas at Stracathro.'

They travelled by diligence, the huge, lumbering French stage coach, which attained only 6 or 7 m.p.h. Henry particularly enjoyed it when the whole body of the diligence was hoisted off the wheels and deposited, complete with passengers, upon a railway truck to speed its progress wherever one of the new railways had been built. But sometimes they hired their own carriage or, to visit Chamonix, a 'char-a-banc', which 'is a mountain vehicle, and may be compared to the half of an Irish car, with a roof to it'. In the Swiss mountains they walked 'the 1st day, 16 miles, the 2nd, 18, the 3rd 18 (very difficult) and the 4th 23 (more difficult still)'.

The young schoolboy revelled in it all. Early on he recorded: 'We had also heard that France was not an interesting country, but we all were enchanted with it.' The enchantment was to last all his life.

They missed nothing – in Zürich, Zwingli's bible and Lady Jane Grey's letters; at Coire, 'some paintings by Holbein, the bones and skull of two saints, all set in jewels, a piece of the true cross (?) . . . etc'.; Madame Taglioni's villa on Lake Como and the residence of the Duke of Melzi, where 'we were favoured with a distant view of the Duchess'; and the Colosseum, where 'a long train of monks and others' going round the chapels and stations, chanting and praying, seemed to him to give 'a fine effect, but rather seemed discordant with the building'. He saw for the first time what he called the 'dull, sad beauty' of Venice, found the Piazzetta 'a fairy, a dream-like place', but did not care for the mosaics in St. Marks.

In Florence he saw a hirsute monk 'who reminded me of Glasgow in connection with the prize oxen at the Highland Society's Cattle Show'. In Rome, he was surprised to see 'two *negro* priests out taking an airing', and told his sister that 'a Cardinal is a priest with a red cap and a purple cape, lolling in a carriage drawn by horses with red plumes, driven by a coachman with a cocked hat, and with two men in cocked hats standing up behind'. He saw the Pope 'borne on a fine chair, supported on two poles, carried by fourteen men in red; and two immense fans . . . carried behind him. He is a kind, pleasant looking old gentleman, and gave the crowd his blessing as he passed. (We being a part of the crowd, got some of it, of course) . . . the real manger (?) was brought up the church by an archbishop.'

This lowland Presbyterian boy was not impressed by the pomp of Roman Catholic ceremonies. He found the smell of incense 'most sickening'. He spent Christmas in Rome and noted that 'the ceremonies . . . certainly were uncommonly fine but without the smallest particle of devotion'. He enjoyed then, as later, the contrasts between the sublime and the ridiculous:

> . . . the finest bit was when Pio was at the altar, saying mass, and when he raised the host, then everyone of the 'Noble Guard' knelt down on one knee, dashed his naked sword to the ground, and raised one hand to his helmet. . . . The 'Patriarch of Jerusalem' was standing there near the altar, and . . . there is the fellow just at this *tip top* bit, blowing his nose, and wiping his moustaches, with a dirty, dark coloured, common pocket handkerchief.

He found the crowds of indulgence seekers on the steps of the Scala Sancta 'a most humiliating sight, to see rational beings degrading themselves thus, but rich and poor, in velvet, silk and satin, and in rags, coming in carriages or on foot, all sorts go up.'

He did not forget to tell his sister about the public cemetery:

> Every day a large pit is opened (they have one for every day of the year) and all the poor who have died that day, are conveyed to that large pit . . . and are hurled in. Then at the end of a year the pits are cleared out. It is a very disgusting system and one which would be enough to stimulate a man to get out of poverty.

At Leukerbad he was surprised to find public baths, 'where gentlemen and ladies all together bathe in long flannel gowns. They sometimes remain there for 8 hours, and there are floating tables with refreshments, books, newspapers, etc. so that they cannot weary'. They had some harmless books they carried burnt at the Neopolitan frontier, and suffered a good deal from fleas in the inns, though in Italy, 'We remark here, that in the meanest, poorest, filthiest inns, the walls are, if not well, yet carefully painted with trees, landscapes, flowers, imitation of drapery etc.' In one 'James had a sizeable saucer to wash in (!) and when he gave it to the "camerere" to throw out the dirty water, he coolly threw it out on the floor of the next room.'

They saw a priest at Varese catching small birds and selling them for 1d. each, and nearly had their pockets picked.

Already he hated violence and cruelty, as he did all his life, and in Italy he was horrified to see a man who had caught a large rat, steep it in turpentine and set fire to it, 'and there was the poor beast running about, and roasting to death, with a great crowd of men in great enjoyment of their nice sport'.

The Columbarium, or tomb of the old families of Rome, with niches filled with ashes and bones, put him in mind of the dovecot at Stracathro.

They saw enormous numbers of churches and art galleries. From Genoa Henry wrote: 'have been very moderate in the church way, having only seen four.' They began, in fact, to suffer from a surfeit, so that when they got to Messina, in Sicily, 'we were delighted to find that we had at last got into a place where there was little or nothing to be seen'. Nevertheless they saw the Duke of Hesse Darmstadt reviewing the Austrian troops in the Piazza of St. Mark's in Venice, and the twenty-year-old Emperor Franz Josef in Vienna. In Berlin 'we had in the train with us the Prince of Prussia ... with his son who were returning from London. ... Their valet was in the carriage with us, with the young Prince's helmet – so that, someday, when we hear of him as King, we may say that though we never travelled with him, we once travelled in company with his hat.'

In Vienna on May 15, 1851, they went 'to a place ... called the Beer Hall, where we heard the great musician J. Strauss play all evening. The music was very fine and we enjoyed it vastly', but when later they went back to hear him play a second time in the Volksgarten 'the music was not so good as the last night, the evening was cold, and there were not many people, so we did not stay long'. In Naples they saw 'a most disgraceful brawl between two women'. They bought some souvenirs. James was 'much pleased with a copy of the noble equestrian statue of Marcus Aurelius, on the Capitol, but he does not see where it could be put at home'.

Of all the paintings that he saw, that which he most admired was Guido Reni's portrait of 'Beatrice da Cenci' in the Barberini Palace. To Louisa he wrote:

> This lady was provoked to murder her father, and was executed at the age of seventeen or eighteen. As she mounted the scaffold, she turned round her head, and Guido painted this from having seen her there. There she is turning round her pale but lovely face to you, draped in white, with a white turban on, with her auburn locks straying down about her face, and you would almost think you saw her. It is small (only giving the head and shoulders) but excessively beautiful.*

On the other hand he thought poorly of the tapestries made from Raphael's cartoons.

For one who was later to be a gourmet in the heyday of Edwardian cuisine he had some peculiar gastronomic experiences. He enjoyed the whitings from the Adriatic and the cockles in Naples, and recorded an occasional menu:

> Hotel de la Poste, Novara. Nov. 1st 1850.
> We had an Italian dinner here, which I give:
> 1st course – slices of raw sausage; celery; pickles; fresh butter
> 2nd course – soup
> 3rd course – boiled veal; fried liver; hot sausage and vegetable; mess of potatoes
> 4th course – little birds roasted, truffles; raw fish; stewed pears
> 5th course – cheese; apples; grapes; biscuits.

Wherever possible they dined at the table d'hôte. From Genoa he wrote: 'it is very dull work without them; as it is only at the "Tavola Rotunda" as the Italians call it, that one meets anyone.'

The brothers sent home a variety of things – wine, macaroni,

---

* This picture is now in the Galleria Nazionale d'Arte Antica in Rome. The Director, Professor Italo Faldi, tells me that the figure is not Beatrice Cenci but a Sybil and that the best critical opinion now considers that it is not by Guido Reni.

earthenware, Leghorn bonnets, a Parmesan cheese, marble and bronze replicas.

On his return from the continent of Europe, in 1851, Henry Campbell entered Glasgow University. He was still only fourteen. Here he won a gold medal for Greek but took no degree, going on at eighteen to Trinity, Cambridge. He went to France in the summer of the next year, 1855, and saw Napoleon III. 'If his features are coarse,' he recorded, 'they are at all events not strikingly or offensively so.'[2] He gave himself dinner at Frascati's and the bill can only arouse the envy of later travellers ('demi-bout d'Ordinaire, Potage, 3 plats et dessert, f2.50'). On the back pages of the journal of this trip he wrote down a number of jokes and stories, and quotations of passages he liked from *In Memoriam, As You Like It* and Gray's *Elegy*.

He was at Cambridge as an undergraduate when the Indian Mutiny broke out in 1857. The following year he was twentieth Senior Optime in the mathematical tripos, bracketed equal with Lord Frederick Cavendish, who, like him, was, briefly, Chief Secretary for Ireland and who was stabbed to death in Phoenix Park in 1881. Henry was later described by that curious Kingsman, Mr. Oscar Browning, as having been, as an undergraduate, a 'strong, hearty, sensible Scotchman, intelligent but not prominent in conversation, popular but not much known'.[3] Like those other Trinity men, Lord Hartington and Arthur Balfour, he took no part in the Union.

At Cambridge he took only a Third in Classics but retained ever after a fondness for the felicitous Latin tag, and knew his way about the classics in a way that is now rare.

At twenty-two he joined the family firm in Glasgow, J. & W. Campbell, warehousemen and drapers, run by his father and his uncle William. In 1860, at twenty-four, he became a partner. This was one of the first firms to use, most successfully, fixed cash prices in place of bartering. A German observer had described the business in the 1840s:

> I visited the greatest warehouse of manufactured goods in the town, that of the brothers Campbell, who employ no fewer than two hundred clerks in their establishment. . . . Of all the goods sold here, none interested me more than the Scottish checked cloth, or tartan as it is called. . . . The owners of this great establishment, the Messrs. Campbell, began with only a hundred pounds capital. They are now among the richest people in Glasgow, and one of them is

Lord Provost of the city . . . the receipts of this house amounted in the year 1834 to £433,021 sterling, an amount probably unequalled by any other similar retail dealers in the world.[4]

The firm still exists as part of Campbells and Stewart & McDonald Ltd. of Glasgow.

This was the basis of the affluence and comfort which Henry Campbell enjoyed all his life, but he himself took little active part in the business and acquired a reputation for indolence. He read Herbert Spencer, that fervent advocate of the rights of the individual against the state, and somewhere about this time, rather mysteriously, he branched right away from the Tory principles held throughout their lives by his father and his elder brother and became a Liberal. This sudden conversion used to puzzle some of his colleagues. Augustine Birrell, for example, later wrote, 'How C.B. became a Liberal, I never knew. Certainly not by prayer or fasting or by a course of hard reading.'[5]

Possibly it was at Cambridge that he grew enthusiastic about Liberalism. More probably he was influenced by his uncle William who, though remaining on excellent terms with Henry's father, had, at the time of the disruption of the Church of Scotland in 1843, broken away and become a Free Churchman and a Liberal.

When staying with his elder brother James in 1860, the year he became a partner in the firm, Henry met Charlotte Bruce, a former school friend of his sister-in-law's. They took to each other at once and, after her second visit to the James Campbells, they became engaged. He was twenty-five and she twenty-eight. They were married in London, at All Souls', Langham Place, in September. 'Charley', as he called her, was the daughter of a distinguished soldier who died in 1832, the year she was born. He fought in the Napoleonic wars, taking part in the capture of Demerara and fighting in the Peninsula, and ended life as Major-General Sir Charles Bruce, K.C.B. His wife, also called Charlotte, was a Forbes from Argyllshire.

Until her marriage, Charlotte lived with her widowed mother in the Isle of Wight and had much of her education in France. She appears from her photographs to have been a fairly plain girl with rather a severe expression. She had, however, a keen sense of humour. Though, sadly, they had no children, it was an exceptionally happy marriage and they were deeply attached to each other. Throughout their lives every interest was shared between them. They both spoke excellent French and often spoke it to each other.

Charlotte was very fond of her elder brother Herbert, who had served in the East India Company's armies, had distinguished himself during the Mutiny, and was now Chief of Police in Oudh.

With Herbert Bruce, Henry had a long correspondence.[6] Bruce sent the young Glasgow businessman long accounts of cotton prospects in India and of the general situation there. Henry wrote Colonel Bruce long letters, which have not survived, but which evidently gave his views on home politics and on the progress of the American civil war. Colonel Bruce was impressed by them. On one occasion in 1862 he wrote: 'The American news you gave me was especially interesting and I perceive that your conjectures are almost always correct and sometimes very different to what the Press would seem to indicate',[7] and on another the same year:

> I very highly appreciate your letters upon the Policies and Parties of the day, and it is quite refreshing to a rusty old Indian to receive such letters – It so happened that at Breakfast on the day your letter arrived I was talking to Sir Bartle Frere. . . . We both agreed on the soundness of your views and the ability with which you demonstrate them.[8]

Henry described Glasgow society and sent *Mill on Liberty* to Bruce, who in return described the awfulness of Calcutta society, and recounted the frontier operations of Sir Neville Chamberlain against the Akhoound of Swat and the Swatees. In February 1864 he wrote: 'What did you do to fascinate Mrs. Hilgers? – she writes in immense raptures regarding you and Charlotte. In a letter just received she says "what a pity it is that this nice broad-minded couple live in cold, foggy and rainy Glasgow amongst a set of bigotted, narrow-minded Scotchmen".'[9]

Henry and Charlotte began, with their honeymoon on the continent, their lifelong habit of spending six weeks' holiday on the other side of the Channel in the autumn.

In Paris they usually stayed at the Hotel Meurice in the Rue de Rivoli. It was a famous hotel in those days. Recording its advantages, Galignani's *New Paris Guide* noted that 'the linen is washed three miles out of Paris, and is not beaten or brushed, to save soap, as is the custom generally in France'. They tried out the restaurants and cafés, and tramped indefatigably round cathedrals and churches, though Charlotte had her reservations about some aspects of sightseeing: 'Rather tiresome like all museums' is a phrase that occurs in her journals. In Paris they went to the Théâtre Français and the Théâtre des Variétés, the Cirque de l'Impératrice and a café chantant. They journeyed mostly in the coupé, or front part, of a diligence.

Both Henry and Charlotte kept journals of these continental trips, on some of which Louisa joined them. Charlotte's recorded the debit as well as the credit side of the tourist's experience: 'I did not fancy the soup much, having seen the woman wash the spoons of the previous diners in it. . . . Horribly swindled by the diligence people. . . . Out of spirits, our feelings terribly lacerated.'[10]

However, there were compensations. A good dinner, she noted, restored their serenity after these upsets, and in Saragossa she was even 'much struck with the good looks of the assistant sacristan'. They went to Domecq's wine vaults, bought some sherry and saw flamenco dancing at Granada. Henry also noted down his comments: 'Lüchow, 29 June, 1862: A nervous and fragile man named Walsh officiated. Mild platitudinarian discourse on Eucharist.[11] Bagnères. H. de France Rather scrambly. . . . Landlord well-meaning, but of the cigar-in-mouth, laissez-aller sort.'[12]

In 1860, having driven up to Fiesole, he wrote: 'Lovely view. . . . Florence sleeping on the Arno and the soft tone of the olives brightened by the white villas and cottages so plentifully scattered over the valley.'[13]

Two years later, in Provence, he recorded: 'Arles seemed a busy, clean, nice sort of place – the women very good looking – dark eyes, regular features, and good complexions.'[14]

In 1864 they were in Spain. Henry went to a bullfight:

> The fight had already begun, and two horses were lying dead in the Arena. . . . This is a disgusting scene: we saw one horse run across the arena with its entrails out, fall and die – another with a perfect torrent of blood gushing from a wound in its side, leaving a broad trace on the sand. . . . On the whole, disgust and indignation prevented my appreciating the skill and grace displayed . . . but I have no difficulty in conceiving how by custom this feeling would wear off. . . .[15]

The same week, in Cordova, they 'went out through the court of oranges, with trees laden with green oranges and lemons. Drove across the Roman Bridge over the Guadalquivir – Moorish flour mill, still used – pigs lying in the stream. Everything southern and hot.'[16] But France was his first and greatest love.

In Biarritz, in July 1862, Charlotte noted, 'H. amusing himself watching Bathers. Funny old woman afraid of the water.'[17]

Forty-five years later, as a Prime Minister nearing the end of his life and fighting a losing battle against heart disease, Henry was to revisit Biarritz. By then Charlotte was dead. His memory must have gone back many times to those early, contented days of their youth.

CHAPTER 3

Parliament

I N 1865 Henry was invited to stand for a Glasgow seat, but he was slow in making up his mind and lost the chance. On August 18 that year Colonel Bruce wrote to him from India, saying that he was glad that 'your thoughts have now been seriously turned to the proper direction, and I can only repeat . . . that the sooner you get into Parliament the better. I am quite sure you *ought* to be in Parliament – indeed you ought to have been there two years ago. . . .'[1]

Henry's next chance of a seat came about in a curious way. The constituency of the Stirling Burghs included the old Scots capital of Stirling; Inverkeithing, the port for the Baltic trade and a shipbuilding and quarry working centre; Culross; Dunfermline, the home of Sir Patrick Spens, where Charles I and his sister, the 'Winter Queen' of Bohemia, were born; and the fishing centre of South Queensferry; the parts that today surround both ends of the Forth bridges. It had, earlier in the century, been represented at Westminster by Lord Dalmeny, the local grandee, with whose son, the fifth Earl of Rosebery, Henry Campbell came into political conflict in the nineties.

Since 1865 the seat had been held by Laurence Oliphant, a traveller, author and occasional diplomatist who, as Chargé d'Affaires in Japan, had been cut about when defending the Embassy with a hunting crop against a nocturnal Japanese swordsman. This man, regarded as unusually brilliant and attractive, had fallen under the influence of one Thomas Lake Harris, the head of a Spiritualist community in the United States. On May 8, 1867, John Bright recorded in his diary: 'Mr. Oliphant called. Long conversation on his change of views and life, and on Mr. Harris, American Spiritualist. Very curious and interesting. . . .'[2]

Oliphant was carried away by Mr. Harris's doctrines. His constituents gave him a broad hint that his resignation would be in order, and were gratified when he took it. In April 1868 he applied for the Chiltern Hundreds and departed for Brocton, Lake Erie, accepting Harris as a spiritual guide and working for his bread as a farm labourer. This left a vacancy in Parliament, and early in 1868 there was a by-election for the Stirling seat.

Henry Campbell, described as a 'spruce, well-groomed Radical out of a Tory nest',[3] had already addressed his first public meeting in the Music Hall of Dunfermline in 1867, where the chairman, a shoemaker and old Chartist called Thomas Morrison, an uncle of Mr. Andrew Carnegie, had aroused the merriment of local Whigs by asserting that the speaker would one day be Prime Minister.

He stood for the Stirling seat as a radical Liberal. He acquired the services of an agent, a Glasgow lawyer named Gordon Smith, who busied himself in dissipating the suspicion that Henry was a Tory in disguise. The Stirling Burghs were an overwhelmingly Liberal constituency, and no Tory normally bothered to stand. The county Tory newspaper could only find seven subscribers in Dunfermline. So the contest, if there was one, was between Liberals of different shades.

In his first speech to the electors, Henry declared himself in favour of household suffrage, the secret ballot, a national and compulsory system of education, the disestablishment of the Scottish and Irish churches, and the abolition of primogeniture. Although one dour Scotsman said: 'He'll nae doe for us, mon; why, he jokes wi'out deeficulty', he was pronounced to be 'sound in the fundamentals'.

His family made no complaint about his defection to the other party. They believed in independence of judgement. The affection and business partnership between Sir James Campbell and his brother William Campbell of Tullichewan was unclouded by the fact that the latter had become a Free Churchman. Henry told the Stirling electors:

> I am the son of a staunch Tory and I am not here to say a word in excuse for that fact, or to apologize for being the son of my father. On the contrary, there is nothing I am prouder of than my close connection with one who has always been respected in Scotland, even by those who have been most bitterly opposed to him. But if you wish to draw any augury from my close connection with Sir James Campbell, this I would have you believe – that possibly the staunchness may run in the blood, that I may inherit his tenacity

without inheriting his principles, and that as my father, through a long public life, through good report and through evil report, in fair weather and in foul, has stuck to his party and his principles, so his son in like manner will stick to his.[4]

After a vigorous election, Henry was narrowly defeated by his opponent, John Ramsay of Kindalton, a wealthy Free Church distiller who was a Liberal of a more cautious, Whiggish stamp. There was a riot in Dunfermline when Henry was not allowed to speak to his supporters from the window of the Town Hall after his defeat.

At the autumn election, the last held with hustings, nominations and open voting, but on the new register, with the numbers casting their votes increased from one thousand to four thousand, Henry tried again against Ramsay. This time his agent was a local man, Mr. Alexander Macbeth. The election was a rough one. Personalities and local antipathies came into it and there was a stiff fight. Speaking on the eve of the poll, Henry said: 'I rejoice that the working classes have been endowed with a share – a great share – I will even say a preponderating share – of power and responsibility'; and of the plan to disestablish the Irish church he said: 'I sincerely hope . . . that the first fruits of that policy will be that we have gained the confidence of the Irish people.'[5] His supporters alleged that Ramsay, who was known to have a horror of draughts, had made only one speech in his months in Parliament – 'I'll thank ye to shut that window.'

This time Henry was successful. The majority of 71 against him under the £10 franchise was turned into a majority of 519 for him under household suffrage. Even his Tory father must have been proud when the Glasgow city fathers entertained the successful candidate at the Western Club.

So began his forty years' association with the Stirling Burghs. He began at once the task of healing the wounds of the election, showing that talent for reconciling differences which he was to need so badly when he was leader of the Liberal Party thirty years later. From this time on he paid an annual visit to the five burghs to hold what he called a 'colloquy' with his constituents, having a public meeting in each and meeting the leading citizens informally at the house of a prominent supporter. In those days these annual meetings between a Member and his constituents were serious affairs. His supporters described him as a model Member, taking trouble to understand their problems, alive to their prejudices and always ready to support their interests. But he spent very little time in the constituency and sometimes he found it hard going. Thirty years later, in a letter to Bryce, he said: 'I hardened my heart and thoroughly *did* my constituency which is a good thing over. There was desperately little of novelty. . . . I feel as a man feels when he leaves a barber's shop, or (may I say) a confessional, which is much the same thing.'[6]

Nevertheless he was never one of those M.P.s who get caught up and absorbed in the business of the House of Commons and gradually become cut off from what is being thought and felt outside.

In London the Campbells set up house at 60 Queen's Gate. For a young man with a devoted wife, secure convictions, a fund of good sense and an agreeable amount of money, it was a good time to come into Parliament. Among other Liberal newcomers were W. V. Harcourt and Charles Dilke.

At that time a large number of M.P.s were financially independent. So much was this so that Bagehot, writing in 1872, said: 'The spirit of our present House of Commons is plutocratic . . . its most prominent statesmen are men mostly of substantial means, but they are mostly, too, connected more or less closely with the new trading wealth.'[7]

The party machines, as we know them, hardly existed, and party discipline was loose. Members had their own strong views and had no fear of expressing them and voting as they pleased. No majority was secure, no man could be taken for granted. This gave Parliament, and individual members, greater standing and prestige than they enjoy to-day, when the power of the machines and the Whips tends to snuff out individual choice. The position of an M.P. then was something like that of a United States Senator today. The House was, for the young Henry Campbell, a congenial atmosphere.

He spoke little at first, but when he did speak – largely but not always on Scottish questions – he took trouble and was brief and effective, with the cheerful iconoclasm of a reformer. As one who had only modest academic achievements, he lambasted the universities, which afforded 'a minimum of education at a maximum of cost'. Perhaps he had himself in mind when he said that what a young man gained most was knowledge of the world, which he obtained, not from the university system, but from mixing in society with his contemporaries.[8] In 1869 he put down an amendment to an Education Bill in favour of compulsory school attendance.

The Parliamentary party of which he was now a junior member was led by a genius. But Mr. Gladstone was wrapped up in Ireland and little concerned with the management or future of his party. In his first Parliamentary session, that of 1869, Henry watched Mr. Gladstone, then at the height of his powers, carrying through the Irish Church Bill in five months in the teeth of furious opposition from Conservative, Protestant, aristocratic and clerical opinion. He supported the Education Act of 1870, which brought in universal elementary education, adopting the principle of compulsion urged in his amendment the year before, and set up the board schools; the Ballot Act of 1872, which introduced secret voting; and the abolition of religious tests at Oxford and Cambridge, passed in the teeth of bitter opposition from Anglican churchmen.

At a dinner one night he took part in a discussion about the alleged enormity of voting an allowance to Princess Louise on her marriage to the Marquis of Lorne. John Stuart Mill maintained that the Duke of Argyll was rich enough to provide for a royal daughter-in-law without help from the taxpayer. Henry, asked for his opinion, said that, as a Scotsman and a Campbell, he thought Scotland entitled to get what she could out of England, and that he was only sorry the vote for the allowance had not been larger. 'Mill looked daggers at me,' he said later, 'and seemed to be wondering who was this flippant Philistine who had found his way into the Holy of Holies.'[9]

He spent only three years on the back benches as an obscure private member whom, a Dunfermline journalist noted, 'Mr. Gladstone passed in the lobby as though he were a stranger'.[10] In 1871, when he was only thirty-five, there came a change in both his official and his private life.

Firstly, at the request of Cardwell, the War Secretary, he was appointed Financial Secretary at the War Office. Secondly, his wealthy uncle, Henry Bannerman, died, leaving him a life interest in his estate at Hunton, near Maidstone, provided that, within eighteen months, he assumed 'my surname of Bannerman either alone or in addition to his usual surname, but so that the name of Bannerman shall be the last and principal name'.[11] This act of posthumous arrogance irritated Henry Campbell and angered his wife, who was never reconciled to the name of Bannerman, and who for many more years signed herself, and was known as, plain Charlotte Campbell. He wrote to Lord Spencer as late as 1884: 'I see you are already tired, as I have long been, of writing my horrid long name. I am always best pleased to be called Campbell *tout court*, and most of my old friends do so. . . . An alternative is C.B.'[12] But he pocketed his pride in a sensible Lowland way and inherited the property, which included a number of valuable farms. As the main house was occupied, he took over as a country house another large and comfortable house on the estate called Gennings, with brick gables, and a great sweep of lawn sloping down to a lake, surrounded by the apple orchards and hop fields of Kent. He kept this till 1887. Henceforward he was to be known to the world as Henry Campbell-Bannerman. As his surname was such a mouthful he soon became generally known as 'C.B.'

CHAPTER 4

Cardwell and the War Office

'THE WAR OFFICE', wrote Florence Nightingale, is 'a very slow office, an enormously expensive office, a not very efficient office, and one in which the minister's intentions can be entirely negatived by all his sub-departments'.[1] To this office C.B. now went. It was housed in a group of buildings in Pall Mall, full of dark staircases, where the Royal Automobile Club stands today.

In his twenties he had had a brief and not very serious experience of military matters in the 1st Lanarkshire Volunteers, as the Captain of a company manned by staff from the family firm. Now he began a connection with the Army which was to last throughout his political career. The *Manchester Guardian* wrote: 'Mr. Campbell-Bannerman fell in love with the war office. . . . It was characteristic of his Scotch fidelity of temperament that he stuck to it through good and evil report.'[2]

He had two widely separated spells as Financial Secretary, the first from 1871 to 1874 under Cardwell, and the second from 1880 to 1882 under Childers. Of these it is likely that the first was much the more enjoyable. He was young and enthusiastic and he had an exceptional chief, one of those rare ministers who can use a relatively brief spell of office to make large and permanent changes. This can only happen when a minister has first-rate advisers, has the confidence and support of the Prime Minister, and has himself the determination, the tenacity and the skill to get his measures accepted by his colleagues, his party and the House.

Cardwell had all these, and he was a man of exceptional ability. In his photographs a handsome, severe, intellectual face looks out critically from the surrounding penumbra of whisker. Lord Northbrook, a Baring, was his Under-Secretary.

Cardwell and Northbrook decided to appoint a Financial Secretary to look after the estimates, the funds of the War Office and the Army Pay Department. It was this appointment that C.B. was given in 1871. He began work in a political tradition, based on the principles of Sir Robert Peel, that attached the greatest importance to the principles of retrenchment and economy – a practitioner of which was called, in those days, a good 'economist'. The post of Financial Secretary was consequently an important one.

C.B. was soon on the most cordial terms with his chief. Moreover he had the enormously valuable and stimulating experience of working in a department at a time when great changes were being made. These changes have passed into military history as the Cardwell reforms. They were, like most radical changes, bitterly opposed. As Lord Wolseley later wrote:

> Except those who worked with and for Mr. Cardwell few knew the difficulties he had to overcome when all 'Society' and almost the whole Army was against him. . . . Never was Minister in my time more generally hated by the Army and by almost all its old-fashioned and unthinking officers. And yet . . . I can think of no man whose . . . great services entitle him to be remembered with such gratitude by all ranks of the Army. . . .[3]

Cardwell abolished the purchase system, under which promotions and regimental commands were bought and sold. There was even a tariff of regulation prices, laid down in 1766 (£6,700 for a lieutenant-colonelcy in the Foot Guards, £3,500 for one in a marching regiment of foot, £1,750 for a lieutenantcy in a cavalry regiment, £550 for one in an infantry regiment).[4] Later the prices were raised, but in any case the actual market prices were much higher. By 1865 Cox and Co., the army agents, reported that the usual price of a lieutenant-colonelcy in a cavalry regiment was £14,000. Promotions were acquired at an auction room in Charles Street.

Under this system the efficient but poor officer remained a subaltern or a lieutenant, while his affluent but not necessarily competent colleague rose quickly to high command. But earlier statesmen had supported the system, Wellington arguing that the officers obtained by it were 'the best officers in the world, and that to compose the officers of a lower class would cause the Army to deteriorate,'[5] and Palmerston that the Army should be 'connected with the higher classes of society', which could only be done 'by allowing members of high families . . . to get on with greater rapidity than they would by mere seniority'.[6]

Cardwell put an end to the system, though he encountered strong opposition in the House of Commons, one member reminding the House that Colonel Pride, who had purged it in 1648, and Oliver Cromwell were non-purchase officers.[7] The opposition of the House of Lords was overcome by use of the Royal Warrant, the Lords thereupon passing a vote of censure, which was deferred for ten days on account of Goodwood.

Army reform was very much of a live issue, and a subject of endless controversy, throughout C.B.'s public life. Most of the disputes had their origins in the changes brought about by Cardwell. C.B. was often in the thick of them.

In many parts of the world today power is constantly being seized by army leaders in coups d'état, and parliamentary and civilian regimes overthrown. Indeed whenever a democratic regime has shallow roots, there is a risk that, when discontent is widespread, the army will step in. In the seventeenth century this had happened in England. The Army, under Cromwell, had destroyed a King and then turned on Parliament. After the Civil War the fear of military and Royal domination over Parliament persisted for many years. It was for this reason that, until 1955, the Army Annual Act, the first passed by each successive Parliament, began always with the words: 'Whereas it is illegal for the Queen [or King] to keep a standing army in time of peace . . .'. In effect the Army is still, under the annual Order in Council which has to be approved by Parliament, created afresh each year. This is one of the cornerstones of the constitution, on which the supremacy of Parliament rests. Hence the revolutionary nature of the plan evolved by Bonar Law, Lord Milner, Sir Henry Wilson and Edward Carson in the Ulster crisis between 1910 and 1914, when they thought of getting the House of Lords to amend or reject the Army Annual Bill, so depriving the Liberal Government of legal control over the forces of the Crown.[8]

Cardwell found that although in theory he was supreme, in practice he had to share control of the Army with the Commander-in-Chief at the Horse Guards.

The Commander-in-Chief had, since 1856, been that formidable but genial person His Royal Highness George, Duke of Cambridge, Earl of Tipperary and Baron Culloden, a grandson of George III, born in Hanover, who held this office for no less than thirty-nine years. A vast, bucolic, Falstaffian figure, known to the War Office staff as the 'dear old Duke', he was a problem for all Secretaries of State for War, including, in time, Campbell-Bannerman. He was, in fact, devoted to the Army and was known as 'The Soldier's Friend', but as he grew older he became increasingly intolerant of change, particularly of such things as promotion by merit rather than seniority. He spoke scornfully of 'pwogwess'. He had a morganatically married wife, Mrs. FitzGeorge, a former actress, in Queen Street (and three young FitzGeorges all born out of wedlock) and a mistress, Mrs. Beauclerk, in Chesham Street, whom he visited in a phaeton drawn by a splendid pair of horses. He had enjoyed the rapid promotion then reserved for Royal personages, being made a Brevet Colonel at nineteen, a Major-General at twenty-six and Commander-in-Chief at thirty-seven. But he was no desk soldier. He had commanded the First Division, composed of the Guards and the Highland Brigade, in the Crimea, in the days when this involved riding in front of it on a horse and leading it personally into action. He had had to do this at the Alma in 1854 under a heavy fire of grapeshot. As he wrote to Mrs. FitzGeorge: 'The moment was an awful one. I had merely time to ask Sir Colin Campbell, a very fine old soldier, what was to be done . . . he called to me "put yourself at the head of the Division and lead them right up to the Battery." I followed his advice.'[9]

At Inkerman, where he had his horse shot under him, he was reminded of the importance of mundane matters like supply. Gallantly urging the Guards to rally, face the enemy and fire a volley, he was met with the unanswerable objection that they had no ammunition.

As a ceremonial commander of the Army he was excellent, but it was perhaps a pity that he retained for so long more active responsibility, including the personal control of most promotions and appointments. Like his cousin the Queen, with whom, in 1838 and 1839, his name had once been linked, he pushed the Royal prerogative to the extreme limit, but was prepared to beat a tactical retreat when it came to a confrontation with ministerial and parliamentary authority. He believed that the Army was the Queen's Army and that the Commander-in-Chief held it in trust for her. As he wrote to the Queen in 1858: 'Once allow the command of the Army to pass out of the hands of the Crown, which it would do if the Commander-in-Chief were abolished, and the Army becomes a Parliamentary Army and would become dangerous to the State.'[10]

He argued that the Secretary of State did not command the Army (which was true) but also that the Commander-in-Chief must, to some extent, be independent of the Secretary of State. This was clearly incompatible with the doctrine of the full responsibility of the Secretary of State.

The struggle went on for many years. Writing to Lady Bradford in 1879, Disraeli said:

> The Horse Guards will ruin this country, unless there is a Prime Minister who will have his way, and that cannot be counted upon. . . . You cannot get a Secretary of War to resist the cousin of the Sovereign, with whom he is placed in daily and hourly communication. I tremble when I think what may be the fate of this country if, as is not unlikely, a great struggle occur, with the Duke of Cambridge's generals.[11]

Fifteen years after that the Duke of Cambridge was still in command, and it fell eventually to C.B. to bring about his retirement in 1895. It is fair to say that the generals appointed by his successors were not much more successful than those he chose. Our record in the early months of the Boer War was a good deal worse than in the Crimea. But the problem of selecting good generals in time of peace has baffled successive generations.

The Commander-in-Chief at the Horse Guards was in 1868 still in practice his own master on all but money matters. Communications between his office and the Secretary of State's were conducted by letter, and the Secretary of State had no responsibility for such matters as the appointments and promotion of officers in the Army. Cardwell brought everyone under one roof in Pall Mall and organized the War Office in three departments – military, under the Commander-in-Chief, supply, under a Surveyor General, and financial, under C.B. as Financial Secretary.

Among the other changes made in C.B.'s first spell under Cardwell were the transformation of recruitment, which had always been a problem, and the raising of the pay of the private soldier to a shilling a day with his rations. In the Peninsular War we had had to enlist regiments of Hanoverians, Germans, Sicilians, Greeks, Corsicans and even French prisoners of war, criminals and deserters, and in the Crimean War we had German, Italian and Swiss foreign legions. It was a costly and wasteful system – the bounty for each man was some £40 – and produced nothing like enough men. Service was very hard, with years abroad in wretched climates, and few returned, so it was no wonder that 'to go for a soldier' was looked on as equivalent to banishment or death. Cardwell introduced the system of short service – twelve years in all, part with the colours and part with the reserve – in place of the old long-service system, so that much younger soldiers took the place of the old, hard-bitten, hard-drinking soldiery. His object was to create, for the first time, a proper reserve of trained soldiers. Whether it was an improvement or not was fiercely argued about for the next thirty years. C.B. was himself a convinced Cardwellian on the issue. But the problem was, in truth, an exceedingly difficult one. Bagehot was one of the few men at the time who recognized its dimensions; as he put it: 'the English try to defend without any compulsion – only by such soldiers as they persuade to serve – territories far surpassing all Europe in magnitude, and situated all over the habitable globe.'[12]

After C.B. had joined the department in 1871, Cardwell set up the linked-battalion system, under which each regiment had one overseas and one home battalion. He also based each regiment on a fixed depôt in a county or city, giving it a firm basis of local pride and patriotism, and grouping with it the local militia and volunteers. This was a system which lasted till the late sixties of the twentieth century, when it began to be dismantled under the stress of successive contractions in the strength of the Army. It was a system altogether different from that which existed in Europe, which was designed to produce large continental armies on a basis of compulsory service. Cardwell's view was that England should have a small but efficient and well provided Army, which could be expanded when the need arose.

C.B. came into close contact with the small and able group of young men in the War Office who worked out the details of the Cardwell reforms – Sir Ralph Knox, a brilliant man quite unable to bear fools gladly, Colonel Sir Garnet Wolseley, then, at thirty-eight, Assistant Adjutant-General, General Adye, the Director of Artillery, and a thirty-year-old Captain in the Topographical and Statistical Department, Evelyn Baring, the future Lord Cromer.

Not surprisingly, he found working in such an atmosphere exhilarating, and conceived a vast admiration for Cardwell which lasted all his life. He was allowed his head and his suggestions were listened to. Early on, in January 1872, before he had learnt that results are achieved by ministers if they work with, rather than against, officials, he sent a note to Cardwell, adding in the covering minute:

I have written this paper for *your own reading* only, and have felt all the more free on that account. Had I taken counsel first of the permanent officials I fear I should have had all the enthusiasm (such as it is) taken out of me by their objections to most of my proposals. And as I have great faith in the *trueness* of a fresh outside view in such matters, I have thought it best to go straight to you with my ideas.[13]

He was not the first, or the last, young minister to conceive that officials are usually negative and defeatist. But he very soon found out how to work with them effectively, certainly before he went to Ireland in 1884.

In 1872 the Campbell-Bannermans moved to 117 Eaton Square, and found themselves conveniently next door to Cardwell. In the same year, Northbrook was appointed Viceroy of India and left for Delhi, taking his kinsman Evelyn Baring with him as private secretary. Cardwell was urged by his friend Colonel Napier Sturt to take the twenty-five-year-old Lord Rosebery as his successor. It would have been curious if Rosebery and C.B. had served together as juniors in the same department at this early stage. But it was not to be, and the appointment went to Lord Lansdowne.

Years later, in 1906, Lord Esher wrote to another Liberal Secretary of State for War who was setting out to reform Army administration, R. B. Haldane, when C.B. was head of the Government and Prime Minister. He said: 'I go back to Cardwell as an example and an illustration. Why did he succeed? Because he faced unpopularity and dealt with Army Reform on great broad lines.'[14]

C.B. was fortunate to begin his official career under such a chief. He learnt from Cardwell that courage and determination, and the will to do what seems right and to stand up to vilification and abuse, are the qualities needed by the statesman whose work is to last. It was an experience he was never to forget. Cardwell's own career, however, was ending, and within twelve years he was to die insane.

CHAPTER 5

The Junior Minister

C.B. remained at the War Office throughout 1872 and 1873.

In these years little went right for the Liberal Government. The dissenters, who were normally among the essential supporters of the Liberal party, had been outraged by the Education Act, which they looked on as far too favourable to the Anglicans. The Anglicans were incensed by the Irish Church Bill and the abolition of university tests. Some minor scandals, negligible by twentieth-century standards, hurt the standing of the Government. Some ministers had been far from successful. The constituents of Mr. Ayrton at the Board of Works had, in 1871, passed a resolution that 'his rude, coarse demeanour, both in and out of Parliament, has made the borough of the Tower Hamlets a byword throughout the United Kingdom'.[1]

Reporting to his constituents, C.B. recognized that the Government was nearing its end, but quoted to them the lines:

> Their setting sun sheds forth a glimmering ray
> Like ancient Rome majestic in decay,
> And better gleanings their worn soil can boast
> Than the sour vintage of the opposing host.[2]

In January 1874 Parliament was dissolved and the Liberals went to the country, campaigning on the pledge to abolish the income tax. It availed them nothing and the electoral disaster was spectacular. The Conservatives came in with a substantial majority. Gladstone resigned, refusing a peerage. C.B. found himself in opposition for the first time after five and a half years in Parliament and two and a half in office. For the next six years his party were to remain in opposition. The election brought for the first time a number of Irish Home Rulers into the House of Commons, who grouped themselves under a Protestant lawyer, Isaac Butt, and in 1877 claimed for themselves the name of a distinct party. It also brought in two notable newcomers, A. J. Balfour and Lord Randolph Churchill.

C.B. was able to enjoy the carefree life of the Opposition benches. He lectured to the Dunfermline Literary Society on Michelangelo, whom he called 'the perfect gentleman', and on Spain. He was full of praise for the indolence of the Spaniard:

> Leave him to his repose and his cigar. . . . What a contrast . . . does this present to the busy, struggling, pushing and driving world in which *we* live, where idleness is looked on as a crime, and where every man is trying with all his might to better his condition. . . . It is positively refreshing to find a great nation on the opposite tack, who . . . ask only to be left alone. May it not be that we too much neglect this contemplative, restful, placid side of life?[3]

At any rate C.B. himself did not neglect it. But on occasions he could bestir himself. In May 1874 the House was debating a vote of censure on Lord Sandhurst, who was accused of having improperly drawn full pay and allowances for seventeen months when he had been absent from the command in Ireland. The debate became heated when a Conservative member named Horsman accused the opposition of the 'shabbiest and dirtiest' of tricks, since, he said, they had used Lord Sandhurst to help push through the Army Purchase Bill, had made him a peer to enlist his help in the Lords and, having brought him to London, had 'in order to reduce the estimates and swell the surplus, with a pistol at his head, extorted from him' sums of money which he was said to have 'returned'. The Conservative benches cheered rapturously, and the House became so excited that the next speaker was howled down. Henry Lucy, reporting the debate for *Punch*, recorded that 'the inclination of the House being decidedly adverse to hearing him at all, Yorke, after some vain struggling, sat down, and Campbell-Bannerman presented himself at the table.' It was clearly a tricky moment. Lucy's account continued:

> the ex-Financial Secretary to the War Office was suffering from a severe cold. His observations, therefore, were brief, but manifestly, in the view of the majority of the House, they conclusively disposed

of Horsman's statements. If the late Government had acted from shabby and dirty motives of economy, Campbell-Bannerman said, then his Royal Highness the Commander-in-Chief and the Adjutant-General must be supposed to have been actuated by the same desires, for no step in the proceedings had been taken by the War Office without . . . receiving the seal of their approval. As for the pistol-at-the-head performance . . . the fact was that the money returned by his lordship had been paid over to the officers who had in his absence performed his duties; and finally, if it were true that the late Government had made Lord Sandhurst a peer in order that he might help them through the Lords with the Army Purchase Bill, all Campbell-Bannerman could say was that they were very unfortunate in the speculation, for when his lordship had taken part in the debates in the other House, he had spoken against the Bill . . . he declared, amid general cheering, that there was no imputation on the character of Lord Sandhurst, and expressed the hope that Anderson would withdraw his motion, which he did.[4]

It is clear that, despite his cold, C.B. on this occasion, in the course of a short speech, entirely transformed the general feeling of the House.

The next year, 1875, Gladstone laid down the Liberal leadership, writing in a public letter to Granville: 'at the age of sixty-five, and after forty-two years of a laborious public life, I think myself entitled to retire. . . .' No one could then have foreseen that this was a mere temporary withdrawal, and that another nineteen years were to go by before he finally gave up the leadership of the party. As it was, Hartington was elected to lead the party in the Commons. C.B. was one of those who backed him in preference to Forster.

But Gladstone was unable to take a back seat. In March there was a debate on the Regimental Exchanges Bill. C.B. spoke, saying that exchanges would 'work evil in the army' and would be giving 'a direct money value to the patronage of the Commander-in-Chief for an appointment to a home regiment'. He argued that it was 'not desirable that men should be induced to enter the Public Service for gain, but to do their duty to their country'.[5] Then, unexpectedly, Gladstone intervened. Disraeli wrote to the Queen: 'Mr. Gladstone not only appeared, but rushed into the debate . . . the new Members trembled and fluttered like small birds when a hawk is in the air.'[6]

The hawk refused to fold his wings. Gladstone would not retire from public life and confine himself to cutting down beech trees at

Hawarden. He entered into battle with Disraeli on the Eastern question. In September 1876 (a year in which he published *Homeric Synchronism: an Inquiry into the Time and Place of Homer*) he brought out his celebrated pamphlet *The Bulgarian Horrors and the Question of the East*.

C.B.'s sympathies, too, were firmly with the oppressed Christian subjects of the Porte. He described Disraeli as the *esprit damné* of the Government, whose three favourite tones of levity, mystery and swagger were all unfortunate.[7] Disraeli, meanwhile, had acquired the Suez Canal shares to prevent the French acquiring exclusive control of the route to India and the East, a transaction that both Gladstone and C.B. criticized. C.B. also condemned the Admiralty circular which directed British ships in foreign waters to surrender runaway slaves, a circular that caused a loud outcry.

In May 1877 Gladstone put down some resolutions urging the country to join Russia in coercing Turkey. Hartington objected and the party risked a split. Dilke recorded that, while many wavered and changed sides, 'Campbell-Bannerman was frankly with Lord Hartington from the first'.[8] In the end Gladstone gave way.

When the Liberals had been defeated, Cardwell had gone to the Lords. This left C.B. as the principal spokesman in the Commons on military matters. He was conscientious but unspectacular. In March 1878 he wrote to Hartington when a motion about guns was up for discussion giving six reasons why muzzle-loading guns were to be preferred to the new breech-loaders: 'Long and patient enquiry with overwhelming weight of authority had led to the adoption of muzzle-loaders. . . . Strength, safety, simplicity, economy, all in favour of muzzle-loaders. Rapidity of fire at least equal.'[9] This did not display him at his most prescient.

T. P. O'Connor, an Irish member and a personal friend of C.B.'s, later described him thus:

Seated on the Front Opposition Bench, regularly but not too frequently, speaking only when a War Office vote was under discussion, and then speaking with hesitancy, without much emphasis, and without any of the prestige of great position and commanding oratory, he never attracted to the House a large audience, never raised a ripple of disturbance or enthusiasm on its surface; and when the dinner-hour came, and there was nothing associated with his old departmental activities under discussion, he quietly slipped away and went off to his home and his friends.[10]

He was not perhaps quite as indolent as this description suggests. He nearly always spoke with knowledge and common sense on Scottish questions when they came up. But he made little mark in the House.

The six years of Conservative government between 1874 and 1880 mark the high noon of British imperialism. They were the years of the acquisition of Cyprus, the annexation of the Transvaal and the Zulu War. Disraeli arranged for the Queen to be proclaimed Empress of India in 1876. C.B. was unimpressed. 'We cannot', he said, 'add to the lustre and dignity of the Crown of this realm, the most ancient and august in Europe, by tricking it out in a brand new title.'[11] He was worried lest the ancient title of Prince of Wales might be replaced by that of 'Prince Imperial'.

He settled down into the routine of Parliamentary life which, from 1878, began to be complicated by the Irish tactics of obstruction. His father died in 1876, leaving Stracathro to his elder son James and to C.B. his property in Brunswick Street, Glasgow, £25,000 and the silver in his house in Bath Street. Louisa had died three years earlier.

C.B. was now a relatively wealthy man and in 1878 moved to 6 Grosvenor Place. He had turned forty the year before. He had been ten years in the House of Commons and had a good knowledge of Army matters. But he did not make a splash there and even in his own field he was not asked to take a leading part. In March 1877, for example, Childers wrote: 'Two days ago Hartington asked me if I had any objection to take up Army affairs, nobody but Campbell-Bannerman knowing anything about them on our bench. . . .'[12]

The House of Commons is the forum where political reputations are made. Its essence is a state of continuous, though often artificial, warfare between two parties, conducted according to well-understood rules. Those who make rapid political reputations are those who are seen to distinguish themselves in these contests. The qualities needed are a certain brutal toughness – for a case has to be made in the face of up to three hundred critics anxious for your downfall – fluency of speech, quickness of wit and an eye for the weak spot in the opponent's armour. It is in a way like cockfighting. The rival gamecocks are sent forward, they skirmish, and finally one or other succeeds in tearing his opponent to pieces. The fighting cocks of Parliament are dangerous to those who take them on. They develop great skill at the game. And so they rise swiftly to commanding positions in their parties. When their party is returned to power they naturally expect, and are given, the chief Cabinet posts. Such were Arthur Balfour and Lord Randolph Churchill on the Conservative benches, and Joseph Chamberlain, who, according to Asquith, had 'extraordinary powers of Parliamentary swordplay',[13] on the Liberal side.

The House of Commons rapidly assesses these fighting qualities, and no one acquires a major political reputation there without showing marked ability. But the system has one great drawback. The talents required to defend a party's policies, good or bad, and to pulverize and destroy the opposition's case, are not the same as those required by a Cabinet Minister who is charged with the management of public affairs. The system of selection may, and sometimes does, bring into high office men who have great debating ability but defective judgement, and it tends to exclude, or at any rate to hold back, those who possess qualities of judgement and good sense which are needed to conduct the affairs of a great nation, but lack the gladiatorial qualities necessary for parliamentary success. Only a few exceptional people possess both sets of qualities.

Balfour wrote: 'We habitually assume that anyone who is competent to debate must be competent to administer and anyone who is competent to administer must debate; and we assume it, though the examples of John Bright and W. H. Smith stare us in the face.'[14] Macaulay too, maintained that 'parliamentary government is government by speaking'. He remarked that the 'accomplished and ingenious' orators Charles Townshend and Windham would, in a perilous crisis, 'have been found far inferior in all the qualities of rulers to such a man as Oliver Cromwell, who talked nonsense, or as William the Silent, who did not talk at all'.[15]

This explains why a man like Campbell-Bannerman was eclipsed by more agile debaters, was kept in minor office, took so long to reach the Cabinet and reached the highest office only when he was old and his health was failing. In party debating terms in the House of Commons it made sense. In terms of managing ability and wisdom in council it did not.

C.B. was one of the most genuinely modest and least ambitious of politicians. Indeed it is in a way surprising that, being so modest and easy-going, he chose to go into politics at all. The House of Commons naturally attracts those who seek power and glory and celebrity, like Disraeli, who told John Bright, 'We come here for fame!'[16] This has been true of many notable men since. It was true only to a very limited extent of C.B. Yet his absorption in politics lasted all his life.

In 1879 Mr. Gladstone embarked on his Midlothian campaign under the auspices of the young Lord Rosebery. When he visited Dunfermline C.B. was there on the station platform with a parcel of the local linen for Mrs. Gladstone. The 1880 election was a famous victory for the Liberals, who won over a hundred seats from the Conservatives. C.B. himself was re-elected by a vast majority, his Conservative opponent withdrawing before polling day. The Queen, mortified by the result, sent first for Lord Hartington. But she was eventually compelled to accept Mr. Gladstone, now over seventy, as her Prime Minister. So long as he wished to play an active part, no one else was prepared to try to form a Liberal government. The Government was predominantly Whig, and the great landowning nobles occupied most of the leading posts. Indeed so consistently was this the case, under both Disraeli and Gladstone, that one can only question Mr. Asquith's assertion, in his Romanes Lecture on the Victorian age, that it was 'an era when England was ruled by the middle class'. This particular administration did however contain the two radical leaders, Chamberlain and Dilke, who were from the start at odds with the Whigs.

In the House of Commons Sir Stafford Northcote led the Conservatives in a humdrum way, but this Parliament saw the emergence of the Conservative ginger group below the gangway, 'the Fourth Party', comprising Lord Randolph Churchill, Drummond Wolff, Gorst and Balfour. C.B. was outraged by the obstructive tactics of the Fourth Party and the Irish Nationalists. Speaking in 1881 at Dundee, he said:

> The noblest representative body in the world is thwarted and insulted by men who do not conceal the fact that their object is to degrade and defile it. We see introduced into it the manners of the mob and the taproom. We see its leader, the foremost Englishman of his day, who has occupied a conspicuous position in Parliament and before the world for well nigh fifty years, treated with personal insolence by men whose Parliamentary experience can be counted by hours.[17]

Despite his modesty, C.B. must have been disappointed when he was only given again the Financial Secretaryship at the War Office, to which he had first been appointed nine years before. He had been thirty-five then; he was now forty-three. Moreover there was no Cardwell to work for, but instead Hugh Childers, a much less interesting man, 'without whom', Asquith later wrote, 'it was one of Mr. Gladstone's foibles to think that no Liberal Cabinet was adequately equipped'.[18] Harcourt called Childers 'cold as ice and as impassive as dough', but C.B. who, unlike Harcourt, had a positive genius for getting on with people, enjoyed the sunniest relations with him both officially and socially.

At the War Office, Childers carried out no large reforms and, as a military historian puts it, 'was content to leave the organization of the army more or less as he found it'.[19] In 1884, he described C.B. to Gladstone as 'an excellent economist and administrator'.[20] The files of the War Office for this period bear witness to the correctness of this judgement. C.B.'s notes often have a shrewd, worldly, down-to-earth touch. He was also one of those ministers who remember to say 'thank you'. 'I am greatly obliged for the pains which have been taken . . .' is the sort of phrase that occurs frequently. Courtesy came naturally to him.

He was at the War Office throughout 1880 and 1881, a year that saw the outbreak of fighting with the Boers after Mr. Gladstone had declined to return the Transvaal to them, in the erroneous belief that the 'great majority of the people of the Transvaal were reconciled to annexation'. C.B. later described the attempt to force direct rule on the Boers as a disastrous blunder. There followed the catastrophe of Majuba in May. After that the Liberal Government did what they had better have done before, and gave the Transvaal back its independence. Inevitably, however, it now looked like a concession from weakness.

In 1881 the struggle between Crown and Parliament over the control of the Army broke out again over the appointment of Sir Garnet Wolseley, like C.B. a determined Cardwellian, as Adjutant-General. The appointment was strongly opposed by the Duke of Cambridge and by the Queen, who argued that under the Royal Warrant only the Commander-in-Chief (who disliked Wolseley) could propose appointments. However, it went through. In the same year Wolseley went off to Egypt to deal with Arabi's revolt and defeated him at Tel-el-Kebir, receiving as a result the thanks of Parliament, £30,000, a barony and promotion to full General. C.B. wrote from Marienbad to congratulate him, and in his reply Wolseley said, 'I hope we have now silenced for ever all the old fogies who have for some years past talked so much nonsense about young soldiers and the iniquity of those who favoured Army Reform.'[21]

In May 1882 C.B. succeeded Trevelyan as Parliamentary and Financial Secretary to the Admiralty. The First Lord, Northbrook, with whom he had served at the War Office, was in the upper House, so C.B. had to answer for the Admiralty in the Commons. In reply to one letter of congratulations he wrote: 'It is of course a great piece of promotion, and being my own Master in the House will make it much more interesting: but it is a shocking grind to have to get up all the complicated technical details of a service of which I know nothing.'[22]

He worked hard, nevertheless, at the detail of his job. His private secretary, who became Sir Gordon Voules, wrote later, 'One of his favourite phrases was "I don't think we need publish this urbi et orbi" so much good work was hidden in oblivion.'[23] Northbrook thought highly of his work. C.B. and Charlotte went round the dockyards to see for themselves how the men and women working in them were treated.

Politically, moreover, the post became important, as an agitation was got up in 1884 about the allegedly unprepared state of the Navy. C.B. had told the House of Commons the year before that the Government were not disposed to 'embark on a new career of Naval Expenditure, and possibly set the example of a fresh international rivalry on the sea'. Now the public was to be 'aroused' by a well-organized press scare. The men behind this agitation were a curious group. There was H. O. Arnold-Forster, then twenty-nine, a knowledgeable but humourless person who specialized in military affairs, Reginald Brett, the future Lord Esher, at this time secretary to Lord Hartington at the War Office, W. T. Stead, editor of the *Pall Mall Gazette*, a journalist and crusader of great flair but with erratic judgement and an addiction to stunts, and Captain J. A. Fisher of H.M.S. *Excellent*, the future First Sea Lord. Arnold-Forster was the original moving spirit; Stead saw a chance for a sensational campaign based on official information, and Fisher provided the information, hoping to see the campaign result in a bigger and better Navy and the confusion of the Gladstonian 'economists'. The naval Lords added their support and gave private interviews to Stead. Fisher, characteristically, told him, 'You have got enough in your wallet to break half the officers in Her Majesty's Service if you split.'

The first *Pall Mall Gazette* article, 'The Truth about the Navy' by 'One Who Knows the Facts', painted a dark picture of a Navy starved of funds, undefended ports and a lack of torpedo boats. The campaign created a stir. Public opinion was stirred up effectively and Tennyson published in *The Times* a frantic poem addressed to Northbrook. One stanza ran:

> You – you who had the ordering of her Fleet,
> If you have only compass'd her disgrace,
> When all men starve, the wild mob's million feet
> Will kick you from your place –
> But then – too late, too late.

The former First Lord, W. H. Smith, called for a committee of enquiry. C.B. was not easily rattled, but realized the political dangers. On October 2 he wrote to Childers, now Chancellor of the Exchequer. The first paragraph of his letter has a delightful period flavour:

> . . . I wrote to Lord Northbrook last week, judging that although he is not to be troubled about ordinary Admiralty matters, he ought to be consulted on the general Parliamentary question of Naval policy which is now being discussed. But I see that he has gone to Upper Egypt, so that it may be some time before he can reply, and it is not to be expected that he will give any detailed statement of opinion. . . .[24]

He went on: 'Although I do not believe that the hysterical excitement of the *Pall Mall Gazette* extends far beyond London, there is sufficient interest and anxiety felt in the country to prevent the question being shelved or poohpooed.' He suggested to Childers that the case might be adequately met if naval expenditure were increased 'by half a million to a million'. It was an astute and well-timed departmental move. Childers saw C.B. on October 6. C.B. promised to send him a paper reviewing expenditure since 1866 but alarmed him by saying that the facilities in England for making armour plate, torpedoes and guns were far inferior to those in France. The Cabinet were shaken, and C.B.'s calm presentation, which carefully understated the case, pointing out that he had found no trace in the Board of sympathy with the scare, but drawing attention to the political hazards, was effective. He warned Childers that 'the Opposition will support a motion insisting on the Navy being strengthened, and whatever its motive may be (as to which I have my ideas) many of our people will join them'. The

Cabinet swiftly authorized a supplementary naval programme, not of one million, but of three. Three million pounds went a long way in those days, and out of it two battleships and thirteen cruisers were built.

In October 1884, however, at the age of forty-eight, C.B. was at last given major office, being appointed to that graveyard of reputations, the Chief Secretaryship of Ireland. Northbrook wrote from Cairo:

> I am in despair at hearing . . . that you are going to leave the Admiralty for Ireland. I suppose I ought to congratulate you, as the position is one of the most important in the Government and it is a real privilege for any one to work with Spencer. But it is a severe loss to us all. . . . You may feel assured that you have made your mark at the Admiralty, and that you will be very much missed there. . . .[25]

His constituents did not require his presence for his re-election, necessary in those days after appointment to any new office.

There was a difficulty in replacing him. One of the Prime Minister's secretaries, Edward Hamilton,* noted on October 21:

> I went this morning by Mʳ G's wishes to see C. Bannerman over the question of his successor. . . . It is an exceedingly difficult matter – an 'impasse' according to Bannerman. He says that Brassey is distinctly incompetent as an administrator & is not competent to represent the Admiralty in the H. of Commons. On the other hand, if Brassey is not promoted from the Civil Lordship . . . he will resign: and his retirement would be a great blow just at the moment . . . because he has hoodwinked the public into believing that he is the one great civil authority on naval affairs. . . . I fear C. Bannerman's opinion is confirmed by the Naval Lords.[26]

The Government could not afford a resignation, so Brassey was promoted.

Wolseley wrote to C.B.:

* Hamilton was a lifelong friend of Rosebery, with whom he had been at Eton. He was all his life a Treasury official, and was twice Private Secretary to Gladstone (1873–4 and 1880–5). He went about a great deal in society and knew and corresponded with many leading political figures. His very interesting diary (1880–1906) is in the British Museum.

Dongola – Nubia
22 November, 1884

From this far off oasis in the midst of this great desert, I send you my greetings. . . . Your acceptance of the position shows you to have a stout heart, the first qualification required for effectively dealing with my countrymen. . . . The task before you is more difficult than that of taking a small army to Khartoum. . . . I congratulate Ireland and the Govt. upon having you to rule that unfortunate country. . . . You have the *misfortune* . . . to be a Scotchman which to the Irish Nationalist is worse even than being an Englishman. . . .[27]

Rosebery wrote:

I have hesitated whether to write and congratulate you, because I doubted if the exchange of an office which you liked for the most disagreeable post in the public service was a subject for that sort of thing. However I write to wish you joy on one ground alone, that you have now an opportunity of displaying those great talents which I have long known you to possess, but which have never yet had fair scope. . . . May I add a humble hope that you will add some excellent Irish stories to your inexhaustible Scottish repertoire.[28]

C.B.'s secretary at the Admiralty thoughtfully presented him with a pocket revolver.

Part 2

Ireland

CHAPTER 6

The Chief Secretary

'If you choose to go to the west of Ireland, I suppose you'd find the Atlantic. But nobody ever does go there for fear of being murdered.'

Mrs. Hurtle in Trollope's 'The Way We Live Now' (1875)

Mr. HAROLD MACMILLAN, when he was Minister Resident in Algiers in 1942, used to tell young officers that the British must think of themselves as Greeks in the Roman Empire of the Americans and supply the experience and the brains, while America supplied the big battalions.[1] Looking back on the long, sad history of our dealings with Ireland, it is difficult to resist a degree of scepticism about our political sagacity or our capacity to deal adequately with this problem on our doorstep which has plagued us for so many years. Winston Churchill spoke nearly fifty years ago of 'the power which Ireland has ... to lay her hands upon the vital strings of British life and politics and to hold, dominate and convulse, year after year, generation after generation, the politics of this powerful country'.[2] Never was this more true than during the forty years of Campbell-Bannerman's public life. In 1884, when he was appointed Chief Secretary for Ireland, he became directly involved in the struggle when it was in one of its periodic eruptions of savagery and bitterness.

There was no simple explanation for this state of affairs. Ireland was involved in a permanently uneasy relationship with England. As Grattan put it: 'She can never unite because of the Channel – She can never separate because of the ocean.' The crisis which came to a head in the 1880s had a number of causes. There was established in Catholic Ireland an alien, Protestant, aristocracy, the 'ascendancy', which was supreme throughout the eighteenth century. These families, who gave us many of our most celebrated soldiers and judges and built beautiful houses all over Ireland, became intensely Irish, after their own fashion, and were often fiercely opposed to the Government at Westminster, but they never became one people with the native Irish.

In the eighteenth century they did, however, have their own Parliament on College Green. This was a body of considerable distinction. Its short history came to an end with the savage rebellion of 1798, of which the best-known leaders were Protestants. Thereafter the union with Great Britain was carried through by Pitt and Castlereagh, and the old Kingdom of Ireland ceased to be. In retrospect, this act of union, described by Gladstone as having been 'obtained against the sense of every class of the community by wholesale bribery and unblushing intimidation'[3], seems a major error.

There was a chasm between the poverty of the native Irish and the wealth of the ascendancy which produced continuous tension. Disraeli, by far the most perceptive Conservative, realized this and in the House of Commons in 1844 asked what was the Irish question:

> One says that it is a physical question; another a spiritual. Now it is the absence of the aristocracy; now the absence of railways. It is the Pope one day and potatoes the next . . . they have a starving population, an alien Church, and in addition the weakest executive in the world. . . . What then is the duty of an English Minister? To effect by his policy those changes which a revolution would effect by force. . . .[4]

He was not listened to.

John Bright, who visited Ireland in 1849, made two revealing entries in his diary:

> August 23. At Skibbereen into the market-place. . . . Saw a young woman having a basket or skip of turf for sale. She asked 1½d. for it. We had it weighed: 62 lbs. – cutting, drying, carrying 8½ miles for 1½d., and a woman standing by said she would take 1d. for it.[5]
>
> August 29. Longfield: bullet-proof windows and doors; yard with high walls; large doors, bullet-proof. Lord Hawarden's agent riding with armed men going before, inside fences, to protect him.[6]

As some saw it, the fundamental difficulty was religious. The future Lord Esher wrote in 1880: 'The Irish question is and has always been a religious question. . . . If the Irish were Mahommedans or Hindus we should have no difficulty with them. . . . We shall do no good in Ireland until we admit there the supremacy of the Catholics.'[7]

It was in deference to this line of thinking that Gladstone had disestablished the Church of Ireland. But there was no sign of any diminution of discontent. And Ulster made it clear that it was invincibly determined to remain part of the union and not to come under the domination of the Catholic majority.

Others held that the trouble was primarily economic and agrarian. As in England, there was agricultural distress, but the Irish people nearly all lived off the land. Their complaints were, fundamentally, the same as those of the Scottish crofters, who also had their Land League advocating non-payment of rents. They had no security of tenure, and there were too many people trying to get a living from stony soil in a wet climate. Their holdings were far too small. The agricultural depression which began in the seventies made it impossible for them to pay their rents in full, and the landlords were under inexorable economic pressure to organize their land into larger units and to go over to stock raising. This led to the miserable cycle of evictions and reprisals, which assumed the dimensions of a land war.

But the mainspring of Irish determination to be rid of the English was a new feeling of nationalism. It was, perhaps, Gladstone's fatal error that for so long he shut his eyes to this, the true nature of the Irish problem, and thought he could solve it by redressing church, land and educational grievances. The tide of nationalism was sweeping over Europe. The Irish, or rather all the Irish except the million Protestants of Ulster, found their leader – the least likely of men, a landowner from County Wicklow with an American mother, a scion of the ascendancy and a Cambridge graduate, Charles Stewart Parnell. Like Isaac Butt, whom he displaced – of whom Mr. Gladstone said that, but for his being a drunkard, a swindler, and devoid of principle, Butt would have been a good fellow[8] – Parnell was a Protestant. He was impassive, autocratic and ruthless; a lone wolf, a 'man of iron', as T. P. O'Connor called him (except where women were concerned), 'with a disregard that amounted to positive contempt for all Englishmen'. He had many drawbacks. O'Connor said he was 'a dreary and a costive speaker' and added: 'It was one of the abiding terrors of those quite close to Parnell in hours of crisis that his brain might also give way and his end might be the same as that of his ancestors. The truth is that Ireland was led – and consummately led – by a madman of genius.'[9]

Asquith said that 'he was not well read even in Irish history'.[10] But he was a born leader of men. Winston Churchill thought him 'the last great leader who could hold all the Irish', and held that 'as a Protestant he was probably the only one who might eventually have conciliated Ulster'.[11]

When the Liberals returned to power in 1880 they faced a serious situation in Ireland. As in England, the harvest in 1879 had been a disaster and the collapse of agriculture threatened landlords and tenants alike, making good relations between them hopeless. There were 10,500 evictions of tenants for non-payment of rent in that year alone and 2,590 recorded 'outrages'. In the same year the boycott movement began. 'Moonlighting' and cattle maiming were widespread. Parnell and other Land League leaders were arrested in November, but released again because a jury could not be persuaded to convict them. There was strong pressure for tough measures, but Harcourt told Gladstone that 'Campbell-Bannerman (a very shrewd and sensible man) took credit to the Government for not having been frightened into resorting to measures beyond the present law'.[12] The Liberal Government finally decided to introduce both coercion and land legislation. In the teeth of Irish obstruction, which in January and February 1881 reduced Parliament to chaos, counter-measures were resorted to and after a non-stop sitting of forty-one and a half hours the Speaker brought the debate to an end, introducing the 'closure' for the first time.

In old age, James Bryce wrote of this:

> It now seems to me to have marked the end of the old, dignified, constitutionally regular, and gentlemanly House of Commons. . . . The stoppage of business by the Irish party had become intolerable. . . . The Closure was inevitable. . . . It has helped to reduce the credit and character of representative government; but representative government could not have continued longer without it. . . .[13]

There were only two practical policies for Ireland – wholehearted conciliation or wholehearted coercion. The natural instinct of most Liberals, and certainly of those who, like C.B., belonged to the central Cobdenite tradition, was to try conciliation. But there were also ministers who thought there was no alternative to coercion. The chief of these was Harcourt who, as Home Secretary, saw the police reports and had the fullest knowledge of the campaign of murder and intimidation conducted from New York by Fenians like O'Donovan Rossa, whom the United States Government did nothing to stop. Harcourt argued that 'all the measures of conciliation which we have passed or proposed have absolutely failed. . . . They have only been regarded as signs of weakness and inspired fresh demands which will never rest short of absolute confiscation of the property of the landlords and a total separation of Ireland from England. . . . I feel very strongly that the time is come when we must put the iron heel of government on the head of these foul conspiracies.'[14]

In October 1881, just after Gladstone had declared that 'the resources of civilization against its enemies are not yet exhausted', Parnell told an audience at Wexford that an Irishman who threw away his arms would have 'placed himself in the power of the perfidious and cruel and relentless British enemy'. The Liberal Government decided that enough was enough and Parnell, Dillon and Sexton were arrested under the Coercion Act and imprisoned in Kilmainham jail. C.B. fully supported this step and told his Scottish constituents, who did not care for the Irish, that the excesses in Ireland were due, 'not to the peasantry, but to some loose, ill-conditioned, untraceable persons'.[15]

The Irish themselves were filled with the joy of battle. A recent historian, Mr. F. S. L. Lyons, has pointed out 'a crucial fact about politics in an unsophisticated country – that colour, movement, emotion and legend have great power over simple men. Each clash with Dublin Castle, each riot, each baton charge, each imprisonment, was celebrated as an incident in an unending crusade'.[16] Ultimately coercion failed in Ireland, as it has failed elsewhere when practised by British governments, and for the same reason. Parnell himself later told Asquith: 'It is a great mistake to suppose that Ireland cannot be governed by Coercion.' Asquith asked if it had not been proved to be an impossibility. 'Perhaps it has,' Parnell replied, 'but that is because, under your English party system, neither party can be trusted to make the policy continuous.'[17]

The Liberal Government did not care for coercion and Parnell did not care for being shut up in Kilmainham jail. There were, therefore, the makings of a deal, and a settlement was negotiated through Chamberlain and Captain O'Shea, Parnell's colleague and the husband of his mistress. Parnell agreed to cooperate with a policy of appeasement and was released on May 2, 1882. The Lord Lieutenant, Lord Cowper, and the Chief Secretary, Forster, resigned and were at once replaced by Lord Spencer and Lord Frederick Cavendish. The latter reached Dublin on May 6, and was stabbed to death that evening with his Permanent Under-Secretary in Phoenix Park.

The reaction in London was one of horror. Parnell said in the House that the crime had been 'committed by men who absolutely detest us' and wrote to Gladstone offering to apply for the Chiltern Hundreds. The post of Chief Secretary was offered to Dilke on May 7, but he refused to accept unless he was given a seat in the Cabinet, declaring that the offer was 'an insult' and that 'it was obvious that I could not consent to become a mere mouthpiece'.[18] Gladstone was shocked at his refusal. The choice then fell on Trevelyan, who held the job for two years. A distinguished and sensitive man, his experience of the Irish almost drove him off his head. The Irish constantly threatened him and even sent word that they intended to mutilate his boys at school.[19] His hair and the eyelashes of one eye turned quite white.

A new coercion bill did little to stop the killings. There were explosions at Westminster Hall, the House of Commons and the Tower. The *United Irishman* in New York called daily for more murders. Spencer even had to face a situation when the whole of the Dublin police force resigned. To the Victorians it was a profound shock to have this mindless anarchy across St. George's Channel. They were, not surprisingly, quite unable to understand its causes.

A new factor in 1884 was the extension of the franchise to the working class in the countryside which brought in the 'mud cabin vote' of the Irish peasants, thereby making it certain that nearly all the Irish seats would be held by the Nationalists.

The man who now rode this whirlwind, the Viceroy of Ireland, was Earl Spencer, one of the last of the great noblemen who had dominated English public life for so long. He was known as 'the Red Earl' from the colour of his great beard, and by his opponents as 'Foxy Jack'. Margot Asquith wrote of him:

> Lord Spencer was . . . prejudiced, insular and simple . . . adored by all the neighbours, farmers, and owners of covers in Northamptonshire, and . . . an unrivalled Master of Foxhounds. His lean lanky figure, loose reins, red beard, keenness and courtesy, made him a notable figure in any company, and though arrogant and authoritative, I never saw him lose his temper. . . . I never saw him open a book. The only time books were mentioned he said to me in a deprecating voice that he had no time to read. 'What with the stables, the kennels, and politics, how can I read – ! but I enjoyed that book "Jane Eyre" – you know . . . by George Eliot.'[20]

On July 11, 1884, Edward Hamilton wrote in his diary: 'Poor Trevelyan got terribly abused last night in the House. He is too sensitive

– his nervous system is too highly strung – for his present place. He can't stand being "bully ragged" by those Irish blackguards. . . . He must, if he is not to break down, be relieved.'[21]

Two months later Spencer wrote to the Prime Minister from Dublin:

> I have slowly come to the conclusion that in the public interest it is most desirable that Trevelyan shd. be relieved.
>
> He did admirably until the worry of Irish affairs in & out of the House of Commons affected his health & nerves . . . his judgement is seriously warped. I feel he has lost his nerve with Irish M.P.s.
>
> He may be bolstered up to appear in the House, but I seriously fear that he may break down there, in the face of the attacks to which the Irish Govt. will be constantly & persistently subjected. . . .
>
> Either S. Lefevre or Campbell-Bannerman could fill the post with success. . . .[22]

The post was offered first to Shaw Lefevre, but he refused, partly because of doubts about the wisdom of coercion. Hamilton noted on October 10: 'The obvious man next to Lefevre for the Irish Secretaryship is C. Bannerman; but those who know him best feel sure he would decline to exchange his present congenial post at the Admiralty for the horribly thankless office of Chief Secretary.'[23]

Harcourt's son Lewis, or 'Loulou' as he was called, noted in his journal on October 8:

> Spencer is willing if necessary that the new Irish Secretary shall be in the Cabinet, but Lord R. Grosvenor said – 'Oh no, it is much better that he should not be in, so that if he gets into a mess with the Irish in the House of Commons, it is much easier to throw him over. . . .'[24]

C.B. had taken Charlotte for a holiday by the sea at Thurston, near Dunbar, when he received a telegram from Spencer asking him to meet him in Edinburgh. At the meeting Spencer offered C.B. the Chief Secretaryship, but C.B., after reflecting for an hour or so, turned it down, confirming his decision in a letter the same day:

> On thinking the matter over quietly and taking as clear a view of it as I can, I am only confirmed in the opinion I expressed to you

that it would not be wise for me to accept. . . . I know the limit of my own capacities, and I should be greatly afraid that I should fail to discharge my duties successfully, and at the same time I confess I should be hampered by want of belief in the system I was called upon to defend. . . .[25]

This was the decision that had been expected.

Spencer replied, expressing regret and adding:

> I flattered myself that you might (notwithstanding your modest diffidence and your want of faith in the system of Irish Government) have consented to try and work with me in Ireland.
>
> But I must not press you more. I will send your letter to Mr. Gladstone, and all I ask of you is this, if after a night's reflection you feel justified in arriving at a different conclusion, pray telegraph at once to Mr. Gladstone at Hawarden and to me at Ballater or Perth some words like 'Ready to meet you' which I will understand and will prepare him for also.[26]

Spencer told the Prime Minister that C.B. 'professed entire ignorance of Irish affairs & said that he had never faced any formidable Parliamentary foes, that he had no confidence that he would succeed etc. etc. I used all the persuasion which I could. . . . I fear however that he will not change his mind. I greatly regret this as I liked extremely his views & manner. . . .'[27]

That night C.B. did change his mind. As always, Charlotte was for the bolder course. Years later C.B. told his own Chief Secretary, Augustine Birrell, what had happened:

> I went home . . . consulted my wife, and having been instructed to telegraph, telegraphed refusal. . . . I then proceeded to write a letter giving my reasons why, and I found a difficulty amounting almost to impossibility to get these excellent reasons into a letter. Then arose my domestic adviser and said 'See you not why you cannot write the letter? – because it is a false letter. Your conscience is always telling you, as you write, that you ought to accept.' After a grand conseil de nuit, therefore, I telegraphed the next morning recanting my refusal. And this little manœuvre remained a mystery to Spencer, and to a greater than he, Mr. G. Thus is a woman ever a man's superior in intuition, and in self-sacrifice.[28]

Mr. Gladstone had not, however, been primed, and telegraphed back: 'Do the words "meet you" mean an affirmative, if so, it is in time, reply forthwith please.'

C.B. had in fact already written to the Prime Minister, saying that he was willing to do his best. His diffidence was in marked contrast to Dilke's refusal of the post on the ground that he would be a 'mere mouthpiece'.

C.B.'s acceptance was just in time, but it was a near thing. Gladstone had jumped at a suggestion by Hamilton that Sir Henry James might be appointed, and on hearing of C.B.'s refusal had instructed Hamilton to waylay James at the station and offer him the place with a seat in the Cabinet. This was countermanded in the evening. James had to be told a false story about why he had suddenly had a peremptory summons. Spencer and Lord Richard Grosvenor, the Chief Whip, tried to get Mr. Gladstone to appoint James after all, but he had already obtained the Queen's approval and told them on the 21st that it was too late to change.[29] Hamilton, although he had been very keen to see James appointed, nevertheless wrote of C.B., 'I believe he will do excellently well.'

So C.B. became Chief Secretary. Replying to Rosebery's congratulations, he wrote, 'I carried, in truth, the line "nolo secretariari" to the extremest point permitted by decency, not to say honour. Having undertaken it, I have got to go through with the business. . . .'[30]

Childers wrote to his son on November 12: 'Trevelyan left the Irish Office simply because his health and strength had broken down, and not in the least as a concession to the Nationalists. His successor – who has nerves of iron – will be much more formidable to them. . . .'[31]

This forecast turned out to be true. Ralph Knox wrote from the War Office:

> As promotion is dear to us all, I congratulate you on your move, but the Paddies still more.
>
> If a good and kind heart, and the commonest of sense can quiet the green isle, you are the man to do it.
>
> Whatever may be the result of your labour there, I feel confident that you will gain the love of all.[32]

C.B.'s appointment was received without enthusiasm by the Irish. Speaking in Glasgow in December, Tim Healy said:

How would Scotsmen like to be ruled by an Irishman sent over
from the sister island – an Irishman, it might be, whom you greatly
admired, myself, for instance? . . . yet I venture to say that I have as
much knowledge of Scotland as Mr. Campbell-Bannerman has of
Ireland. . . . Mr. Campbell-Bannerman is one of those who have
the insufferable egotism for the sake of a couple of thousands a year
to go over and pretend to rule five millions of people, not
one of whom they saw before, on whose shores they have
never landed, and of whose history and feelings they are entirely
ignorant.[33]

The appointment, though some friends referred to it as a bed of
nettles, was in fact a turning point in C.B.'s life. Asquith wrote:
'Events showed that C.-B. was right to take the chance; he became
during those months for the first time a distinctive figure in the
House of Commons; and his keen humour and imperturbable
temper made him an invaluable asset to his colleagues and his
Chief.'[34]

He was still very little known. One day he met two members in the
House who were discussing the new Chief Secretary. 'At all events,'
said one of them, the proprietor of the Dublin *Freeman's Journal*, 'everybody seems agreed that he is a sufficiently dull man.' C.B. was delighted,
while the Irishman was much embarrassed.[35]

A writer in the *Spectator* later wrote of C.B. that, when he became
Irish Secretary, he

at once showed that he knew how to hold his tongue and keep his
temper. The Irish Member who declared that the Minister responsible for this country ought to have 'the heart of an iceberg and the
hide of a rhinoceros' might have almost found his ideal in Mr.
Campbell-Bannerman. No taunts worried or annoyed him. If he
was asked absurd and insulting questions, he did not, like poor Sir
George Trevelyan, flame up about his being 'an English gentleman'.
He sat doggedly on, and treated the Irish Party like one of the mists
of his native land – a tiresome phenomenon, but not one to be overcome by indignation or denunciation. He took the abuse like the
attendance at the office, the journeys to Dublin, and the other disagreeable incidents connected with the post – that is, as things to be
endured with the minimum of fuss. Mr. Campbell-Bannerman, in
a word, lay as low and kept as 'snug' as possible.[36]

One Irish Nationalist member, T. P. O'Connor, who, in 1881, had declared that 'the deadliest foe to Ireland is a Liberal Minister', wrote:

> The Irishmen found that they had met with a very tough antagonist in the new man. When they were confronting Mr. Forster, they could make even that rough and rude giant writhe. . . . Mr. Trevelyan's face would shrivel up almost with visible pain . . . and it was expected that Campbell-Bannerman, much less known, with a much smaller reputation, would prove a far easier prey. But the real Campbell-Bannerman was unknown to the Irishmen and to the House generally. Up to this time people had thought of him simply as one of the industrious, painstaking, eminently respectable, and eminently dull officials who are chosen by every Government for the smaller places in the official hierarchy. It was expected that he would meet Irish wit with dull, unimaginative answers, and that he would be, so to speak, roasted alive. What turned out to be the fact was that Campbell-Bannerman had wit as ready as that of any of his opponents, that he had immense force of character; above all, that he had unfathomable, unreachable depths of imperturbability. It might have been self-confidence, it was probably indifference; but there was no human being who seemed so absolutely impervious to attack. . . . There was nothing to be done with a Chief Secretary like this. He laughed at vituperation; he was jaunty under a cyclone of attack.[37]

The same story was to be repeated just over twenty years later when C.B. became Prime Minister. Then again most people expected him to be a plodder, lacking sparkle, panache and imagination, and once again people were astonished that he was, when it came to the point, an exceedingly good performer, in full command, and with his own brand of wit and urbanity.

C.B. wrote from the Irish Office to his new chief on November 2:

> Dear Lord Spencer,
>   I think my best way is always to write frankly and without reserve or timidity my opinions on things as they come up. But I wish you to understand that I have no false pride or dignity in the matter and that I of course expect you to set aside or correct or overrule with the greatest freedom. I am not dogmatic by nature,

although I sometimes fear I write in a dogmatic tone, and I hope
I am always ready and ever glad to be convinced.

Yours very truly

H. Campbell-Bannerman.[38]

Spencer reassured C.B. about his 'dogmatic' opinions – C.B. had
sent him a long and carefully argued note about salmon fisheries – and
there was thereafter a perfect understanding between them.

C.B. went to Dublin in November and was sworn of the Privy Council.
Both he and Charlotte, being severely practical people, were concerned
about the drains at the Chief Secretary's Lodge and far more anxious
about this than about the risk of assassination. They discovered that the
well which supplied the water was only three yards from the cesspool.
They were not prepared to establish themselves in Dublin until this was
checked. 'Tainted water', C.B. wrote severely to the Viceroy, 'is bad
even for horses.'[39] However, it was put right, and after he had come
back briefly to face the embattled Irish Nationalists in Parliament, the
Campbell-Bannermans went over to Dublin in January 1885, travelling
in a special train from Kingstown. Writing to Wolseley on January 10
from the Chief Secretary's Lodge in Phoenix Park, C.B. said:

> I am not conscious of any special qualifications for the task, un-
> less it may be these – a light heart & a thick skin. If the one carries
> me through the course of legislative difficulties & failures which are
> inevitable, while the other escapes being penetrated by the fiery
> darts of the Evil one (i.e. Mr. Biggar & Co.) I shall do well. One
> consolation I have; that while nothing that can be said or done will
> conciliate ces messieurs, anyone who has to confront them has the
> goodwill & sympathy of all England & Scotland.[40]

Things were still far from safe in Dublin, and Charlotte recorded
that when Henry stayed until seven in the evening talking to Spencer
at Vice Regal Lodge he was 'well scolded by every one for being out so
late even with his protectors', and that, when they went into Dublin
to dine with the Lord Chancellor, 'we were accompanied by two cars
going there were 3 police on each and returning 4 on each car. A pleasant way of dining out.' Charlotte had to be formally presented at a
'drawing room' and noted that 'there were some very good looking
people at it, Lady Kildare, Lady Ormonde, Lady Kilmaine were among

80

the beauties'.[41] Henry was taking stock, and wrote to Gladstone on the 23rd saying: 'I think most of us here agree . . . that any Bill dealing with Crime should be accompanied by some important remedial measure.'[42]

In those days the Viceroy was still provided with a mounted escort. One of the officers in charge of this was a young captain of the 5th Royal Irish Lancers, Jack Sinclair, just back from the fighting round Suakin in East Africa, where he had taken part in the last cavalry charge in which lance pennants were used. What Sinclair saw in Ireland made him a Liberal, and soon after he abandoned the Army for politics. He saw a good deal of C.B. in Ireland and was to be much with him in later days, becoming first his Parliamentary private secretary at the War Office; then his Scottish Whip; from 1895 to 1905 his chief political assistant; then his Secretary of State for Scotland in the Cabinet of 1905; and finally his literary executor.

C.B. kept a close eye on the actions of the Irish administration which he had to defend in the House. He warned Spencer in November that he would have trouble over a man who 'was in the end tried merely for being a Fenian',[43] and the same month said: 'With regard to jury-packing . . . I think the House generally wd. wish that extraordinary care shd. be taken against the wholesale "setting aside" of catholics, such as is alleged of many cases, & undoubtedly has happened in some.'[44]

He struck in the House his own note of relaxed, genial indolence mingled with shrewdness and irony. When there was an artificial fuss by the Irish Members about the timing of a speech he had to make introducing a measure, he remarked:

> No one can dislike making a speech more than I do on any occasion; but . . . it is the practice on a question of first-class import-ance always to make a statement upon its introduction. I have no desire to make such a statement for my own satisfaction; and I can say that if on Tuesday the Bill comes on so late that it would be unreasonable to detain the House with a speech, I will be glad to introduce the Bill without a speech at all, and to leave the Bill to the acumen of Hon. Members opposite. . . .[45]

A government spokesman could scarcely be more accommodating.

He told Spencer in November, 'Generally I am pretty confident in my own estimate of the feeling of the House *in a matter with which I am familiar or in regard to which I have watched events.'*[46] He had been sixteen years in the House and had a good idea of what it would, and what it would not, take.

The Parliamentary work of the Chief Secretary was heavy. He had to answer streams of questions from the Irish Members on crimes and outrages, proclamations, prohibitions of meetings, prisons and riots – and on such matters as the Land Commission, insufficient accommodation in lunatic asylums, inflammatory language, the alleged misconduct of emergency men, festivities at Dublin Castle during the lying-in-state of Cardinal M'Cabe, and the opening of a Freemasons' Lodge at Bantry. Pressed by Parnell on Orange addresses to the Prince of Wales in Londonderry, he began cheerfully: 'I am neither an Orangeman nor an Apprentice Boy'. But he had to confirm, under questioning by Sexton, that in the third quarter of 1884, 489 families, comprising 2,389 persons, had been rendered homeless through evictions.

A Liberal colleague, George Russell, recalled that:

> ... He was not a good speaker; but he invariably mastered the facts of his case. He neither overstated nor understated and he was blessed with a shrewd and sarcastic humour which befitted his comfortable aspect and spoke in his twinkling eyes even when he restrained his tongue.[47]

He had other responsibilities, including, for example, the control of the Secret Service Fund in Ireland and of the Detective Department. His knowledge of the conspiratorial aspect of the Irish Nationalist movement quickly became extensive. Murders and outrages – there was, for example, an explosion at the Admiralty in April – were still being organized from the safety of the United States, but in February O'Donovan Rossa, one of the chief culprits, was shot and wounded by a young Englishwoman, Mrs. Iseult Dudley, in the street in New York City. C.B. himself had several letters from a man called Pigott, asking for money to keep the bailiffs out of his house, and hinting at information he could give. He enquired about Pigott's reputation, and was told by his advisers that he was a scoundrel with whom he should have nothing to do. *The Times* and the Conservative Attorney-General who, two years later, were to try to use Pigott's evidence to discredit Parnell, would have done well to be equally cautious.

C.B. got on well with Spencer, who told him: 'I like extremely your minutes – they are clear, comprehensive and short', and tried to get him a Cabinet key, but failed as Mr. Gladstone did not want to create a precedent.

In December he was back in Scotland. He wrote to Spencer:

> I had nothing to say to my constituents on Friday and I think I effectually said it. I had to make *some* allusion to Ireland, and I thought the most innocuous line to take was . . . that if the Irish were gradually allowed to have things as much their own way as the Scotch, there would be no inconsistency or danger to the Union in it. I found however that my countrymen have no interest in the subject beyond a wish to see the disloyal people put down and kept down. There is no love lost between the two countries![48]

Meanwhile the water was getting rougher in the House of Commons, where Lord Randolph Churchill and Arthur Balfour were now supporting the Irish assaults on the Government.

In those days ministers outside the Cabinet were told little about what went on inside it. C.B. therefore had the not altogether satisfactory experience of defending in the House, against storms of invective, policies he had only a modest voice in framing and about which, as his original letter to Spencer had made clear, he himself harboured doubts. That he was able to discharge the task so successfully indicated that he had become a hardened Parliamentary performer.

He sent Spencer accounts of the Irish debates – for example: 'I am bound to add that the House of Commons sometimes (and generally on a personal question like this) becomes like the herd of swine into which the devils entered, and then no reason prevails',[49] and telling him of Harcourt 'intervening with a forcible speech which doubled the heat of the discussion and increased the waste of time in about the same ratio'.[50]

He was, for Spencer, an ideal representative in the House. When a row broke out over the case of an accused policeman, C.B. wrote: 'You can always depend on me to stand to a decision when I know it is yours.'[51]

But he sometimes found the going difficult, writing, for example, in May: 'The difficulty of giving no grounds for being thought tricky, and yet of giving as little room as possible for the evening's amendments, is extreme.'[52]

A memorandum he addressed to Spencer was circulated to the Cabinet. In it he wrote:

I have a strong conviction that stopping meetings does, in the vast majority of cases, far more harm than good. But I cannot set my opinion against your experience of troublous times, and I can conceive that, without the power of proclaiming meetings in extreme cases, the Executive would feel, and would really be, helpless. . . .[53]

In March he introduced a Bill to extend elementary education in Ireland, pointing out that he had advocated universal compulsory education since 1869. A few days earlier, questioned about the teaching of Irish history in Irish schools, he said that it did 'appear to him somewhat extraordinary that the history of Ireland should be excluded'. This was, he pointed out, due to the enormous difficulty of finding an impartial work on the subject.[54]

Consulted about the post of Lord Chancellor of Ireland, he wrote to Spencer, 'Do not be too sure that Lord Fitzgerald wd. not take it. The very day the late Chancellor's death was announced the Fitzgerald family left cards at my house. Why so suddenly civil?'[55]

He and Spencer were concerned to keep the temperature down between the Nationalists and the Orangemen during the visit of the Prince of Wales in April. C.B. wrote: 'I should have more faith in the closing of the whiskey shops than anything else, even the sending of troops.'[56] Considering the state of the country, the visit went off well. C.B. met the Prince, then forty-three, and Princess Alexandra when they arrived in the royal yacht at Kingstown, and travelled to Dublin with them. Charlotte noted that when the Princess was made a Doctor of Music at the University her academic robes, worn without a bonnet, made her look like a boy and that she 'was evidently greatly entertained at her own appearance'.[57]

There was, however, an incident at Mallow involving Mr. William O'Brien and his supporters which annoyed the Prince. Cork, as feared, produced more demonstrations.

The Prince's private secretary, Francis Knollys, told C.B. that he was appalled by the attacks but that 'Lord Spencer assures me that I should get accustomed in time to these sort of things being said'.[58] At any rate he was able to report that the reception at Belfast had been 'quite excellent' and that at Londonderry 'likewise most enthusiastic'. Here the Chief Secretary's problem was different. He wrote to Spencer saying that he had consulted two authorities about a proposed Orange address to H.R.H. – 'They say', he reported gloomily, 'that we may dismiss any idea that if the Orangemen have set their hearts on an address any power on earth will get them voluntarily to abandon it.'[59] The Prince's safe departure was a profound relief to C.B. The risks had been considerable. The *United Irishman* in New York had printed a letter offering $10,000 for the body of the Prince, dead or alive. The following month Spencer tried and failed, as Gladstone had failed before him, to persuade the Queen to allow the Prince or one of his brothers to become a non-political Viceroy in Ireland.

The next problem was whether to renew the Crimes Act, which expired in August. C.B. took soundings for Spencer on whether the criminal law for the whole of the United Kingdom might be toughened up to the degree required to cope with Ireland. Though he was initially optimistic, believing that 'England will stand a good deal with this object',[60] in the end, not surprisingly, this was found impracticable. In May Gladstone wrote to C.B. asking him to prepare 'the draft of a Bill with a judiciously chosen title, to succeed the Crimes Act (or rather displace it)' and to get out a statement showing the comparative state of agrarian crime and of convictions. C.B., as unflurried as ever, was in Paris on holiday, but the job was done. Indeed two Bills were prepared. He wrote to Spencer in June:

> What we arranged before the holidays was that Harcourt was to submit both Bills to Mr. G. for his choice. Not only was this duty left to Harcourt but it was loudly claimed by him. He has, however, done nothing and denied to me last night that this had ever been suggested. . . . Mr. G. took (to me) exception to the title, 'Trial and Constabulary'. He expressed a particular dislike to the word 'Constabulary'. He also thought the Bill too long. . . .[61]

These arrangements over the Bill and its title might appear semantic but they were important, for things were at breaking point in the Cabinet, and if either the Whigs or the Radicals were pushed too far, there were certain to be resignations.

C.B. was at one with Spencer in recommending a Land Purchase Bill, unpopular though this was with men like Morley on the left. 'I am more and more satisfied', he wrote to Spencer on March 26, 'that whatever is done or left out, we must have a Purchase Bill. I began with a strong prejudice against it (unless in the most limited form) but I think it is quite necessary in the interests of the landlords, and in order to shut the door and end the question.'[62]

Chamberlain now produced his scheme for a 'Central Board' in

Ireland, an effort to solve the Irish problem by a municipal version of Home Rule. On April 30 he circulated a box to Trevelyan, Lefevre and C.B. giving details of it. C.B. minuted:

> I am not sure how far I am invited to give an opinion.
>
> I am personally not afraid of going great lengths – the length of something like a 'Grattan's Parliament'. . . . But this scheme, it appears to me, would put the so-called Irish Government in a position, not only intolerable to itself, but impossible.
>
> The Central Board, elected by the mass of the people, would have a weight, and assume an authority, inconsistent with an independent Executive. The Chairman of the Board and the leading men in it would altogether overshadow the Minister. The situation would be impossible; we must go further and have a separate Irish Ministry, if we go this length.
>
> County Boards are a matter of course; but, although I have no prejudice against a radical change, I cannot see my way to the Central Board. . . .
>
> The Education Bill might well wait for the Establishment of County Boards. I doubt that the Catholic Bishops really wish Education to be controlled by an ordinary representative body of laymen; but if they acquiesced, I should be glad of it. . . .
>
> 30/4/85.[63]

Chamberlain's Central Board was favoured by Gladstone as the next practicable step. But, as Chamberlain's biographer records, 'Spencer, Campbell-Bannerman and the "Castle" threw their whole weight against the limited revolution. That settled it.'[64] On May 9 the Cabinet rejected it, whereupon the Radicals said they would not have the Land Purchase Scheme. The Cabinet was hopelessly divided, with Chamberlain and Dilke wishing to resign.

On March 19 C.B. told Spencer that he had heard that late one night the Conservative Whip, Rowland Winn, had been seen talking furtively to Parnell. A deal was in fact being made between the Conservatives and the Irish Nationalists, which was to result in the Irish switching their support to the Conservatives and defeating the Liberal Government.

On June 8, in a vote on the budget, the combination was made effective in a division, and, with Irish help, the Conservatives beat the Government by 264 to 252.

Lord Randolph Churchill was, for a short time, an uncertain factor, but C.B. advised Spencer on June 17: 'I do not believe for a moment that Randolph will carry his pranks too far. He will not quarrel with his bread & butter so far as to prevent the formation of a Govt.'[65]

This opinion proved to be correct. After seven months, C.B. was a private member once more. But his short tenure of the Irish Office had transformed his reputation. He was now a man of some consequence. With Spencer he had formed a firm friendship which lasted the rest of their lives.

CHAPTER 7

Home Rule and the Liberal Split

'We ought not to presume to legislate for a nation with whose feelings and affections, wants and interests, opinions and prejudices we have no sympathy.'

Charles James Fox

THE crisis about Home Rule came suddenly. Before 1885 no important politician had contemplated a Parliament in Dublin. The Union was regarded as indissoluble. In 1871 Gladstone had himself declared flatly that if Ireland were given Home Rule, Scotland and Wales would be just as much entitled to it, and had added: 'Can any sensible man, can any rational man, suppose that at this time of day, in this condition of the world, we are going to disintegrate the great capital institutions of this country for the purpose of making ourselves ridiculous in the sight of all mankind?'[1]

But in the second half of 1885 Lord Salisbury's government itself began to toy very gingerly with the idea of Home Rule. Lord Randolph Churchill dropped hints. The new Conservative Viceroy, Lord Carnarvon, whom Disraeli used to refer to as 'Twitters', condemned coercion, advocated a generous settlement on Home Rule lines and had a secret meeting with Parnell in an empty house in Hill Street.

C.B. had spent the autumn of 1885 at Marienbad and was returned unopposed at the November election of that year. In his election address he wrote:

I am desirous of seeing at the earliest possible moment a large extension of local self-government in Ireland; but I would give no countenance to the scheme of those who seek to injure this country, as they would assuredly ruin their own, by separation under one name or another.

It was, not unreasonably, argued later by his opponents that this and other passages indicated that he was opposed to Home Rule in the sense in which it was generally understood. Indeed, when, in the House next year, these words were flung in his teeth, he admitted that by that time he had shifted his ground. It is fair to say, however, that Home Rule meant self-government within the Empire and was held to be equivalent to separation only by its opponents. C.B. was certainly doubtful (rightly, as events showed) about the practicability in terms of British politics of re-establishing a parliament in Dublin. He was convinced that the problem could not be settled unless both main parties agreed on the broad lines of a settlement.

Only on December 14, 1885 did the Salisbury government finally reject Lord Carnarvon's plea for a Conservative Home Rule Bill, mainly because Salisbury did not want to repeat the experience of Peel over the Corn Laws. That put paid to Gladstone's unselfish but forlorn hope that Home Rule might be brought in as a Conservative measure and passed with Liberal support, as Catholic Emancipation had been. C.B. had shared that hope. Now there was a new situation. He had an urgent message from his late colleague in Dublin:

16 December 1885

Althorp
Northampton

My dear C.B.

I really must see you before the week after next.

You are the one person I want to talk out the Irish Question with. Any day Mr. Gladstone may write to me or see me, & I am in real anxiety. . . .

I had a very long talk with Goschen yesterday & frightened and horrified him I expect greatly. . . .

Yrs. very truly
Spencer[2]

A week later, two days before Christmas, C.B. made his views public. A report appeared in the *Daily News* of an interview he had given in which he said that the Irish question must be dealt with, and that Mr. Gladstone was bound to face the situation, but that Mr. Gladstone was not likely to draw up detailed legislation without consulting his colleagues, which he had not done. 'In my opinion,' he continued, 'the best plan would be for the leaders of the two political parties to confer together to ascertain whether some modus vivendi could not be arrived at by which the matter could be raised out of the area of party strife.' As matters stood it was for the Conservative Government to take the first step. C.B. said that he sincerely hoped, however, that their proposals would be such as could be accepted by the Liberals.[3]

The Queen's Private Secretary, Henry Ponsonby, wrote ten days later: 'Campbell Bannerman's suggestion that there should be a union of parties to deal with the Irish question always seemed to me the most practical and when I told H.M. of it she agreed.'[4]

But Salisbury's decision had ruled out that possibility.

The Radicals were going their different ways. Chamberlain was operating more and more independently of Gladstone's leadership. Dilke had been cited as a co-respondent by Mr. Donald Crawford on August 5 and was therefore temporarily out of active political life. Gladstone himself had gone to Norway in the autumn, and had finally made up his mind that Home Rule was the only answer to Ireland's problems and that it must be put through, cost what it might. In November the general election produced a House of 335 Liberals, 249 Conservatives and 86 Irish Nationalists – a dead heat as long as the Irish continued to support the Conservatives. On December 17 Gladstone's intentions – an Irish Parliament, wholly responsible for Irish affairs, but combined with the maintenance of the supremacy of the Crown and the Imperial Parliament – became known to the world by way of his son Herbert's disclosure to the press – the 'Hawarden Kite', as it was called – producing, inevitably, a good deal of shock and dismay. Liberals had, very quickly, to decide, each man for himself, whether they would support Gladstone in trying to pass Home Rule or break with him and stand firm for the preservation of the Union.

C.B. spent Christmas at Althorp talking to Spencer, and while he was there he came to grips with the issue. This was a turning point in his political life, as it was in that of many leading Liberals, and the letters he wrote at the time, far longer than his usual brief and businesslike notes, show how he reasoned out his position. The first is one he sent to Spencer from Gennings, his home in Kent, on December 27:

> The two great points on which my doubts fasten are the finality of the scheme and the possibility of carrying it out. . . . I think we ought to have . . . better evidence . . . that it would be accepted as satisfactory and final. Can we depend on the moderates standing

firm? They would have some evil days, between the angry loyalists on one hand and the Fenian extremists on the other. . . .

Then as to practicableness. I do not imagine that public opinion at present would support it, unless both parties agreed.

If there is no agreement, ought the proposal to be mooted . . .? On the whole I think not. If things are left as they are, the Government may struggle on, and opinions would ripen gradually. But with a number of prominent public men giving open support to the proposal of a separate Parliament, it would be impossible to administer Ireland, and people in this country would at once fall into one or other camp on the subject. The question would be compromised and prematurely forced; and we might find ourselves, before we knew how, in a civil war in Ireland.

My hopes rest, therefore, more than ever on some entente between the two parties.

The whole prospect is most perplexing and bewildering, and I do not know that my muddled cogitations are of much value. I confess that I find my opinions moving about like a quicksand.[5]

A few days later he wrote again, saying: 'Surely the Govt. cannot face the world if they leave Ireland as it is, with the "no Government" which prevails. They must say what they propose to do.'[6]

Another letter, sent to Northbrook on Boxing Day, contained an acute and realistic assessment of the chances of a solution:

The prospect . . . is still bewildering, if not appalling. I have seen Lord Spencer . . . I think I am a good deal more timid than he is . . . and our choice is between modest reforms and a separate Parliament with a separate Govt. . . . Now whatever difficulties or dangers may attend a separate Parlt., it does not create the condition of antagonism in administration which I dreaded in the scheme of last summer. It also, in the main, rids the House of Commons of the Irish obstructives. . . . We can hardly expect that improved County Govt. will satisfy the public mind in Ireland. And how is fresh agitation . . . to be met? The Landlords' party having ostentatiously thrown away, last summer, such powers as they had, we cannot expect public opinion here, and especially Liberal public opinion, to support any exceptional legislation of the kind we have been accustomed to rely upon. There is thus no obvious alternative to the grant of a Parliament.

The conditions to the establishment of a separate Parliament are these: _

(1) It must be accepted publicly by Parnell & Co.

(2) We must have reason to believe that it will be final. This is the point on which I have the greatest doubts. . . . Some authorities say it will; but I should fear it will not satisfy the English-hating Americans (for instance), whose money keeps the whole agitation going.

(3) Some security must be taken against the complete spoliation of landowners.

(4) The control of police must of course go over. . . .

(5) We must provide for all our officials. . . .

There remains three questions:

(6) Would this lead to civil war or religious feuds? If so, this would be a strong reason against it. I do not believe it would.

(7) Would it ruin Ireland by driving all capitalists and their money out of the country, and destroying her credit? This I think a more likely evil than my (6).

(8) Will English and Scotch public opinion support the idea? I doubt it. It would if the true facts were known, but they are not, and the decision will be largely governed by sentiment. The proposal certainly could not be carried by our party if the others raised the country against it.

The gist of my opinion, therefore, at present, is:

(a) A separate Parliament is not open to the objections fatal to a National Council.

(b) There is no alternative to it.

(c) Its details can be adjusted.

But:

(d) We must be sure that it will satisfy (or as sure as you can be in politics), and

(e) Public opinion in this island will not support it unless it is put forward by the leaders of both parties. . . .

Possibly these two conditions make the whole proposal incapable of realization at present. . . . I can hardly doubt that some members of the Govt. at least must see that things cannot go on as they are, and that no change but a big change can meet the necessity of the case. I confess that my hope lies in their being able to bring about some joint action between the parties.

My views have thus shifted onwards since I saw you. . . .[7]

C.B. and Trevelyan stayed with Northbrook for a few days and C.B. wrote again to Spencer on January 8, 1886. By this time he had become pessimistic about the success of any Home Rule plan, and said:

> A separate Parlt. will be opposed by the Tories and most Liberals and Radicals. I do not see how this opposition can be easily overcome. It is based rather on English and Imperial than on Irish grounds, and I think, indeed, that those of us who have had to do with Ireland and know the hideous difficulties of its government . . . are naturally disposed to take too light a view of the dangers to the Empire of the alternative to which we deem ourselves driven.

If this was so, he said:

> the scheme of a separate Parliament is impracticable for the moment. And if it is not practicable, it seems to me it ought not to be mooted. It is not as if any of us thought it a good thing in itself, or beneficial either to Ireland or England. On the contrary, if the Irish people would only be quiet and reasonable, they have very few grievances and these would be readily removed, leaving to the country the immense advantage of a close connection with England. We regard Home Rule only as a dangerous and damaging 'pis aller'. What good then can be done by declaring for it; and what effect will be created except to weaken still further the . . . chance (if there is any) of a quieter and less revolutionary solution? It appears to me that we are very much in the position of a beleaguered garrison. Some of us may think that we should do well to come to terms with the enemy, but if the majority are for trying their fortune and resisting, it is not either necessary or right that we should hold out a little white flag on our own account. It would be quite different if we thought that the Parnellites were right in principle; we might be bound in conscience to declare for them. As it is, the country being unwilling to take the step which we may consider in the long run unavoidable, ought we to urge it, when we ourselves dread it, and above all when the attendant safeguards are apparently unattainable?

> Is it possible after all to hope that Mr. Gladstone may appear and produce a scheme of Home Rule, free from all the defects and guarding against all the evils which ordinary people like me see and dread? This would be indeed a triumph and no prejudice would

stand in the way of its being accepted. But it is a task almost more than human.[8]

It was.

Sir Edward Russell of the *Liverpool Post* recorded that about this time C.B. and Mundella were talking in the Lobby of the House of Commons. Mundella said: 'I have come to the conclusion that Home Rule has got to be accepted, and that that and that alone can clear everything up.' C.B. replied: 'Yes, you are just in the position of a man who, in the language of the Salvation Army, has found Jesus. He has been in great perplexity and distress and he feels that everything has been made straight and right by this one thing.' According to Russell, C.B. was astonished when Mundella subsequently said that his friend Campbell-Bannerman declared that he had 'found salvation' long ago. 'Finding salvation' became, in the context of Gladstone's conversion to a belief in the inevitability of Home Rule, one of the less happy Liberal political cant phrases.

The suggestion that light, in the form of a conviction about Home Rule, suddenly dawned independently on the leading Gladstonian Liberals in December 1885, or the early days of January 1886, is clearly absurd. It was Mr. Gladstone who suffered what Sir Philip Magnus has aptly described as one of his 'seismic' conversions. His principal colleagues were faced with a choice, which they took in accordance with their convictions and their view of the right answer to the appalling problem of Ireland.

In many ways Spencer was the key man because of his unique authority and his long experience of the Government of Ireland. Gladstone said that he doubted if he could have taken up Home Rule without Spencer's support. The Prince of Wales wrote to Ponsonby on January 31: 'If Ld Spencer is "talked over", I lose for ever all the high opinion I have ever held of him as a politician & a man of honour.'[9] But Spencer had made up his mind and did not need to be 'talked over'. A continuation of coercion was impossible. The only alternative was Home Rule.

On January 21, 1886, the Queen's speech, written by Salisbury, said that she was 'resolutely opposed to any disturbance' of the legislative union with Ireland. On January 26, Hicks Beach – 'Black Michael' – announced a new Coercion Bill. The Irish went over again to the Liberals and the Salisbury Government was defeated.

Gladstone, at seventy-six, became Prime Minister for the third time and made his confidant John Morley Chief Secretary. But the Liberal Party split apart on the rock of Ireland. Hartington, Goschen and Henry James had voted for the Conservatives on the need for coercion and seventy-six others, including John Bright, abstained. None of them would now join Gladstone. Those who took this line included Derby, Northbrook, Selborne and the Duke of Argyll. One result, which was to be of great importance in the early nineteen hundreds, was that the House of Lords became overwhelmingly anti-Liberal. Another was that the long domination of the Whigs – the patrician wing of the Liberal Party – came to an end. As Morley wrote in his life of Gladstone: 'With a small number of distinguished individual exceptions, it marked the withdrawal from the Liberal Party of the Aristocratic element.' Joseph Chamberlain wavered. At first he joined the Government, but Gladstone gave him only the Local Government Board, which wounded his vanity, and he was unhappy about both the Home Rule Bill and the Land Purchase Bill. He and Trevelyan resigned on March 26. C.B. himself reached the Cabinet for the first time as Secretary of State for War but Mr. Gladstone still did not place much reliance in him and, despite his recent experience as Chief Secretary, he was not included in the Cabinet Committee which drafted the Home Rule Bill.

Gladstone introduced the Government of Ireland Bill on April 8 and the Land Purchase Bill on the 16th. He fought for both like a tiger, but he must have known that the cause was almost hopeless. The Home Rule Bill had moreover the serious defect that it made no special provision for Ulster. Reginald Brett had noted in his journal on May 20:

> Since the introduction of Mr. Gladstone's Home Rule Bill the storm has raged. Many private friends have gone down into the deep. With a rump of his old following the 'Grand Old Man' has held his own . . . all the argument, all the authority, all the social influence are against Mr. Gladstone. This only drives him to fight the harder; and among the despondent hosts, he, with his 76 years of conflict behind him, alone is full of confidence and indomitable pluck.[10]

C.B. made a major speech on the second night's debate on the second reading, on May 13. It was generally expected that he might be going to announce concessions to the dissentient Liberals.[11] There had been much argument about whether, under Home Rule, Irish Members would, or would not, sit at Westminster. The Bill excluded them. C.B. was put up to say that, under the principle of no taxation without representation, when any move was made to create or increase a tax, 'the Irish Members shall be summoned and restored to their full position in this House'. This was hardly a concession likely to make much impression and it was, in fact, received with derisive jeers by the Opposition. But C.B. took the opportunity to set out his views on the central dilemma of Home Rule.

He spoke immediately after a searching criticism of the Bill by Sir Henry James, who had been Attorney-General in the previous Liberal government, and began:

> I am but an uninstructed layman and unqualified therefore to analyse the elaborate constitutional argument to which we have listened. But there were one or two things in the course of his speech which were, at any rate, within the scope of my comprehension. . . .

After this characteristically modest opening, he set out to develop his argument, saying that the Government's decision to propose the creation of a statutory Parliament in Ireland, with full control of Irish affairs, was 'the gravest and most startling event, in the political life of any man among us'. *The Times* commented next day: 'This is candid, at all events.'

He pointed out that the position had been changed because the Conservatives, during their brief tenure of power, had renounced any intention of renewing the Crimes Act, while doing nothing to satisfy Irish aspirations: 'They allowed things to drift until at last our rule in Ireland, which had been disliked, came to be despised as well. . . .' The Conservatives had 'by their conduct really made it well-nigh impossible, even if it were desirable, at any time to re-enter upon a course of coercion.' Moreover the general election had demonstrated 'the growing spirit of hostility to our rule in Ireland'.

He went on:

> No strengthening of legal powers, no exercise of law, whether exceptional or ordinary, can operate in check of a growing national feeling such as this . . . the object it has in view – which is the self-government of Ireland – is one which is in conformity with equity, reason, and common sense . . . we are called upon to go a step fur-

ther, and . . . we ought to try whether by yielding to the wishes of the Irish people we may not take the shortest way to bring quick and good government to that country.

The only solution was to 'give the Irish people, in one form or another, the self-government they desire'.

There, in quiet and sober words, spoke the man who was, twenty years later, to give self-government to Botha and Smuts in South Africa. He believed that it was wise to be generous and that you made a friend by giving a man, or a nation, your trust.

He admitted that his own views had not been consistent:

> I am not ashamed to confess that my opinion on the subject has fluctuated. I would go further, and say that I have nothing but surprise, verging on pity, for any man tolerably well informed on the difficulties of Irish Government who was ready comfortably to settle himself down at once to a conclusion on this matter without having gone through many changes and modifications of opinion . . .

Referring to fears that the Roman Catholic majority would oppress the Protestant minority, he said: 'I do not believe it. I refuse to believe that Ireland is to be the one exception to all the free nations of Europe in which minorities of one religion enjoy perfect toleration. . . .'[12]

On the benches behind him Sir Alfred Pease noted in his diary: 'Sir Henry James continued the Second Reading debate . . . a marvellous example of arduous and intricate research for excuses for his opposition . . . Campbell-Bannerman followed with a sensible speech – he is no orator – a jolly, lazy, sort of man with a good dose of sense.'[13]

The Times thought that C.B.'s 'attempts to impart perspicuity to the dark sayings of the Prime Minister's speech were not brilliantly successful'.[14] Sir Richard Temple, a political opponent, thought his speech was 'vigorous in parts' but 'halting on the whole' and complained that 'it did not show nearly as much intellectual culture as many of the speeches made on his side'.[15] It was perhaps deficient in intellectual fireworks, but it was an honest speech and a wise one.

Two days later Lord Salisbury, whose views on Ireland were plain, declared: 'You would not confide free representative institutions to Hottentots.' He put forward his alternative – 'government that does not flinch, that does not vary, for twenty years'[16] – something that the vagaries of British parliamentary democracy rendered a vain hope.

In the House the debate continued. On the 17th a member taunted C.B. with what he had said before he 'found salvation'. C.B. rose to protest. He admitted that the quotation was accurate, spurning the politician's usual refuge of saying that he had been misquoted, but said, rather lamely, that it was 'stronger than he would now like to endorse', a remark that aroused laughter in the House, and that it was 'an indiscreet expression', out of harmony with the 'gist and tone' of the rest of his speech. C.B. was never at his best in defending himself from attack in the House. Cross said that at all events the passage appeared to express the opinion of the right honourable gentleman at a time when his views had not been 'corrupted and warped by the pressure of some of his colleagues'. This was a legitimate debating point, but it did not represent the truth.

The split among Liberals ran right through the country. In his constituency C.B. found that people in Culross were 'rather strong against a separate Parlt.' And his own agent in Dunfermline, John Ross, asked to resign because of his opposition to Home Rule. C.B., however, persuaded him to stay on,[17] and wrote to him on April 28, saying:

> I have passed myself through all the stages of hope & fear, doubt, misgiving, confidence, dismay, abhorrence – & I do not know what more . . . it took me from June to Christmas . . . to reach solid ground. . . . Since that time, I cannot say that I have had any doubt upon the main question. . . . I have no reason to be surprised that people are at first alarmed, bewildered, or repelled by our proposals. But I hope they will not act upon early impressions. . . .[18]

He had hopes, which were to prove vain, that some of the dissenting Liberals might return to the fold. On May 19 he wrote to his friend Provost Yellowlees in Stirling: 'I may also say (confidentially) that Chamberlain himself is showing great signs of anxiety to get back under the umbrella.'[19]

In fact, Chamberlain's opposition to the Home Rule Bill was powerful and effective. Feelings ran high in London. But the end was inevitable, and the defeat of the Bill, by thirty votes, came on June 8. Ninety-three Liberals voted with the Conservatives against it. Thereafter they were known as Liberal Unionists.

C.B.'s support for the Bill was given in the hope that it might produce a final settlement. As he said in a letter to Sir Henry James: 'It was an indispensable condition that we should be reasonably certain that if we gave self government it wd. settle the question and put an end to agitation.'[20]

The effort failed, and instead the Liberal Party was broken into two, and left struggling for many years.

At the general election which followed they were heavily defeated. The majority of 30 against Gladstone on the division was turned into one of 113. In Scotland his supporters were reduced from 61 to 42. C.B. himself was re-elected with a majority of just under a thousand against a Liberal Unionist. When he came out for Home Rule the faith of some of his constituents in him was shaken. He was accused of changing his opinions to obtain office. The local Liberal Party was shattered. But his hold on the voters was too secure to be broken.

On leaving the War Office he received a friendly letter from Wolseley in which, however, Wolseley expressed his Unionist views and was critical of Gladstone. C.B.'s reply, sent from 6 Grosvenor Place on August 1, 1886, reveals a good deal both about his own attitude and about Gladstone as seen by a close but detached observer. He wrote:

165050

... I am distressed by the rest of your letter. Surely you do not take for gospel all the rubbish that does duty on platforms about the disintegration of the Empire & so forth. That is meant only for the groundlings. No one surely believes that to give the Irish the management of their own affairs will break up the Empire – if so, what a rotten state that venerable structure must be in!

And then as to Mr. Gladstone. I have never been a toady and worshipper of his. I never had much to do with him, or much opportunity of intimately observing him, till the last two years. But I am bound to say that the nearer I have come to him, & the more behind-the-scenes I have got, the higher has been my respect & admiration for him. As to this latest effort on his part – so far from it serving his vanity and self-interest, he knew and feared from the first that the chances were enormously against success, that he risked power and position & party strength in advocating his new Irish policy; but he believed it to be the right policy and worth the risk, and he believes this still.

I know that you will believe that I am honest in this opinion of him, and that I have not been without opportunities of judging. He has, no doubt, been very kind to me; but I have never gone out of my way to please him or to draw his approval. I am quite independent of him. But I confess I am grieved to hear the imputations

99

that are made not only upon his wisdom, but on his integrity and purity of motive, and I cannot fail to protest against them whenever I have a chance.

All this will pass over. Before many years are past, when the Kingdom is really United, when Ireland is contented & peaceful, and the fruits of the policy he has first advocated are being reaped, you will be one of those who will crown his bust (metaphorically) with wreaths of gratitude. Of this I have no doubt, and the prospect takes the sting away from much that is said now. . . .[21]

C.B.'s hopes were vain.

CHAPTER 8

Ireland: The Last Twenty Years

C.B. was fifty in 1886. The traumatic events of this year had a profound effect on his own prospects as well as on the future of the Liberal Party itself. 'Except for the three years between 1892 and 1895,' Asquith later wrote, 'when a Liberal Government lived almost from day to day on a composite and precarious majority, it may be said that the Irish controversy kept the Liberal Party out of power for the best part of twenty years.'[1] That twenty years was to take them well into the twentieth century, and when the party did finally come back in triumph, with C.B. at its head, he himself was nearly seventy, with a dying wife and an ailing heart. It may be convenient to consider at this point C.B.'s association with Ireland in the last twenty years of his life.

The situation after 1886 was an uncomfortable one, for both the Gladstonian Liberals, like C.B., and the Liberal Unionists, now their mortal foes, sat side by side on the same benches, and when speaking used the Parliamentary forms for colleagues of the same party, so that Chamberlain would refer to Gladstone as 'My Rt. Hon. Friend', while speaking in terms of bitter reproach. From this time on the ex-radical Chamberlain became an ever stronger force on the anti-Liberal side, and in the nineties it was he who dominated the Unionist Party. But at heart he was never a Tory. As Margot Asquith observed: 'It seems strange to me that the leaders of the great Conservative party have so often been hired bravos or wandering minstrels with whom it can share no common conviction.'[2]

C.B. kept in close touch with Gladstone, who corresponded with him in December about what might be done now that there was a 'deplorable change in the state of Ireland since the cup of hope was dashed away from the lips of the people'.[3] He took no direct part in the round table conference of 1887, the abortive effort to heal the split in the party, but Chamberlain complained to Harcourt in February about 'the speeches of such men as Stansfield, Campbell-Bannerman and Sir C. Russell', saying that 'the tone of these speeches is disagreeable in the highest degree'.[4]

C.B. was absurdly euphoric about the political outlook, writing on July 29, 1887: '. . . Things are going first rate all over. You never knew people in such a pitiable, disheartened, humiliated plight as the Govt. & their followers. They have lost belief in themselves, and are going fast down the hill. . . .'[5]

The Irish leaders recognized what the Liberal Home Rulers had tried to do. John Dillon said in Dublin: 'In spite of all we have suffered from the English democracy in the past, in their present attitude they have established a claim to our friendship and our gratitude.'[6] There are no certainties in retrospect, but if it had been possible to pass Home Rule in 1886, England might perhaps have been able to have the same sort of relations with Parnell and Dillon as she was able to have, later on, with Botha and Smuts as a result of C.B.'s policy of reconciliation.

Meanwhile C.B. took his part in opposing Government measures in the House, and on occasion was formidable and effective. He spoke on the Irish Crimes Bill in 1887 and this time Sir Richard Temple thought his speech much better than that of the previous year, adding: 'My impression is that he has not the fluency and readiness necessary for a real speaker, but that when well-loaded and primed he can go off pretty well as he did on this occasion.'[7]

In July 1887, when Balfour moved the second reading of his Irish Land Bill, C.B. claimed that, after six months, a 'tumult of evictions would burst upon the country'. He told the House what evictions meant: 'Aged men, sickly women, and starving children are turned out on the hill side while their wretched cabins are committed to the flames.' He took full advantage of his recent expert knowledge to deliver a powerful and detailed criticism of the Bill, comparing its stilted language with the real situation:

> . . . you will have the county courts in some of the poorer districts administering the assets of 100 or 1,000 wretched hand-to-mouth men, whose whole assets are a bit of bog land and a few pieces of what by courtesy may be called furniture, perhaps a pig, and two or three hens, and the whole of this complex and cumbrous machinery is to be set up in order to manage such a farm. And

for this a whole host of official persons are to be appointed. Let the House picture to itself a little farm. The Court is to permit the tenant 'to remain in possession of such of his property' – his pig and his poultry – 'as may be necessary for the profitable working of the holding so long as may appear likely to result in the realization of money available for the payment of his debts or of such a proportion thereof, or composition thereof, as shall appear to the Court just and equitable' . . . I leave it there. A more ridiculous proceeding I never knew. . . . Multiply those cases by thousands and imagine what condition the country will be in. . . .

He claimed that the Government had fulfilled the Scriptural maxim, 'From him who hath not shall be taken that which he seemeth to have'.[8]

The Dublin *Freeman's Journal* praised him for putting the case for the Irish leaseholders in the House 'with so much earnestness and power'.[9] Even *The Times* was impressed, admitting that 'Mr. CAMPBELL-BANNERMAN's vigorous description of the working of the elaborate machinery of the Court in relation to a small Irish holding was hardly overdone', that C.B.'s case had been, 'we must say, very forcibly argued', and that he had drawn a lively picture of the inconvenience and absurdities of the Bill.[10]

After the failure of Gladstone's Home Rule Bill, the Irish question would not go away, but continued to haunt British politics.

C.B. viewed with astonishment the antics of *The Times* in using forged letters in an attempt to discredit Parnell in 1889. 'Everyone is a-gape', he wrote to his cousin, 'to find that all the Times have to rest on is the word of Pigott, who was a notorious man even when I was in Dublin. . . . How the Times and the Attorney General can have trusted such a man is inconceivable.' He thought that the affair would be bound to damage the Government – 'they are so mixed up through Webster and W. H. Smith (that respectable old impostor) with Walter and the Times.'[11]

Salisbury, who led the Conservatives, wrote to Carnarvon in March 1890: 'Rightly or wrongly, I have not the slightest desire to satisfy the national aspirations of Ireland.'[12] But Gladstone never lost hope. He talked to Parnell at Hawarden in January 1890, and C.B. was among the colleagues who saw and initialled the record of those talks. Some other Liberals of good judgement were optimistic. Asquith, for example, wrote of 1890: 'The stars seemed at last to be fighting in their courses for Home Rule . . . the political prophets predicted a substantial Home Rule majority in Great Britain.'[13] But on November 17 these expectations were shattered. On that day Captain O'Shea obtained a decree of divorce against his wife, citing Parnell as co-respondent. Six years before, in October 1884, C.B. had been sent by Dilke a letter he had had from O'Shea in which he said: 'I am for certain reasons rather more dangerous to attack than any other Irish member. . . .'[14]

Now O'Shea had exploded his mine. Parnell offered no defence and the evidence, which was not contested, made him appear treacherous, dishonest and untruthful. There had been plans for a meeting at Dalmeny that month between Rosebery, Gladstone, Parnell, Harcourt and C.B. These had to be abandoned. Gladstone himself had warned Parnell the year before:

> The back-bone of the Liberal party lies in the Nonconformists of England and Wales, and the Presbyterians of Scotland. These men have a higher level and a stiffer rule of action than the Tory party. As my own standing ground is not wholly theirs, I say this with some approach to impartiality. They have strong Protestant prejudices. . . .[15]

C.B. was clear about his Scottish constituents' views and wrote to Harcourt from Belmont three days after the verdict:

> To the best of my observation and information, the feeling among our own people in Scotland is very strong against Parnell remaining as the recognized head of his Party. There is here a strong undercurrent of distrust of the Irish character, and this recent exposure strengthens it. . . . Whether they are right or wrong, my belief is the Scotch will not tolerate Parnell in his position of quasi-partnership with the Liberal leaders. . . .[16]

Gladstone's immediate reaction was the same. He wrote to Acton on November 17: 'The Parnell business is terrible. It seems that he is to go on. . . . There comes back upon my mind the saying of the old Aberdeenshire peasant "It'll na dae" . . .'[17]

The Irish members, ignorant of the depth of English and Scottish feeling on an issue of this sort, re-elected Parnell on the 25th as their leader for the session. There was consternation among Liberal members. Gladstone at once published the letter he had given to Morley to show to Parnell, saying that 'his continuance at the present moment in the leadership . . . would render my retention of the leadership of the Liberal party, based as it has been mainly upon the prosecution of the Irish cause, almost a nullity.'

There followed the famous meetings of the Irish party in Committee Room 15, Parnell's furious struggle to retain his position, and the split between the majority of the Irish members and the Parnellites. Harcourt told Gladstone that opinion was

absolutely unanimous and extremely strong that if Parnell is allowed to remain as the leader of the Irish Party all further co-operation between them and the English Liberals must be at an end. You know that the Nonconformists are the backbone of our Party, and their judgement on this matter is unhesitating and decisive. . . . I have a letter from Campbell-Bannerman who takes the same view as to Scotland.[18]

A week later Harcourt gave Gladstone some further advice on relations with Parnell. 'It is a very dangerous thing', he wrote, 'to approach an expiring cat.'[19] Gladstone knew, however, what the fall of Parnell meant for his plans to settle the Irish problem. Tim Healy wrote to his wife on December 8: '. . . Gladstone tore his ex-Cabinet asunder on Friday night trying to get them to let him give "assurances" before Parnell was deposed. He almost cried, Campbell-Bannerman says. . . .'[20]

C.B. himself made his own position quite clear. Speaking at Dumfries on December 17 he said that 'Parnell, by his conduct, had made it absolutely necessary that he should disappear from the field of public life'. The Home Rule policy was by no means doomed, although 'Mr. Parnell had shown by his acts that he was unfit to be a leader of a political party'; for what he had done was not only

a breach of the moral law but the exhibition of a shiftiness of character and want of straightforwardness, and an unblushing attempt to employ for the interests of his own personal cause those fires of racial animosity between the peoples of the two islands, which it has been the prayer of the best men in the three countries to assuage and extinguish.

Next day, at Culross, he said that the only solution for Ireland was to allow the Irish people to have the management of their own affairs;

but he warned that if the Irish kept Parnell as their leader, 'a very serious blow would be struck at the Home Rule policy, and the hour of granting Home Rule would be postponed'.[21]

The answer came quickly. At the North Tipperary election the Parnellite candidate was decisively defeated. The Roman Catholic Church had sat on the fence for a while, Archbishop Walsh first declaring that 'in the selection of a political leader it was no part of the duty of a party to consider moral questions'. But a fortnight later the hierarchy came out decisively against Parnell, saying that he had attained 'a scandalous pre-eminence in guilt and shame', and his political doom was sealed. Not long after he died.

In 1892 came the general election. Hamilton had written:

> Unless Mr. G. gets a real swinging majority of 80 to 100, he will never be able to carry Home Rule; and if he gets a majority of only 30 to 40 including the Irish, it would be useless for him to propose a Bill at all: indeed he ought not to attempt even to form a Government.[22]

In fact the results gave the Gladstonian Liberals a majority of only forty, for though they had 81 Irish Nationalists with them, they had 46 Liberal Unionists against them.

Dillon found Gladstone 'much cast down by the election results'. Moreover, the smallness of the Liberal majority made it certain that the power of the House of Lords would be used ruthlessly against another Home Rule Bill. Gladstone told Dillon 'with great sadness that in view of his age and of the way in which the election had turned out he had no longer any hope of being in at the death'.[23] But the indomitable old man was not finished yet. He was eighty-three and had been sixty-one years in Parliament, but he formed his government – with C.B. again as Secretary for War – and proceeded once again to work out a Home Rule Bill. Dillon said after Gladstone's death: 'Above all men I have ever known or read of, in his case the lapse of years seemed to have no influence to narrow his sympathies or to contract his heart. Young men felt old beside him. And to the last no generous cause, no suffering people, appealed to him in vain.'[24] That tribute was as just as it was eloquent.

Gladstone presided over a Cabinet Committee to draft the Bill, with Morley, Spencer, Herschell and Bryce. Harcourt, whose views on Ireland were not very different from Lord Salisbury's, was not asked to be a member, but Loulou noted that his father said that 'he must have some man there who would have some regard to the views of the English people on the question'.[25] Gladstone's Private Secretary, Sir Algernon West, wrote on November 18: 'Saw Harcourt who said it really was necessary that some man of common sense should be on the Home Rule Committee. . . . C. Bannerman, a hard-headed Scotsman, should be on it.'[26]

C.B. was duly put on.

The outlook was dark. Dr. Jowett wrote from Balliol in December to Margot Tennant: 'The Ministry have very little to spare and they are not gaining ground, and the English are beginning to hate the Irish and the priests.'[27]

In Ireland itself the difficulties were more formidable, especially in the north, since Lord Randolph Churchill had played 'the Orange Card' six years before. Wolseley wrote to his Commander-in-Chief, the Duke of Cambridge, from Dublin on April 23, 1893, saying:

> Of this, Sir, I beg of Your Royal Highness to be quite assured, and that is, that Ulster is determined to resist, and will fight *à outrance* if at any future time she be cut off from England and placed at the mercy of a race which her people hate as much as they despise it. . . . The general belief in the North is that our troops, if ordered to fire upon men who will meet them with shouts of 'God Save the Queen', will fire over them.[28]

C.B. underestimated the strength of feeling in the Protestant north. He described the agitation there as 'Ulsteria'.

In 1893 the second Home Rule Bill was introduced. As Secretary for War C.B. was told of the Army's anxieties about their position under Home Rule. Would they be obliged to obey, say, a call from the Mayor of Cork to put down what he considered an unlawful assembly? He recognized that these difficulties were substantial. On the main issue Unionist feeling ran high. Members of the Stock Exchange assembled in three detachments and marched to the Guildhall, where they publicly burnt the Bill to the singing of the National Anthem. Salisbury, who described the Irish members as 'eighty foreigners', said in a speech at Belfast that 'those Irishmen who were commanded by Archbishop Walsh and Mr. Healy represented the enemy with which England had contended for centuries.'[29] C.B. and Lord Randolph Churchill occupied most of one evening in the debate but C.B. said little new. When Lord

Welby suggested beforehand to C.B. that he should take part in the debate, as finance was of the essence, he replied cheerfully: 'Come to me, an old soldier, to take part in a financial debate, why I should not know a Consol in the street, if I met him.'[30] The Bill passed the Commons but was duly killed in the Lords by 419 votes to 41. When the peers came out after the vote at 3 a.m. they were greeted by crowds cheering, singing *Rule Britannia* and letting off fireworks. No one objected to the Lords frustrating the intentions of the Commons. As was said at the time, 'not a dog barked'. Gladstone's colleagues would not let him go to the country and the Irish Party broke off their alliance with the Liberals.

In 1894, when Rosebery, in his first speech as Prime Minister, caused a storm by describing England in relation to Ireland as 'the predominant partner', he asked C.B., in some perplexity, why this remark had stirred up such a shemozzle. He pointed out that it was, after all, true. C.B. used to enjoy telling this story afterwards. It showed, he said, how little political and parliamentary education Rosebery had had if he thought it a sufficient defence of any public utterance that it was true.

For some years thereafter Home Rule was a dormant issue. Not until February 16, 1899, ten days after C.B. had been elected to the leadership of the Liberal Party, did John Redmond, by then leader of the Irish, move an amendment to the Address in favour of the 'legislative independence' of Ireland. C.B. declared that, though the Liberal Party remained the only party attached to the principle of Irish self-government, they claimed the right to say when and how they should apply that principle. They were, he said, practical men, and refused to give a promise that Home Rule should be the first subject with which they would deal on their return to power. He went on to say that any Irish Parliament must be 'subordinate and not an independent body', and added that there was no formal alliance between the Liberals and the Irish Party, but that the 'alliance, in the sense of sympathy and the desire to co-operate, was as strong as ever it was'.[31] This cautious line was approved by the great majority of English and Scottish Liberals.

At the National Liberal Federation in March 1899, C.B. 'astonished his hearers by the warmth of his defence of Home Rule, asking how they could abandon this Irish policy so long as they called themselves Liberals', and adding: 'We will remain true to the Irish people as long as the Irish people are true to themselves. Twice we have essayed to embody this policy in a statute, and twice we have been foiled.' But he was careful to add again that he would not make it the first item of any Liberal programme. 'I repudiate the necessity, the expediency, aye, and the possibility, of any such promise. Putting aside the question of wise or unwise, I declare it to be impossible.'[32]

When the South African war broke out the uninhibited support of the Irish for the Boers alienated large sections of the Liberal Party, and of the public in England and Scotland. When, for example, Brodrick, as Secretary for War, announced the capture by the Boers of Lord Methuen, with his guns and baggage, the Irish members, it was observed, 'burst into hilarious cheering, Mr. Swift MacNeil, like the hills known to the Psalmist, clapping his hands for joy'.[33] They were not forgiven.

It was only after the turn of the century that Rosebery made a determined effort to get the party to abandon Home Rule altogether. This was the significance of his demand at Chesterfield in December 1901 that the party should 'clean the slate'. He told C.B. at that time that he was opposed to Home Rule in any form. The demand to drop Home Rule was steadily resisted by C.B. He, Spencer and Morley remained faithful to the old policy, but, unlike Morley, he realized that to proclaim it too loudly and to propose an early third Home Rule Bill would provide the Conservatives with exactly the issue on which they could reunite their party, split after 1903 by Chamberlain's advocacy of protection. In 1905 he persuaded the other Liberal leaders to agree to his 1899 formula – a continued commitment to Home Rule but a gradualist approach – the 'step by step' policy he set out at Stirling on November 23, 1905. Redmond, too, was persuaded to accept this.

It has been argued that this was a surrender to Grey and Asquith and excluded Home Rule from the benefits of the 1906 Liberal victory.[34] But this involves making the very questionable assumption that the House of Lords could have been overwhelmed. In fact, the compromise was politically realistic, given the known attitudes of the House of Lords and the British public. C.B.'s line was fully supported by the cool judgement of Lord Crewe, who argued that the party should stand by Home Rule as the ultimate objective but that for the time being it was supremely important to get the largest possible majority for Free Trade.[35] It was Rosebery's repudiation of the step-by-step policy in his speech at Bodmin on November 25, 1905, which marked the final breach between him and his disciples.

The problem had been to reconcile the party's commitment to the Gladstonian policy, and belief in it as the ultimate solution, with the continued reluctance of the English electorate to see the Union disrupted and an unfriendly self-governing Ireland set up on their doorstep. Many Liberals had become convinced, after the long years of opposition, that in electoral terms Home Rule was a major stumbling-block.

C.B. held that Home Rule could not be abandoned simply because it was politically inconvenient. It was based on principles – belief in the virtues and efficacy of self-government, appreciation of national sentiment and recognition of the overwhelming demand of the Irish people in election after election. This demand could only be met by the creation of a local Parliament, even though this might not, for the present, be within the realm of practical politics. Spencer, too, said that if the Liberal Party were to give up Home Rule he would not belong to it.

The Liberal Imperialists, and in particular Asquith in 1901 and Haldane right down to the end of 1905, urged that the party should commit itself in advance to refuse office unless given an independent majority free of Irish support. C.B. refused to give any such commitment and wrote to Herbert Gladstone as late as November 1905:

> I wish Mr. Haldane would not go on shouting that we must have a clear majority without the Irish. It may be true, but it is not conducive to effort in our favour on the part of the Irish; if I were one of them I should gravely resent it. This friend of ours – such a wonderful intriguer and diplomatist we are told – has no more tact than a hippopotamus.[36]

In October 1905 Morley demanded that the party should put Home Rule in the forefront of their programme. Asquith told Herbert Gladstone that if this received any countenance from C.B. it would do 'incalculable and perhaps fatal mischief'. A majority in the next House of Commons could only, he thought, be secured if it was clear that a Liberal government would *not* introduce a Home Rule Bill in the next Parliament. Such a bill 'will be at once chucked out by the H. of L., and will wreck the fortunes of the party for another twenty years'.[37] C.B. was for a middle course. He wrote to Herbert Gladstone, saying:

> It was surely unnecessary (and may be inconvenient) to declare absolutely that nothing in the way of home rule shall be attempted in the whole course of the next parliament. That there would be

time or opportunity for anything like a full-blown home rule bill is utterly unlikely: but we do not know how circs. may change. . . .

There may be some . . . hostile feeling about H.R. in some so-called liberal quarters where we may look for votes . . . but this would be a mere fleabite compared to the loss of belief in our sincerity on the part of the mass of real liberals.

We have come through it before, by being straight and discreet and we can do it again. But we must let this little breeze . . . blow over.[38]

Not for nothing did C.B. have thirty-seven years of political experience behind him.

The Irish leaders still did not know at first hand where C.B. himself stood. As usual he went for the autumn of 1905 to the continent, spending the second half of August and all September at Marienbad. On October 30 T. P. O'Connor wrote to Redmond: 'C.B. is not in London; I believe he is not even in England yet; the last heard of him was from Vienna. But he must come home very soon now; and the moment he does I will put you in communication with him.'

C.B. got back from his travels on November 12. As soon as he was back the Irish leaders made contact. Redmond recorded:

Breakfasted with C.B. (T.P. O'C. also there) at 29 Belgrave Square 14 November 1905. He sd. he was stronger than ever for Home Rule: It was only a question how far they cd. go in the next Parlmnt.

His own impression was it wd. *not* be possible to pass full Home Rule, but he hoped to be able to pass some serious measure wh. wd. be consistent with & wd. lead up to the other.

He wd. say nothing, however, to withdraw the larger measure from the Electors.

He wd. speak his mind plainly on the question to his own constituents on the following Thursday week.

He did not mind the Rosebery crowd & felt quite independent of them. . . . J.E.R.[39]

Nine days later C.B. spoke at Stirling, and said:

My opinion has long been known to you. It is that the only way of healing the evils of Ireland, of . . . giving content and prosperity to her people, and of making her a strength instead of a weakness to the Empire, is that the Irish people should have the management of their own domestic affairs.

But, he went on:

> If I were asked for advice ... by an ardent Irish Nationalist, I would say, 'Your desire is, as mine is, to see the effective management of Irish affairs in the hands of a representative Irish Parliament. If I were you I would take it in any way I can get it, and if an instalment of representative control was offered to you, or any administrative improvements, I would advise you thankfully to accept it, provided it was consistent with and led up to your larger policy. . . .'[40]

This definition of Liberal policy, although it provoked final repudiation of C.B.'s leadership by Rosebery, won general approval from the party. Even Morley, surprisingly, read it 'with the utmost satisfaction', while the *Freeman's Journal* welcomed it. Thereafter Home Rule ceased to be an important issue in the election, becoming merely 'Balfour's bogey'.

Mr. F. S. L. Lyons has written:

> It may seem surprising that the Nationalist leaders should have accepted, apparently with reasonable equanimity, a formula which was much more designed to paper over Liberal cracks than to satisfy Irish needs. One reason why they did so may simply have been that they liked and trusted Campbell-Bannerman who, they knew, had remained loyal to the Gladstonian conception of Home Rule through all the changes and chances of the last few years. That he still remained loyal to that conception Redmond and T. P. O'Connor were evidently prepared to believe after their meeting with him on 14 November, and because they believed this they believed also his diagnosis that Home Rule would have to wait.

Lyons adds, however:

> The acceptance by the Irish leaders of the step-by-step policy had in it the seeds of danger. For one thing, their dependence on one man – Campbell-Bannerman – was too great, since that man, had they but known it, had little more than two years to live.[41]

King Edward VII at Marienbad:
underneath is an example of the King's handwriting:
'Trusting that you are benefitting from the mountain air   E.R.'

C.B. and Sir Gilbert Parker (M.P. and novelist) at Marienbad

Belmont:
as it was
in C.B.'s day

No. 6
Grosvenor Place
C.B.'s London
home

Balfour resigned at the beginning of December 1905, hoping to rally his party on the Home Rule issue. Immediately Redmond wrote to the new Prime Minister, C.B., from Dublin on December 5, stressing the 'vital importance' of the choices for the Irish places in the new Government if Ireland was to be administered in harmony with Irish ideas before 'any attempt to carry out a serious reform of the system of Irish Govt.'.[42] The man C.B. chose for Chief Secretary was James Bryce.

The Irish trusted C.B. Justin McCarthy wrote on January 19: 'I have great faith in C.B. personally and I do not even find fault with him because he refuses to show his hand just now too fully on the subject of Home Rule.'[43] But it was twenty years since C.B. had been Chief Secretary and Gladstone was forming his determination to bring in Home Rule. The leading Liberals were tired of Ireland. The will to settle the problem by granting self-government within the Empire had largely gone. So, though the 1906 election produced such a landslide for the Liberals that they were given a majority of over a hundred in the House over all other parties combined, not much was done for the Irish. The Liberals were no longer dependent in any way on the support of the eighty-three Irish Nationalists. This meant that they could decide for themselves what to do about Ireland, and when to do it. But it soon became plain that the House of Lords was in a belligerent mood, and would undoubtedly kill a Home Rule Bill as it had in 1893.

When Bryce got to Dublin he proved too gentle and scholarly for the tough and exacting job of dealing with the Irish, despite the help he had from his formidable Permanent Under-Secretary, Anthony McDonnell. This man was a Catholic Irishman, who had made his name in India and was known by some as the 'Bengal Tiger' and by others as 'The Fiend'. C.B. had described him to Asquith in 1904 as a man he did not know personally but who 'appears to be a man peculiarly suited to his place in Ireland', though he also told Buchanan that he was a difficult person. Bryce was soon hopelessly bemused and bewildered and was glad to be moved to the Embassy in Washington at the beginning of 1907. After some hesitation, C.B. appointed Augustine Birrell to succeed him.

Earnest, idealistic Liberals advanced with hope and goodwill on the Irish problem, but were, more often than not, left 'hanging on the old barbed wire'. Balfour, whose lack of any feeling at all had made him a singularly successful Chief Secretary, so much enjoyed the guying of the

English Liberal in Ireland in the person of Thomas Broadbent in Shaw's play *John Bull's Other Island* that he saw it five times, and on one occasion took C.B. as his guest.[44] No doubt he took a sardonic pleasure in confronting an old Liberal Chief Secretary with a caricature of a politician who shared his beliefs.

The 'serious measure', which C.B. had told the Irish leaders he hoped to pass, was the Irish Council Bill of 1907. C.B. told the King's Private Secretary on January 17, 1907:

> It has been generally expected that in the coming session we shall promote a bill constituting a representative body dealing with Education, Poor Law, and other local matters, and so far relieving the 'Castle' and the House of Commons. There are many people in and out of Ireland, who would welcome such a change, without being partisans of what is generally understood as 'Home Rule'. 'The Castle' is not popular with anyone but its own officials. Bryce elaborated a scheme, and a Committee of the Cabinet considered it: but nothing has been decided, and now we must allow the new Chief Secretary to make himself master of the case. . . .[45]

Bryce's plan did not find favour with the Irish leaders. He had written to C.B. in October 1906, to say that Redmond was, not surprisingly, 'profoundly disappointed' with it. 'He thinks that it could not bring him any nearer his ultimate goal, and conceives that the creation of a new body in Ireland, created irrespective of the existing Irish members, would fatally reduce the importance of the latter.'[46] Dillon and Sexton were equally discouraging. Two days later Bryce told C.B. that 'they care more for a showy bird (very much) in the bush than a plump little bird in the hand'.[47] The Bill, little changed, was introduced by Birrell in May 1907. C.B.'s private secretary, Arthur Ponsonby, noted that Birrell's speech was 'not very good. The truth is that those of our men who are keen on Ireland would like Home Rule & those who are not are bored.'[48] A. G. Gardiner described Birrell as bringing in the Bill 'in the accents of defeat' and went on:

> The key was minor, the terms apologetic. When at the close Mr. Balfour rose and said, 'The right hon. gentleman has brought in a Bill which the House does not believe in, and which, I venture to say, the right hon. gentleman does not believe in himself', you felt that he held the winning hand.[49]

Lloyd George, brought in because by then Bryce had become totally discouraged, explained to Redmond in November 1906 the fact of political life presented by the obstacle of the House of Lords. The Bill, which C.B. himself described as a 'little, modest, shy, humble effort to give administrative powers to the Irish people',[50] provided for an Irish elected Council of a hundred members controlling the principal departments of State and to be given £5 million to spend. T. P. O'Connor welcomed the plan. In a speech the year before in Philadelphia he had described C.B. as 'one of the bravest and one of the most upright and one of the most consistent politicians that ever ruled in England', and proclaimed: 'the hour of Ireland's deliverance is at hand'.[51] Redmond himself was reluctant to turn down flat the first instalment of a limited form of self-government coming from a Campbell-Bannerman government, and he made an eloquent and moving speech on the plan, but he was profoundly disappointed. Ponsonby described to his wife 'Redmond's appearance and demeanour in the House. Instead of his usual bold bossing piercing look, he sat with a pale face turning aside from the Govt. benches, He is not at all happy.'[52] The reaction in Ireland was hostile and the proposal was rejected by a Nationalist Convention in Dublin, much to the chagrin of O'Connor, who felt that his standing with the Liberals and C.B. was involved. So the Bill died. Birrell offered to resign but C.B. would not agree to let him go. Morley wrote drily to C.B. on May 23: 'Ireland is a sorrowful business. How they could even pretend to accept such a trumpery bill, I could never understand; tho' I didn't tell them so.'[53] Bryce and others believed that the Bill had foundered on the rock of clerical opposition to lay control of education. It would have put Irish schools under the control of an elective Irish body. Bryce wrote that what was essential was:

> getting the schools out of the hands of clerics, whether Roman Catholic or Protestant. It was because the bishops and priests feared this that they gave such vehement, and successful, opposition to the Bill. It was a small measure and full of imperfections. But it might have done some good, if people had tried to work it fairly. . . .[54]

To the King C.B. wrote: 'It was an honest attempt to improve the system of administration by enlarging the powers and enlisting the direct help of the Irish people and if it did not please them the Government have no desire to proceed with it.'[55] In September he wrote to Asquith about a proposal by Lord Aberdeen to prosecute some

Irish M.P.s, saying: 'I am dead contra: Neither of the two men has any importance but if proceeded against they wd. become heroes.'[56]

C.B. was now in the last year of his life, and the problems of Ireland would soon trouble him no more. But Ireland, denied Home Rule and perennially disaffected, was still full of unrest. There were serious riots in Belfast after police and soldiers were attacked in the Cullingtree and Falls Roads in August. Four people were shot and 6,000 troops had to be brought into the city. Elsewhere in Ireland there were outbreaks of cattle-driving and cattle-maiming, murders and bomb explosions. C.B. told the King on January 23, 1908: 'Especially in Galway and Roscommon, mobs of peasants have driven the cattle from land let for grazing. . . . The result is a disorderly condition with which it is almost impossible for the police to cope. . . .'[57]

Two of Carson's relatives were murdered in the presence of a jeering crowd as they left church on a Sunday. Carson declared, 'If you are not prepared to govern Ireland according to the ordinary conditions of civilization that prevail in every country, then go out of Ireland and leave us to govern ourselves.'

In 1908 the Irish Nationalists determined to try again and in January Redmond and Dillon drafted a Home Rule resolution. They hoped that C.B. might himself be persuaded to introduce it. They saw Birrell, who wrote after consulting the dying C.B.:

> I have seen the P.M. on the subject of the resolution . . . he demurs to the words 'vital and urgent' as giving unanswerable force to the reply: if it be both *vital* and *urgent*, why in God's name don't you *do* something!
>
> He also thinks that from a *tactical* point of view the advantage to the *United Kingdom* of withdrawing Irish affairs from Westminster ought to be suggested. . . . I think he is right, as he usually is in such matters. . . .[58]

Redmond was not satisfied and asked to see Birrell and if necessary C.B. Birrell replied on January 26:

> As you may guess, it is not easy in C.B.'s state of health and circumstances to thrash anything out with him, and I am nearly worn out with the attempts I have made.
>
> I have succeeded in obtaining *some* access to him and his mind. . . . He thinks it would be *disastrous* to use words which would give

force to the contention that 'he and his' were in favour of an *independent* Irish Parliament. . . . The P.M. thinks before he could ask his friends to support any resolution this must be made plain.[59]

It was C.B.'s last recorded word on Ireland. Redmond was one of the last men he spoke to in the House before he retired to Downing Street to die.

The Irish leaders mourned his departure. In December 1907 William O'Brien had told C.B. that he was 'perhaps the best living example of what a brave and honest life can do to make us all think better of human nature'.[60]

C.B. had to leave the Irish problem unsolved, mainly because the House of Lords still had its veto unimpaired. With South Africa this was circumvented by using an Order in Council, but such a device could not be used to dissolve the Union. So the problem passed to his successors, and C.B. did not live to see the curbing of the House of Lords by the Parliament Act of 1911, its rejection of the third Home Rule Bill of 1912, which nevertheless, under the Parliament Act, became law in 1914, and the Ulster agitation led by Carson and Bonar Law. He was spared, too, knowledge of what came after – the Easter rising of 1916, the growth of Sinn Fein and the wiping out of the Irish Home Rule Party in 1918, the bloodshed and burning of 1920 to 1922, and the settlement of 1921, a botched solution, made by men weary of strife.

It was not fortuitous that in 1939 Smuts, who had never forgotten C.B.'s generosity and trust in 1905, brought South Africa into the war on England's side, in the face of bitter opposition from Herzog and the Nationalists, while the Republic of Ireland stayed neutral. When England fought for her life, the ports of South Africa – and Ulster – were open to her, but those of the Irish Republic were not, despite the appeals of Mr. Churchill. In a letter to *The Times* in January 1970[61] Captain Roskill, the historian of the war at sea, said that 'without the bases in Ulster we could hardly have survived and had we enjoyed the use of the Eire bases, many Allied ships and seamen's lives would have been saved, and perhaps the Atlantic Battle won earlier.'

There are many ifs in history, but it is sad that the bold and generous policy C.B. carried through in South Africa was never given a chance in Ireland.

Nicholas Mansergh has written that the South African settlement of

1907 'made a profound and lasting impression upon John Redmond. Time and again I have noticed how in his letters and in his speeches at critical moments he recalled Campbell-Bannerman's generosity and its reward. Do to Ireland, he was urging Asquith even as late as 1916, as your predecessor did to the Dutch republics and you will reap that same reward.'[62] He said that Redmond would like to have been the Irish Botha. Things did not work out that way. Perhaps if the honourable, generous, large-minded Redmond had come before the implacable Parnell, instead of after him; if the crisis in Ireland had not coincided with the rise of imperial sentiment in England; even if Parnell had not become involved with Kitty O'Shea, there might have been a happy issue. But, as in one of Hardy's novels, a malignant fate was always against a solution, and though C.B. had in 1905 come through long experience of the problem to supreme power in England, with a massive majority at his back, and though he knew what had to be done, he was powerless to do it.

Part 3

C.B.'s Way of Life

CHAPTER 9

A Vanished World

I N later life C.B. was described by Arthur Ponsonby:

> Caricatures and newspaper gossip had given me the idea of a heavy . . . rather unattractive person. I found on the contrary that, with rather a heavy build and a rather old fashioned Victorian appearance, he had a particular sparkle . . . and an attractive voice with a rolling r. He was light in hand, in fact, and to my relief I found he had an acute sense of humour which I should never have suspected from the dull colourless figure by which he seemed to be represented publicly. . . .[1]

And T. P. O'Connor wrote of the 'transparent honesty . . . written . . . all over the face. The broad and somewhat short and typical Scotch face . . . the stout, robust, well-knit figure, above all, the large eyes – light blue or grey, and open, lucid, fearless, and steady.'[2]

The life that C.B. and Charlotte led was a life of ease, comfort and routine, lived before telephones, aeroplanes, quick-lunch counters and washing up.

C.B. was never a very rich man, but he was well off and he had no children. Because he lived in large houses and drew an income from the family business in Glasgow and other investments there, besides what he had been left by his uncle, he was reputed to be enormously wealthy, but this was not so, and in the last years of his life, when his expenses were heavy, he had to borrow two amounts of £2,000 and another of £700 from his brother to make ends meet, paying him 4 per cent interest on the loan.[3] His brother, who had taken over the business, was much better off and left a quarter of a million when he died. C.B. bothered very little about his financial affairs and spent money freely. The bailiff of his estate in Kent had ten children, and when he died is said to have left them £10,000 each. A great deal went on new cottages for tenants and not much was left to the owner.

Nevertheless C.B. and Charlotte did themselves well. They lived in very large houses. Their houses and gardens were kept in an immaculate way that is now hardly ever seen. But C.B. was unlucky to live before the days of central heating. In 1906 he told his friend Lord Haliburton that he had been unwell at No. 10 Downing Street – 'I think it is chiefly due to the cold of this rotten old barrack of a house.'[4]

In those days the well-to-do regularly ate too much and their consumption of food and wine was, by present-day standards, staggering. Even of John Morley, who was regarded as something of an ascetic, it was recorded that 'at dinner he rarely drank anything but champagne'. C.B. was an authority on food and remained interested in it throughout his life, perhaps on Meredith's prescription that 'Kissing don't last: cookery do!' His tastes, however, were simple. He once described his ideal meal as 'mutton broth, fresh herring or salmon, haggis, roast mutton, grouse, apple tart, strawberries – maistly Scotch'.[5]

His life followed an absolutely regular routine. He would come down from Scotland in January for the opening of the session. For the next five months or so he would be in London, attending the sittings of the House, entertaining and being entertained, and, when in office, looking after the affairs of his Department. He often lunched at a club, and belonged to the Athenæum, Brooks's, the Oxford and Cambridge and the Reform. At Easter he would often go across to Paris for a few days. A French newspaper wrote on his death: 'Il adorait Paris et rien ne l'amusait comme de flâner . . . perdu dans la foule et philosophant à l'aventure.'[6]

When he found London oppressive he would go down to Dover, where he stayed at the Lord Warden Hotel and used to sit on the end of the pier. There, he said, he could get the maximum of ozone without the nuisance of getting into a boat. Occasionally he would cross the Channel briefly for the pleasure of a French luncheon at the Gare Maritime at Calais. Lord Mersey, who met him at Dover in 1901, found him 'an amusing talker with an amazing knowledge of French literature, both classical and modern', noting: 'Such British decadence as there was he considered as partly due to under-feeding'.[7]

In June or July he would be off to Scotland and at this time of year he took to the platform, and went round making speeches to the large public meetings which, before television, satisfied people's needs to see and hear their political leaders. He slipped easily into Scots speech – of the Perthshire rather than the Glasgow variety. In the first week of August, he took Charlotte for five or six weeks to Marienbad. The greatest pleasure they both had was travelling. They enjoyed it like children off on a holiday. After Marienbad there would be a week in Vienna and Innsbruck, or Salzburg and Milan, or Lucerne and Berne, followed almost invariably by a few days in Paris. After Paris they came back to London about the end of October, where they spent a month or so before going back to Scotland. There C.B. would have some local friends in to shoot the covers once or twice. Having disposed of the pheasants he would spend Christmas in Scotland before going back to London for another session.

The routine gradually became fixed and immutable. Marienbad became a yearly fixture after 1872 and Scotland after he had acquired a house there in 1885. He was content to keep, like a tram, to his pre-scribed route. He never visited the United States or any part of the British Empire overseas, never went to Ireland, except when he was Chief Secretary, and never in his life left Europe. Once his doctors suggested to him that he might try Egypt in the winter but, he wrote, 'we do not grue to it'. He took the minimum exercise, neither riding nor even playing golf, and never walked far if he could help it. He felt no need to escape the Scottish winter. He wrote from Scotland in 1905 to a Liberal colleague, Ellis:

> I ran about Italy for a year when I was a boy, but have not been there much since: and on the whole I prefer in winter a climate where it is not 20 degrees warmer on one side of the street than on the other. We are colder here, it may be, but our cold is better distributed.[8]

This may have been so, but his diary shows that he and Charlotte were constantly being laid up with colds. He was born too early to become, like Mr. Balfour or Mr. Asquith, a believer in the weekend habit.

After four years at 60 Queen's Gate, C.B. and Charlotte moved in 1872 to 117 Eaton Square and in 1878 to 6 Grosvenor Place, a very large house on the corner of Halkin Street looking across to the gardens of Buckingham Palace. This he took on a lease at a rent of £185 a year. It was a town house on a scale which would now be suitable for a fair-sized Embassy. In 1972 the Gulf Oil Company sold the lease of this house for more than £2½ million. It was the Campbell-Bannermans' London home for nearly thirty years.

In 1904 they decided to move again. Grosvenor Place was beginning to become noisy by the standards of those days. The point of decision came when a hansom cab fell into the basement area. Charlotte's nerves, she declared, wouldn't stand it. Jack Sinclair wrote in June:

Crowds in London for Ascot: you never saw anything like the Park on Sunday. I walked down . . . to lunch with C.B.: they are house-hunting: and after luncheon, he and I chartered a hansom, and took a non-stop comparative survey of his various possible houses – south side of the Park – north side – Park Lane, Portland Place, Grosvenor Square, Belgrave Square. . . . We guided the driver by umbrella-semaphore, and at first he thought we were clean off our heads. I want him to go to Berkeley Square: but at present Belgrave Square is first favourite.[9]

Finally at the end of September C.B. took another lease (his third) from the Grosvenor Estate, this time of 29 Belgrave Square, where, just over a year later, he was to interview his colleagues and make up his administration. He described the move as 'slipping round the corner for the sake of the quiet'. The sixty-three-year lease cost him, in those days, £4,816 and the annual rent was £170. After Grosvenor Place, it seemed to C.B. 'a small house'. They moved in early in 1905. They were there for only twelve months before they made their last move to 10 Downing Street, the house in which C.B. died.

From these houses he would take his brougham, drawn by the same favourite horse for fourteen years, or a hansom cab ('eighteen pennorth of danger' as he called it) to the House.

Like everyone else who lived in these great houses, the Campbell-Bannermans had a score or so of servants – a butler, a first and second footman – three in the dining room, as the phrase went – a cook, and a range of maids from the lady's maid and an old Scotch housemaid to the humble tweeny. Arthur Ponsonby wrote of C.B. that 'all his servants were devoted to him and with the older ones he was on very intimate terms'.[10] In those days the ladies who ran these vast establishments used to address each other on the subject of servants with quaint formality, as if they were negotiating with foreign governments. Communications like this passed between them:

Mrs Graham Murray presents her compliments to Lady Campbell-Bannerman and is glad to be able to give James Roberts an excellent character. He is *perfectly* sober, steady and honest, clean, active & most obliging & knows his duties thoroughly. . . . He has been 2½ years with Mrs. Graham Murray as second footman & she is exceedingly sorry to part with him. He leaves of his own accord, as he wishes to get on.[11]

and:

Dear Mr. Campbell-Bannerman.

Edwards a Coachman who lived with us for close upon ten years tells me that you will be expecting to have his character from us . . . Alas after the influenza he had been decidedly the worse as they call it – so we parted with him – Happily he has taken the pledge and looks a different man. . . . it is fair to say he was one of the very best of servants first rate driving and a neat and clever coachman . . .

Believe me
Yours sincerely
Cath Gladstone.[12]

The large number of servants meant that when the establishment was running smoothly, entertaining on a large scale was no problem, and could be done with the minimum of wear and tear. At the Campbell-Bannermans the food was pretty good. Four or five large dinner parties a month for eighteen or twenty people were normal during the London season.

They went out as much as they entertained themselves. In the summer of 1881, Charlotte's journal records:

31 May . . . to Mrs. Gladstone's reception.

14 June . . . in the evening to 'Patience'. [They saw it again on the 25th.]

17 June . . . to see Sarah Bernhardt in 'Frou Frou'.

21 June Had a party in the evening & Hungarian Band, about 350 present.

22 June Dine at 34 . . . afterwards to Devonshire House.

24 June Had a dinner party 20 . . . after dinner went on to the Queen's Ball.[13]

Lady Monkswell, who went out a great deal, described one evening at the Campbell-Bannermans as 'very splendid' and another time wrote: 'Campbell-Bannerman is *delightful*. . . . The dinner & flowers did everything money could do – some groups of splendid roses.'[14]

The dinner parties were sometimes for men only, so that politics or Army affairs could be thoroughly discussed, and there were frequent after-dinner receptions at one of the great London houses – Holland House, Spencer House, or at the Roseberys at 38 Berkeley Square. On one occasion C.B. had to cry off a dinner with Bryce because he had been bidden to dine with Armistead to meet Gladstone and 'This is not quite a royal command: but it is an arch-angelic command'. Like other wives, Charlotte spent a lot of time driving out to pay calls, and receiving callers at home. The political hostess was much in evidence in this period. They often went, for example, to Lady Hayter's in Grosvenor Square. She gave a large party two or three times during the session, mainly for Liberals, but the parties came to an end when, during the Rosebery administration, Sir Arthur Hayter failed to obtain the colonial governorship after which he hankered.

Henry Lucy met Mark Twain at the Campbell-Bannermans. Margot Tennant went there with her fiancé, H. H. Asquith, soon after their engagement, met the Gladstones there and was lectured by the wives on the duties of the wife of a possible Prime Minister.

On the whole, C.B. and Charlotte were conservative in their choice of friends. In Scotland they had their neighbours, while in London the list of guests extended each year. At the dinner table C.B. was at his best. It was recorded of him in the early nineties that: 'He does not take a prominent part in debate in the House, but in private circles he delights and adorns he is known as a man bubbling over with natural humour.'[15]

Although they entertained so much the Campbell-Bannermans never at any stage aspired to belong to what was called 'Society'. They were happiest together. At the end of her life, when Charlotte was very ill, one of C.B.'s secretaries wrote to the other: 'The two get on so splendidly together when she is in anything like good form & are so completely happy in one another's society that I don't believe the case is quite so desperate as it strikes you as being.'[16]

Charlotte's poor health and shyness prevented her from going much to stay in the great country houses of the time, and C.B. would not go without her. In her later days, she had the misfortune to become enormously fat, so much so that she had to be helped to dress by her two maids. Despite this she was very fussy about her clothes and bought most of them from Worth. After one dinner at Grosvenor Place Lady Monkswell wrote in her journal, 'Poor Lady C-B, who has not known a day's health for years & weighs perhaps 18 stone, was dressed in a most magnificent white satin, which would have looked extremely well on a girl, & was covered with jewels.'[17] Neither of them had any inclination for the sparkling insincerities of smart people. They lived quite apart from the world of house parties such as those at Panshanger, Wilton and Taplow, or from the raffish London world of the 1880s, when Hamilton was writing in his diary about Dilke being 'extraordinarily free & easy with ladies', and about the Prince of Wales's favoured young girls, who were known as 'H.R.H.'s virgin band'.[18]

Perhaps, left to himself, C.B. might have gone more into society, for he had great social gifts. Moreover, though he recognized that what he called 'the heavy metal' of the Liberal Party were the salt of the earth, he had to admit that their entertainments were apt to be sticky, and after Charlotte's death in 1906 he found the dinners and lunches he was then invited to greater fun. But he told Lord Rendel that he agreed that 'the efforts of the Liberal Party to shine in London entertainments were worse than useless', and that 'Haldane and Asquith were both handicapped by their social proclivities'.[19] Ponsonby noted that Charlotte 'detested the society into which – to his undoing, as C.B. always thought – Asquith had been drawn by Margot'.[20] Spender, in his book *The Public Life*, wrote that C.B. 'never disguised his opinion that London society was bad for Radical politicians. You couldn't, he used to say, be perpetually in the company of people who thought your opinions disreputable without wishing to tone them down to prove yourself respectable'. Spender added that politically 'nothing stood Campbell-Bannerman in better stead than his reputation of being a quiet Scot who preferred the society of his own kind'.[21] In his reluctance to mingle socially with members of the other party he was at one with Lord Salisbury but differed entirely from Salisbury's nephew Arthur Balfour. C.B. told a deputation of Montrose Liberals in 1903 that members of the House of Commons 'were subject to little temptations of their own. They were living in London and away from their electors, and they were subject to certain social influences – the influence of the atmosphere of London and of the clubs, which was never very favourable to stalwart Liberalism.'[22]

Augustine Birrell, who knew C.B. in his last years, noted that he never mixed freely in society with 'the other side':

This [Birrell said] was not from morosity, for he was one of the most companionable of men, but from the habits of his life, and his detached way of regarding his fellow-creatures; thus, for example, he remained to the end of his days impervious to the almost historic 'charm' of A.J.B. He simply could not see it; and thus was left unaffectedly and completely unmoved. Just as John Bright or Harcourt never really wanted to become Baronets, so C.B. was well content to live quite outside many circles of interest.

None the less he could order a dinner, and discuss it, with any man in Europe, and he once told me that he was able when in opposition (from having been Secretary of State for War) to discern the signs of the times, and the impending fate of Ministries, by the showers of cards left on his hall-table by his old military friends, scenting their provender from afar.

He was indeed one of those good men at whose feasts it is always a pleasure to sit.

C.B. . . . had no objection to being alone in the company of a French Novel or Memoir, with a good dinner either before or after those periods of seclusion.[23]

Besides his London house, C.B. had, for all but the first three of his forty years in Parliament, a large country house. For the first sixteen years this was Gennings, the house he had inherited in Kent. In 1884, however, he and Charlotte began looking for a house in Scotland, which would be near his family and a base for the nursing of his constituency. In December they found Belmont, a property near Meigle in Perthshire. It stood in Macbeth's country, between the Grampians and the Sidlaw Hills, not far from Glamis. On the estate was only the burnt-out shell of a white, battlemented eighteenth-century house. They rebuilt it inside and added on as much or more again, in the ungainly style of the eighties, with immensely high chimneys. They planned the grounds so as to look their best in winter, when they were there; laid out a flower garden in the shape of a coat of arms; made great sweeps of lawn and a path beside a plantation, which caught the setting sun and had a view over the valley. When Charlotte was in London, a white gardenia was posted to her daily from Belmont.

They both loved Belmont, which became their true home, and both of them now lie in the little churchyard at Meigle. Meigle today is no longer the quiet village they knew. Now the church is kept locked and the fish lorries thunder through on the main road from Aberdeen to Perth. People come sometimes to see the Pictish stones in the museum and the curator, who knew nothing of Campbell-Bannerman, remarked grimly to me: 'I reckon politics then was much as politics is now.'

Belmont still stands, but has become a home for old people. The vast walled kitchen garden – more than two acres for a family of two people – has become a tree nursery. Some of the great trees which C.B. loved remain, including a copper beech by the house. When he passed those of which he was particularly fond he would, in a whimsical way, bow to them and wish them good morning.

In its heyday Belmont was a spacious, comfortable house. C.B.'s furniture was nearly all French, some of it original eighteenth-century pieces, which came from châteaux in provincial France, and others copied from furniture he had admired in the Louvre and elsewhere by the ébéniste Henri Dasson and the cabinet makers of the house of Durand. It was elegant, elaborate and beautifully made. There were quantities of flowers and palms, a collection of Sèvres china, bronzes and candelabra, Aubusson carpets and a huge Meissen cock C.B. had had made. There were some good nineteenth-century Dutch pictures, including a grey, shadowy, twilight river landscape by Matthew Maris.[24]

Belmont was not a beautiful house. The courtyard of the old house was covered in with a coloured skylight to make a vast and remarkably hideous hall. There was a grandiose staircase, and on the walls there is still the pattern of thistles painted by French artists. The drawing room was, however, an agreeable, well proportioned room, and the rooms on the ground floor opened into each other in an attractive way. It was all on a large scale. It was indeed a very substantial establishment for one man of radical views and his wife.

C.B. was attached to the grey African parrot he had bought the year he entered Parliament. He called her his 'political godmother'. He kept her for forty years and she outlived him. He also loved his horses. Once he was driving a friend at Belmont, who said to him, 'I wonder you don't keep a motor, Sir Henry'. C.B. said nothing, but when he pulled up he went to the horses' heads and stroked them, while they nuzzled up to him. To his friend C.B. remarked quietly: 'That's why I don't keep a motor.'

Originally C.B.'s letterhead was:

BELMONT CASTLE
MEIGLE
N.B.

But with the revival of Scottish national self-consciousness it became unfashionable to talk about 'North Britain' and in 1889 C.B. changed 'N.B.' to SCOTLAND.

When he was in office C.B. often took his work up to Belmont. Sir Gordon Voules, who was his private secretary at the Admiralty, recalled that he was so busy there on the Naval Estimates 'that he nearly drove his two keepers – Fozzers he called them – to despair. They used to call every morning to know when he would shoot his covers – but during all the time I was with him he never fired a gun.'[25] In fact C.B.'s sporting enthusiasm was reserved for billiards.

Belmont was, in those days, readily accessible from London, especially after the opening of the Forth Bridge in 1890. C.B. used to tell his friends that if they left London at noon, the train took them straight through to Alyth Junction by the evening, whence a carriage took them to Belmont in ten minutes.

C.B. liked everything French – French food, French furniture, yellow-backed French novels, French caricatures, French bulldogs, of which at one time he had a kennel of about thirty, which harassed the butler and, later, his private secretary, who had to defend himself with a fireguard when handing round tea. Now and then he took one over to Paris to see, as he put it, the city of its birth. He read and re-read, in French, the novels of Balzac, Flaubert, Anatole Françe, Zola and De Maupassant. His copy of France's *Sur la Pierre Blanche* was marked and scored in many places. He was amused by Hernant's *Les Transatlantiques*. He also enjoyed Bret Harte and he loved Burns's poems.[26]

Besides being at home in French, he knew a good deal of Italian and German. According to Lord Acton, he spoke German 'with a smart Viennese accent'. In fact he was a man of genuinely European culture, who was comfortable talking European languages and at ease with people from many parts of continental Europe. He told a story well and was a good mimic. But he seldom discussed abstract subjects.

C.B., a portly man, liked to take his ease, preferring to sit a long time over luncheon and to end meals, in the Scots fashion, with gingerbread and butter.[27] He had the foibles of a childless but deeply affectionate man. It was recorded of him that he 'had a great collection of walking-sticks. . . . To these he would talk affectionately under his breath, as he selected the one to be taken for an airing, murmuring words of consolation to the ones to be left behind.'[28]

The personalities of C.B. and his wife were quite different. C.B. himself was genial, easy-going, amusing and sociable, very much a man of the world. Margot Asquith called him 'essentially a *bon vivant*, a *boulevardier* and a humourist'.[29]

Charlotte was very different. She was shy, nervous, retiring and altogether lacking in self-confidence. She had few close friends of her own. Most of her life she was extremely stout and T. P. O'Connor remarked on the 'somewhat grotesque contrast' between her bulky physique, which suggested a tough, jolly person, and the reality of continuous ill-health and social timidity, revealed by her 'nervous and anxious eyes'.[30] She was a very plain woman and had none of the reassurance that comes from being generally admired. She came to believe, as her cousin noted, that 'no one could possibly care for her society', and she depended completely on her husband, whose devotion and affection for her impressed all who knew them.

Her influence over him was very marked. He knew that she was the one person in the world who put him before everything else, and that she had more steel in her make-up than he had. At every turning point in his life it was her decision that counted. He used to call her his final Court of Appeal. He had, moreover, a great respect for her acumen. She was not an intellectual woman but she had a sharp wit. According to O'Connor: 'Whether she was as intelligent as he thought, may be open to question; she was certainly a very cultivated woman . . . and she . . . was able to create a beautiful house and an orderly household.'[31] This was true. Anyone who went to their houses remarked on how perfectly everything was managed.

For the friends she did have she would do anything. So far as her husband was concerned she had a sharp instinct which told her at once who was his friend. She recognized hostility instantly, whereas her kindly and genial husband did not, or when he did, usually chose to disregard it.

As a wife Charlotte was possessive and demanded a great deal of attention, but this C.B. never grudged. Arthur Ponsonby suggested that she was both jealous of and for C.B.'s career. She took, however, a keen interest in politics and shared C.B.'s sardonic attitude towards many of his less admirable colleagues. She had, according to Lady Pentland, a wry Scots humour. C.B. talked over everything with her. He gave all his colleagues nicknames, or if he couldn't think of a suitable nickname referred to them by the name of their houses or their constituency. This enabled him to preserve discretion when talking political gossip with Charlotte in front of the servants. Lord Salisbury was 'Old Sarum'; John Morley (most appropriately) 'Priscilla'; Haldane 'Schopenhauer'; the massive W. V. Harcourt, after his house in the New Forest, 'Malwood', 'The Malwood Philosopher', 'The Nymph of

Malwood', or just 'The Nymph'; Rosebery 'Son Eminence Grise' or 'Barnbougle' after his castle on the Forth; Dilke 'The Forest of Dean'; Spencer 'Spec'; and King Edward VII 'Jupiter'.

These two were devoted to each other, and they were, all their lives, inseparable companions. Charlotte once said of C.B., in a moment of emotion, that the truest praise one could give him was that he was a really perfectly good man.

C.B. was seldom away from Charlotte for long, so he did not often need to write her letters. But, when he was a member of the Government in the nineties, he had to go for three years running in the late autumn to Balmoral as Minister in Attendance on Queen Victoria, and when he was there he wrote to Charlotte every day, and sometimes two or three times a day.[32]

These letters are extremely affectionate. He addressed her as 'Dearest Moust', 'My own darling diddy' or 'My own pet' and signed them 'Your loving true Poo Ole', 'Your loving bin D.', or 'Your old homespunbin D.'. Often they contained phrases like 'Goodbye darling. I never loved you so much as now, & I loved you before ever I saw you'. They were the letters of a man who was entirely devoted to his wife and used to sharing all his news with her. They also gave an entertaining picture of life at the castle.

The first, on October 22, 1892, said gloomily that it was 'Siberia! Snow all round . . .', but went on: 'I have a snug little bedroom (only) but comfortable, with turret as dressing room: on ground floor, south exposure. My neighbours are the Lady in Waiting & the Maid of Honour! . . .'

He faithfully recorded the domestic details and even drew little charts to show her who sat where at every meal. He told her that 'the house is all carpeted & curtained in tartan' and said loyally – or perhaps sincerely – 'It looks very well.'

On the 24th he wrote:

> The amusing thing is the way the suite lament the dullness. Certainly the actual dinner is triste enough, every one half whispering to their neighbour. It seems however I need not have sat in my room all afternoon yesterday. Lady Downe has *implored* me to come to the billiard room (where they sit) for afternoon tea, which she says is the only bright hour of the day & I think they are all so sick of each other they jump at a stranger.

Nobody could be more thoughtful, kind, sensible & charming than Ponsonby. I do not think Major Bigge (who is here also) wd. adequately replace him. . . .

'The Queen', he said on the 26th, 'is always either very serious or all smiles. They have Curtis's band, which plays beautifully in the evening in the corridor – Österreichische and Hungarische – really first rate.' On the 23rd he wrote:

It has been a perfectly dreadful day. Snowing ever since 10 a.m. . . . I drove to church at Crathie with Sir H. P. & Miss MacNeill, & we occupied the big seat in the 'breast of the loft'. . . . My companions envied me my nice fur coat!

It is the funniest life conceivable: like a convent. We meet at meals, breakfast 9.45, lunch 2, dinner 9: and when we have finished, each is off to his cell (at least I to mine) & there is no common life except round a table. About 7 a man comes round & says whether I am to dine with the Queen. I hardly expect I shall tonight. So, in this weather, I spend the whole day alone reading in my room. . . .

The Castle is all intersected by long narrow passages, ending in baize doors and I could not find my way without help . . . all the talk, even in the suite's room, is very subdued – a good deal of criticism of what 'she' will or will not do. Lady Downe & Miss McNeil (who is an elderly Argyllshire McNeil) are very nice. Yorke is the groom in waiting & a Miss Lambert the Maid. Whether she is of the Irish lot I do not know – she is not like the type – plain & pale faced. . . .

My room is very comfortable, about the size of the bird room at Belmont. . . . I have a good fire and five new candles each night. But my, when one does not get out, it *is* dismal. . . .

On the 27th Lady Downe took him for a walk in the snow on the other side of the Dee. C.B. learnt that her husband, who had commanded the 10th Hussars, was unemployed, and reflected that no doubt the Secretary of State for War was a desirable acquaintance. That night he dined with the Queen and they listened to Curtis's band, which C.B. enjoyed, as did the Queen, who, he noted, 'kept remarking that it was "*quite* charming", "*so* beautiful" etc.' A discussion began as to whether the band were all English or Viennese, and C.B. told the Queen that he had discovered that they all came from Kentish Town.

In a later letter C.B. wrote: 'Here is Mr. Curt von Kentish Town's card: which keep, for if we ever wanted anything of the sort we could not do better.'

On the 28th he wrote: 'I had a long & very animated conversation with the Q. – all about the commands. I was quite fatigued at the end of it.'

So ended the 1892 visit. He was presented with an inscribed copy of *Leaves from Our Journal* and told Charlotte, 'so I bring my prizes home from school'.

C.B. did indeed find favour. Henry Ponsonby wrote to him on October 31: 'I think you made a very good impression on the Queen as you listened to her and encouraged her to speak openly which she hesitates to do with those who seem convinced that what she is going to say is wrong in their view before she says it.'[33]

October 1893 found him back again at the Castle, ruefully writing: 'That it shd. come to this again! I feel as if I had never been away: the same room, the same atmosphere!'

But at any rate some of the people were new. There was Lady Ampthill, 'a big fair haired woman of about 45, a sort of improved type of Ida Forbes, with her nose stuck on at an angle: pleasant enough, noisy & outspoken', and the Duchess of Fife – 'the most extraordinary long nosed slip of a little thing, like a Scotch terrier'. And there were private theatricals and a notable visitor:

> Dinner was hurried over & we went into the drawing room, & then the Empress Eugénie was announced. She does not go to plays, but came under the rose to this rehearsal. The Q. not only rose to receive her but trotted off with great agility to the door of the room & out into the corridor to meet her. The Empress had a lady with her – a *very* plain stout woman, like a Dame de Comptoir. Then . . . off we all marched to the Ballroom where the stage is erected. . . . The servants were all ranged round the room on the back seats. . . . I sat with my knees in the Empress's back. She gives one the idea of a maitresse femme in some respects, & it was odd to look into the back of her head & think of all she had been & all she had come through. It was odd also to watch the two old ladies together. They spoke French.

C.B. thought the play creditably done but suffered from the 'interminable entr'actes'. At supper afterwards he sat next to the

Princess Aribert, whom he described as 'tall, élancée, fair, long faced, diaphanous, delicate-looking, but fresh'.

He liked best of all Sir Henry Ponsonby, 'a perfect old brick – so natural & unaffected through it all: he makes it endurable'. He enjoyed exchanging stories with Ponsonby. He relayed to Charlotte one Ponsonby told him about Mrs. Gladstone:

She wrote this year to Borthwick, who is at Birkhall – 'Dear Lord Borthwick, will you let my son in law Mr. Drew fish in your waters at Invercauld.' To which the answer had to be, 'Dear Mrs. G., I am not a Lord, I do not live at Invercauld, & I have no fishing.'

Some actors and actresses arrived to give a performance, Forbes Robertson, the Bancrofts and Hare. 'You shd have seen Bancroft's bow!' wrote C.B., adding, 'They seemed very scared & yet had the aplomb of the stage.'

He even wrote to Charlotte before breakfast, saying that he was beginning work on a speech – 'I mean to have a good turn at *speechie*: but it has not come to the spit & sputter stage yet.'

On the 25th he and Ponsonby went for a drive and 'we danced the most amusing chassez-croisez with the Q. . . . the more we tried to avoid her the more she ran into us, & she passed us *three* times. When she passes we pull up & stand up uncovered etc. The third time the Q laughed aloud, it was so ridiculous.'

C.B. did not share the Queen's enthusiasm for amateur theatricals – 'Nothing new here,' he wrote, 'play, play, play: and Court Circular. Little else talked about.' Next day he complained – 'It is really dreadfully slow & there is great difficulty in making conversation outside the subject of these plays.'

On another night he wrote: 'I sat next to Lady Kennard . . . a conspicuous person. . . . Thank goodness the end approaches. . . . Let us hope I may some night dine with the H'hold which is more lively. . . . Goodbye my own dear. You are *never* out of my thoughts. Speechie is getting on.'

On Saturday there was at least one new visitor, Lady Constance Lytton, 'a strange maypole with a hatchet face, very ungainly, but modest clever unaffected so far as I can judge. Rather a more dégagé party altogether than usual. . . . The Q. very merry over some old Aunts of hers who when she was a girl used old fashioned pronunciations – obleege, goold for gold, ooman for woman, ospital for hospital etc. etc.'

It was the same routine in 1894 – 'Bigge has been in my room for half an hour gossiping. We are in mourning for the Czar, therefore no music after dinner, but he says "the family" like it & think we can mourn to music, so it is to begin again tomorrow.'

His duties were negligible. Very occasionally there was a Council, and once he had to be present, as a Secretary of State, when a newly appointed Minister to Mexico had to drop on one knee in the corridor and kiss hands. There were the usual members of the Household – 'Miss McNeill, plaintive as usual, and Miss Mary Hughes (shewing her years a good deal)', and some new arrivals, Lady Tennyson, 'a pleasant lively person of the English type', Lady Blythswood, whose 'beauty is as you know of the Jezebelian order', and Lady Antrim, 'very like Albert Grey'. He had found, on closer acquaintance that 'Bigge is exceedingly nice & even more expansive than Sir H.P.'

The service was taken by 'little Dr. Macgregor . . . a born preacher & actor, with nothing of the ecclesiastic about him, an amusing cultivated man-of-the-world'. He found Lord Carrington, with whom he went for a long walk over the moors, excellent company, but missed the London newspapers – 'I don't believe they read any but the Morning Post & the Aberdeen Tory paper!' He got on very well with Princess Louise and Princess Beatrice. 'It is really', he said, 'a different thing when the Princess L. is here.' The Queen told him that the new Czar was going to give his uncle Bertie a cavalry regiment as a surprise on his birthday. C.B.'s comment to Charlotte was: 'A new uniform for Tum!'

In the drawing room the Queen spoke to him about the Kaiser:

screwed up her face about him, said he had no heart, he had behaved very badly to Caprivi: & the other day when news came to him of the Russian Emperor's death it found him dining with a big party & when he heard it he jumped up & drank to the health of the young Emperor. Not a word of grief or sympathy. I do not know if I told you that she wants to give a Regt to the Russian Emperor, and I suggested to her last night that it might offend the German Emperor, who at present is the only one so honoured, – she said 'I do not care if it does'.

CHAPTER 10

Marienbad

FOR more than thirty years C.B. and Charlotte went every year to the spa of Marienbad in Bohemia, so that in time their annual arrival there became one of the events of the place. When they began to go there in the early 1870s it was a little-known watering place, though Goethe had stayed there in 1820, conducting a romance with a girl fifty years younger than himself, while Chopin and Richard Wagner used to compose there. In their last years, however, and particularly after the Prince of Wales began his visits in 1899, it became very fashionable.

People have an inexhaustible interest in their health, and belief in the therapeutic powers of natural mineral springs lasted for many years. In England the fashion began in the eighteenth century, and many towns grew up round mineral springs. Apart from Bath itself, Buxton, Cheltenham, Harrogate, Leamington, Malvern and Tunbridge Wells were among the most important, but there was a time when many lesser places laid claim to the possession of healing waters. Within a small area of mid-Wales the names of Llandrindod Wells, Builth Wells and Llangammarch Wells testify to past enthusiasms, and even in Hampstead the names of Well Walk and Well Road indicate where past generations drank the waters.

In the nineteenth century many of these English spas decayed, but, with the building of railways, spas on the continent became accessible to English people in search of health, change and recreation. Gastein, Carlsbad, Kissingen, Homburg, Wiesbaden, Aix-la-Chapelle, Ems, Vichy and Baden-Baden were at the height of their reputation at the end of the nineteenth century and in the first few years of the twentieth.

A 'cure' of three or four weeks at one of these spas was the remedy pre-scribed by doctors in England, France and Germany for eleven months of over-eating by the well-to-do of late Victorian and Edwardian days. The routine suited them well. They dieted, more or less, and drank the waters, which were supposed to benefit their livers. A band woke them early in the morning, they took their glass, strolled about, met their friends, sat in cafés, walked in the forests round about, went to the theatre or shopped, took baths at the spa in peat or 'mineralized mud', and felt that while enjoying themselves they were doing themselves good. Whether the effect was physical or psychological did not matter. It may to some extent have been a matter of faith – one contemporary saw a parallel between Marienbad and Lourdes.

Marienbad was visited in its heyday by fifteen thousand people every year. It was a village in a Bohemian valley, eight hundred miles from London, surrounded on three sides by hills covered with pine forests. There were three main springs, the Kreuzbrunnen, surrounded by a colonnade, the Carolinenbrunnen, which smelt slightly of sulphur-etted hydrogen and was covered by a Greek temple set in a grove of alder and fir trees, and the Marienbrunnen, where the escaping carbonic acid gas produced a constant hissing noise. From these springs came the healing waters, clear, sparkling and bitter. They belonged to, and enriched, the nearby abbey of Tepl. The monks of this abbey wore white cassocks and, in sunny or cold weather, black top hats. They spent alternating two-year periods in seclusion or in the world. C.B. said that their costume was emblematic of their lives, the white cassock standing for their two years' seclusion and the top hat for their two years in the world.[1]

A contemporary authority on spas, Dr. Sigismund Sutro, wrote that 'Marienbad owes its virtues chiefly to the sulphate of soda, and is indicated in plethora, and for persons of luxurious habits'.[2] Such were, in great part, the people who flocked to it. It lay some two thousand feet up, halfway between Eger and Pilsen, where the beer comes from. There was a long central street, the Kaiser-Strasse, a building called the Brunnenhalle, where those taking the cure could walk in wet weather, and a Stadthaus. There were churches of all denominations, including a Russian Orthodox church with golden onion domes and an English church. There were a number of hotels, the old-fashioned Klinger, where the Campbell-Bannermans always stayed, unmoved by King Edward, who in 1906 remarked: 'I don't know whether this old barrack is a fit abode for the British Prime Minister', the newer and palatial

Weimar, where the King stayed, and, next door, the Grünen Kreuz, preferred by Admiral Fisher.

All sorts of people came to this tiny place, and most of them enjoyed it immensely. Fisher, who called it 'beloved Marienbad', and who managed to go there and back, staying for three weeks, for £25, wrote:

> At Marienbad I met some very celebrated men, and the place being so small I became great friends with them. If you are restricted to a Promenade only a few hundred yards long for two hours morning and evening, while you are drinking your water, you can't help knowing each other quite well. . . . I almost think I knew Campbell-Bannerman the best. He was very delightful to talk to.[3]

The routine of drinking the waters could be varied by taking mud baths in a substance described by Dr. Sutro as 'a brown, bituminous, unctuous mass, intermixed with decomposed vegetable fibre'. It is agreeable to think of large Edwardian gentlemen and ladies wallowing in this like hippopotami before resuming the social round.

To this Nirvana came a fine selection of the entries in *Who's Who* and the *Almanach de Gotha* from all over Europe. Among them were Princess Ferdinand of Bulgaria, Grand Admiral Tirpitz, Mr. Oscar Browning from King's, Arthur Pinero and the actors Squire Bancroft and Beerbohm Tree, the Vienna correspondent of *The Times*, Wickham Steed, the Princesses of Saxe-Weimar, Württemberg and Mecklenberg-Schwerin, and the ageing Lillie Langtry. Here also came Slatin Pasha, a Viennese gentleman turned Moslem, who had fought the Mahdi with Gordon and been the Mahdi's prisoner for twelve years, the Turkish Grand Vizier Hakki Pasha, Princess Dolgorouki, once morganatic wife of the Czar, Sir Ernest Cassel the financier, the art dealer Duveen, and the Russian journalist Madame Olga Novikov, a friend of C.B.'s and of Mr. Gladstone's. Another friend of C.B.'s was General Gallifet, the French cavalry general and hero of the last despairing charges of Sedan, who was Minister of War during the Dreyfus case, shot down the Communists in 1871 and had a silver plate over part of his stomach covering one of his many wounds. He was followed from Paris by a bevy of beautiful women. There were some of the Ambassadors from London, including Count Mensdorff and the Marquis de Soveral, King Edward's great friend, called by C.B. and his friends 'the blue monkey', Sir Rufus Isaacs and the young Lloyd George. Here too came the diplomatist Sir Horace Rumbold, who once knocked a man down when he was asked for his ticket on a train, such a question implying that an Ambassador might be trying to travel without one, and who on the strength of his acquaintance asked C.B. in 1900 to guarantee a banker's loan of £800. In 1894 there even arrived so unlikely a person as the Irish leader John Dillon. Lord Rosebery went there after his wife's death; Mr. T. P. O'Connor was to be seen sporting an immense flowered handkerchief and a huge silver snuff box. Sundry Russian and Polish Jews in kaftans and side-curls mingled with society ladies in huge Edwardian hats. Indeed almost everyone seemed to be at Marienbad except the Czechs, who actually lived in Bohemia.

They all had, very broadly, the same social background, so that although they came from all parts of Europe they got on well with one another and mixed easily. The relations between them had that touch of formality and ceremoniousness which makes it easy for men and women of different nationalities to mingle comfortably.

C.B. went to Marienbad primarily for Charlotte's sake. She was very often in indifferent health. The doctors could find nothing fundamentally wrong with her but she put on a lot of weight and was constantly suffering from one ailment or another. She loved Marienbad and it undoubtedly did her good. They stayed there for six weeks or more and then usually went on to the Austrian Alps for a 'Nachkur'. They put themselves in the hands of the spa's most famous physician, Dr. Alfred Ott, and later of his son Ernst, fair, slim and elegant, the very pattern of a society doctor. They had great confidence in both the Otts and an affection for them too. The elder Ott stayed with them in London. The younger, who took over the practice in 1897, also looked after the King. His financial affairs fell into disorder soon after both the Campbell-Bannermans were dead. He neglected his wife and family and took to morphia, an addiction of which he died miserably at Udine during the First World War.

To C.B. and Charlotte, however, he was an unmixed blessing. When Charlotte reached Marienbad she began to feel better. In September 1899, for example, C.B. wrote to his cousin: 'I am glad to say my wife, who was very low in health when we came, and who did not show much improvement for the first few days, is recently immensely better – nerves better, pulse, walking power & everything. Even the Dr. is quite astonished. . . .'[4]

Charlotte was not the only person to find this. Lord Fisher, for example, suffered from dysentery:

When all the doctors failed to cure me, I accidentally came across a lovely partner I used to waltz with, who begged me to go to Marienbad, in Bohemia. I did so, and in three weeks I was in robust health. It was the Pool of Bethesda, and this waltzing angel put me into it, for it really was a miracle, and I never again had a recurrence of my illness.[5]

Enthusiasts began drinking at the Kreuzbrunnen even in the half-light of the early morning – between 5 and 6 a.m. But social life was also intense. At the theatre there were undemanding entertainments, like *Fledermaus* or *The Merry Widow* or recitals by Yvette Guilbert. One could have breakfast served by the mädchen at the Dianahof, sip coffee or lunch at the Café Rübezahl, on a hill overlooking Marienbad, which had majolica gnomes scattered under the pines, dine at the Stem off Wiener Schnitzel and Schinken, go to Wagner concerts at the Bellevue, a 'dairy café' on the edge of the forest, or listen to Beethoven in the woods.

Only an hour and a half away was Carlsbad, with another strange assortment of personalities – Clemenceau, the Russian Foreign Minister Izvolsky, Dr. Jameson of the Raid and the singer Adelina Patti.

At Marienbad C.B. and Charlotte met and made friends with Princess Louise. C.B. advised her where to buy her coffee and how to roast it. Thereafter he and Charlotte used to dine with her at Kensington Palace.[6]

Lady Wolseley, the general's wife, came to Marienbad rather earlier with her daughter Frances and gave Charlotte some names of dressmakers and makers of bonnets in London. She too stayed at the Hotel Klinger and wrote thence to her husband in September 1889:

The band begins to play just outside this Hotel at 6.30, & after that there is no peace. I drink 3 glasses, with intervals of 15 minutes, then take an hour's walk in the woods, then come home to tea & dry bread. . . . We find Lord Shand an intolerable bore and do all we can to shake him off. The C. Bannermans are friendly and harmless. The Bishop of Salisbury and Mrs. Wordsworth are *dirty* & he has horribly soft hands . . . beginning to talk at 7 a.m. is very exhausting. . . . This place wd. bore you to death. It is extremely pretty . . . just like the scenery of an operetta, but the performers are those of a *burlesque*, grotesque from fat.[7]

In another letter she wrote: '. . . We continue to find the Campbell-B.'s quite the nicest people here and had quite an affectionate parting with them.'[8]

C.B. was pained by the morals of his countrymen. He wrote to Herbert Gladstone in 1899:

I do not know how it comes to pass, but in this small Society of English people, quite half of the ladies either have already been, or are qualifying themselves for being, divorced: and a considerable number of the men are helping. I am not at all particular, but this makes a difficult situation in so small a society.[9]

A little later he wrote to his cousin:

All, all, are gone: our sweet countrymen & women, all off to their native shores, leaving no regrets behind them, but an evil name for scandals & loose living such as the poor Austrians (who do not pretend to much morality) have never seen equalled. Lords & Ladies & others have no right to come out to a quiet place like this & disgrace their country. I confess I have had more pleasure in consorting with the little colony of French people. They were, oddly enough, almost without exception on the side of Dreyfus. I hope the English will not lose their heads over that business: to carry indignation too high would do infinite harm. We were all specially interested here because General Gallifet is a constant comrade, & we are almost personally proud of the pluck & judgement he has shown.[10]

In 1900 he told his friend Ralph Knox:

We . . . are delighted to be here again. Our country people are fewer than usual: and there are one or two who I suspect are now studying the routes from here to Homburg, as The Object of Their Worship is to be found there and not here. Dieu merci!

Our only notabilities are my old friend General Gallifet, and the august Duc d'Orléans, from whom the British matron gathers up her skirts as he passes.[11]

Two years later: in a postscript to a letter to Sinclair, he wrote: 'Monseigneur Philippe d'Orléans in the adjoining rooms, but usually out of them with a Miss Mary Dalton whom I have not seen but who I hear is an American singer, well stricken in years and not well favoured.'[12]

King Edward VII went twice to Marienbad as Prince of Wales, and as King from 1903 until 1909. He, too, greatly enjoyed it, and his yearly presence helped to make it a social Mecca. It is recorded of the King that he 'used on his morning walk to greet a certain pretty shopowner named Fräulein Pistl, who sold Styrian hats under the colonnades. From time to time he was kind enough to buy one of her hats, which she had to deliver to him personally at the hotel.' The King made his household buy her hats and even the visiting Haldane was prevailed upon to acquire one.[13]

One September, before the King's accession, C.B. wrote to his cousin:

> Our most illustrious guest, the Heir Apparent . . . has enjoyed his stay and got good from it. He has kept to the diet & lost a lot of what our Dr. calls 'bad stuffs'. He is off today to Copenhagen. I asked him did he travel by Berlin? He drooped his right eyelid & said No, he would pass near it by Magdeburg. How his kindred love the 'shouting Emperor'.
>
> We have seen a new realization of the true saying that wheresoever the eagle is there will the carcasses be gathered together. Whether on account of the Prince's presence or not, the English & American society here has contained an extraordinary number of tainted ladies – including five divorcées and about ten others of various degrees of doubtfulness. The decent people were almost in a minority & we thought of wearing our marriage certificates as a sort of order outside our coats. . . .[14]

In August 1904 a letter to Bryce told the same story: 'We have the great man here with a cloud of bluebottle flies buzzing round him. It is worse than ever – he is recklessly abandoned to the society of a few semi-déclassé ladies and men to match. He is however civil enough to decent people: and follows the cure loyally. . . .'[15]

Next year, however, he told Sinclair that the King was 'less evilly surrounded than in other years . . . the doubtful ladies rather out of it. . . .'[16]

But the pace of royal social life was exhausting. In September 1905 C.B. wrote to Herbert Gladstone:

> The King is gone, and now one can breathe. While he was here it was one round of unceasing parties, and for the last fortnight about half of my meals have been taken in his company: and in the case of the evening meal this means beginning at 7.30, eating plain food but far too much, a trying mixture of court restraint and jollity; then while the dismal mysteries of bridge are being performed sitting making difficult conversation with one's fellow non-players and at 11 getting home to bed.[17]

The King dieted, but still allowed himself trout, grouse, aubergines and peaches, though wine was replaced by the waters of the Kreuzbrunnen. He normally adopted the style of the Duke of Lancaster, and would appear on the parade about 8 o'clock, walking between his equerry, Sir Stanley Clarke, and his assistant private secretary, Captain Frederick Ponsonby. He and C.B. wore the holiday rig of a suit with a short coat, a grey Homburg hat and a stiff collar and carried walking sticks.

After breakfast the King bathed in the Neubad. On the birthday of the Emperor of Austria, Franz-Josef, in whose dominions Marienbad lay, he dropped his incognito and, attired in the white uniform and green plumed hat of an Austrian Field-Marshal, attended, as King, the Emperor's birthday service, afterwards taking the salute at a march past of veterans.

On occasion the King went shooting, the worldly abbot (who duly received a K.C.V.O.) sending a monk round neighbouring estates to net partridges to put down near the abbey so that plenty of birds would be shown to the royal gun.

Not surprisingly, the King's efforts to avoid publicity and the attention of the crowds were of little avail. When he complained about being bothered by the crowds, C.B. replied: 'It would not be agreeable to you, Sir, if they did not take any notice at all.'[18]

Marienbad greatly helped C.B. to get on to good terms with the King, who was suspicious of him after his attacks on the Government during the Boer War. Arthur Ponsonby wrote to Herbert Gladstone early in 1906: 'I hear from my brother that C.B. was a great success at Marienbad. The K. was a little shy of him at first, but C.B. shone at the first luncheon with repartees, jokes and gastronomic appreciations, and

C.B. *by F. Sargent, 1893*

Hartington *by F. C. Gould*

he became a frequent guest, finally entertaining the K. himself.[19] Ponsonby's brother Fritz recorded of C.B. that

> the King thought he would be prosy and heavy, but found to his surprise that he was quite light in hand with a dry sense of humour. He told several amusing stories and was very good company. After this a sort of friendship sprung up between the two and the King seemed to like the straightforward way he had of stating his convictions without fearing that his opinions might be distasteful to His Majesty.[20]

On one occasion, after he had been at Marienbad during one of the King's visits, one of C.B.'s private secretaries, Henry Higgs, showed him an illustrated paper with a sketch of the King talking very earnestly and striking his hand in his palm while C.B. listened gravely. Around them in the gardens of the Kurhaus the visitors stood in a ring at a respectful distance. The picture bore the title 'Is it Peace or War?' C.B. looked at the picture and said solemnly, 'Would you like to know what the King was saying to me?' Higgs said he would. 'He wanted to have my opinion whether halibut is better baked or boiled!'[21]

In the easy and unconstrained atmosphere of Marienbad C.B. was seen at his best. He was good-humoured, equable and amusing. He himself rarely took the cure but he mixed with the crowd and carried his glass, even if it contained a milder draught than the Kreuzbrunnen waters.

All the years that C.B. went to Marienbad he kept lists[22] in his diary of the people he met and got to know there, and these annual lists show the growth of Marienbad as a fashionable centre, while at the same time C.B. was rising slowly from the obscurity of 1872 to the eminence of 1906. Marienbad was also the place where he and Charlotte formed many of their friendships. At first there are only a few well-known names – Lady Holland, the Spencers, the Bernstorffs, rather mysteriously 'Stanhope & Tolstoy' in 1884, 'Fisher R.N.' from 1889. Then from 1894 the list becomes more exotic – the Grand Duke Michael, the Duc d'Orléans, Mrs. Langenbach (a Viennese lady married to an Englishman), the Duchess of Dino and Princesse Galitzine, Lord Charles Beresford and his wife, the Princesse de Montglyon, the Shah in 1900, Hardinge in 1902. There is no list for 1903 but from the next year it starts with the King.

C.B. never tired of Marienbad. Ponsonby wrote in 1906: 'He

simply loves the place as he has been here every year for nearly 30 years & every old woman & shopkeeper greets him & he goes up & shakes hands with them.'[23] In one letter to Mrs. Langenbach C.B. wrote: 'I hope you are not suffering for your unfaithfulness to Marienbad last year. You would have found many sad changes: among others, Mme Fischl incapacitated and the business sold! Tout passe: tout casse: but I do not find that tout lasse.'[24]

Marienbad has slipped behind the Iron Curtain in communist Czechoslovakia, and is now called Marianské Lázně. The great Edwardian hotels have fallen into decay and are filled with Czech party workers and officials. Ichabod.

CHAPTER 11

The Member for Stirling

FOND though C.B. was of Marienbad, it was only an annual inter-
lude. The centre of his working life was the House of Commons.
He was a member of it for forty years. When he came to it, as a
young man, it was dominated by the contests between Gladstone and
Disraeli and the orations of John Bright. When he ended his days in the
House, it contained men of an entirely different epoch – Lloyd George,
Winston Churchill and F. E. Smith, Ramsay MacDonald and Hilaire
Belloc.

He loved the House of Commons, and was a stickler for old Parliamentary practices. He was, for example, one of the last members who
wore a hat in the House, uncovering to hear a direct message from the
Queen, but keeping it on, as Gladstone, Lowe and Hartington had
done, 'all', as C.B. held, 'the vieille école', when a message was read at
second-hand from the Chair.

In his young days C.B. sat on the cross benches, near the Peers'
Gallery, facing the Speaker. The House was still to quite a large extent
an aristocratic assembly, though there were an increasing number of
men like himself whose fathers or grandfathers had made money in
business, so enabling their offspring to give their minds to public affairs.
The character of the House was constantly changing, sometimes
markedly so, as after the elections of 1868, 1885 and 1906. But he was
at all times at home in its atmosphere. He bridled when a friend of
Lady Aberdeen's described political people as men 'of the baser sort',
and told her that 'there is quite as much honesty, nobility, sacrifice, and
so on, in political as in ecclesiastical circles. I am not sure that I would
not go further and say that – but no; better not.'[1]

For the first twenty years of his career the Whigs, who comprised about a thousand families, owning large estates, formed the right wing of the Liberal Party, their representatives being mainly noblemen like Granville, Hartington and Argyll. The split over Home Rule in 1886 put an end to them and there are various candidates for the title of the 'Last of the Whigs'—Lord Hartington, Lord Spencer, or even Sir Edward Grey.

C.B. himself, who was described by one observer as 'a tallish, well-nourished man' who 'always reminded the House of a plainly dressed Captain O'Shea',[2] began as a Radical, a young, earnest Lowlander, anxious to see big changes, one of the impatient young men of the left. But he soon moved to what might be called a left/centre position. Once there he drifted no further. With the later Radicals on the left of the party in the eighties, Joseph Chamberlain and Dilke, with their tinge of republicanism and their thoroughgoing *dirigiste* programme of social reform, he had little in common; nor with the extreme liberalism of Wilfrid Lawson. Still less did he sympathize with the wearisomely cynical radicalism of 'Labby', the somewhat shady Henry Labouchere, a rich ex-diplomatist and theatrical manager who thought the worst of everyone, edited his own paper, *Truth*, and held court in the smoking room of the House. But C.B. never felt the lure of imperialist romance. He deeply distrusted Chamberlain, whom he described as the Opposition's 'evil genius for he is always guided by his spite and is therefore a poor tactician'.[3]

He remained constant to the Cobdenite and Gladstonian philosophy, with a strong feeling of respect for the rights of the individual as against the state, derived from Herbert Spencer.

On the benches opposite, after Disraeli had withdrawn to the upper House, C.B. observed the placid leadership of Stafford Northcote and W. H. Smith. Both had a good deal in common with C.B. himself, but when W. T. Stead remarked to Balfour on the similarity between C.B. and W. H. Smith, Balfour replied: 'I quite agree, but he is much cleverer than W. H. Smith.'[4]

There also was the reassuring figure of Henry Chaplin, 'the Squire', a cross between Squire Western and John Bull, who hunted six days a week and kept four packs of hounds. He was a man with whom the horse came first, so much so that, when he became engaged to a daughter of the Duke of Sutherland, his first thought was how to provide her with a mount, and he wrote: 'you will no doubt understand, my dear child, that it is of importance to me to know whether you are under or over 15 stone – no, I meant 14, for I do not suppose you are more than that, although there is no knowing what time may do for you.'[5] C.B. saw, too, the rocketing rise of Lord Randolph Churchill who, as his friend Lord Rosebery wrote, was in the wrong party, his 'Tory democracy' being 'simply Liberalism under another name', and the emergence of Arthur Balfour. The Irish members – Parnell himself, the fanatical Biggar from Belfast, the eloquent but interminable Sexton, the brilliant but vicious Tim Healy, the urbane T. P. O'Connor – were his antagonists in 1884–5, but he remained on good terms with them and they liked him.

He had, of course, his dislikes. He did not like Goschen, whom in a moment of anger he once called 'that vile intriguer Göschen, with his big bribes all round'.[6] H. J. Massingham wrote of him: 'C.B. hated the superior person; hence his life-long aversion for Mr. Balfour.'[7] Arnold Morley he never cared for, nor Sir Charles Dilke, of whom Margot Asquith once wrote: 'After hearing him talk uninterruptedly for hours and watching his stuffy face and protruding eyes, I said to Laura: "He may be a very clever man, but he has not a ray of humour and hardly any sensibility. If he were a horse I would certainly not buy him." '[8]

Among the Conservatives he was fond of Walter Long. He told the Master of Elibank that he thought that Long would one day lead the Conservatives. Elibank thought that C.B. and Long were much alike.

C.B., until he became Prime Minister, when, as many witnesses testify, he astonished both sides of the House by his Parliamentary performances, was never much of a speaker or debater, especially if he was put off his stroke by hostile criticism. He stuck too close to his written text, spread out on the despatch box. He used loose sheets of notes, written out in his own hand, with new points and points to emphasize marked in red chalk. He often held these notes up close to his eyes, as he was short-sighted. He usually took great pains and spent a lot of time on the texts of his speeches, for he was not a quick worker. It was said that he read more of his speeches than any previous front-rank minister but that, typically, 'he never made the faintest attempt to conceal what he was doing'. He had not the quickness or the attacking verve of Balfour or Chamberlain, nor the massive forensic vigour of Asquith. This was one reason why he was so consistently underrated. Massingham wrote that 'his voice, though agreeable, lacks the fulness of note that the dramatic flight requires'.[9] But he was described as a very fair House of Commons speaker who did not bore members by the excessive length of his speeches. One critic wrote in 1895:

Mr. Campbell-Bannerman has himself to thank if he is not better known and better understood. There are very few abler men in the

Government or the House of Commons. But he makes no fuss and no show. He does not sufficiently sacrifice to the glorified spirit of self-advertisement which presides over the new era. He cannot always get up moral steam. . . . But . . . when he speaks people listen, attend, and are convinced.

This was true, but it took a long time before he was given a real hearing. He was always a popular man in the House – Stead wrote of him in 1908 that he had gone through life without making a personal enemy.[10]

He thought that politics had deteriorated during his lifetime. In October 1900, he wrote in a letter to Sir Ralph Knox: 'You say politics is a dirty trade. It did not use to be so: it is since certain gentlemen have come into it, e.g. R. Churchill, Chamberlain, Brodrick etc. that these dirty attacks are made. Formerly there was loyalty and solidarity: but now there is none. . . .'[11]

He was seldom caught up in the excitement and fever of politics. Indeed he told Knox in 1896: 'I habitually avoid controversy and hate it, and shall not poke my nose into the thing if it is not absolutely necessary.'[12] He was never rattled, never panicked into rash and inconvenient courses, never tempted into trying to take a quick trick. He had the unhurried worldly wisdom which one might expect from the best type of old family solicitor. He was naturally indolent. Arthur Ponsonby said that 'he was punctual but too easy-going. He told me that he had never read a Bill or a Blue Book through.'[13]

Officials found him easy to work with. One of them later wrote:

He took official life very easily without in any way neglecting any of its duties or shirking any of its routine work. . . . He had an extraordinarily methodical mind which enabled him to get through the maximum of work with the minimum of labour – either mental or physical. . . .[14]

Knox was sent a pin with a star sapphire on it to remember C.B. by after a spell at the War Office. 'There is a sobriety about it,' C.B. wrote, 'which is in harmony with your stern financial character!'

C.B. also looked with a cool eye on the prizes of great office. Typical of his attitude was the letter he wrote to his cousin on August 15, 1892, just after becoming a Cabinet Minister for the second time:

. . . It is the first time I have had to do with making up a Government, and it is a most sickening job. Everything has to be discussed and considered, and the secrets of all hearts laid bare. Even yesterday (Sunday) they scoured the clubs for me, and finally tore me away from a French novel in a cool library to advise as to the mode out of a dilemma. I take as little to do with it as I can. . . .

I expect we shall go down to Osborne on Wednesday, and I see nothing to prevent my slipping away with my wife to Marienbad on Saturday or Sunday. The next few weeks are the dead season in all the public offices. . . .[15]

There was no affectation in this. It represented his real outlook, described in confidence to a close relative and friend. It is scarcely the note of a man burning for personal glory or filled with a desire to re-arrange other people's lives for them. Two days after receiving the seals of office on this occasion C.B. did indeed leave for Marienbad.

His colleagues, in fact, had considerable difficulty in prising C.B. away from Marienbad or luring him down from Scotland when there was work to be done in the House of Commons. He had a strong tendency to lurk off if his presence was not absolutely imperative. Once, when he was a junior Minister, he was intercepted by one of the Whips, Lord Kensington, and rebuked with the words, 'The hireling fleeth.' 'He fleeth because he is an hireling,' replied C.B. placidly. He told the wife of another Whip, Whiteley, in 1906: 'Personally I am an immense believer in bed, in constantly keeping horizontal: the heart and everything else go slower, and the whole system is refreshed. . . .'[16]

When he became a senior Minister, this tendency increased. Sir William Harcourt, whose burdens in the House of Commons he was supposed to share, wrote to him at Belmont on the last day of 1894:

Xmasing now being over . . . I really hope you will awake to the fact that there is an institution called H.M.'s Govt., that there are such things as Estimates, and that one day there will be a H. of Commons.

A week later he added:

I am extremely sorry that any one should be put to inconveniance and most of all you. Scotland is a 'far cry', but then as a compensation it occupies more than half the Government, and till we get Home Rule for Scotland it is almost inevitable that Ministers should be occasionally in London.

We began this Govt. with a declaration that there were to be

Cabinets *once a week*; we have got down now to *once a quarter*, and I suppose if we survive we shall have ½-yearly & perhaps yearly meetings . . .

In my recollections of Govts., Ministers are always in town all November and Jany., and I do not see how administration can be carried on upon any other footing. . . .

I am urgently in need of your strong sense and judgement to help me in controlling the extravagance and looseness of other Departments.[17]

C.B. replied amiably to this blast, explaining that he had been addressing some public meetings in Scotland:

My view of it is rather that I have been sweating in the stoke-hole to keep the steam up, while certain other people have been lolling in the smoking-room or enjoying the breezes on the quarter-deck. Mine have been meetings without plum-pudding unless that word can be figuratively applied to the varied but stodgy oratory of the War Minister.

He also claimed that he had had Knox, the Accountant-General at the War Office, up at Belmont for some days and that they had been going through the estimates.[18]

Next year he was asked by the Queen to go to Nice at Easter as Minister in Attendance. He wrote to Harcourt: 'It is not the manner I would select for spending a holiday but on one or two occasions I have made difficulties and got off and this time it would be well to "bow my head". If the holiday was too short for so long a journey I suppose I could bulge over a day or two in moderate limits.'[19] Harcourt wrote sharply: 'We can have no "bulging over". This first footman work must be done by the drones of the other place. What else do they exist for. . . .'[20]

There are a number of notes in the Harcourt papers like this:

10 Downing Street
4 October 1894

Dear Sir William,
The Cabinet sat for about an hour and a half this morning. . . .
C. Bannerman did not turn up, and nobody has heard of him. . . .
Yours very truly
G. H. Murray.

C.B. was indeed of a passive disposition, at the opposite end of the world from those politicians who enjoy activity for activity's sake. He looked with a cool and amused eye on the follies into which their restless energy led them. They, for their part, were apt to despise his inactivity. But as, in an imperfect world, the choice is often between doing nothing and doing harm, a cautious and quietist approach in politics may have something to commend it.

In those leisurely days, C.B. was not alone in his relaxed attitude to his responsibilities. Among his letters, for example, is one from General Sir Redvers Buller in 1894, written from Devonshire when he was Adjutant-General and C.B. Secretary of State for War. It begins: 'The news that you will be at the office Wednesday, Thursday & Friday has come rather upon me like a bomb shell: as I have private theatricals here on Thursday & Friday & a dance on the Friday night after them. . . . I had rather calculated that Scotland would hold you from New Year's day till twelfth night. . . .'[21] Another, four days later, said: 'I am very much obliged to you for allowing me to be away at this moment from London, for my poor wife is in a great taking with the house full, theatricals and a dance and no one to help her.'[22]

Throughout his career C.B. remained faithful to the Stirling Burghs and they to him. All the efforts of his opponents could not dislodge him. In 1887 the party managers made an effort to persuade him to fight one of the more doubtful Scottish seats at the next general election. Those suggested were Forfarshire, Central Glasgow and Dunbartonshire. At the first he would have been, rather awkwardly, on the home ground of his Conservative brother at Stracathro. Dunbartonshire, though he thought he could win it, did not attract him. The great challenge was the Glasgow seat, where there was an enormous Conservative majority, which the party managers thought that he, but hardly anyone else, might pull down. But he told his cousin that he was not going to run his head against a stone wall and, after two years' cogitation, he finally decided against it. Moreover he had warned Mr. Gladstone that if he left Stirling the seat would probably be won by a Unionist. He then thought about West Perthshire, commenting to his cousin: 'Old Currie is a horrid old fellow for an antagonist: but just because he is a horrid old fellow they want him out.'[23]

He was invited to stand by a large number of local electors but decided that the 'toil of it and the expense' would not suit him and that what was really needed was a 'rough sort of fellow, who could hit hard and go in for crofters and all that' if 'that old wretch Curric' was to be opposed effectively.[24]

At one stage he had trouble with the Secretary of the Liberal Association in Dunfermline, a Mr. Ireland, who accused him of giving up his independence by accepting office and favouring Stirling over Dunfermline, and reproached him with 'the indifference which it is said you manifest to your Constituents or as some style it your cavalier treatment of them, contenting yourself with one flying visit in the year of an hour or two's duration which is the only intercourse you have had with your constituents for some years. . . .'[25] C.B. was unruffled, regarding Mr. Ireland as a poor guide to Dunfermline feeling and as a man who for some reason harboured a grudge against him. But he certainly spent the minimum of time on cultivating his constituency.

In 1886 he told the Duke of Cambridge: 'I have no fear as to my own election which ought to be a very hollow affair but it is necessary to attend to it and not to have the air of taking it as a matter of course.'[26] In 1903 he wrote: 'I expect to be in Scotland at Whitsuntide & have a meeting at Perth. At these odd times however I seldom invade the constituency, as I have never found much good done by it, & it gives trouble to people.'[27]

In Stirling in the eighties, however, he had to be watchful. After the Home Rule split, he wrote: 'all the old Ramsayites have left me and are vicious Unionists', and of Ramsay himself he said: 'I should not wonder if the silly old fellow actually thinks of opposing me. I saw him there yesterday. He gave £1,000 to the Burgh the other day for Education, & must have had a sinister motive for so unnatural an act.'[28]

Two years later he wrote: 'The Unionists . . . are to have no less a person than Hartington to rouse their enthusiasm at Stirling, with all the Primrose dames, special trains & cheap tickets set in motion to gather an audience. I do not expect he will do us much harm.'[29]

He didn't. Next month C.B. wrote that Hartington had been 'deadly dull & disappointed them all'. On his home ground C.B. was indestructible. He was also entirely in tune with his constituents. One of them met him in the street and said to him: 'Sir Henry, I like you very much, but I would rather vote for the Devil.' C.B. promptly replied: 'As your friend is not a candidate, you might just as well vote for me.'

C.B. was a thorough Scot, and a very typical one, as was Charlotte. C.B.'s food, his jokes, his closest friends were all Scots, and it was in

Scotland that he preferred to live. He called it 'the best side of the Tweed' and, oddly enough, repudiated what he held to be the Sassenach illusion that whisky is the national drink of Scotland. 'Claret', he maintained in the House of Commons in 1899, 'is the very special drink of Scotland.'

The *Manchester Guardian* thought that 'if his life had been ordered in accordance with his own wish he would have devoted himself, like Burns, to do something for "puir auld Scotland's sake" '.[30]

But he had, on the whole, a poor opinion of the Highlands. He wrote to a colleague in October 1905:

I seldom venture as you have done into the wilds of the Scotch Highlands. They are not the working & really dominant part of the country: I find the humdrum lowlands interesting enough: and I keep my temper even by avoiding even the sight of the shooting tenant & ghillie-dom which is the curse of Celtic Caledonia.[31]

As a politician who was much caught up in the controversy about Home Rule for Ireland he could not escape pronouncing on the claim from his own country. In 1889 he had set out his views in detail in a letter to Donald Crawford:

My own conviction is that it is only by local parliaments & local executives in each of the three kingdoms that we can settle H.R. at all. And on the whole, although there will be difficulties, the advantages will outweigh them. . . . I am therefore ready (but not anxious) for it: and my experience is that *everywhere* I go the body of a meeting favours Scotch H.R. . . . It is not a doctrine imposed on the people by us for our purposes: it is a genuine growth of popular opinion.

At the same time . . . I think we should deprecate the idea of cumbering & bedevilling the Irish question by a simultaneous demand for Scotch Home Rule . . . but the one will involve the other as sure as eggs is eggs.

It should be pointed out . . . however that Scotch Home Rule involves *English* H. Rule; and that not one in a thousand Englishmen has ever grasped the idea of having a local Parlt. as apart from the common Imperial Parlt., so that Scotch Home Rule must wait until the sluggish mind of John Bull is educated up to that point.

Nothing rash, but nothing discouraging, is therefore, I think, what ought to be our motto. . . .[32]

In 1894 he voted for a resolution in the House of Commons 'that it is desirable, while retaining intact the power and supremacy of the Imperial Parliament, to establish a legislature in Scotland for dealing with purely Scottish affairs'.

He became extremely knowledgeable about Scottish opinion, from his own experience and from his wide circle of Scottish friends. By 1889 he was regarded as one of the foremost Scottish M.P.s. Morley and others used to consult him as a matter of course on Scottish questions.

In 1897 his friend Thomas Shaw wrote an article in the *Nineteenth Century* on the needs of Scottish education and was thrilled when, as a direct result, Andrew Carnegie offered £1 million for it. Shaw went first to consult C.B., whose reaction was, he tells us: 'Lord, Tammas, this beats a'! That blessed little essay of yours which you sent round to us – well, it went into the waste-paper basket. And now here is the whole affair. Yes, of course, I'll be a Trustee.'[33]

Later Carnegie modified his scheme, so that there would be no general exemption from fees, but only on special application on grounds of poverty. C.B. and Shaw were both irritated, C.B. saying that 'the professor lot' would put obstacles in the way and try to 'grab for their own university', so that university education would remain primarily a class institution, and the great mass of the Scottish people would be left outside.

Scotland would not be Scotland without the kirk. All his life C.B. was in favour of disestablishment and disendowment of the Church of Scotland, and he was in the minority who voted for disestablishment in 1886. But he had little time for the extremists, writing to Bryce in October 1904: 'The "wee Frees" are a poor lot – no men of standing and no ministers of any save the narrow Highland type: but they have the cleverness and cunning of that type.'[34]

He feared these influences in the field of politics too. In 1890, after a by-election, he wrote: 'Ayr was a bad business. . . . It was in Oban & the other Highland Burghs that we were beaten: & the Auld Kirk did it. . . . This is rather disgusting: but the Highlander is a rum politician. . . .'[35]

There were other types of Scotsman he did not much care for. In another letter to his cousin he told him that 'you & I & the rest of us are quite unworthy of mixing with the small lairdies of Stirlingshire, and we ought not to expect to have our names mentioned in such august company. . . .'[36]

He was always in favour of more power and responsibility for local authorities in Scotland. In taking this line he was making a genuine effort to increase local powers and was not hoping for any party advantage, for, as he told Bryce in 1904:

The fatal thing is that County Councils in Scotland are nearly all Tory. The areas are so large that the body of the people and their possible representatives are excluded because they could not attend. Payment of travg. expenses wd. help a little.

At present it is all Lairds and farmer-toadies carefully selected and reduced by flattery and snobism to a pulp.[37]

In his day the *Scotsman* was an extreme Tory paper. C.B. wrote of it to Mr. Gladstone in 1886: 'There is no limit to the Scotsman's malignant distortion of facts',[38] and fifteen years later, in 1901, he took the same view, saying: 'I have for many years pursued the course of ignoring the virulent ravings of that paper, and I do not think I have lost by it!'[39]

Looked at in the round, C.B.'s was a strange way of life. Ample means meant that it was easy and comfortable. Not only was he not troubled by the worries about money that afflict most people, and able to do whatever he liked, but he lived, all his life, in a spacious and luxurious atmosphere - large numbers of servants, good food, good horses, large, well furnished rooms, good hotels, first-class railway carriages. This undoubtedly played a part in making him so relaxed and genial a person. But in other ways it was a life that many people would find dull and limiting – a fixed and immutable routine, no adventures to distant parts of the world, no spice of danger, no passionate absorption in any great project, not even any sport or game pursued with more than tepid enthusiasm. But it exactly suited a man who was by nature indolent and easy-going, and whose wife was disabled by ill-health and nervousness from taking any difficult and unexpected road. And of excitement there was to be plenty in the political life that C.B. had taken up when he came to London. Indeed, in that world he was to have as rough a passage as any man of his generation, and was to show that under the soft exterior there lay a man of tough fibre.

Part 4

The Secretary of State

CHAPTER 12

The War Office Again

'I knew in that old building half a score of Secretaries of State. . . . Those among them who made the fewest mistakes were those who tried the fewest changes: bad as the old machine was, it went better with oil and leisure than it did with grit and energy.'

Sir William Butler in his Autobiography[1]

C.B.'s few months of dealing with Irish affairs had markedly increased his reputation. In November 1885, Hamilton stayed at Iwerne Minster in Dorset, seeing electric lights for the first time. He noted in his diary: 'Lord Spencer formed a very high opinion of the qualifications and powers of Campbell Bannerman while he held the post of Chief Secretary. I am not surprised: and it is quite conceivable that Campbell Bannerman may take a great jump in the political world. . . .'[2]

As usual, Hamilton was right. Within two months, in February 1886, C.B. was in the Cabinet. True to form, he and Charlotte refused to take things too seriously. On the Wednesday afternoon they went to the circus at Covent Garden and on the Friday to the new operetta, *The Mikado*, which they very much enjoyed. On the Saturday C.B. went down with his new colleagues to Osborne to receive the seals of office, and before long he was summoned to Windsor 'to dine and sleep'. He had finally become one of Her Majesty's 'confidential servants'.

C.B. probably had little idea how much his elevation to the Cabinet, at the age of forty-nine, had been due to royal influence and how little to Mr. Gladstone's choice. In fact royal intervention had been decisive. When C.B. had been Financial Secretary he was one of the few politicians who seemed sensible and agreeable to the Duke of Cambridge, and the Duke's favourable opinion had become known in the Royal family. So had his highly unfavourable opinion of Childers.

When the Government changed the Prince of Wales wrote to the

Queen's Private Secretary, Sir Henry Ponsonby, saying: 'Should Mr. Campbell-Bannerman be moved up higher I know that the Duke of Cambridge would gladly see him at the War Office.'[3] Ponsonby replied next day thanking the Prince for his 'very valuable' suggestion, but saying:

> I fear however that he is not to be in the Cabinet though I think The Queen would have been glad if this arrangement could have been carried out.
>
> Mr. Gladstone proposed Childers and Her Majesty . . . positively refused this, so positively indeed that Mr. Gladstone eventually promised to reconsider the question.[4]

Ponsonby was given the task of ensuring that the unwelcome proposal was dropped. He arrived in London to find Gladstone closeted with Childers, and the subsequent interview was not an easy one. Reporting the talk about Childers to the Queen, Ponsonby wrote:

> Mr. Gladstone . . . enquired what were the reasons your Majesty disliked him. Sir Henry Ponsonby could only say he was much disliked at the War Office and Admiralty, and that your Majesty could not possibly consent to his going to either Department again.
>
> After some discussion Mr. Gladstone said he wished to please your Majesty to the best of his power, and therefore at a great sacrifice would give up Mr. Childers and would select the gentleman named by your Majesty, Mr. Campbell-Bannerman, for the War Office.[5]

Royalty was triumphant. The Queen noted in her journal: 'Mr. Campbell-Bannerman, a good honest Scotchman, to the War Office',[6] and the Duke of Cambridge wrote to her on February 9 expressing his grrtitude,

> not only on my own account but specially as regards the interests of the Army, that you insisted on Mr. Campbell Bannerman coming here as Secretary of State, in preference to Mr. Childers. The former is a very nice calm and pleasant man, well known to all here and who knows the War Office work, & with whom I have no doubt I shall be able to get on very smoothly and well.[7]

After eighteen years in Parliament, C.B. had at last arrived.

As yet he was little known. The press gave him a tepid welcome, though the *Daily News* wrote that his few months as Chief Secretary were full of promise: 'He then displayed a certain *sang froid*, withal courteous, that baffled obstruction, and made the creaking wheels of Irish administration proceed with unusual smoothness.'[8] At Gladstone's request he made his youngest son Herbert Financial Secretary.[9]

As soon as he took up his duties, in the old building in Pall Mall that he knew so well, C.B. was faced with a demand from the Prime Minister to know why the Army Estimates were to be increased. C.B. sent a minute to the Chancellor of the Exchequer, Sir William Harcourt, explaining the demands arising from the occupation of Egypt, the increase of forces in India and other commitments, saying that he could reduce the amount left by his predecessor but that he feared that an increase over the 1885 estimates would still remain.[10]

Harcourt, however, was determined to cut expenditure to the bone. He was horrified that the combined naval and military estimates left behind by the Conservatives amounted to £30 millions. (What he would have thought of a defence budget of £2,000 millions cannot, fortunately, be imagined.) He insisted on reductions, threatening to resign if he did not have his way, and was supported by Gladstone. The estimates were reduced by £3 millions.

On February 15 C.B. attended his first Cabinet. Another newcomer was John Morley who, after only three years in the House of Commons, had become Chief Secretary for Ireland. C.B. found himself sitting next to Gladstone. 'I sat down timidly,' he said, 'like a *fausse marquise*, abashed to be under the wings of the great man'. But Gladstone waved a hand towards his colleagues, and said: 'You'll do, you're cantie and you're couthy.'[11] This pithy, though patronizing, utterance was in fact an accurate assessment of C.B. Eight years later, when he was said to be the only member of the Rosebery administration who was on speaking terms with all the others, some of his principal colleagues could have done with a little of his 'couthyness'. Mr. Gladstone, who had been a member of many Cabinets—he had held office under William IV – knew the value of a man being able to rub along with others. He had recommended his son to C.B. as 'competent and conformable'.[12]

C.B. was now brought into close contact with the leaders of the party, among them the rumbustious, brilliant, bullying Harcourt, full of scandalous stories, a tremendous performer in the House – a heavy-weight in every sense of the word – and Lord Ripon, born in No.10

Downing Street, a convert to Roman Catholicism, described by Mr. Gladstone as 'a model statesman of the second rank'. C.B. took to him at once. There was John Morley, very much the intellectual and man of letters in politics. C.B.'s friend Lord Spencer was Lord President of the Council, Granville Colonial Secretary, Rosebery Foreign Secretary and Chamberlain briefly, until he resigned in March, President of the Local Government Board.

At this first Cabinet the Army Estimates were discussed, and C.B., as a newcomer, was hardly in a position to make a stand against the demands for reductions made by the Prime Minister and the Chancellor of the Exchequer. Harcourt's son Loulou noted in his journal:

> . . .W.V.H. at Cabinet from 2.30 to 6. He carried his point that the Army and Navy Estimates are not to exceed those of last year. C-B took it well, but Ripon rather cross. In the middle of the discussion W.V.H. threw a note across the table to Chamberlain – 'Why the devil don't you support me in this?' Chamberlain replied by note 'I saw you were getting on swimmingly so I seized the opportunity to take a short but refreshing nap.'
>
> John Morley, asked by W.V.H. what he thought of his first Cabinet, replied: 'I think it very dull.'[13]

Harcourt was not content to let matters alone after his success. Ten days later he drew attention to French military economies, adding: 'As Carlyle says "Great art thou, oh Bankruptcy"!! What a good thing for the world it would be if all nations were altogether insolvent. How much less mischief they would do.'[14] C.B. wrote on the back of this: 'You are very cruel after the ruthless sacrifices you have imposed on us. . . . No doubt great would be the use of bankruptcy; it might even make a Treasury and a Ch. of Exchequer unnecessary? But even beggars will fight, so that a War Minister (without salary) would still survive.'[15]

Although he was so acceptable to Royalty, C.B. knew that a good deal of the trouble at the War Office was due to the increasing resistance of the Duke of Cambridge to any form of change. The office of Secretary of State was recognized to be a grave of reputations. Dilke and Chamberlain had scribbled notes to each other in Cabinet in 1884. Chamberlain had urged Dilke to consider taking on the job, saying: 'I have the lowest opinion of army administration. . . . It is most ludicrously inefficient.' Dilke replied: 'The Duke of Cambridge and the old soldiers and the Queen would make it very nearly hopeless.'[16]

The Queen was indeed a problem, as C.B. was soon to find. Her long experience gave her a great advantage in dealing with her Ministers. C.B. once tried to get her to agree to a plan and she replied: 'I remember Lord Melbourne using the same arguments many years ago, but it was not true then and it is not true now.' C.B. said he felt like a little boy talking to his grandmother. Some years later Lord Esher put his finger on the particular trouble that C.B. encountered:

> The Navy is a constitutional force. . . . The Army is a royal force and, while the Queen never interferes with the Navy, she interferes very much with the Army. As she listens to soldiers rather than to Ministers, the task of the Secretary of State for War is never easy. . . .[17]

C.B. began, wisely, by writing to Ponsonby, saying: 'I hope you will assure Her Majesty that it is my great desire to do all that is required for the efficiency of the army . . . to the maintenance of which I will devote all possible care.'[18]

In the House his first experience as a Secretary of State was an odd one. Mr. Howard Vincent moved for an increase in the capitation grant for the Volunteers. This was a reasonable suggestion, but Gladstone, much to the surprise of his supporters, suddenly rose and launched into a passionate protest about its unconstitutional character and declared that he would never accept orders from the House of Commons to increase public expenditure. C.B. was unmoved by this outburst. The *Annual Register* recorded that 'the Secretary for War, Mr. Campbell-Bannerman, somewhat threw over the argument of his chief. He admitted that financial difficulties existed in some corps which he hoped to remove.' A man who, after only a few weeks in the Cabinet, could, in the House, 'somewhat throw over' what Mr. Gladstone had just stated with considerable vehemence was clearly a man with a mind of his own.

C.B. had to explain to the Queen, and then to the House, the changes he was making in the deployment of the Army and the introduction of new weapons. He extracted funds from an unwilling Treasury with which Wolseley, the Adjutant-General, was able to set up an enlarged Intelligence Department under Brackenbury, whom Wolseley described as '*the* cleverest man in the British Army'.

He had to consider a new appointment at Suakin. Conscious of the need to avoid imperialist adventures, at this time of rampant jingoism, he wrote to the Duke of Cambridge: 'Against Kitchener . . . I understand he is rather apt to . . . create occasions for himself. Whereas we want quiet at Suakin. But he is a capable man. . . .'[19]

Kitchener was appointed.

No detail escaped the Queen. The new rifle had to be sent up to Balmoral and demonstrated for her. Writing to the Palace, C.B.'s private secretary reminded them that 'it went to Balmoral (absit omen) the last time Her Majesty was there, and . . . the cartridges jammed, and broke. This . . . was owing to the cartridges being old ones which had been repeatedly refilled.'

Fortunately, this time, it 'behaved admirably' and the Queen was much interested in seeing it'.[20] C.B. wrote to the Queen about the Army's quota of honours, saying that 'although the number allotted to the Army is usually exceeded it has been customary to borrow from the Navy, the number allotted to which Service is considerably in excess of requirements.'[21]

In June, asked about a possible honour for a certain Lieutenant-Colonel Gildea, he minuted:

> I know nothing about him except that he is an exceedingly pushing and fussy person, who whenever any small war takes place keeps writing to the 'Times' and starting funds. . . . Their administration furnishes a field for the benevolent exertions of a number of fine ladies, and this sort of thing seems to be Col. Gildea's *métier*.[22]

C.B.'s first spell in the Cabinet was however a very brief one, for the Government resigned when the Home Rule Bill was defeated and the next six years were spent in opposition. In those years he entered fully into the spirit of what Arthur Balfour called 'the monotonous fury of Party controversy'. As a member of the Opposition front bench with special experience of military questions, he spoke mainly on these, corresponding a good deal with Mr. Gladstone about political tactics. In 1888 he was chairman of a House of Commons committee on naval expenditure which included the young Sir Edward Grey and Lord Charles Beresford. Beresford led the minority which voted against C.B.'s chairmanship. The committee went exhaustively into questions of naval policy, including the design and armour-plating of ships, and questioned at length the First Naval Lord, Admiral Hood, and other witnesses.

In the same year C.B. strongly opposed a suggestion by Lord Randolph Churchill that civilian control of the Army should be reduced, arguing that the responsibility of Parliament must be retained intact, and that any other system would result in expenditure getting out of hand. He wrote drily to Gladstone of 'Lord R. Churchill, whose economy often becomes very thin in quality when no glory is to be gained and when party interests pull the other way'.[23] C.B. was a consistent critic of increases in military spending. He held that the Army had a strictly limited purpose. Speaking in the House on March 11, 1889, he asked:

for what purpose our Army is maintained. . . . Military policy obviously depends upon foreign policy. Both political Parties profess one principle of foreign policy, which is that, while willing to give friendly advice, we shall entirely abstain from any interference in Continental politics. What is the inference, as affecting our military policy, to be drawn from that fact? It is that we must abandon definitely all idea of placing on the Continent the six or ten, or perhaps 15 or 20 Army Corps which Continental interference would imply, and that we should restrict our Army to the protection of India and our Colonies and to our own domestic defence.'[24]

In 1888 he was nominated by Gladstone to be a member of the Royal Commission set up to enquire into the administration of the naval and military Departments. This became known as the Hartington Commission, after its chairman. Besides C.B., its membership included Lord Randolph Churchill, W. H. Smith and General Brackenbury. Its secretary was an engineer officer, Major Clarke, who was later to play an important part in the reorganization of the Army and to become Secretary of the Committee of Imperial Defence.

C.B. was sceptical about the value of the whole exercise and wrote to Ripon: 'I confess to having regarded this Commission from the first as a farce, and I feel pretty sure that it will produce nothing but smoke. . . .'[25] The first outline of the Commission's conclusions alarmed the Conservative Secretary of State for War, Stanhope, who wrote to Hartington on July 5, 1889, saying that if it was adopted both he and the Commander-in-Chief would have to resign. 'I should be sorry', he added, 'if H.R.H. is condemned and thrown aside. It would certainly be most unpopular with the Army.'[26] But the conclusions were modified, so as to reduce friction with the Duke of Cambridge to a minimum.

The Commission's first report, issued in 1889, rejected the suggestion that a single Minister of Defence should be appointed. Of this C.B. wrote to Ripon on July 18:

> This general scheme is Randolph's, inspired by Brackenbury and others. Hartington seems bitten with it. I confess to being dead against it. It seems to me that it is possible to carry the craze for 'direct responsibility' too far: and that in order that the control of Parliament may be upheld it is necessary to retain & confirm the power of the civilian Minister at the head of each Service . . . the two professional Depts. would be quite too strong for the poor Minister of Defence. . . .
>
> I think however that the two Departments should consult oftener, and in a more regular way, than hitherto: and I would diminish Treasury interference in details. . . .[27]

The Commission recommended instead the establishment of a joint Naval and Military Council. Lord Randolph wrote a dissenting report suggesting that the Secretary of State for War and the Board of Admiralty should be abolished and replaced by a Lord High Admiral and a Captain-General of the Army, who would be made peers, together with a Secretary of State and Treasurer for the Sea and Land Forces of the Crown.

In their second report, issued in 1890, the Commission dealt with the internal administration of the War Office. They reported that there was an excessive centralization of responsibility in the person of the Commander-in-Chief, whose office must be abolished, and that there should, in future, be a Chief of Staff and a permanent War Office Council.[28]

When the Commission was drafting this second report, C.B. explained why he could not wholly agree:

> . . . I am anxious to take the course which will most strengthen the Report . . . in its main direction – that is, deposing the Pope at the War Office, and establishing a Council in his place. What I fear is that your new Chief of Staff will be virtually a new Pope: and therefore I am against him. . . .[29]

He signed the main report, but he remained opposed to the Chief of Staff proposal, both because he had seen how a man like the Duke of Cambridge could block new ideas and discourage the best brains in the Army and because the proposal seemed to him to have about it a dangerous, militaristic and continental ring. He therefore added a separate note, dated February 10, 1890.[30]

In this, he expressed his strong agreement with the main recommendation of the report, but argued that continental countries, which had Chiefs of Staff, were

... constantly, and necessarily, concerned in watching the military condition of their neighbours. ... and in planning possible operations in possible wars against them. But in this country there is ... no room for 'general military policy'. ... We have no designs against our European neighbours. Indian 'military policy' will be settled in India itself, and not in Pall Mall. In any of the smaller troubles into which we may be drawn ... the plan of campaign ... would be left (I presume and hope) to be determined by the officer appointed to direct operations.

He went on to express doubts about staff officers who were supposed to 'sit apart and cogitate'. The officers advising the Secretary of State should be on a level footing in their relations with the Minister. The Board of Admiralty was the model to be copied.

In fact nothing was done by either Conservative or Liberal governments to create a general staff until after the disasters of the early months of the Boer War. The memorandum is important as indicating a fundamental element in C.B.'s thinking. He was essentially a man of peace, a man for conciliation, free trade and self-government for small peoples. He feared that a general staff would drag the country into foreign entanglements and commitments which might ultimately involve England in the catastrophe of a continental war, a danger which she had succeeded in avoiding in 1870, when there was no general staff.

He took the same line when he spoke in the House on the Army Estimates on July 4, 1890. He said then:

... The hierarchy of officers at the head of the Army is arranged perpendicularly, whereas it ought to be arranged horizontally. Every matter requiring decision, every suggestion or idea originated among the capable military officers on the Headquarters Staff, has to pass upwards from grade to grade, and to pass through the Adjutant General and Commander-in-Chief before it reaches the Secretary of State. The consequence is waste of time, circumlocution, a discouragement of independent initiative, and a slackening of the sense of direct responsibility.[31]

Of the plan to set up a Chief of Staff, he said: 'If a Chief of the Staff were to be appointed he would remain shut up in his room by himself, and he would feel bound to justify his existence by inventing magnificent schemes.'

C.B. was concerned to give all the chief soldiers at the War Office direct access to the Secretary of State, so that he could hear all points of view. It was the same desire which, seventy years later, was to lead President Kennedy to talk direct to desk officers in the State Department and the Pentagon. He wanted their views direct, not filtered upwards through the hierarchy.

Although C.B.'s view on this question of a Chief of Staff is often dismissed as absurdly old-fashioned Cobdenite Liberalism, it is fair to remember that, after the creation of a general staff and the Anglo-French staff talks of the early years of the twentieth century, approved by C.B. as Prime Minister, England was drawn into the First World War. It can be argued that there was no choice, but C.B. at any rate had no doubt of what would be entailed if England did take part in a continental war. The village crosses and the school memorials to the hundreds of thousands who died at the age of nineteen or twenty testify to the validity of his apprehensions.

In August 1892, Gladstone formed his fourth administration, to the disgust of the Queen, who had written to Ponsonby on July 26: 'The Queen cannot make up her mind to send at once for that dreadful old man . . . as she utterly loathes his very dangerous politics. . . .'[32]

The Duke of Cambridge was again anxious about whom he might get as a colleague. He feared that Dilke might get the job. 'He wishes,' his friend Lady Geraldine Somerset, a violent Tory, wrote in her diary, 'if one can possibly speak of wishing, in such a choice! – he might get Campbell-Bannerman back again, who at least is personally decent to deal with.'[33] The Duke's wish was fulfilled. C.B. again became Secretary of State for War, telling his cousin: 'I am glad to know that it was generally anticipated, and desired, not only among politicians, but at the War Office and in High Quarters.'[34] It was indeed acceptable to the Queen, who wrote to Ponsonby on August 10: '. . . Sir Henry will if necessary . . . say the Queen will *insist* on Ld. Rosebery as M. for F.A. also on Mr. Campbell Bannerman for the War Office.'[35] It was however reported that when C.B. was asked why he had gone back to the War Office, he replied: 'Did you ever hear of a fellow called

Hobson?'[36] Loulou Harcourt recorded in his journal: 'It was agreed at Spencer's that the only man apparently fitted for every office was Campbell-Bannerman.'[37]

At the War Office C.B. was back among old friends. He again had Lord Sandhurst, whom he very much liked, as his Parliamentary Under-Secretary. The Duke of Cambridge, now seventy-three, was Commander-in-Chief of the Army, as he had been for the previous thirty-six years, and was more opposed to any change than ever. C.B. told him, 'I look forward to my term of office with the greatest pleasure', and added, typically: 'As soon as I can get away I intend going to Marienbad for some weeks as this being the holiday season I imagine there will be no urgent business requiring attention.'[38]

The man who had to do most of the work on the military side was the Adjutant-General, Sir Redvers Buller. He was, in many respects, a military version of C.B. He was much the same age and was a large, bluff, choleric countryman from Devonshire. He had served all over the world, won the V.C. and was a legend in the Army. In 1886 he had been sent to Ireland as Under-Secretary to put down moonlighting and restore order, which he did, while speaking his mind about the conditions which caused it. Although he looked very stupid, like a stranded walrus, he was in fact an able man. Even so critical a man as Balfour wrote that 'Buller was a fine brain in a way – he drank too much though. I don't mean that he got drunk, but he would sit on all night like they did in Ireland in those days. He got through an enormous quantity of drink.'[39] C.B. liked Buller, and had perhaps too uncritical an admiration of him. Later in the year he tried to get him to go to India to succeed Roberts as Commander-in-Chief there. But the plan failed, and C.B. told the Duke of Cambridge: 'He has . . . finally declined. . . . No doubt the personal and domestic inconvenience would have been very great.'[40]

Of the civilians in Pall Mall the most senior was Sir Ralph Thompson, the Permanent Under-Secretary. C.B. got on well with him. Thompson was amused by Buller and once wrote of him to C.B.: 'Buller will be at his country place all next week entertaining a party for the Church Congress! He is a many sided man.'[41] But C.B.'s closest collaborators were the two other senior officials, Sir Arthur Haliburton, Assistant Under-Secretary, and Sir Ralph Knox, Accountant-General, of whom he had the highest opinion, and to whose ability he paid tribute in the House.

Jack Sinclair became his assistant private secretary. C.B. resumed official relations with Wolseley, now in Dublin commanding the British forces in Ireland, and wrote to him three months later:

> I assure you, coming back to the old W.O., I find it much changed, and I fancy your absence is at least an element in the change. It is a fin de siècle War Office, and I gape & stare every day at the things I see done, any one of which would make poor old Cardwell (for instance) turn in his grave, if a merciful softening of the brain had not left him beyond the reach of such influences before he breathed his last.[42]

Wolseley's biographers wrote: 'To Wolseley, Campbell-Bannerman always lent a willing ear. For the soldier who took his profession seriously, he had the greatest respect, and in the special War Office reform, over which he was just now busy, he leaned largely on the best military advice he could secure.'[43]

Wolseley pleaded with C.B. for help in securing promotion by merit, which the Duke of Cambridge, who preferred promotion by seniority or occasional special favour, looked on as heresy. In February 1894 Wolseley wrote from Dublin:

> There is no use in appealing to H.R.H. for over & over again he has condemned promotion by merit as a system. Will you therefore lift us out of the slough of seniority promotion? You can easily do so, & the Army – all that is best in it – will bless you. The Army in general wants a spurt of reform: for there is growing up amongst us a feeling of hopelessness, that zeal, hard work and ability are still kept in the background & that the idle and stupid – whom it is thought have most friends in high quarters – have as good if not a better chance of preferment. The young school want to make the Army a real profession in which the best men may be able by their own exertions to rise to the top, as men do at the Bar, in the Church, as Doctors, Civil Engineers etc. . . .[44]

It was all true enough, and C.B. helped to change it by bringing about, in the fullness of time, the retirement of the Duke. Unfortunately the new generation of military leaders, the 'Wolseley ring' of bright young men, proved often to be not much more effective in the field than the old-fashioned generals. Wolseley's favourite, Colley, had already come to grief at Majuba. Buller, another of Wolseley's selections, was yet to be found out, when, under his command, British forces did so disastrously in the Boer War that the elderly Lord Roberts, who had spent his life in India, had to be called in to take over.

C.B. continued to be on good terms with the Queen, who noted in her journal on October 25: 'Mr. Campbell Bannerman (who is extremely agreeable) . . . dined.'[45] Soon after taking up office again, C.B. wrote a long, tactful letter to Her Majesty. He explained in detail the problems of the Infantry, the furnishing of drafts for India and Egypt, and the working of the Cardwell system. Gingerly he approached his main purpose – 'that a Battn shd be added to each of the Scots Gds & Coldstream Guards, and that the Guards should, while the occupation of Egypt lasts, have two battalions in garrisons in the Mediterranean.' C.B. knew that the Queen had been approached once before about this plan to send her personal Guards on foreign service and had said no. He rehearsed the arguments in its favour, among them:

> As a mere measure of military experience this very limited turn of foreign service in the nearest and pleasantest of all our stations would be both beneficial and agreeable to the Brigade of Guards. In view of recent occurrences it may not be undesirable that the Household troops should be removed occasionally from association and influences which are sometimes pernicious, and should be brought, more than at present, in contact with other branches of the Service.[46]

He wished also to carry his colleagues with him, telling the Prime Minister that his plan 'would be a good stroke of business; it would be popular; would in the end save money; would greatly increase efficiency; and would stop, for the moment, the demand for costly changes.'[47]

C.B. warned Gladstone that securing the Queen's assent would be a difficult task. He was right. But the case was a strong one and, though she much disliked the proposal, Ponsonby thought that she was bound to give way, and wrote to C.B. from Balmoral saying: 'As the proposal about the Guards is recommended by 2 Secretaries of State and all the Staff Civil and Military of the War Office I imagine that the Queen will not raise further objections.' He added, 'She objected because she considered the scheme . . . detrimental to the efficiency of the Service and the military position of the Court.'[48]

The Queen, hard pressed about the Guards, adroitly changed the subject:

Windsor Castle
November 25, 1892.

Dear Mr. Campbell Bannerman,

The Queen says she cannot consent to the obliteration of her own Regt of Cameron Highlanders. Why should they not have a second Battalion?

Yours very truly,
Henry F. Ponsonby.[49]

C.B. was forced on to the defensive. He admitted that this regiment was in an unfortunate predicament, argued that there were too many Highland regiments and pointed out that the Camerons could not get anything like enough men from Scotland and were mainly recruited from the East End of London.[50] Ten days later Ponsonby began the counter-attack: '. . . as the Guards are worn out with sentry duty in London you would not I presume send them to still harder night work at Malta or Gibraltar. . . .'[51]

On December 22 the general advance was sounded from Osborne, C.B.'s status as a Scot being loftily ignored:

The Queen cannot find any soldier who likes the proposed plan of sending the Guards abroad on regular Colonial Duty, which of course abolishes 'Guards' altogether. . . .

At the same time Scotchmen consider the annihilation of the Cameron Highlanders as a severe blow to the National feeling, an unjust return to a Regiment which has distinguished itself by its good conduct and a slight to the Queen. . . .

The Queen hopes you will consider the whole question again, as she feels sure you will not wish to press on a scheme which will not meet the requirements made and which is so universally condemned.[52]

The Queen found allies. A line came to C.B. from Rosebery at the Foreign Office – 'I hope I am not impertinent in expressing the hope that you are going to leave the Cameron Highlanders alone?'[53]

C.B. replied in detail, and Rosebery hoisted the white flag:

Never has such a phalanx of closely knitted argument, statistical and historical, descended on me as in your letter about the Cameron Highlanders – set off as it is by various light 'excursions and alarms', as Shakespeare calls them, of satire and invective. I leave the kilt, my dear C.B., and huddle into my native trews.[54]

Lord Esher was right. The task of the Secretary of State for War was not an easy one. The Queen eventually had her way over the Cameron Highlanders, and Lord Lansdowne gave them their second battalion in 1897. But she was in the end defeated over the Guards, and in the same year the Coldstream and the Scots Guards were given a third battalion each.

In those days a Secretary of State had to deal himself with trivial details which nowadays would not get anywhere near him. In September 1892, for example, C.B. wrote to Harcourt:

> I have called for a special report as to the mode in which purchases of meat for Soldiers' messes are now made, and I think it will be found that your Oxford friend is describing and condemning (a) the old system, or (b) the way in which the Depôt at Oxford is fed, perhaps by some rival butcher who has the local contract. There was a committee on the subject a short time ago on which served Goldsworthy M.P., who looks as if he knew what beef is, and Farquharson M.P., who though a hungry-looking Aberdonian is a doctor. . . . I will see what they say to the growl of your man. . . .[55]

As an administrator C.B. got on well with everyone but took care to exercise a strict economy of effort. Mr. Guy Fleetwood Wilson, who had been a private secretary in the War Office to Hartington, W. H. Smith, and Stanhope, was appointed to the same post with C.B. in August 1892. His experience of working for three previous Secretaries of State gave him a good yardstick by which to judge a Minister. He wrote:

> Mr. W. H. Smith and Mr. Campbell-Bannerman played a game of puss-in-the-corner at the War Office. . . . In one respect the two men were the antithesis of each other. Mr. Smith was perhaps the hardest and most conscientious worker I ever knew, whilst Sir Henry Campbell-Bannerman was distinctly lazy and it was difficult at times to get him to learn his lesson. . . . The fact is he hated detail, and some knowledge of detail is essential even in the House of Commons. On one occasion when I knew he was going to be

attacked in debate by a dangerous opponent I bored him very much by giving him a long lecture on the subject to be debated. He professed to have all the information at his finger ends and went down to the House. I felt some doubts and followed him there, taking with me the general officer in charge of the department concerned, who was a pundit on the subject. Poor Sir Henry gave a deep sigh and settled down in a chair in an attitude of profound attention. The general went into the case ably, clearly and at some length, and when he was three-parts through his statement we were both startled by a loud snore. Campbell-Bannerman was very nearly beaten that evening, and it was chiefly his great personal popularity which saved him. . . . Both Ministers were immensely liked by both soldiers and civilians. . . . Sir Henry did an immense deal of good in improving the relations between the heads of the army and the House of Commons.[56]

One of the soldiers, General Grenfell, who was at the time Deputy Adjutant-General of Reserve Forces, wrote of C.B.:

I liked him very much. He left the administration of the Militia very much in my hands, and only asked me to let him know, from time to time, how the Force was getting on, to enable him to answer questions connected with it in the House of Commons. When I first went into his room I was amused to find him immersed in a French novel.[57]

Naturally his political opponents felt that so easy-going a man could hardly be taken seriously as an administrator. St. John Brodrick, one of his Conservative successors at the War Office, summed him up as a 'popular, prejudiced and elusive Scotchman' and wrote of him: 'Despite being lazy and a *bon vivant*, he was a good business man and an effective speaker, with a touch of humour which, although of advanced political views, he often employed to the detriment of progress, especially with regard to the Army. . . . Needless to say, the Army from 1892 to 1895 made no progress whatever. . . .'[58]

One of his officials, Sir Henry Gibson, gave another view:

He was most courteous and tactful & did not fluster or hustle his staff. He trusted his subordinates implicitly (perhaps too much some times). . . . He was the antithesis of men like Mr. Brodrick or

Arnold-Forster, who had extreme views on military organization &
thought that they knew a good deal more than the soldier about his
own job.[59]

W. T. Stead wrote of C.B. that: 'If he could only be induced to
become a vegetarian, and to read only one French novel a month,
he might depose the Duke of Cambridge, and become famous in
history as the man who created the modern British Army.'[60] C.B. did
eventually remove the Duke. He did not re-create the Army. A major
reconstruction of this sort took more energy and readiness to break
eggs than he possessed.

In the House of Commons he resisted demands for constant
tinkering with Army organization. 'Let me remind hon. Members',
he said on March 7, 'that we cannot in this country indulge a desire for
theoretical perfection in our Army organization. . . . We are tied . . .
by traditions and prejudices and habits which it is hopeless to overcome,
and to ignore which would be fatal to success.'[61] As a lifelong man of
the left, he could tell the Radicals: 'We have to humour the feelings of
those classes from which the Army is supplied.'

But he faced a steady drumbeat of criticism from a regular group
of critics. Dilke, Lord Wolmer and Arnold-Forster began criticizing the
War Office and the short service system as early as 1891. Dilke and the
military publicist Spenser Wilkinson advocated a general staff on the
Prussian model. Dilke was a particular thorn in C.B.'s flesh. He was,
according to Asquith, 'by nature a dull and ineffective speaker', who
'in comparison with men of the brilliance of Harcourt and Chamberlain . . . seemed like a cab-horse among thoroughbreds',[62] but he
acquired by assiduous study a wide knowledge of military matters
which, to C.B.'s irritation, he liked to show off in the House. Asquith
found him as tedious as did C.B., and described his biography wither-
ingly as a 'dullish book in two huge volumes about a dullish man'.[63]
A fellow-member, Sir Richard Temple, wrote that C.B. 'ably with-
stood the severest and longest sustained criticism of the Army that has
been known in this generation . . . with endless interpolations directed
with skill and knowledge from the Opposition side'.[64]

Sometimes he found it rough going. In one letter to his cousin he
wrote:

> We have had a bad week: obstruction of the most impudent
> kind . . . I think it will come all right: & the other side cannot keep

it up to this level when the race meetings & other attractions begin. Still it is a hard fight: I had a dreadful day of it yesterday.[65]

But he was singularly lacking in egotism. He minuted in February 1893 that the memoranda accompanying the estimates had 'grown into rather vainglorious and sometimes party-coloured documents; and I think the more they are reduced in character the better'.[66]

C.B. was a conservative in Army matters: at any rate he believed in resting four-square on the reforms brought in twenty years before. In moving his first estimates on March 11, 1893, he paid a tribute to the man he admired above all others, his old chief Cardwell, who had faced prejudice and obloquy, but whose 'achievements in Army reform' were 'such as no Army reformer, in this country at all events, has ever produced, or is ever likely to produce again'.

Now, he argued, the system being established, the thing was to allow it to work, and 'to leave it alone; distinctly I say to leave it alone. . . . There is nothing so pernicious to the Army as perpetual change, perpetual oscillation both of theory and practice.'[67]

He was unmoved when Dilke tried flattery, saying in March 1893:

> It is time that a capable Minister, like the present Secretary of State for War, should insist . . . on being allowed to deal with this question. He has considerable advantages. . . . He is extraordinarily popular – extraordinarily, not in the sense that he does not deserve his popularity, but because it is universal. He is popular with the Army of all ranks, from the Commander-in-Chief downwards; he is popular with his colleagues, and with this House; and if ever there was a man who had a chance of distinguishing himself by inaugurating . . . a revolutionary scheme of Army reform, it is the right hon. Gentleman.[68]

But the right hon. Gentleman had no use for any revolutionary scheme. Moreover he maintained the view he had expressed in opposition about the limits of the use to which the Army should be put. On the same day as Dilke spoke, C.B. told the House:

> What do we want two Army Corps in this country for? Surely not for foreign service. Who is going to send two Army Corps to the Continent? Is there any man in the House who would think of sending an Army Corps on the Continent to engage in a Continen-

tal war with one of the great European nations? Such a possibility
I dismiss from my mind altogether. What we want our Army for
is to garrison India and the Colonies, to defend the shores of this
country, and to supply those small special expeditions which are
from time to time sent out to the small wars, in which, unfortunately, we are often engaged.[69]

In other words Army operations were to be restricted, in the main,
to those which were described as the product of the 'skill of Sir Garnet
at thrashing a cannibal'.

He resisted, too, in language which has a fine old Victorian ring,
Dilke's demand for 'great military manœuvres':

> Has my right hon. friend forgotten that the enclosed nature of
> this country, cut up into small fields with hedges and ditches, pre-
> cludes manœuvres on a large scale? I say you cannot pass great
> bodies of troops over them without doing considerable damage to
> the owners and occupiers of property, which the country would
> not stand for one moment.[70]

Next day, having, it was said, 'had recourse to the strong measure of a
Saturday sitting', he was able to give a more considered reply to the
critics, 'readiness of reply', as one writer suggested unkindly, 'not
being one of the War Minister's characteristics'.[71]

Sometimes he was aroused by some detail. A member complained
of the state of the drains at the Tower and in Wellington Barracks.
C.B. replied at once:

> If there is anything I myself have served an apprenticeship in, it
> is drains. I served that apprenticeship when I had the honour of
> being Chief Secretary for Ireland, and the locality of my service
> and knowledge was the Phoenix Park, Dublin. I am certain that
> whatever the drains and cesspools in the Tower or the Wellington
> Barracks may be, they are a mere trifle compared with what
> existed, in my time, in the Chief Secretary's lodge.[72]

He dealt with Parliamentary questions in a bland, almost casual
style. On March 11, 1893, in reply to Mr. Digby, he said: 'As to these
questions respecting the Yeomanry force I have not had time to get
information, and I shall be obliged if hon. Members will postpone
them'; and, pressed by Mr. Long as to when he would be prepared to

answer: 'Oh, in a few days I will answer them, so far as the information in my possession allows it.'[73]

Such Ministerial insouciance is rare.

Harcourt continued to send blasts to C.B., couched in the intemperate and hectoring style that did so much to alienate his colleagues and consequently to prevent his ultimate succession to the office of Prime Minister. In one letter to C.B., he described 'the unfortunate manner in which business is conducted at the War Office' as 'really like the Russian administration'.[74] In another, he wrote: 'If people's private business were conducted as public business is, bankruptcy would follow in 6 months.'[75]

C.B. and Spencer, who was now First Lord of the Admiralty, were both irritated by these blasts. C.B. wrote to Spencer on July 10, 1893:

> I too received the fulmination. I replied that . . . it was the easiest thing in the world to launch fine general declamations against expenditure, but the most difficult thing to check it in detail; that my zeal for this part of my duties would be only slackened if I received thunderbolts of that kind, and that the departments would be reasonable if only 11 Downing Street would be sensible.
>
> I had a reply this morning: 'All right: you keep down your estimates & I will keep down my bile.'
>
> Really, that sort of thing is not business.[76]

But Harcourt was unsubdued, and told C.B. next year: 'We are actually in the condition of a householder whose weekly bills are at the mercy of a French chef over whom he has no control.'[77]

C.B., however, refused to be rattled.

In June 1893, he became involved in the delicate matter of senior appointments, and wrote to the Prime Minister: 'Lord Roberts has just come home, and he is urgent for employment, alleging that (although he has had seven years of the very highly paid Office of Commander in Chief in India) he is very poor.'

He explained that Roberts would not accept the Governorship of Malta or Gibraltar, but demanded that he should be appointed to Aldershot. To this, C.B. explained, there were strong professional objections. He went on:

> Roberts is a peculiar man. He is a good soldier, a capable administrator, most conciliatory towards the civil population, but he is an arrant jobber and intriguer, and self-advertiser, and altogether

wrong in his political notions, both British and Indian. We may expect that he will make a great noise and complaint: and therefore I thought it right that you should know exactly how the matter stands.[78]

He told Ponsonby: 'I have every reason to suspect that the putting forward of Lord Roberts's name is organized by Sir C. Dilke, who poses as a friend of Roberts, and who stayed with him (to everyone's surprise) in India.' Dilke, he added, 'has a great underground influence in the Press, which accounts for much'.[79]

The Duke of Cambridge wrote to C.B. that 'there is no doubt whatever, that Lord Roberts *cannot* and *ought* not to go to Aldershot, & if he does not, it is also quite clear to me, that the Duke of Connaught is the fittest & best General Officer to succeed Wood.'[80] Royalty were sticking together. The Queen told the Duke: 'I . . . am grateful to you both for not allowing my dear Arthur's just claims to be disregarded to suit other people's whims & fancies',[81] and got her Private Secretary to write to C.B., saying: 'the Queen is anxious that a decision be arrived at about Aldershot and that it should now be offered to the Duke of Connaught . . .'[82]

The Duke of Connaught, brother of the Prince of Wales, was duly appointed, despite a further appeal from Roberts, and it was left to C.B. to answer criticisms. A number of service journals said that the appointment was unfortunate, and a leading Liberal newspaper said that it was nothing more than a 'discreditable job'.[83] 'It seems to me,' wrote Ponsonby serenely on September 5, 'you are in a wasps nest about the Aldershot command – Buzzing all round you.'[84] C.B. had told Ponsonby that he was being 'pretty freely bombarded' but, as usual, he was unperturbed – 'I do not anticipate any difficulty, although it is unpleasant.'[85]

He handled the problem deftly, but he did not have an altogether easy passage in the House. It was argued that the appointment was of extreme importance because it was the great military training school of the country. Dilke, as usual, joined in the criticisms of C.B. C.B. took full responsibility for the appointment, and maintained that it was a good one, saying that while it was hardly 'the duty of an officer like the Duke of Connaught to prance a horse in front of the assembled army and to challenge some leader on the other side to single combat', he had been under fire at Tel-el-Kebir and had an excellent record as a soldier. In India 'the Duke actually learnt the language in order to be able to communicate more freely and easily with the native troops under his command'. As to his being a son of the Queen, that was no disqualification: 'We should rejoice at his devoting a useful life to his country.' He praised Roberts but said it would be an indignity to give him the position of a drill-master at Aldershot.[86]

Ponsonby wrote from Balmoral on September 12: 'I congratulate you on the skilful management by which you secured a victory last night. For there is no doubt a discontented spirit afloat and I feared that the temptation to vote against the Duke of Connaught would have taken a good many to vote with Mr. Dalziel.'[87]

Three years before the Queen had enthusiastically endorsed a suggestion by Wolseley that the Duke of Connaught should be appointed as Commander-in-Chief, but had been told by her Conservative Ministers that he must fill other commands first and not, as Ponsonby put it, jump 'into power by what may almost be termed violent means'. The Queen had then instructed Ponsonby to 'see Lord Hartington and Mr. Campbell-Bannerman, so as to be able to hear *what* they want. . . . She suspects that the Government think (most foolishly) Arthur would be as retrograde and old-fashioned as the dear Duke of Cambridge, whereas he is the very reverse, and it is too shameful keeping him out of all important places on account of his birth'.[88]

By now arranging the appointment of the Duke of Connaught to Aldershot, the Queen hoped that an important step had been taken towards getting him made Commander-in-Chief.

A writer in the *Spectator* said the following year that 'though little noted at the time – and herein was its chief cleverness –' this episode was

a veritable masterpiece of Parliamentary management. . . . the Radicals . . . had a particularly good case. . . . It was a command which . . . required an officer of great experience . . . an officer exactly qualified – Lord Roberts – would have willingly taken the appointment . . . the whole thing was exactly what Radical speakers and writers have again and again denounced as Court jobbery. Armed with this excellent case, the young lions of the Radical party proceeded to bait the Secretary for War. Did they move him or embarrass him? Not in the very least. He kept cool, while they grew hot. He was always civil, always patient, but he contrived to turn the edge of every weapon brought against him. Any other man would have made a dozen bitter enemies. Not so Mr. Campbell-Bannerman. He never said a word too much, or a word too little, but kept steadily on, with his head down and his coat up to his ears, as a man does who has got to face a temporary storm of rain. One stroke of management was specially masterly. Mr. Campbell-Bannerman let drop that it would have been an insult to offer such an appointment to Lord Roberts. Off went the hunt in full cry after this false scent. The Duke of Connaught's alleged military incapacity was entirely forgotten in the fervid declarations that Lord Roberts would not have been insulted by the offer, and that Mr. Campbell-Bannerman was deplorably stupid to have thought any such thing. Mr. Campbell-Bannerman only smiled and lay low. At last the Radicals remembered that their object was not to defend Lord Roberts, but to attack the Duke of Connaught. By this time, however, the pack was bored and weary, and had little heart to start running again. Accordingly, the matter soon dropped. . . . Mr. Campbell-Bannerman had come out of the scrimmage with his point gained, and without having made a single enemy. Contrast this result with Mr. Asquith's fate in regard to the dynamiters or the Featherstone riots. He, too, stuck to his guns; but in the sticking he managed to create enmities which are still alive and active.[89]

At this period, what with his troubles this year with the Duke of Connaught, and those which came to a head two years later with the Duke of Cambridge, C.B.'s time seems to have been heavily pre-empted by the affairs of Royal and military Dukes. Although he had managed to get the House to approve the Aldershot appointment, he had had to promise that the office of Commander-in-Chief, for which the Duke of Connaught was supposed to be in training, would be abolished at the next vacancy, as the Hartington Commission had proposed. The Duke of Cambridge noted this with some pain.

Having settled the problem of Aldershot, C.B. had to think about other appointments. They were, in those days, sometimes handled in an odd way. This letter, for example, was despatched to Dublin:

6 Grosvenor Place,
S.W.

10 Nov. 93

Dear Lady Wolseley,

I hope you won't be alarmed, and in any way misunderstand my meaning in writing to you: but I do not wish anything in the disposal of which I have any influence to pass away from your husband if he wishes to have it. . . . I have *no* desire to induce you to shift your anchorage. . . . Still, it has occurred to me that it is possible you might fancy Malta, and . . . I should be most unhappy if, for want of asking, I failed to meet your wishes . . . why do I write to you & not to him? Simply because your comfort is even more concerned than his, and there can be no horrid savour of official relations in such a communication with you. . . .

Very sincerely yours,
H. Campbell-Bannerman.[90]

Perhaps C.B. thought that if he could induce Wolseley to go to Malta, he could then satisfy Roberts by sending him to Ireland. Four days later, however, Lady Wolseley replied, asking C.B. to 'Forgive *very* official paper!', thanking him for 'your *extreme* kindness in giving us this choice', and saying: 'I shall *never* forget the friendly & delicate way in which you have given *me* the choice as well as giving it to Lord Wolseley. It is a very subtle compliment. . . .' She explained that they had decided to stay in Ireland, since although a move would mean 'an escape from the noxious Liffey', it would be 'exceedingly expensive'. She went on:

These considerations are however practically the *fringe* only of the question at issue, the real heart of which is as follows: My General is 60, he feels as active healthy & sound as he did 20 years ago, and he would like to shape his course if possible so as to have as much work, and as much advancement (see how frank I am!) in the remainder of his career as possible & not to throw away a chance of either, by any mistaken move. . . . Lord Wolseley's great hope & ambition is, that when a Royal Personage who was born in the same year as our Queen – 1819 – ceases from whatever cause it may be to be C in C, there may (in the reconstruction of any reorganization that will no doubt take place) be found a place for him at Head Quarters. In 95 when we leave here, HRH will be 77 (at least in his 77th year). We should be leaving Malta in 98. . . .

Having thus asked as plainly as she could that her husband should be the next Commander-in-Chief, Lady Wolseley went on to make another suggestion:

May I, because you have done us one kindness ask you to do us *another* should opportunity occur; I feel I am about to be guilty of that indelicacy. I mean, to bear my General in mind for a future F.M.'s bâton? It . . . would afford us the additional ease of a few hundreds a year, to which *I* who draw the cheques & pay the weekly bills, am by no means indifferent. . . .[91]

Lady Wolseley had made it quite clear how she and Lord Wolseley saw the future. C.B. replied:

I do not imagine that distance, or the tenure of any office, wd. prevent Lord Wolseley being the foremost man for any new arrangement that may be necessary when An Illustrious Person retires.

But I am not surprised that you are not tempted to change your quarters.

On one point you mention, viz. the F.M.'s bâton, let me say this: I have always had this in my eye, and I do not anticipate any difficulty in the person you are interested in going upstairs – the only doubt is as to the company that may go with him! He would be the first up any way!

This is really a very flippant way in which to speak of such a sacred subject, but I know you will forgive me. . . .[92]

Wolseley was duly give his Field-Marshal's baton next year, a year before Roberts. When the latter got his, C.B. forgot to tell the Prime Minister, who sent him the gentlest of rebukes:

My dear C.B.

Why is it de fide with you to make field marshals as Orsini made bombs!

I looked rather foolish yesterday when the Queen found out that I knew nothing about the promotion of Roberts.

Ys ever,
Æ.[93]

Relations with the Queen had now become much sunnier. In February 1893, Ponsonby was writing to Fleetwood Wilson:

You whispered La Reine le Veult and then disappeared in a cloud of Home Rule ladies where I could not follow you.

But I received your laconic despatch on my return to Windsor and gave it to the Queen. Her Majesty was very much pleased and commands me to ask you to thank Mr. Campbell Bannerman for his prompt attention to her wishes. . . .[94]

About this time there was trouble with a member of the War Office staff, who was described as a Hyde Park orator and a man who was always trying to foment trouble. When it was decided to dismiss him, he went to the House of Commons and got the Labour members to take up his case. C.B. sent for the senior official concerned and asked him to reinstate the man. The official pointed out that this would be destructive of all discipline. C.B. then said: 'We cannot have a whole day's debate about it, and the whips say we may even be beaten, can you suggest any way out?' They decided that C.B. should ask Mr. John Burns, the Member for Battersea, to look into the case. Most of the men concerned were his constituents. Burns came to the War Office, conducted a full enquiry, and said that if he had been the man's boss he would have fired him long ago. Politically the move had been effective, and C.B. also marked down John Burns as a thoroughly honest Scot.[95]

In June 1893 pressure was put on C.B. to have Clarke, the former secretary of the Hartington Commission, kept on special duties. C.B. wrote to Spencer at the Admiralty:

Major Clarke has been for years away from his regular Corps duties . . . I . . . finally decided that he must go to Malta. . . . Apparently however he has not been long at his post when he obtains short leave home, and the next we hear is that he and his friends in the Colonial Office think the Empire will perish unless he now goes to Chicago and the American lakes. . . .

He is extremely capable and I am personally most willing to get the best of his services but he must after all take his turn quietly with his brother officers of the less pleasant side of his proper work.

He mars his prospects in fact by being *wire puller issimus* and his ambition seems to be of the restless kind which I saw today described as 'de l'ambition qui se sert de tout, qui se couche plus tard que le vice et se lève plus tôt que la vertu'.[96]

The Queen overlooked no detail. She wanted, for example, to know from C.B. about an incident in Sierra Leone in December 1893, when, by mistake, a fight had occurred between British and

French colonial forces, in which the French commander and three British officers had been killed. The French had mistaken the British white tropical uniforms for Arab dress. C.B. wrote about this affair to Ripon on January 6, 1894:

> The West African incident is most sad, but our officers have behaved with commendable patience & coolness, and came well out of it. . . . I am urging that . . . the account of the French officer picking off our men, should be kept out of the newspapers. . . .[97]

When the Kaiser, at a Court Ball in Berlin, said that he would like to be made Honorary Colonel of a Highland regiment, Rosebery wrote to C.B. from the Foreign Office forwarding the Ambassador's report, and commenting: 'The idea of William as a Highland Colonel is sufficiently comic in itself, but it is rendered inexpressibly so by the fact that he has forbidden the kilt to appear at his Court Balls as being an indecent costume!' Ponsonby told C.B.: 'The Queen thinks this has never been done before in the British Army and does not like it.'[98]

But when the two Sovereigns met at Coburg the Prince of Wales and the Duke of Connaught prevailed upon her to make the offer to the Kaiser, which she did without reference to her Ministers, who were formulating their objections. Ponsonby wrote to C.B. apologizing 'for this unfortunate affair', saying that the Queen 'remembered that you had objected to his being made a Field Marshal last winter', and adding: 'The telegram from Rosebery, Kimberley and you came late but the Queen only said that many things were done without precedent and that no one really objected to his Colonelcy.'[99] No doubt she realized perfectly well that she had acted improperly, but she was not going to admit it.

Meanwhile there were other problems. C.B. tackled the question of the hours of work at the ordnance factory at Woolwich and decided to introduce an eight-hour day. He told Gladstone that 'it should be done in such a way and at such a time as to get for your Govt. the full credit . . . from all I can gather there is no reason to doubt that . . . the same number of workmen with the shorter hours will achieve as much.'[100]

The experiment was an entire success, and other Departments followed the example of the War Office. Only the Fabian Society was sceptical. In an article in the *Fortnightly Review*, written on their behalf by George Bernard Shaw, it was argued that C.B. ought rather to have established a minimum wage on which a family could be maintained in decency. But, Shaw wrote: 'Mr. Campbell Bannerman, with these opportunities, has done nothing, being content with the distinction conferred on his tenure of office by the appointment of the Duke of Connaught to the most important military command in the British Islands.'[101] This was scarcely fair.

C.B.'s Under-Secretary, Lord Sandhurst, was made Governor of Bombay and was succeeded by Lord Monkswell. To his new colleague C.B. wrote:

> I think you will like this office; the soldiers are very nice to get on with, altho' of course they require a little management, & the leading civilians are exceptionally able; while the questions dealt with are remote from ordinary politics & form a little garden to be cultivated apart. . . .[102]

Early in 1894 C.B. was involved in the Cabinet crisis over the Naval Estimates which lasted for two months and culminated in Mr. Gladstone's final resignation on March 3, at the age of 85. C.B. attempted to help compose the difference between Harcourt and the First Lord, Spencer, who backed the senior officers at the Admiralty. These now included the volcanic Rear Admiral Fisher, who later wrote:

> Sir William Harcourt and Sir Henry Campbell-Bannerman were alternately turned on . . . us. . . . Sir William Harcourt . . . was what might be called 'a genial ruffian' . . . Campbell-Bannerman was a more awkward customer. But it was all no use. We got the ships and Mr. Gladstone went.[103]

C.B. was one of those who refused to accept Mr. Gladstone's demand for cuts. So the great man departed at last. Rosebery became Prime Minister and Harcourt continued as Chancellor of the Exchequer.

After these upheavals, C.B. returned to the even tenor of his ways, and in March Lord Randolph Churchill referred in the House to 'the Secretary of State for War, who is slumbering, I am sorry to see. . . .'[104]

In March 1895, introducing the Army Estimates, C.B. said that it was 'quite consistent with the character and *role* of a reformer to wait until our reforms have borne their fruit and not to go on reforming the same field again and again. It is right that we should press the soil around our plant and trim and prune the plant itself; but it is hardly wise to take it up and plant it afresh every year, or even every half-dozen years.' He went on: 'as to the main fabric of our Army system, the truest courage and the best reforming wisdom lies in leaving well alone.'[105]

Dilke was stung, and said derisively: 'The Secretary of State for War is undoubtedly very disinclined to move. He says that Mr. Knox, the Accountant-General of the Army, may be classed as an Army reformer. That throws a certain light on the opinions of the Secretary of State for War. The present Pope is, I believe, under the impression that he is an ecclesiastical reformer. . . .'[106]

The question of official secrets came up. C.B. told Spencer in February 1895 that the War Office had had no recent case of secrets being disclosed, but that 'my people are very anxious to amend the official secrets act. At present, unless evil intention can be proved, disclosure is only a minor offence, liable to a slight punishment – and it is almost impossible to prove evil intent. The act is thus a dead letter.'[107]

C.B. now turned his hand to the reconstruction of the War Office itself. Little had been done by the Salisbury Government on the basis of the Hartington report, and C.B. prepared a scheme of reorganization. Under this, a Defence Committee of the Cabinet was set up, a body which Lord Rosebery afterwards considered to have been the origin of the Committee of Imperial Defence. A War Office Council was established, presided over by the Secretary of State, with the Commander-in-Chief as first military member. The office of Commander-in-Chief was retained, but with the period of tenure strictly limited to five years, a limit which the Queen regarded as a 'deathblow to the cherished fiction that the Commander-in-Chief was the permanent personal deputy of the Sovereign'.[108]

He was to continue responsible for all military matters, but the heads of military departments were given direct access to the Secretary of State. They 'would thus', C.B. told the House in June 1895, 'constitute a deliberative Council, so that the Secretary of State, when he gave his decisions, would be guided and supported by the expressed opinions of all the experienced officers by whom he was surrounded'.[109] The only snag in this arrangement, as Lord Wolseley was to find when he became Commander-in-Chief, was that the soldier who was supposed to have full military responsibility did not have full authority. Wolseley remarked that the Adjutant-General and the Quartermaster-General were no longer his staff officers, but those of a civilian Secretary of State. To the Secretary of State, however, this was not a snag.

CHAPTER 13

The Dislodging of the Duke

O^N the 1st of January, 1895, Hamilton wrote in his diary: 'The New Year is pretty certain to see a change of Government . . . I would lay even money that the change will come about half way – probably on some unforeseen contingency.'[1]

It was a remarkably shrewd forecast.

C.B.'s plan for the reorganization of the War Office was worked out by the spring of 1895, and he now had to approach the most difficult and delicate part of it. The Hartington Commission had recommended the abolition of the post of Commander-in-Chief. His own plan did not go so far, but under his arrangement the Commander-in-Chief would have much reduced powers and authority. It was clear that the time had come when George, Duke of Cambridge, should, at the age of seventy-six, retire gracefully.

The Duke had already expressed his alarm at C.B.'s endorsement of the Hartington Commission's conclusions. Now the time had come to act. But the Duke was not easily removed. He strenuously maintained that the post of Commander-in-Chief ought to be held by a member of the Royal Family. It took six weeks, and the united efforts of C.B. and Queen Victoria, to induce him to retire.

C.B. first talked the matter over tactfully with him and told Rosebery on May 4 that H.R.H. had been 'very voluble, very clever, & very nice. He puts himself entirely in my hands: only he won't go *now*, as he does not wish to be kicked out.'[2]

On the same day the Duke wrote to the Queen:

My Dear Cousin,
. . . there are serious attacks being made in some of the newspapers . . . on myself. . . . It is specially pointed out that my *age* is

much against me, and that if I don't retire voluntarily, I ought to be forced to do so by a vote of the House of Commons. . . . If I felt unequal to perform my duties from age, I should unhesitatingly ask to be relieved of them, but this I do not at present admit, and therefore, it must depend upon you if you wish me to relinquish the high honours that you have placed upon me, as *your* Commander-in-Chief . . .

Your most dutiful cousin,
George.[3]

As Sir Henry Ponsonby had been struck down by a paralytic stroke in January and succeeded by Colonel Bigge, it was the Queen's new Private Secretary who made a note of a talk with the Duke on May 6: 'Mr. C. Bannerman, of whom HRH spoke in the highest terms, is, he knows, in favour of a Board, with the 1st War Lord – to be in a similar position to the 1st Naval Lord at the Adty board . . .'[4] Next day Bigge saw Buller, 'who does not believe in the reality of attack against the War Office & the C in C: thinks it comes round annually like "spring onions". . .' He also saw Rosebery, who 'thinks there is somethings behind the Press Attacks'.[5]

On the following day he warned the Queen that her cherished plan that her son the Duke of Connaught should take over as Commander-in-Chief was not practicable for the time being. She wrote:

saw Mr. C. Bannerman . . . who thought the C in C's retiring . . . a good idea as would stifle spirit of discontent in H. of C. . . . D. of C'ght now succeeding to C in C practically impossible. But after some other General has held it for a term not exceeding 5 years, HRH would then be received with acclamation . . . so far as the *Army* goes no doubt D. of Cght would *now* be welcomed.[6]

Bigge noted of the Queen that 'tho' it had been the dream of her life to see the D of Cght succeed D of Cbdge – would not now press it'.[7]

The Queen saw the Duke of Cambridge on May 7 and wrote in her journal:

His anxiety is to do what is best for the Crown & to maintain the office of Commander in Chief, so that it should never become Parliamentary. He praised Mr. Campbell-Bannerman very much, & said he was ready to do anything for him (G). What he wishes is not to be kicked out by these violent radicals, who have made such attacks on him. I assured him that would not & could not be.[8]

Two days later she saw Rosebery, who told her that 'there was a feeling abroad that George was too old, though he was extremely popular'.[9] On May 12 she told Rosebery that she was prepared to accept the Duke's resignation, provided that the office of Commander-in-Chief was retained, so that the Duke of Connaught might eventually succeed. Rosebery reassured her on this point, but said that he and C.B. thought that the Duke of Cambridge ought to go before the end of the year.[10]

On the 13th Bigge went down to Aldershot to break it to the Duke of Connaught that he was not to succeed, telling him however that the Queen 'hoped to live to see him in that position'. The Duke was disappointed but dignified. The Duchess 'took a more gloomy view, and said it was a case of "now or never".'[11] She was right.

Next day C.B. wrote to Rosebery telling him how matters stood and added the political gossip. Joe had 'made a pitiable exhibition of himself' in the House, and C.B. remarked inconsequentially: 'Odd, is it not, that the H. of C. should appoint a committee to determine whether old Selborne's son was born in wedlock? I should not have had that idea of the old chap myself.'[12] On the 15th Bigge saw the Prince of Wales, 'who at first strongly deprecated yielding to political pressure from obscure Radicals. . . . But after hearing what Mr. C. Bannerman had said . . . H.R.H. said Mr. C.B. ought to know real feeling of H. of C.'[13]

The Queen noted 'the feeling amongst the opposition . . . that it is not right for George to remain on at the age of 76 when other officers had all to retire at 67'.[14] C.B. reported to the Prime Minister:

> The Duke is, I believe, being urged by his own family . . . not on any account to give way in face of vulgar attacks . . . he declares a strong repugnance to resignation, *even if requested by H.M.* . . . it wd. be showing the white feather. . . . He is as fit as 20 years ago, was in the saddle from 10 till 3 at Aldershot yesterday, & went to the Theatre in the evening. . . *But,* he is ready to write to the Q. . . . expressing his readiness to do whatever She on the advice of her Ministers desires . . . he thinks it saves his dignity, and I urged him strongly to take this course *at once.* . . . (He was very much hurt because the P. of W. on the way to the races told him in quite a casual picktooth sort of manner that the Q. had come to the con-

clusion he ought to go. . .). I think it will go right enough: but the fish are rather heavy for the tackle.[15]

The same day, however, the Duke wrote a second letter to the Queen, saying that his Radical critics 'would consider themselves *triumphant* if there was even a suspicion that I contemplated resignation, and this would therefore be a fatal error'.[16]

Next day C.B. reported to Rosebery on a talk with the Queen at Windsor:

> I am sorry to say that my old Duke wrote to her a letter which did not quite tally with what he had told me it wd. be. . . . he enclosed to her a letter he had received from the Duke of Richmond strongly urging H.R.H. on no account to give way. . . . I gather that she is not much impressed with the wisdom of the Duke of R. . . . Bigge had found that Marlbr. House was also recalcitrant yesterday: it . . . was all for no surrender; & references were made to 'this d—d Government'. But Bigge managed to smooth its feathers, and before he left, it was again declaring that the Duke must go.[17]

The Queen recorded:

> saw Mr. C. Bannerman who was very kind & sensible. He believed if George C. were to resign about Nov. . . . things could be so arranged, that he would leave, regretted by the whole nation. Should he however cling to office it might lead to regrettable unpleasantness. . . . I said I felt terribly disappointed about Arthur not succeeding him. . . . Saw George C. which was a trying & painful interview. He was quite calm, but would not see the reason for resigning, so that our interview led to nothing which is very despairing.[18]

C.B. told Rosebery's secretary that he would let him know how matters progressed, but added: 'You are aware that the fat is in the fire!' He was, however, prepared to try again where his Sovereign had failed. She for her part wrote on May 17: 'Mr. C. Bannerman . . . was much distressed about George C., and did not know what could be done. He would try and see who could have any influence over him. Nothing could be kinder than Mr. C.-Bannerman about the whole business.'[19]

The same day C.B. sent Bigge a long letter, beginning: 'Things look very much better than in the morning.'

He explained that he had had a long and frank talk with the Duke, who had explained the distinction he saw between resignation, by which 'he thinks it would be implied that he took some blame to himself . . . that he confessed failure, that he gave way to vulgar attacks', and 'placing himself in the Queen's hands'. C.B. clearly listened patiently and sympathetically and commented to Bigge, 'I gathered that the reason of age is not a very acceptable reason: the acceptable reason is that of a change in the office. . . . There is a refinement in the distinction worthy of the Schoolmen; but I see it clearly enough.' He went on: 'To show how far I got with H.R.H., he discussed at great length with me his successor . . . he strongly favours Buller.'[20]

On May 17 the Prime Minister's private secretary, George Murray, summed up the situation for his chief:

> 10 Downing Street,
> Whitehall S.W.
>
> The Kaleidoscopic changes in the old Duke's humour are rapidly driving C.B. and Bigge out of their minds.
>
> The Queen sent for the Duke yesterday and had an interview with him before dinner, expecting to find him in a submissive frame of mind and ready to take any hint he might get. But the boot was quite on the other foot. He blustered a good deal about the 'Queen's Army' and the wicked radicals and their Press, and finally said that he might be kicked out but nothing should induce him to go of his own accord. . . . This afternoon . . . there was another change. C.B. saw the Duke for an hour, and found him quite tired out with his little run up stream and sulking under the bank ready to be gaffed at any moment. . . . C.B. suggested that his annual trip to Homburg in the beginning of August would be a suitable opportunity; and he seemed quite agreeable. . . .[21]

Rosebery minuted on this: 'C.B. was quite right.' C.B. himself wrote to Rosebery next day:

> At Windsor Bigge & I drew up a beautiful letter for her to write to the Duke. We put it all upon the change of the C. in C's duties . . . I think our phrases could hardly be surpassed. . . . I went to the Queen with this in my pocket. . . . A happy thought occurred to

me, inspired by our excellent old friend Solomon, who is always
getting me out of troubles. The last two months of the year are
dead months ... for ... active military duty: on the other hand they
are the months in which the preparation of estimates for the succeeding year is begun and advanced, & this duty shd. be performed by
the new team, un-dazzled by the expiring Sun: Therefore, let us
say 1 Nov. The Duke's pride is saved, his year is completed, & two
months' acceleration given to the Advent of the other Duke five
years' hence. The Queen was delighted. I whipped out our draft
letter which was cordially approved; I took my leave; and after
Bigge & I had shaken each other's hands & danced round his room,
I took train for London. . . . Thus it stands.[22]

Rosebery replied:

My dear C.B.,
    Many thanks for your charming letters. You seem to have had
a trying but successful time, & could not have done better.
    I am sorry from my heart for the Queen & even for the Duke,
although the vacillations of the latter disprove his allegations of
efficiency.[23]

C.B. had written to the Duke to explain how matters stood – he
preferred to do nothing behind a man's back – but he received a pained
reply:

May 18th/95
I think you will admit, that a loyal & devoted public service to Her
Majesty & the country of 58 years, 39 of which in the high & responsible position of Commander in Chief of Her Majesty's Army,
justify me in assuming, that my personal feelings are entitled to
some consideration. . . . I am deeply grieved & hurt by the suggestion put forward . . . it has the appearance in my mind of almost
summary dismissal. . . .
                    I remain, in deep sorrow,
                    Yours most sincerely
                    George.[24]

On receiving this, C.B. wrote to Murray, mentioning that he had
enlisted the aid of the Military Secretary, General Sir Reginald Gipps:

I understood that the Queen wd. send her letter to the Duke when she had written it large – possibly last night?

But eheu! rerum vicissitudines! I have this morning a pietous letter from the Duke. My letter . . . has cut him to the heart . . . I feel for the poor old boy: and I suspect that it is not so much the date that has hurt him as the proof my letter gave him that the gate of hope is closed. . . .[25]

Murray told Rosebery that the Duke seemed 'tolerably resigned to his fate', adding, inconsequently: 'It is reported from Algiers that the Czarevitch has carried off the Superior of the Carmelite Convent there (young lady aged 30) in his yacht.'[26] It was a relief to contemplate somebody else's tribulations with Royal Personages.

The Queen, meanwhile, made some amendments to the 'beautiful' draft. Bigge sent these to C.B. on the 19th, commenting: 'I think you will agree that they (especially the last eight words) have not taken the stiffening out of the letter! . . . Certainly H.M. is most grateful for your invaluable help and advice.'[27] The letter went to the Duke the same day. It is not difficult to see which parts of it were drafted by C.B. and which inserted by the Queen. It ran:

> Windsor Castle.
> 19 May, 1895.

My dear George,

Since seeing you on Thursday I have given much anxious thought to the question of your tenure of the office of Commander-in-Chief.

I quite appreciate the reasons which make you reluctant to resign the office which you have so long held with the greatest advantage to the Army and with my most entire confidence and approbation. I have, however, come to the conclusion, on the advice of my ministers, that considerable changes in the distribution of duties among the officers constituting the Head Quarter Staff of my Army are desirable.

The alterations cannot be effected without reconstituting the particular duties assigned to the Commander-in-Chief. And therefore though with *much* pain, I have arrived at the decision that for your *own* sake as well as in the public interest, it is inexpedient that you should much longer retain that position, from which I think you should be relieved at the close of your autumn duties.

This necessary change will be as painful to me as it is to you,
but I am sure it is best so. Believe me always,
                    Your very affectionate cousin and friend,
                              Victoria R.I.[28]

The same day the Duke recorded in his diary: 'I must submit as
best I can to the inevitable, but I own that I am disgusted with this, to
my mind, most unjustifiable proceeding, though Mr. C.-B. was most
amiable in all he said.'[29] On the 20th he replied to the Queen's letter,
accepting her decision 'with great pain and deep sorrow', and adding:
'I have now only to express the hope, that . . . my feelings may be
spared every mortification that may be avoidable in making so great
an alteration in my future position. . . .'[30] The Duke was not letting
any one off easily. Bigge told C.B. on the 20th that 'H.M. goes farther
than you did in styling H.R.H.'s views as *nonsense*'.[31] On the 22nd C.B.
told him:

> We now encounter . . . the difficulty I foresaw. A statement will
> have to be made . . . and this necessity may come sooner than we
> should desire. You will have seen that The Times is again to-day
> firing into me. But how can we announce the successor's name six
> months in advance, and without indicating the new organization?[32]

Even C.B.'s patience was beginning to wear a shade thin. At this
stage the Whitsun holiday intervened, and hostilities were suspended
for just under three weeks. C.B. went to recuperate at Dover. Then on
June 11 Bigge, who had been knighted by the Queen on her birthday,
May 24, recorded that

> Mr C. Bannerman . . . says he *must* very shortly make a statement
> in the House of Commons, and if only the Duke will yield, he could
> do this in a way to reflect nothing but praise and credit to his Royal
> Highness. But Sir Arthur regrets to hear this morning from some-
> one who saw the Duke *yesterday* that H.R.H. has become as deter-
> mined as ever *not* to resign. . . .[33]

The Queen was also losing patience, and telegraphed to Bigge:

> It is most urgent that the arrangements about C.-in-C. should be
> complied with forthwith, as I hear a Ministerial crisis is expected at

the end of this month. Mr. C.-B. *must* settle it. Think Duke wrong not to have retired some years ago, and that it is undignified to cling to office.[34]

The Queen's political intelligence was remarkably good. Not only was there to be a crisis, but the Government was to be defeated in ten days' time.

Meanwhile, on the 11th, Bigge wrote two letters to C.B. In the first he transmitted the Queen's message, tactfully adding an exclamation mark after the words 'especially as someone has told H.M. a ministerial crisis *may* occur – !'.[35] In the second he wrote: 'I have been told this morning by *one who knows* that the Duke is more than ever determined *not* to go – and that nothing but *the strongest action* will move him . . . I was told the Queen must order him to retire. . . .'[36]

On the 15th Bigge saw C.B. again, and reported to the Queen that 'he will make his statement . . . either on Thursday or Friday next. He would much prefer the latter date as Thursday is an important day at Ascot: probably many of the military members of the House will be absent and they may suspect the S. of S. of having taken advantage of this to discuss a subject in which they are especially interested.' Bigge continued:

> Your Majesty will perceive that he is ready to state that '*some time ago*' it was arranged that the Duke would resign early in 1896. This will be an answer to those who are inclined to say that H.R.H. is yielding to Radical clamour . . . He fears that the Duke will not allow him to use the word 'desire' in which case he will say 'willingness' – tho' the former expression would be indicative of greater magnanimity.[37]

On the 16th the Duke wrote again to C.B., saying: 'I confess that the whole thing hurts my feelings fearfully. . . . I have now been called upon to relinquish the post in spite of the Royal Warrant, which I believe is always looked upon as a *security*. . . .'[38] The same day Bigge again telegraphed to the Queen: 'Sir A. Bigge has seen Mr. C.-Bannerman and regrets to say things not going smoothly. Duke of Cambridge will not allow first part of statement to be made, as he says it is not true. . . .' On the succession Bigge added: 'Mr. C.-Bannerman . . . asks if your Majesty will approve informally of Buller. Prime Minister, Duke of Cambridge, and Military Secretary all in favour of that selection.'

Bigge told the Queen that the Duke had agreed to retire but had 'raised the question – and in a very excited manner – as to whether he could be legally compelled to do so'. He went on to tell her that C.B. had 'referred the question of a pension to the Prime Minister and to Sir William Harcourt who consider that it would be absolutely impossible to bring such a proposal before the House of Commons – HRH would of course continue to receive £2000 a year as Colonel of the Grenadier Guards. . . .'.[39] The Duke also had an allowance of £12,000 a year from public funds, and a house free of rates and taxes, as a Royal Personage. He would only lose these if he became King of Hanover.

Later that day C.B. wrote to Bigge, saying that the Duke had seen the Prime Minister, and 'the result is, I think, a quieting of the air, and the pacification which comes of despair'. He went on:

> H.R.H. has gone to Ascot, and a Cabinet on Wednesday will decide on the points raised.
>
> The almighty dollar has been most prominent in these recent interviews: the post of dignity having receded. But everyone is willing to manufacture a post, or posts, of dignity if only no power of interference is involved.
>
> On the whole, the state of things is healthy.
>
> I have had the whole matter out with Balfour, who will follow my statement on Friday.[40]

On the 18th the Duke wrote to C.B. from Windsor, thanking him for the 'very friendly terms' in which he had written, but saying that the Cabinet's decision had 'filled me with grief, sorrow, and I must own also with *surprise*' and saying that if he got no pension he would 'look upon myself as absolutely disgraced'.[41]

On the 19th Rosebery told Bigge: 'The Duke, I am afraid, gets worse and worse.'[42] That day the Cabinet decided unanimously against a pension. The Queen had told Bigge on the 16th that she approved of Buller.[43] On the 19th she sent a further telegram:

> . . . The pension would be preposterous. The Military Title Duke of Cambridge proposes would not do either. The Office and Title of Grand Master of the Order of the Bath is in Abeyance as I did not wish anyone to hold it after my husband –
>
> Would that please the Duke?[44]

The Queen was clearly doing her best. On the same day Bigge reported to her: 'Mr. C.-Bannerman will . . . only announce to following effect. No chief of the Staff. Retention of General Commanding-in-Chief, but with functions modified and duties less centralized – . . . Cabinet also decided not to name successor now . . .'

Bigge told the Queen that C.B.'s wish had been to describe his scheme in detail and to announce the decision that Buller would succeed the Duke as Commander-in-Chief in October, but that 'in their present shaky condition the Government does not feel strong enough to act as freely as Mr. C. Bannerman wishes'. 'Mr. C. Bannerman', he added, 'is somewhat perplexed at the decision *not* to now nominate Sir R. Buller, as the necessity for doing so has been one of the strongest arguments to induce the Duke of Cambridge to resign on 1 October.'[45]

Nevertheless, in all essentials, C.B. had finally solved the problem, by what Asquith called 'a felicitous mixture of firmness and tact'.[46] Next day he made his announcement in the House. He paid a tribute to the Duke's long service and said that the Army was proud of him, recognizing in him 'some of the most characteristic qualities of our countrymen'. He went on:

> There are two qualities which, in my opinion, are the most important that any public man, and especially any public servant, can enjoy. One of these is supposed to be inborn, though I doubt it; the other is acquired. They come, in my opinion, before talent; they are better than zeal; they make genius useful; they fertilize eloquence. They are as rare as they are essential; they are constantly spoken of, but never defined. We know them by the vague titles of common sense and knowledge of the world. In the exercise of these great qualities the Duke is a past-master, and it is their possession that has made his influence so great. [47]

C.B. might have been speaking of himself, for these two qualities were peculiarly his.

He went on to say that the Duke's retirement was linked with the introduction of changes in War Office organization. These followed the lines of his own memorandum attached to the Hartington report five years before. There was to be no Chief of Staff, but there would still be a Commander-in-Chief, though with more limited functions and tenure. This officer would be the principal military adviser of the

Secretary of State, and he, with the heads of the military departments, the Adjutant-General, the Quartermaster-General, the Director of Artillery and the Inspector-General of Fortifications, who would each be directly responsible to the minister, would form a council advising the Secretary of State.

The following day the Queen observed to the Prime Minister 'how very satisfactorily Mr. C.-Bannerman had made the statement in the House of Commons'.[48]

The Duke bore C.B. no ill-will, though he referred to Rosebery as 'that blackguard'. He wrote to C.B. from the Horse Guards, saying: 'I am deeply sensible to yourself personally for the very friendly and flattering tone towards myself in making the announcement in the House yesterday afternoon, for which I must offer to you my sincere thanks. . . .'[49]

In his reply, C.B. said that he had been glad to express his appreciation of the Duke's services, adding:

> The incident which occurred later in the evening will probably lead to the severance of my connection with the War Office, but I shall always remain profoundly sensible of Y.R.H.'s kindness and consideration, and proud of the distinguished honour I have enjoyed of serving the Queen as a colleague of Y.R.H.[50]

So ended this extraordinary episode, which, one imagines, must have resulted in the total exhaustion of C.B. and everyone else concerned. It was astonishing that it ended in relative goodwill, and there can be no greater testimony to his skilful handling of delicate affairs.

CHAPTER 14

The Cordite Vote and After

THE 'incident which occurred later in the evening', thus lightly described, was the defeat of the Rosebery Government on a motion to reduce C.B.'s salary. It was in fact the last occasion on which a British government resigned after a defeat in the House of Commons resulting from the defection of some members of its own party; for, with the growth of party discipline, it was becoming rarer for members to vote against their party.[1]

The Government had been living from hand to mouth by tiny majorities, and was itself rent by bitter differences, especially between Rosebery and Harcourt. The Conservatives decided that the moment was appropriate to try to defeat the Government on a snap vote. The occasion came when St. John Brodrick heard that the supply of ammunition and of the new explosive, cordite, was temporarily short. Brodrick consulted Balfour and Salisbury, who entered into the plot with enthusiasm. He then wrote innocently to C.B. saying that he was disturbed about the supply of ammunition, and C.B., not scenting danger, replied, after consulting Buller, saying that there was 'no shortage at all, and no case to be met'. Brodrick was anxious to get the powerful support of Chamberlain, but Chamberlain said that he thought the case was good enough without him. Brodrick, however, who was concerned lest the House should be 'reassured by the cheerful bluff which had carried "C.-B." so far in public life', argued that 'on a question as to the merits of which nine M.P.s out of ten were wholly ignorant "C.B." would get a personal verdict'. Chamberlain was still not convinced and said to Brodrick: 'I think you over-estimate him.'

At question time C.B. was asked about two Highlanders who had died of sunstroke at an Aldershot field-day after an eleven-mile march.

C.B. replied, expressing regret. In a supplementary question he was asked whether he would give the soldiers 'a more reasonable head-gear than the absurd forage cap which they wear at present'. He replied: 'We have taken away from the British soldier my native Glengarry. Perhaps it is owing to that that this melancholy event occurred.' Members laughed amiably. The watchful Brodrick sent a note to Chamberlain, asking what other member of the Government could have made such a joke successfully under the circumstances. Chamberlain saw the point and at last agreed to lend his weight to the attack.[2]

C.B. then made his statement about the Duke's retirement, the important business of the afternoon. After it Ministers and Government supporters trooped out, leaving it to the small group who took an interest in Army matters to discuss the abstruse technical question of cordite. A number of Liberal members were not even in London. Asquith, John Morley and Lloyd George were absent. Everyone expected a quiet evening. Harcourt, strolling on the terrace, is reported to have said: 'Thank heaven! There is one night on which we need not fear a crisis.' But the Conservative whips had taken discreet steps to have a good turnout of members available without alarming the unsuspecting Government whips. A good many Conservative members had agreed to spend a hot afternoon on the terrace.

Brodrick moved to reduce the salary of the Secretary of State for War by £100. He claimed that there was an inadequate amount of cordite and small arms ammunition, and that this constituted a grave national danger. The Financial Secretary, Woodall, replied that there was an ample supply, but he declined to give details. C.B. supported him. George Wyndham supported Brodrick. C.B. spoke again, saying that the position was perfectly satisfactory. He could mobilize three Army Corps 'and we have sufficient ammunition for the whole of them'. He suggested that anxiety was strongest among members who had cordite factories in their constituencies.[3] A colleague, Griffith-Boscawen, recorded that he spoke 'not very happily'.[4] As always, he was at his weakest when speaking off the cuff and under hostile pressure. He had fired his gun with his admirable statement about the Duke. That prolonged affair had taken up all his time and attention. Now he was inadequately briefed to deal with a carefully prepared attack on a complex issue. Moreover, he now had to face the enemy's capital ships. Balfour rose and made a skilful attacking speech. Immediately after him Chamberlain was up. Figures of ammunition, reserves, the amount kept by the Japanese, were quoted and the air was dense with technicalities. Woodall made another speech, but after him Goschen rammed home the opposition case. C.B. had, in defending himself against this surprise attack, made a tactical mistake. As a contemporary described it:

> Mr. Campbell-Bannerman retreated from his impregnable position. Had he still held, on the reasonable assurance of his military advisers, that the supply of small arms ammunition was ample, and refused to budge from that position, the House would probably have been satisfied. But he condescended to particulars, and a question which would otherwise have been one of responsible authority became one of evidence.

According to Fleetwood Wilson, C.B. was 'very badly served on this occasion by his personal entourage, but he was himself to blame as he had had a warning of what might happen'.[5] Another War Office official, Haliburton, said that C.B. was 'called upon to meet the case of the Opposition without preparation or instruction, . . . owing to the forgetfulness of a subordinate'.[6] G. W. E. Russell was surprised 'that Campbell-Bannerman did not somehow or other turn and rend the Tories more than he did, for . . . they had virtually accused him of lying'.[7]

The Liberal Whips had not scented danger until Chamberlain had joined in the attack. Then, too late, they began to try to recall Liberal members. The result was the defeat of the Government on the evening of June 21 by 7 votes – 132 to 125. Everyone was taken by surprise. None of those even in the Chamber itself expected the Government to be defeated, and the first indication of a crisis came when the Ministerial lobby was cleared of members a few moments before the Opposition lobby. The four tellers handed their numbers to the clerk at the table, who filled them in on a slip to be given to the principal teller on the winning side. The paper was taken by Tom Ellis, the Government Whip, and the Liberals cheered. Then Ellis glanced at the figures and handed the slip to the chief Opposition Whip. He, bemused by the situation, handed it back to Ellis, but Ellis returned it again and it at last became clear that the Government had been defeated. The Conservatives cheered wildly and there were cries of 'resign!'.

A colleague recorded that C.B. jumped up, threw his papers into his hat and at once moved the adjournment. He then promptly left the Chamber, saying: 'You must find another Secretary of State.'[8] The Liberals had been caught off their guard. It was an 'off' night, a discussion of the Army Estimates, a tedious subject which most members were glad to escape, and which was, as Asquith later wrote, 'in the safe hands of one of the most capable and quite the most popular of the members of the Cabinet'.[9] His own description of the division was 'a snap vote in a thin House on a side issue'.[10] It had been a carefully organized manœuvre, and the Government, if they had wished, could quite easily have mobilized their strength, demanded a vote of confidence, and reversed the vote. Indeed, at first, some members treated the whole thing as a joke. T. W. Russell suggested in the lobby that a subscription might be got up for C.B.'s benefit.

The Queen wrote: 'I heard with astonishment . . . that the Govt. had been defeated. Did not quite see that this would cause a crisis.'[11] But it was soon apparent that the crisis was a real one. The Government were tired of internal wrangles, and were glad to throw their hand in. Harcourt wrote to Rosebery at 7.30 that evening to tell him of the defeat, commenting: 'It is a *chance* blow but in my opinion a fatal one.'[12] There was an improvised ministerial meeting in Harcourt's library, which lasted till midnight, and a full Cabinet at 11 the following morning. Rosebery, Harcourt, Ripon and Tweedmouth were for resignation. Two Ministers were for remaining, the rest for a dissolution. No decision had been reached at the end of the morning. C.B. lunched at the Oxford and Cambridge Club and wrote a line to Charlotte:

> Cabinet meets again at 4. No decision yet: Resign probably, I think.
>
> The Q has sent R a telegr. that if I tender resign. she will not accept.
>
> I will come out after Cabt.
>
> DO.[13]

C.B. had in fact made it clear to his colleagues the previous evening that he felt bound to resign and he wrote to Rosebery on the 22nd submitting his resignation because the vote 'amounted to a Censure on myself'.[14]

There was a good deal of sympathy for him. Hamilton wrote in his diary:

> By a strange irony of fate, it was the reduction of the salary of by far the most popular Minister in the House of Commons, and

of the man who has not only been long considered to be the best Secretary of State the War Office ever had, but who had just announced his intention of carrying through the most important reform in military administration that has been taken in hand during that generation.[15]

But the Rosebery Cabinet judged that it was impossible for them to continue without C.B., and after the adjourned meeting had decided for resignation, Rosebery went straight to Windsor to inform the Queen. Earlier in the day she had written: 'That the Govt should be defeated by an attack on the most popular of its Members is too extraordinary.'[16]

Loulou Harcourt noted: 'R. explained to the Queen how badly the Tories had behaved – especially to Campbell-Bannerman whom she loves – and thinks he has prepared a bad quarter of an hour for Salisbury and Arthur Balfour.'[17]

After seeing Rosebery, the Queen wrote: 'To him personally it would be an immense relief if the Govt were to go out as the scenes in the Cabinet must have been quite dreadful. His only regret is to leave me.'[18] But, according to John Morley, the aged Gladstone, who, 'in spite of his incessant sighs for a hermit's calm, was always for fighting out every position to the last trench, . . . thought his successors pusillanimous for retiring on a small scratch defeat on cordite'.[19]

Dilke, who did not speak in the debate, but was on this occasion the most prominent Liberal to vote with the Conservative Opposition, continued the alliance on military affairs which he had formed with Brodrick and other Conservatives in 1892. Having taken this course and actually voted, as a Liberal, for the reduction of a Liberal Secretary of State's salary, it is curious that he should have been so chagrined when he was not given a place in the Cabinet by C.B. in 1905. Charlotte indeed never forgave him for his action this day, but almost certainly this vote was not the only reason for his exclusion.

There were others who voted against C.B., with whom he later had excellent relations, for example Leonard Courtney, to whom he gave a peerage in 1906, and George Whiteley, who became his Chief Whip. Dalziel, on the other hand, who had led the attack on the Duke of Connaught, voted for C.B., as did Grey, Labouchere, Bryce, Harcourt and John Burns.

Not all Liberals were sorry about the result. Harcourt was glad to see the Government break up. Birrell described the division as 'a trick, a well-manœuvred assassination, for as it chanced there was when it happened more cordite available . . . than there had been for a long time'.[20] One member, a retired regular soldier, wrote saying:

> Will you allow me – as one of those who voted in the majority last night – to assure you that my vote was not given in any way as intended to cast blame upon yourself. It is no secret that the Army have generally looked upon you as the best War Minister of modern times, an opinion which I cordially share. . . . I could not endure the thought that you might consider me ungrateful for all you have done for the Army and the country.
>
> Believe me, Yours very sincerely,
> Francis Bridgeman.[21]

The Times actually went so far as to say: 'With Mr. CAMPBELL-BANNERMAN personally much sympathy will be felt', commenting:

> Mr. CAMPBELL-BANNERMAN had just effected a grand *coup* . . . when a motion to reduce his salary was carried by a majority of seven. Just when his blushing honours were thick upon him, and he may personally have thought, good easy man, his greatness was a-ripening, there came this killing frost of censure.[22]

The *Manchester Guardian* reported that at the military clubs there was 'the greatest sympathy with Mr. Campbell-Bannerman' who was 'certainly the most popular War Minister of this generation', had shown a real desire to improve the position of the officer and the soldier, and had done much to speed up the rearming of the forces.[23]

C.B. himself wrote to his cousin from the Oxford and Cambridge Club on June 24:

> I can quite understand your all thinking we shd hold on, but it was impossible: and resignation was better tactics than dissolution. I think we are well out of it as things were going.
>
> As to the censure of me I am very proud of it. It was a black-guard business. We have too much ammunition rather than too little: but Kynoch & Co. of which company Joe's brother & son are directors wd. like a larger order, and the Chilworth Company in Brodrick's constituency were unsuccessful in getting any orders at all from us because their prices were prohibitive.

The Adjt Genl. and his Officers strongly support me, both before the vote & since it: but Mr. Balfour & Mr. Goschen spurn my word and his assurances alike. . . .[24]

Buller, who, as Adjutant General, should have been briefing C.B., was at the Hotel Metropole at Brighton, whence he wrote innocently on the 22nd:

I was so sorry for the vote last night because I feel it was rather my fault as I did not inform you with what I myself thought I knew, namely that Mr. Brodrick was going to try to win his spurs over the question – As it was the matter seems to have been mis-understood – We are changing the pattern of small arms, and we are also changing the character of our ammunition. . . . I say that the amount of ammn. we have in hand is by far the least part of the military risk we run . . . so I hold our supply is . . . sufficient. I am satisfied with the position . . . I hope you will treat it as a catch vote taken on false premises.[25]

Buller might have done better to have told C.B. all this before the debate. As it was the affair of the cordite vote long rankled in C.B.'s mind. Chamberlain indeed later said: 'I sometimes think that cordite has entered into my right hon. Friend's soul.' And Rosebery knew that it was a sore subject. Next year he wrote:

> 38, Berkeley Sq. W.
>
> My dear CB,
>   Two or three of us dine together on Thursday at 8.30 here to commemorate the Cordite vote, & its consequences. I wrote to ask you & tore up my note as you took that vote somewhat personally. But now I pluck up courage & write again.
>   Yrs,
>   Æ.[26]

Rosebery now answered C.B.'s letter of resignation, saying:

My only reply . . . is to ask you to permit me to add a letter to the familiar initials, and convert you to G.C.B.
    I hope you will allow me to mark in this way the sense that your Sovereign and your colleagues entertain of the masterly

manner in which you have carried through a great reform in military administration [of] priceless benefit to the country, and which no Administration can recall or reverse.

As to your resignation I will only write what I have already said to you – that you were right to offer it but that no earthly consideration would have induced me to separate myself from you.[27]

A week later C.B. wrote again to his cousin:

I have to go back to Windsor today to be invested. Of course it has a special significance after the circs. of last week: but it is specially meant as a mark of her approval of my conduct of the negotiations about the poor old Duke of Cambridge. She has repeatedly told me that no one except myself could have managed it! That is a little strong, but she is very effusive about it.[28]

According to a relative, C.B. had been sounded about a peerage, but had no wish to leave the House of Commons, and as his nephew Morton Campbell, the only son of his elder brother James, was considered to be a disreputable character, the black sheep of the family, and unsuited to succeed to a baronetcy, that alternative was also dismissed.[29] Writing to congratulate C.B. on the 30th, Admiral Fisher said: 'I've heard your political opponents cursing that you were not made Speaker.'[30]

But C.B. was undoubtedly very sore about what had happened. Lord Monkswell, who went to say goodbye on June 28, found him for the first time really worked up. 'Indeed,' wrote his wife, 'he was in such a rage & poured forth his wrath so unrestrainedly that . . . it was the most startling half hour of Bob's life.'[31]

C.B.'s announcement in the House had not indicated who was to succeed the Duke of Cambridge as Commander-in-Chief, but the Rosebery Government had decided on Buller. C.B. told Balfour and Brodrick. Brodrick asked: 'Are you going to pass over both the Field-Marshals?' – referring to Wolseley and Roberts. C.B. replied: 'Why not? Won't your party support it?' Rosebery then saw Salisbury, who was giving nothing away, and merely said that the appointment was not to be vacated for some months and it would rest with the Government then in power to appoint a successor.[32]

C.B.'s letters to Lady Wolseley had certainly implied that the succession was pretty well assured to her husband, and Wolseley was outraged when he heard that he was not to get the job. He wrote to a friend on July 17: 'Campbell-Bannerman was always such a friend of mine, that his change from me to Buller took me "aback" in a way I had never experienced before. . . . This sudden knockdown blow has been delivered to me *below the belt*.'[33]

It is not easy to say for certain why C.B. had come to prefer Buller. He must have changed his mind some time between 1893 and 1895. Three days before the cordite vote Buller had written to him saying that some time before C.B. had dropped a hint that he might be thought of as the Duke's successor, and that he thought it right to say that his appointment would possibly pain Wolseley. He was himself inclined to think he was 'a better second fiddle than a leader of thought' and he modestly suggested that perhaps Wolseley was better fitted for the place.[34]

C.B. and Rosebery had eventually concluded that they must pass over Wolseley and give the job to Buller, though it was a close-run thing. The Duke had long disliked Wolseley, and they may have felt that it would be too wounding to the retiring Commander-in-Chief to give Wolseley the succession, or they may have hesitated because of Wolseley's forthright Unionist views. This seems the most probable explanation. Wolseley was a radical on army policy, but on other matters his views were strongly conservative, even blimpish. Next year, for example, in a letter to the Duke of Cambridge, he wrote:

> our mode of action in all Foreign affairs is . . . so childish that we deserve to suffer for our folly – we might easily have broken up the United States into two powers in 1862-3 & 4, and had we been true to ourselves & to our own interests we should have done so. . . .
>
> The only bright spot I see . . . is that our affairs are being managed by the greatest man we have had in England since Ld. Beaconsfield's death, by a very great statesman supported by men like the Duke of Devonshire, Mr. Chamberlain & Mr. Balfour. . . . The arch traitor Mr. Gladstone has reached the end of his ignoble career; 'an extinct volcano' that can no long vomit forth destruction to his country. His successor is a poor creature who would be, if he could, like him & who, like him, would willingly sell England for power. But when he tries to roar like a lion, he only brays like an Ass. We have not therefore much to dread from Roseberry [*sic*]. . . .[35]

By then Wolseley had cause to be grateful to the Salisbury Government, which had offered him the choice between being Commander-in-Chief and Ambassador in Berlin, but if C.B. had learnt anything of his views he must have realized that this was not a man whom a Liberal Government would want to establish in the highest military office. After the fall of the Rosebery Government, while the appointment was still in the balance, Wolseley became so desperate that at one point he showed his political colours by having himself put up for the Carlton Club, a move that was quickly stopped by Lord Salisbury.[36] But in due course his anxieties were set at rest, and the incoming Unionist Government decided not to proceed with the plan to appoint Buller.

Knowing that the Liberals had intended to appoint him, and anxious not to be presented with a *fait accompli*, Lord Salisbury hit on the plan of demanding the retiring Secretary of State for War's seals of office direct, and C.B. was pursued about London by Salisbury's private secretary, Schomberg McDonnell, who finally tracked him down at the House of Commons and asked for an immediate transfer of the seals, as it might be necessary to appoint a new Secretary of State that afternoon. C.B. demurred, since the proper practice was that the seals should be surrendered only to the Sovereign, from whom they came. He was strongly supported by Harcourt and by Rosebery, who told him that he thought Salisbury's proceeding unparalleled. Salisbury, who described the whole affair as a 'mare's nest', was compelled to make rather specious excuses. When C.B. and his colleagues went to Windsor to give up their seals, C.B. was given a great reception by the crowd at Paddington. Loulou Harcourt recorded: 'The Queen told Campbell-Bannerman that she thought he had been scandalously treated.'[37] Salisbury eventually made a grudging apology, whereupon C.B. himself sent a letter to *The Times*, explaining what had happened.[38]

The Queen read a long explanation by McDonnell, on which she commented tersely: 'The Queen has read this memo & thinks it does not the least alter the question. It was *quite* wrong and Ld. Salisbury's fault. . . . The Pr. of Wales shd. know this.'[39]

Kimberley remarked that Salisbury had sent his private secretary 'very much as he might have sent his footman to ask for Mr. Campbell-Bannerman's seal'.[40] Salisbury had indeed done C.B. an injustice, for C.B. was the last man to try to take advantage of a technicality to commit his successor. Such sharp practice was alien to his nature.

In due course Wolseley was appointed, but, despite their criticisms of C.B.'s management, the Conservatives then proceeded to adopt almost the whole of his plan of reorganization, which provided for a shift of power from the military to the civilians.

The cordite question came up again in the House on July 2. C.B. insisted on making a speech of self-justification which, according to Loulou, made the worst of his case.[41] Balfour, in his reply, loftily and hypocritically disclaimed 'any wish to revive a controversy originally undertaken with no party object whatever', and said that it was dangerous to appeal to the authority of men who could not be present in the House of Commons to answer for themselves.[42] As often happens, the truth was on one side, and the Parliamentary honours on the other.

The argument growled on for some time, and in August C.B. complained to Haliburton that his opponents were holding him up to public condemnation by speech, poster and leaflet as one who was sending soldiers to certain death. Not unreasonably, he considered this to be 'very scandalous'.[43]

No party has a monopoly of virtue. Six years later Balfour was to startle the House by revealing that, at a critical juncture of the Boer War, there were in the United Kingdom, not the 100 million rounds of ammunition for which C.B. had been censured, but just over three thousand. No member of his party, however, then voted against him.[44]

Despite this rather unreal controversy, C.B.'s reputation at the War Office had been high. General Grenfell, for example, wrote:

> The departure of Mr. Campbell-Bannerman ... was much regretted by us who had worked with him. He had muddled less and done more for the Army than most Secretaries of State. He worked very well with Redvers Buller as Adjutant-General, and had a very high opinion of him. ... We all said our adieux to him with great regret, though I think there were few of us that were not glad to see a Conservative Government in again.[45]

Wolseley himself later said: 'In my experience – a pretty long one now, Mr. Campbell-Bannerman is the most capable War Minister I have known or had dealings with.'[46]

C.B.'s handling of the Duke's retirement showed that when he cared to exert himself he had great resources of skill, patience and tact. Lord Haliburton's biographer wrote of C.B. that he was 'strangely misunderstood and underrated south of the Tweed' and that 'it has been charged against Sir Henry Campbell-Bannerman that in the War Office he acted on the simple principle of letting the permanent officials have their own way. To anyone who knew the quiet, stubborn nature of the late Prime Minister, the suggestion carries its own refutation. . . .'[47]

On July 31 C.B. wrote to Harcourt:

I have learned from the War Office . . . that after considering several schemes for a new organization . . . they have rejected them all and adopted mine. . . . They may of course alter it a little to make it look more or less original . . . they will add £50,000 to the Store Vote for Small Arms Ammunition. This is a very moderate *mus* after all the parturition. . . .'[48]

And when, in August, Lansdowne sent a sketch of his proposals to the Queen, he said: 'Your Majesty will observe that they differ little, in essential particulars, from those put forward by Sir Henry Campbell-Bannerman.[49]

C.B.'s War Office days were now over, but in the years of opposition ahead he was able to speak with authority on military affairs, and, at the end of his life, to preside, as Prime Minister, over a reorganization of the Army as important, in its way, as the Cardwell reforms with which his official career had begun.

At the end of 1897 there began a furious public controversy about the merits of Cardwell's short service system, which was assailed by Arnold-Forster in a series of articles in *The Times*. To Haliburton C.B. wrote on January 6, 1898:

The hornets are all out of the nest and more audacious than ever. What, can you tell me, has happened to the Times?. . . . Is it a new man? And who? Its articles are not only violent, but personally abusive; and though in ordinary politics it has unfortunately caught the tone of the 'Eatanswill Gazette' of late years, and my poor friends are always denounced as knaves and swindlers, I have not seen that spirit applied to 'service' questions until lately.[50]

He wondered whether the leading soldiers who had helped to create the Cardwell system would speak out, 'or will these boar-hounds join the chorus of mongrels and turnspits who are yelping in the press?'[51]

In another letter to Haliburton he said: 'The whole pack are yelping our way: we want the bay of some big hound of authority to get them

The Secretary of State

off. The soldiers must fight the soldiers' battle, or we are done.'[52] But it was Haliburton who argued the case in a series of articles in *The Times*. C.B. was delighted with these.

The House debated the problem when the Army Estimates came up for discussion on February 25, 1898. Brodrick was assailed from his own side by Arnold-Forster, whom he described as one of those who 'denounce and deride' all official explanations. Arnold-Forster was, in the fullness of time, to succeed Brodrick at the War Office. Both of them were singularly unsuccessful Secretaries of State. In the debate C.B. warmly defended both the soldiers, who were frequently praised, and the War Office civilians, who were not. Writing after the debate to Lady Haliburton, whose husband had been ill, he said:

> ... the enemy collapsed entirely on Friday night. There was no trace of the fierce words of the newspaper attack. ... Three nights' debate that was promised shrivelled up into one night sustained with difficulty. One result was that poor I, who had meant to speak on Monday, with a nice Saturday and a possible Sunday for polishing up my tropes, arguments, and epigrams, had to dive into a back room and hastily scramble together some sort of a speech. ...[53]

'Backing of his friends', comments Lord Haliburton's biographer, 'was an obligation which "C.-B." never neglected.'

To Wolseley, the appointment as Commander-in-Chief, which he had coveted so much, proved only dust and ashes. He was not even consulted when Roberts and Kitchener were sent out to South Africa. He got it into his head that, under C.B.'s administration, Buller had plotted against him and, as Buller put it to C.B., 'tried to supplant him in what he held to be his birthright'. Buller was upset about this and in 1899 asked C.B. if he could let him have a copy of the letter he had written in 1895 urging Wolseley's case. C.B. was unable to lay his hands on it, but confirmed to Buller that 'so far from pushing or intriguing, you disclaimed ... any thought of your own advancement ... and advocated the high claims (which indeed were evident) of Lord Wolseley'.[54] Wolseley, for his part, wrote to his wife in 1898: 'Campbell-Bannerman ... was at dinner with the Portsmouths. He seemed a little shy of me, but rallied when I spoke to him as usual – He asked kindly after you, so I forgive him much.'[55]

During the ten years of opposition between 1895 and 1905 C.B.

continued to speak regularly on Army matters. In 1897 he ridiculed the idea of encircling London with a chain of forts, but agreed that it was sensible to defend possible invasion routes. In 1900 he said that he believed conscription to be 'impossible in this country' (wherein he differed from Rosebery, who had taken the opposite view a few days before) and commented that: 'Conscription with the ballot seems to me to be nothing but a combination of the press-gang and the roulette wheel, neither a very dignified nor effective way of defending the country.'[56]

He wrote to W. T. Stead, the journalist, in January 1900, saying: 'The governing truth is that if our Empire is to be Imperial, and if we are to go on pushing, bustling, quarrelling, & hectoring, as we have acquired the habit of doing, our Army is not nearly big enough, and *it cannot be made much bigger on the present system.*'[57]

Next year he urged that commissions should be granted more liberally to non-commissioned officers and not given exclusively to young men from the public schools. He also warned, sensibly, against too much reliance on the lessons of the war in South Africa, since the geographical conditions were peculiar. Then and in 1903 he criticized the 'panic schemes' of the Conservatives and the ideas concocted by St. John Brodrick and the ageing Lord Roberts.

The Conservatives, for their part, regarded C.B. as a hopelessly misguided Little Englander. When he spoke on Army affairs he asked the House to remember that the strength of the Empire was 'derived from its being an Empire of peace and commerce and good relations' and he expressed concern about any departure from 'the policy of prudence' in the direction of 'a military spirit which would alter vitally the character of our nation and Empire'.[58]

Brodrick, who had laid the mine which destroyed C.B. as Secretary of State in 1895, found, eight years later, that the post was a far from easy one. As early as November 1901, Harcourt, in a letter to Spencer, said that Brodrick was hooted in the streets when he accompanied the King.[59] In January 1903, after the Boer War, C.B. said in a letter to Bryce:

You ask about Brodrick's Army Scheme. Certainly attack it freely. It has no friends that I know of – military or civilian.

My own opinion (which need not embarrass anyone else) is that in the War the Office itself did its work exceedingly well (e.g. supplies, stores, recruiting etc.) and the failure was due to

(a) the vanity and self-sufficiency of Lansdowne and Brodrick; their jealousy of others and of each other . . .

(b) the incompetence of some of the generals in the Office (what can you expect? 'Bête comme un vieux militaire' is a proverb). E. g. Evelyn Wood whose amorous subservience to Lady J. and her daughter is the origin of all the sneers about fine ladies.

(c) the fact which could not have been got over that the whole thing was on a scale exceeding anything that the organization ever contemplated.

This last is the main point.

But his proposed Army Corps are preposterous, and there is no sign of a real grasp of what our future needs will be. The truth is we cannot provide for a fighting Empire, and nothing will give us the power. A peaceful Empire of the old type we are quite fit for. . . .[60]

Next month Balfour, the Prime Minister, wrote about Brodrick to Lady Elcho: '. . . his unpopularity now is the most serious menace to the Government. . . . Many good observers think the feeling against St. John so violent that we shall never get through our Army estimates without a fall! He is naturally depressed, poor old boy.'[61]

Brodrick's scheme, propounded in 1901, was for six Army Corps. The young Winston Churchill leapt to fame by denouncing it in a speech which he told A. G. Gardiner he had written out six times in his own hand. Balfour realized that Brodrick had to go, and finally moved him to the India Office, where he was to come into collision with Lord Curzon, the Viceroy, in the autumn of 1903. He paid a tribute to him in the House, which caused C.B. to comment sarcastically on the transfer of such a paragon of a War Minister to the India Office. To succeed him Balfour chose Arnold-Forster, whom King Edward found exasperating and uncouth. Harcourt's sympathies were with the War Office: 'To be handed over to such a tormentor as the conceited prig, Arnold-Forster', he wrote to Morley, 'is punishment enough for all their crimes.'[62] Arnold-Forster was inclined to revert to pre-Cardwell thinking, and to favour an Army recruited of long-service soldiers designed for overseas service. Naturally C.B. opposed this and in his attacks on Arnold-Forster he was joined by Churchill.

The publication in 1903 of the report of the Elgin Commission on the conduct of the war in South Africa dealt a blow to the Conservative

Government. C.B. wrote to Spencer on September 6, commenting on the part Lansdowne and Brodrick had played:

> The Elgin report is tremendous. . . . The fault mainly lies with the ministers: no organization, board or council would have stood their practices. Stanhope, Lansdowne, Brodrick in succession have through their vanity, fussiness, love of acclaim, secretiveness & self-sufficiency, broken down the loyalty and confidence which used to exist & which is essential to *any* system, and have irritated & alienated soldiers & civilians alike.
>
> As B. has been there all through I suspect he is the main culprit. L. is weak and pleasant, but exceedingly secretive and anxious to get the credit for everything: but B. with the same faults is brusque, underhand, & crooked: which L. is not.[63]

To Lefevre he wrote at the same time:

> The main thing is to decide what we want the army for. . . . There could be nothing more pestilent than all this desire to make a military nation of us, even to train schoolboys for war! It makes one almost reconciled to the peaceful arts of golf & football which at present absorb the energies of the nation.[64]

He was also sceptical about the Esher Committee on War Office reform, set up in November 1903. It had Lord Esher as Chairman, and Admiral Fisher and Sir George Clarke as the other members. C.B. was inclined to suspect Esher as an intriguer. Fisher he liked personally but he distrusted his judgement. Two years later he described him to Spencer as 'very bellicose and . . . the worst possible counsellor on anything, at least beyond his métier'.[65] Clarke was the officer C.B. had described as 'wire puller issimus' in 1893. He called it a 'strange committee' and pointed out that none of its members knew anything of Army administration. In March 1904, Esher wrote to his son: '. . . You will be pleased to hear that C.B. called us a "damned dictatorial domineering Trio". The Prince of Wales is delighted with this description.'[66]

In June C.B. wrote to his friend Robertson:

> What a collapse of their great Army scheme: it has absolutely broken down on the ground of expense, and they are all at sixes and sevens over it. Very agreeable to me, who have from the first

ridiculed their methods and plans, and counted on failure when they had shipped all the men of experience and given the thing over to tyros, ignoramuses, and pushing journalists.

Tommy Bowles says what could you expect from

(1) A financial courtier (Esher)

(2) A Times leader-writer (Clarke)

(3) A Cingalese sailor (Fisher, whose mother was a native woman in Ceylon) and

(4) 'Our Mr. Arnold-Forster', from Cassell's.

It is a big breakdown, and far more than enough to wreck a Ministry.[67]

The covering letter under which the committee submitted its final report, insisting that their proposals should be accepted as a whole, C.B. described as 'a mixture of the Pontifical and the hysterical'.[68]

In the House he pointed out that Army expenditure had increased under the Conservatives from £18 million in 1895 to nearly £37 million in 1904. In January 1905, Lord Carrington told C.B. that 'the King . . . is very outspoken about the W.O. "Chaos" as he calls it'.[69] In April C.B. wrote to Haliburton about Arnold-Forster:

A.F. is done. The House was nearly unanimously against him: his own people even stronger than mine. . . his colleagues gave him no support. His metallic voice, sour visage, & dogmatic egotism bored when it did not irritate. . . . It is quite understood that his scheme is dead.[70]

Writing to Ripon, he criticized 'the "Service Members" all whose opinions seem to me wrong, & to be the mere repetition of the gossip of messrooms & clubs'.[71]

1905 saw the final end of the Conservative Government. Balfour afterwards told his biographer, Mrs. Dugdale, that the main reason why he delayed his resignation was to get the 18-pounder gun into production – 'The re-arming of the Field Artillery I considered vital for the safety of the Empire and worth risking a débâcle in the Unionist Party and I was determined not to go out of office until we were so far committed to the expenditure that no Liberal Government could have withdrawn from the position.' Mrs. Dugdale recorded this conversation but did not think it worthy of inclusion in her biography of Balfour. Her scepticism seems justified.[72]

When C.B. became Prime Minister in December 1905 he sent Haldane to the War Office, remarking drily: 'We shall see how Schopenhauer gets on in the kailyard.' Two months later he wrote to Haliburton from 10 Downing Street:

> I was pleased (and surprised) to hear from my most philo-sophical friend the S.S.W. the other day that he has been consulting you, & he was able to tell me that you are very sound in your Army views – thoroughly Cardwellian. . . . This is hopeful! He had even heard of our Knox and wd. like to have a talk with him: I told him I would bring this about if I could.
>
> I never discuss things with him: but I have warned him against talking and speaking in public too much, and above all agst. dogmatism and swagger; and advised him whatever he does to give the credit of it to the soldiers, and never to seem to be making capital for himself. In short, to be as unlike his two predecessors as he can. . . .[73]

His friend T. R. Buchanan was given C.B.'s old post of Financial Secretary. In his *Autobiography* Haldane records that Buchanan 'was one of the most loyal of comrades, but very orthodox as a Liberal. Sir H. C.-B. had made him Financial Member at the War Office in order, I think, to make sure that I should not run wild'. But C.B. was not for economy at any price. He was for keeping the Army's 156 battalions of the Line.[74] Today we have just over fifty.

Haldane was an unusual War Minister. He began by telling the Army Council that what he had in mind was 'a Hegelian Army'. This, not unnaturally, baffled them, but in fact he turned out to be one of the best Secretaries of State for War since Cardwell. He created the British Expeditionary Force that helped to stop the German advance in 1914. Fortescue, the historian of the British Army, described that force as 'incomparably the finest army which this country had ever put into the field', and says that Haldane 'built up on the German model a striking force of the Regular Army, small indeed but perfect to the last detail'.[75]

The striking force consisted of six divisions and one cavalry division (the 'old Contemptibles') – in all some 160,000 regulars, with fourteen divisions of territorials in second line. Haldane also formed a General Staff, and, this time, in the darkening state of Europe, there was no protest from C.B., though there was at last created the post of Chief of

Staff, later to become the Chief of the Imperial General Staff. C.B. no doubt realized that, with the growing German menace, involvement in a European war might be inevitable, much as he loathed the prospect. Colonel Omond, in his *Parliament and the Army*, comments: 'The general principle adopted by Haldane and his advisers was to complete the Cardwell Scheme.'[76]

Here perhaps lies the key to C.B.'s warm approval and support for Haldane's work. The name Cardwell was still something of a totem to him, as his shrewder colleagues realized. Use of that magic name produced in him a Pavlovian reaction in favour of their proposals. Asquith, for example, wrote to him on January 9, 1907: 'We had a useful meeting of the Cabt. Commee on the Army scheme yesterday. I think it can (in its main features) be maintained, as proceeding on Cardwellian lines. . . .'[77]

The same day Haldane also wrote to C.B., saying:

> General Ewart's suggestion about carrying to its completion Cardwell's scheme of a third battalion has worked like magic with the Generals. They . . . expressed themselves as . . . very hopeful of this scheme being the best piece of work done for the Army that has been done since Cardwell's time.[78]

In fact C.B.'s support was unstinted from the start, though in 1907 he made Haldane reduce the Army Estimates. After introducing these in March 1906, and pleasing C.B. by a tribute to Cardwell, Haldane wrote to his mother: 'Old Sir H. C.-B. is about the most enthusiastic and warmest.'[79] When Haldane sat down C.B. went over to him and said, 'Not only a splendid speech but an historical speech.'

While Brodrick and Arnold-Forster had made enemies on every side, Haldane, purring softly like a great cat, soon had the whole military machine on his side. Lord Hankey described him 'seated at ease in the Secretary of State's chair at the head of the great table in the Army Council room at the War Office, smoking a cigar poised delicately on the two prongs of a tiny silver fork he always used for the purpose',[80] and Edmund Gosse, even more vividly, as 'pacing up and down his room, with his heavy legs alternately thrown in front of him, with his odd elephant- or rather tapir-like movement'.[81] Gosse, like others, was enthusiastic about Haldane – 'The sweep of his mind always amazes and exhilarates me. He seems like Thought itself made flesh, pale, ponderous and bland . . . our one great intelligence in public life'.[82] C.B. looked on him with a cooler eye, but he recognized his qualities as well as his defects. For, despite his love of mystery and intrigue, Haldane was an outstanding administrator. One of his most attractive traits was his patience with, and respect for, soldiers who knew their job but were not as articulate as the average politician.

C.B. knew, too, the political importance of the success of Haldane's plans. Haldane wrote in a letter to J. A. Spender in November 1907: '. . . as C.B. said to me today, "Beat them we must, for an agitation for Compulsion is the inevitable result of failure!" '[83]

Balfour, now Leader of the Opposition, opposed the Haldane reforms, including the creation of an expeditionary force. This did not stop him writing to Haldane in 1914 demanding that the Expeditionary Force should be at once mobilized and embarked. Balfour's opposition to Haldane's plans makes it hard to accept his view that Liberals were irresponsible and that the defence of the country was only safe in Conservative hands.

Immediately after taking over the War Office in December 1905, Haldane told Esher that C.B. had given him a free hand. He went on to talk of the Committee of Imperial Defence – the C.I.D. – which had been set up by Balfour in December 1902, using as a basis the Cabinet Council originally proposed by the Hartington Commission and established by Rosebery, C.B. and Spencer. Balfour attached great importance to the Committee and never missed a meeting.

C.B. had had serious doubts about its usefulness. In the House on March 5, 1903, he said that he was inclined to think that Service representatives should not be full members of the Committee, as this might interfere 'with that Ministerial and Cabinet responsibility which constitutes the foundation of our system of Government'. He also drew attention to 'the strange absence of the Chancellor of the Exchequer from the Committee'.[84] In a private letter the same month to Lefevre he said: 'This precious Defence Committee is utterly mischievous, but I at least managed to secure that it was to be accepted by the House as a purely tentative & experimental body, and also that its decisions were not to be held binding on subsequent Ministers.'[85] But now Haldane told Esher 'that C.B., although he admitted he did not like the institution when it originated, accepts it as a *fait accompli*, and will preside over it and use it'.[86] Haldane later told Hankey that he had 'begged the life' of the Committee from C.B., who had agreed to its continuing provided that Haldane kept an eye on it.[87]

On December 13, 1905, Esher wrote to the King describing a talk with C.B. about the C.I.D.:

> Sir Henry admitted that he had originally been prejudiced against it as an Institution but he had determined . . . to . . . work it. . . . He admitted . . . that he had also looked with suspicion on Lord Esher's committee for the Reconstitution of the War Office . . . it was 'his weakness to poke fun at people' although he should not be taken too seriously.
>
> This was quite a charming 'amende honorable' and Lord Esher at once felt that future relations would be very pleasant. . . . Sir Henry then . . . spoke very confidentially and quite openly about his colleagues and their characteristics & his difficulties and all this with much humour & shrewd discernment of character.
>
> Your Majesty would have been much amused at the very good natured fun which he poked at Mr. Haldane . . . and his energy in commencing within twelve hours to grapple with the most difficult problems, and his (Sir Henry's) quite affectionate but humorous appreciation of Mr. John Morley's 'rather feminine & old maidish sensitiveness'. . . .[88]

Two men of the world had made contact, and had hit it off admirably. A month earlier Buchanan at Belmont had noted that C.B. did not like Esher. But C.B.'s suspicions were now set at rest, and soon after he invited Esher to attend the Committee regularly, which he did up to 1914.

At the end of 1906 Haldane's plans were ready, and it was necessary to gain C.B.'s approval before putting them to the Cabinet. Once again Esher was brought in. Three letters he wrote to his son tell the story:

> Dec. 18th
> . . . Tomorrow I am to see C.B. about the Army – and our Report. He wants to understand the drift of Haldane's scheme, and has not been able to understand Haldane's rhetorical rendering of it. So I must try my hand in dry prose.

> Dec. 19th
> Yesterday morning I had a long talk, quite an hour, with C.B. He was most genial, and listened to everything I could tell him about Haldane's scheme. He put his finger, in that quiet way he has,

upon the weak points. I think that he will back Haldane. If that is so, our fat friend stands a good chance.

March 7, 1907

. . . The only other event of importance is that Haldane has got his Army scheme through the Cabinet. Campbell-Bannerman, whose flair is excellent, says 'the public neither knows nor cares about the details of an Army scheme, but as Haldane shows £2,000,000 decrease in cost, and has got a definite scheme, they will say "give him a chance".' This is a true diagnosis.[89]

Buchanan helped to keep expenditure down, saying of Haldane to C.B. in December 1907: 'It is not that he is extravagant, but he likes to be before the public from week to week starting new schemes, and you can't do that without spending money.' He said that Fleetwood Wilson, C.B.'s old private secretary, was indispensable at expounding to others 'the vague utterances of the S. of S.'[90]

Looking back in 1919, Haldane remembered C.B., whom he had once struggled so hard to displace as leader of the party, as 'very sympathetic and helpful to me'.[91] Haldane needed sympathy and support from his chief. Like most War Ministers, he ran into powerful opposition, aggravated by what Esher noted as a weakness, that 'in wanting to please everybody, he satisfies no one'.[92] By the end of 1907 he had lost the support of the King and of a number of his Cabinet colleagues. But C.B. and Asquith backed him up and gave him 'quiet support . . . that enabled me to hold on'.[93] An early speech of Haldane's in January 1906, when he had spoken of 'an obligation higher even than economy', which was provocative to radicals and economizers, gave C.B. an opportunity to twist the tails of his former Liberal Imperialist critics, and he wrote to Asquith at the Treasury:

I fear our philosophic friend has not learned the trick of accurate and guarded official language.

What he asked me was, could he say in the City that I was in favour of an efficient army, notwithstanding what I said at the Albert Hall about armaments.

I gave him full leave to make that perfectly platitudinous and truistical declaration; and pointed out that A.J.B. had no foundation for his argument that reduction of extravagant expenditure implied reduced numbers and lessened strength.

I do not mind it a bit myself. . . . But I do not wish the Ch. of the Ex. to think that I gave any one a 'free hand' to foreshadow increases in Army expenditure.[94]

Asquith replied:

I read with a cold shudder that particular sentence in our friend's speech, and inferred that (by what Hegel calls the 'dialectical process') the Idea had received a good deal of expansion since it left you. But I don't think that any harm has resulted. . . .[95]

They were agreeable days when Ministers made a habit of exchanging their thoughts in this way in manuscript letters.

C.B.'s personal staff were less tolerant than their chief. In September 1906, one of his private secretaries, Vaughan Nash, wrote to the other, Arthur Ponsonby: 'Haldane's war trump is like a philosopher learning a penny whistle. Why can't he shut up. He will madden C.B.'[96] But C.B. was not maddened. He was amused but also impressed. In February he told Sinclair, a strong critic of Haldane's plans:

R.B.H. left all the papers on the Army. . . . He dwelt on the fact of the *Cardwell* system being maintained. . . . All is . . . for the best – the soldiers delighted; the Volunteers everywhere enthusiastic; Grey and Asquith very warm for it: Burns and J.M. most appreciative. Every bolt hole was thus stopped. I could only congratulate him, and hope it would turn out a success. . . . He thus rides on the storm and directs the whirlwind.[97]

After the success of Haldane's proposal at the conference of Colonial Prime Ministers in April 1907, that there should be an Imperial General Staff, C.B. told Haldane that he had made a hit in choosing his War Minister. In October 1907, Crewe wrote to C.B. from Dalmeny, saying: 'Haldane is here, quite in his element, being compassed about' by a great cloud of Lord Lieuts; to whom he is explaining the Army Act. I have not joined the symposium.'[98]

In the House in August 1906, C.B. said:

I have never been strongly prejudiced in favour of the Committee of Imperial Defence. I was always afraid it might get beyond its proper bounds, that it might interfere with the responsibility of the Cabinet and the Ministers charged with the two great Departments .... I confess that I have modified my opinion in this respect. . . . My experience of this Committee has been most satisfactory.[99]

But C.B. could hardly be called an enthusiast for the Committee. In 1907 Lord Mersey wrote:

One of the Secretaries to the Committee of Imperial Defence says that C.B. pays much less attention to it than Balfour did. I remember C.B. saying to me when it was set up, that it had a wrong tendency and ought to be abolished. Fisher never comes but sends D.N.I.; Esher attends but is mal vu at the F.O. as he is supposed to repeat things to the King which Grey resents.[100]

Sir George Clarke, however, who was the Committee's secretary in C.B.'s day, wrote numerous letters to him on all kinds of defence questions and, when he left the Committee in September 1907, wrote to C.B.: 'It has been an honour & a pleasure to serve under you, & I shall cherish the memory of this time. I could well understand that you at first felt misgivings about the Committee. . . .' He concluded: 'You have got more out of it than Mr. Balfour whose intentions did not reach accomplishment.'[101] Clarke was critical of Haldane's plans, of the *Dreadnought* design and of a proposal to do away with the militia, and put his views direct to C.B., who, by mistake, sent some of his letters about the *Dreadnought* on to the Admiralty, where Fisher saw them, was outraged and got Clarke moved on to be Governor of Bengal. In one of his letters, in May 1907, Clarke sent C.B. an extract from a letter from a German saying that Germany was dominated by Prussia and was preparing for a war against England.[102] It was a timely warning.

Clarke wrote of C.B. that he was a man 'whose natural bent and training did not dispose him to enter deeply into the matters which seemed all-important to me; but who had an open mind always calm and receptive. . . . While, as Prime Minister of the Empire, he showed defects due to absorption in domestic policies, he had great qualities too little recognised.'[103]

C.B. was not a man to harbour resentments and his last letter to Haldane, who had intrigued long and energetically against him in opposition, said:

. . . Let me most sincerely and warmly congratulate you upon the great success you have wrought out of your complicated problem. . . . It is a great triumph to have carried such a large body of opinion with you, and I hope you will have as much satisfaction while you proceed to carry out and superintend the working of the details of your *magnum opus*.[104]

Old friends were taken care of, too. On August 8 Haldane announced the appointment of the Duke of Connaught to be Field Marshal Commanding-in-Chief and High Commissioner for the new Mediterranean command. If he could not be Commander-in-Chief in England, that was the next best thing.

For over thirty-five years C.B. had been involved, on and off, in military affairs and the question of Army reform. Now, at the end of his life, he was leaving the War Office in good hands, and the Army in a state of high efficiency. In less than seven years after his death it was to face, in 1914, its greatest and most terrible challenge, and to succeed superbly.

Part 5

C.B.'s Accession to the Leadership

CHAPTER 15

Nearing the Summit

I N February 1894, a fortnight before Mr. Gladstone's final resignation as Prime Minister and eighteen months before the cordite
vote, an article in the *Spectator* said:

> It is interesting to note the flutter of surprise which has run
> through the country at Mr. Campbell-Bannerman's speech against
> the House of Lords. To the plain man who does not worry about
> magazine-rifles and Army grievances, the figure of the Secretary of
> State for War is the merest shadow. No wonder, then, he rubs his
> eyes, and asks, – What sort of a man is this Mr. Campbell-Bannerman
> and why . . . does he speak with authority, and not like the ordinary
> Ministerial nonentity; why, in a word, does he make one feel that
> . . . one ought to know more about a man who speaks with such an
> evident sense that his opinion is a very important matter? The
> explanation is that, though the public at large has not realised the
> fact, Mr. Campbell-Bannerman is one of the five most important
> men in the Gladstonian Party, and that if the three most important
> had to be named, they would, in spite of all appearances, be Lord
> Rosebery, Mr. Morley, and Mr. Campbell-Bannerman, – not Lord
> Rosebery, Mr. Morley, and Mr. Asquith. So important, indeed, is
> the position occupied by Mr. Campbell-Bannerman, that it has
> been freely said in the inner circle of Gladstonians, that if Mr.
> Gladstone retired, he would be the only person capable of stilling
> 'the fierce conflict of sects and factions . . .' which is certain to succeed
> the political absolutism of the present *régime*. 'Mr. Campbell-
> Bannerman is the only man who could do it, but he could,' is what
> is frequently said by those who point out with despair how Sir

William Harcourt could not serve under Lord Rosebery, nor Lord Rosebery under Sir William Harcourt; how Mr. Morley is impossible as a Prime Minister; how Mr. Asquith's elevation would set loose a tornado of jealous indignation; and how Lord Spencer and Lord Kimberley are compromises who might be blown to pieces by an article in an evening paper. Mr. Campbell-Bannerman is, in a word, the 'dark horse' of the Gladstonian Party, and a 'dark horse' on whom a great many knowing people are inclined to put their money. . . .

Close observers may have noticed . . . that he has been gradually gaining a position of great influence in the House of Commons. Besides doing his departmental work with ability, and avoiding all needless conflicts with the military experts on the one hand, and the Radicals on the other, he has been always ready to help his colleagues and his party in moments of difficulty. Whenever the coach has seemed like sticking in the mud, there has been the cheery but never garrulous Scotchman, the man who always inspires confidence, and never raises envy or malice, ready to lend a hand and set things going again. There has been no self-advertisement, no parade, only the persistent diffusion of a general sense of capacity, moderation, geniality, and common-sense carried to the ninth power. . . . Nothing can long prevent such a man coming to the front in an English deliberative Assembly. . . . A curious piece of self-revelation . . . is to be found in a little speech made last week by Mr. Campbell-Bannerman at a luncheon at the Liberal Club in Newcastle-on-Tyne. Mr. Campbell-Bannerman was drawn into a definition of Liberalism. He might have been expected at the present moment to define it after some one or other of the cant phrases of the day, such as 'trust in the people', or 'justice and brotherhood'. Not a bit of it. He was content with pitching a very much lower note. 'Liberal politics,' said Mr. Campbell-Bannerman, 'meant the politics of common-sense.' . . . It is easy to understand why Mr. Campbell-Bannerman never makes enemies, never stirs up strife, never hates and never gets himself hated, and if he or his Party are assailed, takes his punishment with the utmost coolness and good-humour. To do otherwise would be to show lack of common-sense. . . . It must not be supposed, however, that Mr. Campbell-Bannerman has nothing but common-sense and the genial and businesslike cynicism which so often accompanies it. . . . He is . . . a man possessed of a political judgment . . . a capable administrator, a persuasive if apparently unattractive speaker, and possesses the instinct for managing the House of Commons. . . .

It may well be that the 'dark horse' of the Liberal Party, and not Lord Rosebery or Sir William Harcourt, will succeed Mr. Gladstone.[1]

The writer's forecast was wrong. It was Lord Rosebery who became Prime Minister next month. Nevertheless it was an unusually perceptive assessment, and the writer would perhaps have been less incredulous than most, if he could have been told that within four years Lord Rosebery, Sir William Harcourt and Mr. John Morley would have all eliminated themselves from the leading counsels of the party, leaving the field clear for C.B. to be elected as leader.

In 1884, the year Edward Grey was sent down from Oxford for idleness, C.B. had been recruited to the Irish Office, as was later said, as a 'dose of oxygen' to help revive the fortunes of Mr. Gladstone's second government. Since then he had been a man of some consequence in the party, and by 1895 he had become an important person in it.

At one time Sir Charles Dilke had seemed likely to go to the top. Hamilton had written in July 1885: 'Mr. G. & Lord Hartington removed, Dilke seemed alone to possess qualities to lead.'[2] Had he done so, there would have been no future for C.B. But the Crawford divorce case put an end to his prospects. The following year the Home Rule split knocked another potential leader out of the running. Hamilton wrote then of Chamberlain: 'If he had stuck to Mr. G., the mantle must have fallen upon him.'[3] But he had gone over to the enemy. C.B. remained in the field, and as early as 1889 John Morley wrote to him saying: 'You'll be greatly wanted by your party one of these days.'[4]

But he was still not very well known in the House, since he spoke mainly on the Army Estimates, the normal audience for which was only twenty to thirty. In the eyes of most people he still seemed a secondary figure in comparison with Rosebery, Harcourt or Morley.

The Liberal Party itself had been dreadfully wounded by the Home Rule split of 1886, which had lost it Hartington, Chamberlain and many others, and thereafter floundered for twenty years in search of a unifying philosophy and policy. Its support came primarily from Scotland, from the Free Churches, from the universities, and from those working men who had the vote. It appealed to idealists and to moralists. But in a country that was increasingly under the influence of Imperialist ideas, the party was hard put to it to formulate a clear and persuasive programme.

There were new and difficult issues which had to be faced. There was, for example, the question of how far the state should carry its intervention. C.B.'s early mentor, Herbert Spencer, had regarded state intervention with horror. 'How is it', he said, 'that Liberalism . . . has grown more and more coercive in its legislation?' In 1885 Gladstone wrote to Lord Acton of modern Liberalism that 'its pet idea' was '. . . taking into the hands of the State the business of the individual man'.[5] To Gladstone this was wrong. In 1892 he wrote gloomily to the Queen: 'A moderate Liberal is becoming a thing of the past.'[6]

At the root of Liberalism was the principle of even-handed justice for all. According to G. M. Trevelyan, Edward Grey said that 'the real root of Liberalism is fairness'.[7] L. T. Hobhouse described Liberalism as 'the open mind, the value – almost the sanctity – of the "other fellow's" point of view'.[8] Trollope said of the conscientious Liberal: 'What is really in his mind is, - I will not say equality, for the word is offensive, and presents to the imaginations of men ideas of communism, of ruin, and insane democracy, – but a tendency towards equality.'[9]

C.B. himself said:

> What do we mean by this Liberalism of which we talk? . . . I should say it means the acknowledgement in practical life of the truth that men are best governed who govern themselves; that the general sense of mankind, if left alone, will make for righteousness; that artificial privileges and restraints upon freedom, so far as they are not required in the interests of the community, are hurtful; and that the laws, while, of course, they cannot equalise conditions, can, at least, avoid aggravating inequalities, and ought to have for their object the securing to every man the best chance he can have of a good and useful life.[10]

The problem was to apply these principles to the changing social pattern of late Victorian and Edwardian England, an England in which voting habits were changing too.

Once Hartington and the Whigs were no longer part of the Liberal Party, but allied with the Conservatives, the propertied classes, instead of dividing themselves equally between the two parties, tended increasingly to support only the Conservatives. Later on the skilled workmen tended to drift away to support Labour candidates. If the 'haves' were to vote Conservative, and the 'have-nots' Labour, the days of the Liberal Party were clearly numbered.

The real threat to the future of Liberalism was the rise of Socialism, offering working men a more drastic alternative to Conservatism. *Fabian Essays* came out in 1889, the first Labour members took their seats in the House in 1893, and in 1895 the Prince of Wales made his well-known remark: 'We are all socialists now-a-days.' Nevertheless, after 1886, the support for the Liberal Party in the country was increasingly identifiable as working-class support. It was the sad fate of the Liberal Party that, despite this, the higher counsels of the party were increasingly dominated by able middle-class professional men, like Asquith and Haldane, who were carried away by the tide of Imperialism in the nineties, instead of applying their minds to adapting the party to new circumstances. The next generation, Lloyd George and Winston Churchill, tried to do so, but by then it was too late, and the threat of war was coming to overshadow every other question.

Like other Liberals, C.B. believed wholeheartedly in representative institutions and Parliamentary government. But in his day enough members put their own convictions before party loyalty to make the House of Commons effectively responsive to public opinion – as the Liberal Party had found over Home Rule. It was only after his death, when the party machines became all-powerful, that the sensitivity of the House of Commons to what was really thought in the country began to be more doubtful.

The Liberal Government of 1892 to 1895, which began as Gladstone's fourth and last administration and ended as Rosebery's only one, was a brief interlude in two decades of Conservative rule – from 1886 until the end of 1905. During that interlude the Liberals could form only a weak government, at the mercy of the Conservative majority in the House of Lords. They were reduced to the dispiriting policy of 'ploughing the sands'. This government was described by Asquith, who, like C.B., was a member of it, as 'an object lesson in the difficulties of attempting to carry on government without an independent majority in the House of Commons'.[11] Passing legislation in the Commons, which everyone knew would be killed in the Lords, the policy of 'filling the cup', was clearly futile. In July 1893, C.B. wrote to his cousin: 'A bluish look out here. We have such a lot of opinionative chaps who are ready on any excuse to fly off, & it is thought we shall be beaten.... A defeat wd.... be a fatal blow to the Government....'[12]

Mr. Gladstone formed his government, after the disappointing result of the 1892 election, in August of that year. C.B. went back to the War Office. Newcomers to the Cabinet were Asquith, Acland, Fowler, Bryce and Arnold Morley. The Lord Chancellor was Herschell. Of him C.B. wrote: 'Herschell is a very good fellow: but my experience is of all Lord Chancellors that they are the most impracticable of public officials.'[13]

Rosebery again became Foreign Secretary. He was reluctant to join, saying that he had come to the conclusion that public life did not suit him, that his ambition was dead and buried with Lady Rosebery and that he wished to live the life of a recluse. C.B. told his cousin: 'Rosebery will be in: but he is in wretched health and has refused & been overpersuaded ten times over. He is . . . in a morbid condition of mind & health.'[14] There was the same hysteria about Rosebery's hesitations as there was to be thirteen years later over Grey's. One of Salisbury's private secretaries said that if Rosebery did not come in there would be a European war in a year, and when he did come in Hamilton wrote: 'A national calamity has been averted.'[15] But, in retrospect, Mr. Gladstone thought this appointment a serious mistake, writing of Rosebery: 'He showed himself in the Uganda business to be rather seriously imbued with that territorial greed, which constitutes for us one of the grave dangers of the time', and 'the fatal element in this appointment was his total and gross misconception of the relative position of the two offices.'[16]

Harcourt had moreover protested to Gladstone that 'More than half . . . the places of greatest emolument and dignity are assigned to the Peers . . . this arrangement will give rise to great discontent in the House of Commons. . . . Campbell-Bannerman . . . expressed strongly the same view. . . .'[17]

C.B. was now important enough to be consulted about the choice of a Secretary of State for Scotland. Loulou recorded on August 14:

> Gladstone was keen to appoint Bryce to the Scottish Secretaryship, but there was a general protest and he was told he must give it to Trevelyan. Marjoribanks agreed and Campbell-Bannerman was sent for, who also said it must be Trevelyan, and this was ultimately settled.[18]

Next year he was consulted about the Viceroy of India, and gave his voice for Elgin, who was appointed. He did not know that he himself had been considered. Gladstone and Knollys had both independently suggested him but it was agreed that he could not be spared.[19]

There developed inside the Gladstone Government serious differences on Imperial policy. These were mainly between Rosebery, who proclaimed that the nation was 'pegging out claims for the future',[20] and such men as C.B., Harcourt and Morley, who were thoroughly opposed to what they thought of as expensive and wrong-headed Jingoistic adventures.

Much has been written about the complex and elusive character of Rosebery. Benjamin Jowett described him to Margot Tennant in 1889 as 'Very able, shy, sensitive, ambitious, the last two qualities rather at war with each other – very likely a future Prime Minister.'[21] Esher, who knew him very well, called him 'a queer fish' but recorded in his journals an agreeable picture of him at work in 1893:

> . . . Rosebery reads everything. Did his boxes in the billiard room. He was humming a tune and suddenly discovered it to be 'Rule Britannia'. He said it was desirable the Foreign Secretary should hum 'Rule Britannia' while doing his boxes in order that he should not lose heart.[22]

Between Rosebery and C.B. the contrast could not have been greater. Rosebery was an earl and a patrician. He had three princely houses – Dalmeny, Mentmore and The Durdans – and a group of lesser residences – the old castle of Barnbougle, 38 Berkeley Square, 'Rosebery' at Gorebridge and the Villa Rosebery at Posillipo, not to mention the yacht *Zaida*. He kept a racing stable and amassed a great collection of books and letters. He had been married to a Rothschild who brought him £100,000 a year.[23] He was moreover a glamorous public figure, a splendid orator, a man filled with a sense of history, an enthusiast for the Empire, the darling of the press and of those who liked patriotism tinged with romanticism, a mysterious and exciting person, unpredictable, stylish, a real bobby dazzler. A later generation can sense something of his quality by reading his books, especially his brilliant essay on Lord Randolph Churchill. C.B. himself said of him: 'Rosebery excels in the art of letter writing.' He was eminently 'twopence coloured'. But he had very serious drawbacks as a politician. He was cloudy, enigmatic and self-centred, and in the end even his staunchest supporters despaired of him. Desmond MacCarthy wrote 'Rosebery is a mist.'[24] Moreover he was almost certainly in the wrong party. When he wrote of his friend Lord Randolph that he was at heart a Radical, who had landed by mistake in the Conservative Party, he was in a sense describing his own position in reverse. At twenty he had had trouble in making up his mind to which side to commit himself. He might have followed Disraeli. He would perhaps have been happier if he had. He was outraged by Harcourt's death duties budget in his own government of 1894, which Asquith and others regarded as a landmark. On Imperial affairs, on Ireland, on land questions, he was much more in sympathy with Conservative than with Liberal thinking. As he grew older this tendency increased. When Esher dined with him and Morley at the Carlton in 1912 he noted afterwards: 'But what a Tory is Rosebery. "Property" on the brain . . .'[25]

C.B. was the reverse of all this. He came from the Scottish commercial middle class, not the Scottish aristocracy, from Glasgow High School, not Eton. Far from being glamorous, he was regarded by most people who did not know him as a dull man, an ordinary, penny plain, run-of-the-mill, bourgeois politician. He was a poor speaker, wrote no books, kept no racehorses, was always entirely predictable, was little interested in the Empire, and seemed at one period to be constantly running down the actions of British troops. About C.B.'s Liberalism, however, there were no doubts. Ever since he had broken away from his family he had remained unshaken in his devotion to Liberal principles. He had also the virtues of courage, patience, imperturbability, reliability and, above all else, good sense. Herein lies the true explanation of why C.B., with much more ordinary equipment, was ultimately successful, while Rosebery was not. Gladstone, in whose Cabinet they both were at this time, summed up the matter by saying 'that Rosebery was one of the ablest as well as one of the most honourable men he had ever known, but that he doubted whether he really possessed common sense'.

At this time Rosebery had a high opinion of C.B. E. T. Cook, the editor, stayed with him at his Epsom house, The Durdans, and wrote in his diary: 'I strolled about in the grounds with Campbell-Bannerman . . . R. said of C.-B. he might almost do anything if he had ambition to, but apparently he hadn't.'[26]

Rosebery exerted a strong attraction for the new, middle-class, imperially minded Liberal intellectuals, who had been influenced by Seeley's *Expansion of England*, first published in 1883 and constantly reprinted in C.B.'s lifetime, which described the Empire as 'a vast English nation' and declared that as soon as distance was abolished by science, 'Greater Britain' would become a reality and would 'belong to the stronger class of political unions'.[27] This was the inspiration of Alfred Milner and his friends. In 1885 Edward Grey, R. B. Haldane, and Arthur Acland entered the House, and a year later they were followed by Asquith. All of them were, to some degree, Imperialists. C.B., however, was not affected by the new expansionist theories or by the then fashionable ideas of Anglo-Saxon 'racial' superiority. In his 1885 election address he wrote: 'I am strongly opposed to a meddlesome foreign policy.' Moreover he still looked at these matters as one brought up in a business family. In a letter to Wolseley in January 1885 he wrote:

the forward policy is the popular one at the moment. One thing I do not quite agree in is the denunciation of Bismarck . . . our instructors . . . have given us a picture of Bismarck looking over the map of the world, & fixing on places here & there which he will summarily annex. But they omit to see that he merely follows German Commerce. He does not seize virgin soil in some arbitrary way. The fact is the English Commercial people have allowed German traders to supplant them, on the coast of Africa, in Polynesia – even in our own Colonies, in India, in China. It is not our stupid old Govt. that have been remiss & caught napping, it is the bumptious, ignorant, thriftless Englishman who has been cut out by the steady, quiet, educated German: and where the German commercial interest predominates, there Bismarck not unnaturally says the German flag (if the Coast is clear) shd. fly. Our conquests in India & elsewhere were made as much by the trader as by the soldier: we are as good soldiers as ever, but it is in the arts of peaceful commerce that we have fallen behind.[28]

He believed, too, that the next Prime Minister must be in the House of Commons. In August 1893 Sir Algernon West wrote: 'walked to church with Campbell-Bannerman, who thought Harcourt first favourite for Prime Minister, though people did not trust him. They would not have a Lord, and the Scotch had lost faith in Rosebery's Liberalism. Of course Harcourt's faults were transparent and not real.'[29]

The differences in Mr. Gladstone's last government arose from three main issues:

First there was the question of Uganda. The Imperial British East

Africa Company, which was trying to open up the country, was spending £80,000 a year and making only £35,000. Its representative, Captain Lugard, returned to England after three years of exploration and fighting. Salisbury bequeathed the problem to the Liberals. Rosebery was determined to keep Uganda. The Cabinet decided, however, that the evacuation must go on.

C.B. wrote to Harcourt on September 27, 1892:

> As to Uganda I am certainly against any new undertaking being given; it will be a bottomless pit if we get into it. . . . From all I can learn the Germans are pretty sick of their share of the Equatorial Paradise. If we can't withdraw our stakes let us at least not plunge heavier. There can be no doubt about the feeling of the Party – excepting only the pietistic sentimentalists who have neither numbers weight nor loyalty.
>
> A lot of our Scotties are (I am sorry to say) pretty keen about Blantyre, Nyassa etc. but I am not aware that they care at all about the more Northern districts.[30]

To Gladstone himself he wrote on October 6: '. . . I mentioned to Harcourt that Lugard . . . is looked on as a lunatic: a sort of Gordon on a smaller scale; who thinks his mission is to go across all Africa with a flag.'[31]

C.B.'s views were shared by most of his colleagues, but Rosebery threatened to resign if he did not get his way. Sir Gerald Portal was sent out to enquire and report, although he was a known advocate of retention. Rosebery gave him private instructions 'not for a moment to consider withdrawing from Uganda, except as a matter of form'.[32]

In March 1893, Labouchere moved a reduction of £5,000 – the cost of Portal's mission – from the vote for the diplomatic services and challenged the Government's East African policy. He denounced Rosebery as the 'high priest of jingoism'. But the Conservatives naturally backed Rosebery, who was simply continuing Salisbury's policy, so Labouchere was overwhelmingly defeated. Portal remained in Uganda during 1893, and in August was instructed by Rosebery, who was acting directly against the wishes of the Prime Minister and a majority of the Cabinet, to make treaties to protect the British position. Rosebery's position was, however, very strong, as the Liberal Party could not afford, with their precarious majority, to lose him and his supporters. So they had no alternative but to acquiesce in what he was doing, with as good a grace as they could muster, especially as it was clear that the time for Mr. Gladstone's departure was approaching, and Rosebery seemed the most likely successor, despite C.B.'s view that 'they would not have a Lord'. Eventually the Cabinet agreed to a protectorate after Rosebery had become Prime Minister.

The problem of Egypt was equally difficult. The Cobdenites in the Cabinet would have liked to see a British evacuation. Rosebery was determined to back Cromer and stay. In January 1893, the Khedive carried out an anti-British coup d'état and Cromer asked for more troops and authority to take counter-measures. Gladstone told Harcourt that 'they might as well ask him to put a torch to Westminster Abbey as to send more troops to Egypt'.[33] But once more Rosebery made it a resignation issue and once more he prevailed. He wrote to Cromer: 'There is a Cabinet on Monday, and if you do not receive the powers you ask on Monday evening, the Foreign Office will have passed into other hands.'[34] Rosebery was politically indispensable and he knew it. The French hoped for a negotiation leading to a British withdrawal, but Rosebery would have none of it, and, baffled and frustrated, the French began to work out the plan for a dramatic coup on the upper Nile which was to lead, five years later, to Fashoda.

Mr. Gladstone, despite these concessions to a forward policy of which he deeply disapproved, was still full of vitality, even though he was eighty-four. In November 1893 C.B. told his cousin that 'Mr. G. is in enormous spirits – I have just had ten minutes of him, – laughing & joking & exuberant!'[35] But his time was nearly up, and C.B. told Lady Monkswell that Gladstone's deafness was so bad that he could hear next to nothing at Cabinets, when everybody tended to talk at once.[36]

It was the third issue which proved fatal to Gladstone's leadership, that of the 1894–5 Naval Estimates. Most of his colleagues, including C.B., thought these reasonable, but Gladstone called them 'outrageous' and 'in my judgement only fit to be accepted by men "drunk or mad"'.[37] In a minority of one on this issue, and suffering from cataract, he decided to give up at last. C.B. felt that it was time the old man went, but he had come to have a deep admiration and affection for him. Four years later he ended a letter, 'with an ever grateful heart for all your kindness to me'.[38]

Gladstone replied: 'You refer in terms of undeserved warmth to our old relations. But I am not conscious of ever having done anything for you beyond what was strictly due to an old upright and very distinguished colleague.'[39]

Gladstone's final departure was attended with an emotional scene in the Cabinet, but C.B. told Lady Monkswell at the same dinner party on March 15: 'He is not dead yet... & might astonish them all if in the middle of one of these speeches he were to appear on the back benches.'[40]

Gladstone, despite his anger about the estimates, proposed to recommend Lord Spencer as his successor, a choice that C.B. would have welcomed, but the Queen did not seek his advice, and asked Rosebery to form a government. The party being in power, it was thus she, and not the party itself, who chose the next leader. But she could only do so if her choice was acceptable to the other party leaders. The key was the attitude of Harcourt.

Harcourt was sixty-seven and Rosebery only forty-seven. Harcourt's political experience was far greater, and he had shown himself to be a forthright and effective Parliamentary debater and an able administrator. He was a tough, downright, no-nonsense Englishman, intensely patriotic, who saw things in black-and-white terms and always went straight to the point. His greatest drawback was his inability to rub along with others or to keep a hold on his naturally blistering tongue. Gladstone once told Lord James that he had had in the course of his Cabinet life sixty-five colleagues, and that Harcourt was far and away the most troublesome. Birrell wrote that 'in the House we all delighted in his swashing blows, and shared to the full his own pleasure in them. His gurgling chuckles at his own wit greatly relieved the "drip, drip" of debate.' He called him 'a good, old-fashioned parliamentary bruiser'.[41] Asquith wrote of his 'extraordinary combinations of great intellectual power with childish character and bullying disposition', and held that though 'there was something essentially lovable about Harcourt's nature . . . yet, to tell the naked truth, he was an almost impossible colleague, and would have been a wholly impossible Chief . . .' for 'his lack of any sense of proportion, his incapacity for self-restraint, and his perverse delight in inflaming and embittering every controversy, made co-operation with him always difficult and often impossible'.[42]

Asquith's verdict explains why his colleagues were prepared to see him passed over for the much less experienced and much younger Rosebery. Harcourt's son Loulou worked night and day lobbying in his father's cause. But his father's temperament defeated him. C.B. always respected Harcourt and liked him personally, but he, too, had suffered under the lash of his pen and tongue. Lord Crewe wrote:

General Sir Garnet Wolseley
*A portrait by C. Sohn at the Staff College, Camberley
belonging to Her Majesty the Queen*

Sir Redvers Buller

'Campbell-Bannerman could get on with anybody, but he had been bullied over his Army estimates and, as I knew at the time, did not want to see Harcourt ruling at No. 10 Downing Street.'[43] Finally Harcourt himself refused to make a fight of it by declining to serve under Rosebery.

Loulou's journal recorded the evolving crisis:

> Feb 21st 1894. . . . Morley says there seem to be two possible combinations:
> (1) Rosebery Prime Minister
>   WVH Chancellor of the Exchequer
>   C-Bannerman Foreign Office.
> (To this I said I thought Rosebery leaned towards Kimberley for F.O., but Morley has told R. that he cannot have the P.M. and the F.O. both in the Lords, even though in different hands.)
> (2) WVH Prime Minister
>   Rosebery Foreign Secretary
>   Fowler Chancellor of the Exchequer, whilst – as J.M. put it – 'I should be washing the dishes in the Irish back-kitchen, whilst the quality were feasting upstairs.' . . .
> J.M. . . . says that Campbell-Bannerman . . . and others would prefer W.V.H. to Rosebery. . . . J.M. said 'If your father, for any reason, were to stand aside, Campbell-Bannerman would lead the House of Commons, supposing that I assented to it. . . .'
> Feb. 22. . . . Morley thinks the Queen will be anxious for Rosebery to retain the Foreign Office; that the Royal Family always have rather an exaggerated notion of the importance of Foreign Affairs. . . . W.V.H. dined with Campbell-Bannerman to meet the Gladstones, Asquith, Margot and her family.[44]

Three days later, Rosebery recorded:

> February 25th. Asquith came. He and C. Bannerman had been listening to Marjoribanks. He had been summoned to Harcourt yesterday to listen to a long memorandum. It set forth that the P.M. should be in the H. of C. But that he if it were the general wish would lead the H. of C. under conditions: 1. that he should take independent decisions in the House; 2. that he should see all F.O. despatches; 3. that he should have some control of patronage; and another which I forget.

I remarked that it might be difficult to serve under Harcourt, but that it would be still more difficult to serve over him. Marjoribanks also said that there was a growing feeling in the H. of C. against a peer. I said I was delighted to hear it. – Might it grow! Asquith and Campbell-Bannerman came to see me. Both, I could see, much disquieted by E. Marjoribanks' tidings.[45]

On March 3 Marjoribanks told Hamilton that 'he considered it to be a *sine qua non* that the Foreign Office should be filled by a Commoner like Campbell-Bannerman; it was impossible that the highest places in the Government – the First Lordship & Foreign Secretaryship – should be held by Peers'.[46] But five weeks before, Hamilton, who knew Rosebery intimately, had, after dining with him at The Durdans, written of the Foreign Office:

> . . . if he got a competent & loyal man like Lord Kimberley to do the drudgery work, he could retain the conduct of all the really important foreign business in his own hands. People abroad would know that he controlled the foreign policy of this country. . . .[47]

Loulou's journal continued the story of Cabinet making:

> *March 2nd.* . . . R. . . . had meant at first to make Kimberley Foreign Secretary, but Morley said it was impossible . . . and R. then consented that Campbell-Bannerman should have the F.O. W.V.H. said he would sooner have J. Morley at the F.O. than anyone, but J.M. said this was impossible on account of the Queen and also because he had no great house etc . . . he will have to stay in Ireland. . . .
>
> *March 3rd* . . . Morley tells me that Rosebery is very determined that on giving up the F.O. it should be occupied by Kimberley and not by Campbell-Bannerman. . . . J. Morley says . . . that it is quite impossible to have the P.M., the Foreign Secretary and the First Lord of the Admiralty in the House of Lords. I pointed out to him what his and W.V.H.'s position would be in debates in the H. of C. turning on Foreign Policy. . . . If C. Bannerman were Foreign Secretary they would have him constantly on the spot for . . . consultation on . . . policy, but if they have E. Grey as Under-Secretary they can only ask him for information as to facts. J. Morley fully and warmly admitted the absurdity of this position,

saying 'I fear I am bound to admit that it seems to me that Rosebery desires to make the Foreign Office a secret bureau controlled by himself. . . .'

. . . Marjoribanks says R. is very stiff about being allowed to nominate his own Foreign Secretary and is now thinking of putting Spencer in that place and Campbell-Bannerman at the Admiralty. . . .

. . . J. Morley announced here at 5.40, very angry at the idea of Spencer *or any Peer* being put at the F.O. He said he did not think he could join the Government under the circumstances. . . . The moment J.M. left . . . Rosebery arrived. . . . Rosebery said he had accepted the Queen's command to form a Government but on the absolute condition that he should nominate and select the Foreign Secretary. If this was not admitted he said he would not be Prime Minister, but was quite willing to remain as Foreign Secretary under anyone else. He proposed to make Kimberley Foreign Secretary, as being the best man suited to the place and infinitely superior to Campbell-Bannerman, whom R. treated with scorn. R. used all the old arguments against a Foreign Minister in the House of Commons, hard work, danger of heckling etc. . . . WVH . . . told Rosebery that the question of the Foreign Secretaryship was such a serious one that he must take time to consider it with John Morley . . . before he accepted the lead of the House of Commons. . . . Campbell-Bannerman entirely agrees with W.V.H. and J.M. about the difficulties of a Foreign Secretary in the House of Lords with the Prime Minister . . . if J. Morley, W.V.H. and C.-Bannerman stand out on this subject Rosebery will throw out the Government and offer to take the F.O. under W.V.H. as P.M. . . . There would be an outcry if Rosebery were displaced and W.V.H. substituted and the public would never understand the importance of the point on which it was done, so I think the thing must go on on Rosebery's terms and we must make the best of it. . . .

March 4th . . . They (R & WVH) had a long talk about the Foreign Secretaryship, WVH saying . . . that he had no doubt that (apart from being a Peer) Kimberley was personally the best man for the post and better than any available man in the H. of C. . . .

March 5th . . . At 11.30 WVH went to the F.O. to meet Kimberley, J. Morley and C-Bannerman. . . . It was several times suggested to transfer C-Bannerman to various Offices, but he said – 'Why can't you leave me alone, when I am quite happy and doing very well?'

C.B., Kimberley, Morley and Harcourt discussed other appointments, and agreed that, as Marjoribanks had just succeeded his father and gone to the Lords as Lord Tweedmouth, Tom Ellis should succeed him as Chief Whip. When they agreed on Fowler as Secretary of State for India, John Morley, according to Loulou, 'flew into an uncontrollable rage; said "then I vote against him" and bounced out of the room'.[48]

So this most unhappy of governments was formed. Thereafter Rosebery and his acolyte, Kimberley, conducted an Imperialist foreign policy, while a resentful and suspicious Harcourt made scenes in the Cabinet. The compromise was a thoroughly bad one.

Morley told Edward Hamilton in May 1894 that Rosebery's only chance would have been 'the most complete accord with the Leader of the House of Commons, such as Campbell Bannerman or I . . . would have given him'.[49] Morley also told Hamilton later the same year that Kimberley 'proved to be as malleable as clay in the hands of R.; and R. was practically Foreign Minister himself as well as Prime Minister'.[50]

As it was, C.B. remained Secretary for War. His one chance of being Foreign Secretary had gone. In many ways this was perhaps a pity. From the political and party point of view C.B., as a Foreign Secretary in the Commons, might have held the Cabinet together. He got on well with both Rosebery and Harcourt, and his own views, though tending towards those of Harcourt and John Morley, were not inflexible or extreme. He might have prevented the clashes between Rosebery and Harcourt, mainly over foreign policy, which made this government a misery for its members.

C.B. might also have made a very good Foreign Secretary, and was in some ways more suited to this office than to a primarily administrative Cabinet post. In contrast to a man like Edward Grey, who knew almost nothing of Europe, and whose French was rudimentary, C.B. spoke fluent French and was thoroughly at home in Europe, far more so than most of his colleagues. He was well used to rubbing shoulders with Frenchmen, Germans, Austrians and Italians, understood how their minds worked and where their outlook was different from ours. Moreover in the Foreign Office his passivism might have been a positive advantage. He would not have yearned to meddle, a course that so often does harm, but would have been content to wait on events, keeping always in view the need to understand the passions and convictions of other people. Under him there would have been no dramas and no adventures, but the interests of this country would have been in the hands of a man who was shrewd, calm and wise. But the tradition that the Foreign Secretary should be in the Lords – between 1868 and 1905 no commoner held the post – Rosebery's low estimate of C.B.'s capabilities in this field, and his own opposition to Imperialist policies, prevented him from getting the post.

The Rosebery administration was in trouble from the start. After Rosebery rashly said of Home Rule that 'England as the predominant member of the partnership of the Three Kingdoms will have to be convinced of its justice and equity',[51] C.B. had to tell him the following night 'that the Government had been beaten at 8 – by Labouchere and by two' on the Address. This was reversed but the Government limped along with tiny majorities, especially after the Parnellites under Redmond went over to the Opposition, and morale was poor. This was reflected outside. C.B. told Bryce in December: 'I have found among my constituents much exhaustion and sickness of politics, and much reluctance to tackle any big job, even the Lords.'[52]

Morley, disgusted at not getting the Foreign Office or the India Office, sulked and wrote to Rosebery saying: 'I propose to confine myself strictly and absolutely to the business of my department, *plus* attendance at Cabinet councils, *plus* steady obedience to the call of the whips for my vote.'[53] Harcourt, much to Morley's chagrin, took him at his word and in a letter to C.B. wrote: 'I shall have very heavy work over the Budget this next month and shall much want aid and relief in the House of Commons. I hope you will be willing when I am unable to be there to take my place. . . .'[54]

To Rosebery, Harcourt wrote the same day: 'I have asked Campbell-Bannerman to take the lead in the H. of Commons in my absence. . . . He is the person most fit for that business by seniority, temper and aptitude. . . .'[55]

Harcourt, having been let down by Morley over the leadership, was probably only too glad to snub him now. Rosebery replied on March 9: 'May J.M. not be hurt?'[56] C.B. accepted Harcourt's proposal. But Harcourt appears to have funked an explanation with Morley. Next month Loulou recorded: 'No-one seems to know whether the House in W.V.H.'s absence is being led by C–B or J.M. . . .'[57] Morley demanded the job back, and got it through Rosebery's intervention. On April 7 Loulou was writing:

Tweedmouth . . . told W.V.H. that C–B is rather sore at being replaced by J.M. as Deputy Leader. . . . W.V.H. told Tweedmouth that he had nothing to do with it and that it was entirely a put-up affair of Rosebery and Asquith and that he should tell C-B so. . . .

Two days later Loulou wrote:

> J.M. said to WVH this evening – 'I know you want to have Old Campbell-Bannerman as your Deputy Leader and I shall write to you tomorrow morning to beg you to take him and disregard me.' WVH replied theatrically that he had nothing to say, that he dare not express any opinions on any subject, that he lived in an atmosphere of intrigue, in which the prominent figures were Asquith and Acland, that he feels he is being constantly undermined in all he does. WVH spoke to C-B on the subject and found him sore with Rosebery about it. W.V.H. said that it was entirely contrary to his wish that J.M. was doing Deputy Leader and that the whole thing had been done by Rosebery & Asquith. C-B was very good-tempered about it and has no grievance against WVH in the matter.[58]

It was scarcely a happy ship.
In his diary on July 4, 1894, Hamilton wrote:

> . . . I dined this evening at C. Bannerman's and came away with Herbert Gladstone. I asked him what the feeling of the House was about the succession to Harcourt, should he go or have to go. He himself evidently considered . . . that J. Morley would suit the radicals best: what they want is a man of real earnestness and strong convictions – Campbell Bannerman might, Herbert G. thought, be handier, but he would not be serious enough, or impress people enough with his own belief in the articles of the radical creed; while Asquith has not had sufficient Parliamentary experience, and is suspected a little of preferring society and amusement to the House of Commons and work. Such was Herbert G.'s opinion – and he said it was an unprejudiced one, – for he had lost his real interest in politics now & did not much care whether he gave them up or they gave him up. He had many other interests – (the chief one being the cello) – and was not ambitious. . . .[59]

Next month he wrote, in summing up the Parliamentary session: 'Campbell-Bannerman has improved his chances of succession to the leadership of the House of Commons, partly because of his own popularity and handiness, & partly because John Morley has not exhibited greater qualifications for leading.'[60]

Two days before Hamilton had dined with Asquith at Brooks's and wrote: 'Asquith spoke in the highest & most appreciative terms of Alfred Milner, whom he had known ever since Balliol days. He hoped that A. Milner might go higher. . . .'[61]

Alfred Milner, then working in the Inland Revenue, was indeed to go higher.

As time went on the personal differences in the Cabinet grew deeper. Rosebery suffered from terrible insomnia and complained bitterly of lack of support from his colleagues, particularly Harcourt, though he blamed C.B. and Asquith less than the other leading Liberals in the Commons. In February 1895, things got so bad that he threatened to resign. C.B. thought that Harcourt was principally to blame. Harcourt lacked any restraint and continually assaulted Kimberley's forward policy in blasts that C.B. used to call 'gales from the south-west'. C.B. told his cousin that the Government's principal difficulties were: 'Intrigues of Dilke and Labby, and sulks and despondency of a certain great man of my near acquaintance. The last is very bad and is the cause of woes innumerable. The Prime Minister is most patient and good-natured, but his difficulties on this ground are prodigious.'[62]

Three years before the Rosebery Cabinet was formed Rosebery himself had written, in his book on Pitt:

> It would be too much to maintain that all members of a Cabinet should feel an implicit confidence in each other; humanity – least of all political humanity – could not stand so severe a test. But between a Prime Minister in the House of Lords and the leader of the House of Commons such a confidence is indispensable . . . unity of sentiment is the one necessary link that makes a relation, in any case difficult, in any way possible.[63]

Now Rosebery was Prime Minister in the Lords and Harcourt led the Commons. But there was no confidence between them. Rosebery told C.B. that Harcourt was insufferable, but that Morley was worse – 'a petulant spinster'.[64] Asquith wrote that 'Cabinet life under such conditions . . . was a weariness both to the flesh and the spirit', though C.B.'s 'flashes of cynical humour now and again lightened the scene'.[65]

In 1899, Asquith, in a letter to C.B. recalling this administration, wrote: 'Is there any member of it, in either House, who wishes to see it assembled again for any purpose under Heaven?'[66] Those outside the Government thought just as poorly of it. R.B. Haldane told Beatrice Webb in January 1895:

> With the exception of Acland, none of the Ministers are doing any work: Rosebery sees no one but Eddy Hamilton, a flashy fast Treasury clerk, his stud-groom, and various non-political fashionables; Sir W. Harcourt amuses himself at his country place and abroad, determined to do nothing to help Rosebery; even Asquith, under the dominance of his brilliant and silly wife, has given up attending to his department and occupies his time by visiting country houses and learning to ride![67]

This was a caricature. But the truth was that a government so constructed could not work. Rosebery himself was disgusted with the business. He later wrote: 'I am bound to say that I have had a revolting experience of the higher positions in British government and that it will take some time to wash out of my mouth the taste of the last administration.'[68]

C.B. himself felt the strain and blew off steam on occasion. Labouchere, in a letter to Loulou written on March 3, 1895, said of Rosebery: 'Bannerman ... bitterly complained of being treated by him as a schoolboy, and being summoned to Cabinets suddenly for no reason. He said that for a word he would resign. . . .'[69] Labouchere added that the Radicals in the House thought that in the Cabinet 'Bannerman represents sound Scotch common-sense'. Rosebery, despite his view of the impossibility of C.B. as Foreign Secretary, recognized his value to some extent. When, for example, he discussed the possibility of Harcourt's retirement with Esher, Esher noted:

> If Harcourt goes ... who is to lead the H. of C.? Morley would expect it; but is he sufficiently in agreement with the Prime Minister? Very much the reverse, on Foreign Politics and some social questions. He is quick tempered and very sensitive.
>
> Campbell-Bannerman is physically and mentally the best qualified. Asquith has not enough experience as yet, and is viewed askance by the Irish. These are R's criticisms. I think he is inclined to Bannerman. A good man; but very undistinguished compared with the others.[70]

C.B. slogged on at his job at the War Office and endured the Cabinet disputes, Rosebery and Harcourt by now being scarcely on speaking terms. He told a Hawick audience that the main objects of the party were to establish Irish Home Rule, to disestablish the Church, and to 'deal with' the House of Lords by asserting the supremacy of the Commons. His political optimism remained strangely undimmed. On February 12 he told his cousin: 'How are things going? First rate, if some of our great people wd. only see it. It is of course a tight fit & needs close steering. . . . I do not say we shall be very triumphant but we can peg along.'[71]

Nevertheless he found it a weary road. He was fifty-eight, and it was clear that before long the Government must be defeated and that the party might then face a long spell in the wilderness. He was tired of wrangles. Then suddenly, in March 1895, there came the prospect of release in a way which, he thought, would exactly suit Charlotte and himself.

CHAPTER 16

The Speaker's Chair

C.B. had often been thought of as a possible and even a probable Speaker. He had nearly thirty years' experience of the House of Commons. He was one of the most agreeable of members, and he combined ability and knowledge of the House and its ways with an entire absence of the more rancorous type of partisanship, which makes some men a red rag to their political opponents. He was described at this time as 'among the ablest, certainly the most popular, member of the Government'.[1] In 1883 the Liberal Government proposed that he should succeed Speaker Brand, preferring him to Childers, Goschen, Dilke and Courtney, but they offered it first to Arthur Peel, one of Sir Robert Peel's sons, who unexpectedly accepted and held the post for twelve years. Now Peel decided to retire. Loulou Harcourt noted:

> *February 27th* . . . we are at our wits end to think who we can put in his place. W.V.H., Ellis and G. Murray all think Arnold Morley would be best. . . . The other names which occur to us are Edward Grey, Haldane, Campbell-Bannerman. . . . WVH circulated a box to the Cabinet asking them to meet in his room at the H. of C at 4 today . . . C.B. at once sent a note saying that if a new Speaker was wanted he was willing to take it. Of course he would be excellent, but he would be a great loss to the Government. . . .
>
> *March 1st.* WVH . . . is amused by a suggestion that Mr. G. should be offered the place. He says the only objection is that Mr. G. would allow no-one else to speak. . . . I told WVH this evening that I thought he ought to beg Campbell-Bannerman *not* to ask for the place; that I believe he does so because he has been ousted from the Deputy Leadership of the House by John Morley; and that if

WVH said he looked to him (C.B.) to be his Deputy in Opposition the thing might be managed. I told W.V.H. that J. Morley and Asquith are respectively too weak and too strong for the place of Deputy Leader and that the latter is not very popular with our people owing to his rather brusque manners. . . .[2]

Another diarist, Edward Hamilton, wrote on March 5:

The two men principally spoken of in Cabinet circles for the Speakership are C. Bannerman & Arnold Morley. The first might be accepted by both sides; but the nomination of the second would pretty certainly be contested . . . So it is quite likely that Courtney may be put up; he is . . . lacking in presence and has not too plentiful a supply of H's; but he has great experience as Chairman of Committees, and the Unionists could hardly oppose him.[3]

Loulou's account continued:

March 8th . . . WVH went to see C-B this morning; he is still in bed with a touch of the lungs, and expounded to him the view of the impossibility of a member of the Government being made Speaker. C-B received all this amiably and silently, making no protest. WVH does not even now feel quite sure whether C-B's letter asking for it was meant seriously. . . . A. Morley . . . was very indignant at C-B having asked for it. . . .

March 9th. WVH wrote a long Memo. on the Speakership which arrived at Courtney as the necessary man, and sent it to Rosebery, who read it at once and returned it with a note saying that he agreed. C-B is touting all his colleagues for the place. . . .[4]

The Times wrote on the 9th that 'The man best suited for the Speakership among the Ministerialists is undoubtedly Mr. CAMPBELL-BANNERMAN, but it is doubtful whether the office, with its severe obligations, would have sufficient attractions for one who may be at no distant day the leader of his party, if he remains in political life.'

Loulou was not alone in being surprised at the direction of C.B.'s ambition. Birrell, for example, when he heard the report, thought it absurd, and commented: 'How it would have bored him!'[5] But C.B.'s desire for the post was real and deep. His doctor had warned him that physically he was five years older than he had been twelve months before, and he longed for a recess free from the need to make speeches.[6]

The same day that Harcourt sent his memorandum to Rosebery, C.B. himself wrote to both Harcourt and Rosebery. In the letter to Harcourt, he argued that the Liberals ought to nominate a man of their own, and that Courtney's nomination would be 'very badly received by our people in the House of Commons', adding, of himself: 'My ambitions do not permanently lie, nor do my powers, in a fighting direction; and despite my rumbustious aspect I do not think I can go on long with *active* politics. . . . What more fitting therefore than the calmer life?'[7] His letter to Rosebery set out his position with clarity and frankness:

You may remember that when we had a talk in Berkeley Square last summer I said I 'fancied' the Speakership. The fancy persists. . . . Harcourt . . . suggests Courtney. . . . Courtney's nomination, would be pusillanimous and would be popular in *no* quarter of the House. We passed him over for Chairman: we are going to win his seat. I expect our people wd. be *furious*.

All this is impersonal: now let me speak of myself.

For me, wd. be I believe the fact that my nomination wd. be more acceptable to the opposn. than that of any other man of our own. Without being conceited, I believe this: & the Times today confirms it.

Against me, appears to be the notion that I have a high value to my friends & that I may be a leader. That is not my opinion, nor *is it my intention*. I could not stand the wear & tear of being higher than I am. I am not young, & my doctor warned me two days ago that I was older than my years, & that I *must* take it easier & have more absolute holiday. I doubt therefore my being able to go on in active fighting politics: & the Speakership wd. precisely fit.

What is before us? If we win at the General Election, we go on merrily & I am not missed: if we lose there are 6 years of opposition – that wd. see me out. I am all for the 65 years' rule: and Asquith & the younger men will be fully ripe at the end of that time.

I do not touch on the question of fitness, on which I have no opinion except that I think I could do it. But I have a strong personal desire to turn into this channel, and I know that you & many of my colleagues will give this fact full weight.

It is the first time, I think, that I ever pushed myself; and if it were not a serious matter with me I shd. shrink from doing it now. . . .[8]

Two days later Loulou noted:

We hear from Tweedmouth that CB is pressing very strongly for the Speakership . . . some of our Radicals . . . consider that Courtney is not enough of a man of the world for the place: The Tories also are very hostile to Courtney and swear that if he is proposed they will run Mat. White Ridley.[9]

The same day C.B., whose judgement of feeling in the House was being fully borne out, wrote again to Harcourt, maintaining that the Liberals could not, without fatal loss of prestige, 'go to the enemy for a Speaker', and crisply pointed out the disadvantages of Courtney.[10] But, for once, Rosebery and Harcourt were united, believing that the loss of C.B. would be fatal to the Government. Rosebery's reply to C.B.'s letter was emphatic:

Very secret   11 March, 1895
                                                10 Downing Street,
                                                    Whitehall.
My dear C.B.

. . . your letter . . . greatly distresses me; for there is no human being to whose personal views I should wish to pay more attention.

But no minister, and of all ministers least of all you, can be spared to fill the Speakership. The fabric of our Government is delicate & tesselated enough, it cannot now be touched without risk of ruin.

I need not lay stress on this, for you have long been aware of my estimate of your value.

Please therefore do not any further press or entertain an idea which I sincerely believe to be disastrous on this score alone, without using other arguments. . . .

I may mention to *you* that the Queen spontaneously expressed her sense of your indispensableness to me to-day.[11]

Next day the Cabinet met. Loulou recorded that they '. . . discussed the Speakership and agreed definitely that they would not propose any member of the Government. C-B was intentionally absent from the Cabinet. . . .[12] Next day, March 13, Loulou wrote:

> R . . . says he agrees to Courtney but thinks C.B. ought to be present (at a special cabinet meeting) to state his own case. . . . All the Cabinet except R and C-B came to WVH's room at 4 o'clock.
>
> They decided . . . that WVH is to make the offer of the Chair to Courtney at once. . . .
>
> As soon as the Cabinet was over WVH went to see C-B at his house and broke the decision to him. C-B fought hard against it but very amiably. He said he felt six inches higher in his own estimation from the discovery of his universal popularity and the general belief in his indispensability. WVH said that was exactly why the Government could not afford to lose him and that they could not face any reconstruction. . . .
>
> C-B had a cut and dried plan of how he was to be replaced – A. Morley to be Sec. for War, Sydney Buxton to be Postmaster General and E. Grey to be made a Privy Councillor as a salve for non-promotion.
>
> WVH pointed out that such a scheme would drive J.M. to distraction as he is determined to be a Secretary of State and practically admits that his desire for this has had much to do with his opposition to Courtney and support of C-B.
>
> WVH and C-B parted in great amity – both unconvinced, but C-B understanding that the offer is to be made to Courtney.[13]

But C.B. was not reconciled to the decision Harcourt had forced through. He told Lucy that Harcourt, whom he described as '*capable de tout*', had threatened to resign if the Cabinet put him forward. Lucy afterwards recalled that 'for one naturally inclined to take genial views of men and things, C-B was exceptionally bitter on this unexpected interference with a cherished plan'.[14] He had encountered surprising reactions all round. His constituents grumbled at what seemed to them the possible disenfranchisement of the Stirling Burghs, and some of them sourly suggested that he might be attracted simply by the prospect of a pension.

His supporters in the party begged him not to go into the Chair. T. R. Buchanan wrote: 'We cannot afford to lose you either in the House or out of the House. For equally selfish reasons the Tories and

the Times want you to be Speaker, for they will get a first-rate Speaker
& at the same time deprive us of one of our best men.'[15] As against this,
his position in the House had been made clear in a remarkable way. As
he told his agent:

> Tories, L.U.'s, Irish and Liberals were all unanimous for me. . . .
> I am the only man whom all would support, and the personal
> expressions of feeling I have had from all quarters would surprise
> you as they have surprised me. . . .[16]

Harcourt made the offer to Courtney on March 15, but Courtney
found that not only some of the Radicals but the Tories, the Irish and
even his own group, the Liberal Unionists, were against him. So, a disappointed man, he had to withdraw. On the 15th C.B. was heard from
again. Loulou noted:

> C-B is not at all reconciled to his position. He came down to the
> H. of C. yesterday and had rather a strong interview with J. Morley
> and Spencer in the former's room, in which WVH joined. C-B
> complained of being badly treated by his colleagues and is much
> annoyed at not getting the Speakership. . . . WVH has written to
> R . . . that he can be no party to any reconstruction of the Govern-
> ment and that if such is to take place he cannot be a member of it.[17]

The Conservatives now let it be known that, although Sir Matthew
White Ridley was their candidate, if the Government chose to put
forward C.B., they would make no difficulties. Loulou added: 'C-B
comes tomorrow to make a final appeal to WVH about the Speakership but he is determined not to give way.'[18] Next day, March 16, he
wrote:

> The interview with C-B took place this morning and WVH
> explained very clearly that nothing could induce him to consent to
> the appointment of a Minister. . . . C-B went away still unconvinced
> and is going to see R. at The Durdans. W.V.H. wrote a Memo. and
> letter on the situation to R. today in which he begged him to do his
> best at convincing C-B of the impossibility of his wishes.[19]

C.B. went down to Epsom to see Rosebery next day. They went
for a long drive together to Box Hill. Hamilton was staying at The
Durdans and wrote in his diary for Sunday, March 17:

R. has been spending most of the day with Campbell Bannerman who came down after breakfast to talk over the matter of the Speakership, on which he himself has apparently set his heart. Indeed, he had thought of resigning if his claim were passed over. However he seems to have behaved wonderfully well and R's talk with him has smoothed him down. He is thoroughly loyal to R. R. took the line with C.B. of saying that he was indispensable to the Government, of hinting that the next lead of the Liberal party in the House of Commons would be assured to him, and of pointing out that the chorus of approval at the idea of his being nominated to the chair was far from being disinterested. I feel sure he will on consideration waive his claim. . . . R. is just as strong as Harcourt about the inconvenience, if not fatality, of any Ministerial reconstruction. If Harcourt carried out his threat of resigning, J. Morley would probably follow suit from mortification at not securing the lead which certainly would not fall on him. So C.B.'s nomination to the Chair might deprive the Government of the services of three of its foremost members. . . .[20]

Rosebery reported to Harcourt:

I have had an interminable talk with C.B. . . . I cannot tell whether I have produced any impression. . . . But in any case we must bring this affair to an issue one way or another. It is impossible to allow the points of the various candidates to be canvassed like those of a slave auction for another three weeks. . . .[21]

In a letter to Gladstone Rosebery said: 'C. Bannerman greatly hankers after the chair, & all the Tory journals from the "Times" downwards extol him for the place for a very obvious motive. But it is impossible to spare him – one of the most loyal unselfish capable colleagues that ever man had.' He concluded the letter: 'A pretty kettle of fish, & no lack of perfidious cooks to stir it into a witches' cauldron. My love to Mrs. Gladstone.'[22]

C.B. came back to London on the Sunday evening with Rosebery's private secretary, Murray, still hoping to be able to convince his colleagues. Never before had he been so obstinate and so determined. Probably after his doctor's report he had promised Charlotte that he would try to put into this port.

Two days later, however, his hopes of tranquillity were finally snuffed out. Loulou wrote:

March 19th. WVH went to the Cabinet at 12 and returned at 1.15. He says C–B has surrendered at discretion. . . . He behaved very well and actually drew up the statement to be given to the Press of his reasons for refusal. He suggested 'that Mr. C–B had declined to be nominated for the Speakership owing to the representations of his friends and colleagues'. WVH said he thought the distinction between *friends* and *colleagues* would be unfortunate and that we might at least appear to the world to be friends *though* colleagues. . . .[23]

Harcourt wrote the same day to the Queen, saying: 'A great desire has been expressed on both sides of the House that Mr. Campbell-Bannerman, who is universally popular, should be nominated', but told her that the Cabinet 'regarded the reconstruction of the Government which would have been the necessary consequence of the removal of Mr. C-Bannerman as so serious a blow that it would probably be fatal to the Administration'.[24] The Queen, at Nice, minuted to Bigge on March 23: '. . . Even if Ld. R. had not been so strong abt Mr. C. Bannerman *She* wd. have never allowed Mr. C. Bannerman to leave the Cabinet. . . .'[25]

The quest for a Speaker continued. Haldane was approached but, though flattered, refused it. Gladstone, now a private member, said that in his view the man best qualified was Harcourt. Hamilton saw Gladstone on the 26th and, though it was now irrelevant, the great man

. . . went seriatim through his objections to Courtney – (1) Courtney was not gentleman enough for the purposes of the Chair (2) He was wanting in sound judgement and a faddist (3) He was overweeningly self-confident (4) He neither would, nor indeed would know how to, consult with others (5) He had on one occasion shown a tendency to run not quite straight. . . .[26]

Next year Gladstone justified to Lord Rendel his description of Courtney as a faddist by saying that he was a 'lover of paradox, the advocate of women's franchise, minority votes, bimetallism and the rest'.[27]

But Courtney was now out of it. The Conservatives stuck to Ridley, and the Liberals had to scrape the barrel to find a candidate. Eventually they settled on Gully, an obscure M.P. and Q.C. It was variously said that he was proposed as a joke, and that Labouchere, seeing a good-looking man walk past, asked who he was and, finding he was a Liberal, declared: 'That's our man.' Murray wrote to Knollys on March 28, with the detachment of one private secretary writing to another: 'Gully seems to be the best man – He is a grandson of the prize-fighter & a son of the Dr. who had something (I forget what) to do with the murder of Mr. Bravo. So he has a distinguished pedigree.'[28]

Gully had seldom appeared in the House and most members had no idea who he was. But Rosebery was unconcerned, writing to Hamilton on the 29th: 'I hate seeing a man of real ability imbedded in that pompous tomb.'[29] Harcourt asked Birrell to second his election, saying he was asking him to do it as 'I am told you actually know Gully'. Balfour, proposing Ridley, said that Gully was 'absolutely unknown to them in his Parliamentary capacity. Mr. Gully had never opened his lips in debate. . . .' Harcourt replied and in his speech said of C.B. that it would have been contrary to all Parliamentary precedent to propose a Cabinet Minister for the office of Speaker. Gully was elected by a majority of eleven.

Mr. Gladstone had the final word. He thought that C.B. had been ill-used, and told Hamilton that 'it was not fair to exact from a member of the Cabinet such a sacrifice as that which had been exacted from Campbell-Bannerman. He was certain C.B. was eminently fitted to occupy the Chair, and he made light of the difficulties about re-construction of the Cabinet.'[30] A year later he was still of the same opinion. In February 1896, he told Lord Rendel that he 'thought it not only a great wrong done to a most loyal colleague, but an injury to the party that Campbell-Bannerman should not have been allowed to take the Speakership'. Gladstone considered, wrote Lord Rendel, that, in dissuading him, the Cabinet had pushed the claims of colleagueship too far, and beyond any right or propriety. He said that he had been sorely tempted to write to Campbell-Bannerman to urge him to take the post.[31]

But the chance had gone. C.B.'s bid for freedom had failed. Henceforward he was to remain chained to the oar of party conflict, and in that service he was to die at his post.

CHAPTER 17

Rosebery Departs

T HE cordite vote of June 1895 brought to an end C.B.'s second spell as Secretary of State for War and the life of the Rosebery Government. The election which followed was a disaster for the Liberals. To his cousin, at the end of July, C.B. wrote: 'It is a regular rout: & we must just lie low & keep quiet for a time.'[1]

He was particularly hard hit by the defeat of Jack Sinclair in Dunbartonshire. But bigger political fish had suffered too. Both Harcourt and Morley were out. Ten years of Conservative rule and a forward Imperial policy, culminating in the Boer War, lay ahead. Salisbury became Prime Minister, Balfour leader of the House and Chamberlain Colonial Secretary. Despite the Queen's staunch Conservatism, there is this note in the journal of her friend Randall Davidson, then Bishop of Rochester:

> *Windsor Castle. Sunday night. 7 July 1895.* I dined both last night and this evening with Her Majesty and had a good bit of talk. She is not specially happy I think at the change of government. In her heart I think she *personally* likes Rosebery, Bannerman, Spencer and Fowler better than their successors. . . .[2]

C.B. and his colleagues now faced a long period of Opposition. There were, as always in a great party, many elements of weakness. On March 24, 1896, C.B. burst out to the editor of the *Dundee Advertiser*:

> . . . let me ask a question about the D.A. Why does it (its London man especially) play the game of Dilke? He has no following but

three in the party (Dalziel, young Allen & McKenna) – the party *will have none of him*, but he is an insatiate intriguer. He dines & otherwise nobbles the press men in the lobby, who sing his praises.

We have had lately the ludicrous cabal got up by him, Labby & Philip Stanhope: each one has his personal grudge agst the late Govt – & wd. rather defeat & thwart *us* than help the Lib party or injure the Govt. Yet the correspondents talk of them as 'the Radicals' & hold them up as patriots. That view is not taken by the honest rank & file here. . . . I can only say that the whole dirty tissue of intrigue so revolts me (& others) that the temptation is great to chuck the whole affair. You should hear for instance honest John Burns or Tommie Burt giving their mind on these gentlemen. whom the D.A. treats as heroes!

For heaven's sake read this *yourself only* & burn it: I shall not be happy till I hear it has gone up the chimney.[3]

But the first question that now had to be decided was who was to lead the party. In fact it took three and a half years to settle it, and the not infrequent public initiatives of Mr. Gladstone after his retirement did not make things any easier.

C.B. had tried hard to eliminate himself by taking the Speakership, but he had failed. In 1895 the two leading figures in the party were Rosebery and Harcourt. Now that they were in opposition Rosebery saw no need to keep up even a façade of cooperation. He wrote to C.B. on July 27 saying: 'It is not possible that the strain of partnership can be carried on any longer.'[4] In August the two men ceased to have any dealings with each other.

In October Rosebery resigned the leadership. In a letter to Ellis, the Chief Whip, published in the newspapers of October 8, he said that it was necessary to 'clear the air. . . . Scarcely from any quarter do I receive explicit support. . . . When I speak . . . I must speak my mind, and speak it without reference to party . . . the leadership of the party, so far as I am concerned, is vacant.' Next day he spoke at Edinburgh, saying that a leader in the Lords could only succeed if he had very exceptional loyalty and support, which he had not had.

Among the reasons Rosebery gave for his resignation were his differences with many Liberals and with Mr. Gladstone on the Eastern question and on the wisdom of intervention to compel the Turks to behave in a civilized way. On this C.B. was entirely with Rosebery. He wrote to him a day or two later:

Hotel Terminus
Paris. 15 Oct. 95.

My dear Rosebery,

I had to limit myself to a brief telegram when I heard of your coup because the Vienna papers merely gave the fact & now that we know more about it and every penny a liner has had his say, there does not seem any occasion to re-discuss it. I must say that it must be most gratifying to you that you have the sympathy & approbation of all parties & countries, and of by far the larger number of Liberals. One may say 'felix opportunitate demissionis', also; for the prudent view of the Armenian question blends satisfactorily with the implied protest against disloyalty of the domestic kind.

Often as it has been asserted, by yourself among others, that most Liberals or Radicals are for active interference in Turkey, I cannot believe it to be true. I cannot but think it is only a small remnant who follow Mr. Hugh Price Hughes & Mr. Channing. And there is some irony in the fact that the Ex. Prime Minister whose main alleged fault in the eyes of some one could name was that he was too Jingo, Imperialist, & Great Englander, resigns because he cannot agree with those of his followers who are willing to plunge us in a wanton war. . . .

Yours,
H. C.-B.[5]

But Harcourt commented on Rosebery's departure: 'I believe he funked the future which he saw before him – that he felt called upon to say something on politics in general and give a lead, and that he did not know what to say and so took up his hat and departed.'[6]

Eleven years before, when Rosebery had refused a seat in the Cabinet, Hamilton had recorded some prescient doubts of Mr. Gladstone's: 'Mr. G. . . . fears that this sort of hesitancy of mind & angularity of disposition betrays weakness of character. . . . Mr. G. is afraid that his hopes as regards R's future may not be realized. . . .'[7]

Rosebery had privately told Asquith in a letter of October 6: 'I hope that, very soon, you will replace me.'[8] This was natural. Asquith was the outstanding man in the Commons who shared Rosebery's Imperialist views, and, shortly after this, Rosebery made his view public, declaring that Asquith had 'that rare combination of head and heart which, in my humble judgement . . . will conduct him to the highest office of the State'.[9]

Rosebery, however, was not in a position to nominate his successor. In the leadership stakes Harcourt, as Liberal leader in the House of Commons, now possessed the field, but no move was made to promote him to the formal leadership of the party, though the *Daily Chronicle*, Labouchere and a handful of Radicals advocated this. Meanwhile Kimberley took over from Rosebery the leadership of the Liberals in the Lords. C.B. thought well of him and described him later to Aberdeen as 'a brave, unselfish, clear-headed straight man',[10] but he was not a big gun politically.

Harcourt was still a dominant figure in the House, although he was now sixty-eight. C.B. was, like Harcourt, firmly opposed to the rising tide of Imperialist and Jingoist sentiment, with which he did not as yet associate Rosebery, and which he described with distaste to Knox as 'Rule Britannia screeching'.[11] In November he even made the not very sensible suggestion that to disabuse other powers of their suspicions we should renounce Cyprus or give 'some other evidence of disinterestedness'.[12] But, as long as Harcourt dominated the scene, C.B. was content to keep out of the limelight, and Lucy wrote that 'Sir Henry Campbell-Bannerman, unfortunately only too ready to make the most of the opportunity, has gratefully retired into the background, a place where he has the company of that promising young statesman Sir Edward Grey'. Lucy considered, too, that Asquith, in returning to the bar, had 'committed an act of political suicide unparalleled in recent history'.[13]

CHAPTER 18

The Jameson Raid

*'Those of you who will be in public life during the next twenty years
will have experience of the mischief he can do.'*
W. E. Gladstone, talking about Joseph Chamberlain in 1886.[1]

JOHN MORLEY was not always favoured with the gift of prophecy.
In 1887 he had asked a friend: 'Why are you going to South Africa?
Nothing of interest can ever occur there.'[2] In fact, events of the
greatest interest were to occur there before the turn of the century.
Indeed they were to dominate Imperial politics for the last ten years of
C.B.'s life.

The first of these events took place at the beginning of 1896. On
New Year's Day, *The Times* carried a report under the headline

DR. JAMESON CROSSES THE FRONTIER WITH 700 MEN

and published what purported to be an appeal from the English
'uitlanders' – non-Boers living in Johannesburg – which said that 'in
the event of conflict thousands of unarmed men, women, and children
of our race will be at the mercy of well-armed Boers'. Dr. Jameson had
started on his famous raid into the Transvaal Republic. The *Evening
News* headlines ran:

IS CHAMBERLAIN BLUNDERING?

KRUGER HAS CUT THE WIRES, AND
WE DO NOT KNOW WHAT IS GOING ON
AT JOHANNESBURG.

UNARMED ENGLISH AT THE MERCY OF THE BOERS

THE LAST CHANCE FOR BRITISH PRESTIGE
IN SOUTH AFRICA.

At first opinion in England was appalled by this assault on an independent state under British suzerainty. Then the Kaiser's telegram of support to Kruger on January 3 produced an angry reaction. On that day came the news of the surrender of Jameson's party to the burghers at Doornkop. Two days later Rhodes resigned as Prime Minister of Cape Colony.

The romantic view of the Jameson Raid persisted for some time. On January 11 the new Poet Laureate, just appointed by Lord Salisbury, published in *The Times*, which paid him £25, his memorably bad verses on the affair, some of which ran:

> There are girls in the gold-reef city,
> There are mothers and children too!
> And they cry, 'Hurry up! for pity!'
> So what can a brave man do?
> If even we win, they'll blame us:
> If we fail, they will howl and hiss.
> But there's many a man lives famous
> For daring a wrong like this!
>
> So we forded and galloped forward,
> As hard as our beasts could pelt,
> First eastward, then trending northward,
> Right over the rolling veldt. . . .

As the *Daily Telegraph* was later to say: 'Mr. Alfred Austin has a clearly-defined talent, the limits of which are by this time generally recognized.'[3]

But it was not long before the truth began to emerge, despite the hope expressed by Chamberlain, in a speech on January 21, that there would be 'less excessive interest' concentrated on the Transvaal, and that 'the recollection of recent sensational events' would soon pass away. The publication of the Transvaal Government Green Book of captured documents and the Cape Committee of Enquiry soon revealed the broad outline of what had happened – an attempt, organized by Cecil Rhodes and the British South Africa Company, or, as it was usually called, the Chartered Company, with the help of Alfred Beit, Dr. Rutherfoord Harris and Rhodes's brother Frank, to engineer an uitlander rising in Johannesburg, to overthrow President Kruger, and make the Transvaal either an independent state looking to Britain or a

British territory under the Union Jack. W. T. Stead, the editor, got the true story from Rhodes when he came to England – that he had not authorized the Jameson Raid itself, but that a rising was to take place in Johannesburg and that the Chartered Company's force was to come in and restore order, since 'a successful rebellion of the uitlanders would have meant an English in lieu of a Dutch Republic, which would have meant the nucleus of a United States'[4] of South Africa.

The whole affair was permeated by a sort of amateur dottiness, an inability on the part of any of those concerned to realize that revolution is a serious life-and-death business. Stalin or Nasser would have laughed at the bungling improvisations of these stock-exchange conspirators.

Rhodes's position was described later by Milner as 'Rhodes uncontrolled, in the ... position in which he was before the Raid, with a H. Commissioner practically nominated by himself, in his pocket, and the British Government simply following his lead. ...' Milner recognized Rhodes as a big man, but was acute enough to realize that his great fault was excessive haste, and that he was 'too self-willed, too violent, too sanguine and in too great a hurry ... not patient by nature, and ... desperately anxious to have another slap at old Kruger. ...'[5]

It was unrealistic to imagine that a romantic Imperialist coup of the sort Rhodes wanted could be brought about with the help of the Rand mine-owners. The men Michael Davitt later described in the House as the 'fine old English gentlemen for whom the British Empire is going to war ... – Beit, Wernher, Eckstein, Rouilot, Barnato, Adler, Lowe, Wolff, Goldmann, Neumann and Goertz'[6] – were not going to run great risks for the Union Jack. The organization was laughably casual. One of Jameson's men, Stacey-Clitheroe, took with him lists of all the conspirators and the key to the code in a box which the Boers captured and which became celebrated as 'die trommel van Bobby White'. The manager of *The Times*, Moberly Bell, who was in the know, and whose brother-in-law was one of Jameson's troopers, telegraphed to his correspondent, Younghusband, on November 21: 'I want to impress upon Rhodes that we hope the *New Company* will not *commence business* on a Saturday ... because of Sunday papers.'[7] It emerged that the 'women and children' letter published in *The Times* had been written weeks before and left undated.

It was clear, even then, that the whole affair had been a monumental fiasco, and worse, that it had done irreparable damage to confidence and cooperation in South Africa between the British and the Boers. What was not then known, but only suspected, was the extent to which the High Commissioner in Cape Town, Sir Hercules Robinson, and the Colonial Secretary, Chamberlain, were implicated. We know now, following the opening of the Bower papers in Cape Town in 1946 and the researches of Dr. Jean van der Poel and Miss Ethel Drus,[8] that they were both heavily involved. Lady Milner recorded years later that 'the High Commissioner knew every detail of the arrangements, and as the time approached his train was kept in readiness for him to start at a moment's notice'.[9] Chamberlain's secret knowledge is now generally accepted, though both he and Rhodes were taken by surprise by Jameson's sudden decision to go in *before* any rising had taken place.

But at the time none of this was sure. The Government's complicity in illegal and aggressive conspiracy was widely believed but not established. The opportunity for the party of Opposition was clear. If they could bring home to Chamberlain the charge of complicity, they might discredit the policy of Imperialist adventure and destroy an opponent who had, ten years before, done such damage to their party by his apostasy over Home Rule. The arch-renegade was now the dominant figure on the Government benches and had been mixed up in smash-and-grab Imperialism of a type they deeply distrusted. The radicals scented blood.

The opportunity was allowed to slip by, and this remains a puzzle, as does, for example, the failure of the Conservative Party to do any damage to the Asquith Government as a result of the Marconi scandal in 1912. Possibly in both cases there was something of a trade-union spirit among the politicians – what the French call the 'république des camarades'. Harcourt and Chamberlain had been friends for thirty years. Possibly it was, in Harcourt's case at any rate, a patriotic feeling which drew the line at dragging his country's affairs through the mud. At any rate the dagger was there, and the leaders of the Liberal Party conspicuously failed to grasp it.

In July Jameson and his officers were tried and sentenced. The night before he went to prison Jameson dined with the Asquiths in Cavendish Square. But the Queen's speech in February had had to promise a 'searching enquiry'. The Government first proposed a Royal Commission, but, unaccountably, Harcourt pressed for a select committee of the House of Commons. This meant inevitable delay because a select committee could not sit during the recess. Moreover, as Chamberlain himself did not fail to note at the time, 'the House of Commons never suspects its own Committee, and has a pious confidence in their honour and efficiency. I doubt whether they would be the most successful tribunal for arriving at the truth. . . .'[10] The proposal was duly accepted and the committee was appointed in August. The members of it included Chamberlain, Harcourt, C.B., Sydney Buxton, Labouchere and George Wyndham. C.B. was not an enthusiastic participant. On August 5 he wrote to Harcourt: 'You, of course, understand that if there is any difficulty about the member to serve on the S. African Committee, I am quite ready to stand aside. I only went on at your request; and the role of Jonah would not touch my amour propre in any way.'[11]

The committee's hearings on the Raid began, in a room off Westminster Hall, in February 1897, in a blaze of publicity, the Prince of Wales and other leaders of society coming to listen and making little secret of their sympathy for Rhodes and Jameson – two years before, the Prince of Wales and the Duke of Fife had resigned from the Travellers' Club when Rhodes had been black-balled.[12] The hearings went on for five months, the committee usually sitting twice a week.

Rhodes was the first witness. His friends were worried at the start. Esher wrote to Stead on February 19: 'Alas! Rhodes was a pitiful object. Harcourt *very* sorry for him; too sorry to press his question home. *Why* did Rhodes try to shuffle after all we had told him? His advisers are fools and knaves, some of both. . . .'[13]

C.B. questioned Rhodes on February 23, asking whether the expectation of a visit to Johannesburg by the High Commissioner had been held out as an inducement to 'subscribers'. Rhodes was evasive and, as one report put it, 'wandered off into the Cretan question'. In the luncheon break journalists gaped at the spectacle of the great empire builder tackling stout and ham sandwiches. After giving his evidence Rhodes departed for South Africa. On May 30 the press reported that 'Mr. Cecil Rhodes, having cleared the road . . . of the numerous bodies of Matabele, arrived in safety at Bulawayo, and was received with great enthusiasm'. His Imperial mission had been resumed.

On March 16 C.B. questioned Schreiner, the Cape politician, about the Afrikaner Bond. Schreiner told him that England must not 'in any way in any degree . . . minimize the gravity and importance of what has taken place', and ten days later agreed with C.B. that the most deplorable result of the raid was to magnify differences between Boer and Briton.[14]

On the 26th C.B. confronted Jameson himself and asked him in what capacity he thought the High Commissioner was to have gone up to Johannesburg. Jameson replied, 'To mediate. He knew nothing about the force . . .' C.B. suggested (with good reason) that Jameson had implied to his officers that he did have official backing and that the High Commissioner was being 'used'. Jameson's reply was a shuffle.

Four days later C.B. questioned Newton, the Resident Commissioner in Bechuanaland, and Colonel Frank Rhodes. He asked the latter 'what this abortive insurrection from first to last cost?' and was told about a quarter of a million pounds. He got Frank Rhodes to admit that the 'women and children' letter had been asked for by Jameson. C.B. quoted a telegram from Jameson which referred to delays in Johannesburg and described them as 'all mean fear'. Later he examined other leaders of the rising that never happened, among them Lionel Phillips and Charles Leonard. On April 2 he questioned Major Willoughby, who had told Sir Redvers Buller that he had taken part in the raid, as a serving officer, in the honest belief that what was being done was 'with the knowledge and assent of the Imperial authorities', a statement on which he declined to elaborate.

On May 25 C.B. first took on the enquiry's most interesting witness, Miss Flora Shaw of *The Times*, the future Lady Lugard, beginning with an exchange which was typical of the kid-glove methods of this committee:

> C.B.: I understand you would rather not answer questions as to your relations with or your communications to *The Times* newspaper?
> Miss Shaw: I would rather not.

When Miss Shaw was recalled on July 2 C.B. asked why *Times* correspondents in Europe had had to be briefed on Transvaal affairs:

> C.B.: Is it a usual process that *The Times* correspondents are used not only to gain information for the readers of *The Times* in this country, but to propagate certain policies in foreign countries?
> Miss Shaw: I think that is perhaps rather going into the question of what is done in *The Times* office, which it was agreed I might be allowed not to answer. . . . It seemed to be necessary that every representative of Great Britain should be as fully informed as it was within our power to make them of the situation.

The representative character of *Times* correspondents, in the eyes of those who work for *The Times*, has seldom been so clearly defined.

C.B. questioned Miss Shaw about the interview with Fairfield, a senior official at the Colonial Office, after which, using her code name of 'Telamones', she had telegraphed to 'Veldschoen' (Rhodes) saying that she had 'special reason to believe' Chamberlain 'wishes you must do it immediately'. She argued, disingenuously, that it had been only a casual observation by Fairfield and that 'it was my special knowledge of the situation which led me to communicate, not anything that he said to me'. Miss Shaw, whose poise was unshakeable, drew a veil of ingenious interpretation over the truth. C.B. was not wholly convinced. He went on:

> 'You recognized, I should think, that these words . . . are very definite and pointed?'
> 'They are,' replied the imperturbable Miss Shaw. 'That must partly be attributed to the code.'

C.B., who told his friend Knox at the War Office on July 5 that he hoped 'to be off to Mid-Europe, to get the acids of the South Africa Committee washed out of me',[15] later told W. T. Stead:

> Flora Shaw bewildered the Committee. She was extremely plausible, very voluble, and always spoke in such a debonair, offhand way that they felt that after all if Flora Shaw's telegrams can be explained away so easily, what was the use of asking for any more. . . .[16]

It was not then known that many of Flora Shaw's telegrams had been drafted by Moberly Bell, the manager of *The Times*. The *History of The Times* concedes that 'It is not possible now to doubt that Miss Shaw used her woman's wits rather to conceal than to reveal'.[17]

In July 1897 the committee reported, censuring Rhodes and the unfortunate Imperial Secretary at the Cape, Sir Graham Bower (whom we now know to have agreed to let himself be made a scapegoat for patriotic reasons) and clearing Chamberlain and the High Commissioner.

In the debate that followed C.B. defended the committee which, he claimed, had 'exposed the whole story, the manufactured revolution, the lavish expenditure, with such futile results, and the ludicrous but inevitable collapse'. It had 'showed how from first to last it was the creation of Mr. Rhodes and his friends, and how shallow were the pretences by which it was sought to hoodwink British feeling'. He emphatically denied that he had been a party to any attempt to cover up for the Colonial Secretary – 'I received no communication, I entered into no collusion.' He pointed out that Chamberlain had declared, on oath, that 'he had no part in any connivance with, or cognizance of, the scheme of Mr. Rhodes – I introduce the words "on oath" not to add force to the word of the Colonial Secretary, but surely it adds to it something of solemnity'. Discussing the 'special reason' telegram, C.B. said, with rather patronizing innocence: 'One forgives the lady who sent it in consideration of her zeal and excited temperament . . . she probably . . . did not realize the very pointed meaning which such an expression would have when received in South Africa.'

The lady realized perfectly well. C.B. went on to draw one lesson: 'The Government must have learnt how dangerous it was to entrust the administration of a great territory to a trading company – or rather not to a trading company, but to a speculative financial company.'[18]

Up to a point the committee had unravelled a good deal of evidence and secured the production of a number of curious telegrams, but at that point it stopped short. Rhodes's solicitor, Hawksley, a member of the Liberal Party, defied the committee and refused to produce the other 'missing telegrams'. On this C.B. later told Stead:

Of course I remember that Mr. Hawksley was giving evidence very freely when he was stopped, and had he been allowed to go on, he would probably have told us exactly what had taken place between him and the Colonial Office. That vote, therefore, I would not give again, if I had the opportunity.[19]

Labouchere got diverted into a blind alley trying to prove that the whole thing had been a racket to manipulate the stock exchange. Stead recorded C.B. as saying in 1899 that:

Labouchere had done more to render the Committee abortive than any other man. He was continually running about declaring that he had got wonderful evidence in his pocket which when it was examined always came to nothing; and . . . he irretrievably damaged his own case and what with Harcourt determined that nothing should come out, and Labouchere never knowing how to bring it out, the Committee was at a loss.[20]

Labouchere had misread entirely the character of Cecil Rhodes, whose true motives were revealed in the telegram he had sent to Flora Shaw on December 30, 1895, which the committee did see and publish: 'Inform Chamberlain that I shall get through all right if he supports me, but he must not send cable like he sent to High Commissioner in South Africa. To-day the crux is, I will win and South Africa will belong to England.'[21]

The note is unmistakable. It was never that of a mere stock-exchange manipulator.

One fundamental error was to include on the committee Chamberlain himself, which was equivalent to letting a thief be a member of his own jury. *The Times*, commenting on Chamberlain's version of a talk he had had with Rutherfoord Harris just before the raid, wrote on May 1, 1897: '. . . every one will accept MR. CHAMBERLAIN's account of the incident, and believe his simple and straightforward tale.'

The Times's touching faith in Chamberlain's veracity was not widely shared then or later.

From the first there were suspicions of a whitewashing operation and the Boers, for their part, never doubted that the British Government had been behind the raid, and accordingly began a massive build up of armaments. The *Annual Register* for 1897 noted that

> . . . the representatives of the Opposition, Sir William Harcourt, Sir H. Campbell-Bannerman and Mr. Buxton, were, after Mr. Rhodes had unaccountably been permitted to quit England, willing to allow the breakdown of the proceedings. . . . To a very great extent the inquiry had been obviously factitious, but in whose interest concealment was considered necessary remained undivulged. It was surmised that reasons of State had been found which outweighed party considerations, and that the leaders of the Opposition had been privately convinced that the alleged grounds were sufficient for the course adopted.

J. A. Spender wrote in his memoirs that the committee 'was from beginning to end a disaster' and described it as a 'hushing-up in public'.[22] But there is no evidence that the Opposition members were nobbled, and C.B. always firmly denied that they were. Certainly he himself was not. Many believed, however, that there had been a deal. One Conservative, Lord George Hamilton, said in the House in July 1897:

> With that enquiry some of the responsible leaders of the Opposition were associated, and they behaved as Englishmen always behaved in positions of responsibility. They sought no party ends, and they declined to push the enquiry to a point which would endanger the supremacy of the British rule in South Africa.[23]

Harcourt believed that Chamberlain was innocent of complicity in the raid itself. Brought up in an older school, he found it hard to believe that a Secretary of State could be guilty of conspiracy and perjury. C.B. shared this feeling. When Harcourt died Wilfrid Blunt wrote in his diary: 'He was straighter than most of his fellow politicians, and when he condoned the Jameson Raid at the inquiry, I believe it to have been out of loyalty as a Privy Councillor to the Queen.'[24]

In his 1899 interview with C.B. (which is mostly a record of what Stead said to C.B. about Chamberlain's guilt), Stead quoted C.B. as saying:

> . . . he had no idea the telegrams went so far . . . he did not know . . . whether Harcourt was . . . in with Joe in the matter. All he knew was that Harcourt had an extraordinary influence over men. He . . . hypnotized them, and he had known over and over again, when acting with Harcourt, the rest of his colleagues give in to him and accept a policy which they strongly disliked, because of his overmastering influence, and also because they knew that if he did not get his way, he would be extremely nasty. He said that Harcourt was still entirely on the hush-up line, and did not wish anything to be said; that there were two men chiefly responsible for the failure of the Committee to discover anything; Harcourt was one, and Labouchere was the other.[25]

Twenty-five years later Sir Graham Bower explained to Spender why he had agreed, at great personal cost, to conceal the truth:

> No one with any knowledge of the position in Europe & in South Africa could . . . have contemplated with equanimity the awful consequences that would have followed a disclosure of all the facts. You may if you wish say truth must prevail *Fiat justitia ruat*

The Duke of Cambridge

L. Salisbury in House of Lords
1895 —

fe Cornell, years

Salisbury in the House of Lords,
listening to Liberal speeches, 1895

coelum and condemn me and the officers for the concealment of truth. But do you realize that if the truth had come out millions of men would have died.[26]

Bower's fears were probably exaggerated, but there is no doubt that he was sincerely convinced of their validity. Of Harcourt Bower wrote:

> We all believed he knew. Sir Robert Meade said 'Harcourt & Chamberlain are friends & have mutual confidences.' Flora Shaw said 'It is impossible that these men can be ignorant of what is known in every newspaper office in London.' Was Harcourt ignorant? My belief is that he suspected the truth but thought it politic to attack & ruin Rhodes ... & to ruin me as a scapegoat. He thought that if he did this he could whitewash Chamberlain. I make no complaint. I was a willing accomplice in the deception.[27]

Many in the Liberal Party, especially the Radicals, were far from satisfied, and at the end of July they forced a debate, on a motion of Philip Stanhope's, regretting the inconclusive nature of the report and the acquiescence of the committee in Hawksley's defiance. Harcourt defended the report, and said that he believed in Chamberlain's innocence. C.B. was reluctant to ally himself with Stanhope, whom he regarded as an extremist. To Stead in the talk which has been referred to he said 'that Phil Stanhope had told him that Mr. Hawksley had said that the correspondence would prove the complicity of the Colonial Office. But – he said – Phil Stanhope is not a good man to take charge of such a case'.

Chamberlain astounded the House, and further undermined Harcourt's position in the Liberal Party, by declaring that Rhodes had done nothing which affected his personal character as a man of honour: this despite the unsparing condemnation of Rhodes by the committee, of which he had been a member. The Government declined to remove Rhodes from the Privy Council, to which he had been appointed by Rosebery in January 1895. It was just under a hundred years since Charles James Fox had been struck off the Privy Council merely for giving, at a dinner, the toast of 'Our Sovereign, the people'. Standards had changed.

This was the occasion when Mr. Abel Thomas, the member for Carmarthen East, was said to have been sitting in the House with the missing telegrams in his pocket, ready to produce them (as Chamberlain allegedly knew) if Chamberlain's statement was not satisfactory to Rhodes's friends. Both Harcourt and C.B. felt that they had been fooled. The *Manchester Guardian* was so incensed that it wrote: 'It is the most lamentable lowering of British standards of public honour and official conduct that has ever been witnessed.'[28] *The Times*, however, welcomed the conclusion of a debate 'which ought never to have been begun', praised Harcourt's 'statesmanlike speech', and approved the resolution of Harcourt and C.B. 'to terminate investigations and controversies, which can serve no possible good purpose of a practical kind'.[29]

The main result of all this was the disillusionment of the Liberal Party with Harcourt.[30] He stayed on as leader in the Commons for the rest of 1897 and through 1898, but his authority had gone. Most of the other leading Liberals who had not been on the committee thought it had been a deplorable business. Rosebery enquired hopefully: 'Will the indignation die out, or does it spread? I have never read a document at once so shameful and so absurd. One would laugh, did one not cry.'[31] Ripon wrote: 'Harcourt has been completely sold by Joe.'[32] Buxton thought that Harcourt had '*very seriously* damaged his position as leader'.[33] Morley wrote to Spencer on October 15: 'The S.A. Cttee was certainly a scandalous mess and I shall never have a more vexatious job than the lame vindication of it which I felt bound to attempt for the sake of W.V.H. and C.B. We shall not get over it for many a long day.'[34] Earlier he had written to Harcourt: 'I am not an alarmist, but I think our wretched broken party will founder, if we leave your report lying in the dirt, where it now is.'[35]

C.B. had written the same month to Stead: 'I am far from saying that the S.A. Committee shewed either the wisdom or the penetration that it might have shewn . . . but . . . there is nothing to justify the attribution of evil motives to its members.'[36] Writing later to Bryce in January 1900, Asquith described the committee's part as 'humiliating and disastrous', adding: 'But both Harcourt and C.B. were consenting parties, and we confined ourselves (most foolishly as I now think) to private protests.'[37]

C.B. should logically have shared the odium with Harcourt, but he did not. The committee's report was known to have been largely Harcourt's work. It was he who had been outmanoeuvred by Chamberlain and it was his standing which suffered. C.B. was looked on simply as a colleague who had acquiesced in Harcourt's decisions. In this affair his natural indolence and unassertiveness had been to his advantage. Later he was suitably cautious. In November 1899, for example, he wrote to J. E. Ellis: 'I had a long interview with Stead. . . . He left it with my conscience etc. etc. to decide how I could help in extorting the truth & clearing off the blot. . . .'[38] He declined to take the bait.

On three later occasions the raid again became an issue – in 1899, in 1900 and again the following year.

In the 1899 debate Stanhope challenged Chamberlain to lay on the table the correspondence between the Colonial Office and Hawksley. Chamberlain replied that he declined to satisfy the 'spiteful curiosity' of the Radicals, but that he would, if necessary, show the correspondence privately to Harcourt and C.B. Not surprisingly, they were not prepared to have their hands tied in this way. C.B. was helped by Chamberlain's attack on his 'insinuations' and by Chamberlain saying that he much preferred Harcourt's frontal attack.[39]

The 1900 debate followed the disclosure in the *Indépendance Belge* on January 5 of documents stolen from Hawksley's office, which showed that the Colonial Office had attempted in 1896 to get Rhodes removed from the Board of the British South Africa Company, that Hawksley had, on Rhodes's behalf, had a hand in the selection of the members of the Committee of Enquiry and that Hawksley had written to Albert Grey of the Chartered Company in February 1897, saying that 'Mr. Chamberlain will have no one but himself to blame . . . if the cables of the last half of 1895, or rather the negotiations of that period' were revealed.

C.B. wrote to Harcourt beforehand, saying that 'our people who are on the scent of a Rhodes–Chamberlain collusion' were sure that nothing short of a revival of the enquiry would do, as they wanted Hawksley to be re-examined and Albert Grey to be questioned.[40] But in the House Chamberlain defended himself vigorously and, as usual, in Parliamentary terms, effectively. C.B. took a cheerful line, as a former member of 'this much-maligned committee', beginning by saying that 'I do not think I have heard any one say a good word of that committee except the members of it themselves.'

He dealt at once with 'a suspicion which we heard of at the time, and which has bubbled up occasionally in the debate to-night – a suspicion that among the members of the committee there was something known, that some understanding had been communicated to them, some arrangement come to . . .' and said: 'I can only say for myself . . . that

I heard nothing, I was told nothing, I did not hear of anyone else hearing anything.'

He skilfully avoided getting too heavily involved in the defence of the committee's actions by taking a line of amused detachment: 'Then it was said that we should have called over Mr. Rhodes. You may call Mr. Rhodes from South Africa, but will Mr. Rhodes come?'

Of the other star witness he had this to say in retrospect: 'When the Miss Flora Shaw telegrams were examined they did not contain anything – I will not say there was nothing of a mysterious and odd appearance – which was not capable of being explained in some kind of satisfactory way by a clever witness.'

He declined to lay the blame on Hawksley, who wrote him a warm letter of thanks afterwards. But this time, mindful of the strong feelings of Liberal backbenchers, he pressed for a new enquiry, saying:

> Matters do not now stand exactly as they stood then. Let me say at once that if this was a question of some alleged misconduct of a Minister some years ago I should think it hardly worth the while of the House of Commons to reopen an old controversy. But this is a much more serious matter. It is not the conduct of the right hon. gentleman individually that is concerned. It is the estimate formed by the world at large, and by our neighbours in South Africa, and by our own people, of the character of British Ministers, of the British Government, of the British Parliament, and of the British people. Undoubtedly this inquiry was an inconclusive inquiry . . . it is the Colonial Secretary's strange conduct which has to a large extent encouraged and fanned the feeling of suspicion and uneasiness which exists.

Chamberlain had defended Rhodes, saying that as one entering into revolutionary measures, he must be expected to tell falsehoods. Of this C.B. said:

> . . . this is not the case of a private person; it is the case of the Prime Minister of a colony, of a public servant. . . . Surely the right hon. gentleman never intended to imply that conduct such as that was consistent even with a decent standard of honour. Can we wonder that the extraordinary exculpation of Mr. Rhodes by the Colonial Secretary obliterated the exculpation of the Colonial Secretary by the committee . . . and left doubts and suspicions as to the relations

of the Colonial Office with the conspirators in South Africa? Can
we wonder that it made the report seem to the world only a great
imposture and hypocrisy? . . . I myself attach little importance to
opinions of the Press which may be actuated by all sorts of motives,
but what I do look at is the opinion of cultivated, intelligent,
educated men, and . . . in the opinion of such men throughout
Europe the character of this country has not come quite clean out of
transactions connected with the Jameson Raid. . . . What a relief
would it be to show to the world what it does not now believe,
that, Government and people, we had no part in the iniquitous
folly of 1895, and that, Government and people, we are alike
anxious and determined that all the truth shall be known. . . . If you
huddle up the matter, if you stand on rules of Parliament, precedent, and propriety, you increase suspicion in the world that there
is something to conceal.[41]

The motion for a new enquiry was, however, killed by the Conservative majority, some Imperially minded Liberals like Fowler and Grey
walking out before the vote.

In the same year a correspondent in the *Spectator*, later revealed as
Charles Boyd, a journalist friend of Rhodes, suggested that the Liberals
on the committee had not pressed home the case because Rhodes had
given £5,000 to Liberal Party funds in 1891 on condition that Egypt
was not evacuated. C.B. at once wrote to the *Spectator* to say that 'the
story is from beginning to end a lie, and that your deductions are
therefore also false'. He told Robertson that the allegation was 'a
palpable mare's nest! For Rhodes was not spared at the enquiry, on the
contrary he was condemned in measured terms which . . . were, substantially, dictated by Harcourt and accepted by Chamberlain.'
Undoubtedly C.B. and Harcourt knew nothing at all of any contribution to party funds by Rhodes, still less of any deal with him on policy
(though Rhodes told Rosebery about the payment in 1895).

Arnold Morley, who had been Whip at the time, wrote to C.B. on
October 15 to say that he had never heard of the contribution and
pointing out that Rhodes's money had gone to the National Liberal
Federation, which was outside the control of the Parliamentary Party.
C.B. sent copies of Arnold Morley's letter to all members of the former
Liberal Cabinet. He must have been embarrassed when Rhodes two
months later published the original correspondence in the *Spectator*,
showing that he had sent £5,000 to Schnadhorst, the Liberal Party

organizer, making two conditions, firstly that it should be secret, and, secondly, that the cheque should be returned if the party brought in a Home Rule Bill without Irish representation at Westminster. Egypt was mentioned in a postscript, in which Rhodes said: 'It would be an awful thing to give my money to breaking up the Empire.'[42]

Harcourt drafted a letter dealing with these charges and sent it to C.B. who replied that his leaning had been towards silence but that he thought Harcourt's letter 'such a masterly exposure of the scandal' that he inclined to publication. He added a little advice on drafting:

> I would trim it a little in the matter of adjectives, do not you think? 'Malignant' especially is rather frequent. (Substitute 'vindic-tive' for some of them.) Also you say 'you understand the Spectator professes to be respectable'; and again you are 'told it once bore a decent character'; the sneer is well placed, but is not once enough?[43]

Three days later, however, C.B. thought better of his agreement to publication and decided that silence would be the better course. He wrote accordingly to Harcourt, who expressed disappointment at being baulked of his 'flogging' and suggested that C.B. was 'flinching'. C.B. denied this but expressed a reasonable doubt 'whether by chang-ing the line of contemptuous silence good would be done'.[44] He had by now discovered from Herbert Gladstone that no trace existed of the money being paid to the National Liberal Federation. Schnadhorst was dead, and clearly, as C.B. warned Harcourt, they could be 'in for an ugly squabble with the S. family if we published any denial'. So Rhodes was allowed the last word. C.B. told a correspondent, 'Whoever may be affected . . . it will not be me! I quite agree with you that the main evil of the Raid Enquiry failure was that it left the impression of there being a desire to cover things up – which to the best of my knowledge was not the case.'[45]

By 1904 C.B. was declaring in the House that the Jameson Raid would never have occurred under a Liberal Government. 'Certain men in South Africa,' he said, 'who had designs of their own felt that now a friendly hand was on the helm and we had the Jameson Raid. . . . It was the "jumping off" ground at Pitsani which was refused by a Liberal Government, but granted by the more favourable authorities that had succeeded them.'[46]

CHAPTER 19

The Choice of Leader

A the end of 1897 C.B. and Rosebery were still on good terms.
When Rosebery received the freedom of Stirling he said in his
speech: 'There is none I am prouder to be on the same list with
than Sir Henry Campbell-Bannerman.' But they moved politically in
different circles. Meanwhile, disillusioned with Harcourt, the party was
frankly at a loss about the leadership. As Asquith told Milner in
January 1898 they were 'bewildered by the problem of choice' having
been 'accustomed for more than a generation upon both sides to
leaders who are obviously marked out for the post'.[1]

On December 20, 1897, C.B. spoke at Edinburgh and criticized
what he called programme-mongering. It was poor tactics to give
information to the enemy. A little reticence, he argued, tended to
success, and, pointing out that Liberals had had sad experience of an
'unauthorized programme', he remarked that 'burnt bairns dread the
fire'.[2]

1898 was, however, the year that finally brought the leadership
question to a head. In May Gladstone died. In the autumn C.B.
talked politics with other English visitors to Marienbad, telling his
cousin:

> I have been all among Tories . . . with the one exception of
> Labby, who is not a man but a monkey. All . . . have but one mind.
> Suspicion of Ld Salisbury, hatred of Joe . . . and contempt for most
> members of the present govt. And one after the other have dis-
> closed a desire to see Rosebery at the head of affairs. It is an odd
> situation. . . .[3]

But the Liberals had worse problems. On November 5 Bryce wrote to C.B. saying that the party was in a parlous state, and adding:

> After you left the H. of C. in July there were such murmurings and mutterings about leadership, or the want of it. Now the discontent has spread to the country, and we stand to lose a good deal if the present disorganization continues.
>
> In the heart of Scotland (where I was a fortnight ago) they are keen to have Rosebery back again.[4]

On that day the newspapers published an exchange of letters between Harcourt and Morley. Harcourt's said: 'My resolution is fixed to undertake no responsibility and to occupy no position the duties of which it is made impossible for me to fulfil.' He declared that a 'party rent by sectional disputes and personal interest is one which no man can consent to lead, either with credit to himself or advantage to the country', and continued: 'I am not, and shall not consent to be, a candidate for any contested position. I will be no party to such a degradation in the tone of public life . . . a release from vain and onerous obligations will come to me as a welcome relief.'

Morley's reply, which was couched in enigmatic terms, expressed sympathy with Harcourt, whose leadership had been 'incessantly made matter of formal contest and personal challenge'. But it left Morley's own intentions obscure.[5]

Two days before, Harcourt had written to his chief colleagues to inform them of his intention. His letter to C.B. said that discussion of the leadership question had made the situation intolerable, but thanked him for his support. C.B. replied saying that he had been abroad and then at Belmont, 'so that I was quite unaware of the negotiations or confabulations to which you refer. The silly newspapers have of course been saying all sorts of silly things.' He added, however, that he was not astonished at Harcourt's decision and concluded: 'The party is indeed in a queer condition and no one can see what the end of it all will be.'[6] Harcourt said to Morley of this letter that it showed C.B. as 'jolly, good humoured, & "careless of mankind"', and commented: 'I doubt if they will capture that sagacious fish.'[7] To Loulou he wrote on the same day: 'Dear old Kimberley is very good, and so is the philosopher C-B. You will observe that they and Bryce express no surprise.'[8]

The party as a whole, however, were bewildered. The reasons for Harcourt's decision to give up at this point were unintelligible to them.

Harcourt was apparently exasperated by persistent attempts to discuss the leadership in, for example, the Scottish, Home Counties and National Liberal Federations. Early in December the *Daily Mail* even had a competition for suggestions for a new Liberal programme and a new leader. Press criticism was getting under his skin. His devoted son Loulou, who had been a great prop to him, had become engaged to be married. But above all he clearly felt increasingly isolated in the battle against the demon of jingoism. Kitchener had defeated the Mahdi at Omdurman on September 2, 1898. Three days later Major Marchand and a French party arrived at Fashoda on the Nile and Kitchener pushed on south, meeting him there on the 19th. From then, until November 4, when the French gave way and ordered Marchand to withdraw, the country hovered on the brink of war with France. Rosebery and his friends strongly supported the Conservative Government. Harcourt and Morley had already been talking of resignation in July, but the Roseberyite pronouncements increased their anxiety to go, and they agreed on this in principle at the end of September.

Even C.B., usually so devoted to France and so much opposed to foreign adventures, was stirred to protest by Fashoda. Speaking at Stirling on November 24, he said that the crisis had been due not to the French people at large, nor even primarily to the French Government, but mainly to the initiative of a small but influential knot of French politicians who supported an aggressive colonial policy:

> The great mass of the French people . . . . have no hostile feeling to this country. But both from the geographical and political standpoint the French claims in mid-Africa are unsound. . . . The very same set of men who instigated the Fashoda expedition are busy in the East plotting and contriving, with the assistance of one or two Russian emissaries, to induce the Abyssinian monarch to come down from his mountains with his warlike hordes, and bar the progress of the British up the Nile. The Abyssinians, whose barbarism is not changed very much for the better by a thin crust of nominal Christianity, are to be launched by Prince Henry of Orleans and the educated gentlemen of Paris who share his views into the Nile Valley, in order to meet and encounter and defeat or thwart the object of the British and Egyptian soldiers who are moving up the valley for the purpose of rescuing the whole country from savagedom and restoring order and decent government. . . . The French have from the first embarrassed our action in Egypt,

and now that has culminated in this great abortive intrigue. . . . Can anyone wonder that even the quietest among us are filled with hot indignation and that we range ourselves as one man in determining to resist the aggression? I believe that the Fashoda incident would never have occurred if Lord Rosebery had been our Foreign Minister at the time.[9]

One rubs one's eyes in reading this highly uncharacteristic utterance by C.B., which could well have been made by someone like Edward Grey. Perhaps he had come to look on Monsieur Hanotaux, the French Foreign Minister, as a French version of Chamberlain. To Harcourt, it must have been the last straw to have a leading colleague, usually reckoned as a down-the-line Cobdenite, uttering Imperialist sentiments of this sort and, worse, putting in a laudatory reference to Rosebery.

Harcourt's decision may possibly have been a tactical move on the principle of 'reculer pour mieux sauter'. If so it was ill-judged. Or it may have been that he was simply tired of the weary task of rolling a stone uphill. Morley intended his own letter to leave the position open as far as he himself was concerned, but, being published with Harcourt's, it was universally interpreted as indicating that he, too, was renouncing any claim to the leadership. To his intense chagrin, all his colleagues so read it, and none of them asked him for clarification. Morley resented this, and for a time turned away from active politics to write his life of Gladstone.

So now Rosebery, Harcourt and Morley had all, within a short space, ruled themselves out, and the leadership was open.

Grey, the most active of Rosebery's disciples, spoke on the day the letters appeared, deprecating any hurried decision. He clearly hoped that Rosebery might be prevailed upon to come back. But what was above all needed was someone who could unite the two sides of the party. The *Manchester Guardian* asserted that the real reason for Harcourt's decision was the fundamental divergence of view within the party between Cobdenism and Palmerstonianism.[10] These two wings now made themselves heard. Dr. Spence Watson, Chairman of the National Liberal Federation, said on the 16th that the Liberal Party 'would never wrap themselves in the filthy rag of a spirited foreign policy',[11] while on the same day Asquith gave a reasoned definition of Liberal Imperialism.

On December 15, the day after the publication of the letters, Bryce wrote to C.B., saying:

You are the person who will best unite the party and be followed by our men in the H. of C. with the most general satisfaction. This has been pretty clear for a good while back: and so far as I can hear, it is the general sentiment now. I earnestly hope you will be moved by it. The post is one nobody could possibly desire, and it would be a sacrifice on your part to take it, but you have always – if you will let me say so – been so self-sacrificing in the interests of the party that one ventures to hope you may be prepared to undertake this further service: which we should all be bound to try to render as little onerous as such a post can be.[12]

C.B. replied:

I hardly care to even indicate what I think of a certain pair of letters. Knowing all we do, I am sickened by them as I am sure you are. . . . As to the future I quite appreciate what you say; but the present circ[es] greatly aggravate the situation. Could an arch-angel take the place, with two men sitting round the corner ready to pounce at any moment? It is a far worse position than Hartington with W.G. in the offing after 1874: for he had not retired in dudgeon and nourished no grudge. . . . I have *no* ambition or desire to be prominent: and will joyfully fall into any arrangement except two: one, reinstatement, which is I hope out of the question; the other, having things put on *me* that I cannot do justice to.[13]

C.B. did not change his mind about the action Harcourt and Morley had taken. Two months later E. T. Cook recorded that he pitched into them both at a Reform Club meeting – 'He saw no reason why an old gentleman shouldn't retire because his son, on whom he leaned, married. But why those two gentlemen should retire making insinuations against those they left behind, he couldn't imagine.'[14]

There seemed to be no one obviously cut out for the leadership. F. W. Hirst wrote: 'There is a surprising lack of fighting qualities in our Liberal leaders. . . . They mostly have either big brains and faint hearts or small brains and large hearts. A friend remarked to me to-night – "We have plenty of men for a sticky wicket, but no fast bowlers".'[15]

But in practice the choice now lay between C.B. and Asquith. C.B. was sixty-two, Asquith only forty-six. C.B. had proved himself an effective administrator, a sagacious politician and a genuine Liberal.

He was the man the rank and file preferred. A recent historian has written:

> His colleagues underestimated his staying power and plain horse sense. Although he lacked the intellect and oratorical power of many of his colleagues, he had none of the obstructing sensitivities of Rosebery and Morley, nor Harcourt's rudeness and unwillingness to consult. With neither friends nor bitter enemies on the front bench, he was not crippled or blinded by personal feeling, and he possessed a political toughness which his contemporaries failed to appreciate.[16]

But to the leading men in the party what was more immediately apparent was that Asquith was a more effective Parliamentary performer – indeed one of the best debaters of his time – who could be relied on to hold his own, and more, in conflict with Balfour and Chamberlain in the House and on public platforms. He was also the leading representative of a new generation.

The two men were a striking contrast. Asquith, who had made his reputation as Home Secretary in the early nineties, was a man of obviously superior ability. C.B., with a far less vigorous intellect, relied on his native shrewdness. Asquith was a good example of the limitations of mere ability without much imagination or instinct. He was to go badly wrong on the Boer War, and, by giving the Liberal Party, later on, a middle-class, intellectual, Imperialist colour, he opened the way for a separate Labour Party, which spelt the end for the Liberal Party. That shrewd judge, Lord Esher, wrote: 'Asquith's mind is a perfect instrument, and he takes points after the manner of a trained lawyer. But he lacks some element of character; perhaps hardiness. I should say he was a soft man; and his chin *recedes* when an attack is possible or imminent.'[17] Stead described Asquith as 'a forensic gladiator who never made a heart beat quicker by his words, and who never by any possibility brought a lump into his hearers' throats. . . .'[18]

Asquith was a moderate Imperialist, and, as such, preferred by all who followed Rosebery or were affected by the tide of Imperial feeling, now at its height. He was supported by a large number of leading Liberals, including Ellis, Ripon, Tweedmouth, Spencer, Grey, Haldane and Dilke. Some of them urged him to recognize that he was the proper successor. He, however, was not anxious to stand for the leadership at this stage, for the simple reason that, with his large family and with his

wife's expensive tastes,* he did not think he could afford it. He recorded at the time:

> It is impossible for me without a great and unjustifiable sacrifice of
> the interests of my family to take a position which – if it is to be
> properly filled – would cut me off from my profession and leave me
> poor and pecuniarily dependent. On public and party grounds, I
> doubt whether at this moment and under existing political condi-
> tions, I would not render as good service as second in command as
> in the position of leader. From every point of view I thought that
> the best choice our party could make was Campbell-Bannerman.[19]

On Saturday, December 17, after making a carefully non-committal speech to a huge meeting at Birmingham, Asquith talked it over
with Ellis and Haldane, and convinced them that, 'in the first instance
the lead ought to be offered to Campbell-Bannerman, whom I and all
would loyally support'.[20]

Asquith's son Raymond wrote in a letter to R. C. K. Ensor on
December 22: 'The Whips lunched here the other day and *offered my
father the leadership*; but he defers to C.-Bannerman, being a poor man
and dependent on his practice at the bar.'[21] Having made up his mind,
Asquith was not a man to dither. He wrote at once:

> This is a pretty kettle of fish! The sum and substance of my
> reflections upon it all comes to this: what a pity it is when big
> causes and interests get into the hands of grown up children who
> will not play in the same nursery! . . . My object in writing is to say
> at once, & without any ambiguity, that I earnestly hope you will
> see your way to take the lead, & that if you do you will receive
> from me – and I believe from all of us – the most loyal & energetic
> support. I am strongly of this opinion, on every ground – public &
> personal: tho' I confess it has not at first sight a very friendly look to
> urge a man into such a position.
>
> In any case, I most strongly trust that you won't at present
> commit yourself to anything in the nature of a definite refusal. . . .[22]

---

* Asquith had married the brilliant Margot Tennant, his second wife, in May
1894. When I acquired a copy of Asquith's first book, *Studies and Sketches*, I found
written on the fly leaf, in Asquith's hand 'Margot with all love 2 Feb 1924'. The pages
of the book were still uncut, which is perhaps a commentary on the vanity of human
aspirations.

C.B., who was at Belmont, replied the following day:

> I have felt all this week that you and I wd. be taking precisely
> the same view of the performance of the twin brethren. I do not
> wish to dwell upon it: . . . You have located it well in speaking of
> the nursery. . . . How much more dignified and easier it wd. have
> been if the big man had written a simple note to Ellis, alleging
> advancing years, failing sight, loss of Loulou, etc., etc., as reason for
> not going on. . . . From all I hear it has been badly taken in the
> country – especially the antistrophe of Melibœus. The situation is
> hideous. . . . I am not my own candidate, and will do my best to
> help another far more merrily than I shd. ask help for myself. I
> really do not know what may come of it. . . . But the big salmon
> will always be sulking under his stone, and ready for occasional
> plunges which will not always be free from a sinister intention. . . .[23]

Labouchere, meanwhile, had written to 'the big salmon', saying:
'I know Campbell-Bannerman very well, and always see a great deal
of him at Marienbad. He is a pawky and cautious Scot. But he never
got over your not agreeing to his being Speaker.'[24]

This, like much that Labouchere wrote, was misleading. C.B.
nursed no grudge against Harcourt because of the Speakership. What
he did resent was Harcourt's suggestion that he had had to give up a
thankless task because of the disloyalty of his colleagues.

John Morley wrote to his friend Dilke, saying: 'My own opinion
is strong for C-B. He is a Tory, perhaps, but . . . he will hold his own
(quietly) against R., if R. goes against Radicals in H. of C. But I have
some doubt whether health will permit. W.V.H. and I should get on
much better with C.B. than anybody else.'[25]

Tweedmouth went up to Belmont to take soundings. He wrote
from Haddo House, Aberdeen, to Haldane on December 22 saying
that he had found both C.B. and Charlotte in a sorry case from bad
colds. He reported of C.B.:

> . . . on the whole I gather that his inclination would be to accept the
> responsibilities of leadership and to put his back into it always pro-
> viding that he is allowed to do so by his doctor. Unless however he
> (Maclagan is the man) pronounces him sound and fit for the job he
> will not touch it. . . .
>
> I think he quite concurs in our views as to what is wanted of a

leader and thinks he could do it with perhaps a little apprehension of Harcourt's tongue but the question of health and strength to endure is a serious one and I have my doubts on this point. . . .[26]

The same day Fowler wrote to C.B. saying: 'I am satisfied that *you* will be the choice both of your colleagues – *all* of us & of the party – Asquith, Bryce and myself the only survivors of the ex Cabinet in the Commons will I am certain render you a united loyal & consistent support. . . . I do sincerely hope you will accept the generalship of our diminished forces.'[27]

In the light of Fowler and Asquith's subsequent conduct these protestations of loyalty and consistency have a somewhat hollow ring.

On the 24th Spencer wrote a long letter to Asquith from Althorp. He said he had given Morley dinner and found him 'almost hysterical because I had in a speech praised the eloquence of Rosebery's language'. He said that he wished Asquith would lead, but understood his private difficulties, adding:

> Of course H.C.B. will be an excellent Leader, but I fear that his health is hardly strong enough for the constant attendance which the Leadership should impose on a man.
>
> What you quote of his letter to you certainly looks as though he might undertake the duties.
>
> With your hearty support he will no doubt succeed, for he has many qualities admirably fitting him for successor to Harcourt. . . .[28]

On the same day Grey told Buxton that though it would be best for Asquith to lead, if he would 'cut the Bar altogether', C.B. would 'carry this thing on very cleverly & in very pretty style, but he would not make the running as Asquith might, & he is delicate in health'.[29]

In later years a story began to circulate about the nature of Tweedmouth's mission to Belmont. In February, 1912 Austen Chamberlain wrote:

> I have just recently heard an odd bit of gossip about the choice of Campbell-Bannerman as leader of the Liberal Party, first on the authority of the late Lord Wolverhampton and secondly on that of McKenna. It is to the effect that after Harcourt's resignation the Liberal leaders held a meeting to consider who should be invited

to take his place; that they were all agreed that Campbell-Bannerman was not the right man, but that it would be discourteous to pass him over. Finally Tweedmouth said: 'Let me go to C-B with an invitation from you, and I undertake to get him to decline it.' This was agreed to, but after the interview Tweedmouth returned to say that he had been unable to secure a refusal from C-B, who, on the contrary, insisted on accepting. It was suggested by McKenna that Tweedmouth had seized the opportunity to make his own terms and secure for himself the post of First Lord of the Admiralty![30]

This may, or may not, be true. Certainly on January 1 Tweedmouth wrote to C.B. from Beauly suggesting a dinner at which 'you could find yourself the unanimous choice of those present and you could then have the opportunity of making very clear the terms and conditions on which you could accept the onerous and responsible duties to be placed upon you'.[31]

There now occurred a curious episode. Asquith himself was probably sincere in wishing to avoid succeeding to the leadership at this stage. He knew that, with the party hopelessly split on many questions, it was a weary and unprofitable task. He knew also that C.B. was a far from robust sixty-two, so that he himself was bound to succeed sooner rather than later. In the meantime the hectic social life on which Margot insisted needed to be paid for. But Margot herself wanted to see her husband take the leadership, and thought that her rich father, Charles Tennant, might be induced to provide the necessary income. She decided to put this idea to him through an intermediary, and the man she chose as a go-between, was, of all people, the leading Conservative in the House of Commons, Arthur Balfour. She wrote to him asking him if he would persuade her father to provide her husband and herself with an income to replace the £5,000 to £6,000 a year which Asquith earned at the bar and which he would lose if he became leader and had to concentrate full time on House of Commons affairs. Balfour accordingly wrote to Tennant saying that Asquith would obviously hesitate to give his full time to politics if this adversely affected Margot's comfort. Tennant, however, took an unexpected line, saying that he wasn't worried about the money but, as a Liberal, believed that C.B. was entitled by seniority to the position of leader, and would do nothing to prevent him getting the post. So Margot's hopes were disappointed.[32]

C.B. now received a friendly letter from an unexpected source:

27 Dec 98   Cloan Den, Auchterarder
                                                    N.B.

My dear Campbell-Bannerman,

For myself I feel as if a pile of featherbeds had been lifted from me, and I look forward to the possibility of a close attendance in the house under your leadership with unadulterated satisfaction. . . . I am not at all sure that the movement towards Mentmore will go on at its present pace. People will begin to say that they must see where Liberalism comes in, and our friend may have to show himself a trifle more hum-drum. . . .

Yours sincerely
R. B. Haldane.[33]

This, suggesting that the writer was really a partisan of C.B.'s and casting doubt on the wholeheartedness of Rosebery's Liberalism, was a singularly disingenuous production, even for Haldane, but C.B. replied on the 29th:

. . . no one desires prominence less than I; no one wd. with more willingness than I serve as 2nd or 3rd Mate; but if you and others who understand the party think that I could be most useful in any particular position and if this came to be evidently the general wish, I should be ready (with some muttering between the teeth) to bow the head and do my best. That is, subject to the question of health and I have hopes that will be got over. . . .

I see no reason why we shd. not fight away and do it effectively. If there is a little less of the ponderous gladiator style . . . that in itself is no inconsiderable gain![34]

Haldane was not as detached from Rosebery as he suggested. He wrote to him on January 4, saying that C.B. 'is evidently quite keen . . . & does not mean to have his allotted cubic inches encroached upon by the ponderous figure of the Resigned One – or to be disturbed by the sharp elbow of the Unresigned One'. He added: 'I see no reason why the new arrangement should not work – Asquith will support it in a very friendly way.' Referring to Margot's approach to Charles Tennant, about which he clearly knew, he said: 'Indeed, as CB has a warm supporter in the Bart, he would find difficulty were he otherwise disposed. But he is not.'[35]

On the last day of 1898 Asquith wrote to C.B.:

I hear (through Tweedmouth) that you are thinking of taking counsel with your doctor as to the future. This is, no doubt, a prudent step, but I hope that, in describing the burdens & responsibilities of the post, you will not forget to tell him that you have the assurance that these exactions will be lightened as far as possible by the co-operation & loyalty of others.[36]

This assurance was to be proved false a hundred times in the period ahead, when the Liberal Party displayed a singular lack of either co-operation with their leader or of loyalty to him. However, C.B. replied to Asquith on January 2, 1899, saying:

You write very kindly of the future, in case I should find myself in the horrid position: and I need not tell you that I should not entertain the idea of it for a moment were I not sure that I should have more help from my colleagues than I could give to the thing myself. . . . my standing medical counsel . . . tells me that he knows no reason a priori why I should not undertake the duties.[37]

To Bryce he wrote deploring the 'set things have taken in favour of my nomination', but adding:

Facing the prospect now, though I hate the idea of my being in so prominent a place, and although it involves an entire change of my domestic plans and ideas, I confess to you that I look forward to it without fear, and with a confident expectation of some actual enjoyment. For the more we think of it the more clearly we shall see, my dear Bryce, what an incubus we have been living under, not for recent years only but for a dozen years. That incubus has removed itself: and those of us who remain can realize a friendship and hearty comradeship which we have never had, at least in an unimpaired form.[38]

Whatever hopes Harcourt may have had of being recalled to the leadership he seems now to have abandoned, and he departed for a long holiday in Italy. But a letter to his constituents was published in *The Times* on January 4. It was a turgid document, explaining, at some length, that he did not propose to make a political statement at that moment. C.B. wrote to his cousin:

Another letter! and apparently not a forgery this time. A very nasty letter of the same old kind – bad English, bad taste, bad feeling, bad tactics. . . . I think he must have lost his head: but open mischief is meant by him, Labby, Dilke, Stanhope, with Joe C. in the background. Never mind, we will drive on & be hanged to them. I am much mistaken if this letter will not be much resented. And what will poor dear J.M. do? Write a letter also? The whole thing is sickening.[39]

An old enemy reappeared on the scene. Dilke was reported in *The Times* of January 6 as telling his Gloucestershire constituents that it seemed 'pretty clear that Sir Henry would be unanimously elected by the Liberal members to be their leader', but that he regarded him 'as not only not advanced in his views, but in the whole trend of his mind . . . one of the most conservative members that occupied a seat upon the Liberal benches. In his administration of the War Office, he was more than any one else who had ever been in Pall Mall severely inclined to let things alone.' Dilke said that he wished 'to express his doubts in advance with regard to the permanence of a Campbell-Bannerman leadership', though 'personally there could be no better choice', since 'whatever his policy might be, his Scottish wit was calculated to put the best face upon things and to recommend them both to Parliament and to the country'.[40]

A letter came to C.B. from Rosebery, at Mentmore, saying:

I have no doubt that there will be a universal wish that you should accept, and universal pleasure that you face the matter in so manly a spirit. . . . You will be few, but you will be absolutely united, cordial and loyal – I mean the four leaders . . . for the first time in years there will be a handful on the front bench working like a good team, unjealous, with real and friendly and eager co-operation. . . . Good luck to you – and I think you will have good luck.[41]

C.B. wrote to his friend Donald Crawford on January 10:

. . . as days roll on it becomes more & more likely that I may be in for this ugly thing. . . . My own belief is that though we have some camstrairy deevils, the party as a whole is sound enough . . . it necessitates a complete change of my . . . plans, for I have been for some time engineering a way of escape, instead of plunging deeper. . . .[42]

Bryce was delighted that C.B. was willing to take 'the post of danger', and in a letter to C.B. on January 13 wrote: 'What I hear leaves me in no doubt that you are the choice of the immense majority.'[43] C.B.'s reply reflected his growing confidence and Bryce wrote again on the 16th, saying, 'Your letter does me good. It is like a fresh breeze.'[44]

C.B. was now briskly businesslike. He wrote to Asquith again on January 17 about arrangements for a party meeting, which should, he thought, be at the Reform Club – 'Anything else wd. be a confession of weakness and of decadence. . . . To go to another Club wd. be a slap on the cheek of the Reform, and we should get all our men black-balled! The alternative is a Committee Room, which wd. be to sink to the level of the Irish. . . .'[45] Asquith agreed, but said that he would have to repudiate publicly Morley's suggestion that 'nous autres are wallowing in the mud of Jingoism'. Fowler also agreed but warned C.B. that there might be difficulties as he thought a majority of the committee of the Reform Club were Liberal Unionists and that some Liberals didn't belong, 'such as Perks who was blackballed'.[46]

On the 17th *The Times* commented:

It has been generally assumed by the organs of the Opposition that SIR HENRY CAMPBELL-BANNERMAN will be chosen, without dispute. . . . We do not know why the party appear to have agreed to set aside the claims of SIR HENRY FOWLER, but the fact is plain enough. MR. ASQUITH, it is believed, is unwilling to sacrifice his career at the Bar for the shadow of authority over a divided party, and, even if he were to overcome his objections, it is by no means certain that he would command the support of the Opposition as a whole. The selection of SIR EDWARD GREY would be admirable from the national point of view. . . . But it . . . has been regarded from the first, by practical politicians, as altogether out of the question. By a process of exhaustion, SIR HENRY CAMPBELL-BANNERMAN's name is left as that of the leader who . . . divides the least. Unfortunately, as MR. GOLDWIN SMITH says, in a letter we publish this morning, 'It is not a leader that is wanted for the party, but a party that is wanted for the leader.'

In the present circumstances of the Opposition, we do not think they could select a better spokesman than SIR HENRY CAMPBELL-BANNERMAN. He has a high Parliamentary reputation on both sides of the House. . . . He is a man of wealth and position, a capable debater, with a large amount of experience in administration as well as in Parliamentary life, with an imperturbable temper and conciliatory manner, a *persona grata* to his opponents as well as to his allies, and, in many ways, peculiarly adapted to conduct a disorganized party through a period of transition. While the Radicals are waiting for the 'evolution', as SIR WILFRID LAWSON has put it, of the new leader, SIR HENRY CAMPBELL-BANNERMAN will 'mark time' respectably and even with dignity. He is not a 'little Englander', but, on the other hand, he is not a pronounced Imperialist. . . . SIR HENRY CAMPBELL-BANNERMAN will probably be found in a strongly intrenched position 'on the fence' . . . For the moment there is nothing that can be done by the leader of the Opposition . . . except to criticize the conduct of the Government where it seems to be necessary and to support it where that is clearly for the public interest. These modest functions SIR HENRY CAMPBELL-BANNERMAN is quite competent to discharge. . . . If 'evolution' should bring a leader with more commanding claims to the front . . . SIR HENRY CAMPBELL-BANNERMAN is not the person to stand in the way of a necessary change. . . .

If SIR HENRY CAMPBELL-BANNERMAN has a defect it is that he is not prone to excess of activity. . . . It is . . . likely that he will turn out to be . . . a 'warming-pan', from which . . . neither 'light' nor 'heat' can be expected. Nevertheless, a 'warming-pan' has its uses. . . .

Labouchere wrote to Loulou in the same vein on the 31st, saying that he had seen a letter from 'some Scotsman, who in explaining that the Radicals of Glasgow are against Rosebery, kindly compared C.B. to a wooden Scotsman, as fit to lead a party as any one of those who do duty before the shop of a vendor of snuff'.[47]

On the 17th Morley spoke at Brechin, saying darkly that 'cross currents' had compelled Harcourt to resign. Morley said that he himself had not resigned, for he had nothing to resign, but had 'decided independently of Sir William Harcourt, but on similar grounds, that he could no longer take an active and responsible part in the formal counsels of the Liberal party'. T. P. O'Connor wrote that Morley 'was an older and more powerful Liberal leader than Mr. Asquith, and he had a far bigger position in the party than Campbell-Bannerman. And Campbell-Bannerman suddenly emerged from obscurity into the full blaze of . . . the Leadership. . . . But Morley groaned internally instead of striking out for his own hand.'[48] Spender, who knew him well, noted that Morley had had very serious ambitions to lead the Liberal Party, ambitions that were closed by C.B.'s election. He was not even consulted about the choice of Harcourt's successor. According to Spender he used for several years afterwards to speak sourly of C.B. as 'that worthy man'.[49]

C.B. himself realized that his election was inevitable. Grey wrote to him on January 23 saying: 'I haven't been near London for ages, but I hear & read that you are to be our new leader, and if you consent there can be no doubt about the willingness of all of us to give the best backing we can.'[50] C.B. may have remembered these words, rather grimly, in the next six years. On February 3 he wrote to J. E. Ellis: 'there is no room for shirking, and . . . I am enough son of my country, and have enough of the "Shorter Catechism" still sticking about my inside, to do my best with a thing if it comes straight to me.'[51]

Soundings were taken among Liberal members of the House of Commons. One of them, A. A. Provand, a Glasgow merchant, wrote of C.B. that he was 'undoubtedly the most popular and best liked front bencher on our side'. He argued that it was a mistake to have doubts about C.B. because he was not a ready speaker. Gladstone had been far too ready and fluent, so providing ammunition for opponents like Lord Randolph Churchill. Provand hoped that C.B. would follow the example of W. H. Smith, 'who successfully led the House for years and never . . . got off more than a few sentences of housemaid's English'.[52]

On February 6 the party meeting was held in the smoking room of the Reform Club. C.B. was elected leader unanimously, in what Asquith described as 'a temper in which relief and enthusiasm were curiously blended'.[53] The left – Labouchere, C. P. Scott and Atherley-Jones – made a declaration of continued confidence in Harcourt, but few really wanted him back, and support for C.B. was general.

Congratulations poured in. George Russell wrote: 'Ave Caesar. . . . This is better than the Speaker's chair',[54] the editor of the *Stirling Journal*: 'They are not typical Scotsmen who spend sixpence or more on congratulatory messages – let me send mine by post',[55] Acland: 'Edward Grey was here a few days ago and I could see that he was quite in spirits about working under you.'[56]

C.B. must have felt that he had really arrived when he received on the day of his election a letter from 10 Downing Street:

My dear Campbell-Bannerman,

I hear you & I are to face each other over the Table of the House:
– as the first incident in the new and I trust not disagreeable relationship, it falls to me to send you a copy of the Queen's speech. I need
only add that it seems rather duller (if possible) than usual.

Yours ever,

Arthur James Balfour.[57]

The *Annual Register* noted that C.B.'s acceptance speech at the party
meeting 'made a distinctly favourable impression on his hearers'. Even
The Times thought it displayed 'geniality, good-humour, and a toler-
able wit'.[58] In this speech, which Asquith later described as 'admirable',[59]
C.B. said of his election:

> It is an honour which is immensely enhanced by the fact that it
> comes to me from a body of public men among whom, or among
> their predecessors, I have lived and moved through over thirty
> years of political life. . . . I am well aware – no one is better aware –
> that I am poorly equipped for the duties of that position in com-
> parison with some distinguished men who have gone before me;
> but there is one thing in which I will yield to none of them –
> namely, in my devotion to the Liberal party and my faithful adher-
> ence to Liberal principles. . . . I declare in the strongest terms that I
> am, above all things, a loyal son of the House of Commons, and that
> I place before all interests, even the interest of the great historic
> party to which I am proud to belong, the maintenance and the
> advancement of the name and fame and power of the great Assembly
> to which we all belong.[60]

C.B. also described himself as 'well known to be a person of a
pretty tolerant and easy-going disposition'. On this, Asquith later
wrote: 'He was that, but also a great deal more. . . .'[61] Morley, who
thought that C.B. was 'far too sagacious and experienced a man not to
be wide-awake to the formidable difficulties to which his sterling sense
of public duty was exposing him', wrote of him: 'with no other
leading Liberal of our time did diplomacy, transitory tactics, expediency of the hour, weigh lighter in the scale against principle'.[62]

According to Lord Crewe, Rosebery 'cordially approved'[63] the
result. Rosebery wrote to C.B., saying, 'If I may say so, you could not
have made a better start. . . . All this will give new life to the party.'[64]

G. W. E. Russell remembered it as 'a most remarkable meeting, for we were unanimous, a most remarkable thing for an assembly of Liberals'.[65] Unanimous it was, but the Liberals were determined to preserve the right to say and do precisely what they liked, whatever the new leader might think.

So C.B. replaced Harcourt, not, it is true, as official leader of the whole Liberal Party, for in those days there was no such post when the party was out of office, but as leader in the House of Commons. It did not necessarily follow that he would become Prime Minister if the party were returned to power. Rosebery was still available, and his supporters looked on C.B. as a mere stopgap. Spencer too had ambitions to be Prime Minister. C.B. told a friend that he had no desire to be Prime Minister, and was willing to serve under Spencer, and to Spencer himself he wrote on December 12, 1899: 'The only thing I demur to is the implication that I am "leader". I only fulfil that function with my commoners and have honestly not the slightest idea of, now or ever, doing more: they are an unruly herd enough, and more than I can manage without going outside for a larger flock.'[66] But he was now nevertheless the effective party leader. He was a very different sort of man to Harcourt. Mr. James Pope-Hennessy records that Crewe thought Harcourt inferior in political judgement to C.B., and quotes Crewe as writing:

> Having known both intimately, I regard C.B. as having been gifted with a far finer political mind than Harcourt was, though the latter had to do with more exciting affairs on a bigger scale, and was probably associated with a greater number of interesting people.[67]

But the immediate prospect for C.B. in February, 1899, was hardly dull or unexciting. He had come to the head of a turbulent and deeply divided party, which had baffled the efforts of both Rosebery and Harcourt to control it. As a writer in the *Nation* was to say in April 1908: 'He came to the rescue of Liberalism when it was a mere hulk, floating captainless and rudderless on the waste of waters.'[68] The skies were rapidly darkening in South Africa. As Leader of the Opposition, C.B. was to have as difficult a task as has ever fallen to the lot of the holder of that most frustrating and unrewarding of posts.

Part 6

The Leader of the Opposition

CHAPTER 20

The Boer War

'A war of unprecedented dimensions was raging, at the time of which I speak, in the sub-continent of South Africa.

The President of the South African Republic, thinking the moment propitious for a conquest of our dominions, had invaded our territory after an ultimatum of incredible insolence, and, as though it were not sufficient that we should grapple foe to foe upon equal terms, the whole weight of the Orange Free State was thrown into the scale against us.

The struggle against the combined armies which had united to destroy this country was long and arduous . . . the Commander-in-Chief himself, Lord Roberts . . . in less than three years from the decisive victory of Paardeburg imposed peace upon the enemy. Their territories were annexed in a series of thirty-seven proclamations, and form to-day the brightest jewel in the Imperial crown.'

Hilaire Belloc – 'Mr. Clutterbuck's Election'

AGAINST all the odds, C.B. had become leader of his party. Abandoned by two successive leaders, it now sorely needed a period of calm to repair damage and restore a reasonable measure of discipline. But the new leader was not to be given any such chance. A crisis lay immediately ahead.

This was the Boer War, an issue on which the Liberal Party almost broke itself apart. It began in 1899, and dominated British politics until the middle of 1902.

It is odd that the rights and wrongs of this distant war should have aroused such furious controversy within the party. Essentially what Chamberlain, now Colonial Secretary and the moving spirit in the Unionist Government, and Milner, the High Commissioner – who described himself later as a 'British race patriot'[1] – were trying to do was to create a united British South Africa, speaking English and firmly and irrevocably lodged within the British Empire. This could only be done if the Dutch in South Africa – the Boers – could be induced to submerge their separate identity. They were few in numbers – there were only 30,000 burghers in the Transvaal. So their absorption did not appear impossible.

Milner himself began as a Liberal and social reformer, and was a highly intelligent and forceful man. He went out to South Africa from the Board of Inland Revenue in April 1897, when he was forty-three. Like Rhodes before him, he had begun by using tact and conciliation. But he soon found that the problem was more difficult than he had thought. In a letter to Asquith in November 1897, he said:

> In spite of Majuba, in spite of Jameson, I remain firmly of the opinion that, if it were not for my having some conscience about the treatment of the blacks, I personally could win over the Dutch. . . . You have only to sacrifice the 'nigger' absolutely and the game is easy. . . . Deep down in the heart of every Dutchman in S. Africa is the ideal of a white land-owning aristocracy resting on slave labour (of course the word 'slave' is carefully eschewed, nor do they exactly want slaves, but simply the cheap labour of the black proletariat *without any rights of any sort or kind*). . . .[2]

As time went on Milner became increasingly unsympathetic to the Boers and, like Rhodes, increasingly impatient when faced with the rigid obstinacy of Kruger. John Buchan, who worked for him in South Africa, wrote later: 'He was not very good at envisaging a world wholly different from his own, and his world and Kruger's at no point intersected. There was a gnarled magnificence in the old Transvaal President but he saw only a snuffy, mendacious savage.'[3]

Moreover, like Rhodes, Milner, though born and schooled in Germany, had a mystical view of the role of the British race. Sir Edward Grigg later wrote of him: 'His whole political philosophy was based on the conception of race, which was in his view the key.'[4] Rhodes had in the end resorted to the short cut of force. The result had been the Jameson Raid and his political nemesis. Milner took the same road. Faced by an unyielding Kruger, he adopted a hectoring and impatient line, and told Chamberlain in February, 1898: 'I should be inclined to work up to a crisis.'[5] He proceeded to do just that, broke off the Bloemfontein negotiations in the summer of 1899 and forced the issue, so making war inevitable. It was a war which could have been avoided. But Chamberlain and Milner wanted quick results. Once set on a course, we are apt to be impatient with those who oppose us and do not fit into our plans, whether we are faced by a

Kruger, a Nasser, a Carson or a De Gaulle. We tend to lack the imaginative sympathy which would tell us why these leaders cling so tenaciously to their positions, and hence to underestimate their sincerity and determination. Moreover in this instance the leading role on the British side was being played by Milner, who was described by A. G. Gardiner as having 'the spirit of a Torquemada, ruthless, unbending, fanatical'.[6] So we became involved in what Massingham called 'a blood feud with one of the most obstinate races in the world'.[7]

The Boers spent large sums on arms after the Jameson Raid. They were first with their ultimatum on October 9, 1899, and began hostilities by invading British territory in Natal on the 11th. This cut the ground from under the feet of those, like C.B., who criticized Chamberlain and Milner and understood the feelings of the burghers in the small states of the Transvaal and the Orange Free State, and fulfilled Milner's wish that if war came, 'we must seem to be forced into it'.[8]

The Liberals had to work out a line in a country which was filled with patriotic fervour and where there was a natural call to close ranks and to resent any criticism in wartime. C.B. was a patriotic man himself and, having served so long at the War Office, set his face against criticizing the Army or the British soldier. He was clear that it was the Unionist Government's policy which must be attacked.

But a number of leading Liberals had been infected with Imperialist enthusiasm. Chief of these was Rosebery, who defined Imperialism as 'the larger patriotism', and whose supporters in the party came to be known as the Liberal Imperialists and by C.B. as the Liberal Imps. They had acquiesced in C.B.'s election to the leadership, but regarded him as simply a stand-in for Rosebery. The *Manchester Guardian* later observed of C.B.: 'Here was an easy-going creature, it was suggested, that would keep the nest warm for a bird of more brilliant plumage to be welcomed back to its natural home all in good time.'[9]

The chief Liberal Imperialists were Asquith, Grey, Haldane and Fowler. They admired Milner and thought the British cause a righteous one – 'We are in the right in this war. It is a just war. It is a war which has been forced upon this country,'[10] Grey declared in the House. They thought that the Liberal Party ought to support the Government. E. T. Cook was their chief supporter in the press.

Against them were ranged the old Cobdenite radicals – Bryce, Channing, H. J. Wilson, Bob Reid – by and large men of somewhat lesser standing in the party and in Parliament, but with the retired leaders W. V. Harcourt and Morley behind them and H. J. Massingham their eloquent spokesman in the press. Later they were joined by the young Lloyd George. The fact that the war, instead of being short, sharp and glorious, dragged on for four unhappy years, with a toll of humiliations and increasing resort to brutal methods, strengthened their case as time went on.

Between the two groups a great gulf yawned, and in that gulf C.B. tried desperately to hold the party together and prevent any formal split or any takeover of the machinery of the party by either group. He was intrigued against by his colleagues, some of whom laboured openly to displace him, and would not even sit with him on the Opposition front bench. He was sneered at by most of the press and excoriated by society, but he set his teeth and kept at it. That he succeeded in holding the party together, and, in the fullness of time, in forming a government representative of all sections and leading the party to the greatest electoral triumph in its history, is his most remarkable political achievement. No one in 1899 or in the first three years of the new century would have regarded such an outcome as conceivable.

Sir Robert Menzies has written that 'the duty of an Opposition, if it has no ambition to be permanently on the left-hand side of the Speaker, is not just to oppose for opposition's sake, but to oppose selectively'.[11] No one knew this better than C.B., but he had a good many militant colleagues who had no such realistic view, and he was even more troubled with colleagues of note who wished only to applaud the Government, and whose opposition was so selective as scarcely to be opposition at all. No man was ever worse supported.

On February 7, 1899, C.B. spoke for the first time in the House as Leader of the Opposition. His speech was a marked success. Hamilton wrote: 'Many formed high expectations of him as leader, but he has surpassed those expectations ... he was tip-top.'[12] Balfour, no admirer of C.B.'s, wrote to the Queen, as Leader of the House, describing the debate:

Sir H. Campbell-Bannerman ... spoke ... extremely well: somewhat more aggressively perhaps than is usual on such occasions, but this was perhaps not unnatural ... he apparently aimed at proving that no weaker or more vacillating foreign Minister than Lord Salisbury had ever existed ... his criticisms ... at times were grossly unfair. But they were very well delivered and full of humorous touches and eloquent passages: it was a good beginning to his term of leadership. ...[13]

Morley, writing to Harcourt next day, said: 'C.B. was very clever – easy – amusing – and a success, as we knew he would be.'[14] Spencer wrote to C.B., saying that it was 'delightful to see the joyful faces of your followers, & the effect which your shells had on the enemy'.[15] Years later, the *Manchester Guardian* wrote:

> Those who heard Sir Henry's first speech as leader of the Opposition are never likely to forget the sensation it caused – the look of pained resentment that came into the faces of Mr. Balfour and Mr. Chamberlain as they realized that the new man was actually attacking them, even holding them up to derision, and the flutter of excitement on the Liberal benches as the new man's following awoke to an elated sense of their champion's unexpected prowess. From that moment, in the eyes of all good Tories, dates Sir H. Campbell-Bannerman's metamorphosis from a passable type of *bonhomie* into an embodiment of political wickedness.[16]

C.B. had surprised those who wrote him off as a mediocrity. But it was a false dawn. On the 13th he spoke again and this time he was much less effective. Labouchere, a very sharp critic, told Harcourt:

> Yesterday . . . he not only made tactical errors, but a very poor and ineffective speech, to which Balfour replied by a very effective one. . . . Balfour told me that Bannerman's speech was pitiable. He seems to be a man who is not ready. When speaking without preparation, he bungles over his sentences and he certainly does not manage to hold the House. . . . Altogether I should say that Bannerman is not regarded as a success. . . .[17]

The Imperialist and anti-Imperialist wings of the party both hoped to be able to capture the new leader to the discomfiture of their opponents. On February 24 he had, for the first time, to give a public indication of where he stood. Morley denounced the Government's policy in the Sudan, and was strongly attacked by Grey. When C.B. rose the House quickly filled & there was, as one reporter put it, 'a crowded circle of faces eagerly watching Sir Henry painfully pacing the perilous slack rope'.[18] Morley told Harcourt:

> Nobody knew . . . what he would do. He said to somebody that he should not make up his mind until he rose. We listened for

quarter of an hour; without an idea which way he would go. I made sure he would go with Grey. No, he came with me!! Immense sensation. One of the most dramatic things I have yet seen. A.J.B. said to me afterwards – 'Could not have been worse done. He ought to have taken a line firmly and strongly in his speech, if he was going to vote with you.' Quite true. . . .[19]

When C.B. concluded his brief speech by saying he would vote for Morley's amendment there was a moment's silence, then a cheer from the Opposition and a burst of laughter from the Ministerial benches. He dropped back into his place and smiled genially. Morley was jubilant and told Harcourt next day that 'the Liberal jingoes are very wroth with him, which is as one wishes it to be'.[20] They were indeed. Haldane told Rosebery: 'The events of tonight have formed an odd commentary on your hopeful view of C.B. The blow which his action has dealt to his authority is more serious than any one who is not of his followers in the House can realize. It is a very bad business . . . Labouchere is going around triumphant. . . .'[21]

The vote split the party. 58 voted with Morley and C.B.: 15 or 16, including Grey, voted with the Government. C.B. himself wrote a letter of explanation to Rosebery:

> I did it on a balance of advantages, and as the best way of out-witting the little clique. The truest representation of my opinion would have been to walk out: but this always has a mean effect. . . . On the whole I thought what I did (however distasteful) was the best. . . . It was however a painful moment. . . .[22]

Rosebery replied:

> I am as you know a member of the E. Grey minority. But as regards a parliamentary situation you are incomparably a better judge than I am. . . .
>
> I cannot tell you how much I enjoyed our talk on Thursday. It is a pleasure to be able to converse with an old friend, without being anathematized as an intriguer![23]

Morley wrote to C.B. saying: 'The difficulty of the moment was undoubtedly pretty sharp, and I should like to say how warmly I recognize your courage in facing it.'[24] Labouchere, writing to Harcourt on the 28th, said: 'C.B. has, for some reason, a strong dislike of Grey, and he has often told me that he has never been able to understand how anyone can suppose him to be likely to become a Leader. This possibly influenced him to a certain extent. . . .'[25]

In any event a watershed had been passed. In the same letter Labouchere added: 'C.B. is generally beaten in debate by Balfour, and our side does not like this.' Morley told Harcourt just over a month later that 'some people are already becoming gently critical of C.B., "not magnetic", etc. etc. Before the year is out we shall see the same shabby game being played, of which *you* know more than enough. . . .'[26]

C.B. attended the House regularly. Labouchere noted that he 'sits solidly there, but speaks seldom', and a few days later, in March, that he 'looks very much bored'.[27]

One result of his election as leader was that he was now asked to address huge party meetings all over the country. Travelling to these by train, often from Belmont, was an exhausting business, but C.B. found it a novel and stimulating experience to address five or six thousand cheering partisans, and these meetings exhilarated him and gave him some idea of the real support for his ideas in the country, whatever might be the opinion held in London society or in the offices of *The Times*.

On March 8 he spoke to one such meeting of the National Liberal Federation at Hull. He said that Liberals were not afraid of the responsibilities of Empire. But they were opposed to 'the vulgar and bastard imperialism of irritation and provocation and aggression, of clever tricks and manœuvres against neighbours, and of grabbing everything even if we have no use for it ourselves'. In the same speech he criticized the rise of the 'steady and relentless tide of expenditure', and said also that it was a very serious fact that thousands of Nonconformist young men and women were shut out from the teaching profession 'unless they were content to stifle their consciences or to alter their opinions'.[28] Rosebery, who was away yachting in the Mediterranean, wrote from Lesbos to Hamilton, saying: 'Campbell Bannerman's speech at Hull I thought as a speech quite excellent', and from Messina to Ronald Munro-Ferguson, that it was 'one of the cleverest I ever read', adding of its author: 'Remember that he is thoroughly straight, a gentleman, a friend of yours, a Scot, and do not be too hasty to despair of him or even criticize him.'[29]

In those days, when Foreign Secretaries sat in the Lords and the arcane mysteries of foreign affairs were supposed to be too delicate to be exposed to irresponsible questioning by private members in the House of Commons, the Conservative Government would not agree to the Under-Secretary at the Foreign Office, who sat in the Commons, answering any supplementary questions. C.B. declared that the Under-Secretary 'speaks in the House of Commons with a muffled voice, because he is all enwrapped with cotton wool lest peradventure some reckless questioner should require an answer from him which he has not had several hours to prepare'. Later, on June 5, he supported the vote of £30,000 to Kitchener and praised his services in the Sudan, but deplored the desecration of the Mahdi's tomb – such treatment of a former enemy had an air of vindictiveness 'which is surely unworthy of this nation'. It was 'an infraction, not only of sound policy, but of good feeling, good taste – and I would even say of good manners'.[30]

In April he had to take his first administrative decision. Tom Ellis, the Chief Whip, died suddenly. C.B. thought Herbert Gladstone, the son of the great man, would be the best successor. Asquith agreed, though he pointed out that Herbert Gladstone was 'naturally inclined to a slack – if not lazy – existence',[31] and Gladstone was appointed. He turned out to be hardworking and assiduous but lacking in judgement and too much inclined to seek peace at any price within the party.

The crisis in South Africa now began to cast its shadow on affairs. On May 5 Milner sent home a highly coloured despatch describing the uitlanders as being 'thousands of British subjects, kept permanently in the position of helots, constantly chafing under undoubted grievances and calling vainly on Her Majesty's Government for redress'. On May 31 Milner and Kruger met at Bloemfontein in a last attempt to settle the problem peacefully. 'It is our country that you want,' said Kruger as he wept and put his head between his hands. On June 17, three days after the publication of Milner's despatch, C.B. spoke at Ilford:

> Some of the newspapers . . . talk freely of the probability, and even the necessity of war. . . . I can see nothing in what has occurred to justify either warlike action or military preparation. The people of this country have no hostility to the people of the Transvaal, and no desire to humiliate them or deprive them of their independence. But the outlanders have not the municipal government, the police protection, the organized maintenance of order, the even-handed administration of justice, which in all civilized communities are regarded as the very elements of civil right and civil freedom.[32]

This was a carefully balanced statement, but *The Times* asserted that it had increased the danger of war – presumably because they thought it would encourage the Boers to be uncompromising.[33]

Three days later, Chamberlain asked to see C.B. Not until February 5, 1904, did C.B. reveal what then took place, when he described it to the House of Commons in these words:

> It was on June 20, 1899. The right hon. gentleman . . . came to my room. He told me that he wished to submit to me, and of course to those with whom I acted, certain proposals that the Government were contemplating. The first of them was to send out 10,000 men to the Cape, and the right hon. gentleman asked whether the Opposition would join in recommending that step to the House and to the country . . . the right hon. gentleman went on to say, 'You need not be alarmed. There will be no fighting. We know that those fellows' – that was the Boers – 'won't fight. . . . We are playing a game of bluff.' I think I ventured to express frankly to the right hon. gentleman my opinion that such a policy was unworthy of the country. If I did not say that, I felt it; but at all events I said that it was a rash and dangerous policy, that it was dangerous to begin a course of bluff when you did not know what it might lead to. . . . we could only reply that the responsibility for a great movement of troops such as that lay entirely with the Executive Government, and that we were not prepared to relieve them of any part of the responsibility. . . .[34]

This talk had a profound influence on the line C.B. took during the war. As he subsequently explained: 'That declaration of the policy of the Government sunk into my mind and remained there.' It was a 'declaration that a game of bluff was being played, that there was no sincere expectation or intention of using actively any forces which might be sent out'.[35]

Chamberlain said in 1904 that he did not remember having used the word bluff. This may have been so, but it was undoubtedly the sense of what he had to say. C.B. made a note of the conversation the same day. Chamberlain had given him a telegram, which quoted an unnamed authority, said to know the mind of the Boers, as saying that they would give way without striking a blow if the Government backed their demand by strong and unmistakable pressure of force, but that if there was the slightest vacillation, their backs would be stiffened and they would give nothing. C.B.'s note ran:

I urged the apparent danger of this course, that it might inflame Dutch feeling instead of allaying it, and that, intended though it might be as a mere piece of bluff, if the bluff was not successful it meant war. He said that . . . he himself was striving, and always had been, for a peaceful settlement. But he was afraid that a demonstration of the kind indicated would be necessary. It would, however, be a game of bluff and it was impossible to play that game if the Opposition did not support the Government.[36]

Chamberlain had, since 1895, played the game of bluff very successfully against the French in West Africa. In the light of what he said to C.B. it is odd that he should have written to the Queen on October 12, saying: 'Mr. Chamberlain has long felt that the differences between this country and the Transvaal could only be settled by force, and he is glad that the inevitable conflict has now been commenced by the Boers. . . .'[37]

There is no doubt that C.B. carried away from this conversation a very strong, and disagreeable, impression of what Chamberlain was trying to do in South Africa.

He was strengthened in his doubts by letters he had from Sir George Clarke, the soldier, who wrote: 'Preparations are going on to a much greater extent than is generally known. . . .'[39] and, '. . . there is nothing to fight about, nothing worth the bones of a single grenadier. The uitlanders do not want the franchise and have never scrupled to say so. . . . We have not a friend in Europe. As soon as we begin to shoot the Boer farmers, we shall be universally execrated.'[38]

Clarke was not alone in these views. Esher, for example, wrote to his son: 'It looks as if the Government will cave in to Chamberlain. In that case there will be war. Such a horror – and a crime too.'[40] Lord Salisbury himself had written to Chamberlain in April 1897: 'I should look with something like dismay to a Transvaal war.'[41] But the forceful Colonial Secretary had disregarded his chief's well-founded anxieties.

On July 18 C.B. said in the House that

he could see no ground for surprise at the stubborn resistance made by the burghers, and especially by President Kruger, to the proposal to admit Outlanders to the franchise . . . the Boers had 'trekked' into the Transvaal to live by themselves, and now they felt themselves swamped by the newcomers, however much it increased their prosperity. Then there was the Jameson raid, which the Boers could not forget. . . . There was a certain strangeness in the idea that we should go to war to enable our fellow-citizens to give up their own citizenship in favour of another . . . at present there was no case, even for a threat . . . of war.[42]

After the debate, on August 1, he told Sir George Clarke, with misplaced optimism: 'we have reason to believe that the wiser hands in the Cabinet have got it in charge. Still, it is a gunpowdery business.'[43] He took care to keep in touch with Rosebery, who wrote on July 8: 'I am always delighted to see you, and will let you know if I come to town. But don't talk of reporting to me! Generals don't report to Chelsea Pensioners!'[44]

C.B. was finding his form as leader now. He had a strong case, which he thoroughly understood. He was beginning to score points too. One day in the House he quoted a letter written by Lord Kimberley in 1881 criticizing the 'disposition in members of our party to maintain that the Empire can be and ought to be maintained without ever resorting to force'. The Imperialists were delighted at this denunciation by a Liberal leader of the failings of Liberals. But a contemporary report added:

> Before the laughter and cheers of the jubilant Ministerialists had subsided Sir H. Campbell-Bannerman was observed standing at the table in almost apologetic attitude.
>
> 'I think,' he said meekly when silence was restored, 'that letter was written when the right hon. gentleman was a member of the Cabinet.'
>
> It was now the turn of the Opposition to laugh and cheer, and they responded with a will. For once in a way Mr. Chamberlain was put out. During the last dozen years he has grown so familiar with the sudden apparition of ghosts of his dead self that he has accustomed himself to disregard their importunity. To-night he feebly made answer, 'I do not see the point.'
>
> The House did, and rudely laughed again.[45]

But C.B. was hamstrung by the lack of unity among his supporters. The battle in the party between the Imperialists and the anti-Imperialists was gaining momentum. The Imperialists succeeded in capturing the *Daily Chronicle*, and removing from it their most formidable critic, Massingham, who fled to the *Manchester Guardian*.

Rosebery was, for the time being, quiescent. Morley, writing to Harcourt on August 20, said: 'They sounded Ld. R., but he, "having retired does not think it fair to meddle with C.B.'s responsibility".'[46]

On August 26 Chamberlain spoke at Highbury of the 'sands running down in the glass'. The sands might be running down, but C.B. was, in accordance with his invariable habit, at Marienbad, where he had been since the 8th and was to remain, despite the anxieties of his colleagues, until September 25.

Cheered by the fact that Charlotte was, as he told Sinclair, 'amazingly better, quite eine andere Frau',[47] he had not as yet fully settled in his mind the rights and wrongs of the South African crisis. He wrote to Sinclair on September 10:

> I think Kruger by his methods has done much to invite sharp treatment; whether these methods be the result of suspicion of our sincerity or the mere cunning of the crafty old animal . . . undoubtedly he has set quiet and unprejudiced people at home against him, and whatever provocation he may have received from Joe's hectoring the fact . . . will make it difficult to denounce vigorous action.[48]

But five days later he wrote to his cousin:

> I remain, as I have always been, of the opinion that the Transvaal thing was pure bluff from end to end. In fact Joe told me so, though that is rather a reason for believing he wished for war: but the game is a vulgar game, & even if a settlement came (as I believe it will) it will leave angry feelings behind.[49]

He refused to believe that the country was really headed for war. But he was aware that, as he put it: 'The Transvaal question covers the sky.'[50] He told Gladstone: 'The negotiations have been bungled: bungled because of the application to them of too much cleverness and too little honesty.'[51]

On the 22nd he wrote to Sinclair from Marienbad:

> On Tuesday last I was knocked off my feet by a telegram from the Transvaal Committee (which on being boiled down precipitates Mr. C. P. Scott) of 16,000 words, the biggest telegram ever received in this place; they very nearly had a general holiday proclaimed, with fireworks etc.

This telegram demanded my opinion and called upon me to save my country, and it contained the full transcript of the Boers' last despatch, which, I may add, I could see in the Vienna papers. I concocted an innocuous reply.[52]

The Chief Whip wrote to him on September 21 advising him to return. But he refused to be hustled, and replied blandly, saying: 'We leave this on Thursday for Berlin for a day or two & will work homewards . . . but we shall be riding at a single anchor & could quicken our movements homewards at any time.'[53] Only, in fact, on the 25th did C.B. start wending his way very slowly homewards, stopping at Frankfurt on the 25th, Mainz on the 26th and Brussels on the 28th, and telling Sinclair: 'We shall haul in or slacken our cable according to what we may hear, but I rather wish to work in a day or two in Paris if possible.'[54]

By the time C.B. had reached Mainz, Asquith was beginning to get worried, and he told Gladstone on the 27th: 'It is impossible to take any joint action until C.B. arrives: if he can be hurried back he should be.'[55]

On the 28th C.B. wrote to Bryce from Cologne: '. . . Evidently our people are wandering. . . . Joe is foiled: his bluff has not answered. . . . He has driven our friends in the Free State into prospective hostility.'[56] On the 30th he wrote to Herbert Gladstone from Brussels: 'Jesse Herbert kindly telegraphed to me last night the gist of the Cabinet decision. It is a clear case of the fat in the fire: to hurl such a catalogue of demands at Kruger's head is of course war.'[57] On October 2 Morley, who was of a much more excitable turn of mind than C.B., wrote to Harcourt: 'Herbert G. . . . is in despair. C.B. is (or was) at Brussels: does not see what the fuss and hurry is about: what is there to say etc. etc. etc.'[58]

C.B., leaving Charlotte in Paris, finally got back to London on October 3, and there was a meeting of the Liberal ex-Cabinet at 6 Grosvenor Place the following day. On the 6th he spoke at Maidstone. He said that war was being spoken of as inevitable, but that no one appeared to be able to answer the question, 'What is it that we are going to war about?' He said that he regarded the idea of such a war with horror. He quoted Clarke's remark about the difference between a five- and a seven-year qualification for the franchise not being worth the bones of a single British Grenadier, and said that the man in the street and the newspapers took a very light view of the situation, judging that there would only be a short, sharp, exciting and interesting encounter 'between our forces and a brave, but happily limited, community'. He pointed out that what was really important was good feeling between the British and Dutch in South Africa, and warned that 'a war undertaken and conducted in this manner will have raised and will leave behind it . . . racial enmity and anger which it will take generations to overcome'.[59]

Having delivered himself of this utterance, C.B. went back to Paris and rejoined Charlotte. Harcourt thought the speech strong, clear and sound[60] but was concerned about C.B.'s emphasis on British paramountcy, and wrote to him on this point. In his reply, C.B. said:

> If you ask me my own opinion, I hold this 'franchise' movement as the biggest hypocrisy in the whole fraud. It was designed in order that
>
> (a) Kruger, seeing the real drift of it, might refuse it, and supply a direct ground of quarrel;
>
> (b) If he accepted it, it would mean that not being able to get in by the front door they would get the area gate opened and get possession in this way of the country;
>
> (c) The innocent Briton would be gulled by the flavour of legality and of civilized progress in the word 'franchise'. . . .
> Then as to the general power or responsibility of this country, it is no doubt vague, but I think it is substantial. . . .
> It is analogous, surely, to the right of the Powers of Europe to try and stop misgovernment in Turkey, which endangers general peace? . . .[61]

To Gladstone C.B. wrote: 'I have a long blast from W.V.H. raising portentous legal problems about "paramountcy". I have sent it to Asquith, as indeed the writer suggested.'[62]

Harcourt sent C.B.'s letter on to Morley, who said in his reply:

> I have no intention whatever of taking any counsel with C.B. or his colleagues. . . . All that time, when criticism might have been useful, they were silent. . . . I cannot consent to cut my coat according to the cloth that men of this kidney may choose to provide. Therefore you must go to C.B. without my company, and without my proxy. . . .[63]

C.B. wrote from Paris to Spencer on the 8th, saying: 'I have not much hope of the business, for old Kruger's ideas of the meaning of "independence" are quite different from ours.'[64]

On October 11 the war began. At once Rosebery spoke out, saying: 'In the face of this attack, the nation will, I doubt not, close its ranks and relegate party controversy to a more convenient season.'[65]

In the House C.B. said that the Opposition would vote supplies and powers necessary to secure a rapid and effective prosecution of a war rendered absolutely necessary by the terms of the Boer ultimatum and the subsequent invasion of the British colonies. But he pointed out that the country was 'entering on a war directed against a European people, a people of a race akin to our own, a Christian people, a Protestant people. . . . a war between white men in South Africa, in addition to all the evils of a foreign war, has greatly the character of a civil war'. He asked too how it was that the efforts of the Government to settle the controversy had failed, and suggested that the Government had played a game of bluff, 'not a very worthy game for a great country at the best . . . an impossible game on so large a scale as this'. He went on: 'Of all the people in the world against whom such a game could not be played with success I should select the Dutch. . . . The Boers have, like all of us, some good qualities and a good many bad ones, and among their qualities . . . they are stubborn, they are self-sufficient, they are unimpressionable, they are shrewd, and they are brave. . . .'[66] Balfour denied that the Government were bluffing – 'We have the cards and we mean to play them.' Writing to the Queen about the debate (from the point of view of a participant), Balfour said of C.B.'s speech that it

. . . exhibited a peculiarity which Mr. Balfour has more than once observed in his Parliamentary utterances. He began with an excellent and patriotic statement to the effect that he and his friends were prepared to support the Government in any proposals financial and military which might be deemed necessary for the successful prosecution of the war. Unfortunately, he spoiled the effect of this commencement by appending to it a feeble and somewhat captious criticism of the action of the Government in sending out troops and in their conduct of the negotiations. Mr. Balfour was therefore compelled to make a controversial reply which under existing circumstances he would have been glad to avoid.[67]

The Queen herself noted in her diary: 'Sir Henry C. Bannerman did not speak as patriotically as he should have done. But Ld. Rosebery wrote an admirable letter the other day, supporting the Govt. Mr. Asquith also made a good speech at Dundee.'[68]

Philip Stanhope put down an amendment expressing 'strong disapproval of the conduct of the negotiations'. Though the Liberal leadership abstained, 135 Liberals voted for it. Even some Conservatives were uneasy about Chamberlain's policy. The most notable dissentient was Sir Edward Clarke, a former Solicitor-General, who conducted a damaging cross-examination of Chamberlain in this debate and concluded: 'I am bound to say that the more I read of the correspondence and learn the circumstances of the case, the more I am convinced of the errors in the negotiations, and that this lamentable war is absolutely unnecessary.'[69]

From the beginning C.B. regarded the war as 'Joe's war', a phrase he used in a letter to his cousin on October 25.[70] If it went well, 'all the glory would be his', but if it did not, the responsibility would be his also. But some of his colleagues were taking a very different line. Grey said at Glasgow on October 25 that, after most careful study of the blue books, he was convinced that the war was inevitable, that it was not sought by us, and that it was forced upon us by the Government of the Transvaal. It is not surprising that Chamberlain regarded Grey as 'representing the best characteristics of the Opposition'. Another Liberal who spent a whole month studying the Transvaal blue books was Haldane. As a result he told Beatrice Webb that he 'was convinced that Milner was right, and that war was from the first inevitable'.[71] Seldom has the danger of forming opinions solely from blue books been more clearly demonstrated. On October 27 Rosebery said at Bath: 'I believe the party of Liberal Imperialism is destined to control the destinies of this country.' A separate Liberal Imperial faction was beginning to emerge.

C.B. was filled with gloom about the prospects. He wrote to J. E. Ellis on November 1: 'This war is going to be a bigger mess than you & I thought & prophesied. And now we are told to trust the man at the helm. He is the man of all others whom I don't trust.'[72]

He was particularly concerned about the line Rosebery was taking in public. In private Rosebery seemed not unreasonable. C.B. wrote to Ripon on October 27: 'I sat next to Rosebery on Wednesday at a dinner and found he was by no means of the opinion of Grey Haldane & Co.'[73] But what Rosebery said on the platform was another matter. On the 10th he wrote to Bryce:

I greatly fear . . . that recent events have strengthened the Government . . . the ordinary man, even if a Liberal, is saying: 'the disclosures since the war began of the vast war power of the Boers, far beyond anything that could be necessary against a raid or a revolt, shows that they meant mischief against *us* . . . this explains their insolence and their ultimatum; and it shows that they must be put down.' Thus . . . insinuations against capitalists, or hole-picking in J. Ch.'s diplomacy lose all effect.

In effect, Joe and Milner claim the credit of having unmasked batteries which had been erected and pointed against the Empire; we need not care now how they did it: they have delivered us from a great peril: they must be supported, and it is a mean thing to snarl at them.

What do you say to that? The very difficulties of the war, and strength of the enemy, help the Government in the country![74]

On November 3 the *Daily Chronicle* published a report of a conversation between Milner and Mr. J. T. Molteno, a member of the Cape Parliament, a month before, just before fighting began. In this Molteno recalled Milner as saying: 'Well, Mr. Molteno, it is no use; I am determined to break the dominion of Afrikanderdom.' Milner denied that he had said this but only that the Transvaal Republic and its sympathizers 'aimed at maintaining throughout South Africa the predominance of a single race, while we were contending for equality'.[75] After this disingenuous explanation Asquith pressed C.B. to support Milner, but to C.B. Molteno's account rang altogether too true.

He had an opportunity of saying what he thought in public when he spoke in the Free Trade Hall in Manchester on November 15. He said then:

There were some words published the other day, astounding and ill-omened words, attributed to the highest representative of the Imperial authority in the Cape – words which I cannot believe to be authentic, but which would account for all the trouble we are having. . . . It must be some hideous mistake . . . because these words represent not merely a departure from but the very antithesis to . . . a sound policy.

In the rest of his speech C.B. praised the courage of our own troops – pointing out, as an old Secretary of State for War, that they were the young short-service soldiers produced by the system he had helped to create – and praised also the courage of the Boers. He quoted Lord Randolph Churchill's description of the increasing friendship between

Dutch and English at the Cape in 1891, and pointed out that the war would 'give fresh bitterness to old jealousies and revive hatreds which ought to have expired'. His conclusion was that 'any solution would have been better than a war between Europeans at the Cape, and no mere assertions of its having been inevitable all along will relieve from the shoulders of her Majesty's Government the burden and blame of having led us into it.'[76]

The Manchester Liberals told the Chief Whip that C.B.'s visit was an unqualified success and that he himself had made a most favourable impression.[77] M.P.'s who were there said they had never heard him speak so well. *The Times*, however, which gave full support to Chamberlain and was never a friend to C.B., was severe on his speech:

> . . . The public have long watched with amusement the wobblings of SIR HENRY CAMPBELL-BANNERMAN. . . . Something or other has now upset the balance . . . SIR HENRY CAMPBELL-BANNERMAN has come down from the fence at last, and . . . has come down upon the wrong side and pretty much of a heap. His speech yesterday . . . reached vituperation and incoherence . . . the leader of the Opposition . . . more than insinuates that there was a foregone determination to bring war to pass; yet at the same time he labours to show that the Government made no preparation for war; and, finally, to make confusion worse confounded, he says they did make preparations, but only with intent to 'bluff'. . . . One utterance, however, may make us all very thankful that SIR HENRY CAMPBELL-BANNERMAN was not in power when things became critical. He says the first duty of the Government was to keep us out of war in South Africa, and that they stand condemned by the fact that war exists. He is utterly wrong. The first duty of the Government was to maintain the interests of the Empire, by peaceful means so long as they could be made efficacious, but by war if war became necessary.[78]

Asquith thought that C.B. had gone too far in condemning the Government and his friend Milner, and protested. Morley, however, was pleased, and to him Harcourt wrote saying:

> C.B. has put his foot down well on the right side of the fence and has cut the painter of the dinghy in which Rosebery, E. Grey and Fowler may drift off by themselves. I hope this will settle the question of where the centre of gravity lies.[79]

On the 17th, in another letter to Morley, Harcourt wrote of C.B.:

> He was bold and good. I never think you do that worthy Scot
> full justice. Mr. Gladstone used to delight to sing Mrs. J. Woods'
> song in the Milliner's Bill:
>
> > 'No matter what you do
> > If your heart's only true
> > And his heart was true to Poll.'
>
> A circumstance you will no doubt record in *The Life*. C.B.'s
> heart is true to the Liberal Poll. . . .
> I have written to applaud him. It is a shot between wind and
> water to the recreants and the shaky ones. . . .[80]

C.B. duly received this pat on the back, and told Spencer: 'I have
a letter from W.V.H. making his scimitar whistle over the heads of
H.H.F., Grey & R. each in his turn!'[81]

Despite their differences on this and other occasions during the war,
however, C.B. and Asquith never drew too far apart, and the bridges
between then were never pulled down.

On the 24th C.B. was at Birmingham, speaking on Chamberlain's
home ground or, as he put it to Spencer, 'supra Dunghillum chanti-
cleeri'.[82] He had gone at the invitation of Mr. George Cadbury, after
getting Gladstone to make enquiries about him, 'as I fancy there are
Cadburies and Cadburies'.[83] In this speech he ridiculed the idea of
'making the Boers love us by soundly thrashing them'. He expressed
his satisfaction 'that Sir Alfred Milner had given, as he himself was sure
he would give, the most explicit and complete contradiction to the
sentiment imputed to him to the effect that he sought the overthrow
of Afrikanderdom'. The Government's talk of a gigantic conspiracy
throughout South Africa for the overthrow of our dominion he described as 'a mere and obvious afterthought'. He described his own
outlook as 'common-sense Imperialism'.[84]

C.B. threw back in Chamberlain's teeth what he had said in May
1896:

> A war in South Africa would be one of the most serious wars
> that could possibly be waged, and it would be in the nature of a
> civil war. It would be a long war, a bitter war, and a costly war. It
> would leave behind it the impress of a strife which I believe genera-
> tions would hardly be long enough to extinguish. To go to war

with President Kruger in order to force upon him the reforms in the internal affairs of his State would be a course of action as immoral as it would be unwise.

No Liberal could have put the case more succinctly, and C.B. rubbed it in later when Chamberlain claimed that 'there was not one single man who was entitled to the slightest confidence or even pretended to be an authority upon the subject who anticipated the prolonged resistance which we have incurred'.[85] But Chamberlain's words had been spoken before Milner took the bit between his teeth. C.B. told his cousin on November 19: 'The real arch-offender is Milner – but we can't get at him.'[86] To Herbert Gladstone he wrote that 'it is doubt of Milner that is the unpardonable sin'.[87] It seemed to him that Milner had gone hopelessly wrong and he could not understand how some of his colleagues, like Asquith, Grey and Fowler, admired him so uncritically. He attributed it to a perverse Balliol solidarity. A. G. Gardiner observed long afterwards: 'Balliol did not come well out of the Boer War.'[88]

Milner was by temperament a ruthless autocrat, poles apart from a genuine Liberal. Ilbert, Clerk of the House of Commons, was once in the same house-party with him and told Bryce that 'it distressed us to find that all his sympathies were with the Raiders. We little thought that he was destined to be the Strafford of South Africa.'[89]

C.B. thought well of Sir William Butler, a radically-minded soldier who had been the general commanding at the Cape and had strongly opposed the moves towards war, which led to his being removed by Milner. Butler had also been right about the size of the military task we faced. Indeed part of the indictment of Milner is that he removed the ablest soldier in South Africa at the outset of the war, simply because he was out of sympathy with Milner's attitude to the Boers.

C.B. wrote to J. B. Smith on November 27: 'I do not mind the abuse of the newspapers. . . . But my difficulty has been to keep the Party decently together. If some of my colleagues had their way there would have been open revolt. . . .'[90]

Meanwhile Brassey, one of the lesser Liberal Imperialists, had written to Milner on November 28, saying:

> After C.B.'s attack on you on Nov. 15th and his speech of Nov. 24th I am quite clear that he is a man who ought never again to have a large share in the Government of the British Empire. He is

such a good fellow personally that his way of dealing with the Molteno interview is quite incomprehensible. . . . Whether the Liberal Party is going to be rent in twain on this War is an open question. Personally, I think it may be; but there is no doubt which side will have the upper hand in the end. Rosebery says in a letter I had from him two days ago: 'The Liberal Party – which is Imperialist in the true sense – has got to fight for its existence against the Rump or Little Englanders. The fight is one of a giant against a dwarf and therefore should not be very formidable.'[91]

Rosebery underestimated the opposition and above all he underestimated C.B. A. G. Gardiner wrote:

It was Campbell-Bannerman's good or evil fortune always to be underrated by clever people. They mistook his character and they mistook his understanding. They regarded him as a genial, good-natured, but simple-minded man, whom circumstances had pitchforked into an eminence for which he was entirely unfitted. It took years for them to discover that behind that plain and unpretentious exterior there dwelt, as in the case of Lincoln, one of the firmest wills, one of the most sagacious minds, and one of the noblest and most disinterested characters that have appeared in the long record of British politics. Harcourt . . . was content to have so stout a figure blocking the path to a Rosebery revival. . . .[92]

As the end of November drew near the rift within the party grew wider. Asquith made a speech on the war, the tone of which struck Harcourt as 'especially unfriendly to C.B.' and as containing an 'emphatic endorsement of Milner's policy'.[93] Morley said of this speech: 'Of course it is *directly* in the teeth of C.B. – and leaves C.B. alone with Bryce. . . . It is a speech for the war, and for the government – and pours the last drop into the cup of Liberal mischief. . . . Undoubtedly with Asquith, Fowler, and Grey in a cave, they will have the preponderance in speaking power over C.B. . . .'[94]

C.B., however, declined to panic. Writing to Spencer on November 30, Bryce said: 'C.B. with whom I am staying to-night here is in good spirits, and says that he found the Manchester people, tho' somewhat divided and wavering when he arrived, rallied quickly and fell into line. . . .'[95]

The Liberal Party were nevertheless in deep trouble, and Chamberlain was able to write with some complacency to Milner on December 6:

The Liberal Party as a whole have behaved extremely well. . . . Rosebery and his supporters have now spoken out well, but they preserved absolute silence until it was quite clear which way the tide was going. . . . Campbell-Bannerman, who wobbled at first, has succeeded in climbing down on the wrong side – that is the Morley-Labouchere side – of the fence, but he has lost influence, and I do not think there can be any serious attack upon us, except, perhaps, for the military conduct of the war, and, later on, upon the settlement.[96]

C.B. had been at Belmont since the end of October, occasionally sallying forth to deliver a speech and coming up to London when it was absolutely necessary. He took the temperature in his constituency and wrote to the Chief Whip on December 7:

Coming home, I spent an hour or two at Dunfermline among my constituents. There is a good deal of war fever, and they are a little bewildered by the buckets of contempt and abuse poured on by the Scotsman and other papers. I do not think, however, it goes very deep: but for the moment there is a coldness.[97]

Two days later he wrote: 'For the present I think we must sit tight & keep our hatches closed, without any swopping of horses (I would work in a few more metaphors if I could find them).'[98]

Gladstone, as Whip, had his eye on more mundane matters, such as the temperance question and the Liberal Party's relationship with the liquor trade. He told C.B. that 'Haig (distiller) throws up his candidature in S. Derbyshire', and that '*We cannot afford* to lose the Gilbeys and all their grocer clients, the Whitbreads, Eversheds, Buxtons, Beaufoys and other men. . . .'[99] But C.B.'s mind was elsewhere.

The war had gone badly in South Africa. Instead of a cheerful campaign against a 'brave, but happily limited community', Kimberley, Mafeking and Ladysmith were all under siege, Dundee in Natal had been abandoned, and two battalions of British infantry, with four guns, had surrendered at Nicholson's Nek outside Ladysmith. Now in December, the last month of the old century, there came the 'black week', a series of humiliating reverses. On the 10th General Gatacre fell into a trap at Stormberg and lost two guns, 89 killed and wounded and 633 others taken prisoner. Next day Lord Methuen's advance towards Kimberley was stopped at Magersfontein. The Highland Brigade, caught at dawn in close order after a night march, was shot to pieces and bolted, their commander, General Wauchope, being killed. Worst of all, on the 15th, Sir Redvers Buller failed hopelessly in his bid to cross the Tugela river in a frontal attack on Colenso, losing eleven hundred men killed, wounded or prisoners and eleven guns, though he had 18,000 men to Botha's 6,000. Lieutenant Roberts, only son of the Field-Marshal, was killed trying to get away the guns. It became clear that the war was to be no picnic. The Unionist Government awoke to the seriousness of what they had undertaken and the sixty-eight-year-old Roberts was despatched to take over from Buller as Commander-in-Chief, with Kitchener as his Chief of Staff. Esher wrote to Harcourt on December 18:

. . . Buller telegraphed an absolute non possumus on Saturday, in regard to the passage of the Tugela. His supersession is the reply. It may restore the morale of the Army which has been rudely shaken. But *what* a national fiasco so far! . . .
     And what a justification of the unfortunate Butler! However, it is all too wretched to write about.[100]

Ian Hamilton soon wrote to a friend from South Africa: '*Buller is no use. He is indeed far, far worse than useless.*'[101]
     On December 19 C.B. spoke at Aberdeen to an audience stunned by the destruction of the Highland Brigade. He shared their feelings, but said again that 'Mr. Chamberlain is mainly answerable for the war. It is the natural result of his persistent policy.'[102]
     On December 23 he wrote to Stead: 'I cannot . . . take so despairing a view of our resisting powers, though the present panic and the extraordinary measures being pursued – including the sending out of two new Generals – would justify the notion that we are in extremis.'[103]
     Now, at this dark moment, a ray of light broke through the clouds. A letter arrived from Asquith:

20 Cavendish Sq.
20 Dec 99.

My dear CB
     I must congratulate you on your speech at Aberdeen in which I thought you handled the question of 'differences' with much skill & tact.
     The said differences, wh. relate entirely so far as I know to the

interpretation of the past, & involve no issue of principle or policy, have, of course, been magnified & distorted to the highest degree for purposes of obvious mischief. I have kept as silent as I could, & when I had to speak what was in my mind I pitched it in as low a key as I could. . . .

Yours always
H. H. Asquith

The generals seem to be neither able to win victories nor to write intelligible accounts of their defeats.[104]

C.B. must have realized at once the political significance of this letter. Its friendly tone at this moment meant that Asquith, despite his admiration for Milner and despite the gulf that separated him from men like Morley, was determined not to break with C.B. He had his feet much more firmly on the ground than either Grey or Haldane, he knew Rosebery's limitations as a practical politician – which they had yet to learn – and he could see that the war the Liberal Imperialists had backed was going very wrong. His position was a key one, and his support for C.B. was crucial.

Bryce continued to be a faithful supporter, though inclined rather more strongly than C.B. towards the 'pro-Boers'. On December 22 he wrote:

> I have been feeling so strongly all through these eleven months what a splendid example you have shewn us all – if you will permit me to say so – of unselfish and single minded devotion to the interests of the party as a whole. But for you, we should have been in small pieces by this time. . . .[105]

C.B. replied on Christmas Day with some more scathing comments on Milner: 'The thing that strikes one is, apart from the rights and wrongs, what a . . . weak undignified tone there is about the High Commissioner . . . his whimpering petulance is characteristic of narrow-minded obstinacy. . . .'[106]

CHAPTER 21

The Struggle against the Liberal Imps

'I believe there is no permanent greatness to a nation except it be based upon morality.'

John Bright, 1858

C.B. saw the twentieth century in at Belmont. His main assistants at this time were Vaughan Nash, a journalist, who had, with Massingham, been driven off the *Daily Chronicle* and who did research for his speeches, and Jack Sinclair, who kept in touch with all types of political opinion from Rosebery to Keir Hardie. He wrote to Birrell on January 5:

> ... how ugly our country has come to look in the sight of its best friends. All the weaknesses & worst faults of poor John B. carefully brought to the front. . . . This can only be redeemed by his best qualities being applied to the settlement afterwards ... but we shall not get those qualities auspice Josepho.[1]

The Conservative Government had hopelessly miscalculated the size of the military task in South Africa, disregarding Sir William Butler's warnings. The staff they sent out initially to run the railways in a region the size of Central Europe consisted of one officer, one batman, one horse and one groom.[2] On January 8 C.B. commented to Spencer:

> There never was such a heap of misfortunes and difficulties, bringing discredit & shame as well as danger upon us.
>
> Even all this random enrolment of yeomen & huntsmen & ghillies & colly dogs, creditable though it is to the adventurous spirit of our countrymen, is proof of our being about, after some ten weeks of war, at our very last gasp – militia regiments going on active service! We were never reduced to that even in the Crimean War. . . .

Politically also it seems to me that the whole situation is changed, for the success of the Boers makes annexation in any form impossible even if we beat them in the end. The whole world would cry shame on us. But if we don't annex, then for what have we been fighting, & what will the Rhodes party have gained? Their whole policy presumed an early collapse of the Boers.[3]

But C.B. was concerned because some Liberals were only too ready to be diverted from the main issue of the political responsibility for the war to attacking the details of military organization. When Dilke submitted an amendment to the Address, C.B. wrote to Gladstone saying: 'I do not think Citizen Dilke's amendment covers the ground. It is admirably fitted as a peg on which to hang up for public admiration the intimate knowledge of facts possessed by its originator – but that is not our sole object.'[4] To Bryce on January 11 he wrote: 'The real question *now* is the conduct of the Government . . . their neglect of the information supplied to them, their criminal levity and recklessness, and their total miscalculation of the probable issues. It is on these they must be attacked; and the guns and horses and transports are the merest red-herrings. . . .'[5]

He kept an eye on the intrigues of the more ardent Liberal Imperialists – 'our excellent Haldane,' he told Gladstone on January 21, '. . . was busy laying pipes and pulling wires and wigging ears all the time he was down here at Xmas'.[6] He wondered whether to invite Harcourt and Morley to his 'speech dinner', telling Gladstone: 'Our big friend is so overpowering & all-pervading not to say overbearing, that his admission wd. restore to us our old trampled condition. . . . Still . . . if front bench is the test, why not the twins? Echo answers, why?'[7] He decided to invite them, and, in his next letter, said: 'I have written to the fair Malwoodina, and I hope that bulky nymph will not be coy.'[8]

There were signs that even the Liberal Imps were unhappy about some of the Government's statements. Grey wrote to C.B. on January 20 admitting that 'an awful mess has been made, and the tone of Balfour's speech at Manchester & the cool information that the Govt. are not responsible for anything and are not to be blamed for the unhappy entanglement at Ladysmith are intolerable'.[9] C.B. accordingly worked out an amendment to the address that both he and the Liberal Imperialists could support, and got Lord Edmond Fitzmaurice, a man he described to Gladstone as 'as straight as a reed in his action and as sound as a bell in his views',[10] to move it.

Milner's friends now regarded C.B. as beyond the pale. A certain James M. Rendel wrote to him from the Reform Club, of all places, on February 9, saying: 'Even that poor "trash" Campbell-Bannerman will have to be quiet now. . . . They say that Joubert has told his men to take particular care not to shoot the English generals. I think that we here should take the most tender care of Campbell-B.'[11]

But another friend of Milner's, Philip Lyttelton Gell, told him that he had talked to Haldane, who had asked him '(very seriously!) . . . whether *you* might not have so far alienated Dutch feeling, that (Oh! Good Lord!) it might be politic for you to leave the settlement to some-one else. . . . Of course I went for him remorselessly . . . it may be worth an occasional effort to refute silliness.'[12] This was the first of a number of signs that Milner's supporters in the Liberal Party were beginning to have doubts about the wisdom of their hero.

Other men in positions of responsibility took the same line as C.B. Arthur Nicolson in the Foreign Office, for example, wrote to his wife: 'I do so thoroughly loathe and detest this war – and feel that it has done irreparable injury to our reputation. I can hardly bear to think of it.'[13]

When the House met in February, the Opposition vote of censure failed. Balfour reported to the Queen on the 7th:

> After a large number of speeches had been delivered, two of them (by Mr. Lloyd George and Mr. John Burns) of extraordinary violence, Sir H. Bannerman rose to conclude the debate for the Opposition. His gifts, which are considerable, do not specially qualify him for this kind of effort; he had no easy duty to fulfil, and it cannot be said that he rose to the occasion.[14]

There is an uncharacteristic note of slight desperation in the letter C.B. wrote to his cousin on February 9:

> We have had a stormy time & worse is in front of us.
> Most people one meets, of all politics, denounce the war, & its authors (Rhodes, Joe, & Milner) but they have nobbled almost the entire press: [in the margin he scribbled bitterly: 'How many shares in Rand mines have all those editors & pressmen got given to them. Panama was not worse.'] Joe has trampled on his colleagues and any one who whispers a doubt is abused like a pickpocket . . . a lot of our people have not the pluck of a flea and funk the newspaper abuse.

What is still more annoying is all the intriguing that is going on *in certain quarters* among one's 'own familiar friends' – but of this I cannot write. I have done all that mortal can do to keep them together: but I am at the end of my tether now, & if they wish to join the Tories or form a fine Party of their own, let them go & be. . . . It is a' ane to Dandie.[15]

C.B.'s depression was only temporary. As a matter of fact there were still three and a half years of conflict with the 'Liberal Imps' ahead. But there was another reason for his discouragement. In the same letter he told his cousin: 'my wife prostrate with neuritis & unable to lie or to sleep'. It was a rough life.

'They are destroying the unity and power of the Liberal Party, and are making its leader an object of commiseration.' Those words might well have been written in 1900, but were in fact written by John Bright in his diary for 1867. The Liberal Party was fatally prone to tear itself apart.

C.B. wrote to Spencer on February 19:

> I cannot say we are in a pleasant condition here.
> 1. There are some who really disagree with my opinions – i.e. with the established principles of Liberalism.
> 2. There are those who 'funk' their constituents and the war fever.
> 3. There are intriguing partisans who introduce the personal question: and these cease not day nor night.
> If these causes mean splitting up, then the split must come. . . . as to myself, I am half-surprised to find that as I go on I get more and more confirmed in the old advanced Liberal principles, economical, social, & political, with which I entered Parliament 30 years ago: and if all these gentlemen can't stand my principles, they must do without me! That would not break my heart.[16]

But the Unionists were also beginning to show signs of strain. Philip Gell wrote to Milner: 'Nothing . . . has hit the Government more seriously than Arthur Balfour's speeches at Manchester this week. The Nation has simply risen in wrath at the extraordinary superficiality and ineptitude and blank ignorance which they have betrayed. . . . Whether the Ministry will fall, God knows!'[17]

At the end of February, however, Roberts and his massive reinforcements began to show results in South Africa and on the 27th Cronje surrendered at Paardeberg. Next day Lord Selborne said in a letter to Milner: 'The Govt. seems to me parliamentarily very stable, more owing to the fatuous incompetence of Campbell-Bannerman than to anything else.'[18]

Noisy patriotic feeling in England was running high. John Burns, the Labour leader, had to defend his front door with a cricket bat against a yelling Jingo mob which smashed his windows and threatened to loot his house. On March 15 C.B. raised in the House the breaking up by thugs of pro-Boer meetings and the wrecking of Quaker shops at Scarborough. Balfour's disdainful reply irritated the House.[19]

Later in March C.B. was ill and Grey had to deputize for him at a meeting of the National Liberal Federation at Nottingham, saying on that occasion of his leader: '. . . had anyone else been in the position, a man of less self-sacrifice or a man less devoted to trying to preserve the unity of the Party, I am not sure that by this time there might not have been a split which was beyond recall and beyond repair.'[20]

On June 1 C.B. summed up his attitude to the war in a letter to the Chief Whip: 'I have never uttered a pro-Boer word: I have been anti-Joe but never pro-Kruger. And it is as clear as a pikestaff that the countries must be in form "annexed".'[21] Putting the same argument to Ripon, he added: 'if this is so, I see no good in boggling over it: better to accept it frankly'.[22]

This question had now ceased to be academic. Just a week later Roberts entered Pretoria. The time had come to define the position of the Liberal Party. This C.B. did in an important speech he made at Glasgow on June 7. He said that the two Boer states must in some form become part of the British Empire and that the objective must be the harmonious cooperation of the two European races in South Africa. This could only be achieved by applying Liberal principles. Now he was entirely specific, and laid down the policy which, as Prime Minister, he was himself to follow six years later when he had at last obtained power:

Let us restore as early as possible and let us maintain those rights of self-government which give not only life and vigour but contentment and loyalty to every colony which enjoys them, the rights of self-government . . . which I for my part . . . think, would work effectively for cordial conciliation between communities much nearer home.[23]

C.B. was saying what he deeply believed at a time when it was extremely unpopular to advance such views. As in the case of Ireland, self-government within the British Empire, not independence, was what he advocated. But in this same speech he denounced Salisbury for having declared, at a banquet in the City, that 'no . . . security is within our reach so long as we leave a shred of real independent government to either Republic'.[24]

Even some of the Liberal Imps applauded him. Haldane wrote from Paris to say how much he liked his speech – 'Its directness, and the plain line of policy which it indicates for the Opposition . . . should tend to bring all sections of the Opposition together. I am sure that many besides myself will appreciate the skilful way in which you have cleared a path.'[25]

But the Conservatives, who were in power, were not so farsighted and could see no alternative to the formula they had tried in Ireland – years and years of 'resolute government'.

Milner's own view had been forcibly expressed in a letter to Gell in April: 'About things political *don't yield to the temptation* to leave a vestige, or fragment, of a Boer state anywhere – not even in the Zoutpansberg. *Delenda est*, even if it takes 2 years of guerilla warfare. We owe it to the unborn generations. . . .'[26]

Balfour, in another one-sided account of a Commons debate on South Africa he sent to the Queen, observed contemptuously that 'Sir H. Bannerman concluded the debate in a characteristically colourless oration'.[27] At this stage C.B. was no match for Balfour as a debater. Massingham described him as 'a poor, almost an embarrassed speaker; the best in him was almost pathetically inexpressive'.[28]

Herbert Samuel, who entered Parliament as a young Liberal in 1902, wrote that C.B. was 'rather like a stout, amiable City man, called upon to face, with nothing better than a walking-stick, a lithe fencer with a nimble rapier.' 'Yet', he added, 'C.B. was at times surprisingly effective, and always imperturbable.'[29] Margot Asquith wrote that C.B. 'was as much stimulated as Mr. Balfour was irritated by his opponent, and, considering the inequality of their intellect, they made a fair duel. Sir Henry's patent sincerity constantly pierced the armour of Mr. Balfour's insolent detachment, and the Tories who took him to be a guileless person found themselves confronted by an unforeseen combination of pawkiness and courage.'[30] L. S. Amery wrote of Balfour:

It was always a delight in his House of Commons days to watch the puzzled look on the face of the Liberal back benches as, with both hands on the lapels of his frock coat, he gently pulled to pieces their most cherished eternal verities, and then philosophically contemplated them as interesting specimens of human muddle-headedness. This analytic, dissecting habit . . . infuriated simple-minded opponents like Sir Henry Campbell-Bannerman. . . .[31]

According to J. A. Spender, Balfour had considerable success in 'guying' C.B. Spender wrote of C.B.: 'Even his best friends had been obliged to admit that few other men of his abilities could make such bad speeches as he did when thrown off his stroke or confused by interruptions.'[32]

Balfour could not resist jeering at C.B. Nor could Salisbury, who at a public dinner affected to have forgotten his name.[33] But as a friend wrote at the time of his death:

What I think went far to establish his popularity was the sneering contempt with which the Unionists in the House, on platforms, and in the press, always treated him, as though it were almost an outrage that so plain and simple a man should be the leader of a great party.[34]

But Balfour was, in a way, the least of C.B.'s problems. It was calculated that at this time there were in the House 62 Liberal Imperialists, supporting the war; 68 firm Liberal opponents of it, led by Harcourt, Morley and Lawson; 30 moderates, led by C.B.; and 27 others.[35] It was hardly surprising that the Unionists, with the war apparently won, began thinking in terms of a general election. A debate on South Africa on July 25 revealed starkly the Liberal disarray. An amendment moved by Sir Wilfrid Lawson was supported by Sir Robert Reid, the former Liberal Solicitor-General, Lloyd George, Courtney and Labouchere. Chamberlain attacked his critics in his usual sharp and effective way. C.B. said that he would not vote for Lawson's amendment, as he disagreed with the extreme views of the mover: But equally he would not vote against it, as that implied approval of Chamberlain's policy. 40 Liberals, including Grey, voted with the Government, and 31 for Lawson's amendment, while 35 followed C.B.

and walked out. The vote was a very embarrassing one for C.B. and rumours that he was going to resign a thankless post were widespread. For a few days such a move appeared to be imminent. Gladstone told Morley in the House: 'I believe that tomorrow morning, I shall be looking out for a new leader for the party.'[36]

Morley wrote to Harcourt on July 28 in a sour vein. His letter showed no understanding of the problem C.B. faced in the party, and clearly indicated Morley's limitations as a politician:

> . . . I am a charitable man, but I don't find any tears flowing for C.B. He belongs entirely to our political school. . . . His one chance was to be both straight and firm. . . . He agreed with us who opposed the war: has done all along. What was gained by hiding his agreement? His want of pluck has emboldened Perks, Haldane & Co., and his trimming and wavering is more answerable than anything else for the present mess. . . .[37]

On the other wing, Haldane had reported to Rosebery on the 25th:

> The old split of October re-appeared. C.B. . . . insisted on a general abstention – The party refused to acquiesce. . . . Asquith (who was with us but did not vote) & Grey think that C.B. was riding for a fall. He may change his mind in the morning but our impression is that he means to resign & set off for Marienbad on the advice of Maclagan his good physician . . . if you choose to emerge & lead those Liberals who may be called 'Lord R's friends', with Asquith & Grey as Lieutenants in the House, I think things will work out. . . . We have the machinery & the Whips & the future. . . . Of course C.B. may change what was his mind tonight, but I do not think so. He tried to do the impossible. It now remains to consider another way.[38]

The Unionists were jubilant. The ineffable Rendel wrote exultantly to Milner on the 28th:

> I hope you were satisfied. . . . It was a big victory, so big as to be nearly a disaster, for a disaster it would have been to have displaced Campbell-Bannerman. As long as he is leader, the party he leads is pretty well doomed to impotence. . . . The party nostrum is to find a form of words which will nominally reconcile two totally

divergent lines of thought. But it wants a very able quack to use it, and though Campbell B. is a quack, I don't think he is a very able one. Therefore may his shadow never be less![39]

Chamberlain was also delighted. He could now, he thought, disregard C.B., and he took no account of a man like Bryce whom he had described earlier as 'just a snivelling professor'.[40]

Bryce might be derided by the Unionists, but he was not a man to desert his chief in his hour of trial, and he went round to give C.B. a drop of encouragement. C.B. wrote to him next day: 'I cannot help sending a line to say how very kind it was of you to come round here last evening. I assure you it gives me great support to know that there are a few, and yourself prominently among them, who understand my position and feelings and with whom I am entirely in sympathy.'[41]

Harcourt, too, was not a man to run for cover when the fire grew hot. On August 18 he wrote to Spencer:

> . . . The mess that had been made by the folly of Lawson on one side, the malignity of the Roseberyites on the other was so bad that as you know they had made the position of poor C-B intolerable which was what the latter (Roseberyites) aimed at. I therefore plucked up my courage to give him a helping hand. . . .
>
> . . . I did not think it was possible that anyone could have been worse treated than I was but I admit that they have exceeded themselves in their conduct towards C-B. . . . I am afraid the poor fellow feels his position keenly but we must do what we can to keep him in the saddle – he is an honest Liberal *without any* adjective a thing which can be said of very few in what is called the Liberal Party. There is not a man on the Front Bench I think except myself who is really loyal to him and very few behind.
>
> The Roseberyites put him in, in the hope and expectation that he would be the alter ego of R. and when they found they were mistaken they determined to oust him. . . .[42]

Harcourt said of C.B. at this time: 'He is like the Tsar who was followed by the assassin of his predecessor and preceded by his own.' C.B. had indeed reached the nadir of his fortunes as Leader of the Opposition. Margot Asquith, writing to Milner on July 9, said: '. . . I feel *strongly* tho. entre nous that C.B. is *not* the man to lead us & that Rosebery has done infinite harm . . . thanks to quarrels in our ranks and the varied attitudes on the war taken up by some we shan't make much of a show at the Elections.'[43]

The Liberal Imps now set up a body called the Imperial Liberal Council. The moving spirit was R. W. Perks, the member for Louth, a solicitor, who had made a fortune out of contracts for the Manchester Ship Canal and the Severn Tunnel, and was a prominent Wesleyan.

It was perhaps fortunate for C.B. that Balfour was also going through a bad patch. There was a debate at the beginning of July on the unsatisfactory medical arrangements in South Africa. C.B. pointed out that for every man who had died of wounds in South Africa two had died of enteric fever. Balfour's response was petulant and received in chilly silence by his own side.[44] Next month, on the same issue, Balfour lost his temper altogether, and the Unionist Chief Whip admitted that he 'was completely unhinged last night'.[45] It must have been a relief to C.B., with all his troubles in his own ranks, to see his chief opponent floundering uncharacteristically in this fashion.

In South Africa, where there were now a quarter of a million British soldiers, the war should by rights have been over. The Unionist Government said so. Balfour talked of 'the war now happily drawing to a close', and Mr. Chamberlain said flatly: 'The war is over.' But the Boers apparently did not understand the rules of the game. Although Roberts issued a proclamation in August that all burghers who had not taken the oath would be treated as prisoners of war and 'transported or otherwise dealt with as I may determine', they carried on highly effective guerilla operations with their commandos. The Conservatives did nothing to encourage them to come to terms, Salisbury repeating that 'we can never allow, and never have allowed, that any shred of independence can be left'.[46]

Gladstone, guessing correctly that the Unionists would try a snap election, was driven to distraction by C.B.'s usual autumn absence at Marienbad. He wrote to Robert Hudson, his deputy, on August 18:

> The political position is just maddening with C.B. away. The whole party waits for the smallest scrap of inspiration, but it is all smothered in a Marienbad mud bath. The situation is grotesque. . . . Our efforts to find a leader are about as successful as Tommy Atkins' efforts to shoot a Boer.[47]

Hudson said that he supposed it was no use hoping that Rosebery would come to the rescue. Gladstone replied: 'I have some hope of R.

yet. *Most* unfortunately C.B. is away unbelieving in an Autumn election.'[48] A week later he wrote disgustedly to Hudson: 'Today I have a letter from C.B. – he stays at Marienbad till Sept 15, & then goes on elsewhere unless he has to come home. . . . I am sick of rebuffs.'[49]

At the end of August Gladstone had a letter from Asquith about Rosebery, in which he said: 'I spent Tuesday night at Mentmore. . . . I am sure no good would be done by formal approaches from C.B. or anyone else (least of all from C.B., whom R. regards as discredited & moribund).'[50]

In September came the expected dissolution. The Unionists were unable to resist the opportunity of celebrating the defeat of the Boer armies and the fall of Pretoria by holding a general election which, given the state of public feeling and the disarray of their opponents, might be expected to confirm them in office for another five years. The Liberals were in no fit state to go to the country. Bryce complained to C.B. that the Tories were quoting Asquith and Fowler against them, adding that 'Imperial Perks seems to be still on the warpath', and that 'Haldane might be better occupied than in cracking up Alfred Milner, for the first requisite to better things in S. Africa is to get that gentleman out of it'.[51]

But C.B., who was back in England on September 22, was anything but downhearted, 'especially', as he told Gladstone, 'that *labour* is with us'.[52] To Bryce he wrote on the 30th:

Everything seems prosperous. Last night a *tremendous* meeting in St. James's Hall – and all our people say they have not for years had such a feeling as there is in London.

. . . The Unionists very glum. Joe has overshot the mark, and three things damage him – the election trick, the publication of private letters, and the shares in contracting companies. I hear the last is having great effect.

Then A.J.B. is drivelling – and the others nowhere.[53]

Public meetings, at which he was always given a great reception by rank and file Liberals, played a big part in keeping up C.B.'s morale in these difficult times.

The remark about the publication of private letters referred to the Government's action in publishing some letters from correspondents in England which had been captured in Bloemfontein. C.B. was old-fashioned about such matters and was genuinely shocked. He described it as a 'scandalous and unworthy act' and said that a private individual who published private letters would be excluded from the society of honourable men.

His election address said that the war had come home to citizens of every class, and spoke of the need for educational reform and for the brushing away of 'sectarian cobwebs'. In a speech in London on September 29 he also asked: 'What in the world have schools to do with either church or parson?' He had not lost sight of domestic issues, and earlier in the year had told Gladstone that 'London is a great field for us' and urged him to support the London County Council, who were 'fighting against monopoly & money-power & "gentility" combined'.[54] He was concerned, too, about the party machinery, and on September 30 told Lefevre: 'the organization has been accaparé by the Imperialist side of the party'.[55]

The election which followed, known as the khaki election, was not by any means the total disaster for the Liberals that some of them expected. Gladstone had even said at Leeds on September 18 that they had no chance of winning, a curious pronouncement for a Chief Whip. The party made a considerable effort to pull itself together and bury its differences, though Haldane told Beatrice Webb that the Liberals 'would reform after the election, with Rosebery as Leader, Asquith as first lieutenant and Perks as organizer; "Then money will flow in and everyone who dreams of a peerage or a baronetcy will send in his cheque" '.[56]

The campaign was an unusually bitter one. The Liberals attacked Chamberlain for his family interest in Government contracts. His theme was that every seat lost to the Government was a seat gained by or sold to the Boers. Winston Churchill had a poster at Oldham which ran:

BE IT KNOWN
THAT EVERY VOTE GIVEN TO THE RADICALS MEANS
2 PATS ON THE BACK FOR KRUGER
AND
2 SMACKS IN THE FACE
FOR OUR COUNTRY[57]

Rosebery described it as a 'wanton' election and denounced Chamberlain's slogan, particularly when used on behalf of an 'obscure candidate' who was opposing his right honourable friend Sir Henry Campbell-Bannerman. Asquith's view was that 'Rosebery has not improved his position. He was afraid to plunge, yet not resolute enough to hold to his determination to keep aloof.'[58] In this same letter he was uncharacteristically violent in his comments on Joseph Chamberlain, comparing him unfavourably with Disraeli: 'We have seen the worst fit of vulgar political debauch since 1877–78, with the difference that the orgy was then presided over by a man of genius, whereas now the master of the feast has the manners of a cad and the tongue of a bargee.'

In all the circumstances the Liberals did better than they might have expected and, though defeated, did not lose by a very large margin. The Unionists came back with a majority of 134, only 4 more than before the election. C.B.'s own majority at Stirling was cut to 630 by a Liberal Unionist. As usual, he was unruffled. On October 10 he told Ralph Knox: 'on Saty. you will be out, waving Union Jacks. . . . Thank God I am in quiet country fields, where Union Jacks are unknown.'[59] Ripon wrote to thank C.B. for his 'admirable speeches', adding: 'I was also delighted with your well deserved snub to those impertinent fellows who call themselves Liberal Imperialists.'[60] C.B. wrote to J. E. Ellis on October 14:

> . . . we shall never have so many adverse conditions again; and in the circs. we have not done badly. Scotland has been horrid: for one thing the Catholics voted against us for the first time – this is the main cause of the reduced majority in my own case. . . .
>
> We have now to dry our clothes & restore our health after the hurricane & storm; the ship will want some repairing, but she will be all right if the crew work together. Let us hope![61]

Next month he gave his views to Spencer:

> We heard a great deal of the election bringing Liberals together. I doubt it. The only thing is that my flock will not be in such a nervous fright for their seats . . . possibly, therefore, a little more courage may be shown. . . .
>
> The difference in the party . . . is not great so far as it is genuine. . . . There is of course a fringe of extremists at either end. But it is not allowed to remain natural: it is blown up into a mighty Schism – pro R. and anti R. The former are more insidious and deadly. As long as he hangs on our flank we are paralysed. . . .[62]

He said to Ripon:

We cannot shut our eyes or ears to the fact that Milner has close friends very near to us. I have heard them spoken of as the 'Balliol set'. They include Grey, Asquith & Haldane; and it is my conviction that one of the main influences causing the determined support given by them to the Govt's S.A. policy has been Milner-worship.

I must frankly say that the impression left on my mind is entirely opposite. I think he was the worst man possible for his position . . . sensible & solid people regard him and his influence with the gravest mistrust.[63]

The Liberal Imps were in no way inclined to bury the hatchet. Grey wrote to Munro-Ferguson on October 18:

I think my word to R. will be that if he doesn't come out into the open in the next two years his chance will be gone anyhow, and that he may at any time get an ultimatum from some of us that we are not going on any more without him. If C.B. goes on as leader, the only choice will be either to go full steam ahead on one's own line, or else to chuck it. . . . I don't care to fight for my own hand; there is nothing in C.B. to fight for. . . .[64]

Munro-Ferguson, a determined Liberal Imp, resigned as Scottish Whip, and C.B. was glad to replace him with the faithful Jack Sinclair.

The Imperial Liberal Council now came out into the open with a resolution declaring that the time had come 'to clearly and permanently distinguish Liberals in whose policy with regard to Imperial questions patriotic voters may justly repose confidence from those whose opinions naturally disqualify them fron controlling the action of the Imperial Parliament of a world-wide community of nations.'[65]

This was a direct challenge to C.B.'s leadership. Harcourt heard the alarm bell, and told Morley: 'I am making a declaration of loyalty to C.B. I think he has deserved it, and he is the only buffer against the Perks conspiracy who are longing to dismiss him, which they shall not do if I can help it. . . .'[66]

C.B. himself reacted sharply, and on October 23 published a 'letter to a correspondent', in which he said that when a sectional organization

. . . proclaims as one of its first objects that all Liberals who do not belong to it, and whom it chooses to proscribe, should be excluded from the party, the case becomes intolerable. . . . In what may be styled Imperial policy there is absolute harmony among four-fifths of the Liberal Party and it cannot be for any useful public purpose that it is sought to manufacture a division. . . . Such tactics, and the spirit which they display, are fatal to our usefulness as an Opposition, and no party could exist in vigour and efficiency within which they were pursued and tolerated.[67]

He told Gladstone: 'I never saw a more audacious piece of mischief than the Perks manifesto',[68] but to Harcourt he also said: 'I think the manifesto is a happy incident, as showing quiet Liberals through the country something of the spirit of the men we have to deal with.'[69]

It was a help to him that his opponents had walked unwarily and overplayed their hand.

One of the surprising things about this period is the virulence of C.B.'s Liberal opponents. Arthur Ponsonby, who became C.B.'s private secretary, wrote later:

To be frank, the Imperialists disliked C.B., and C.B. disliked the Imperialists. I mean personally. . . . Haldane and Grey acted together. Their animosity against C.B. was pronounced and undisguised. They thoroughly disapproved of his attitude on the Boer War, despised him as an inferior intellect, and thought he would discredit the party. They were constantly thinking of how he could be shelved. . . . One objection to C.B. as Prime Minister in their eyes was that C.B. was not 'in society'. C.B. never . . . blew his own trumpet. . . . He had no ambition for power, no desire to be Prime Minister, no wish to oust anybody.[70]

To Lord Ripon, whom he greatly respected, C.B. permitted himself a rare outburst about the state of public opinion:

I confess that the thing which concerns me most is to find that Chamberlain *pays* with our countrymen. They worship a forcible man and a clever man, and if his methods are vulgar, dishonourable, unfair, they only smile and approve. The lowering of the standard of public life is a far worse evil, because it is more permanent, than toryism, jingoism, or any other heresy; *panem et circenses*: money spent in the country, flags to wave, bluster to shout for – that is the object: let right and honour and freedom go and be hanged! The *commencement de siècle* morals, apparently![71]

The Chief Whip was not proving much of a prop and stay and was now wobbling dangerously. J. E. Ellis told C.B. on November 7 that Gladstone wanted him 'to commit yourself publicly *without delay* to support of the Government in their "settlement" viz. Crown Colony admin. – with A. Milner at Pretoria as Administrator. I told him I hoped you would do no such thing'.[72]

C.B. fully agreed.

On November 12 the Imperial Liberal Association held a dinner at the Hotel Cecil. Brassey said that Rosebery was the leader who could 'best promote the union of all sections of the party'. Perks, who seems similarly to have been devoid of all sense of humour, called for unity on the front Opposition bench. Gladstone was now urging C.B. to enlist Rosebery's cooperation. C.B. was prepared to try to do this, but told Gladstone: 'I will hold the door wide open, but I shan't ring the dinner bell or hang out a flag of distress.'[73]

On the 15th C.B. spoke at Dundee. He began by saying: 'The election was a false election. We know it, and our opponents know it, and the best men among them are ashamed of it.' He referred to Chamberlain's 'vote for the Boers' slogan, which, he said, 'reached a depth of infamy in party malice'. There followed some gibes at Chamberlain – 'I am afraid if you look into any Parliamentary list you might find that there are one or two sitting members for Birmingham still left who have not been made Privy Councillors, and even they must by-and-by be exhausted.' Then he turned to his main theme:

> It is the merest calumny to say that we are indifferent to our Imperialist interests. It was to a great extent Liberal enterprise that founded the Empire. . . . But one of the surest ways of consolidating its strength is to avoid those blatant pretensions and that aggressive spirit which some seem to mistake for patriotism. . . .

He went on to quote Wolseley in praise of the Cardwell reforms, carried out under a Liberal government, which had enabled Britain to send so large an army to South Africa, and could not refrain from citing Lord Lansdowne as saying that the despatch of this army would not have been possible but for the scheme of reorganization, 'which he found when he went to the War Office having been elaborated by his Liberal predecessor, whoever that may have been, and which he took *en bloc* and published and put into force'.

Then came the invitation:

Lord Rosebery, to our great regret, went out of public life four years ago. None of us ever rightly understood why. . . . The door has always been open for Lord Rosebery's return. We should welcome him and rejoice to see him standing among his own comrades, and taking his share in carrying on, as he so well can, the work which they have been endeavouring to prosecute under the most unfavourable circumstances during his absence. Of one thing you may be quite sure, that Lord Rosebery will never come back to put himself at the head of a section. . . .[74]

It was not a very warm invitation – in the circumstances it could hardly have been so – but it had been extended. Harcourt thought the speech 'bold, able and effective . . . if he will sustain himself at that level nothing can shake him'.[73] The Liberal Imps, however, were not sure how far it could be regarded as an olive branch.

Grey wrote a civil letter to C.B. defining his position as a Liberal Imperialist and saying that the 'name and action are the natural result of men like Labouchere, Massingham, and the "Speaker" group claiming to be the only true Liberals'.[75]

C.B. sent a conciliatory reply, saying that he had no objection to their expressing their opinions, but had only condemned the actions of the Liberal Imperial Council. Of that, he told Grey: 'My whole theory of the party and its management implies complete toleration of all shades of opinion, and it is because this body set up exclusive claims that I found it – after considerable patience – necessary to rebuke it.' He went on to appeal to Grey:

Is it not worthwhile for us to consider how far we can come to-gether instead of working for division? I have over and over again suppressed my own views, and stood the racket of abuse for 'sitting on the fence' and pusillanimity, and I should have thought that others might be content in the general interest to do the same sometimes.

He argued that only one fifth of the party gave trouble. It comprised 'the wilder men at each flank'. 'Most Imperialist Liberals', he suggested, 'are in the 4/5ths, just as are most of the older school.'[76] In his reply, Grey said:

I feel deeply the self-sacrifice and chivalry with which you have tried the policy of compromise for the sake of unity; but I think that it has resulted in increased vitality of both extremes, each is contending for the ascendancy, one in the hope of getting you entirely on their side and pushing Rosebery further off; the other in the hope of bringing Rosebery back as leader. Anything would be better than the continuance of this exhausting uncertainty. . . .[77]

An apparent emissary from Rosebery did go to see C.B. at Belmont. This was Leicester Harmsworth, a millionaire Liberal Imp M.P. and a brother of the future Lord Rothermere. A less suitable man could hardly have been chosen. C.B. described him to his agent as 'the sort of man who is to me abhorrent apart from his politics'. Harmsworth asked if C.B. would serve under Rosebery. C.B. replied: 'Certainly, if I was willing to serve at all, and if his policy was sound.'[78]

To Sydney Buxton he wrote on November 21:

It was absolutely necessary to trounce this pretentious L.I. Council. I . . . could not sit quietly & let these fellows take command of the ship and order out half the crew.

But I said nothing against their opinions – in fact I share them, cum granis, being I hope a Liberal & also an Imperialist enough for any decent man. But when you put the two words together, L. and I, it is like pouring one part of a Seidlitz powder into the other. . . .

As to the troublesome R., it is time he must be in or out: as long as he is merely looking over the wall, there will be no peace for us. . . . Grey and his very superior set must be content not to be asserting their superiority at every turn. . . .[79]

Asquith was fussed about criticism of Milner. He wrote to Gladstone on November 26: 'I have told C.B. that to countenance an attack on Milner wd. be to split the party at once into fragments: this being the argument which appeals to him most. He suggested to me – characteristically enough – that a "via tertia" might be found: I suppose between attack & defence. . . .'[80]

The Dunfermline Liberal Association declared its continuing confidence in C.B. and he was described as a 'pillar steadfast in the storm'.

When Parliament reassembled in December, C.B. attacked the Government's policy of unconditional surrender, and urged generous treatment of the burghers. He spoke in vain. He told Gladstone on December 26: 'I am not an *enragé* Imperialist, but I am a sort of all-round Home Ruler. . . .'[81]

The Struggle against the Liberal Imps

So ended 1900. It had been a tough year. A determined challenge to his leadership had been fought off, but the party was still without any sense of discipline or common purpose. C.B. thought it best still to ride it on a loose rein, and allow personal views full play, however disruptive they might be. But he was determined to resist any attempt to capture the organization of the party. The party itself had lost an election and so faced five more years of opposition. It was a bleak prospect.

CHAPTER 22

Methods of Barbarism

'I can't understand what that miserable Campbell-Bannerman is up to: but thank heaven the Radicals will never get in again.'
Siegfried Sassoon, quoting his Aunt Evelyn, in 'Memoirs of a Fox-Hunting Man'

WHEN 1901 opened, C.B. felt that the time had come to take a stand and that no more concessions should be made to the Liberal Imps. South Africa was depressing. He told Ripon on January 9: 'I agree with all you say as to the black outlook and the Slough of Despond in which we are wallowing at the Cape. . . .'[1]

The anti-Imperialists received a substantial boost in January when a pro-Boer syndicate bought the *Daily News* for around £100,000. This entailed the departure of the Roseberyite editor, E. T. Cook, and was a counterstroke to the capture by the Imperialists of the *Daily Chronicle*. The new coup was organized by Lloyd George with the help of Cadbury money. C.B., writing to Harcourt on January 10, described it as 'a happy change. We shall now have something besides the Westminster Gazette that we can read.'[2] But two days later he told Harcourt: 'The ugly element is the indisposition of our people to speak . . . the only willing speakers either Lib. Imps opposing or cold watering, or Extremists playing the devil.'[3]

Politics were becoming increasingly bitter. On the 8th Lord Carrington wrote to C.B. about a banquet the Liberals were boycotting 'as it would be impossible for any of the party to sit down under Chamberlain's chairmanship & it would be a mockery to drink his health'.[4]

On the 18th he warned Bryce that 'we must be very careful not to take any line which might seem to be anti-British, for our countrymen, though sick at heart, are all the more touchy and obstinate, and if we are to have any influence we must not run counter at this moment to the policy in which the national dignity seems involved'.[5]

In addition to his political worries, C.B. continued to suffer the heavy burden of Charlotte's illness. He told Bryce that she was suffering greatly from 'gouty neuritis' and that the pain prevented her sleeping.

Bryce had some advice from Goldwin Smith in Toronto: 'Rosebery is a very bright star; but I am afraid he will do nothing but twinkle to the end. You had better stick to Campbell-Bannerman, who, though not great, has borne himself pretty well, it seems to me, through this business.'[6]

On January 22 Queen Victoria died. C.B. paid his tribute in the House on the 25th, speaking of the understanding between the Queen and her subjects. He was the only speaker to mention Queen Alexandra. King Edward VII acceded to the throne. C.B. and the new King, who were much the same age, had enough in common to make it easy for them to get on.

On February 9 C.B. had a letter from Bryce, describing Rosebery's views, and replied:

Thank you for your letter. It is most interesting in unfolding the views of 'son éminence grise'. I can however over-trump you, for I lunched yesterday with the Cardinal Prince himself.

There was not much in it all. Perfectly friendly, deeply interested, but immovably aloof . . . on S.A. . . . he was not nearly so one-sided . . . as those who cluster round his name.[7]

To Ripon he wrote: 'I lunched in Berkeley Square yesterday. I should say he is not steadfast & unmovable, but unmovable without being steadfast.'[8]

In February, and again in March, C.B. lunched with Merriman, the South African politician, whom he described to Bryce as 'a most taking and effective envoy'.[9] He told Ripon that Merriman had seen Chamberlain and 'found him ignorant and obstinate'.[10] In February, too, a new member made his maiden speech. C.B. sent him a line of congratulation and the member replied:

105, Mount Street
W.

Dear Sir Henry Campbell-Bannerman,

It was a great pleasure to me to receive your vy kind note: and I regard it as a great honour that you should have written it.

Yours vy truly,
Winston S. Churchill.[11]

Although the Liberals were still disunited, Chamberlain's attacks on all of them, including the Liberal Imps, were so savage that they had the effect of drawing them together. C.B. told Ripon: 'I have no complaint to make of the way I have been met even by the extremist men – Lloyd George, H. J. Wilson, C. P. Scott, Channing, Pirie &c.'[12]

When he spoke he stressed the need to offer the Boers reasonable terms, condemned the policy of unconditional surrender and denounced the burning of Boer farmhouses. Balfour in reply said that C.B.'s policy was apparently to give the Boers full representative institutions as soon as hostilities were over. This, he said, would be 'absolute insanity'.[13]

C.B. 'cordially seconded' the motion in the House granting £100,000 to Roberts to support the earldom to which he had been raised as a reward for winning the war. He had been approached on behalf of the Prince of Wales, as he then was, who thought the original proposal of £50,000 mean. The war however was, sadly, not won, but was now entering its grimmest, guerilla phase.

In February negotiations between Kitchener and Botha at Middelburg failed, and there was no alternative but to resort to the policy of 'clearing the country'. 8,000 blockhouses were built and a vast network of wire fences erected. The systematic burning or wrecking of the farms of burghers who had gone on commando was now intensified. Houses and furniture were burnt, gardens torn up, orchards cut down, cattle and sheep slaughtered. The homeless women and children were then collected into camps, improvised by the army, often in unsuitable places. 4,000 Boer women and 16,000 Boer children were to die in these camps.[14] A member of the Inns of Court Volunteers, Lionel Curtis, wrote:

> I cannot control my wrath as we go down the line and see the poor little homesteads in ruins. . . . What fool in his folly has taught us we could prevent men from brigandage by making them homeless. . . . Charley Rankin . . . told us he had been with a column who marched across the Free State east from Kroonstadt with orders to burn every farm indiscriminately. . . . It will take more years than I shall live to wipe out this stain. . . We are doing things that 100 years ago Wellington would have none of and which a year ago we should have said were impossible. Thank God X sees the sin and folly of it, but wrong has been done and more will be done before he can stop it.[15]

X was Milner. Milner himself, however, was increasingly bitter.

Just now [he wrote to Gell] the men still fighting us . . . and they are, for the most part, the lower class of the people . . . – are degenerating into absolute savagery . . . the clearer the rottenness, corruption, and virtual barbarism of the whole Boer system becomes, the more affectionate, and even gushing, the attitude of the ultra Liberals in England towards people who conspicuously trample every principle of Liberalism under foot. Every crime against Liberalism and humanity is pardonable in the eyes of those gentry on one condition, which is that it should be committed by an enemy of their country.[16]

Gell told him of signs of wobbling, even among Conservatives and Liberal Imps, and said: 'Grey goes off to Leonard Courtney – meets Merriman, – and comes back shaken and wobbly – talking as if Merriman's opinion was a serious ground for reconsidering our position. . . .'[17] Kitchener wrote drily to the Secretary of State for War, St. John Brodrick, on March 22: 'We are now carrying the war on to put two or three hundred Dutchmen in prison at the end of it. It seems to me absurd and wrong.'[18]

C.B. was elected President of the 'Eighty' Club and, speaking on March 2 at Oxford, advocated 'conciliation and friendship, not domination and ascendancy – because the British power cannot, there or elsewhere, rest securely unless it rests upon the willing consent of a sympathetic and contented people.'[19]

In March Harcourt wrote to Loulou that he had been to the House for the Army estimates – 'C.B. was quite sound in his argument but not sound in his wind, as he had a bad cold and was hardly audible, so I thought it right after dinner to reinforce his attack.'[20] One may be confident that Harcourt was audible.

The King was disturbed by C.B.'s attacks on the Government's South African policies and decided to urge Rosebery to come back and resume the leadership of the Liberal Party. On March 5 Salisbury's private secretary, Macdonnell, wrote to Knollys saying:

I have told Lord Salisbury of the proposal . . . that, in the event of Lord Kimberley's lamentable illness ending fatally, the King should send for Lord Rosebery, and ask him, in the interest of the Country, to resume public life and the Leadership of the Opposition.

The proposal is so novel and the personal considerations involved are so delicate that Lord Salisbury, as Leader of the Government, feels that he is almost the last person to express an opinion upon it; the very peculiar conditions of the Opposition, with which in its details he is imperfectly acquainted, would make him a bad adviser in such a matter: . . .[21]

The King saw Rosebery on the afternoon of the same day and may have tried to persuade him to come back. If he did he failed.[22]

So C.B. remained in possession. In May he spoke to the National Liberal Federation at Bradford. He said that the whole country was longing for peace, and that when a settlement did come there should be no trace in it of resentment or vindictiveness. He took issue with Lord Selborne, the First Lord of the Admiralty, who had spoken of 'hysterical nonsense as to conciliation' and had said that it would be better to have a 'gradual growth of mutual self-esteem'. This 'incomprehensible language', C.B. said, was extracted from Lord Selborne under the shock of which he started back in horror from the idea of conciliation. 'What a sentiment', he declared, 'to come from a Minister who has been engaged in the conduct of delicate affairs.'[23] It is not perhaps surprising that five years later C.B. had doubts about Selborne's suitability to continue under a Liberal government as High Commissioner in South Africa. On the same occasion Lloyd George described C.B. as 'the only leader whom we as Liberals recognize in the House of Commons: Sir Henry Campbell-Bannerman has, we all know, a sane head directing a thoroughly warm heart'.[24]

On May 24 Milner arrived in England on leave. Grey was among those who went down to Southampton to meet him. He was given an extraordinary reception, driving in state to Marlborough House, where he was received by the King and raised to the peerage. Chamberlain even tried to get him met by a royal carriage.[25] On the 25th Milner made a typically harsh speech:

It is hard that some of the busiest men in the world should . . . be put to inconvenience merely in order to prove . . . that the people of this country will not allow themselves to be bored into abandoning what they have spent millions of treasure and so many precious lives to attain. . . . I do not know whether I feel more inclined to laugh or to cry when I have to listen for the hundredth time to these dear delusions, this Utopian dogmatizing, that it only required a little more time, a little more tact, a little more meekness, a little more of all those gentle virtues of which I know I am so conspicuously devoid, in order to conciliate – to conciliate what? Panoplied hatred, insensate ambitions, invincible ignorance.[26]

Grey spoke up strongly for Milner,[27] but Morley described him as an 'imitation Bismarck'.[28] C.B. deliberately kept out of the public argument, but his sympathies were with Morley. At this stage C.B.was very far from regarding his own future Foreign Secretary as a sensible and solid person.

Milner took a great deal of trouble to keep his friends in the Liberal Party informed of his thinking and was rewarded with their uncritical support. This paralysed C.B.'s efforts to oppose effectively the Chamberlain–Milner policy in South Africa.

According to Beatrice Webb, the stand Asquith took this year was largely under the personal influence of his old friend Milner. Her own sympathies were wholly with the Liberal Imps and against what she and Sidney Webb saw as 'the "retreat" of the Liberal Party within the old lines of Gladstonianism, under the leadership of Campbell-Bannerman nominally, but of the pro-Boers actually'. C.B. himself she described as 'a weak vain man who all along has been in his heart pro-Boer'. After meeting him at a dinner in 1900 she wrote that he was 'a quite stupid person for a leader – well suited to a position of wealthy squire or a sleeping partner in an inherited business'. What the Webbs were doing, in their own words, was 'debunking Gladstonian Liberalism in order to clear the way for Fabian collectivism'.[29] In the circumstances it is odd that the previous June the Liberals should have tried to rope in Sidney Webb as a candidate at a lavish banquet given at Tweedmouth's house, at which Webb was seated next to C.B. The Webbs' judgement of the leading Liberals was as wrong as the party's judgement of them. To have selected Rosebery as an apostle of collectivism was particularly ludicrous.

In December 1900 the daughter of an Archdeacon in Cornwall sailed for South Africa. Miss Emily Hobhouse went out for the South African Women and Children Distress Fund. When she got there she bullied the authorities to let her travel round the concentration camps, where 60,000 Boer women and children were now confined. She swept round like a flame, ordering about the officers in charge of the camps, organizing the beginnings of cleanliness, sanitation and clean water, and bringing hope into the lives of broken Boer women. She was another from the same quiver as Florence Nightingale.[30] Horrified by what she saw of the results of the Army's policy, she came back in the same ship as Milner, and as soon as she got back she went round telling her story to anyone who would listen. She came to see C.B. In 1923 she wrote down her recollections of this meeting:

> The interview . . . remains vivid in my mind. Of all whom I saw at that time . . . he alone . . . seemed to have the leisure and the determination to hear and understand everything. . . . I was enabled to pour out to him more fully than to anyone else I met the detailed horrors of those camps. For nearly two hours he listened with rapt attention now and then putting a question to elucidate a point. As I dwelt upon the wholesale burning of farms and villages, the deportations, the desperate condition of a burnt-out population brought in by hundreds in convoys, the people deprived of clothes, bedding, utensils and necessities, the semi-starvation in the camps, the fever-stricken children lying . . . upon the bare earth . . . the appalling mortality . . . – he was deeply moved – and now and again murmured sotto voce 'methods of barbarism, methods of barbarism'. He was right. . . . He left the abiding impression of a man who spared no time or pains to arrive at truth and in whom wisdom and humanity were paramount.[31]

C.B. was profoundly impressed by Miss Hobhouse and the account she gave him. He realized that here was not simply an hysterical do-gooder, but a woman who knew what she was talking about and who was telling the truth. This was the reality behind the bombast, the true cost of the war in which 'Joe' and Milner had involved us and which Grey and Haldane applauded. He had the imagination to realize, as Asquith, Grey and Haldane never did, what it was like for a Boer woman to stand, with her children round her, and watch British soldiers burn down her barns and her home, shoot her sheep and cattle, and hack down her orchard trees, after which she and her children were driven off to a camp with little food and bad water to live or to die as luck might have it. His deep anger was aroused. If they knew what was going on his countrymen would not, he knew, tolerate it for a minute.

Lloyd George had raised in the House the 'appalling state of things' in the camps on May 24. He pointed out that in February and March a quarter of all the children in the camps – 261 out of 1,100 – had died. Brodrick, replying, claimed querulously that he could not remember all the statistics, 'with the immense labour I have to undergo at present', said that 'no doubt there are hardships, war is war', and that 'I do not pretend that the accommodation and food represent in any case luxury'.[32]

Now came a chance for C.B., boiling over with indignation as a result of Miss Hobhouse's account, to say what he thought. On the evening of June 14, a dinner was given to him and to Harcourt at the Holborn Restaurant by the National Reform Union. When C.B. spoke he said of the Government's policy:

> What is that policy? That now that we had got the men we had been fighting against down, we should punish them as severely as possible, devastate their country, burn their homes, break up their very instruments of agriculture. . . . It is that we should sweep – as the Spaniards did in Cuba; and how we denounced the Spaniards! – the women and children into camps . . . in some of which the death-rate has risen so high as 430 in the thousand. I do not say for a moment, because I do not think for a moment, that this is the deliberate and intentional policy of His Majesty's Government . . . at all events, it is the thing which is being done at this moment in the name and by the authority of this most humane and Christian nation. Yesterday I asked the leader of the House of Commons when the information would be afforded, of which we are so sadly in want. My request was refused. Mr. Balfour treated us with a short disquisition on the nature of the war. A phrase often used is that 'war is war', but when one comes to ask about it one is told that no war is going on, that it is not war. When is a war not a war? When it is carried on by methods of barbarism in South Africa.[33]

When C.B. died, a writer in the *Manchester Guardian* recalled 'as though it were yesterday' listening to that famous speech:

> He was evidently suffering from strong suppressed emotion. He began his speech on a very mild diplomatic note, but gradually became hotter as he went on. For once in a way he was speaking without notes, and that perhaps explained what followed. For suddenly he raised his voice and broke out into that passionate passage of the denunciation in which he described the war in South Africa as being conducted by 'methods of barbarism'. It was the only time that I ever saw him moved completely out of himself. . . .[34]

As so often, the press did not at once spot the importance of this passage in C.B.'s speech. They, and Liberals like Asquith, were at first more concerned about Morley's impromptu speech on the same occasion, which claimed that only those who shared the views then expressed were in the main stream of Liberalism. But the newspapers soon woke up to the challenge of his words. When they did, a Niagara of obloquy descended on C.B. Here, it was claimed, was a former Secretary of State for War insulting the British Army, the British soldiers and the generals. The man was a traitor, he was on the side of our enemies, he was unfit ever to lead a British government. An Episcopalian clergyman wrote to him from his Scottish parsonage:

> Sir,
>   You are a cad, a coward, & a murderer, & I hope you will meet a traitor's or a murderer's doom.[35]

C.B. thought this 'pretty stiff'.

The *Morning Post* said that it was a humiliating reflection that the sympathy of the nation with its soldiers could not protect them from 'these insults', which were 'as false as they are vexatious'.[36] *The Times* wrote: 'The Boers ... will not understand how slight a possibility there is that Sir Henry Campbell-Bannerman and his party will become responsible, for a long time to come, for the control of British policy.'[37] Rudyard Kipling denounced the

> Mildly nefarious
> Wildly barbarious
> Beggar that kept the cordite down.

Even C.B.'s friends, like Spencer, thought the phrase 'methods of barbarism' unfortunate, because it could so easily be twisted and represented to be an attack on the Army, rather than an attack on the Government's policy. Lord Crewe wrote that the 'phrase was of course seized on as an attack on the humanity of our soldiers, whom the speaker should have expressly exonerated before he used it'.[38] People outside the Government were not to know that, eight months before C.B. posed his conundrum, Milner himself had written to Chamberlain describing the policy of burning houses indiscriminately as '(1) barbarous, and (2) ineffectual'.[39] Lord Salisbury was told by his private secretary that the King was distressed at C.B.'s utterances, and wished to send for him and ask him to be very careful to avoid any language which might be interpreted abroad, or in South Africa, as encouragement to the Boers, but Salisbury advised the King not to do this.[40] Rosebery was consulted by the King on the same point on July 8 and gave the same advice, which was accepted. In *The Times* Lord Crewe defended C.B. against the charge that he was attacking the Army, but Lord Hugh Cecil insisted that he was doing so and commented: 'There is no more ungraceful figure than that of a humanitarian with an eye to the main chance', a jibe that in this case was wide of the mark. Winston Churchill joined in the correspondence, supporting Cecil and arguing that: 'When, therefore, Sir Henry Campbell-Bannerman speaks of "methods of barbarism", his charge applies to generals abroad not less than to Ministers at home. When he declines to press his charge against the generals, it is evident that either his logic or his courage is at fault.'[41]

The Unionists were, in fact, having a field day at C.B.'s expense, and some of his friends urged him to explain away or modify his criticisms. He declined to budge. Indeed in the House on the 17th he repeated the challenging words, saying: 'I never said a word which would imply cruelty . . . on the part of officers or men in the British Army. It is the whole system I consider, to use a word I have already applied to it, barbarous.'[42]

Predictably, Haldane defended the system of the clearances and the concentration camps. The intellectual approach to the problem was singularly chilling. C.B. voted for Lloyd George's motion on the camps and Miss Hobhouse's report, but the Liberal Imps declined to vote with him. Altogether fifty Liberals abstained.

C.B. was not the first Opposition leader to take a critical line in wartime. When he died the *Globe* said that he had 'rivalled and surpassed the exploits of Fox during the American War, and of Lord Holland and Brougham during the Peninsular'.[43] The *Saturday Review* also compared him to Fox. But not quite everyone thought he was taking an impossible line. Andrew Carnegie wrote to him on June 25, saying: 'As one who wishes my Native Land well – & would save her from disaster, I hope that she will never have to undertake the task of suppressing the Dutch. It can't be done, they are too much like the Scotch.'[44]

Mr. A. J. P. Taylor has written that 'Campbell-Bannerman re-united Radicals and Liberals by a stroke of genius. His attack on "methods of barbarism" switched the argument from the causes of the war to the way in which it was being conducted.'[45] This is to impute a political purpose to C.B. It seems doubtful whether he had such a purpose. He was simply protesting straightforwardly against something which deeply shocked him. Moreover there was to be little sign of Liberal unity in the next two years.

The Liberal Imps regarded the Holborn Restaurant speeches as amounting to a virtual declaration of war on them, and they determined to hit back. Rosebery himself wrote on June 20 to Spender:

> To me the banquet is a sinister event. There was nothing unforeseen and unexpected about it. C.B. knew exactly whom he would meet and met them. Moreover he made them a speech such as they might have made themselves. I do not see therefore how a schism can be avoided. Indeed I think it must have been in the minds of the organizers of the banquet to bring one about. . . .[46]

C.B. wrote to Ripon on the 22nd: 'What a week we have had – what scarps and counter-scarps, what an outburst of Milnerism! On the whole I think it tells for good, & I am more "cœur léger" than I have been for months.'[47]

There now ensued the somewhat ludicrous episode of mutual denunciation within the party at a series of public dinners. Asquith delivered a trenchant blast at the Liverpool Street Station Hotel on June 20 and plans were announced to give him a congratulatory dinner at the Hotel Cecil. C.B. wrote of this to a Liberal M.P.:

> I need hardly say that in ordinary circumstances I should have been delighted to hear of, & even to take part in, such a recognition of his merits. . . . But in view of . . . the frankly expressed intentions of its promoters, I could not but regard it as a serious assault on that Party unity which it ought to be our desire – it certainly is mine – to preserve. I have therefore been obliged to make known my objection to the proposal.[48]

Asquith wrote disingenuously to Gladstone: 'The dinner, as you may imagine, was no idea of mine, but it was put to me in such a way that I did not feel able to decline. The distinct understanding was that it was to be *in no sense* anti-C.B. . . .'[49]

As Henry Lucy put it:

> To dine or **not** to dine, that is the question. Whether 'tis nobler to suffer the slings and arrows of the outrageous John Morley, or, to

take a room at the Hotel Cecil, invite Asquith to dinner and make things hot for our pro-Boer brethren. Thus did Shakespeare in a little-known folio edition forecast the dilemma of the Liberal party today.

The Holborn Restaurant gathering, Lucy wrote, 'posed as the only and original Liberal party (N.B. – No connexion with the shop next door . . .). Mr. Asquith picked up the glove, and vigorously flung it back in the face of the challenger. Now the hot bloods of the party are for war to the knife – and fork.'[50]

C.B. was described by the more extreme Liberal Imps as 'the incubus' – a man who must be got rid of at any cost. He was, however, unmoved. Gladstone wrote to his brother on the 28th: 'Dear old C.B. is *not* the man for a crisis. He sits on the sofa, and is rather humorous. . . .'[51]

Gladstone was now doing his utmost to support C.B. He reported 'a pretty stiff ten minutes with Grey at 2 a.m. this morning'. He thought that Asquith had got into a hole about the dinner and that the need was 'to save A. from his friends'.[52] About this time C.B. said:

I don't want to form a Ministry, or to be a member of the Ministry. I have no ambition to serve, and this struggle has destroyed the health of my wife and my domestic peace, but I will not give way until I see Liberalism through the wood and the cause in the hands of men who have the true faith.[53]

Hamilton, who met him at a dinner on July 4, found him 'in high spirits and quite belligerent', and noted, 'He did not care a damn what people said of him, what concerned him . . . was the intrigues that had taken place.'[54]

He now decided that the crisis in the party had been reached. His predecessors, Rosebery and Harcourt, had laboured on under grievances they regarded as intolerable until they had flung out of the leadership. Their mistake, he thought, was not to have had it out openly with their opponents. He determined not to repeat this mistake. On July 2, in a speech at Southampton, he announced that the party was in a critical position. Lloyd George was impressed, writing: 'C.B. is doing well. His speech last night was excellent. He is showing his mettle and winning the respect of friend and foe.'[55] Asquith scented danger, and began to back-pedal, telling Gladstone on July 5, 'I shall do all I can to keep the peace'.[56] Then C.B. moved. He called a meeting of all Liberal M.P.s at the Reform Club for July 9. His critics were to be faced, and faced at once, with the choice of confirming his leadership or of finding someone else acceptable to the party as a whole. *Punch*'s political correspondent wrote of the Liberal leadership:

> The post was not tempting to any one as long as there was anywhere to be had the sweeping of a street crossing. Least of all men was it attractive for C.-B. Of assured position, wealthy, popular, disposed to enjoy the quiet things of life, he was the last man to hanker after a position that . . . soured the milk of human kindness even in the breast of Sir William Harcourt. . . . How has Sir Henry Campbell-Bannerman been treated by the party for whom he made colossal sacrifice? The question is answered in a single word. Abominably. . . . That C.B. has so long borne what has come to be the indignity of the post of Leader of the Liberal Opposition is crowning testimony to his impregnable good humour, his patience and his courage. But even a Campbell-Bannerman will turn at last. . . . Hence the meeting at the Reform Club on Tuesday. . . . There is no difficulty in forecasting its result. C.-B. is as indispensable to the Opposition today as he was in February two years ago. . . . He must stay where he is, because there is no one to replace him, a fact that makes meaner and more amazing the ingratitude with which he has been treated since he gave up to the Liberal party what was meant for Marienbad and Meigle. . . .[57]

So indeed it turned out. C.B.'s move was successful. The Liberal Imps who, although they supported the Government on South Africa, were hostile to the Conservatives and to Chamberlain on other issues, and had been unsparingly lashed by Chamberlain during the election, had nowhere else to go. C.B. addressed the meeting plainly and frankly:

> It becomes necessary for me to ascertain . . . whether I still retain your confidence . . . which is absolutely indispensable to any effort that I may make. . . . Our friends in the country . . . are discouraged, and they are mystified. If you go among them . . . they say: 'What on earth is the matter, that you people in the House of Commons cannot agree . . .?' Well, gentlemen, I am here to say to you deliberately and emphatically that we shall never restore healthy efficiency to the Liberal party in the House of Commons unless these cabals

are put down. . . . You know me; you know my faults, and my good points, if I have any. You know my views on all public subjects. . . . It is for you to say whether I enjoy that confidence which my position necessarily requires.[58]

The result was a substantial strengthening of C.B.'s position. Solid representatives of middle-of-the-road Liberal opinion came forward and spoke and a resolution of confidence was passed unanimously. Asquith and Grey had no alternative but to support it, and thereby to commit themselves publicly to C.B.'s continuing leadership. Asquith said that the differences in the party were real and could not be ignored, and he claimed to know nothing of any 'cabals'. Grey made a speech full of self-pity, pointing out that 'the best years of my life are slipping away'. C.B. made it plain that he had no objection to free expression of opinions, but would not tolerate any separate organization.[59]

In his speech C.B. had once more set out his own position on the main question at issue between him and his critics, that of South Africa. He said:

. . . let us promise that so soon as ordinary social conditions are re-established on the ending of the war, after a short interval of irregular government, the free, independent system of colonial self-government, so familiar to us, shall be set up, leading ultimately, if the several states so desire, to a federal constitution in South Africa.

Once more he was charting the future for his colleagues.
On July 13 he wrote to William Robertson:

. . . We have had an awful fortnight, but it has all ended well for the moment. . . .

The Asquith dinner is a stupid blunder. They cannot make it innocent, do as they like; it has the taint of its origin about it: and, honestly, every single man I have spoken to condemns it and wishes it given up. *This includes A. himself*, but he is so thirled to Grey and Haldane that he seems unable to offend them by openly renouncing it. . . . It is a striking picture of the obstinacy of the two I have named, and also of the weakness of A. I suspect Milnerism is at the bottom of it! but those gentry have made A. their tool in a great plot against me.

As to the interests of the Country (apt to drop out of sight in these quarrels!) they go from worse to worse. The prospects in S.A. are appalling . . . the policy of devastation and clearing the country is admitted to have failed. And what to do? No great change, I expect, will be made till Parliament is up and no questions can be asked.[60]

On the same day he wrote to a correspondent in Stirling, Mr. J. B. Smith:

The War Press made it out as a mere matter of personal good nature towards me: it is far more than that: it is the defeat of a determined effort for division . . . the wiser heads in the Govt. (e.g. Hicks Beach) are in something approaching despair. But the newspapers go on raving, & the mobs shouting.[61]

Milner told Haldane what he thought of the Leader of the Opposition:

C.B. really is too *revolting*. For absolute concentrated essence of the foolish and mal-a-propos, commend me to his recent utterances on the Transvaal question. Bêtise no. I to call his own countrymen 'Barbarians'. Bêtise II, to exaggerate the importance of the Boers in South Africa and treat the British as non-existent. Bêtise III – and most colossal of all – to make 'amnesty to rebels' a plank of his programme. . . . It is really is too sickeningly idiotic. What have we done as a nation, that our vital interests should be, even in the least degree, at the mercy of a trifler like that? But there. Personally I mean to keep my hands off him, out of regard for you and the difficulties of the good men and those who are still tied to him, however loosely.[62]

CHAPTER 23

The Widening Breach with Rosebery

ON July 16 Rosebery reacted to the Reform Club meeting and defined his position in a letter to the City Liberal Club, published in *The Times*. He said that after five years of self-imposed restraint he now felt himself free to speak. 'Not that I desire to re-enter the arena of party politics, far from it; I shall never voluntarily return to it.' He went on: 'If the war be unjust and its methods uncivilized, our Government and our nation are criminal and the war should be stopped at any cost. If the war be just, carried on by means which are necessary and lawful, it is our duty to support it with all our might. . . .' Rosebery argued that this was no transient difference:

> Fox . . . opposed the great war with France. But, in spite of his vast abilities and his splendid charm, he split his party . . . and excluded it from power for nearly 40 years. The truth is that statesmen who dissociate themselves from the nation in a great national question, such as a war, in which all strive and suffer together, dissociate themselves for much longer than they think. . . .

He described the Liberal throne as 'the most uneasy that has existed since the partition of Poland', said that the differences between the opinions of a man like Sir Wilfrid Lawson and a man like Sir Edward Grey, 'both honoured names in Liberalism', 'cannot by any conceivable compromise be reconciled', and that until the Liberal 'crew make up their mind towards what point they are to row, their barque can never move, it can only revolve'. The effort to pretend to keep up unity in the party was an 'organized hypocrisy'.[1]

Two days later he made a speech to the same club. He attacked the line taken by C.B., Harcourt and Morley at the Holborn Restaurant and said of the Reform Club meeting: 'I am glad of any vote that recognizes the trying situation in which my old friend Sir Henry Campbell-Bannerman has been working for the party; but I do not believe that by any such resolution . . . you can get rid of the fundamental division that exists in the Liberal party.'

He said that he did not despair of seeing the party, 'purged from all anti-national elements', proceeding in the work of domestic reform. Finally he described his own rôle: '. . . For the present . . . I must plough my furrow alone . . . but before I get to the end of that furrow it is possible that I may find myself not alone. . . .'[2]

He gave his supporters no warning of these utterances, in which he took his stand unequivocally against C.B. on the war. The second altogether stole the thunder from the dinner to Asquith the same evening, attended by Sidney Webb, whose wife described it as 'a scratch assembly'.[3] The theme of this was Liberal support for a just and necessary war. No one mentioned C.B. Asquith, Grey and Fowler spoke at it and Grey presided. But, typically, Rosebery had disregarded the problems of his followers. Even *The Times* was constrained to write: 'To denounce his own party on the one hand and the Government on the other, and to say, in the same breath, that he was going to retire from public life did not seem to us worthy of a statesman to whom the nation might fairly look for the conduct of its affairs.'[4]

Meanwhile, C.B. had appeared with Lloyd George on a platform at Pontypridd. The quick Welsh audience enjoyed his sallies and Lloyd George praised his 'magnificent speech', saying:

> . . . it is a great thing for us to have a leader with a cool head and a stout heart. Sir Henry has led us with patience, with skill, with courage, and with that hopefulness that is essential to every good Liberal. There is another qualification about him which people seem to forget and overlook when seeking for Liberal leaders; he has the one great and essential qualification in a Liberal leader of being a Liberal himself.[5]

On August 2 C.B. expressed anxiety in the House about farm-burning and the hatred being aroused by the concentration camps. Chamberlain's reply was so rancid that even Grey was moved to protest. But Grey still supported the Government on the substance of the question, and Channing, writing to C.B. on the 7th, described Grey's speech as 'the climax of logical & moral unreason & incoherence'.[6]

C.B. stuck to his guns and at Peckham on August 7 explained 'why I have denounced and, heaven helping me, will continue to denounce, all this stupid policy of farm-burning, devastation, and the sweeping of women and children into camps'.[7] Chamberlain continued to pour scorn on him. At Blenheim on the 10th he said of his old party: 'Fifteen years ago they were a great and powerful and a united party, and they were led by Mr. Gladstone. Today they are a rump and they are led by Sir Henry Campbell-Bannerman.'[8]

Different views have been expressed about the effect on the Boers of Liberal criticism of the Government at this time, and specifically of C.B.'s attacks, culminating in the speech at the Holborn Restaurant. The extreme case against him is put by Lord Roberts's biographer. He quotes the speech by Sir Michael Hicks Beach on October 10, 1901, when he said:

> The real cause of the prolongation of this war has been something which, on my word, I believe could never have been seen in any other country in the world. It has been the speeches in Parliament of British members of the House of Commons, doing everything they could against their country and in favour of her enemies.

Mr. James comments on this: 'Innumerable quotations from speeches by Sir Henry Campbell-Bannerman, John Redmond and others, all of which were circulated among the Boer commandos, could be adduced in support of this contention.'[9]

To accept this view, it is necessary to believe that in time of war, even a distant colonial war posing no threat to the United Kingdom, the only patriotic attitude is 'my country, right or wrong', and that had it not been for the Liberal criticism of the Government, the Boers would soon have abandoned their guerilla war. There is no evidence at all that the Boers would not have continued to resist, as they did, to the last possible moment. Only a refusal to recognize the essential toughness and determination of the Afrikaner could lead one to suppose that their will to resist was really affected by speeches made by politicians in opposition six thousand miles away in England.

What C.B.'s speeches did do was to give some of the Boer leaders a feeling that England did not consist entirely of people like Milner, Chamberlain and Rhodes, that the tradition of Bright and Gladstone was not dead, and that there was still a chance that a self-governing South African state, governed if necessary by a Boer party, could exist within the loose framework of the British Empire. This was what Botha meant when he said to J. A. Spender in July 1909: 'Three words made peace and union in South Africa – "methods of barbarism".'[10] Spender recorded that Botha

> . . . went on to speak of the tremendous impression which had been made upon men fighting a losing battle with an apparently hopeless future by the fact that the leader of one of the great English parties had had the courage to say this thing, and to brave the obloquy which it brought upon him. So far from encouraging them to a hopeless resistance it touched their hearts and made them think seriously of the possibility of reconciliation.[11]

C.B. was, as usual, at Marienbad in the autumn. From there he wrote to Bryce on August 29 about a speech by Asquith on belligerent rights: 'That our friend who came to the rescue of the Govt . . . should have stooped so low shews how far the religio Milneriana can carry a man. I fear it shews also a vicious determination to stick at nothing in his, and his friends', separation from us. I agree that it is the worst symptom yet disclosed.'[12]

To Gladstone he wrote on September 12: 'The old war appears to rub along in the accustomed style. I wish Kitchener would not in a despatch speak of the "total bag" consisting of 67 Boers killed, so many wounded, so many cattle . . . etc . . .'[13]

In the September issue of the *Nineteenth Century*, Sidney Webb wrote: 'The new generation have lately witnessed Sir Henry Campbell-Bannerman piecing together the Gladstonian rags and remnants. . . . Lord Rosebery is the only person who has . . . called for a completely new outfit'. Webb denounced Gladstonian Liberalism as 'thinking in individuals' and as hostile to the State, and called on Rosebery, Asquith, Grey and Haldane to produce a policy of 'National Efficiency'.[14] C.B. said in his letter to Gladstone: 'We have had the benefit of instruction by Mr. Sidney Webb, and survived it. . . . I fear I am too old to join that academy.'[15]

On the 19th, on his way back to England, he wrote to Harcourt from Vienna, saying: 'I regard the time before us as exceedingly critical, and the question will arise whether an open split can be avoided. . . . I hope you will open your batteries again. . . .'[16] He proposed, however, to stop for only two days in London, and Harcourt, urging him to stay for a third and receiving no reply, wrote indignantly to Morley on October 2:

> His casualty and indifference does himself and his supporters great injustice. I regard Asquith's speech as a regular declaration of war. The Perks gang are evidently determined to navigate their own ship. . . . If C-B is not to abdicate he must put his foot down or forever hold his peace. . . .[17]

Morley was equally impatient. He replied to Harcourt: 'It is quite certain that the Perksians, using Asquith's brains, are now going to make a desperate push to the front. Nor do I see how under the banner of so slow a leader as C.B. we are to make an effective fight. . . .'[18]

On October 1 an article on the Liberal Party by Dr. Joseph Parker appeared in *The Times*. He said of C.B.:

> He was . . . suddenly called upon to carry the heavy end of a heavy beam, and if he has staggered under it for a moment now and then who has any right to upbraid or reproach him. Sir Henry . . . has deported himself with marked ability and with all but unparalleled forbearance and courtesy. He has not been treated with adequate loyalty.

Beatrice Webb wrote in her diary:

> . . . the Liberal Party seems cleaved into two equally unpromising sections – Rosebery appealing to the grey mass of convictionless voters on the broad and shallow ground of Empire and efficiency; C-B relying on every description of separatist interest, on all the 'antis' – anti-war, anti-United Kingdom, anti-Church, anti-capitalist, anti-Empire. Both combinations seem to me equally lacking in health and vigorous root principles.[19]

This judgement was hardly fair to either group.

The Government proclaimed September 15 as the date for the close of legitimate hostilities in South Africa. The Boer commandos overlooked this proclamation and the war went on. A statement by the Lord Chancellor, Lord Halsbury, that only 'a sort of war' was now going on was regarded as particularly inept. Chamberlain was more grimly determined than ever, and declared:

> I think the time has come – is coming – when measures of greater severity may be necessary, and if that time comes, we can find precedents for anything we may do in the action of those nations who now criticize our 'barbarity' and 'cruelty' . . . in Poland, in the Caucasus, in the Franco–German war. . . .[20]

This statement did not make things easier for the Foreign Office. Sir Harold Nicolson wrote in his life of his father that it was only when the Boer War began 'that the full effects of Lord Salisbury's policy of splendid isolation could be gauged. Great Britain woke up infamous. British opinion was shocked to discover over-night how much we were disliked.'[21] Many aspects of Unionist policy were indeed now beginning to look questionable.

Privately, too, Chamberlain was less sure about a tough policy than he pretended to be in public. On November 4, for example, he wrote to Milner:

> If we are really asked to authorize greater severity, a case must be made for us. . . . The result of this strange with-holding of necessary information is that pro-Boers are able to talk of the 'methods of barbarism' practised by British generals with the approval of the British Government, and we have no information at our disposal which would enable us to justify the shooting of a single Boer.[22]

Milner had now taken over the camps from the military. He told Haldane that they were a 'sad fiasco'. He put in charge of them a young man who had contested Lloyd George's criticisms in the *Spectator*. His name was John Buchan. They found the children, as Buchan wrote, 'dying like flies', but with characteristic energy they revolutionized the whole system and greatly reduced the death rate.[23] Milner's letter to Chamberlain admitted that 'the black spot – the one very black spot – in the picture is the frightful mortality in the concentration camps. I entirely agree with you in thinking that while a hundred explanations may be offered and a hundred excuses made, they do not really amount to an adequate defence.'[24]

In October, the main Liberal leaders, including Asquith and C.B., had addressed the same audience in Scotland. Morley wrote to Harcourt on the 20th:

> Tweedmouth has been giving me an account of the Edinburgh meeting. It listened to A. with attention, but without . . . any signs of enthusiasm. Grey was much more warmly received, not for what he said, but for himself. But without question the heartiness of the meeting was for C.B.   T. pointed this out to A and G, and assured them that they could not get on an inch against C.B. or without him. On the other hand is convinced that if C.B. were to take any steps against them, he also would find that the bulk of the party would not like it.[25]

This seems to have been a correct assessment by a man who, as a former Chief Whip, knew how to judge party feeling. Tweedmouth regarded the situation as a stalemate, but Harcourt pointed out in his reply that 'as Bismarck said *beati possidentis* and if C.B. will only stick to it he will be *beatus*. He is however unfortunately shaky.'[26]

Now that Harcourt had given up any responsibility for directing the party's policy he had relapsed happily into the position of a back-seat driver and wrote voluminously to C.B., supplying him with arguments on South Africa and other problems. On the 25th he told Morley: 'I sent my "cram" to C.B. a few days ago. He has the merit of generally being better than one expects. . . .'[27]

On the same day C.B. spoke in his constituency at Stirling. 'My business', he said, 'is to keep the head of the ship straight, whatever be the theory of navigation which possesses the minds of some members of the crew.'

Then he dealt with South Africa, beginning with a tribute to the Army:

> If the war was not ended long ago it is not for lack of any courage or capacity in our soldiers, who, from first to last, whether on the stricken field under the spur and incitement of a great battle, or in the miserable weary drudgery and obscurity of more desultory warfare, always displayed those unequalled qualities which gave them a foremost place among the military forces of the world.

He soon turned to the crucial question of the settlement, and quoted an old song about the departure of the Grenadier Guards for the Crimea where they were to fight 'side by side with our old traditional enemies, the French'. As they marched over Waterloo Bridge, the song ran:

> Bridge of Waterloo, name of happy omen,
> For the staunchest friends are wrought
> Out of the bravest foemen.

This jingle from the distant days when he was seventeen exactly expressed C.B.'s philosophy. He went on: 'Why can we not do it in South Africa? Because our ministers have barred the way.'

He repeated his criticism of the way the war was now being conducted by Kitchener: The whole country in the two belligerent states outside the mining towns is a howling wilderness. . . . When the war is . . . ended . . . the 50,000 prisoners of war will, of course, return to what by some sort of irony we may perhaps be permitted to call their home.'

He quoted a rash phrase by the Unionist Civil Lord of the Admiralty. This man, perhaps the 'most obscure member of his Majesty's Government', had said, 'to finish a war was one thing, to subdue a race another'.

C.B. concluded: 'Was not one Ireland enough? These methods, this policy, this spirit, which have worked such havoc in South Africa, what are they but the very spirit and policy and methods which England has offered to Ireland through many generations, with the result that we now see before us. . . .'[28]

Unlike his colleagues, C.B. recognized that the Government's policy might permanently alienate the Boers. Indeed some of them did become irreconcilable – Hertzog, for example, two of whose children died in the camps.

Harcourt thought that 'C.B. . . . acquitted himself well at Stirling . . . his speech had courage and sense'. He remarked that 'C.B. has so completely exhausted my "cram" in his speech that I find little more to suggest'.[29] Morley, as usual, was more critical: 'I think what C.B. said was right in itself but I agree that though the aim is good the powder is weak. However, we must fight with what weapons we have. . . .'[30]

C.B. himself was in good heart. He wrote to Ripon on October 30:

The revolt of our 'Lib. Imps' – the *Chartered* Company as I call them – has failed: the Asquith demonstration squib fizzed off the wrong way; and, for the present, things go well. But how painful to be obliged to set oneself against one's most intimate colleagues.

. . . I do not see how frank coöperation can be resumed after this projected mutiny.[31]

John Morley was staying with C.B. and Charlotte at Belmont for the first four days of November. On his return to London he wrote to Harcourt: 'C.B. when I told him that R. was thinking of a concentration govt. which should include C.B. himself, said – "Very well – if he takes the right line in policy, I should have no objection to co-operate." '[32]

On the 13th C.B. wrote to Harcourt, saying:

Everything I hear in Scotland is satisfactory. Even the Scotsman complains that we have 'captured' the local associations. A novelty, that when the official organization passes a resolution of confidence in the leader it is 'captured'! Considerable doubts and misgivings as to the ploughman, but disposition to welcome him if the furrow is straight – not otherwise.[33]

On November 19 C.B. spoke at Plymouth. He denied that he had 'ever uttered one syllable which could be twisted into encouragement of the Boers' – an answer to an accusation by Salisbury – and accused the Government of trying to hunt the enemy to death – 'with the result that the war is in its third year'. This time he did not hesitate to put the blame where he believed it belonged: 'For my part I despair of this peril being conquered so long as the present Colonial Secretary is in Downing Street and as long as the present High Commissioner is at Pretoria.'[34]

Harcourt told Spencer two days later: 'I must say I give great credit to our C-B for the plucky way in which he is fighting his corner and he seems to me to show to great advantage contrasted with the rest. I thought his Plymouth speech as good as could be. . . .'[35]

Harcourt was constantly, and obviously genuinely, praising C.B.'s platform speeches. These never soared to heights of eloquence, but were closely reasoned and had a ring of common sense.

Asquith was still a long way from C.B. on the war. In a speech on the 23rd he claimed that the war had to go on because the Boers were fighting for independence, 'the thing which even Sir Henry Campbell-Bannerman has recognized as impossible'. He also put his name forward as a candidate for the presidency of the 80 Club in succession to C.B. and became a member of the Imperial Liberal Council. Morley asked Harcourt:

. . . I wonder how Asquith's new move strikes you. To me it seems rather grave for C.B. I suppose it is meant to be a *riposte* to C.B.'s speeches last week. It was certain he would have to do something, but this looks like the worst thing he could have done – to join a sectional organization formed inside the party, with the avowed design of countering the leader of the party.

It makes it more difficult than ever for C.B. to carry on, and I am sure, from his tone and temper when I was at Belmont, that it will *provoke* him extremely. . . .[36]

Harcourt replied: 'I believe both in speech and in act he is evidently bent on making C.B.'s position impossible.'[37]

C.B. however was buoyed up by the reception he got in the country. He told Ripon on the 28th that in north Lancashire he had found 'zeal, enthusiasm, loyalty . . . it is a wonderful change: we must just hold on and trust that the country will come to its right senses'.[38] He was amused too by the fact that Rosebery, to whom the Liberal Imps looked to save the situation, was taking so long to produce his panacea. He wrote to Gladstone on November 29: 'What I find occurs to some people is that when a saviour of society comes to the rescue of the empire he usually takes less than six weeks to tie his shoes & pack his trunk. Perhaps he does not know what to put in his trunk!'[39]

The Liberal Imps were, however, still in full cry against him. Grey spoke in Glasgow on November 28, and *The Times* wrote next day:

. . . he made it quite clear that the Liberal party he wants to see re-established is not the Liberal party of Sir Henry Campbell-Bannerman and the pro-Boers . . . it would have been too absurd for Sir Edward Grey to follow in the track of Sir Henry Campbell-Bannerman. That futile politician was further very conspicuously thrown over when Sir Edward Grey scouted the notion that representative institutions can be set up in the annexed territories as soon as the war is over, and pointed out that it is impossible to negotiate with the Boers, since they do not accept any basis except restoration of the Dutch Republics. . . . Sir Edward Grey strongly approves of Lord Milner as the right man in the right place, possessing the confidence of the British people and the respect of both races in South Africa.[40]

There was, at any rate, no doubt as to where *The Times* stood.

By early December, Harcourt thought that C.B. was secure. On the 8th he wrote to Morley: 'C.B. is finally fixed in the motor machine of the Party, and Perks & Co. will find it impossible to displace him.'[41] Nevertheless a clash seemed inevitable, and like an old war-horse, Harcourt was aroused: 'I think our dear C.B.'s Dunfermline speech very good – worthy of the "blood red wine" of its Kings. The issue is now fairly joined. I see Grey & Asquith are now announced to assist at the Rosebery Meeting. . . . It is plain we shall have to fight the Trojans for the plucky C.B. I feel sure that his courageous course will rally great support for him. . . .'[42]

The party managers noted that support for C.B. among the rank and file was undiminished. Robert Hudson told Gladstone early in December that at a meeting of the National Liberal Federation at Derby, there had been a 'marked feeling of enthusiasm' for C.B. though there was 'weariness and disgust at our own internal dissensions'. Gladstone passed this report to Rosebery, and told him:

> The enthusiasm of the rank and file, speaking generally, is with C.B., though I think most men strongly disagreed with his phrase about methods of barbarism. Our people say that he has done the work in the country and that for 2 years he has faced almost single-handed A.J.B. and Chamberlain in the H. of C. This can never be forgotten. On the other hand those who differ with C.B. on the war are strong in ability and in money. . . . Either section beyond question can wreck the other. . . .[43]

There was however no real doubt now that the grass roots of the party were solidly for C.B.

CHAPTER 24

Chesterfield and Berkeley Square

WHEN Bryce returned from abroad, C.B. wrote to him from Belmont describing the manoeuvres of Rosebery and the Liberal Imps:

> We have passed through a most exciting and critical time while you have been away, and it is a great pity you have not been able to follow it.
>
> 1. Open mutiny: full steam on.
> 2. Chief mutineer disappoints followers: fiasco.
> 3. Loyal crew see *at last* what game is; rise like one man against mutineers.
> 4. Outside Potentate, in whose interest mutiny appeared designed, twigs failure: cold water applied.
> 5. Working Captain tours in England and elsewhere: ignores mutineers, talks about object of voyage and rocks ahead. Everywhere enthusiastic confidence.
> 6. Potentate aforesaid says he must save the country – urgent and critical – hang the plough; can no longer stand aside; will in six weeks be ready to utter the words which will save us from ruin. Takes some time, naturally, to think what will be most popular.
> 7. Dec. 13: Six weeks not yet up: still thinking. General fuss: importance of position greatly relished by potentate. . . .[1]

Bryce replied saying, 'All agree that your campaign & particularly your plain speaking, has done great good, & that the rally to you is clear and strong.'[2]

Rosebery

W. V. Harcourt *by F. C. Gould*

C.B. was referring in his letter to an announcement which had been made early in November that, in view of the serious position of national affairs, Lord Rosebery had felt constrained to accede to the invitation of a Liberal association at Chesterfield to address its members, so that he could throw his opinions into the 'common stock'. For six weeks there was mounting speculation about what he was going to say, and few political speeches have been more eagerly awaited. Rosebery was, if nothing else, a master of publicity.

The speech was made on December 16, the occasion being organized by Perks on behalf of the Liberal Imps. By then, the excitement was intense. C.B. wrote in the morning to Mr. Donald Crawford:

> Belmont Castle, Meigle, Scotland
> Die Fest. Beat. Archib[i]
> apud profanos 16 Dec. 01.
>
> *Entre nous*
>
> This is indeed the appointed day – the 4th or 5th Advent of a new Messiah, though I fear in this case neither Virgin nor Holy Ghost has much to do with it.
>
> What a characteristic business all along. The announcement (carefully pipelaid) – What ho, to the rescue! – but no immediate action. The case well-nigh desperate, (otherwise why leave the stilts so recently taken in hand?) but six weeks preparation necessary. Six weeks of fuss and of genuine enjoyment – never did anyone get so much out of the penny-a-liners before. And now, the fatal hour!!
>
> It is a' ane to Dandy – I do not see that his allocution will matter much to anyone but himself – . . .
>
> We shall see . . . as usual I do not care a dump either way.[3]

The Chesterfield speech turned out to be a two-hour exposition of the cogitations of the lonely ploughman. On South Africa, although Rosebery defended the policies of the concentration camps and martial law, his views were not so very different from C.B.'s. According to Lord Crewe, Rosebery thought some of his friends had 'gone too far in their canonization of Milner'.[4] Rosebery criticized Milner's determination to avoid a settlement and asked the Government to remember Lord North and the revolt of the Netherlands against Philip of Spain. He suggested a meeting 'at a wayside inn' of two representatives of each side to begin negotiating a settlement. He criticized 'Toryism . . . in Liberal circles':

There are men who sit still with the fly-blown phylacteries of obsolete policies bound round their foreheads, who do not remember that while they have been mumbling their incantations to themselves, the world has been marching and revolving, and that if they have any hope of leading it or guiding it they must march and move with it too. I hope, therefore, that when you have to write on your clean slate, you will write on it a policy adapted to 1901 or 1902, and not a policy adapted to 1892 or 1885. . . . It is not to Party that I appeal. I appeal to Caesar . . . the tribunal of public opinion and common sense. . . .[5]

He also preached Sidney Webb's doctrine for Liberals – that of 'efficiency'. There could be little doubt now that Rosebery wanted the party to rally to him, and expected to be the next Liberal Prime Minister. But, as always, he did not propose to come down into the arena to contend for the leadership. The party must come to him.

C.B. had had no advance warning of the line Rosebery was to take, though he had known for a long time that Rosebery did not share his disciples' enthusiasm for Milner. On the day the speech was made he wrote to Channing: 'I have received no communication whatever from first to last: any more (less) than if I had been playing Kitchener to their De Wet.'[6] It was a fair comment on the relations between the Liberal Imps and the man whom they had joined in confirming as leader only five months before.

The *Westminster Gazette*, edited by J. A. Spender, was in no doubt about the political significance of the speech:

Did Lord Rosebery join hands with Sir Henry in the great work of conciliation? No. He stabbed the Liberal leader under the fifth rib. . . . The Liberal Imperialists cling all the closer to Lord Rosebery, who in his speech denounced their South African policy, and flung mud at their god of idolatry, Lord Milner. The truth of the matter is that Lord Rosebery . . . will never allow any man to sit unmolested upon the throne which he abdicated. . . . If Lord Rosebery is not to rule, there shall be no King in Israel.[7]

On December 17, the day after the speech, C.B. wrote to Sinclair, saying: 'It leaves things no better than before: the same mystery, the same underground enmity, the same unsettled uncomfortable position.'[8]

The same day Gladstone, whose aim was to bring Rosebery and

C.B. together, and who was much less percipient than the *Westminster Gazette*, wrote to Spender:

> Here is a possible basis for an alternative Govt. . . . You probably know C.B.'s mind as well as I do. It is plastic yet tenacious. I wish you would write to him or see him & urge that . . . we should attack the Govt. next month on the lines of R's proposals. . . . Should he take R in a crabbed or hostile spirit I believe he would be left almost high & dry. . . . I want him to reap all the honour & reward due to him for his services & I can't help thinking that if we miss this opportunity we shall be written down as small & foolish people. . . .[9]

Gladstone also wrote a long letter to C.B. himself suggesting that 'we ought to sink differences', since there was 'so much that is broad, generous & wise in what he says . . .'.[10] C.B. replied on the 18th:

> I have your meditations upon Chesterfield. I agree that the views on peace & war . . . are not unreasonable: though it is unfortunate that they run counter to the very two things our people in the country care most about – Milner & Camps. I also agree that Aaron, Q.C. and Sir E. Hur, who were there to hold up the prophet's hands, must have held up their own at some of the things they were expected to swallow, and did swallow with avowed gratitude. So far so good. All that he said about the clean slate and efficiency was an affront to Liberalism & was pure claptrap – Efficiency as a watchword! Who is against it? This is all a mere réchauffé of Mr. Sydney Webb who is evidently the chief instructor of the whole faction. . . .
>
> What is a flyblown phylactery?
>
> Flyblow is the result of a fly laying the egg from which maggots come in meat: no fly out of bedlam wd. choose a phylactery (if he found one) for such a purpose.[11]

To Spencer he described the 'clean slate' part of the speech as 'not only mischievous but silly – mere Sydney Webb and water: it must be read in the light of Webb's September article'.[12] Spender, however, despite what he had written in the *Westminster*, was impressed by Gladstone's view, and went to see C.B. to try to persuade him to make an advance to Rosebery.

Meanwhile Edward Grey (or 'Sir E. Hur'), who had been at Chesterfield, was deeply stirred. He wrote to Sydney Buxton, saying of Rosebery that his 'attack upon the Govt. is the true line of attack, but it is utterly spoilt . . . by C.B. and the "pro-Boers". I have made my last speech upon the Reform-Club-compact platform, and shall speak next time entirely on Rosebery lines. . . .'[13]

On the 21st Grey wrote to Spender, saying:

> Rosebery knocked four bad points, dear to all 'pro-Boers' on the head. They are
>
> 1. That martial law in Cape Colony should be denounced.
> 2. That the war is being carried on (on our side) by methods of barbarism.
> 3. That the Govt. should make overtures of peace.
> 4. That Milner should be recalled or superseded. . . .
>
> These are the four points on which C.B. asks us to concentrate; I disagree with them all. . . .

Grey went on:

> I think now that we ought to have split at the Reform Club in July: those of us who wanted to attack the Govt. on Rosebery lines could then have ignored C.B. As it is with our leader going on the pro-Boer tack, we have had to guard ourselves. But the thing can't go on. If C.B. closes with the Rosebery line *he must drop what is* inconsistent with it.

In a long postscript Grey argued that the Liberal Party was 'discredited, dissipated & ruined because, except for Asquith, every one of our leaders let the "hissing factionists with ardent eyes" run the whole party unreproved in a time of national crisis'.[14]

Rosebery's Liberal colleagues in the House of Lords were not, however, carried away. Ripon wrote to Spencer on December 22:

> The mode in which R. treats C-B is to me most unsatisfactory and, as you say, ungenerous, and I am afraid we must see in it a readiness to back up the intrigues of Haldane and Co. I take it that at this moment their foremost wish is to get rid of C-B. . . . This, it seems to me, we must firmly resist. C-B under almost unparalleled diffi-

culties has done excellent work for the Party . . . we must stand by him.[15]

The old guard of the party were closing ranks. But the Liberal Imp militants still hoped that Rosebery's speech would result in a reconstituted party. Haldane wrote of it to Milner the same day:

> It was part of his art that by being critical he has detached the Centre Liberals from C.B. . . . and made continuity of policy an assured thing. . . . we ought to be able to repulse heavily any attack C-B may make. . . . I would not for a great deal be in the latter's boots. . . . The Opposition instinct in the constituencies has inclined the wirepullers to go with C.B. Though I do not for a moment doubt that he has failed to get hold of the bulk of the Liberal voters.[6]

There was a strong element of wishful thinking in this analysis. Urged on by Spender and others, C.B. had decided to have it out with Rosebery. The first effort misfired. He told Harcourt on December 22:

> Pondering over the situation I came to the conclusion that it would be very desirable that I should beard the Douglas in his halls, and today I went up to Berkeley Square. But he was out, so I left a card and came away.
>
> The main reason was . . . the . . . accusation brought against me . . . that I am the obstacle to the return of R., and it was . . . necessary to dispel the illusion. . . . I suspect he won't come as a Liberal back to the L. Party, and this ought to be understood. . . .[17]

Next day C.B. did see Rosebery. He lunched with him in Berkeley Square and afterwards the two of them had a frank talk. C.B. described the interview in a letter to Harcourt written that evening after he had gone down to spend Christmas at the Lord Warden Hotel at Dover:

> I propounded the great enquiry, what does it all mean? and I gathered that it does not mean what the quidnuncs suppose. He has left the L. Party . . . he is not (in ecclesiastical phrase) 'in communion with us'; active co-operation is impossible. Ireland especially stands in the way. . . .

On the war, is not aware what other people have been saying; took his own line. Is against Milner, against the policy of harshness, believes he himself could make peace to-morrow.

What did he mean when he said he would do all in his power? This was if the country called on him, not the Party. His cards are on the table. Is he going to play them? Yes, by activity in the House of Lords.

The conclusion is no change, no return, no coalition with old friends.

All this very amiably and quietly stated.

I neither urged nor even suggested anything; merely made enquiries as to the meaning of things. . . .

J'y suis, j'y reste.[18]

To Lefevre he said that Rosebery was 'dead against' Home Rule '*in any form*'.[19]

C.B. knew that he was now fighting for his political life. He bestirred himself to an unusual degree, writing fully to his chief political colleagues and to influential newspaper editors to explain and justify his position and keeping copies of these letters in his own hand.

On Boxing Day 1901, for example, still down at Dover, he wrote to C. P. Scott of the *Manchester Guardian*:

I am stranded here . . . and . . . not fully informed of what is going on. But I am told that the M. G$^{n.}$ is saying that our only hope lies in a coalition between R. & the 'Lib leaders', and thus is following up the general cry that it rests with us (or me!) now to accept or refuse a splendid offer. I am constrained therefore to give you *in the strictest secrecy*, a hint. . . .

You are all on the wrong tack: there has been no offer of help to the Party – it was to the Country. He will not join in: even on the War. There never has been (with one exception which we all know of and which will not stand in the way) any unwillingness on our part for his return: this is absolute. The impediment is that *he won't*.

His friends are busy putting it the other way, whether from ignorance or from malice: and great mischief comes of it. Yet at present I am barred from telling what I know and thus taking all possible ground of blame off myself. What was said last week about the War was substantially what I have been saying for months & getting abused & intrigued against for. . . .

You may safely take your line founding upon this: but for heaven's sake don't allude to it, unless you can evolve it from the speech itself.[20]

Grey was still in an excited frame of mind, and on Christmas Eve had written to Gladstone on much the same lines as he had earlier to Spender: 'I don't think the Reform Club arrangement can stand any more, and if it goes, there goes with it on my part the recognition of C.B.'s leadership: unless of course C.B. can for the sake of union take the Rosebery point of view as a whole.'[21] Gladstone sent the letter on to C.B. at Dover, writing himself, in an effort to turn away wrath:

> The enclosed letter from G. reached me this morning. The spirit moved me to reply at some length for G. reveals, in my opinion, all the chief weaknesses which prevent him from being a useful leader of men. He plumps for R. expects you to drop everything he doesn't like, and the condition of his help is that everyone whose views on S.A. are not his or R's . . . should cry Peccavi.
>
> Yet I have tried to write as Moderator pointing out that he is talking without knowledge of your views on Chesterfield. So please don't treat the letter as at all final. . . .[22]

C.B. was, not surprisingly, outraged, and replied to Gladstone:

> I return Grey's letter. I am hardly equal to characterizing it – impertinent is the word that comes uppermost. It shews the spirit and I fear this may be recognized as irreconcilable. . . . The whole thing is unreal – egotism masquerading as patriotism!
>
> His letter is on all fours with what Ronald & Haldane have been saying in Scotland, and these three are no doubt solidaire. I do not believe A. is with them except it be by force majeure. I think it would be most desirable that you should see Asquith and I hope you would discover him to be in a better spirit. . . .
>
> The whole thing is utterly odious for honest people to have to deal with. . . .[23]

As always, C.B. realized that Asquith was the key man.
Ripon and Bryce were given a full account of the talk with Rosebery.

Ripon replied approving the position C.B. had taken up, and adding:
'I am not ready to wash off our slate all the principles of the Liberal
Party & to surrender at discretion to a Dictator – If R wants to come
back to us it must be on terms of which one of the foremost must be
the honest recognition of your position.'[24] Bryce's comment was:
'That Grey would revolt and depart was to be expected. He won't carry
any one with him. A. might, a few: but ¾ to ⅘ of our H. of C. people
will stand loyal.'[25]

In another letter, written on January 2 to Gladstone, C.B. commented on the printed version of the Chesterfield speech, which came
out that day with a preface by Rosebery claiming that its policy appeared to have received 'a large mead of general approval', but saying
that 'spade-work' was needed to ensure that the 'wave of popular
adhesion' was not 'lost in space'. C.B. said:

> I do not at all like the preface to the published speech. If it
> means anything it means war: if he & his friends are to organize –
> against whom? Did you ever hear of an entrenchment erected by
> spade-work for the purpose of preventing a wave losing itself in
> space? . . . But perhaps it is all froth & fume: it does not appear to
> be seriously taken by the papers. . . .[26]

He had told Spender on New Year's Day:

> You will have seen that we are not left to gnaw the bone of Chester-
> field. . . . He won't join; won't consult; won't do nuffin . . . why
> should the public be told that a noble patriotic statesman wd like
> to save his country but certain selfish curmudgeons won't have
> him. I told him it was most unfair to allow this impression to
> prevail.[27]

Spender replied on the 5th: 'After the plunge the reaction. It is
always so with Lord R. His views on S.A. prevent him from working
cordially with the Lib. Imps. & the fear of breaking them from working
with the rest of us.'[28]

Gladstone, whose aim seems to have been to get C.B. to take his
cue altogether from Rosebery, poured out his complaints to Sinclair,
claiming that C.B.'s attitude wanted grip, that C.B. was refusing to
consult the Front Bench 'because of the move against him by Asquith
in chief', and that he ought to 'give a strong lead on the R. lines against

the Govt.' He said that, as Chief Whip, 'either I must do nothing, or put forward candidates the great bulk of whom would openly or avowedly be anti-C.B.'.[29] Sinclair replied saying: 'You have been eating too much plum pudding or mince pies or something', and pointing out that C.B. was 'dead against a split' and willing to make almost any sacrifice to avoid one.[30]

On Christmas Day Morley told Harcourt: 'We are now coming, I do believe, to the edge of Niagara.'[31] Harcourt replied:

> C.B. seems to be full of fight and I do not see why he should not do very well . . . and we ought to give him all the support in our power.
>
> I have received today – and accepted – the invitation to his King's Speech dinner and I earnestly trust you will do the same. He deserves it and we ought to let the public know by this formal act that we stand by him whatever others may do. . . .

Two days later Harcourt wrote to C.B., saying of Rosebery:

> . . . his absolute *non possumus* or rather more volumus leaves you in a very strong position.
>
> His terms are . . . 'unconditional surrender' of the Liberal Party and the Liberal creed. The next word evidently lies with the Perksites. It will be for them to say whether they are 'knights of the clean slate' . . .[32]

Grey now wrote direct to C.B.:

> I want to tell you where I stand after the Chesterfield speech. . . . My position is this – if you & Rosebery work together, I have no more to say & no new departure to make; if on the other hand you & he decide that you cannot co-operate I must say this: that I go with him.
>
> Please don't think that I say this from personal motives; it is because I find in all he has said about S. Africa full scope and authority for all I want to say and nothing from which in essentials I differ. And as far as my action can have any influence in making difficulties for you, subsequent experience since the summer has made me think that I should make fewer difficulties by being independent. . . .[33]

C.B. was slightly mollified by this direct approach, which was at least honest and straightforward, and writing to Gladstone on the 4th, said: 'I enclose a letter from Grey, and my answer. His letter is in more reasonable & less pugnacious terms than what he wrote to you, so I hope your expostulations have had their effect. We are getting near Philippi now. . . .'[34]

As the war went on, however, C.B. grew increasingly impatient of the attitude of 'Master Grey' as he called him. Indeed Grey's judgement throughout the war was sadly at fault. G. M. Trevelyan's view was that

> Grey, indeed, went further in his applause of Milner than was consistent with his own Liberal views. For he always said and meant that Boers and Britons must be given full self-government when the war was over, whereas Milner objected violently to that course when the Liberals took it in 1906. Grey found out ere long that he had been mistaken in two personal judgements which had largely affected his action at this period – in his belief that Campbell-Bannerman would always be hopelessly incompetent as a Parliamentarian, and in his belief that Milner was not only a great administrator and a devoted servant of the public (as he certainly was) but a wise and liberal-minded statesman. There is no doubt that Grey's conduct during the Boer War was one reason why the more advanced sections of the Liberal Party in later years regarded his foreign policy with constant distrust. He made his mistakes and paid his penalty.[35]

Grey was an intensely upright and patriotic man, but in these years, perhaps under the influence of the rather strange ideas of his first wife, he showed himself anything but sagacious.

In the face of Rosebery's inaction, and C.B.'s refusal to give up his convictions, Grey's revolt collapsed. The other side of the party were firmly behind C.B. Lloyd George told a *Pall Mall Gazette* reporter that C.B. had 'enormously strengthened his hold upon the public during the last two years, and especially the past six months'. The reporter 'glanced at the window with a mute appeal for breath', but Lloyd George stuck to his view, saying, 'you may look as surprised as you like', and went on to say that C.B. carried with him the centre and bulk of the party, was 'beginning to strike the Liberal imagination', and that 'though he has never been a fighting man, he has the courage of a dogged sort' and 'has obtained a triumphant series of meetings'.[36] But C.B.'s real concern was directed elsewhere. On January 6 he wrote to Gladstone:

> On Saturday night I wrote about Grey. But Asquith is the man of real importance, and it seems to me absolutely necessary that we should now know what his position is. It is essential that we should have an aye or no answer from him, and if he is friendly he should be informed of what R. said to me. . . .[37]

Asquith, in fact, had, like Gladstone, and unlike C.B., failed to grasp the real meaning of the Chesterfield speech. He had written to Gladstone on January 5:

> When I heard Rosebery's speech . . . I began to hope that we had reached the psychological moment, & that there was a real chance for united & reconstructed action. . . . I at once urged upon E. Grey (who assented) the desirability of saying or writing nothing in a contrary sense.
>
> Unhappily, an incalculable, & as I fear a fatal, blunder in tactics followed. In my opinion C.B. ought, at once, or at any rate without any avoidable delay, to have publicly pronounced in favour of the Rosebery line.
>
> But he let the opportunity slip – with the result that every kind of fiction & misunderstanding has been allowed to fly about through the air & (what is worse) to poison the springs. . . .
>
> As to the Rosebery–C.B. interview – whatever actually passed, the diverse reports, which have come to me from both sides, are such as to make one despair of writing contemporary history. . . .[38]

It is typical of the blinkered attitude of the Liberal Imps that even so intelligent a man as Asquith should have had no hesitation in saying that it was a fatal blunder for C.B. not to have come out at once in support of Rosebery's views, most of which C.B. had described at the time as 'pure claptrap', and with which he was in profound disagreement. But Asquith's position in the party was, as C.B. well knew, of the first importance. C.B. hesitated for a fortnight before writing to him but finally did so on January 7, keeping a manuscript copy, and describing the interview with Rosebery in the terms he had already done to Harcourt, Bryce, and Gladstone. He added:

The whole situation was completely discussed at the interview . . .
R. is resolved to maintain a position of independence. Of course I
will do nothing to shut the door, but this disposes of the hopes
founded on the Chesterfield speech, and it is not I but R that stands
in way of unity that was hoped for. You now know the whole
story. . . .[39]

Asquith replied in friendly but non-committal terms.

C.B. and Rosebery both thought that the other was inspiring one-
sided press reports, and both of them grew heated on the subject. C.B.
talked of 'a tissue of multi-coloured lies in the papers', and told Gladstone: 'For the rest of my life, two rules of conduct: 1. Never have an
interview with any one. 2. Always have three men present – one at
each door & one under the table.'[40]

Rosebery, for his part, thought that C.B. was responsible for 'the
inspired rubbish visible in the newspapers', and there was a chilly
exchange of letters on the subject between them.[41]

Both men, in fact, protested rather too much, for both had taken
steps privately to brief sympathetic members of the press.

CHAPTER 25

Courage Rewarded

Aᴛ the beginning of 1902 it was generally thought that the Liberal Imperialists would, sooner or later, take over the party, either making C.B. conform to their views or forcing him out of the leadership. Not many shared Harcourt's view that he would weather the storm. But C.B. had already shown that he was made of tough material, and he did not intend to be disposed of. He was now fighting back strongly, and he knew that he represented the broad mass of Liberal voters, particularly the working men in the constituencies, and that Asquith, Haldane and Perks did not. So he continued to fight on two fronts – against Chamberlain's unsparing attacks and against the Chamberlainites in his own party.

After Rosebery's speech at Chesterfield, Asquith, Grey and Haldane hoped that now at last the man they regarded as the proper leader of the Liberal Party would abandon his lonely furrow, emerge from his self-imposed isolation and claim what had once been his. And C.B. would have acquiesced if Rosebery had been prepared to accept the fundamental Liberal doctrines. He told Gardiner later: 'I liked Rosebery, and took the leadership always hoping to see him back.'[1] But Rosebery made no sign, and once more wrapped himself in silence and mystery. G. W. E. Russell wrote of him: 'We have had fourteen years of picturesque eloquence about things in general; ill-timed interventions in current politics; speeches which required letters to explain them, and letters which could only be elucidated by speeches.'[2] More and more Liberals were coming to feel the same sense of exasperation with Rosebery. And it was beginning to be shared by really influential Liberals like Asquith.

The Imperialists included some unlikely people. G. K. Chesterton, himself a 'pro-Boer', wrote: 'The leading Fabians were nearly all

Imperialists. Mr. and Mrs. Sidney Webb were in that matter strong Imperialists . . . even Bernard Shaw . . . was quite definitely an Imperialist. . . . Mr. H. G. Wells . . . went out of his way to scoff at the indignation of the Pro-Boers against the Concentration Camps . . .'³

But from his distant vantage point in Toronto, Goldwin Smith wrote to Bryce: '. . . Campbell-Bannerman seems to me to have been rising of late. He would be ill exchanged for Rosebery, who, though brilliant and attractive, is not a serious person. Rosebery's enigmatic attitude creates a factitious interest in him, but it is a betrayal of his weakness.'⁴

C.B. finally took his line in public in the speech he made on January 13 to the London Liberal Federation. This gathering demonstrated bitter hostility to Rosebery and pamphlets were passed round the audience warning them of a conspiracy to supplant C.B., 'the only Liberal leader', by Rosebery, Asquith and Fowler. C.B., however, said: 'I have always regretted Lord Rosebery's withdrawal from public life, and I have, on several occasions, publicly and privately, urged him to renew co-operation with his old friends, among whom he would be cordially welcomed.'⁵

Meanwhile, on January 8, Milner, speaking in Johannesburg, said: 'The war, gentlemen, will be ended all the quicker if we rely simply on steady pressure without fidgeting about negotiations. It is no use to wheedle; the only thing is imperturbably to squeeze. . . .'

Of the Liberals he said:

> The worst and most dangerous of all the disservices which that party has rendered to our country is that by their eternal clamour they keep the thoughts of their countrymen with regard to South Africa in one particular rut. They will never convert them to pro-Boerism, but they do make the figure of the Boer loom too large in the British imagination. . . . As a nation we really cannot indulge this high degree of altruism at the expense of our friends. . . .⁶

This was odd language for a public servant to use while holding the office of High Commissioner and supposed to be politically neutral.

When Parliament met on the 16th, C.B. was determined that there should be an Opposition amendment to the Address embodying the widest possible measure of agreement. He wrote to Asquith about this and Asquith consulted Rosebery. Neither of them wanted an amendment at all, since they were broadly satisfied with the Government's policy, but Asquith told C.B. that 'for the sake of unity' he would accept an amendment, provided that it was drafted 'to embody the general effect of the Chesterfield speech'.[7] A compromise amendment was accordingly put forward on the 21st, but the Liberal Imps, when it came to the point, would not support it – they simply walked out – and, though he was strongly supported by Harcourt, C.B. was, on this occasion, also attacked from the left of the party. Lloyd George told a crowded House what he thought of the amendment:

> ...it simply... means that one set of gentlemen are asked to support what they regard as a criminal enterprise as an inducement for another set of gentlemen to vote for a proposition they do not believe to be true. My right hon. friend has . . . been captured, and . . . he has been treated by his captors as the Boers treat their prisoners, he has been stripped of all his principles and left on the veld to find his way back the best way he can. I hope it will be a lesson to my right hon. friend . . . on a question of this character, compromise is impossible. I do not deny that opposition to the war has brought unpopularity upon the Liberal party; but, after all, let us face it like men. Let us not try to get out of it by shuffling in this way.[8]

Balfour was able to enjoy himself at the expense of the distracted Liberals – 'unless I do the hon. gentleman's rhetoric a great injustice I think that the epithet "shuffling" was almost the mildest with which his ample vocabulary supplied him to hurl at the proposal which, after all, was made by the leader of his party'. In his winding-up speech C.B. delivered a quiet reproof to Lloyd George which was warmly cheered. He then denounced farm-burning and the whole policy which led to it, which, he said, was 'a gigantic political blunder, driving to present despair and to future exasperation'. But the amendment was overwhelmingly defeated – by 333 votes to 123. *The Times* next day was triumphant:

> SIR HENRY CAMPBELL-BANNERMAN has been left severely alone by the men for whose benefit the insincere preamble of his amendment was concocted. But even this does not measure the depth of his humiliation. He has had the additional felicity of being openly flouted and scorned by the pro-Boers in whom he puts his trust and for whom the substance of his amendment was specially manu-

factured. . . . To wobble and to trim, to blow hot and blow cold, has been the whole policy of SIR HENRY CAMPBELL-BANNERMAN. The end of it all is that men like MR. ASQUITH and SIR EDWARD GREY have not a word to say for him . . . the party to which the nominal leader has pandered amid all his tergiversations treats him with undisguised contempt.[9]

C.B., who knew more about politics than the leader writers of *The Times*, was however himself content with the result, and thought it had damaged the Liberal Imps. He told Ripon on the 24th:

> 1. Grey (and I am sorry to say, Asquith) are much blamed in the party. Their excuse that Chamberlain's speech satisfied them will not stand investigation. . . . They . . . appear to have been grasping for any pretext possible to enable them to vote against, or escape from voting for, the amendment to which they had agreed. . . .
> 2. The Lib. Imps. being broken up is a good thing. Fowler was very cordial to me.
> 3. Herbert G. is gravely offended by the conduct of Grey & Asquith & does not spare them.
> 4. Lloyd George's outburst has greatly angered the party generally, & drove some of that wing – J. Morley & Channing, for instance – to vote for us.
> I see nothing to regret in the whole thing. The centre of the party is enlarged and consolidated. . . .[10]

One newspaper talked of 'the unbridled licence of last night's speech', and commented: 'Mr. Lloyd George has been described as Sir Henry Campbell-Bannerman's evil genius'.[11] But Lloyd George hastened to make it clear in the press that he was not picking a quarrel.[12] Haldane, who, by contrast, was devoid of any scrap of loyalty to the leader he had helped to elect, wrote to Milner about this debate:

> . . . we managed to persuade C.B. to make the amendment which he insisted on moving begin by affirming the necessity of prosecuting the War. As a reward for this we . . . neither spoke nor voted but testified our disapprobation gently by walking out in a body simply!! The advantage of this was that we took out a good many who otherwise would not have gone. Our hands were strengthened by Rosebery having privately but distinctly declared that Chamber-

lain's speech embodied the substance of his own views. . . . C.B. could only whip 123 of whom many were unwilling sheep, into his fold . . . our group . . . are working with Rosebery. He is not an easy or altogether reliable Chief, but he has the touch of genius, and *he is very anti C-B.* in reality, tho' he has tried to minimise our group's split with C.B. for the moment. What he wants to do is to make the split himself when the time comes.[13]

Spencer wrote: 'My heart is very sick as to Liberal politics just now. I see as yet no daylight. . . .'[14] The crux came at the meeting of the National Liberal Federation at Leicester on February 19. There had been stormy discussions in the morning, and in the evening C.B. addressed the gathering. He issued a clear public challenge to Rosebery:

We Liberals have been receiving a good deal of advice lately from one to whom, for my part, I shall always be disposed to listen with respectful and friendly attention. I do not know down to this moment of my speaking to you whether Lord Rosebery speaks to us from the interior of our political tabernacle or from some vantage ground outside. I practically put that question publicly to him a month ago, but he does not answer it. . . . Gentlemen, I am no believer in the doctrine of the clean slate. . . . I am, in fact, wholly opposed to the doctrine of the clean slate. . . . I am equally opposed to . . . the practice and penance of the white sheet. I am not prepared to erase from the tablets of my creed any principle or . . . ideal . . . of Liberalism. . . . I have thirty years and more of Parliamentary life, and I have listened to an endless number of Liberal speeches . . . and have attended an endless number of Liberal meetings, and not only remain through all these years an impenitent Liberal, but with the years have grown more and more convinced. . . . We are to sponge out every article of our creed, but we cannot do that.

He went on to speak of Ireland, the issue on which he and Rosebery were most deeply divided, and said that to abandon Home Rule because it happened for the moment to be inconvenient was not 'a very creditable or even a decent view of the case'.

Finally he said:

. . . it is not numbers that tell in a political movement; it is life and force. . . . What the party requires and desires now is unity of purpose and action. It is the exorcising and forgetting of miserable personal differences, mostly suggested and fostered by a hostile Press, and it is concentration upon our plain duties and doctrines. This is my message to you. . . . Act upon it, and we may be perfectly confident that, whether after a long interval or after a short one, we shall win a triumphant victory. . . .[15]

This was a fighting speech. It was said of it long afterwards that it 'really expunged the policy of the "clean slate", and scattered to the winds a combination based on disregard of the historic purpose of Liberalism'.[16]

C.B. himself was also at the top of his form on this occasion. Robert Spence Watson, the Chairman of the National Liberal Federation, told Morley:

C.B. had really a triumph, and he deserved it. He was like one inspired, & amazed & delighted everyone by his fun, his clever by-play, his solid argument, & his firm powerful statement of his position. A Liverpool man (who shall be nameless) said to me, 'Well Rosebery was not in it with this'. He held his great audience from the first word to the last, and sat down amidst quite a wonderful storm of applause, people leaping to their feet and cheering with enthusiasm.

And it was real good stuff too – the true gospel. I never heard him anything like it before.[17]

He had not long to wait for a response to his challenge. Two days later, on February 21, a letter appeared in *The Times*:

Sir,

In his speech last night my friend, Sir Henry Campbell-Bannerman, asked me if I speak from the interior of his political tabernacle or from some vantage-ground outside. . . . Speaking pontifically within his 'Tabernacle' last night he anathematised my declarations on the 'clean slate' and Home Rule. It is obvious that our views on the war and its methods are not less discordant. I remain, therefore, outside his tabernacle, but not, I think, in solitude.

Let me add one word more at this moment of definite separation. No one appreciates more heartily than I do the honest and well-intentioned devotion of Sir Henry to the Liberal Party and what he conceives to be its interests. I only wish I could have shared his labour and supported his policy.

I am, Sir, yours respectfully,
Rosebery.[18]

Lloyd George said: 'It will compel practically the whole of the Party to rally to "C.B.". The "Rosebery" M.P.s have been treated rather badly, but the constituencies will force them to stand by the Party. There is no room for a third party.'[19]

The radicals were glad that the breach was now open. A correspondent in the *Manchester Guardian* wrote: 'As for leadership in the House of Commons and the country, most of us have increasing confidence in the proved solidity, self-sacrificing disinterestedness, and sturdy loyalty to principle of Sir Henry Campbell-Bannerman. If he be not "brilliant" he is something better, more necessary, more enduring. . . .'[20]

On the 27th an announcement was made that those who adhered to the Chesterfield policy had no intention of severing themselves from the party but that an association had been formed under the name of 'The Liberal League', with Rosebery as its president and, as vice-presidents, Asquith, Fowler and Grey. This body absorbed the former Liberal Imperialist League. It was, of course, designed to try to capture the Liberal Party for Rosebery and his ideas and to displace C.B. He, however, was not worried about the League, and expressed his disdain for it both in private and in public. On March 1 he told Sir George Leveson Gower: 'I believe "Charge, Chesterfield, Charge" is its war-cry and that need frighten nobody.'[21] On the same day he wrote to the chairman of the party in his constituency, J. B. Smith: 'For the present the new League is laughed at in the H. of Commons, except the half-dozen who have got the whole thing up. R. seems universally condemned, and it is fully expected that a few speeches will finish him. In the meantime I shall take a quiet unaggressive line.'[22]

Asquith's son Raymond wrote from Oxford to his friend John Buchan in South Africa expressing a young man's disdain for all this manœuvring:

The bleak futility of our public men on both sides is a thing one never hoped to see outside the neo-Celtic school of poetry. The general effect is that of a flock of sheep playing blind man's buff in the distance on a foggy day. Rosebery continues to prance upon the moonbeam of efficiency . . . but he might just as well call it the Absolute at once for all the meaning it has for him or anyone else. . . . He has started a thing called the Liberal League, which appears at present to consist of three persons – himself, my father, and Grey – backed by a squad of titled ladies. . . .[23]

On March 5, C.B. spoke of the Liberal League with what was described as contemptuous tolerance. He said that it reminded him of Mr. Brodrick's Army Corps, which consisted of officers but no men. He had always been opposed to any sectional organization in the party, and in certain circumstances, he said, it would be their duty to fight such an organization with all their power.[24] *The Times* described this as a declaration of war against Rosebery. The young Winston Churchill wrote to Rosebery on the 7th about C.B.: 'He is always in his place and works harder than anyone on the front opposition bench: but what a vicious speech at the dinner!'[25]

Loulou Harcourt's reaction was different. He wrote to C.B. on the 9th: 'You have not only excited the enthusiasm and gratitude of the Party, but you have acquired a personal affection from them which even Mr. Gladstone did not have.'[26]

Arthur Acland, a former Minister in the Rosebery Government, wrote to Spender towards the end of February: 'Rosebery . . . is so self-centred . . . that it is largely a question with him at bottom of manœuvering and tactics. . . . The dullest dog to whom Liberalism is a kind of *faith* is better in some respects than a man who has this point of view.'[27]

Meanwhile, in South Africa, Milner was enjoying the spectacle of the Liberal leader's troubles. He wrote to a correspondent at this time: 'What a thorough "cropper" he seems to have come, poor man, rolling off the fence into the pro-Boer mire and then trying to balance again, amid universal derision. And "our Joe" how he has been scoring. . . . It is a great thing to see that pluck still pays, and decision, in this wobbly wishy-washy age.'[28]

In April Gladstone sent on to C.B. a peevish letter from Asquith about Parliamentary arrangements, complaining of lack of consultation. C.B. replied briskly: 'There is no occasion whatever for Asquith's hysterical letter. Everything was quite regular.'[29] He was beginning to be surer of his ground, and it was the Liberal Imps who were getting rattled. He was, however, understandably indignant when Gladstone himself proposed to appear at Leeds on the same platform as Rosebery. He wrote to Spencer on May 18:

I am aghast to see that R. is to be 'supported' at Leeds by Herbert G. & Birrell. . . .

(a) R has publicly declared his definite separation from my policy.
(b) he is head of an organisation which is bribing away our agents and intriguing as hard as it can against us in the constituencies. . . .

Yet the Head Whip & the Chairman of the N.L.F. support him.[30]

He made his objections plain to Gladstone, adding: 'The whole meeting in fact has its genesis in the purpose ad majorem R. gloriam. . . .'[31] But he was, as always, a man of great natural courtesy, and he wrote to say thank you to his harassed though politically wobbly Chief Whip for all he had done 'during these dreadful years'; while at the same time conveying a hint that he was, if necessary, dispensable.[32]

Goldwin Smith wrote at this time:

I am conscious of clinging to the ideas that righteousness is the foundation of the State . . . that the greatness and happiness of England are in herself; and that for a commercial and industrial nation, dependent on foreign supplies for its food and raw material, the wisest policy is one of moderation and peace. Just now there is a tidal wave of sentiments opposed to these: but I am old enough to have stood more than once on the dry shore where a tidal wave had been.

I have . . . no doubt that were I now in England I should be heartily supporting Sir Henry Campbell-Bannerman as the representative of genuine Liberalism. . . .[33]

C.B. sometimes boiled over at what he saw as the indifference of his countrymen. To a constituent he wrote on May 10:

. . . we have . . . three great enemies:

(1) devotion to material prosperity, national and individual;
(2) love of sport and of gambling in all forms;
(3) apathy.

These are the curse of our people in addition to drink, and they are perhaps even more widespread and insidious.[34]

On May 31 the Boer War at last came to an end. Two days later C.B. made a short but impressive speech in the House, in which he welcomed the news of peace, and paid tribute to the courage and endurance of British soldiers and of the Boers. On the 5th he seconded the vote of £50,000 to Kitchener, whom, despite his association with the policy of 'methods of barbarism', he praised as a soldier, administrator and negotiator.

The war was over, and with its end the main cause of the furious disputes within the Liberal Party. Against all odds, C.B. had survived. Deserted by most of his front-bench colleagues, reviled as a friend of his country's enemies, plotted against, dismissed as a warming pan, a 'tertium quid', a 'locum tenens', given not even the appearance of loyalty and support by his most prominent political 'friends', it seemed hardly credible that this easy-going, well-to-do bon viveur should have come through three years of savage political in-fighting, not only intact, but actually strengthened in his position. But so it was. No one could now doubt the resilience, the toughness of fibre and the determination of this man. He had set himself to maintain the unity of his party and to preserve its organization intact. Somehow, he had managed to do both. He had, as Massingham later pointed out, been opposed by most of the money and social power in Liberalism. He had had to take on, in Rosebery, the most glamorous political figure in the country, as well as two of the ablest of the younger men in the party, Asquith and Haldane, and a personage respected as the embodiment of the old Whig tradition, Edward Grey. He had done so and beaten them all. But on the principles of his political faith he had not compromised. Only at this distance is it possible to see what an extraordinary achievement all this was. The reward was to come four years later in 1906. It was to C.B. that the Liberal Party owed its very existence in 1902. He had held it together so that it was able, four years later, to win the greatest electoral triumph in its history.

Public opinion now began to swing towards C.B. People began to recognize that he had been right about the war and had spoken out even when to do so had needed courage. Harmsworth asked his agents throughout the country if the political policy of his papers was liked. He was told: 'It won't do to be too hard on C.B. He's getting popular.'[35] A New York newspaper later wrote that his straight-forwardness was 'a lesson to shuffling politicians the world over'.[36]

On July 14 Balfour, who had led the House of Commons for so

long, succeeded Lord Salisbury – 'Old Sarum' as C.B. called him – as Prime Minister. But his leadership, too, was beginning to be challenged, in his case by the supporters of Chamberlain.

Interest now switched to domestic affairs. Inevitably the Boer War had dominated politics since the autumn of 1899, but C.B. did not forget social problems and their importance to the Liberal Party. In December 1901 Dr. Robert Spence Watson had written to him, saying: 'A young friend of mine, one of the York Rowntrees, has written a remarkable & useful book upon "Poverty, a study of City Life", & he has asked me to forward a copy to you. I think that you will like to dip into it for it deals with matters of high importance in a systematic & truthful way.'[37] C.B. read the book and used its conclusions in his speeches.

The Balfour Government had proposed a corn tax which C.B. vehemently opposed as putting a halfpenny on the price of a loaf and as a forerunner of protectionist measures. So in fact it was, as Chamberlain in effect admitted in attacking C.B. at Birmingham on May 16:

Ah! but here Sir Henry Campbell-Bannerman scents mischief. What? Closer relations between the mother country and the Colonies! Cobden, Cobden whom he professes to follow, the great free-trader, made a reciprocity treaty with France, but the idea of a reciprocity treaty with our own children – that fills the mind of Sir Henry Campbell-Bannerman with disgust which he is only able ineffectively to express; and in this he shows once more that lack of imagination, that lack of foresight, which distinguishes and always has distinguished the little Englander and the little Scotchman.[38]

The first sighting shots in the coming battle between Free Traders and Tariff Reformers were being fired. But this time it was the Liberals who were united and the Unionists who were to be torn apart. Chamberlain's speech marked the beginning of the end of the Balfour Government. For C.B. there was at last the prospect of success and of power. But he was sixty-six.

Balfour's Education Bill of 1902 aroused strong feelings and outraged the Nonconformists, being regarded as an attempt to subsidize Church of England schools from state funds and even to 'put Rome on the rates'. It performed the near-miracle of uniting the Liberals in opposing it. Even Rosebery attacked it. It soon began losing by-elections for the Government. C.B. described it in a letter to Bryce in September as 'an attempt to relieve Church funds while retaining Church supremacy. . . . the supremacy of Church interests is incompatible with popular control, and popular control there must be.' We should, he thought:

recognize . . . that the people generally desire that in public schools there should be the means of religious instruction, and then adopt one of three plans

(a) an inoffensive dose of Christian doctrine in all State Schools; supplemented by peculiar teaching of tenets by the sects at separate hours;

(b) purely secular teaching in State schools, supplemented as above;

(c) Option to each locality which of these should be applied.

For myself I dislike a statutory common religion almost as much as a statutory specific religion, and therefore (b) would be my choice. But I am much mistaken if we shall not have to go for one or other of these, and the more courage we have the more chance of success. . . .

All the casual Tories I have met take one line 'Why the —— did they meddle with this hornets' nest? . . .'[39]

C.B. saw the education issue in simple terms. The year before he had told Vaughan Nash that 'the professors, Fabians, philosophers et hoc genus omne take no account of these plain & honest opinions'.[40]

At the end of August Alfred Lyttelton wrote describing the political situation to Milner from the Unionist point of view:

. . . It is probable that the country wd. turn out the present Govt. if they had the chance at this moment. This *is* principally due to the Educ'on Bill. . . . But the Liberals are still in a pretty hopeless condition. Last autumn Asquith and E. Grey failed to dislodge C-B and when Rosebery joined them he reduced their adherents to a lower number than before his arrival on the scene. C-B has reaffirmed all his most objectionable sentiments, and, though his party dislike him, the Briton's loyalty to a man who has taken a work in hand not sought by himself and of a thankless character make him really impregnable. Rosebery is no real good in a fight. . . . Asquith in politics is living on his capital and contributes no new ideas. The austere Radicals of the type of S. Webb who work their skins off and have ideas tho' generally wrong ones have grown to mistrust one who dines so well and so often in the 'frivolous company of decadents'. There is something in this, tho' a week of Asquith's work wd. send most ordinary men to bed for a fortnight.[41]

In the autumn C.B. went, as always, to Marienbad. But now there was little holiday to be had. Charlotte was in continuous pain from neuritis. C.B. wrote: 'Agony has expelled sleep for the last two months. She has greatly benefitted here (as always) in general health, but this frightful thing goes on, & if it were not for the general improvement would have almost made an end of her.'[42] They went on to Baden Baden and consulted specialists, but all to no purpose.

C.B. alone came back to London briefly for the coronation of the new King. Politically things were looking much better. He wrote to Smith in Stirling: 'I do not see how the Gov. are going to get out of their Education troubles', but added: 'the "Leaguers" are full of spite & will do all the harm to us they decently can. Defeated in the open they are intriguing and using their moneybags on the sly'.[43] He wrote to Harcourt on October 11: 'The situation is an exciting one. I only hope the Non. Cons. will stand to their guns. . . .'[44]

He was in Paris in October, consulting the doctors there about Charlotte. He was desperately worried, and wrote to his friend Jack Sinclair on the 12th, saying, 'I do not know what we can do. . . . At present she can neither lie in bed nor sit up (constant pain) and absolutely cannot be left. . . .'[45]

He came back for the autumn session. Rosebery, of whom Beatrice Webb wrote: 'He has no grip of anything except appearances',[46] had published a letter on the 8th maintaining that it was C.B. who had excommunicated him from the party. Some Liberals still wanted C.B. to make a gesture towards him. But he had done with trying to bridge the unbridgeable.

When he got back to London he was still extremely anxious about Charlotte, who, in her distress, became absolutely dependent upon his ministrations. He put her interests first, and as a result was often away from the House, and there was some murmuring that he was neglecting his political duties. But there was at this stage no challenge to his position. The Webbs had Asquith to dinner in November and Beatrice found him 'simply dull. He is disheartened with politics . . . baffled by Rosebery, snubs and is snubbed by C.B. . . . He eats and drinks too much

... and is under no delusion about himself; he has resigned himself to missing leadership.' She saw a lot of Asquith at this time and described him as a 'coarse-grained instrument', with 'hard-headed cold capacity' but with 'neither charm nor personal magnetism'. Grey she dismissed as 'a slight person ... essentially a "stick" to be used by someone else', and 'Imperial' Perks she found 'a repulsive being – hard, pushing, commonplace ... a combination of Gradgrind, Pecksniff and Jabez Balfour'. She and Sidney Webb, however, found the Liberal Imps sympathetic to their ideas of social reform, to which she believed that C.B. was 'really hostile', but she found her new friends far from satisfactory: 'Two months' sampling of the Liberal Imperialists has not heightened our estimate of them' – though the best of them, she thought, was Haldane.[47]

C.B., in fact, had little use for the Webbs. He wrote to Spencer about Balfour's Education Bill on October 9: 'I believe we are all (except the Webb-footed ones) pretty well agreed.'[48]

1903 marked the turning point for the Liberal opposition. The Education Act and the beginning of the reaction from the war had swung the balance against the Government. Labour, too, was an increasingly important force on the Liberal side. At Belmont on January 2 C.B. told a deputation of Liberals: 'We are keenly in sympathy with the representatives of Labour. We have too few of them in the House of Commons.'[49]   On the same occasion he said: 'The Liberal party, high and low, have discovered, if they ever forgot it, that the real road to success ... lies in adhering to the old principles of the party.' He pointed out that 'from 1870 down to the present day we have never had in the Liberal Party the full fighting force of the Nonconformists in England'. The Nonconformist clergy had not put their backs into the political contest. Now at last all this was changed.

In May Chamberlain launched his crusade for Imperial Preference. The Liberals at once united in defence of Free Trade, while the Unionists were split. Balfour was forced onto the defensive and it became a question of how long the Government could last. But a majority of a hundred in the House, and Balfour's extraordinary ingenuity, evasiveness and cunning, enabled him to retain power for two-and-a-half years after Chamberlain had exploded his mine.

The battle for and against Free Trade needs to be considered on its own. But the other aspects of C.B.'s leadership of the Opposition are also worth a glance.

C.B. had for a long time regarded Chamberlain as the real driving force in the Government. Chamberlain kept up his violent attacks on anyone who opposed him. Of C.B. he said: 'If he cannot be a statesman, he might at least try to be a gentleman.' He was now away visiting South Africa and on January 26 C.B. told Bryce:

Evidently Joe will return in triumph, & it will not be altogether easy to be decently appreciative. . . . I regard Joe as the very embodiment of all that is bad in policy and spirit: of all that will wreck and ruin our country & nothing will bring me to say anything else. It is not himself personally or his peculiarities that I object to, but what he stands for politically.[50]

In the same letter he remarked drily on a speech Rosebery had made at Plymouth, ostensibly extempore, as he was reported to have mislaid his notes: '*I have known those notes lost before:* namely at Dundee in '82. The valet had then put them in the wrong portmanteau: have we the same valet in 1903? There are really no bounds to this posing?'

At the end of April C.B. wrote to Harcourt: 'The Non-Con feeling (+ Protestant feeling) is roused as it never was before . . . if we shew the white feather or shirk the real issue we are done.'[51]

Milner was still getting bulletins from his friends. He heard from Lord Selborne on May 25:

The old actors have been a long time on the boards, the old favourite and greatest actor of all has retired. . . . Therefore says the public let us have a turn of the other company. . . . Could they form a government? possibly, if Rosebery and Campbell-Bannerman agreed to serve under Spencer. . . .[52]

Harcourt was depressed about the state of the Opposition. He wrote to Spencer on June 2:

At present the Liberal Party is absolutely derelict as regards all leadership. I had an interview a day or two ago with C-B and was sorry to find him very much broken and shaken not only by his own illness but still more by his mortal anxiety about his wife. . . . Asquith is abroad, Bryce is away, and there is really no one to take charge of the ship. . . .[53]

C.B. himself, though worried to death about Charlotte, was far more optimistic about the political outlook. He was ready to praise any good performances, even by those who were no friends of his. On June 18, for example, he told Harcourt: 'The skirmish we had last night was on a narrow and safe subject. . . . Dilke, Robson, Grey and Hugh Cecil were all excellent.'[54] A few days later he wrote: 'Things are unchanged here: A.J.B. getting exceedingly testy and snappish, and the Party more and more split up and angry.'[55]

On July 21, when some French parliamentarians visited the House of Commons, C.B. addressed them in fluent French, describing Balfour and Chamberlain, who were also present, rather happily, as respectively, the *enfant gâté* and the *enfant terrible* of the Unionist Party.

The Unionist Government had set up a Royal Commission on the war. Spencer and Asquith had both been asked in turn by Balfour to act as Chairman but had refused. Asquith had suggested Elgin, who accepted.[56] In August the country was badly shaken by the publication of the Commission's report which, though moderate and restrained in language, showed that the Government had been quite unprepared, and further damaged its standing.

In August, too, Gladstone, after patient negotiation with Ramsay MacDonald, concluded an electoral deal with Labour to prevent clashes in the constituencies. This arrangement has been criticized by later generations of Liberals. Mr. Jeremy Thorpe, for example, has written that 'the Liberals were to blame for giving room to the Socialist cuckoo in the radical nest. The Herbert Gladstone/Ramsay MacDonald arrangement, which relieved thirty-one Labour candidates of Liberal competition in 1906 without extracting any advantage for the Liberals, was an act of uncalled-for electoral generosity unforgivable in a Chief Whip.'[57] But in 1903 the extent of the Liberal landslide in 1906 was unforeseen, as was the growth of a separate Labour Party, and the arrangement seemed a useful one. C.B. congratulated Gladstone on it. Most of the Labour leaders liked and trusted C.B., but there were exceptions. Robert Blatchford described him in his paper, the *Clarion*, in May as 'an unhappy old drawler of platitudinous flapdoodle'.[58] But Blatchford had been a strong supporter of the war.

Meanwhile Rosebery continued on his own tack, declining to work closely with his supporters like Asquith and Haldane or even to tell them what he was about. On September 30 he recorded in a memorandum why it would be impossible for him to form a government:

I shall always be (and justly) an object of suspicion to the Radical party or rather to the pro–Boer, pro–American, pro–Macedonian and generally hysterical section of it. . . .

There are certain persons – two I think – with whom I could not sit in Cabinet with honour. . . .

My memory, my power of application, my hearing, and my general vigour are all impaired. . . .

In the last seven years, since I left party politics, I have fallen into a solitary habit of life which I should now find it impossible altogether to abandon. . . .[59]

Lord Crewe wrote that 'of the two impossible colleagues, Harcourt was obviously one: the other could only be Campbell-Bannerman'.[60]

The Liberal League remained in being as an engine, though now a somewhat rusty engine, devoted to the overthrow of C.B. and his replacement by Rosebery. But in the new situation, created by Chamberlain's call for Tariff Reform, there was a public reconciliation of a sort in November. Rosebery attacked Chamberlain's proposals and called for unity. C.B. told Gladstone:

I can but repeat . . . that if he returns and bears his share of the work & responsibility I shall be delighted.

But if the idea is that he shd. mount & ride the horse . . . and should dictate what we are to do & say, we cannot of course have him on such terms. . . . I greatly fear from his isolation & his being surrounded by adulating toadies, that may be his view of the proper relationship.[61]

Publicly he extended a cautious welcome to Rosebery, but privately he remained sceptical.

He had had a chance encounter with Rosebery when he was returning from a state dinner at Windsor. He just caught his train, and found himself in the same compartment as Rosebery, whom he described as 'sulky as a bear, never once looked me in the face'.[62]

On November 30 C.B. addressed a great meeting at Newport, and, in this stronghold of the Nonconformists, spoke about the Unionist Education Act, praising the spirit of religious liberty, which 'has been kept alive in the recesses of your mountains', and the stand Welshmen had taken 'against clerical pretentions and political injustice'. He added that Welshmen had 'shown a devotion to higher education . . . second to nothing south of the Tweed'.[63] Words like these, reported in all the local newspapers, spread through the grass roots and helped to focus opinion for the next election. And he enjoyed it. He wrote to Harcourt on December 3: 'I had a tremendous time at Newport: The meetings were splendid, but the streets! I never saw anything like it. The whole place was en fête.'[64]

Lloyd George wrote: 'We are all delighted with the trouncing you gave Balfour for his somewhat imprudent speech at Bristol.'[65] On December 19 Asquith told Gladstone: 'I have a letter from H. Harmsworth (unsolicited from me) in which he declares that he has given strict orders to his staff on the Leeds & Glasgow papers to stop all injurious references to C.B. . . . & to work for party unity.'[66]

On December 29 C.B. wrote from Dover to Bryce, echoing what he had said in 1902: 'But oh! the degraded, apathetic, sport-loving, empty headed, vulgar lot that our countrymen have become . . . a Brassey in the House announces his retirement – why? – because he finds Parlt interferes with his duties as Master of Hounds.'[67]

A new issue had appeared – the employment of Chinese coolies in the mines of the Transvaal. They had been brought in by Milner – in a hurry as always – to get the South African economy going again. Their use was strongly opposed by Botha, Smuts, and the other leading Boers. On the last day of the year, however, C.B. warned Bryce that 'it would be safer for none of us to "plunge" on the Chinese Labour question just yet'. He added:

> Is it not extraordinary how J.C. always plays up to . . . vulgarity and cupidity and other ignoble passions? . . . When he bullies Kruger, when he Mafficks, when he promises preferences & tariffs & wages and work. It is always the same; and he uses the foolishness of the fool and the vices of the vicious to overwhelm the sane & wise & sober.
> What a cheerful thought for New Year's Eve![68]

C.B. was aware of the danger of being branded, however unfairly, as a man who put the interests of his own country last. Writing to Spencer about Tibet in April 1904, he said: 'We shall be told that we are always against our country! I am hardened against this taunt myself, but many of our people may be frightened.' 'Why', he asked Spencer of their Conservative opponents, 'do they always put our country in the wrong?'[69]

But he soon decided that the Chinese labour issue was worth pressing. It was indeed to prove a major political embarrassment to the Government. It encountered the deep aversion of Englishmen from anything remotely associated with slavery, coupled with resentment against the mining magnates who had amassed huge fortunes and were held to be in part responsible for dragging the country into the humiliations and futility of the Boer war. Sir Clinton Dawkins wrote to Milner on March 8, 1904:

> Toujours les Chinoiseries!
> That d—d old C.B. has put down Chinese labour for a full dress debate Monday and the Govt., who are more frightened by a pig-tail than ever was the chastest anchorite by a lady, are again quaking. They have some reason to be. Electorally 'Oriental' labour is most unpopular here at the moment. . . .[70]

The debate took place in the House on March 21, 1904. C.B., who had declared in February his conviction, after a careful study of the evidence, that the allegation about the unavoidable scarcity of native labour had not been made out, and who argued that even if it was, the alternative of white labour ought to be tried, and greater use made of labour-saving equipment, moved a vote of censure. The policy, he said, was an outrage upon the white men in the Transvaal who, 'under the sham and bastard form of self-government that had been extemporized, had not been able to make their views known'. He declared that the state in which the Chinese worked was 'very like slavery – it is so like it that it is almost indistinguishable. Well, these are, at all events, uncommonly like slave laws. "Indentured labour" no doubt sounds better; but do not let us haggle over words: let us see what the thing itself is.'[71]

Milner had, before introducing his Chinese labour policy, secured the agreement of the Liberal Imps at dinners with the Asquiths the previous October. Grey and Haldane had been present.[72] He naturally now felt he could count on their support. Haldane did stand by him and abstained in the vote, but Asquith, with whom loyalty to a person counted for little against political expediency, as Haldane was to find in 1916, joined in the chorus of criticism, saying that as Milner had described the Uitlanders as helots in 1899, how would he now describe the Chinese? Grey wrote to his wife on February 23: 'There is a horrid set being made at Haldane because he abstained from the vote against

Chinese Labour. The Massingham people now count on excluding him from the next government, and they are so elated by things generally that they think they can exclude us all, including Asquith, and have a real Radical government of their own. What a futile thing it would be – all froth!...'[73] L. S. Amery wrote to Milner on February 26: 'I did think you had got Asquith straight on the point, but I am afraid the temptation, with office looming so near and wall paper for 10 Downing Street already selected by Mrs. A., was too much for him.... Haldane won't speak, because he says he is too suspect with his own party.'[74]

C.B. was in good form and early in February Ellis was noting with delight that he had delivered a 'crushing reply to Joe'.[75] Charlotte, though still very weak, had been getting steadily better and this relieved his mind from a great anxiety. But in Unionist circles he was still not taken seriously. On March 4, for example, Lady Edward Cecil wrote to her future husband, Milner: 'Campbell-Bannerman is making every known mistake and lots of new ones of his own – as Lady Lewis once said to me, "fools have so much resource". I understand that his party want him to go to the Lords. Arthur on the other hand must wish to keep him at all costs in the Commons.'[76]

C.B. felt much more cheerful about affairs. He wrote of the Government to William Robertson on March 26: 'Their best and wisest friends wish they would resign: but our Prime Minister is a very supercilious and self-confident gentleman and fancies the world would collapse.'[77]

Milner's contempt for public opinion became less inhibited. In March C.B. was able to ask in the House for an explanation 'of the extraordinary language attributed to the High Commissioner in the newspapers. Lord Milner is said to have declared that he does not care twopence for the opinion of the people of this country. This explains a good deal in Lord Milner's conduct of affairs....'[78]

On February 17 the Governor of Natal wrote to Milner: 'I hope the Bannermen don't get in . . . a Radical Govt. wld. spell ruin to us. I ought not to say this but I do....'[79] Next month Sir Alfred Hime wrote to him from the Natal Legislative Assembly: '. . . I firmly believe the accession to power of C.B. & Co. would be little short of a national calamity.... Chamberlain is a host in himself and . . . knows how to make C.B. squirm and that's what I like to see....'[80] Milner had many supporters among the English in South Africa, whose mood was increasingly despondent. He himself wrote in May: 'Fortunately I don't mind *abuse*, in the very least – rather like it, from certain quarters. If

Morley *by F. C. Gould*

Asquith *by F. C. Gould*

C.B. for instance, were ever to praise anything I did, I shld instantly resign, with a profound sense of failure.'[81]

Rosebery and the Liberal Imps could not forgive C.B. for having thwarted their plans and were still working to do him down. On March 26 Winston Churchill wrote to his friend Lord Hugh Cecil:

> ... at Huntingdon ... there were three or four Liberal candidates for the Eastern Counties. Three of these were ... outspoken Liberal Imperialists. They spoke of C.B. with undisguised contempt and seem to regard a Spencer-Bannerman administration as the greatest disaster that could overtake the country. They told me that there are 80 Liberal Leaguers standing at next election, and as they have so much of the money they have got an undue proportion of good seats.[82]

Imperial Perks had not been letting the grass grow under his feet. This was the organizational challenge C.B. most feared.

In October 1904, C.B.'s old friend Henry Lucy wrote an article for the *Nineteenth Century* suggesting the possible composition of the next Liberal Government. He proposed Spencer as Prime Minister, and among the other members of the Government nominated Dilke as Foreign Secretary, Fletcher Moulton as Chancellor of the Exchequer, and C.B. as Secretary of State for War with a seat in the House of Lords.

> It would be idle to affirm [he said of C.B.] that as Leader of the Opposition he commands the respect of his political opponents or the obedience of his party friends. ... The friendly scheme cherished by affectionate colleagues on the front Opposition bench, whereby after life's fitful fever, represented by thirty-six years in the House of Commons, Sir Henry may rest well in the House of Lords, will, for its realisation, require Sir Henry's more or less cordial acquiescence. If he insists on reversion of the Premiership it will be difficult to withhold it.[83]

This was too much for C.B. When they met shortly after at a dinner, he cut Lucy, whom he only forgave in January 1908, three months before he died. In the event every single one of Lucy's Cabinet post predictions turned out to be wrong.

This was sad. Only a short time before Lucy had described C.B. in the House, coming down on Balfour 'like a falcon on a sparrow'.[84]

That a journalist seeking for a metaphor to describe C.B.'s handling of Balfour in the House should talk in such terms was something altogether new.

Away in South Africa, Milner was growing increasingly desperate. He wrote to Lyttelton on July 25: 'I regard the Opposition, quite frankly, as wreckers . . . and inside information given to them simply would be material supplied to the Powers of Darkness.' He urged that a successor to himself should be appointed soon 'in order that the Enemy may find a decent man in possession, whom they cannot well oust'.[85] The 'decent man' was to be Chamberlain's former No. 2 at the Colonial Office, Lord Selborne.

On July 28 C.B., writing to thank Harcourt for a friendly reference in a speech, added a word of gratitude for 'that constant course of loyalty and (much needed!) assistance and suggestion and advice for which I am indebted to you through these years, and without which I could not have stood out for a month. Be sure that I feel it deeply.'[86] Harcourt had indeed been one of C.B.'s strongest props during the 'dreadful years', and it was one of C.B.'s agreeable characteristics that he never forgot to say thank you.

The following day he received, in reply, the last of his many letters from W.V.H., saying:

> It is very good of you to appreciate so generously the too slight succour I have been able to render you in the most difficult and thankless task which was ever imposed on a public man.
>
> I can assure you it has been done *con amore* and with true sense of the spirit, temper & courage with which you have steered the ship in stormy and treacherous seas. . . .[87]

It was a blow to him when old Harcourt, 'this greatest of Parliament men',[88] as he called him in the old phrase, died on October 1. He was helped, however, by young Harcourt, the indefatigable Loulou. Of him A. G. Gardiner wrote: '. . . those who know most of the intricate story of those troubled years when Sir Henry Campbell-Bannerman was holding aloft the old flag, surrounded by open enemies and cold friends, know how much of the ultimate triumph was due to the astuteness and passionless loyalty of Mr. Harcourt.'[89]

Arthur Ponsonby also testified that 'on our side as a political wire-puller Lulu Harcourt was a match for anyone the Liberal League could produce'.[90]

Lord Ripon was another on whom C.B. greatly relied as a wise counsellor, and Spencer, too, was a pillar of strength. C.B. told Lord Rendel that he had made an arrangement with Spencer early in 1904, under which Spencer was to surrender his claim by seniority to be Prime Minister on the ground that the Prime Minister must be in the House of Commons.[91] Spencer was now getting to be an old man. Edmund Gosse described him as 'very intimidating; one looks up in despair for his face at the top of the white cliff of his great beard'.[92]

Lord Esher, that grey eminence of Edwardian politics, now made a final appeal to Rosebery to come down into the political arena[93] (something that Lord Esher himself consistently refused to do), but it was to no avail.

1904 was the year of the *entente cordiale* with France. This was warmly welcomed by C.B. and Grey, speaking on the same lines in the House for the first time since as long as anyone could remember. In October C.B. moved from Grosvenor Place to his new house at 29 Belgrave Square.

In October, too, when the Dogger Bank incident occurred, and the Russian fleet sank a British fishing boat, C.B. was outraged and fully supported the Government, showing a remarkable militancy in his old age. In December he wrote to Gladstone about a visit to Manchester, where he found 'doubts expressed whether our friend Winston, with all the cleverness and variety of his speeches, is quite the sort of man to capture the quiet non-party voter who went for Houldsworth because of his solidity, and stolidity, and eminent respectability'.[94] A few days later, in another letter to Gladstone, he asked: 'Would it be a useful thing to have Gen. Sir W. Butler as a candidate – He is perhaps our foremost military authority: advanced Radical. Home Ruler. Catholic – no means to spare. He wd. be very useful in the House but like many such people might be a nuisance at times.'[95] Butler was considered seriously but the Liberal policy on education proved to be a fatal obstacle to his candidature.

So 1905 opened, with the Unionist Government in disarray and, for the Liberals, a real prospect of a return to power. On January 22 the King's great friend Lord Carrington wrote to C.B., with whom he was also on excellent terms, saying: 'The King looks on a Liberal Govt. with the greatest serenity.'[96]

C.B. read the news of the Moscow rising and wrote to Sydney

Buxton: 'Russia is dreadful. But what we do not know is what the peasants will do. If they sympathize with and will join the town workmen it is difficult to see how a full blown revolution can be avoided: but I suspect they will side with the "little Father".'[97]

John Morley spoke at the Queen's Hall in March and contrasted Balfour and C.B.:

> When I look at the Prime Minister, going through what are called those admirable feats of dialectics with which he is lowering the character of the House of Commons, I think of what old Oliver Cromwell said. . . . 'Oh, Sir Harry Vane, thou, with thy subtle casuistries and abstruse hair-splittings, thou art other than a good one, I think. The Lord deliver me from thee, Sir Harry Vane!' . . . I say in the words of Shakespeare-' . . . I had rather be a dog and bay the moon than such a Roman.' And, after all, the Prime Minister has only to look across the table and he would see the example that he ought to follow. What would he see? He would see the Leader of the Opposition. We see, thank goodness, that he is not so nimble at dialectics as the Prime Minister; but I will tell you what he has done – the things which the Prime Minister has egregiously failed to do. He has stuck to his principles and he has saved his party.[98]

C.B. wrote to thank Morley (who was also amazed to have warm congratulations from Rosebery) and Morley replied:

> I am rather addicted to history, and I thought I might as well take time by the forelock, and give to the historian his cue in a compact sentence – and a true one.
>
> It is a pity that the brave lady under your roof could not have seen the tumult of enthusiasm evoked. . . .[99]

C.B. told Gladstone that he thought that the Government could hardly 'shamble on' much longer, though he told William Robertson that 'with this conceited, cunning and unscrupulous Prime Minister (– no one else counts) anything is possible. . . .'.[100] He himself, scenting victory at last, was putting his best foot forward. On April 12 Gladstone wrote to Charlotte from the House, saying:

> I must write a line to congratulate you on Sir Henry's splendid speech tonight. Among all sections of our party I have only heard

one opinion. It was a truly great performance to bring together somewhat discordant elements by a clear and courageous presentment of the main facts of the situation.[101]

The party were excited, like hounds closing in on their quarry. C.B.'s animosity towards Balfour, whom he called 'that fellow', increased.

The education issue kept cropping up. C.B. firmly supported the Nonconformists. Once more he had Haldane against him, as Haldane sympathized with Balfour's policy, and on July 14 wrote to his mother: 'I have . . . been trying to prevent Sir H.C.B. from taking a foolish line over our Education Bill – but I cannot. He is very stupid in such things.'[102]

On June 28 C.B. dined with the Carringtons to meet the King. The King was shy of meeting C.B. He still remembered the 'methods of barbarism' speech. A few weeks before Knollys had written to Akers-Douglas, the Conservative Home Secretary, saying that the King agreed that an attack C.B. had made on Balfour was 'gratuitous and ungenerous'. Knollys added: 'H.M. . . . remarks that it is curious that Sir H. C. Bannerman hardly ever opens his mouth without saying something in bad taste. . . .'[103] Now, however, he decided to go, sat next to C.B. after dinner, got on splendidly with him and stayed till one in the morning. Carrington told the King: 'If we come in Sir Henry will make your Majesty a first-rate Prime Minister.'[104]

The end of the Balfour Government was now in sight. On July 20 it was defeated in the House on an amendment of Redmond's to the vote for the Irish Land Commission. When Balfour subsequently announced that he did not intend to resign, his action was denounced by C.B. as unconstitutional. It was recorded that 'language of unusual violence was employed towards Mr. Balfour by Mr. Churchill and Mr. Lloyd George, while even Sir Edward Grey said that there could no longer be that mutual respect which ought to exist between the House and its leader'.[105]

In August Rosebery wrote in a letter to the Duke of Devonshire: 'I do not believe in an autumn dissolution, because I think that Balfour eminently enjoys his position, especially when Parliament is not sitting, and he is free to devote his mind to golf and military tactics: and also because I am sure that he wishes to put the opposition in Downing Street before a dissolution. But I am generally wrong.'[106]

On November 23 C.B. spoke at Stirling on Ireland, setting out the agreed 'step by step' policy. This resulted in Rosebery's speech at Bodmin on the 25th, declaring that C.B. had hoisted the flag of Home Rule and that he must 'say emphatically and explicitly and once and for all that I cannot serve under that banner'. Rosebery's supporters were appalled, since they had agreed to the line C.B. had put forward. Rosebery had signed his own political death warrant, and this time, despite the desperate efforts of his followers, there was to be no reprieve. In fact Balfour mistook the new public difference between C.B. and Rosebery for a renewed split in the party, and chose this moment to resign, in the hope that C.B. would be able to form only a weak government. But he miscalculated. Rosebery was isolated, still down at the bottom of his lonely furrow. Even Grey had just about given him up, though Dorothy Grey was still a devotee, and Trevelyan quotes him as writing in October: 'My wife is much against my going into office; she is one of the few out-and-out Roseberians that I know.'[107] The former darling of Imperially-minded Liberals was not philosophic in defeat. On November 30 Gladstone wrote to C.B.:

> I had a long talk yesterday with Spender, who had been to the Durdans. R. is in a savage and despairing mood. He denounced A. and G. in unmeasured terms, accusing them of having abandoned him, saying he had done with public life, having no party and no friends.... Of course now he is 'sorry he spoke', but he sees no way of unsaying it.[108]

Balfour resigned on December 4, 1905, and the following day the King invited C.B. to form a government. Rosebery was not asked to join it.

CHAPTER 26

The Defence of Free Trade

'I believe in Free Trade because, in the long run and in general, it is the only policy which is technically sound and intellectually right.'
John Maynard Keynes, *Address to the Liberal Summer School,*
Cambridge 1925

So important was the Free Trade controversy in bringing the Unionist Government to an end that it is worth going back a little to consider how it came to have so decisive an effect.

The second half of 1903, the whole of 1904 and 1905, and the election of 1906 were dominated by it. On this issue, which broke the Conservative hold on the Government of Great Britain, swept the Liberals back to power and turned Winston Churchill into a Liberal, C.B. had no doubts. In the doctrines of Free Trade, as laid down by Adam Smith, and upheld by Cobden and Bright, he unshakeably believed. So did nearly all Liberals and the most brilliant of the younger Conservatives. When, therefore, these doctrines were challenged by Chamberlain, still, at sixty-seven, a great political force, C.B. sprang at once to their defence. Chamberlain was a man whose initiatives and methods he profoundly distrusted. This time he was, however, no longer alone and friendless, but in the van of a great and formidable host.

It is an extraordinary fact that the restless mind of one man, Joseph Chamberlain, succeeded in dominating British politics for ten years. From 1895 to 1902 the main issue was his attempt to force the pace in establishing British supremacy in South Africa, the results being the Jameson Raid and 'Joe's war'. From 1903 to 1906 it was his scheme of Imperial Preference and tariff reform.

Chamberlain's famous speech launching the campaign was made on May 15, 1903. Margot Asquith has described how on the morning of the following day her husband came into her bedroom with *The Times* in his hand and said: 'Wonderful news today, and it is only a question of time when we shall sweep this country.'[1] Balfour had taken quite a different line in a speech the same day. C.B. had also spoken at Scarborough, and had said of the Corn Tax that it would be like a 'Chinese wall built round the Empire from the battlements of which we should shout defiance to the world at large'. He went on:

> Is this a new doctrine? Why, it is as old as the hills. It is ... that old ideal of your border towers and castles on the Rhine, and of each little town having its circumvallation of walls. .... In what respect would this great and memorable and unexampled commonwealth of free nations – because that is what our Empire is – be strengthened by leaguing itself against the other nations of the world? The whole spirit of such a policy is false. .... The generation to which we belong – I am not sure that I don't hover about the past generation myself, but at all events let us say the present generation – has had no experience of the working of a system of protection, has never seen the pinch of poverty, of distress, and the lawlessness and disorder which accompanied it when it existed before.[2]

To his chairman he wrote at the end of the month:

> This reckless criminal escapade of Joe's is the great event of our time. It is playing old Harry with all party relations. Hicks Beach will take the lead in denouncing it: he is violently (not to say viciously and even vindictively) opposed to anything in the way of protection, especially from that quarter. Young Churchill too and all that lot are furious. All the old war-horses about me ... are snorting with excitement. We are in for a great time.[3]

C.B. did not exaggerate. Lord Hugh Cecil wrote to Balfour on May 24: 'Like some one in a novel I implore you to pause before it is too late. ... From a party point of view can anything be more hazardous?'[4]

On this issue, too, the Liberal Imps felt as strongly as C.B. Asquith wrote to him on May 20 saying: 'Tomorrow I have to go to Doncaster where I mean to go bald-headed for J.C. and his swindle of a zollverein.'[5] Even Grey was outspokenly critical of the new plan. But privately C.B. wrote scornfully of the Liberal Imps, saying in a letter to Vaughan Nash: 'That section, for their ends, which are mainly personal, exaggerate their zeal in the fiscal quarrel in order to cover their old backslidings. ...'[6]

C.B. was by now an immensely experienced and canny political tactician, and he sensed that too violent and precipitate an attack in the House would only serve to rally the Unionists behind the Government. There were estimated to be fifty of them who were wholly opposed to Chamberlain's scheme, and another fifty who were filled with doubts. His aim was to allow the differences in the Unionist Party to fester unhindered, to allow Balfour's embarrassments to grow and to do no more than poke the fire from time to time. This fully accorded with his own temperamental indolence, but he was criticized by the keener spirits.

In the June debate, which clearly revealed the strength of Free Trade feeling in the Unionist Parliamentary party, he himself said only that the proposal was to tax anew the food of the people, but it appeared that not only was there a submerged tenth in the population; there was a submergeable third. The effect of taxing the food of the people would be to turn the submergeable into the submerged.[7]

C.B.'s hope that playing it quietly would produce a response from some at least of the Unionist Free Traders was not to be disappointed. One of the ablest of the younger men opposite was prepared to co-operate, even if this meant differing from his closest friends. At the end of May, Winston Churchill pointed out to C.B. that 'the position of those Conservatives who are unalterably opposed to the impending fiscal change is one of great difficulty and danger; and I earnestly hope you will consider us in the course you take'.[8]

Churchill's ally, Lord Hugh Cecil, wrote to him complaining that he had not been consulted before Churchill had written to C.B. Few Conservatives, he pointed out, however much they were Free Traders at heart, would be able to bring themselves to vote with the Liberals. He went on: 'An additional but minor objection is that we ought not to act with CB at all. Rosebery & Grey are our friends. We must try & split their party as well as our own.'[9] Churchill sought to persuade Lord Hugh that he must keep a line open to C.B., and on June 3 told him of a talk with Hicks Beach: '. . . I said "utilise CB". He would not do this himself (CB was a fool & did not possess the power to say yes or no); but what I might do was no concern of his. . . . Beach thought Asquith the better man. I disagree. The Leader of the Opposition is the only person who has the power.'[10]

On June 5 C.B. took his stand in a speech at Perth. He began with a metaphor describing the Government's evasions which was, many years later, used with effect by Winston Churchill:

There exists, as we all know, a certain order of fishes endowed by nature with a special means of escaping from the hostility of the hostile and the curiosity of the curious when in danger of pursuit or of a too close, and therefore inconvenient, investigation. These animals can emit an inky fluid, and create a blind confusion around them, under cover of which they may escape the pursuer. What wonder, ladies and gentlemen, if an organism of a somewhat higher intelligence, such as a modern Ministry, may on occasion borrow the tactics of the cuttlefish.

Of Chamberlain's scheme he said: 'We have seen the spectacle that I thought I could not live to witness. We have seen the Prime Minister of the Crown of this great Empire yielding a palpably reluctant and shivering acquiescence.'
He went on:

In this country we know – thanks to the patience and accurate scientific investigations of Mr. Rowntree and Mr. Charles Booth . . . that there is about 30% of our population underfed, on the verge of hunger . . . 30% of 41 millions comes to something over 12 millions – almost identical, as you see, with the whole population of the Colonies. So that it comes to this, that for every man in the Colonies who is benefited, one head is shoved under water in this country. . . . These are terrible figures, terrible in condemnation of this wild and rash project. . . .

Nailing his flag to the mast of Liberal orthodoxy, he declared roundly: '. . . to dispute Free Trade, after fifty years' experience of it, is like disputing the law of gravitation.'[11]
C.B. was criticized in his own party for citing these figures about the undernourished, and so presenting Chamberlain with the obvious line that all this happened under a Free Trade system, which he promptly took. But C.B. had no use for those Free Traders who talked only of Britain's prosperity and said nothing about the millions who still lived in poverty and want. Such complacency, he believed, played into Chamberlain's hands. On the contrary, Liberals must, he thought, put social reform in the forefront of their policy, and give it as much weight as Free Trade.
It was by now clear that the Unionist Cabinet was hopelessly split on the issue, and everything depended on what line Balfour took as Prime

Minister. His characteristic declaration on June 9, that he himself was of open mind and unsettled convictions, took the Opposition entirely by surprise, and C.B. failed to obtain any real clarification when he raised the matter in the House.[12] But even Balfour's ingenuity could not mask the depth of the split. C.B.'s greatest hopes were fastened upon Sir Michael Hicks Beach, who had declared that Chamberlain's proposals might destroy the Unionist Party. As early as May 31 he told Ripon: 'Hicks Beach is going to lead the assault upon J.C. . . . it is he who captains the young Tory anti-protectionists.'[13] He kept closely in touch with Beach, who urged him to avoid an open challenge to the Government, which, he thought, would damage the Free Trade cause by making the wobbly Unionists throw in their lot with the protectionists. C.B. told Bryce on June 7: 'We must join hands as much as possible with Michael and his angels.'[14] Harcourt fully agreed, saying: 'We can no more do without them than Wellington could afford to neglect the Prussians at Waterloo.'[15]

Violet Cecil, writing to Milner from Hatfield on July 1, sought to paint a reassuring picture of the situation from the Unionist point of view, quoting Balfour as saying of C.B. that he was incapable 'even of sitting on the fence'.[16]

By this time the Liberals had settled their tactics and announced that they did not intend to move a resolution in the House, but to concentrate on a campaign in the country. C.B. told Smith in Stirling: 'We are repressing the ardour of our people in the House. . . .'[17]

He was playing a careful game, believing that nothing would happen till October, 'when Joe will go in sorrow not in anger, and will lead an independent crusade in the country'.[18] This was exactly what happened, and was, from the Liberal point of view, far better than forcing the Free Traders out of the Government and leaving Joe in possession. Looking at it from the other side of the fence, Mr. Julian Amery judges that 'the Liberal leaders were wise in their decision'. He quotes a letter from C.B. to his Dunfermline chairman, Mr. William Robertson, explaining the need for caution, and comments: 'The reader will scarcely refuse his salute to the shrewdness and vision with which Campbell-Bannerman and Harcourt led their forces to the defence of their economic faith.'[19]

Three days after C.B. wrote this letter, the resignations from the Government of Chamberlain, Ritchie and Lord George Hamilton were announced. Balfour had come out for a policy of 'retaliation' – that is, taxing the products of countries which taxed ours – and Chamberlain had, as C.B. expected, gone quietly, so as to be free to stump the country.

His son Austen became Chancellor of the Exchequer. There was widespread surprise that the Duke of Devonshire (as Hartington had now become), known to be a convinced Free Trader, did not also resign. As C.B. commented in a letter of September 19 to Smith: 'What a turn up in the Government! . . . This fine idea of Joe freely operating outside, Arthur sympathizing with him and co-operating inside, presents worse dangers than ever to Free Trade. . . . More incidents must follow. . . .'[20] And to Gladstone he commented: 'and the "Jook"! What a contemptible figure he cuts!'[21]

He was in close touch with Spencer, and wrote to him on September 23: 'There is no question that this retaliation business appeals to two unworthy passions – the pugnacity of John Bull, and the selfish interest of individual trades . . . retaliation is only Act I in the drama, leading inevitably to full-blooded protection all round. . . .'[22]

C.B. was right in expecting more incidents. A fortnight later the Duke awoke to the equivocal nature of his position – he had not, he admitted, grasped what was going on around him – and promptly resigned.

C.B. wrote to Vaughan Nash on September 26:

I think the delays in patching up their old tub of a Govt. will only humiliate them still further; and my Egeria at home here declares that they will break down yet. My impression is that 'our Mr. Austen' at the Treas^y, A. Forster in Pall Mall & Milner for the Colonies, wd. be enough to swamp any Ministry. Each of them is an outrage on decency: and so think many Unionists.[23]

In the House of Lords the Duke of Devonshire explained his resignation. Gosse described him graphically on this occasion sinking 'lower and lower at the table, sideways, like a stone figure partly overturned in the sand'.[24]

In public the line C.B. took was to rub in the dubious nature of Balfour's manœuvre. At Blairgowrie on September 24 he asked:

What respect can we have now – can any one have – for a Government the head of which avows his acceptance of a certain ideal, admits that the country is opposed to it, allows a colleague to resign on this express ground, and yet remains in office for the purpose of insidiously paving the way for its acceptance?[25]

This was no mere party cant, but an exact appreciation of the situation. Balfour was managing, by extraordinarily ingenious expedients, aptly described as 'plate-spinning', to cling to office, but at the cost of storing up for his party an increasingly shattering defeat at the polls.

On October 3 C.B. described Imperial Preference as 'the rash and fantastic scheme of so-called fiscal reform – really fiscal reaction – now authoritatively approved both by the intra-mural and the extra-mural portions of the Government'.[26]

On the 15th, at Bolton, he denounced as a 'wicked slander' the assertion that the Empire could only be saved from dissolution by a revolution in fiscal policy. He also charged the Prime Minister, who, he said, agreed with Mr. Chamberlain and yet would not go with him because the times were not yet ripe, with practically acknowledging himself ready to sacrifice the Empire in order to keep his party together and his Government in office. 'This Government,' he said, 'and its noisier supporters, claim the Empire and the imperial idea as almost an asset of their own.' He went on to speak of Free Trade:

> We are satisfied that it is right because it gives the freest play to individual energy and initiative and character and the largest liberty both to producer and consumer. . . . trade is injured when it is not allowed to follow its natural course, and when it is either hampered or diverted by artificial obstacles. . . . We believe in free trade be- cause we believe in the capacity of our countrymen. That at least is why I oppose protection root and branch, veiled and unveiled, one- sided or reciprocal. I oppose it in any form. Besides we have the experience of fifty years, during which our prosperity has become the envy of the world.

He concluded by drawing a comparison between Balfour and one of his predecessors: 'I have been dipping during the last two or three days into a book which has just been published – the life of Mr. Gladstone – written by my friend and your friend, Mr. John Morley...' – it was entirely characteristic of C.B. not to pretend to have read right through this book by a colleague about his old chief:

> . . . I was caught by a phrase . . . Mr. Gladstone was writing to one of his sons. . . . He was . . . preparing . . . a great policy which he believed would work infinite good. . . . And what says he to his

son? He talks of difficulties in his way and then he says, 'But the great thing is to be right.' Not that the great thing it to be successful, not that the great thing is to be popular . . . but the 'great thing is to be right'. . . . These are two Premiers of the Empire. Look, I ask you, upon this picture and upon that.[27]

C.B.'s private estimate of Balfour was given in a letter to J. E. Ellis: 'The contemptible person is the 1st L. of Treasury – never was anything more immoral, dishonest, & unconstitutional, than the rigging up of retaliation as a formal policy while proclaiming adhesion to Joe's. . . .'[28]

On October 16, the Duke of Devonshire joined the Unionist Free Food League, the other leading members of which were Hicks Beach, Goschen, Ritchie and Lord James of Hereford. They were to become known as the Free Fooders.

Three days later, in a letter to Ripon, C.B. said:

. . . From the first I have declared that the enemy was retaliation. The greater scheme runs its head against free food and breaks its neck. Also, the Britisher takes his Colonialism with qualifications, and is a little tired of having our 'over-sea kinsman' trotted out to overawe him.

But retaliation

(a) cultivates the ingrained fallacy that imports are an evil;
(b) captures the Chamber of Commerce sort of man by appealing to his self-interest;
(c) plays up to our pugnacity;
(d) has the air of an innocent compromise. . . .[29]

Unionist difficulties with the Free Food League gave as much joy to the Liberals as their own difficulties with the Liberal League had once given to the Unionists. Beach, however, had wobbled back into support of Balfour's position on retaliation and appeared on the same platform with Balfour on November 13. Some of the angels were still sound, but Michael could no longer be counted on.

In the country all the Liberal leaders were in full cry in attacking Chamberlain, whose biographer records: 'Harcourt thought Asquith too reasoned for the platform and rated Campbell-Bannerman's replies to Chamberlain higher. Most contemporary opinion, however, gave the palm to Asquith; and it was by his relentless pursuit of Chamberlain through the country that Asquith really established his reputation.'[30] C.B. wrote to Robertson: 'Asquith is making some first-rate speeches. (Why did those fellows ever go astray?)'[31]

He himself, when he spoke at Newport on November 30, faced squarely the charge that, on his own admission, poverty was widespread under the existing system of Free Trade:

> Our position is that poverty in a Free Trade country is nothing like the curse which it is in a Protectionist country where every crust of bread is taxed. We are not fanatics. We do not attribute to Free Trade miraculous powers, or claim for it that it can of itself remove the burden of poverty. We leave panaceas to others. But we don't want to see England turned once more into the poor man's purgatory, a place of unalleviated misery for the workman. We don't want another England of the 'thirties and the 'forties . . . the Liberal Party, if it is worth its salt, will take up the cause of the poor man, will stand by the poor man, and see him through this business. . . .[32]

On December 7 he wrote to Bryce:

> I doubt whether – barring individual manufacturers, speculators and loafers – Joe is making much way: I should add fine ladies and 'swells' generally. But these were probably all protectionists at heart already so far as they have a heart and any knowledge.
>
> There is a good deal of doubt what to do with the Free Fooders. . . .
>
> Tweedmouth is full of a scheme for half a dozen voting with us on the Address, resigning their seats and standing as Liberals. A little too melodramatic for John Bull's taste! And after all Winston is hardly worth any increase of complication.[33]

Winston Churchill was not, however, to be dismissed so lightly. On December 21 a letter from him was published in the press, which said:

> . . . Our system of free trade involves two conditions . . . cheap food and honest government. Mr. Chamberlain's victory would deprive the nation of both . . . the time is . . . approaching when . . . free traders of all parties should form one long line of battle against a common foe. . . . All these years we have held up among the nations

the lamp of economic truth. . . . The triumph of protection would set up instead a policy of brag and grab. The defeat of protection – and perhaps you have it in your power to strike a smashing blow – will send forth to all nations a message of peace and goodwill.[34]

Clearly on the great issue of the day nothing divided Churchill from the Liberals on the other side of the House.

Since the Government had a majority of ninety in the House of Commons, it only needed the forty or fifty Unionist Free Traders to vote with the Opposition to bring the Government down. If that had happened in 1903 there might have been strong pressure for a coalition Free Trade government to be led by the Duke of Devonshire or Rosebery. But there would have been opposition to this both from Unionists and from Liberals. C.B. had serious doubts about any electoral pact. When Lord James of Hereford put out feelers to the Liberals he told Gladstone: 'We are to withdraw candidates wherever our local people will allow it, in order to save the skin of the Free Traders. In return the Free Traders are most of them to run away or join the enemy. . . . I fear our people will hardly see it.'[35]

The bitter controversies of Boer War days had faded and politicians of necessity have to have thick skins and short memories. C.B. was now able to consult freely with Asquith on political tactics. He wrote to him on Boxing Day about the Free Fooders, saying: 'It is a ticklish situation for us, but it is life or death to them. We are "the man on horseback"; and while everything should be done to make things easy for them it is they who must draw closer to us, however distasteful.'[36] Asquith agreed, saying of the Free Fooders, 'they look very well in the shop-window but I fear that in most constituencies their voting strength is insignificant'.[37]

Chamberlain made a violent attack on C.B. in December, but this only served to bring the Liberal Imps further back into cooperation with him. Fowler, for example, wrote on December 26: '. . . First let me congratulate you on your reply to J.C.'s outrageous and unprovoked attack at Limehouse. I think that in this speech he out-Heroded Herod in feebleness, folly & rudeness & I think seriously damaged his own position. You said the right thing in the right manner. . . .'[38]

It was a long time since any Liberal Imperialist had come anywhere near suggesting that C.B. was saying 'the right thing in the right manner'.

Chamberlain was now a private member, but the influence exercised by his personality was still immense, and he aroused tremendous enthusiasm or furious opposition. On the issue of tariff reform he faced opposition as implacable from the Free Fooders as from the Radicals whom he had abandoned eighteen years before.

Balfour's position ought now, by any reasonable calculation, to have become impossible. It is a measure of his political agility and adroitness that he was able to keep going for two more years. In the rôle of a hunted fox his ingenuity was marvellous, and time and again he baffled his less nimble pursuers, among them C.B. The game of trying to pin him down, which C.B. was later to describe as 'hunting the fiscal slipper',[39] went on throughout 1904 and most of 1905. But the effect in the country was disastrous for the Unionists, and by-election after by-election showed which way the tide was flowing. C.B. was in good form. After he had spoken at Maidstone, Harcourt told his son Loulou: 'I have written to tell him that in my opinion it is quite the best that has been made on the controversy. Really on the platform he is A1.'[40]

On January 14, 1904, C.B. wrote to James Smith: 'It will be a difficult job to pull the Unionist F. Traders out of the hole, & yet we must & will do it. They are a funky lot!'[41] A month later Winston Churchill attacked the Brussels Sugar Convention as the forerunner of protection, and C.B. referred to his speech as 'brilliant' and as 'the most sustained piece of irony I have ever heard in the House of Commons'.[42] The compliment gave pleasure.[43] Here was one Free Fooder who could not be described as 'funky'. Winston Churchill had, in fact, only three months left as a Unionist. On June 5 C.B. and Lloyd George addressed a vast concourse of twenty thousand at the Alexandra Palace at a Free Trade rally to celebrate the centenary of Cobden's birth. C.B. was described by the *Daily Chronicle* as making 'one of his finest fighting speeches – trenchant, pointed, earnest, eloquent . . . his voice rang with a fervour which kindled overwhelming cheers'.[44] To those who disparaged Cobden as a mere trader, C.B. declared that he had made no riches for himself, but had made his country's fortune.

With them on the platform was Churchill, who also made a powerful speech, heaping scorn on Chamberlain and telling his audience: 'And how is it with the Conservative party? They are not at all pleased with me. They tell me I ought to join the Liberal party.'

Mr. Churchill looked down at his notes, and then again at his great audience:

'It isn't a bad idea,' he added, 'I will consider it carefully.'[45]

Three days later, on June 8, he did indeed cross the floor of the House. His great friend Hugh Cecil was too dedicated a Conservative to take this step. Contemporary opinion in the House was mistaken about the future. Most members thought that Churchill had made a mistake, and that it was Lord Hugh Cecil who was the future Prime Minister.[46] But his constancy led him to political extinction, while Churchill's apostasy led on to glory.

Seven months later, on January 4, 1905, Edward Hamilton wrote in his diary: 'Tonight I met Winston Churchill at dinner. . . . He has completely gone over, & has become a wholehearted Liberal. . . . He is hard at work on his father's life. I like him, but he has not got the personal charm of his father.'[47]

So the battle went forward into 1905. Chamberlain remained the real enemy, Balfour the House of Commons juggler. On January 2 C.B. told J. E. Ellis: 'As to A.J.B. his qualities have been stripped down to Parliamentary cunning & nothing else.'[48]

When Parliament opened, C.B. made what Margot Asquith described as an 'amusing and telling speech', likening Balfour to a general who, having ordered his men to attack, found them attacking one another; whereupon he shrugged his shoulders and said that he couldn't help it if they would misunderstand his orders.[49] But for all his cunning, time was running out for Balfour. To avoid a defeat on March 22 he and his supporters walked out of the House and thereafter three resolutions in favour of Free Trade were carried without a dissenting vote. C.B. said that day:

> Those who have exhausted every wile of concealment, every trench that could be dug, every finesse, every trick by which a little advantage in defence might be obtained, strike their camp, abandon their policy and their pretences, and leave their bewildered followers to take part in a general *sauve-qui-peut*.[50]

Efforts to bring Balfour to bay grew ever more frantic. On May 23 C.B. and Lloyd George joined in a hail of questions to him on whether the Government would discuss Imperial Preference at the next Colonial Conference if they were still in power. Balfour's replies were evasive. C.B. attacked him fiercely and moved the adjournment of the House. After his speech Lyttelton rose but was denied a hearing by the Liberals, who shouted for the Prime Minister. The result was pandemonium, and for once C.B. made no attempt to hold back his followers. In June, when Chamberlain was speaking in the House, Balfour became more and more uneasy, finally turning and whispering to the man next to him on the front bench: 'Oh! isn't this damnable!'[51]

The Liberals were now united. C.B. even wrote to Robertson describing a meeting in Edinburgh, with 'Asquith like a glass of port, and R. like a bumper of champagne'.[52] The Unionists were now all over the place. For three years Lord Hugh Cecil had wrestled for the soul of Arthur Balfour, and many letters had passed between them in which their friendship and courtesy contended with their deep differences on this issue. On July 13 Cecil wrote to express his fury with Chamberlain: 'If you were to die & he became Leader I shd. either join Rosebery or retire, for I certainly differ from R. less than I do from J.C.'[53]

Balfour's reply showed his alarm lest Cecil should follow Churchill across the floor:

My dear Linky,

. . . I do beg you, even if I die, to remain in the party!! It is quite true that, in a sense, you probably agree more with Rosebery than with Joe: – indeed, so far as I know Rosebery's opinions, they do not fundamentally differ from those of the majority of the Unionist Party. It is his great political misfortune that he joined the wrong side.

I doubt, however, whether his health will ever allow him to be the working head of a party in office, and I do not believe that . . . if I were to vanish from the scene, [Joe] would be selected to fill my place. If he were, the Party would, no doubt, for a time be broken up . . . it is within a strong and united Party that the disintegrating effects of Joe's personality and propaganda have the least effect. It is a pity they have been unable to tolerate with greater equanimity my strong sympathy with the colonial ideals which lie, I believe, at the root of Joe's action: Had they done so I should have been in a stronger position to resist the illegitimate accretions with which those ideals are so easily encrusted. . . .

In any case, never talk of leaving the Party!

Yours affectionately

Arthur James Balfour.[54]

Cecil stayed in the party, but his views did not change. On November 7 he wrote to *The Times* saying that Chamberlain's tactics were 'not those of a statesman but of a fanatic'.[55]

Meanwhile C.B. spoke up and down the country, supported by a rising wave of enthusiasm. He attacked the Government and Chamberlain remorselessly, insisting that Balfour's 'retaliation' and Chamberlain's tariff reform were 'inextricably interlocked'. By now he had the Government on the run. Balfour had to resign in December because, as one Unionist put it, 'his party is so hopelessly divided that they could not agree on any pronouncement on the subject'. Fundamentally it was Chamberlain's plan which wrecked the Unionist Party. Free Trade was the main issue in the 1906 election, and on that issue the country gave a decisive answer. As Asquith later wrote: 'The Fiscal controversy was determined by the General Election of 1906, and ceased to be one of the living issues in British politics.'[56]

Part 7

The Plot that Failed

CHAPTER 27

The Relugas Conspiracy

B Y the beginning of 1905 it was clear that the days of the Balfour
Government were numbered. Some thought that Lord Spencer
might be the next Prime Minister – a view Spencer himself did not
actively discourage, though he now had a weak heart. He still looked
on C.B. as his junior. Gosse wrote on February 17 that Spencer 'is not
strong . . . and he is evidently pulling himself up towards the ambition
of being Prime Minister. But the King said to Haldane a few days ago,
"Who told Lord Spencer that I am going to call upon him to form a
Government? I am sure *I* didn't. I am not at all convinced that his
health would allow it." '1

Lord Davey pressed his claims to be Lord Chancellor on Spencer.
According to Gosse, Davey's intellect was still brilliant, but 'his person
is extremely unsympathetic. His long melancholy nose is drawn up in
a perpetual sneer, his parchment cheeks and stealthy hyena-like tread
freeze conversation whenever he makes an appearance.'2 There was
little chance of C.B. choosing such a man.

Others still hoped that Rosebery might be persuaded to come back.
But Knollys told Hamilton that when the King had stayed at Mentmore
Rosebery had advised the King to send for C.B. and Spencer together.3
Rosebery was no longer what he had been. Gosse wrote in April that
his 'appearance is now becoming very extraordinary. The flesh is so
puffy and thick on his cheeks, and his eye-orbits so deep, that it looks
as if he had a face over his face. His colour is unhealthy, a dull deep
red . . . he eats extravagantly, and though he is never "the worse for
liquor", he drinks heavily and continuously';4 and on another occasion:
'Rosebery does not even affect to address the House but speaks entirely
to the Press Gallery.'5

Most people accepted, however, that C.B. had established his position beyond challenge as the leader of the Liberal Party and, consequently, as head of the next government. In January, Morley was staying at Belmont and discussed the composition of the Cabinet with C.B. and Charlotte, writing:

> He would not listen to my *noli episcopari*. 'Within limits, you would have what you like.' I wrote down a list of a possible Cabinet. The upshot was in his mind India for me, Bryce Ireland. The last determination puzzled me . . . I pressed for Labour in the Cabinet in the person of John Burns. Not averse, he thought it worth consideration.[6]

C.B. thought well of Burns, who had mellowed since the 1880's when he had, in a speech, expressed his regret that an attempt to murder the Czar had not succeeded.

On January 29 Hamilton wrote: 'John Morley has been . . . speechifying in Scotland, where he said they were heart-high for C. Bannerman. . . . He (C.B.) had no wish (nor had she) that he should be Prime Minister, but he . . . was like a man in an express train. He could not alight. . . .'[7]

In October 1903 Grey had given a foretaste of difficulties to come, writing to Asquith: 'You must be leader . . . under no circumstances would I take office with C.-B., as Prime Minister, in any Govt. in which C-B was leader in the House of Commons. . . .'[8]

Next year, in 1904, Esher had written to his son:

> Arthur Balfour has no doubt that the King should send for Campbell-Bannerman. . . . He said that he had reluctantly come to the conclusion that Rosebery was hopeless, as he would have been glad, for Imperial reasons, to transfer the Government into his hands. But that as circumstances had shaped themselves, he could only aim at leaving the country . . . in such a state . . . that the new Government would merely have to carry on insured against any dangerous foreign complication. . . .[9]

Balfour had little confidence in the capacity of anyone other than himself to run the country's affairs.

Others too had concluded that C.B. as Prime Minister was inevitable. In 1904 Almeric Fitzroy recorded that 'Haldane saw no alternative to Campbell-Bannerman' but that he expected trouble from

Dilke, 'as he has a following, is not only able, but thoroughly unscrupulous, besides being inclined to put forward the most extravagant pretensions, having the idea that his long exclusion from office entitles him to a kind of cumulative compensation'.[10]

The idea of relegating C.B., or 'Aunt Jane', as they called him, to the Lords, as a figurehead Prime Minister, had obvious attractions for the Liberal Imps. Moreover, given C.B.'s age – he passed his sixty-ninth birthday in 1905 – and his indifferent health, it seemed an objective which might be attained without too much difficulty. As long before as October 1903, Gladstone had been told by C.B. that 'he did not think that he would be able to take any post which involved heavy and responsible work. A peerage and some office of dignity like the Presidentship of the Council would be what he would like.'[11] But this was probably a passing mood of depression.

Haldane quickly emerged as the most active and determined of the Liberal Imps. Gosse wrote in February 1905:

> I dined . . . with Haldane. The confusion of the Liberal Party beggars description. . . . Lord Rosebery has four empty villas at Naples. Haldane says if they could be fitted up, and Ld. Spencer, C.B., John Morley and Ld. R. himself could be deported thither, with orders to the Syndic of Naples to allow them every luxury, but to keep them there, the Liberal Party would be in a perfectly healthy condition. . . . Haldane thinks the only possible solution is to put the Prime Ministership into commission and raise C.-B. to the Upper House as Viscount Belmont. That could exclude Ld. Rosebery of course, but he will be excluded anyhow. . . . Asquith, Haldane and Grey . . . stick together . . . and C.-B. must take all three or none.[12]

Haldane explained in his autobiography that:

> Campbell-Bannerman . . . was genial and popular and respected for the courage with which he had resisted the policy of the Government on South Africa. But he was not identified in the public mind with any fresh ideas, for indeed he had none. What was wanted was . . . a body of men with life and energy and a new outlook on the problems of the State.[13]

Haldane thought C.B. a mediocrity. C.B. thought Haldane a clumsy intriguer. As he put it: 'Haldane always prefers the back-stairs;

but it does not matter: for the clatter can be heard all over the house.'[14] Grey shared Haldane's outlook and was his close ally.

C.B. seemed at first inclined to fall in with the suggestion that he should go to the Lords, but he later told Gladstone that he was resolved not to go there straight away. In fact the Liberal Imps were not the only people to whom the idea had occurred. On February 21 C.B. had had a letter from Labouchere, who said:

> Our very opportunist friend Lloyd George was explaining to me a plan for you to go to the Lords – I said to him that as his object was to be in the Cabinet, he would do well to stick to you, as I had gathered from an observation that fell from you that you were for this – It was an invention of my own, but it converted him, for he came to me afterwards and tried to find out what the observation was, but I only replied that it had quite convinced me that he would be in the Cabinet. This is the best plan to deal with these sort of cadgers. . . .[15]

Trevelyan wrote that Grey was misled by 'the belief that Campbell-Bannerman could not effectively lead the House – a mistake not unnatural to those who had watched him there as leader of the Opposition'.[16] Rosebery was effectively out of it, though he was apparently incensed when he heard that in August Cabinet-making had been going on at Spencer's house and that his name had not been mentioned.[17]

From the middle of August until the end of September 1905, C.B. and Charlotte were, as usual, at Marienbad. C.B. himself had been thoroughly exhausted at the end of the session and had something he described as a 'breakdown'. His doctors found nothing seriously wrong, but told him to clear out of London and take as long and complete a rest as possible.[18] The King, however, was also at Marienbad. C.B. saw him constantly. He had a long, friendly talk with him on the 24th, at which the King said that C.B. 'must soon be in Office and very high Office', and went on to discuss the whole gamut of current problems 'from the Kaiser to College Green'. C.B. told Sinclair that it had been 'all most satisfactory and reasonable. He properly said nothing of the Government as a whole, or of dissolution, but free in denouncing much that they do. At the end, sent messages to my wife and said he was glad to meet and talk to such "old friends". Most significant, and very discreetly done. Quite scared and saddened me.'[19]

For two weeks C.B. lunched or dined with the King nearly every day.[20] He told William Robertson: 'I got so mixed up with the King's incessant gaieties, for which his energy and appetite are alike insatiable, that it was no rest or holiday to me. Thus when at last he was gone . . . my Dr. ordered me to bed and absolute rest for 48 hours. . . .'[21]

C.B. was a profoundly modest man, but it was now apparent, even to him, that in the highest quarter it was regarded as a settled thing that he would, before long, be the next Prime Minister, provided that he could form a government. But whether he would be a real Prime Minister in the Commons, or a figurehead Prime Minister in the Lords, still remained to be determined.

The indefatigable Haldane made up his mind that he would be the man to determine it. In September he and Asquith went to see Grey, who was fishing at Relugas on the Findhorn in Scotland. There, Haldane wrote:

> . . . we agreed . . . that if Campbell-Bannerman became Prime Minister he should take a peerage, and that Asquith should lead in the Commons as Chancellor of the Exchequer. Unless our scheme were in substance carried out we resolved that we could not join Campbell-Bannerman's Government. What we thus resolved on we used afterwards . . . to speak of among ourselves as 'the Relugas Compact'.[22]

Haldane enjoyed being a conspirator. He was even more delighted when he was chosen to bring the King into the plot. 'To place this on a sure foundation', he wrote, 'it was felt that we needed the sympathy and possible co-operation of King Edward, and it fell to me to try to obtain this.'[23] His first step was to write to Knollys at Balmoral, which he did on September 12, saying:

> I have no knowledge of the attitude . . . of Sir Henry Campbell-Bannerman. He is reticent and shrewd and I doubt whether he has uttered a word to those who think they know his mind. . . . He may well hold a sensible view of the position. But it has not always been so. . . . I have just returned . . . from a private consultation with Asquith and Grey. We had, as you know, formed the view strongly that Sir H.C.B. might . . . go to the Upper House leaving Asquith to lead the Commons with Grey by his side. But we have within the last few days been made aware that this course will not be

acceptable to a certain section of the party. . . . Pressure will doubtless be put on Sir H.C.B. to retain his lead in the Commons. . . . Asquith, Grey, and I feel that were this to happen we could in office render no real service . . . and we have decided, in such a case, that it would be best for us to intimate early to Sir H.C.B. that we should stand aside. . . . We believe that the Opposition cannot emerge from its present position unless we can, with our friends and followers, to some extent shape policy. . . .

What is proposed is that Asquith should, in as friendly and tactful a way as possible, and without assuming that Sir H.C.B. is adverse, tell him of the resolution we have come to. We are none of us wedded to the prospects of office. To Asquith and me they mean pecuniary sacrifice. This we do not shrink from in the least, but we ought not to make sacrifices uselessly. Grey delights in his new work, as Chairman of the North-Eastern Railway. But we are all ready to do our best cheerfully under Sir H.C.B. provided we have sufficient safeguards. What we would try to bring about is that . . . Sir H.C.B. . . . should propose to the King the leadership of the House of Commons with the Exchequer for Asquith, either the Foreign or Colonial Office for Grey, and the Woolsack for myself. As to this last I am merely recording for you the wish of the others. I will gladly stand aside. . . .[24]

This letter set out the details of the conspiracy with remarkable candour. Haldane appears to have been innocent of any sense of humour. The picture of himself, Asquith and Grey nobly and public-spiritedly nerving themselves to shoulder the burdens of the Woolsack, the Exchequer, and the Foreign or Colonial Office, of Asquith and Haldane selflessly preparing to make their pecuniary sacrifices, while Grey prepared to scorn the delights of the North-Eastern Railway, is a touching one. To C.B. the letter was relentlessly patronizing – the poor man might perhaps 'hold a sensible view of the position' (that is, surrender to the Liberal Imp leaders) now that he had been shown flattering attentions by the King. He would be able to go away and play with the thirteen Cabinet places left over for him to allocate. He must be disposed of, like an ageing horse, 'with the utmost gentleness and consideration'. It is the letter of a man wholly incapable of seeing himself as others, or at any rate some others, saw him.

It was also a grossly improper letter for a politician who had never held office, still less been a member of any Cabinet, to address to the

Private Secretary to the Sovereign. It was an attempt to involve the King in an intrigue directed against the leader of the Liberal Party by a section of his own supporters. Knollys, however, did not, strangely enough, see it in that light. Like Esher, and others at the Court, he regarded the Radicals with alarm and thought that national interests were only safe in the hands of either Balfour or of the Imperialist section of the Liberal Party. His reply was singularly forthcoming:

> Many thanks for your important and interesting letter . . . which I presume you will not object to my showing confidentially to the King. . . . In the event of his sending for Sir H. C.-Bannerman my belief is that he will strongly urge him to go to the House of Lords as Prime Minister, partly because he would think that Asquith would be the best man to lead the H. of Commons, and partly because he would fear that Sir H.C.B., being a weak or at all events not a strong man like Asquith, would be inclined to give way to pressure from the extreme left, whereas were he in the House of Lords he would not be liable to this pressure to the same extent. If Sir H.C.B. declined to act on the King's suggestion and you and your friends refused to join the Government, H.M. would be placed in an awkward position. A Cabinet of which Sir H.C.B. was the head, without the moderates, would, it appears to me, be disastrous both for the Country and the Party . . . what the King would desire would be the presence of a restraining influence in the Cabinet . . . men like yourself, Asquith and Sir E. Grey . . . would not you be better able to advance the . . . welfare of the Country and the Liberal Party, by joining Sir H.C.B.'s Government, even if he remained in the House of Commons . . . ? At his age it is not probable that he would be able to stand for long the combined duties of Prime Minister and Leader of the House of Commons, and I cannot help thinking that after one session in that House, which would 'save his face' with his extreme friends, he would be glad to move into the House of Lords. I should imagine indeed that if he showed himself unwilling, when forming a Government, to become a Peer, the King might well ask him to give a pledge that he would go into the House of Lords within a certain time, say a year. . . .[25]

One of Haldane's recent biographers describes this as 'the letter of a very wise man'.[26] But considering that the King had just told C.B.

that he proposed to send for him if Balfour gave up, it was surely injudicious, to say the least, for his Private Secretary to enter quite so enthusiastically into a conspiracy against him, and to describe him as 'weak' and a possible radical-based government as a disaster for the country. It was, in fact, just as well that, in the event, the King was wiser and more cautious than his Private Secretary.

C.B.'s friend, T. R. Buchanan, stayed with the Haldanes at the end of September and found the Asquiths there. He reported to C.B. that

> they both recognise, & said so in so many words, that you must be Prime Minister. They would like to shove you into the Lords, but that I told them would be fatal to your position & influence. . . . They accept Lloyd George, are not sure of Winston (Mrs. Asquith dissenting, she believes in him), will shelve Fowler in the Lords, distrust & dislike Dilke, & are afraid of Tommy Shaw & his influence . . . So far as I can judge, they won't, either of them, be divisive elements in a Government after it is formed, but they will try to get it filled with men of their own sort. . . .[27]

Haldane was invited over to talk to the King, and wrote to Asquith from Balmoral on October 6:

> The plan is thoroughly approved in all its details. . . . I think that the K. will ask C.B. to Sandringham in Nov. and say that he doubts, from recent observation, whether any one but a young man can be both P.M. and Leader in his H. of C. . . . This leaves it open to C.B. to think that Ld. S. may be sent for, and later on will enable the K. to suggest a peerage to H.C.B. Meantime both he and Knollys . . . wish you to go into general policy with C.B. but not to go so far as to let him surmise any connection between your conversation and what may done here.
>
> They are fully alive to the importance of secrecy and reticence. . . . If only tongues are held (and I have done all that can be done to secure this) I think . . . that we have secured very cordial and powerful assistance. . . .[28]

Haldane wrote that he 'left the Castle with the feeling that there was no more for me to do, and that the next step must be taken by Asquith when he saw C.-B.'[29] While he was at Balmoral, he had told Esher that 'C.B. has no *intimates* among politicians, and lives exclusively with his old W.O. officials, Haliburton and Knox.'[30]

On October 13 Spencer, while out shooting in Norfolk, had a cerebral attack, which removed him from the running, not only for the Prime Ministership, but for any Cabinet post. C.B. was greatly upset. He had a great affection and admiration for Spencer, and would have counted on him as a major prop of a new government. He described it to Ripon as a 'terrible calamity' and said that he now depended more than ever on Ripon's counsel, 'for I always know where I am with you, and can reckon on sound and honest advice'.[31] Churchill wrote to Rosebery, saying: 'Poor Lord Spencer. It was rather like a ship sinking in sight of land.'[32]

As it became clearer that the Balfour Government was in extremis, Liberals began to wonder what posts they might be offered. Lord Beauchamp's valet declared as his master hurried up to London: 'We shall 'ave Hindia or Hireland, but we don't know which.'[33]

While all this had been going on, C.B. had been staying quietly at Marienbad. He left there on September 28, and he and Charlotte then spent the first three weeks of October at Merano, in Italy, followed by ten days at Vienna and a week at Paris, where there was a letter from Morley saying: 'There are some floating icebergs in the political ocean, but your Sun will melt them.'[34] For a man whose political future was threatened by some of the most powerful figures in his party, acting with the connivance of the Sovereign, it was a singularly unhurried progress. He did not get back to London until November 12. He probably had a shrewd idea of what had been going on in his absence, and as soon as he was back he acted swiftly and effectively to break up the conspiracy.

Next day Asquith, who had agreed at Relugas to tackle C.B., came to see him. He was supposed to persuade C.B. tactfully to agree to go to the Lords as Prime Minister. But C.B. seized, and retained, the initiative, and the interview took quite another course. The most vivid account of it is that left by Margot Asquith:

Henry came into my bedroom at Cavendish Square, where I was having my hair washed . . . tying a shawl round my head ran down to the library, where . . . Henry walked up and down the room and told me all he could remember of his talk with C.B.

He found him in his library in Belgrave Square. . . . They . . . proceeded to discuss Russia and Germany. Henry was glad to find him sound on Germany. He dislikes the Kaiser and thinks him a dangerous, restless, mischief-making man.

Suddenly he said that he thought things looked like coming to a head politically, and that any day after Parliament met we might expect a General Election. He gathered that he would probably be the man the King would send for, in which case he would make no phrases but would consent to form a Government.

Henry said: 'C.B. then looked at me and said: "I do not think we have ever spoken of the future Liberal Government, Asquith? What would you like? The Exchequer, I suppose?"–I said nothing –"or the Home Office?" I said, "Certainly not." At which he said: "Of course, if you want legal promotion what about the Woolsack? No? Well then, it comes back to the Exchequer. I hear that it has been suggested by that ingenious person, Richard Burdon Haldane, that I should go to the House of Lords, a place for which I have neither liking, training nor ambition. In this case you would lead the House of Commons. . . ."' I could see that the impression left upon Henry's mind . . . was that it would be with reluctance and even repugnance that Campbell-Bannerman would ever go to the House of Lords.

C.B. then asked my husband who he thought best fitted for the Home Office; to which Henry replied that that depended upon who would have the Woolsack, and added,

'For that, my dear C.B., there are only two possible people, Haldane or Reid,' and went on to say that Reid had told him in past days that he did not fancy leaving the House of Commons, 'in which case,' said Henry, 'why not give him the Home Office and Haldane the Woolsack?' C.B. answered, 'Why not *vice versa?*'

When Henry told me this – knowing as I do that Haldane had set his heart on being Lord Chancellor, I was reminded of George Eliot's remark, 'When a man wants a peach it is no good offering him the largest vegetable marrow,' but I merely said that I hoped Haldane would not stand out if Reid desired the Woolsack. He went on to tell me that C.B. had then said:

'There are two more delicate offices we've not mentioned, Asquith – the Colonial and the Foreign Office.'

Henry said he thought Edward Grey should have the Foreign Office; C.B. answered that he had considered Lord Elgin for this, but Henry was very strong upon Grey. He said that . . . Grey's appointment . . . would be popular all over Europe. . . .

C.B. said he wanted him for the War Office, but Henry told me – having been unshakable upon this point – he felt pretty sure that he had made an impression, as C.B. ultimately agreed that Lord Elgin would do well at the Colonial Office. . . .[35]

The supposedly sleepy, 'weak' mediocrity C.B. had in fact conducted this crucial interview with masterly skill. The discussion had been throughout on his terms. From the start he took the position that he was discussing the problems of the next government with the utmost frankness and confidence with his chief lieutenant, and Asquith, while pushing Grey's and Haldane's personal claims, simply could not bring himself to press the line of argument about the need for C.B. to efface himself in the Lords, which, in Nairnshire in September, had seemed so sensible, but which looked now, in the cold light of November in Belgrave Square, so shabby, self-centred and unreal. C.B. was treating him, despite his half-hearted support during the Boer War, with generosity and as a friend and ally. He had himself brought up the question of the Lords, only to come down against it. He had offered Asquith his choice of the highest posts.

Asquith was above all else a realist and a practical man. And, unlike Grey and Haldane, he recognized C.B.'s merits. His promise to his friends now looked foolish. Years later Margot Asquith explained to J. A. Spender that Asquith's aim had been to make the new government 'more imperial and less provincial', but she added: 'H. had given Rosebery up after that big meeting in the Station Sheds at Chesterfield as a *hopeless coward* & often said to me 'How I wish old C.B. were an Imperialist . . . I'd a great deal sooner fight for him than for Rosebery.'[36]

C.B., an excellent judge of human nature, knew his man. His approach was well judged and entirely successful. Asquith agreed unconditionally to become Chancellor of the Exchequer. He did so because he now realized that, having been offered the No. 2 post in the Government, he could not justify in public a refusal to join without being exposed to the unanswerable charge that he was actuated solely by personal ambition.

C.B. was now secure in the knowledge that he had the second most important man in the party and best debater in the House committed personally to him. Grey and Haldane, however, were ignorant of what had happened and Asquith did not enlighten them. They still believed that he would, if necessary, stand out with them. But the Relugas compact had been broken up at the first encounter with the prospective victim.

CHAPTER 28

Grey and Haldane

HAVING accomplished his main purpose, C.B. did not linger in London, but travelled north to Belmont, although the resignation of the Unionist Government was now expected at any moment. Tom Buchanan and his wife Emily went to stay with him, and Buchanan kept a diary of those days.[1] He noted that C.B. was firm on the need to take office if Balfour resigned. C.B. himself wrote to Ripon on November 25: 'Many of our people appear to be impressed with the disadvantages of accepting office after a resignation. . . . But it seems to me that these inconveniences would be outweighed by the damping effect on our fighting men throughout the country. . . . They know nothing of tricks and pedantries and judge by facts. . . .'[2]

Next day he wrote to Bryce commenting also on the speech Rosebery had made at Bodmin the day before, in which he had spurned Home Rule and announced his 'final separation' from C.B.: 'What a bombshell in a certain camp (not ours) is Barnbougle's public repudiation of H. Rule. I think he is off his head . . .'[3]

Meanwhile Asquith had written to Gladstone on Saturday the 25th, urging that the party should refuse to take office and should force the Unionists to dissolve.[4] His conscience was perhaps troubling him, for on the same day he wrote a long letter to C.B. in which he deployed all the arguments for making Haldane Lord Chancellor in preference to Reid.[5]

Asquith showed his letter in draft to Grey, so that Haldane would know what he had said and be appropriately grateful.[6] There was, in fact, some force in what Asquith said, but, given his involvement in the Relugas plot and his compact with Haldane, he could hardly be said to be taking a detached view, despite his protestations in the letter that 'what I am going to submit is not in the least actuated by personal, & still less – if possible – by sectional, considerations'. C.B. must have smiled when he read this. He ignored the appeal. Now that he was sure of Asquith, he did not need to worry too much about Haldane, nor did he propose to be dictated to by those who had been doing their utmost to neutralize him. Moreover he had made up his mind that Reid was going to be Lord Chancellor. Reid was a man of great ability – an outstanding classical scholar and a solid lowland Scot, though he was an indifferent advocate. He had a good deal in common with C.B. himself, especially when he was at home with his constituents in Dumfries. C.B. was determined to try to achieve a balanced Cabinet, representing all currents of opinion in the party, and Reid, as an uncomprising Radical, was, in his eyes, an important element in this balance.

At Belmont, this weekend of November 25–6, Buchanan recorded that C.B. was at first annoyed at Rosebery's Bodmin speech repudiating Home Rule, but that, 'after reflection . . . C.B. came to conclusion that R's step had cleared the air, delivered him from the difficulty of having to ask R. to join, and that those most embarrassed would be as they were R's own friends in the party, the Leaguers, particularly Asquith, Grey & Haldane. . . .' He wrote also:

Great pressure to get Haldane on to Woolsack, but he won't do it. Thinks he had better be Home Secretary, Asquith Chancellor of the Exchequer, and second in command, would like Elgin as Foreign Secretary and Grey at the War Office. Again there is pressure to make Grey Foreign Minister. The objections are his ignorance of foreign countries and foreign language: only once been outside U.K. and that was two days in Paris, and secondly, that he takes up decisions suddenly on incomplete knowledge, is obstinate in changing: and that is particularly a drawback in foreign affairs. John Morley a difficulty, but thinks he must go to India, for his sake, not India's. Bryce also a difficulty, wants to put him somewhere where the Tories could not have a daily fling at him. Lloyd George to Local Government Board (he is a little afraid of influence over him). Herbert Gladstone wants to be First Lord of the Admiralty. Thinks Sydney Buxton must have Cabinet, though not on merits, and does not know what to do with him. Fowler to be a peer. . . . For Chief Secretary Redmond and friends don't want H. Gladstone, would like T. Shaw, but doubtful whether he could afford to leave his profession and he will just stick to being Lord Advocate. Aberdeen to be Lord Lieutenant, and if not Burghclere. For Education Lyulph Stanley would be heroic but difficult; thinks probably Reay. For Chief Whip would like Sinclair, but afraid to press on account of wife. . . . John Burns to get a place. . . .[7]

On the 28th Morley wrote to C.B. from the Athenaeum:

> I have just come across Asquith.
> Most *furious* at the 'bombshell'.
> 'Never anything so disloyal. It is us – his own friends – whom he forces into humiliation and capitulation. . . .'
> I have seldom seen a hardened politician so angry. . . . He ridicules the notion of R *now* being able on any terms to come into a Liberal Govnt.[8]

It must have given C.B. considerable pleasure and amusement to read this.

From now on things moved rapidly, and it may be clearer to keep separate each day's events.

Thursday, November 30.

J. A. Spender noted: 'Lunched with Esher (Carlton Grill Room) E. . . . begged me to get into communication with C.B. and tell him to come to London at once.'[9]

Loulou Harcourt wrote to C.B. at Belmont:

> . . . the K. says if you refused he would be compelled very un-willingly to send for Rosebery. So of course you will accept. (By the way I hear that R realises that he has smashed himself in his attempt to smash you, and that he has gone down to Brighton a complete wreck morally and physically.) . . . I hope *nothing* will induce *you* to take a Peerage to start with: if after a year you found the H. of C. too hard work it would be another thing. . . .[10]

C.B. wrote to Gladstone: 'By all I see, I am rather confirmed in my opinion of what we must do. . . . Those who have proclaimed their resolve not to join any Govt. without a majority over the Irish wd be rather in a hole: but that is their affair. Why did they say anything so foolish?'[11]

This was a dig at Asquith.

Gladstone sent a telegram to C.B. urging him to come to London. Esher recorded:

> I lunched with John Morley.... As we parted ... he asked me if I would accept the W.O.! This is ludicrous. To have an offer by one P.M. and a feeler from the other side is an adventure almost unparalleled. And how silly these politicians are.[12]

After this luncheon, Morley went round to the Athenaeum and wrote to C.B., telling him that the King was leaving town for four days on Tuesday afternoon, which would give C.B. 'four days in peace, free from royal *suggestion*, for rigging up your ship'.

Morley continued:

> I said to Asquith just now that the more I thought of it, the less I liked the idea of your going to H. of L. He said 'Very well, then that ought to be settled, because it affects distribution of offices. . . .'
>
> I do hope you will get upon the ground in *good time*. Half of Mr. G's mistakes in his day were due to his obstinate refusal to leave Hawarden until five minutes before important decisions. . . .[13]

In reply to a telegram from Morley, C.B. said he would come up to London. Morley wrote: 'I am truly glad that you are coming. If you refuse, H.M. will call B. back again. In that case B. is going to advise him to try Ld. R.'[14]

At Belmont, Buchanan's diary continued: 'C.B. had a letter from Spender this morning, who had gone down to the Durdans and seen R. He was quite broken in spirit, full of anger, annoyance and remorse. . . .'

He wrote of C.B.:

> During the week past he has been in very good health and spirits, and full of good stories. . . . Had many stories of the way in

which Royal princes plant themselves on people. The Duchess of Teck asking herself and thirty people to lunch with Mundella. . . Francis of Teck coming to stay with Sandhurst at Bombay from Saturday to Monday and stopping five months. . . . At Marienbad this autumn he saw the King frequently. . . . Esher is confidant and go-between (C.B. does not like him). . . . after dinner a letter was read from Haldane who had been with Grey, and they wanted C.B. to make advances to R and explain that he did not intend to introduce any Home Rule Bill. Then all would be well! . . .

After dinner he said that in the watches of the night he had thought it might be a coup to ask Lord Cromer to take Foreign Office. He might not agree to do it, but it would give strength and status to his Ministry, and he would be useful in Cabinet over Indian affairs. I quite agreed and, as an alternative, suggested Monson.* He was rather taken with idea, having been friendly with Monson before war time. Thought it would be a compliment to Diplomatic Service and acceptable abroad. He would be made a peer. He (C.B.) had rather gone off from Elgin being Foreign Secretary . . . and thought he should be Scottish Secretary. He had spoken to Sinclair about the Whips place, and Sinclair agreed. . . . Altogether to-night he has been in excellent fettle and spirits, and though he has some regrets for losing the chance of a quiet life, he takes up the business and will, I hope, go through with it in his own time.[15]

The Liberal Imps wanted Grey as Foreign Secretary. C.B. wanted someone else. Hence the ideas of Cromer or Monson. But the man who really wanted the Foreign Office was Morley. Spender, however, wrote later that, just as it was a fixed point with C.B. that Reid was to be Lord Chancellor, so it was a fixed point that Morley should *not* be Foreign Secretary, and whenever this was suggested as an alternative to Grey, C.B. 'always turned the blind eye'.[16]

The idea of Cromer was an interesting one. Over thirty years before he and C.B. had been young, reforming colleagues in Cardwell's War Office. Now Cromer had an immense reputation as the ruler of Egypt. His appointment would bring in a very able and experienced man of affairs, spike the guns of the Relugas conspirators, and reassure the King. It would go some way to taking foreign affairs out of

* Sir Edmund Monson was sixty-nine and had been for nine years Ambassador in Paris.

partisan politics. And Grey might, after all, have to go to the War Office.

Grey, who was only forty-three, himself enjoyed a surprisingly high reputation, to which his appearance, his ancestry, his gravitas all contributed. Although he had been Under-Secretary for Foreign Affairs, he was, as C.B. pointed out, poorly qualified for the post. Yet a sober man like Spender maintained that any other appointment would be preposterous. Asquith had urged the appointment of Grey on C.B. on the rather curious ground that it would be 'popular all over Europe', disregarding the fact that the Foreign Secretary's task was to protect and further British interests rather than to seek popularity abroad.

Sunday, December 3.

Spender wrote to Arthur Acland asking him to come to town. 'Stumpy' Acland was to play a key part in the events of the next few days. He had been a member of the Rosebery Government, but in 1898 had written to C.B. saying that after serious warnings from his doctors he must withdraw from Parliamentary life. He had added: 'I over-strained my brain when I was about five and twenty . . . & there's not much left now'.[17] Acland was a close friend of Grey's. Now that the promised land was in sight he was beginning to regret his retirement from public life, and on November 30 he wrote to C.B. saying: 'I sometimes think I might be of some use to you in the Lords (this is not an early application for an honour!) . . . It is very hard that there is not some more easy & pleasant way in which the animal that is out at grass could be brought in to do some light work.'[18]

At Belmont, Buchanan went for a walk with Sinclair and wrote that he '. . . does not want to be a Whip, dislikes the work, thinks it too hard, and takes him altogether from wife. But if C.B. presses him he will agree. What he would like would be Chief Secretary, knows Ireland . . . and is good friend to the Nationalists who trust him as an out and out supporter of C.B. . . .'[19]

That Sunday night C.B. finally left Belmont by the night train for London, accompanied by Sinclair. Charlotte remained behind at Belmont.

Monday, December 4.

C.B. arrived at Euston and went to 29 Belgrave Square. He at once began consultations with his colleagues.

Haldane wrote to his mother:

... It is uncertain what may happen to myself. E. Grey came up this morning. He & I completely understand each other. So does Asquith but the former's character shines out at such a time. If he can Sir HCB will give the Woolsack to Sir R.R. I may be forced by public duty (Grey & I agree on this) to go elsewhere. Or he & I may stand out. ... [20]

The wording of this letter suggests that Haldane was now beginning to suspect that Asquith might defect from their compact.

After luncheon C.B.'s first visitor was Grey. This was only a preliminary encounter, but the ever alert Esher noted that C.B. 'saw Grey this afternoon, and met with difficulties, but he is to see him again tonight at 9, when these may be removed'.[21] After his talk Grey went back to Whitehall Court and wrote at once to Asquith:

Just a line before you see C-B to say that I don't want you to risk your personal position more than you think absolutely necessary. C-B gave me the impression that he was quite prepared to form a Government without any of us: he never once suggested that my abstaining would make the formation of a govt. difficult, though I had suggested it might raise difficulties as regards yourself.

If you go in without me eventually I shall be quite happy outside and I shan't think it the least wrong of you to go in. ... [22]

Grey too was beginning to realize that Asquith was not firm in his adherence to the Relugas compact, a fact of which C.B. had been aware for three weeks.

Spender, who had just been to The Durdans, where he had found Rosebery apparently prepared to bury the hatchet, was the bearer of what he later described as 'a characteristically roundabout overture to C.B. which was promptly snubbed'.[23] He wrote later:

The scene is still vividly in my memory. He was wearing a long frock coat with black trousers, and his hat was – rather oddly – on the table beside him with black gloves hanging out of it. The blinds were half drawn, and one might have thought the scene to be set for a funeral. But he was in the highest spirits and overflowing with little quips which never failed him in good times or bad. He said he was expecting a summons from 'Jupiter' ... but in the meantime he was very glad to have news of the 'Lord'. ... Did he come this time with sword or olive branch? I made my unauthorised communication and left him to judge. . . . Then he twinkled all over, as only C.B. could twinkle, and after some moments of apparent reflection delivered his ultimatum: 'Will you please tell Lord Rosebery that within two hours from now I expect to have accepted the King's commission to form a Government, and that being so, I can obviously say no more about the Irish question until I have had an opportunity of consulting my colleagues in the Cabinet.' There scarcely could have been a more skilful answer or the closing of a chapter with a more deadly politeness.[24]

That afternoon the King arrived back in London from Sandringham. At 4 o'clock Balfour saw him and submitted the resignation of the Unionist Government. It had undoubtedly outstayed its welcome, and the *Manchester Guardian* quoted the line: 'When beggars die, there are no comets seen.'[25]

In the late afternoon C.B. received the letter which indicates to a successful politician that he has reached the summit:

> Buckingham Palace
> 4 Dec. 1905
> 4.45 p.m.
>
> Dear Sir Henry,
>   Mr. Balfour having just placed his resignation & that of the Government in the hands of the King, I am desired by His Majesty to acquaint you that he would be glad to if you would have the goodness to come to Buckingham Palace at a quarter to eleven o'clock tomorrow (Tuesday) morning.
>   Believe me,
>   Yours vy truly,
>   Knollys.[26]

No doubt this letter was written out in a hurry, which would account for its being ungrammatical.

The agreeable feelings produced by this letter were, however, soon to be upset. At 10 p.m. Grey called, and announced bluntly that unless C.B. went to the Lords he would not join the Government. After arranging matters with Asquith the month before, C.B. had not expected this, and he was both hurt and angry, though he controlled himself while he listened to Grey, whom he described later as 'all buttoned up and never undoing one button'.[27] Grey found it a relief to have got what he wanted to say off his chest, and in the letter he sent to his wife next day said:

> All is going splendidly so far. I told C.B. that I could take no office unless he went to the Lords and Asquith led in the Commons. He said there would be no question of his going to the Lords at any rate at first. I said then I must stand out: we parted quite cordially; he took my really outrageous (from me to him) proposal in perfect temper and said very nice things. I left him; told Asquith and wrote a letter at midnight to C.B. saying I should not change. So I am in the position of having definitely refused. Of course the situation may change and C.B. give way. I devoutly hope not.[28]

Grey was not indispensable, but to C.B. the danger was that his firm refusal might cause Asquith, who was indispensable, to wobble, and that it also cut across C.B.'s determination to try to construct a government representing all sections of the party, including the Roseberyites.

Tuesday, December 5.

The Times, in a leading article, gave a grudging welcome to the incoming Prime Minister:

> We shall not pretend . . . that we can regard with any satisfaction or confidence the direction of the affairs of the British Empire by SIR HENRY CAMPBELL-BANNERMAN. . . . While the Unionist party remains the sole . . . bulwark against disruption, it has to be admitted that in its present circumstances that party does not form a satisfactory instrument of government. . . . The country wants a change. . . . But though it wants MR. BALFOUR out, it has no particular desire to see SIR HENRY CAMPBELL-BANNERMAN in his place. He takes that place because he is there to take it. . . .
>
> SIR EDWARD GREY would be in the Cabinet the chief guarantee to the country that the rash words of his leader would not be allowed to bring forth fruit in action, and, further, that due continuity would be maintained in foreign politics.[29]

– in other words, that the Liberal Government would follow Conservative policies, the next best thing to a real Conservative government.

Grey now wrote to Asquith: 'One or two things have rankled in the night . . . 1. The discourtesy of forming a Govt. without giving Rosebery the chance even of expressing regret that he can't join it. 2. The slighting of R.B.H. . . .'[30]

C.B. had taken up an offer from Loulou Harcourt to help with arrangements for making up the Government. Among his papers are these unsigned notes in Loulou's handwriting:

Local Govt. Bd: Lloyd George wd. be quite satisfied with this (He would like to be Home Secretary!) but he attaches great importance to being in some office which brings him in contact with Wales – which this would do in local affairs. He thinks Tom Ellis greatly injured himself by having an office (Whip) which divorced him altogether from Wales. . . . I am a little nervous at the idea of J. Burns in charge of the unemployed – this winter too! . . . the feeling against Haldane being in the Cabinet is *very strong* with our rank & file. I don't share it, though *I* have no reason to love him. I expect the K will want him somewhere in the inner circle.[31]

The key to the situation in the party lay with Asquith. C.B. therefore sent for him at about half past ten before he went round in a hansom to the Palace. Once more Margot Asquith's diary described what happened:

On the 5th December . . . C.B. and Henry had a moving interview. *No* one could have been straighter and nicer than Campbell-Bannerman was to him. He told him of the talk he had the night before with Sir Edward Grey. He spoke well of him, but said he was a regular Grey and had all the defects of his qualities. He added that he (C.B.) was well aware that Henry was better equipped to lead the House of Commons than he was; that he easily recognized this; but that, after standing all the stress and strain of the last few years, he did not wish people to say that he had run away when the pinch came – he could not bear the idea that anyone should think he was a coward.

Henry answered that the position was almost too delicate and personal for them to discuss; but C.B. pressed him to say frankly everything that was in his mind. Henry pointed out what a fearful labour C.B. would find the combination of leading the House and being Prime Minister, as they were practically two men's work;

that no one could possibly accuse him of being a coward; that the House of Lords was without a leader, and that it was placing him (Henry) in a cruel and impossible position if under the circumstances Edward Grey refused to take Office; he was his dearest friend as well as supporter, and to join a Government without such a friend would be personal pain to him, as they had never worked apart from one another.

Henry left after this as the King was to see Sir Henry at a quarter to eleven; he said he would return when C.B. had kissed hands.

When they met after the interview C.B. told him His Majesty had been most amiable and expressed himself delighted at hearing he would undertake to form a Government. He warned him, however, by saying that being Prime Minister and leading the Commons at the same time would be heavy work, and added:

'We are not as young as we were, Sir Henry!'

He suggested he should go to the House of Lords, to which C.B. seems to have answered that no doubt he would ultimately be obliged to do this, but that he would prefer starting in the Commons if only for a short time. The King, instead of pushing the matter – which was what I would have liked – seemed to fall in very pleasantly with the idea and shook him warmly by the hand. Knowing that he ought to kneel and kiss hands, C.B. advanced and waited, but the King interrupted by some commonplace remark; when he had finished speaking, C.B. again advanced meaning to kneel, but the King only wrung his hand, at which he felt the interview was over, as to have had another try would have been grotesque. He retired from the presence of His Majesty to Lord Knollys's room and told him he feared he had never kissed hands at all, to which Lord Knollys replied that it did not matter, as he would see that it was properly published . . . next day.

When Henry had finished telling me all this I could see by his face how profoundly anxious he was. He had left C.B. saying that as the matter was one of vital importance to him personally it could not be settled in a day, and that he must be given time to think things over. . . .

Henry ended by telling me he had gone himself to see Grey . . . and had found him in an uncompromising three-cornered humour.

That night at dinner at Hatfield, my husband looked worn out, and I admired him more than I could say for throwing himself into the social atmosphere of a fancy ball, with his usual simplicity and unselfcentredness.[32]

The King wrote to the Prince of Wales, who had been in the habit of talking about C.B., whom he scarcely knew, with great contempt:[33] 'At 10.15 I had a long interview with Sir H. Campbell Bannerman who undertook to form a Government but up till now nothing is settled and he has many difficulties in finding the right people – nothing could be nicer or more courteous than he was.'[34] The King had said his piece, as Haldane had planned that he should, but he had, sensibly, confined himself to dropping a hint, which was not taken. By now C.B. realized, even if he had not done so before, that there was a concerted move to shelve him. But how far it would be carried was still uncertain.

Gladstone saw Grey at 11 and found him resolute to stay out. Grey told Gladstone that 'C.B. for some years had been out of touch with . . . most important movements of thought and action in the country. He could not do justice to them. He was all for conciliating every one, but was not a leader either in council or debate or in character of mind. . . . The new Government should be started by announcement that C.B. would be in the Lords. . . . And R. should be asked to join. . . .'[35]

Tweedmouth saw Spender at the offices of the *Westminster*, and Spender 'promised to write articles which would make it easy for C.B. to go to the Lords on the ground of health'. An hour later, after talking to C.B., Tweedmouth saw Spender again and said that C.B. was very sore and wounded. He told Spender about the King's hint and said that C.B. had instantly realized that the King had been prompted by Haldane and Grey, and that this had increased his repugnance to falling in with their views. 'Was he', Tweedmouth reported C.B. as saying, 'to be dictated to and kicked upstairs by the youngest of the new Ministers, a man who had hitherto been no more than an under-secretary?' C.B.'s indignation against Grey was increasing. Tweed-mouth thought, however, that persuasion was being used with C.B. by 'the senior men' who thought 'that on the whole it would tend to efficiency in both Houses and H.C.B.'s own health & comfort if he could be persuaded to take the peerage'. Tweedmouth added that C.B. 'had not definitely said "no" to the King & had admitted to others that, if there was no other way & the interests of the party absolutely required it, he *could* do it'.[36]

Esher wrote: 'Grey . . . feels that Rosebery gave him his first chance in politics, and he cannot, he thinks, properly desert him. . . . There is a fatal contrariness about the Grey family. . . .'[37] Asquith wrote to Grey:

> I saw C.B. again this afternoon. . . . I gathered from what he said that he was rather smarting from the way in which you had presented the case to him, and that he would therefore regard it as a 'humiliation' now to recede. But the impression left on me was that he would not be indisposed to yield, if something in the nature of a golden bridge could be constructed for him. Do you think you could do anything in that direction?[38]

Grey may well have been puzzled to know what sort of 'golden bridge' Asquith thought he might be in a position to construct.

Meanwhile C.B. had not been letting the grass grow under his feet and had sent a telegram to Cromer in Cairo offering him the Foreign Office. It had, curiously, to be sent to Cairo through Lansdowne, the Conservative Foreign Secretary, who himself wrote at the top of the telegram: 'Sir Henry Campbell-Bannerman asks me to convey the following message to you.'[39] It was a long shot – Cromer had never been active in politics and had refused, at one time or another, the embassies at Berlin, Vienna, Peking and Constantinople and the post of Viceroy of India – but if it came off C.B. need worry no more about 'Master Grey'.

Among C.B.'s friends there was gloom. Buchanan, now back in his house in South Street, wrote: 'C.B. and Sinclair . . . came and dined here tonight. Things going badly. . . . C.B. left us all down-hearted, himself the same. And I much fear he will yield.'[40] C.B. was an old man. He had done his utmost for the party, but now that the promised land was in sight, his chief colleagues seemed to have no use for him and he was being told that he was not wanted in effective command. It is not surprising that he was discouraged.

Wednesday, December 6.

The King left London, giving C.B. a full week before he needed to present a list of the new Government. It was announced that a Royal Warrant had been issued and that C.B. was to be the first man to have the official title of Prime Minister. Up till now the only official title of the King's first ministers had been First Lord of the Treasury.[41]

The Times commented on the prospect that C.B. might go to the Lords. C.B. must have thought that they too were in the plot and his friends like Buchanan assumed that Haldane had inspired the piece. The paper observed that he was 'hardly the kind of Prime Minister to make a successful fight against MR. BALFOUR and MR. CHAMBERLAIN.[42]

The Asquiths were staying with the Salisburys at Hatfield, in the heart of the enemy camp, and coming up to London each day. Margot recorded:

> . . . we motored to London. Henry went at once to see C.B. . . . that evening . . . Henry . . . was much moved in relating what had occurred . . . Henry (to me): 'I said, "It is no use going over the ground again, my dear C.B. I make a personal appeal to you, which I've never done before; I urge you to go the House of Lords and solve this difficulty." I could see that C.B. was moved, but he repeated what you tell me he said to Herbert Gladstone about the arrival of his wife, and that he wished her to be the final arbiter with which our interview ended.'[43]

Asquith had, before making his appeal, put to C.B. a suggestion from Grey, an effort to effect a compromise that was most unlikely to commend itself to him. It was described in a letter from Grey to his wife:

> I held out all yesterday. . . . This morning I offered an alternative, viz. that Haldane should go to the Woolsack and lead the Lords, C.B. remaining in the Commons . . . if either is conceded I must go in. . . . If I stay out, Asquith will have to decide what he does; if he goes in without me his position will be horrid and people will say he has abandoned me in order to have office. If he stays out with me it is considered that the Liberal Party will smash and Free Trade may be beaten at the Election. . . . Your very much harassed and highly wrought E.[44]

C.B. rejected Grey's suggestion. Indeed Grey said that it had only added fuel to the flames. Meanwhile C.B. had had a telegram from Cromer refusing the Foreign Office. Cromer said: 'I really have not the health & strength to undertake this work. I am sure that I should break down in six months.'[45] Loulou Harcourt told Sinclair: 'I am glad Cairo is definitely "off" – I wish Fallodon were firmly "on". I still think Ld E.F. might be a *possible* solution.'[46]

This was the first indication that Lord Edmond Fitzmaurice was being considered as a possible Foreign Secretary. Cromer, for his part, wrote later of his reluctance to become 'engaged in the wordy strife – often sterile of result and to me always distasteful – of Parliament'.[47] There was also another reason for Cromer's refusal, as he explained later to St. Loe Strachey of the *Spectator*. He was afraid that the Liberal Government 'would not improbably lash the English party in South Africa into fury; that they would endeavour to govern South Africa from London and, while proclaiming the principles of self-govern-ment on the house-tops, would themselves violate self-governing principles when the colony wished to run counter to their preconceived ideas'.[48]

In the afternoon the *Westminster* appeared with the first of the articles Spender had undertaken to write easing the way for C.B.'s move to the Lords.

Spender had been a bit nervous about the effect of his article, coming after that in *The Times*, and told Gladstone that this 'would probably lead to a strong protest in certain Liberal papers which would probably stiffen C.B. against the peerage.' He suggested that Gladstone should write privately to certain newspapers saying that it was purely a question of health for C.B.[49] So these busy intriguers set out, with the best of motives, to try to mislead the Liberal press. Later in the evening Spender and Acland concluded that if Asquith agreed to join and C.B. decided to dispense with Grey and Haldane, this 'would be an enormous disaster'.[50]

At seven Charlotte arrived from Belmont. C.B. had told Asquith and Gladstone that he would consult her before he made up his mind. Her word was indeed decisive with him, and he did not simply make her an excuse to shelter behind. On this occasion he seems genuinely to have wobbled. But where C.B. was personally concerned, Charlotte admitted of no compromise. They had always talked things over together. Now he turned to her, and her answer was never in doubt. It was for standing firm and defying those who were trying to force her beloved Henry onto the shelf. After so much uncertainty it was an enormous relief to C.B. to have his doubts blown away. From this time he was a happier man and saw his way clear.

Meanwhile Gladstone and Spender continued their lobbying of Liberal newspapermen. One of those Spender spoke to, A.G. Gardiner of the *Daily News*, was, however, sceptical, and he it was who received the first sign that C.B. was going to fight. Spender hinted that in what he wrote Gardiner should leave room for the possibility of C.B. going to the Lords. Gardiner asked whether that meant that C.B. was yielding. His account continued:

> The reply was equivocal. Even from so friendly a source I was indisposed to accept the invitation to assist the intrigue without learning C.-B.'s actual state of mind. I therefore sent a letter to him by hand, asking him for his view of the 'Times' suggestion. He had just gone to bed when the messenger arrived . . . but he got up and wrote me the following note. . . .

> > '29, Belgrave Square, S.W.
> > 6 Dec, '05.

> 'Secret

> 'Dear Mr. Gardiner, – There has been no such decision taken in any *degree*. Point out the arguments against, but leave it to the discretion of the P.M. – Yours,

> > 'H. C.-B.'

> With that very clear hint of his own frame of mind, I had no hesitation in disregarding the appeal to the contrary made to me over the telephone. At this time Lady Campbell-Bannerman had not returned to London, and the note, I think, makes it clear that C.-B. had arrived at his practically final decision alone. Few men I have known needed less help in making up their mind on fundamental things than he did.[51]

This is an interesting note, but in one rather important respect it is inaccurate. Charlotte *had* returned by the time C.B. wrote his note. It was the first he wrote after he had talked to her.

Morley wrote:

> One evening, while these unedifying transactions were still on foot, Tweedmouth and I left Campbell-Bannerman, cool, patient, half undecided as to his course; we were to return after dinner, and the true counsellor of his life was to arrive from Scotland in the meantime. . . . Returning we found the Minister indescribably exultant. 'No surrender!' he called out to us in triumphant voice, with gesture to match. The decision was iron.[52]

Morley wrote later of Charlotte: 'She was indeed a "valiant lady", and her valour saved us and the party from the very brink of disaster, the famous night when she came from Belmont to Belgrave Square. We were mighty near to the fatal edge.'[53]

Thursday, December 7.

The Times had another leading article: 'The opinion gains ground that Sɪʀ Hᴇɴʀʏ Cᴀᴍᴘʙᴇʟʟ-Bᴀɴɴᴇʀᴍᴀɴ will eventually waive his objections . . . to his elevation to the Upper House . . . it is becoming plain that he cannot otherwise secure the inclusion in his Cabinet of . . . the men . . . upon whom he must depend. . . .'[54]

For once *The Times* was out of date in its information. C.B. had made up his mind. Margot Asquith wrote in her diary:

> . . . at Hatfield . . . when Henry arrived I saw at a glance that it was all up. He told me that C.B. had said to his secretary, Sinclair, that morning at breakfast that he had had a talk with his lady the night before. . . .
>
> 'I don't often make up my mind, Sinclair, but I've done it now – I shan't go to the Lords.'
>
> After Sinclair had told him this Henry went to see C.B.
>
> Hᴇɴʀʏ (to me): 'He looked white and upset and began like a man who, having taken the plunge, meant to make the best of it. He spoke in a rapid, rather cheerful and determined manner: "I'm going to stick to the Commons, Asquith, so will you go and tell Grey he may have the Foreign Office and Haldane the War Office." '[55]

This picturesque account omits one most important point. This is that at this interview Asquith agreed to serve as Chancellor of the Exchequer. C.B. had no reason to look white and upset. His government was no longer in danger. A rather different account was given to Buchanan's wife when she went round to have tea at Belgrave Square next day. C.B. told her what he had said to Asquith:

> 'We must come to business. I have duties as Prime Minister. I am not going to the House of Lords. You must say definitely whether you are coming in or not.' He offered Asquith the Chancellor of the Exchequer. . . . Asquith was in a great state, walked up and down the room, 'See what a position I am in, if I refuse and go to my constituents they will ask why, was it on policy? I must

say no. Were you not offered a good post? I must say "the best",
then it was on personal grounds that you stood out and were
prepared to break up the party? What answer have I?' (And he
would lose his seat.) He evidently was willing to come in. On the
other hand he said, 'if I come in and Grey stands out they will say
at once this man deserted his friends and crawled back into office.'
C.B. contented him with saying that it was not he that had put
Asquith in this dilemma. Asquith said he would go and tell Grey
and see if he could bring him in.[56]

But Asquith failed to persuade Grey, who wrote to his wife: 'So
he goes in. R.B.H., dear man, stays with me. Don't blame Asquith; it
was hard for him, cruelly hard.'[57] Asquith wrote to C.B.: 'I deeply
regret both your decision and E. Grey's. On the assumption that both
are irrevocable, Crewe seems to me for many reasons the best man for
the F.O.'[58]

C.B. was still seeing a stream of callers at No. 29. One of these was
Elgin, to whom he now offered the Colonial Office. Two years before
he had told Vaughan Nash: 'I have always believed in that little Elgin.'[59]
Elgin was a taciturn man, who was an even worse speaker than C.B.,
but he was a good administrator who had been Viceroy of India in the
nineties.

After luncheon the ever busy Spender went round to see Gladstone
who had just learnt of C.B.'s decision. Spender recorded: 'He said at
once that everything had gone wrong. . . . H.G. regarded everything as
lost.'[60] Spender rushed round to see Acland, who agreed to try to
help.

Meanwhile C.B. wrote to Haldane, offering him the post of
Attorney-General, but saying that if he did not want that, 'I shall
gladly make you a proposition of a different nature which would bring
you into the Cabinet.'[61]

Asquith was also writing to Haldane, but his letter said: 'I was
empowered this morning to offer the Foreign Office to E. Grey and an
offer of the War Office will soon be on its way to you.'[62] Asquith then
embarked on a lengthy justification of his defection from the Relugas
compact.

Loulou Harcourt wrote to Sinclair:

It is thought that the situation has changed to the extent of C-B
being forced (by A. & G.) to go at once to the Peers: that Morley

has joined this view in order to get the Ch. of Exch. and that Asquith is to lead the H. of Commons.

Our Radicals are in open revolt: I try to keep them quiet by saying that I don't believe it is true but that I know nothing. I think it would be *absolutely fatal* for C-B to go to the H. of L. *now*: it would be regarded as the triumph of the Rosebery section . . . for God's sake stop this if it is not too late. . . .[63]

Grey, at Whitehall Court, wrote a long letter to C.B. confirming his refusal to come in. This he sent off at 6 p.m. Since he was adamant in his determination to stand out, there remained the problem of the Foreign Office. Esher wrote: 'Cromer has refused, as I knew he would. When Sinclair mentioned Monson – I told him "Polonius" !'[64] Asquith had suggested Crewe; Loulou and Esher, Lord Edmond Fitzmaurice. Another name proposed was that of Lord Burghclere. Morley was appalled that the post to which he had so long aspired might go to one of these comparatively obscure men. He wrote to C.B.:

My last words to you to-night were about taking care in respect of the F.O.

The more I think of it, the more I am *dismayed* at the proposal of either Ld. B or Ld. C . . . they are as yet light weights. It is quite true that Grey is grossly overrated, and that he would be a doubtful diplomatist. Still his name stood high – and you lose something in the public weight of your cabinet. If you fill his place by people of such second-rate public position as B & C, it will be a heavy handicapping for us. . . . You will not misconstrue my motive. My anxiety is wholly impersonal.[65]

At 4 p.m. Haldane, presiding over a committee in South Kensington received his two letters from C.B. and Asquith. He put them in his pocket and went on with his meeting. He felt bound to Grey and intended therefore to refuse office. On his way home he called at Buckingham Gate to see his friend Lady Horner and showed her the letters. She reminded him that he had promised the King not to leave him in the lurch and pointed out that if he and Grey stood out, C.B. might be able to form only a weak government, in which case the cause of Free Trade might be imperilled. Haldane was impressed. He went on to Whitehall Court and found Grey 'lying on a sofa in the library . . . with the air of one who had taken a decision and was done with political troubles'. Haldane told Grey that he intended to refuse office, both in accordance with their compact and from inclination. But Lady Horner had sown a doubt. 'Was it', Haldane describes himself as saying, 'quite so clear from an ethical standpoint that we had quite fully considered the necessities of the King and the Nation?'[66] Clearly so grave a question could not be resolved on empty stomachs. It was now 7 p.m. and the two friends decided first to walk round and see Acland and then to have some dinner. Haldane wrote that Grey was 'much troubled: I think he felt that we were acting somewhat selfishly'.

When they saw Acland, Grey began by saying: 'What *is* the use. I have finally and absolutely closed the door.' Haldane said that he was about to refuse C.B.'s offer, but Acland argued that by standing out they would destroy the prospects of the Liberal Government and damage the country.[67] Then he sent them off to have dinner by themselves. As soon as they had gone he sent a message to Spender asking him to come round and told him he thought he had made a serious impression on the two. They agreed that Spender should get Gladstone to send an immediate message to C.B. begging him to keep the Foreign Office and the War Office open. There was now, for the first time, a prospect that, despite C.B.'s decision to remain in the Commons, Grey and Haldane could be induced to come under starter's orders.

Spender hurried off and saw Gladstone, who promised to communicate with C.B. and 'went on to say that it would be an excellent plan to get Acland into the Lords & make him leader there'.[68] Spender rushed back to St. James's Court and told Acland, who took this as an offer 'that', as he later told C.B., 'I could have high Cabinet office . . . could even, he said, lead the Lords.'[69]

Gladstone wrote at once to C.B., urging him to keep the door open and suggesting that as a reward for his mediation with 'these 2 obdurate minds' Acland might be made Minister of Education and leader of the House of Lords.[70]

Grey and Haldane had gone to dine at the Café Royal. Haldane's account is precise about the moment of truth:

When we had finished some fish we decided that the fact that he had definitely rejected C-B's offer . . . could indeed make a change of attitude disagreeable, but could not alter the moral obligation. He turned to me and said, 'You may do what you please.' I answered that I would go there and then to Sir H.C.-B. Grey said, 'If we enter it is not for pleasure's sake, and we must take the most beastly things. I will take the War Office.' I said the public interest demanded that he should take the Foreign Office, and I would ask for the War Office.[71]

Grey said he would not come in unless Haldane was also in the Cabinet.

So Haldane, leaving Grey, a martyr to public duty, to continue with whatever followed the fish at the Café Royal, went off in a hansom to Belgrave Square to see C.B.:

> I found that he was dining alone with his wife. I said I would wait for him in his study – he came at once. I asked him whether he still wanted Grey. He said he did indeed, but that G. was very difficult. I replied that possibly I might help to bring G. in. I had not answered his letter to myself, but that I could now do so. I did not want to be Attorney-General. He then offered me the Home Office. I said, 'What about about the War Office?' 'Nobody,' answered C.B., 'will touch it with a pole.' 'Then give it to me. I will come in as War Secretary if Grey takes the Foreign Office, and I will ask him to call on you early to-morrow to tell you his decision, which may, I think, be favourable.'[72]

In this curious way was one of the most effective of all Secretaries of State for War appointed. C.B., who had the patience of a saint, received Haldane in a friendly way and promised him the reversion of the Lord Chancellorship if anything happened to Reid. He and Charlotte must have enjoyed themselves discussing this latest development. Charlotte's advice had been right.

But all was not quite over. Haldane went back to Acland's flat and at 10.45 Grey arrived, having been brooding alone over his dinner. He said at once to Acland: 'I have been thinking it all over since Haldane left me and I have come to the definite conclusion that you are *wrong.*' Acland had to begin all over again and only after three quarters of an hour, half an hour before midnight, did Grey finally give way and agree to see C.B. in the morning.[73]

Friday, December 8.

Buckle, the editor of *The Times*, was getting a daily account of developments from Morley. On this morning he came out with the report that Grey had refused office and a leading article in which all the paper's Unionist and Roseberyite prejudices were displayed.

Sir Almeric Fitzroy wrote in his diary:

The writer of the article had evidently received instructions to hammer the rising hopes of the new Administration and deal the Premier as damaging a blow as he knew how – a task upon which he entered in the smashing style with which the traditions of 'The Times' have made its readers familiar for more than a century. . . .[74]

Acland later told C.B. that he was alarmed when he read the article, 'knowing how easily Grey might be upset'.[75] It seems never to have occurred to anyone that C.B. might be upset. It was he, after all, who was the target for *The Times*'s sneers. Haldane wrote to him: 'The "Times" did not help a difficult task this morning, but now that Grey has recognised his obligation he has accepted it very whole heartedly . . . your offer of the War Office . . . I accept; and will do all I can to serve you. . . .'[76]

After breakfast Gladstone, 'also much alarmed', repeated to Acland his offer of the Cabinet and the leadership of the Lords, for which he had no authority at all from C.B. He promised to take Acland to see C.B. in the evening.

Grey duly called at Belgrave Square. According to the account the Buchanans had from C.B. and Charlotte later that day he '. . . made full submission. Said he would take office and bad though his conduct had been on Tuesday, to his credit he said, "Now I have come in I will be loyal to you. If you will forget what I said I will forget what you said." '[77]

At 11.30 Acland heard from Grey that he and Haldane had accepted and at noon the Press Association put out a statement saying that the report in *The Times* was unauthorized and incorrect. In the upper reaches of the Liberal Party the relief and rapture were appropriate to a deliverance from a great national disaster. Margot Asquith, for example, wrote: 'At 12 o'clock Herbert Gladstone came into my boudoir, his face shining with happiness; he opened his arms and said: "It's all right, Margot!" "Not possible!" I exclaimed.'

Even the Foreign Office was carried away, and in response to a telegram from Margot, Louis Malet replied: 'Thank you and God. Suspense awful.'[78]

One might have imagined that the new Foreign Secretary was

some uncanny genius, instead of being a man who had been sent down from Balliol for idleness, had returned to obtain a Third in Law, and spoke no French.

Margot's own comment was: 'So we were all in, and not *one* of us had got what we wanted!'[79]

After luncheon Thomas Shaw, one of C.B.'s lowland cronies, went to see him. He described the interview in a letter to his wife:

> C.B. . . . said with a laugh, 'Do you know it was the comicality of it that I could hardly get over. They were to serve *under* me, but on condition that they were not to be *with* me! . . . this thing began on Monday; and I let it go on for three days; and then I said to each and all of them, "Now look here, I have been playing up till now. . . . But now let me just say – *that it is I who am the head of this Government: it is I who have the King's Command: I am on horseback*, and you will be all pleased to understand that I *will not go to the House of Lords; that I will not have any condition of the kind imposed upon me*. . . ." Grey said, "I cannot face the idea of Lord Rosebery attacking a Government of which I am a member."' As C.B. said that he laughed and said, ' "Dear me, you are a man of distinction, and you are going to be swayed by another man to a course which you can't openly explain in any sort of way satisfactory to yourself!"
>
> 'So,' says C.B., 'they all came in – no conditions; no nothing: there they are.' . . .[80]

Shaw knew that Redmond had asked for him as Chief Secretary, but C.B. told him he was to be Lord Advocate.

C.B. was now in the full flush of victory, and may be pardoned for being a little elated. One observer compared him to the type of Lord Provost who used to be seen in a city like Glasgow: 'When Asquith, Grey and Haldane tried to push the old man out of the way into the House of Lords, he saw through their game at once. It was just such a situation as many a Lord Provost had to tackle and he tackled it in the same way. Without any fuss he put them all in their places and went quietly on his way.'[81]

The wife of one of the three defeated conspirators made a frank comment: '. . . Sir Edward Grey, Lord Haldane, and my husband nearly backed the wrong horse in their choice between service under the leadership of Lord Rosebery or Sir Henry Campbell-Bannerman.'[82] Her husband's relief at the outcome was enormous. He wrote to Haldane: 'I have never spent such a distracting and agonising week. Everything that a man could do I believe I did, to achieve our common purposes . . . I am satisfied that more could not have been accomplished, & there was a real risk of losing everything. . . . The one thing that has dictated my action has been that the election was before, & not behind us.'[83]

In one sense C.B. had, as Esher said, 'won all along the line'.[84] Rosebery had been excluded and none of his friends had stayed out with him, not even his son-in-law Lord Crewe. But C.B. had perhaps conceded more than he need have done. He wanted, and needed to have, Asquith as his Chancellor and No. 2, but he had acquired also a Foreign Secretary with whom he had very little in common, and between whom and himself there was a certain mutual antipathy, supported by a War Minister who had been even more antagonistic. Although he formed a Cabinet which did represent all the main forces in the party, there were obvious elements of weakness in such an arrangement. It is indeed odd that, having made sure of Asquith, C.B. went to such lengths to keep the door open for Grey and Haldane. The key to this was evidently his determination not to have Morley as Foreign Secretary. Perhaps he shared just a little of the doubt Lord Vansittart expressed about Morley:

> He was one of our narrow escapes. Suppose that this vain, intelligent, timid old man, who ran away from the decision of 1914, had been Secretary of State for Foreign Affairs during the vital years that preceded it. You may then give belated thanks for all small mercies, though he and those agonising months are far back among the shades.[85]

But some later wondered if C.B. might not have done him an injustice. Esher told Spender years later that the events of 1914 might have been different if Morley had been at the Foreign Office. 'No one will ever believe that J.M. had a Palmerstonian touch in his forefinger. But he had. . . . C.B.'s diagnosis was wrong.'[86]

If it was not to be Morley, there was no one else available of adequate standing. So in the end it had to be Grey. This was politically the prudent course, but C.B. must have made the appointment *à contre-cœur*, even though it was Grey who was having to eat his words.

Lord Fisher wrote that 'had Campbell-Bannerman only known what a literally overwhelming majority he was going to obtain at the forthcoming Election, he would have formed a very different Government from what he did, and I don't believe we should have had the War'.[87]

C.B. himself confirmed to a friend in 1907 that if he had formed his government after, instead of before the election, the constituencies and the new House of Commons would not have stood for the inclusion of the Liberal Leaguers.[88] Courtney wrote at the time:

> Edward Grey's absurd demand failed, but he and his friends have got a good deal, perhaps the command of the working machine. How has this come about? Largely I think from a conviction on the part of C-B that the Grey section was supported in the country by men enough to cause the loss of a very appreciable number of seats if they were not in the Government in force. And this, I believe, is the truth. Among the professed Liberals up and down the country must be reckoned – more prominent perhaps in their position than their numbers – a good many with respect for names, traditions . . . class ascendancy, men who run after Rosebery while regretfully acknowledging he cannot come in and who put their confidence in his friends. This alliance is necessary for a big majority, though it may weaken its force.[89]

There was also another factor. C.B. was the least vindictive of men. G. W. E. Russell said that he was only too ready to forgive and forget. 'His motto was *Alors comme alors*.'[90]

Those who live by the sword perish by the sword, and those who engage in conspiracy may themselves be brought down by it. Nemesis in various forms awaited the Relugas trio. Grey, the standard bearer of a vigorous imperial and foreign policy, was to see the collapse of all he had worked for in 1914. Haldane was to be dropped by his old friend Asquith, without even a word of thanks, in response to Unionist pressure in May 1915, after a vicious press campaign during which Asquith and Grey did little to help him. Asquith himself was to be the victim of a successful conspiracy organized by Lloyd George in 1916.

CHAPTER 29

Filling the Posts

C.B. was now able to press on with making up his government.

Saturday, December 9.

The Times was put out that its inside information had turned out to be inaccurate. 'Our own statement yesterday morning', it said peevishly, 'correctly represented the condition of affairs at the close of the working day, but by the time it was in the hands of our readers the unforeseen had happened.'[1]

At six C.B. saw Winston Churchill, who chose to be Under-Secretary at the Colonial Office rather than Financial Secretary to the Treasury. In a speech on December 14 Churchill called this 'a small, humble post', and reminded his audience that Lord Hugh Cecil had once described an under-secretary as 'only a stipendiary echo'.[2] The Colonial Secretary, Lord Elgin, was to find Churchill something more than this.

Now that the effort to push C.B. into the Lords had failed, it is ironic that on this day, far away in Vienna, his Marienbad physician and friend sat down and wrote him a letter of advice. Dr. Ott knew, as the Relugas conspirators did not, that there really were good reasons for C.B. not to try, at sixty-nine, to take on too much. Though his spelling was eccentric, his counsel was plain enough, but it reached C.B. too late. Perhaps on this occasion the Gods were kind:

Dear Sir Henry,
 . . . Before I may take the liberty in mixing my not worthy person in your dispositions, I and Mrs. Ott send you the heartiest warmest congratulations. . . . And as I may be as arrogant, as to

call myself, your most *devoted friend* (excuse that expression, to call myself friend, to a man so high in social position. . . . I am very very shoked, to read in the papers, that you have the intention to remain in the house of Commons. . . .

Please do not call me impertinent, in . . . begging you, not to overdo yourself in taking on your *health* – and excuse the 'medical professioner' – also *on your age* such an enourmous burden of work!

I remember very well a time, when you and Lady Campbell-Bannerman were kind enough, to discuss these matters with me, and then I think to remember very well, that we all three aggreed, that for your precious health, the best would be to go in the house of Lords. . . . if you are overworking yourself – . . . then in shorter ore longer time a very bad reaction with all consequences may happen – . . .

always your most devoted
Dr. Ernst Ott.[3]

The Cabinet was now made up, and, at 6.30 p.m. on Sunday, December 10, C.B. went to Buckingham Palace to present his list to the King, who wrote next day to Princess Louise: 'The new Govt. promises to be a strong one – & I find Sir H. Campbell Bannerman charming to do business with.'[4] It was a Cabinet of nineteen. Crewe became Lord President, Ripon Lord Privy Seal and Leader of the Lords, Herbert Gladstone Home Secretary, Sydney Buxton Postmaster-General, Sinclair Secretary of State for Scotland, and Birrell President of the Board of Education. The only appointment that attracted some criticism was that of Sinclair, Stead writing that his inclusion 'was the only thing . . . which looked like a job'.[5]

Rosebery gave a generous welcome to the new government, congratulating C.B. on the position he had achieved which was 'so entirely his due'. He applauded the presence in the Cabinet of four Vice-Presidents of the Liberal League.[6]

Making up a Government is bound to produce its toll of anxieties and disappointments, and reveals unexpected aspects of human nature. All this appears in C.B.'s correspondence. Some opened their mouths wide. Lord Portsmouth, for example, asked for 'some such purely political appointment as the Privy Seal, Chancellor of the Duchy – Board of Works or Agriculture'.[7] According to Gosse, among those greatly disappointed were Lords Reay, Beauchamp (who, despite his valet's expectations, had got neither Hindia nor Hireland), Monkswell and Stanley of Alderney.[8]

At times a man might be in sight of great office, only perhaps to end up with nothing. On the 9th, for example, C.B. wrote to Lord Edmond Fitzmaurice, apologizing for being able to give him no post but offering him a peerage.[9] Three days later Fitzmaurice received a letter from Spender, who did not hesitate to tell him: 'There was a moment last week, to my knowledge, when you were very near being offered the Foreign Secretaryship, & then another moment when there was nothing good enough to offer you.'[10] Fitzmaurice sent a dignified reply to C.B., declining the peerage without a post and quoting his ancestor, Sir W. Petty, who had told Charles II: 'A bare title without some *trust* might seem in the world a Body without soul & spirit.'[11] However, the same day C.B. told him he could after all have a 'trust' in the form of the Under-Secretaryship at the Foreign Office (a post which, as Mr. Roy Jenkins has pointed out, he had held twenty-three years before),[12] so he took the peerage after all.

C.B. had first offered this post to Lord Burghclere, who had been Minister of Agriculture from 1892 to 1895. Burghclere had replied with a long screed expressing disappointment at not now being a 'responsible Minister', making it a condition that he 'should be in as complete confidence as to Foreign affairs with the Government as if I were in the Cabinet', and throwing in a request for a G.C.B., to 'gild my descent on the Ministerial ladder', which would add 'dignity to the office and differentiate me from a waiter'.[13] C.B. did not care for the tone of this letter and chose to interpret it as a refusal, much to Burghclere's distress. ('I do not think you could have read my letter as I certainly never *refused* your kind offer ... all I did was to ask that ... I might be treated ... not quite as an *ordinary* Under Secretary.')[14] C.B. told Ripon: 'We really cannot stand such airs and graces on the part of our friend.'[15] Fitzmaurice remained disgruntled and critical of C.B. At the Foreign Office he was to find himself out of sympathy with both Grey and the permanent officials and without any effective influence.

Requests for jobs and titles flowed in. Some wounds had to be inflicted. One of the saddest was on Bryce, who was sixty-eight, and had been one of C.B.'s staunchest supporters in the dark days. He was bitterly disappointed at being offered only the Chief Secretaryship.[16] C.B. had in fact planned all along to send him to Ireland. He was not alone in thinking that Bryce was ineffective in the House of Commons. Balfour told Gosse in 1905: 'James Bryce ... is only about 65, and I assure you his appearances in the House of Commons are those of a gabbling, foolish, muddled old man. Nobody could be older in mind ... less elastic than Bryce ... Bryce is a startling instance of the uselessness of the higher education.'[17] Nevertheless it is hard to imagine that in 1905 Bryce would not have been a better candidate for the Foreign Office than Burghclere or Fitzmaurice or Monson – or indeed than Grey. And it is sad to think of the chagrin of so stout-hearted and distinguished a man.

A man who was even more disappointed, but with whom it is possible to feel less sympathy, was Dilke. His friend Fitzmaurice wrote to him on December 16 a sour letter, saying: 'Your exclusion is linked with mine in this business, and the joint result ... of the wiles of the "Lowland clans", and very *low* indeed too.'[18] Morley wrote to him on the 10th, saying:

> For yourself. . . . When I opened the matter to C.B. . . . I found him adverse. I resumed it last Monday. . . . He was by that time still more adverse, and even disinclined to listen or to discuss. . . . It was a chose jugée, I think, from the first. . . .
>
> Goodbye, my dear Dilke. To nobody is your absence more truly painful than to
>   Your
>   John Morley.[19]

C.B. never in fact considered Dilke for a moment. This was not primarily because of the notorious scandal which had cut short his career in 1886, nor even, as Dilke believed, because he had been the most prominent Liberal to vote for the reduction of C.B.'s salary in the cordite division of 1895, difficult though it must have been to forgive such an action on the part of a colleague. It is clear to anyone who studies C.B.'s correspondence that he had a low opinion of Dilke. He regarded him as an intriguer who cultivated the press for his own purposes, as a man who enjoyed showing off his own knowledge for reasons of vanity, and as a man who had no influence or following.

Morley had not been an easy man to place. But he was prepared, though without enthusiasm, to accept the India Office. C.B. and Morley were never comfortable partners. C.B. was contemptuous of Morley's vanity and touchiness. Morley for his part despised C.B.'s intellectual powers.

C.B. decided to give Loulou Harcourt the post of First Com-

missioner of Works, outside the Cabinet, but, though he saw him
every day, forgot to mention the fact to him, so that Loulou only
found out from Spender, when they stayed together a day or two
later.

John Burns was the first working man to be included in a British
Cabinet, as President of the Local Government Board. C.B. liked him
and regarded him as a tough, honest Scot. He was merely amused by
Burns's colossal vanity. He told Lord Rendel in 1907 that when he
sent for Burns he said, 'John, I want you to join the Cabinet and take
the Local Government Board.' Burns replied: 'Sir 'Enry, you never did
a more popular thing in your life.'[20]

There was rather more of resignation than enthusiasm in C.B.'s
offer of the Cabinet and the Presidency of the Board of Trade
to Lloyd George. 'I suppose we ought to include him,' he said to
McKenna.[21] But Lloyd George, Reid, Morley, Ripon, Bryce, Sinclair,
and Burns helped to keep the Cabinet balanced against the four
Liberal Imps.

He hesitated before appointing Herbert Samuel Under-Secretary
at the Home Office, and when Gladstone suggested him 'made a terrible
grimace', since he regarded him as a virulent Liberal Imp. In 1903 he
had written of him, 'This gentleman is a little too-too.'[22] But before
long he was referring to Samuel as 'a very level-headed fellow'.

The amiable Lord Carrington, King Edward's great friend, who
had helped to bring his friend the King and C.B. together, was delighted
at being included as President of the Board of Agriculture, and wrote:
'Your kind letter fills me with amazement and joy. . . . I may not be
very clever but I am loyal, and I will do my best to serve you honestly
and faithfully. Lady C. sends you her love & is very happy and very
proud at this moment. So am I.'[23]

Acland, who had taken seriously the hint Herbert Gladstone had
given him, spent the whole weekend, as he described it, 'sitting to
speak metaphorically on the doorstep of 29 Belgrave Square'. No
summons came, and 'on Monday morning I withdrew to the North'.[24]
C.B. thanked him for the part he had played, but he did not share the
almost hysterical relief of those who believed that he had saved the
party from disaster.

C.B. had now to sit down to the distasteful business of writing to
those who had not been chosen, and then to filling the minor posts
and court appointments. One story which went the rounds was
recorded in Gosse's diary:

The standing joke of the new administration is Lord Granard, a blunt-faced black-a-vized young man. . . . His fellow-officers of the Scots Guards played a practical joke on him, by sending him this telegram: 'Would you take under-secretaryship of War Office if offered? If so, call 11.45 tomorrow 6 Grosvenor Place. C.B.' Lord Granard, inexpressibly twitted, accordingly called, was admitted to the presence of the Prime Minister, who said 'And what may *you* want?' Telegram produced, explanations followed, Prime Minister taken with a fit of laughter, poor Lord Granard extremely morti-fied. 'Come, come!' said the Prime Minister, 'it would serve those rascally fellows right if you really were offered office. What do you say to being a Lord in Waiting?' Lord Granard, of course, in the seventh heaven. Unfortunately, he knows very few people and no London gossip. Hence, when he went with the King to the theatre for the first time last week, and the King said 'Take your glasses and see who is in that box,' Lord Granard answered that it was the Portuguese Minister. 'And who is the lady with him?' 'Some common-looking woman, with rather coarse features, Sir.' Presently Soveral came round, and the King said 'Who is that you have got with you?' 'Why! Sir, don't you see...it's Mrs. Keppel!' The King, in a great tantrum, said afterwards 'I don't like to have young men in waiting on me who don't know who people are!'[25]

It is sad to record that, like so many good stories, this is not true. In fact, Ripon had told C.B. on November 15 that Granard was 'un-doubtedly the best of our young men in the House of Lords', and C.B., in his reply, said: 'I hear praises of Granard from all sides.'[26]

Tweedmouth, the worldly old ex-whip, married to Lord Randolph Churchill's sister, turned out, as First Lord of the Admiralty, to be one of C.B.'s least happy appointments. As Lord Vansittart wrote, unkindly: 'Neptune only knows how he got there, for he was patently potty.'[27] As Edward Marjoribanks, he had been a highly competent whip, but he was now past making any useful contribution. But perhaps it did not matter too much. As M. Cambon pointed out to the French Government, his post was less important than one might believe, 'car le véritable chef de la marine anglaise est aujourd'hui comme hier le Premier Lord de la Mer, l'amiral Sir John Fisher'.[28]

So the job was done, and on the afternoon of December 11, in a black London fog, so thick that the King's carriage had to be preceded by a dozen running footmen with flaring torches, the new Ministers went to Buckingham Palace to receive their seals of office, John Burns breaking precedent by turning up in a 'reefer'. In the evening the whole Cabinet dined with C.B. The same day Grey wrote to Margot Asquith, saying: 'My bolt is shot . . . the only declarations of Policy which count are those of the Prime Minister; having entered his Government my statements will be in line with his as long as I am in it.'[29]

Beatrice Webb wrote on December 15:

> It is a strong Government. . . . All the possible actors have been included, and the parts have been skilfully allotted. Our friends the 'Limps' have romped in to the leading posts under Campbell-Bannerman; Morley and Bryce being marooned on India and Ireland respectively. To put Asquith and Lloyd George and Winston Churchill dead in front of Joe on the tariff and the colonies; to place John Burns to look to the unemployed; to give Birrell the Education Office; are all apt placements. But the great *coup* is to get Haldane to take the War Office. . . .
>
> The very day of his introduction to the Cabinet, John Burns arrived, childishly delighted with his own post. For one solid hour he paced the room expanding his soul before me – how he had called in the permanent officials, asked them questions. 'That is my decision, gentlemen,' he proudly rehearsed to me once or twice. . . .
>
> Yesterday afternoon Haldane came in. *He* also was in a state of exuberant delight over his new task. 'I chose the War Office out of three offices. . . . We were really very indifferent,' he added sublimely, 'Asquith gave up a brief of £10,000 to defend the Khedive's property that very week; I was throwing away an income of £15,000 to £20,000 a year; and Grey had no ambition and was sacrificing his fishing. But it was a horrid week – one perpetual wrangle. The King signified that he would like me to take the War Office; it is exactly what I myself longed for. I have never been so happy in my life,' and he beamed all over. And then he poured into my sympathetic ear all his plans. 'I shall spend three years observing and thinking. I shall succeed: I have always succeeded in everything I have undertaken.'[30]

At this stage few thought that C.B. had it in him to make any mark as Prime Minister. Lord Hugh Cecil, for example, wrote to Margot Asquith: 'The new Government makes a good show, better than the late one; the weak spot in this Government is the Prime Minister, in the last it was the one strong point.'[31]

Stead in the *Review of Reviews* had some tart comments on some of the new Ministers:

> If Mrs. Asquith can be prevailed upon to release her husband from the treadmill of society, Mr. Asquith may have enough energy left in two years' time to lead the House of Commons. . . . Mr. Haldane . . . will be afforded an opportunity of proving his quality in other than the subterranean fashion he has hitherto affected. . . . Mr. John Burns is the only gaol-bird in the Ministry.

But of C.B. himself he wrote:

> The honours of the new Administration are his to a degree which must seem almost inconceivable to the Jingoes who for years past have been declaring that the country would never stand a C.-B. Administration. It is now seen that Sir Henry is the chief element of strength in the new Government. . . . He is the hub of the Cabinet. All the spokes centre in him. And he is the hub because he is the solidest, most seasoned, best balanced of all the Liberals. Sir Henry Campbell-Bannerman is not a flighty rhetorician, neither is he an artful dodger. Still less is he a haughty patrician. He is a plain, honest, respectable, good-humoured Scot, wary and canny beyond most of his countrymen. A man standing upon his feet, with a cool head and a warm heart. . . .[32]

The Times was, however, unreconciled, and Leo Maxse's *National Review* expressed an even more full-blooded Tory view next month: 'It may be doubted whether, since Fox, there has ever been one claiming the rank of statesman who has so steadily exerted all his influence against his own country, to stimulate its enemies and discourage its friends, as Sir Henry Campbell-Bannerman.'[33]

Some years later H. W. Massingham wrote of C.B.: 'What was in him was an iron mould of character and a rare capacity, in which humorous observation was a chief part, for testing it, or its absence in others.'[34] These qualities had served him well throughout these critical days.

Part 8

The Prime Minister

CHAPTER 30

The Election of 1906

'All experience proves . . . that there must come a time when both the legislative and executive powers must yield to the popular voice or be annihilated.'

Lord Melbourne, 1831

A PRIME MINISTER'S closest associates are his private secretaries. C.B. appointed three. The first was Arthur Ponsonby, son of the Queen's Private Secretary, who had resigned from the Foreign Office in 1902. He was a strong Radical and stood unsuccessfully for Taunton in 1906. The second was Vaughan Nash, who had been a journalist and had helped C.B. since the early nineteen-hundreds. The third was Henry Higgs, a Treasury official. Ponsonby looked after relations with the Palace and with other Ministers. Nash did the political work, prepared speeches and did research. Higgs dealt with patronage and ecclesiastical affairs.[1]

C.B.'s new Cabinet met for the first time on December 14. At this first meeting Cabinet committees were set up to consider the problems of education and the unemployed. On the 20th, when they met for the second time, they considered the problem of Chinese labour. As a result of Milner's decision to speed up economic development by bringing in Chinese to work in the mines there were about 48,000 coolies in the Transvaal, and 14,000 further licences had recently been issued, 'evidently', C.B. told Jack Seely, 'with a view to rush the question'.[2] The new Cabinet decided that fresh recruitment and importation of coolies should be stopped forthwith, a decision that alarmed the King, who thought that by making up their minds without first consulting Lord Selborne the Cabinet were taking 'a leap in the dark'.[3] C.B., however, told Elgin that 'this was a case of sudden action being required. The large number of licences applied for constitute ample proof of concerted plans which it was necessary to stop.'[4]

The Cabinet decided also to set up a Royal Commission on waterways. C.B. had discussed this a year before with Gladstone, saying that

469

a network of canals would be valuable, but if this were to be established by the State this would be 'a *very* new departure, & wd mean ultimately the taking over of the Railways'. He had feared then that any such proposal would scare 'all the quiet people who live on railway dividends'.[5]

On the 21st C.B. spoke at a great party rally at the Albert Hall. Those present, now at last come into port after so long and stormy a voyage, were unrestrained in their enthusiasm. C.B. himself was given a rapturous reception. As the *Morning Post* later wrote: 'The packed and enthusiastic audience rose to acclaim their new leader as if he were another Gladstone; and as he stood to receive the overwhelming ovation, the big tears sprang to his eyes and coursed down his cheeks. . . . The mantle had fallen on the shoulder of the Prophet.'[6] He delivered a keynote speech for the general election. Lloyd George later described it as C.B.'s best speech,[7] but this may have been more a matter of the occasion than the speech itself, which was comparatively pedestrian. C.B. must, nevertheless, have enjoyed making it, for he was able to lambast the Balfour Government, who had departed in a 'moonlight flitting' and 'run away . . . in the murky midnight of December'. There was the ring of conviction in his characterization of Balfour's methods: 'Tactics! Tactics! Ladies and gentlemen, the country is tired of their tactics . . . they have lived for some years on nothing but tactics and now they have died of tactics.'

He pointed out that a Liberal government was in power but the heavens had not fallen. He gave as an example of the mess the Liberals had to clear up the public quarrel between Curzon and Kitchener in India, in which Balfour and Brodrick had taken part: 'Talk of Imperialism! I know nothing, I can imagine nothing, less like a sense of our Imperial responsibility than the spectacle of this controversy, so rashly raised, so tactlessly handled, so recklessly published.' He reminded his audience that Liberals believed in the 'sacred principle of the subordination of the military to the civil authority'.

The Government, he said, had decided 'to stop forthwith . . . the recruitment and embarkation of coolies in China . . . and their importation into South Africa'.

Turning to foreign affairs, he declared: 'I wish emphatically to reaffirm my adhesion to the policy of the *entente cordiale*. . . . In the case of Germany also I see no cause whatever of estrangement in any of the interests of either people.'[8]

C.B. dealt with home affairs, but, for the leader of a party come to power after twenty years in the wilderness, he had not much to offer in the way of a positive programme. As *The Times* wrote of this speech, after describing the sections on education, licensing and land reform: 'On a level with these great objects, the Premier proceeded, to the surprise of his friends and the amusement of his opponents, to announce that he had appointed a Royal Commission to investigate the subject of – canals!'[9]

Nevertheless the speech was a success, though the French Ambassador, who was present, reported that: 'Le chef des libéraux n'est pas un grand orateur: sa parole manque toujours de netteté et de vigueur.'[10] Buchanan wrote to Charlotte: 'to say what a *first rate* speech Sir Henry made. . . . The Hall is an impossible one for the human voice. But at the beginning he got the audience . . . his hearers knew that he was on the Radical Road, and they were with him & cheered him all the way. It was a great occasion for him & he fully rose to it. . . . I wish you had been there.'[11]

The occasion was also notable for the début of a new champion, Mrs. Pankhurst, the leader of the suffragettes. A. G. Gardiner wrote:

> The spirit of that meeting can never be recaptured in our day. It was the hour of triumph, a moment such as one cannot look for twice in a lifetime. . . . The long reign of Toryism was over and Liberalism was born again after twenty years of obliteration, qualified by one feeble flicker of office without power. We stood on the threshold of a new time. . . . We looked, as it were, under
>
> > 'an arch, wherethrough
> > Gleams the untravelled world.'
>
> . . . Suddenly I became conscious that something unusual was happening. . . . All eyes were turned from the platform to a point in the boxes near me. I looked out and my eyes encountered, hanging from the box next but one to mine, a banner with the legend, 'Votes for Women'. It was the signal of a new attack in the rear. Another Richmond was in the field. The Tory host was in ruins; but the Amazons were upon us.[12]

On December 23 C.B. left for Belmont to spend Christmas there with Charlotte. It was the last they were to spend together. Edward Grey and his wife were also spending their last Christmas together – with Rosebery at The Durdans.

After Christmas, C.B. had to plunge into the activity of a general election, beginning with a speech to his constituents in Dunfermline on the 29th. The main issue was inevitably the question of Free Trade versus protection, and this suited the Liberal leaders. Another issue was Chinese labour, which lent itself to sensational treatment, some Liberal candidates producing hired men dressed as manacled Chinese 'slaves', and Mr. Lloyd George inviting his constituents to consider the horrible prospect of Chinamen working at a shilling a day in the Welsh quarries – 'slavery on the hills of Wales!'[13]

The exuberance of some Ministers C.B. found tiresome. John Burns kept urging the abolition of the House of Lords. C.B. wrote to Knollys on January 13:

> I was greatly relieved by the King's kind message as to J. Burns's most improper speeches.
> That is the worst of the abrupt appointment of men to the Cabinet without serving an apprenticeship in subordinate office. I have had two or three cases of want of discretion already from the 'novi homines' including the S.S.W. [Haldane.][14]

C.B. had himself drafted the telegram to Selborne telling him that the movement of Chinese to South Africa was to be stopped 'until H.M.G. can learn through an elected and really representative legislature, the opinion of the Colony'.[15] C.B. told Asquith on December 28 that he thought this was going well, although, he said: 'I am of course receiving lots of letters denouncing me as bringing ruin to mine shareholders.'[16]

His statement on Ireland at Stirling prevented the Unionists from making much of Home Rule as an issue. The Liberals concentrated on attacking the record of the Balfour Government, on the lines C.B. had charted at the Albert Hall, for reckless extravagance, misjudgement of South African affairs, 'Chinese slavery', the endowment of denominational education and the advocacy of protection. Chamberlain's attempt to brand the new government as essentially a Home Rule and Little Englander administration 'which must exist, if at all, by Irish votes', cut little ice. The election had its bizarre aspects. Lord Montagu of Beaulieu announced that over four hundred candidates, irrespective of politics, were 'generally favourable to the cause of motorism'.

The newspapers, once dismissed by Mr. Gladstone as 'the organs of superficial and transitory opinion',[17] were, in the main, opposed to C.B. In Scotland only the *Dundee Advertiser* supported him. The *Scotsman*, the *Glasgow Herald* and most other important papers were hostile and it was the same story in England. But on voting in an election the press has no influence, as has often been shown both in this country and in the United States.

Parliament was dissolved on January 8, 1906. The same day C.B. issued his election address. This contained more about his opponents' policy than about his own. Their administration, he said, had exhibited a well-nigh unbroken expanse of mismanagement, of legislation for the benefit of privileged classes and powerful interests, of wars and adventures abroad hastily embarked on and recklessly pursued. Protection he described as immoral, oppressive and corrupting. His address contained no word about Home Rule. Margot Asquith noted in her diary: 'Sir Henry Campbell-Bannerman's election address was published in the papers. It was quite good, but not as striking as Robespierre's, which I read the other day.'[18]

On the 9th C.B. spoke at Liverpool, saying that the real issue was Free Trade. He criticized the granting by the Unionists, early in November, of 13,000 fresh licences for the importation of Chinese coolies into the Transvaal and said that he was sorry that the Government could not stop them (having been advised by Asquith and the legal experts that this could not be done without compensation for the mine-owners). Next day he said at Chester that he had never been satisfied either that black labour could not be got or that white labour could not be more largely employed. His doubts were justified. The same day he went on to speak at Wrexham and Shrewsbury. It was a strenuous programme, and at Shrewsbury he had to cut short his speech.

He wrote to Robertson on January 11:

> I expect to arrive tomorrow at 3.37, and shall have to leave for Culross, I suppose at 4.15 or thereabouts; and will gladly have a cup of tea (No. 1) if Mrs. Robertson would kindly allow me. No. 2 will be at the Dundonald Arms, No. 3 possibly at Q'ferry. No. 4 at Perth before midnight. Thus is the combatant sustained.
>
> I had a great time at Liverpool and Chester. Wrexham, among the Welsh, was a prolonged rapture. Shrewsbury a small opposition (from Birmingham, led by a man named Pentland, Joe's leader of roughs) but an enormous gathering, most enthusiastic.[19]

For a man of sixty-nine this was hectic work, but C.B. was enjoying himself.

In those days a general election was spread over about ten days, and the campaign continued as the early results were declared. The first came on January 12, when the Liberals won a seat at Ipswich. Next day there was polling in 35 boroughs. The results were sensational. Liberal or Labour candidates gained 20 seats. In East Manchester Balfour was defeated by a margin of some 2,000 votes and in another Manchester constituency Churchill was elected as a Liberal. In Manchester and Salford indeed, the Unionist representation was wiped out. On the 16th the Unionists lost twenty more seats. Alfred Lyttelton was defeated at Leamington, Brodrick at Guildford and Bonar Law by a Labour candidate at Glasgow. There were 11 Liberal gains in London, 3 in Bristol and more elsewhere. Balfour's brother Gerald was defeated at Leeds. Lord Hugh Cecil who, though a Free Trader, had remained loyal to the Unionists, came bottom of the poll at Greenwich.

C.B. was received everywhere as the conquering hero. On the night of the 16th he was at Glasgow, the city he had left to make his political fortune thirty-eight years before. He dined with the Liberal Club and J. A. Spender recalled how, after dinner, settling down in his chair, C.B. began reading out the election results, giving his delighted audience not merely the names and the figures, but a commentary on the persons involved, putting on his Scots accent when appropriate.[20]

Only a few strongholds held out – the City of London, the universities, the wealthier residential districts of London, Ulster, and above all Birmingham, where there was solid support for the Unionists, a remarkable tribute to Chamberlain from his own city.

On the 19th the county results began to come in. These were only slightly less disastrous for the Unionists. Wales became solidly Liberal and Scotland again predominantly so. It was clear that there was being witnessed one of the largest and most decisive electoral landslides in the country's history. On the 20th C.B. wrote to Ponsonby:

> I have been so busy and so bucketted about that all private correspondence has been made to stand over. . . . What a cataract! and it will probably run quite as high to the end.
>
> We have done splendidly in Scotland. It was a needless humiliation for them to send A.J.B. up to Inverness to counteract my meeting. We travelled there & back in the same train (though at difft ends of it – I never saw him) with exultant crowds at the station, my meeting was greatly bigger than his; and his man was kicked out![21]

Jack Sinclair was staying with C.B. at Belmont for the last days of contest in Forfarshire. When the poll there was declared on January 22, he found he had enormously increased his majority. When his car got back to Belmont C.B. was at the door, both hands held out in congratulation. Charlotte was beaming with pleasure as telegrams kept coming in with the news of one victory after another.[22]

She had not many months to live. After her own physical sufferings, and after seeing her husband battered about in the political arena for so long, it is good to think that she survived to witness his unparalleled triumph in this election..

The results were indeed extraordinary. The Liberals and their allies had gained no less than 229 seats. The representation of the Unionists in the House of Commons was reduced from 369 to 157 (a number that included 25 Liberal Unionists). The Liberals in the new House numbered 379, a majority of 88 over all other parties combined and of 222 over their Unionist opponents. There were besides 83 Irish Nationalists and 51 Labour members, of whom twenty were indistinguishable from Liberals. In Scotland Liberals secured 60 out of 72 seats. In the House the party was entirely freed from any dependence on Irish votes. In practice they could count on over 400 votes in the House. The election had been a tremendous personal vindication for C.B., his personality and his policies.

For Balfour the result was a catastrophe. Lord Newton wrote that it was 'the first occasion on which I had ever seen him seriously upset'.[23] Asquith later wrote: 'His idolators would have scoffed at the idea that so wily a performer could be outmanœuvred by the "plain and simple" Campbell-Bannerman. Yet that is precisely what happened.'[24] Balfour's own comment, sent in reply to a note from Lady Salisbury, which simply ran 'D—n. D—n. D—n.', was: 'If I read the signs right, what has occurred has nothing whatever to do with any of the things we have been squabbling over the last few years. C.-B. is a mere cork, dancing on a torrent which he cannot control, and what is going on here is a faint echo of the same movement which has produced massacres in St. Petersburg, riots in Vienna, and Socialist processions in Berlin.'[25] Balfour's picture of a revolutionary torrent was overdrawn; there were among the successful candidates just twenty-nine independent Labour members, led by Keir Hardie, who included Ramsay MacDonald, Snowden and Clynes, none of them fanatics or men of violence.

In some ways the victory was almost embarrassingly overwhelming. But C.B. was not one of those who were nervous about the immense Liberal majority. He rejoiced at it, and had no doubts about his ability to handle it. So it was to prove.

CHAPTER 31

South Africa

THE first major task facing the new Government was the devising of a political settlement in South Africa. The decisions they took in the early months of their term of office were of great historical importance, but the evidence about how those decisions were reached, and exactly what part in them C.B. himself played, is conflicting.

There never was any doubt about C.B.'s own views. His had been a lone voice when he had said at Glasgow in June 1900: 'Let us restore as early as possible and let us maintain those rights of self-government which give . . . contentment and loyalty to every colony which enjoys them.'[1] He never wavered in his belief that self-government and trust was the right policy in South Africa, as it was, he believed, in Ireland, and he put it forward in speech after speech. Milner regarded this belief as insane, and in his diary on January 11, 1906, described the outlook as 'very black owing to the ignorance and evil dispositions of this wretched "pro-Boer" cabinet'.[2] It was, moreover, a policy about which the Liberal Imperialists had throughout been doubtful and hesitant. They believed in continuity of policy in South Africa, and Haldane in particular urged the importance of this.[3]

When Massingham returned from a visit to South Africa, C.B. asked him to breakfast. Massingham later wrote: 'Long before I had finished my account of their perfect ability . . . to work self-government, I divined that there was no call to persuade "C.B." of or to anything.'[4]

Four years had passed since the end of the Boer War and the conclusion of the peace of Vereeniging, Article 7 of which had promised the Boers representative institutions leading up to self-government 'as soon as circumstances allowed'. Since that time the Transvaal and the Orange River Colony, as it was now called, had been well governed as

476

Crown Colonies by Milner and his 'kindergarten', but without any element of self-government. In March 1905, the Unionist Government had, however, put forward for the Transvaal what came to be known as the Lyttelton constitution, a limited form of representative government, under which all executive responsibility was to remain in the hands of the official, nominated members of the legislature, and the Governor was to be given a veto on any legislation. Nothing had been proposed for the Orange River Colony.

The Liberal Government had now to decide whether to go forward with the Lyttelton constitution, or to amend it, or to scrap it and make an immediate grant of self-government. The Colonial Office were strongly for preserving continuity of policy, but to build on Conservative foundations meant going on, to some extent, with Milner's work. What the Boers really thought about this had been revealed in 1904, when Emily Hobhouse had, without consulting the writer, sent a private letter from Smuts to *The Times*:

> ... the folly, the criminality of it all, is simply inconceivable. ... I sometimes ask myself whether South Africa will ever rise again; whether English statesmen will ever dare to be liberal and generous. ... An awakening will come some day; but I am afraid it may come too late to save either South Africa or the British Empire. ... These people have never loved their country or felt a passion for it in any shape or form. South Africa they regard with unconcealed contempt – a black man's country, good enough to make money or a name in but not good enough to be born or to die in. What is there in common between such people and the Boer, the fibres of whose very soul are made of this despised soil? ...[5]

C.B. wanted a clean break with a policy which produced such feelings in the Boer leaders.

A Cabinet committee had been set up in December to consider the problem. The Lord Chancellor, Lord Loreburn (as Bob Reid had now become), was the chairman, and the other members were Ripon, Elgin (the Minister primarily responsible as Colonial Secretary), Asquith and Bryce. Not much progress could be made during January, when ministers were preoccupied with the election, but on the 30th the committee circulated a draft for amending the Lyttelton constitution.[6]

A number of influential voices were raised in favour of continuity. Milner's successor as High Commissioner, Selborne, argued that the

477

grant of self-government would be a 'leap in the dark', and that the generation of Boers who had fought in the war were irreconcilable.[7] The Governor of the Orange River Colony had declared in November that immediate responsible government 'would be a dire calamity to the people of the Colony'.[8] Colonial Office officials shared Selborne's doubts. The Assistant Under-Secretary, Graham, minuted: 'for all the smooth words of General Botha and others we must lay our accounts with any Boer ministry containing a strong element of irreconcilables', among whom he numbered Beyers and Smuts.[9] The more cautious elements in the new Government thought there ought to be a transitional period.

But there were others who favoured a bolder course. One of these, rather surprisingly, was Grey, who thought it best to have immediate self-government.[10] Another, more eloquent, voice was that of the new Under-Secretary at the Colonial Office, Winston Churchill, who had begun his career in the House of Commons by criticizing C.B. for urging an early move to responsible government,[11] but who was now at one with C.B. in believing that the bold, generous course was the right one. In a memorandum written on January 2 he argued that the Transvaal should be given forthwith a representative Assembly with an Executive responsible to it, saying that, unless this was done, 'What we might have given with courage and distinction . . . in the hour of our strength, will be jerked and twisted from our hands – without grace of any kind – not perhaps without humiliation . . . '[12]

Churchill, as the man who would have to defend the Government's actions in the House of Commons, was allowed to take part in the work of the Cabinet committee, though not himself a member of the Cabinet. On February 4, at Elgin's request, he summarized for the Cabinet the conclusions of this committee. These were that the Lyttelton Constitution must be regarded as unworkable, that full responsible government should be granted and that elections should not be delayed. His paper emphasized the need for an early decision.[13]

Meanwhile the Boers had not been passively awaiting their fate. As soon as the Unionist Government fell, the Boer party Het Volk sent to England their most intelligent young man, the thirty-five-year-old J. C. Smuts, who had been Kruger's Attorney-General and had led a commando in Cape Colony during the war. Selborne telegraphed on December 28 warning the Government that Smuts '. . . is a clever, well-educated man, agreeable to meet, and personally I much like him; but please remember that he is an absolutely unreconciled Afrikander Republican. . . .'[14]

Smuts took with him to England a very able and persuasive memorandum on the Transvaal constitution. It was calculated to strike a responsive chord in a man like C.B., whose very language it echoed, in such phrases as: 'I can conceive no nobler task for Liberal statesmanship than that it may inaugurate in South Africa such an era of trust and goodwill and reliance on the people of the land, and bring healing to the wounds which the errors of the past have inflicted.'[15] It made less impact on Colonial Office officials, one of whom minuted on it: 'Mr. Smuts is a Boer and a lawyer. His Memorandum . . . exhibits all the cunning of his race and calling.'[16]

The nub of Smuts's argument was that 'there may be some danger in trusting the people too soon, but there may be much greater danger in trusting them too late'. He maintained that the issue was not one between the Dutch and the English, but between 'the mine-owners and the permanent population of the land, English as well as Dutch,' that the time for self-government had come, and that self-government must be established on a fresh basis, and not on any adaptation of the Lyttelton constitution.

During the election Smuts stayed the weekend with his Quaker friends the Clarks in Somerset, where an engraving of C.B., which was later to be his, hung in a place of honour. On January 15 he went up to London to try to persuade the new Government to follow the course advocated in his memorandum. To another friend, Margaret Gillett, he wrote on February 1:

> Most of the Ministers I have seen. Kindest of all were C.B. and John Morley . . . I feel certain that the Government mean well, but whether we shall get justice is another matter. If God wills . . . that we shall continue the victims of that Jewish-Jingo gang, and that our fate is to be a martyr people, so be it. . . .[17]

Years later Smuts said:

> The first man I had to see about it was Winston . . . I stated my case. Winston said he had never heard anything so preposterous. He said England had conquered South Africa only three years before, and here was I asking for my country back. He declared he would never stand for breaking up the British Empire, and so on and so forth, with all the embroiderations we know so well. I saw all the other Ministers, too. I made no headway. Morley was sym-

pathetic. He said he agreed with most of what I had said, but that British public opinion would never stand for it.[18]

Then on February 7 Smuts saw C.B. again. They had a conversation which Smuts believed ever after to have been decisive. Smuts gave many versions of the story. In an article he wrote for the boys of C.B.'s old school in June 1948, he wrote:

> The man who wrought the miracle was Sir Henry Campbell-Bannerman, to all appearances an ordinary man, almost common-place to the superficial view, but a real man, shrewd and worldly-wise, but rooted in a great faith which inspired a great action. I discussed my mission with many members of the Cabinet – perhaps the most brilliant Government Britain had had for a long time – and with men among them like Asquith, Edward Grey, Lloyd George, John Morley, and, last but not least, Winston Churchill. Campbell-Bannerman looked the least distinguished in that galaxy of talent. But what a wise man, what statesmanship in insight and faith, and what sure grip on the future! My mission failed with the rest, as it was humanly speaking bound to fail. What an audacious, what an unprecedented request mine was – practically for the restoration of the country to the Boers five years after they had been beaten to the ground in one of the hardest and most lengthy struggles in British warfare. But with Campbell-Bannerman my mission did not fail. I put a simple case before him that night in 10 Downing Street. It was in substance: *Do you want friends or enemies? You can have the Boers for friends, and they have proved what their friendship may mean. I pledge the friendship of my colleagues and myself if you wish it. You can choose to make them enemies, and possibly have another Ireland on your hands. If you do believe in liberty, it is also their faith and their religion.* I used no set arguments, but simply spoke to him as man to man, and appealed only to the human aspect which I felt would weigh deeply with him. He was a cautious Scot, and said nothing to me, but yet I left that room that night a happy man. My intuition told me that the thing had been done. . . .[19]

Sir Keith Hancock has written:

> Smuts always looked upon his meeting with Campbell-Bannerman that night as the crisis, the creative encounter of his political

life. The older he grew, the more vivid grew his vision of it, until it illuminated the whole of his experience. . . . In his memory, Botha and Campbell-Bannerman became linked together with the greatest of political virtues, magnanimity. . . . In moments of doubt and depression he found reassurance in the portrait of Campbell-Bannerman, which hung on the wall behind his desk in the study at Doornkloof. Magnanimity had been achieved, once, at any rate, in the dealings of man with man and nation with nation.[20]

Sadly, there appears to be no record of C.B.'s own impressions of this meeting. But there can be no doubt that in fact Smuts was preaching to the converted. C.B. had always believed that the way to make your enemies friends was the way of forgiveness and trust. In suggesting that this one talk convinced C.B., Smuts was certainly claiming too much, though he may well have gone away with that impression. Certainly C.B. impressed Smuts as a man who was unshakeable in his determination. Smuts referred to him at the time as 'the Rock'. And it was true that it was he who had stood up for the principles of self-government and reconciliation all through the Boer War. In his person he represented, more than any one else, the faith and conviction that carried through the South African settlement. Of this interview, however, the truth would seem to be that suggested by Professor Le May, when he wrote: 'It is probable that the meeting of the two men had its largest consequence in its influence not upon Campbell-Bannerman, but upon Smuts . . . his meeting with Campbell-Bannerman may have altered his opinion of British statesmen.'[21]

The following day, February 8, the Cabinet met. The evidence about what took place at this, the decisive, meeting is conflicting, and constitutes a puzzle which has intrigued historians.

C.B.'s own account, in his Cabinet letter to the King, was scarcely dramatic:

. . . The desire of the Cabinet was to introduce fully responsible government into that Colony at the earliest possible time. Examination and discussion however disclosed the fact that much information is lacking . . . and the Cabinet concluded that it would be necessary, by a Commission or otherwise, to ascertain these data before framing a plan of government. . . . The precise reference to the Commission could not well be settled today, and was deferred to an early Cabinet.[22]

This account did not leave the King very much wiser and, like the official Cabinet minutes of a later period,[23] its bland wording gave very little indication of differences within the Cabinet, still less of who held what view. In fact, however, we know that there was a difference of opinion. Elgin wrote to his wife: 'Rather a disappointing cabinet – but one cannot always have one's own way.'[24] Two days later he wrote to Ripon: 'The result of Thursday's cabinet was unexpected, and as it stands there is no very clear decision . . . the Prime Minister rather took it out of my hands. . . .'[25] This makes it plain that C.B. did make the running in the discussion and that the outcome, though not clear-cut, was not what Elgin himself expected or hoped.

It was Lloyd George who was primarily responsible for the dramatic version of what took place, which was only recently challenged by historians. Sarah Gertrude Millin records, after describing Smuts's interview with C.B., that he

> . . . heard the rest of the story from Mr. Lloyd George, who described the Cabinet meeting next day as the most wonderful in his experience. 'I have made up my mind,' Campbell-Bannerman told them, 'that we must scrap the Lyttelton constitution and start afresh and make partners of the Boers.' . . . He was full of emotion and he moved others too. They decided in a few minutes to give the Boers responsible government.[26]

This version of what he said certainly sounds like C.B. The talk with Smuts, reinforcing his own deepest convictions, may have acted on him as did the talk with Emily Hobhouse four and a half years before. This may have produced on this occasion an emotional outburst, all the more effective for being so rare. Lord Riddell gave a fuller account when he recorded a conversation with Lloyd George in April 1913:

> R.: The South African constitution was the biggest thing established in our day. Who was responsible? Campbell-Bannerman or Asquith? L.G.: Oh, C.B.! He deserves all the credit. It was all done in a ten minutes' speech at the Cabinet – the most dramatic, the most important ten minutes' speech ever delivered in our time. In ten minutes he brushed aside all the checks and safeguards devised by Asquith, Winston and Loreburn. At the outset only two of us were with him, John Burns and myself. But his speech convinced

the whole Cabinet. It was the utterance of a plain, kindly, simple man. The speech moved one at least of the Cabinet to tears. It was the most impressive thing I ever saw.[27]

Lloyd George also told Sir Robert Ensor, the historian, that persuading the Cabinet, in principle, that complete colonial self-government should be granted 'was entirely the veteran prime minister's doing. He made a speech in cabinet so unanswerable as to secure at once the unanimous assent of his hearers, many of whom had till then held a different opinion.'[28]

Historians are now inclined to dismiss this version of what occurred as a 'legend' or a 'myth'. To set against it there is a letter from Asquith to J. A. Spender, written from 10 Downing Street in June, 1912, after the *Manchester Guardian* had said in a leading article that the settlement was due to C.B. alone, and that without him it could not and would not have been done:

> The notion that C.B. was opposed in Cabinet, or 'won it over', in regard to the Transvaal settlement is a ridiculous fiction. Between ourselves, he had little or nothing to do with the matter and never bothered his head about it.
>
> The Transvaal Constitution was worked out by myself, Loreburn, Elgin, Winston, and Sir R. Solomon with the help of Lawson Walton.
>
> There was never the faintest difference of opinion about it in the Cabinet. . . .[29]

It has been suggested that this 'offers the most convincing evidence that Sir Henry Campbell-Bannerman's real contribution to the grant of responsible government in the Transvaal was minor and that the story was for some reason manufactured after the prime minister's death'.[30]

The accounts given by Lloyd George and Asquith, in both cases after the lapse of several years, cannot be reconciled and there is some reason to regard both as somewhat suspect. Elgin's comments have already been recorded. There remain two letters sent to C.B. by his Cabinet colleagues at the time.

Lord Carrington wrote on the same day:

Feb 8 06

You must allow me to congratulate you on having so magnificently saved the S. African situation today. The Party would have been in arms if we had capitulated to Lyttelton and the Mine owners – and you pulled us through entirely, and alone.

Burns and I are very proud of our chief –[31]

Lloyd George himself wrote on February 9: 'I hope you will not regard it as presumptuousness on my part if I congratulate you on the way you saved the Government from inevitable disaster yesterday. It was a magnificent piece of work.'[32]

It is also recorded that Mrs. T. R. Buchanan, 'who was sitting at tea with Lady Campbell-Bannerman that afternoon, remembers the triumphant relief with which Sir Henry came in after the Cabinet meeting, and said to Lady C.-B.: "Well, Ma'am, they've agreed, and I've got it through." '[33] And Arthur Ponsonby wrote: 'I remember his coming out of the Cabinet meeting. . . . They had been all for compromise until C.B. spoke. . . . He was elated but rather exhausted: as he sat down to write his usual letter to the King he murmured something about having "fought with beasts at Ephesus".'[34]

Trevelyan noted that Grey 'always spoke in the highest terms of Campbell-Bannerman's conduct of South Africa as Prime Minister, and it was one of several things that led him, when in office, to feel a real admiration and personal loyalty to this chief, whom in opposition he had so often misunderstood'.[34]

If the version given in Asquith's letter is accepted, it is hard to see why Grey, of all people, should talk in such terms of C.B.'s handling of South Africa; and the letters written at the time by Carrington and Lloyd George, C.B.'s remark to Charlotte and Ponsonby's account, all become unintelligible.

In fact, what seems to have happened is that Elgin put forward the agreed proposals of the Cabinet committee, which were for a draft constitution based on, or at any rate linked with, the Lyttelton constitution. C.B. appears then to have intervened, without previous warning to anyone, in a brief but eloquent appeal to his colleagues to treat the Boers with confidence and generosity, to make a clean break with Conservative policy and scrap the draft constitution produced by the committee, suggesting that instead a commission should go out to work out a basis for a new constitution. This was not what the members of the Cabinet committee were expecting – it was not, so to speak, in the script. But what C.B. said carried conviction and was accepted without a dissentient voice. Having carried the main point of principle, C.B. was content to leave the details to the experts. To this extent what Asquith wrote may be true. And Lloyd George certainly exaggerated in suggesting that a majority of the Cabinet were against self-government altogether, and were converted by C.B.'s speech.

In domestic political terms the decision C.B. had secured demonstrated to the Liberal Party that their Government was making a fresh departure and was not tied to the burden of the Conservative past. But, above all, it convinced Botha and Smuts, who had but four years before been fighting bitterly against us, that they were dealing at last with the England of John Bright and Gladstone. Their response was immediate, and was exactly what C.B. had always claimed it would be. Their friendship and support was given to England for the rest of their lives.

The Cabinet duly decided on February 13 to send a committee of three to the Transvaal to carry out an enquiry on the spot and to prepare a scheme of responsible government. The chairman selected was Sir Joseph West Ridgeway, one of the unsuccessful Liberal candidates in the City of London. Churchill said at Manchester on C.B.'s death that the plan of sending out the Ridgeway Commission 'was entirely his own personal wish and plan'.[36]

On February 26 Milner spoke for the first time in the House of Lords. It was a thoughtful, though bitter, speech. He dwelt on the fundamentally anti-British nature of Boer nationalism: 'That insidious and absolutely consistent enemy of this country, *Ons Land*, breaks into a paean because the Lyttelton–Milner regime is as dead as a door nail.' He finished with the words: 'South Africa, once lost, will be lost for ever.'[37] In the very long run there was force in Milner's argument. Forty-two years after he spoke, Smuts was to be defeated in South Africa and displaced by a Nationalist government under Dr. Malan. But in the short and medium term he was wrong and C.B. was right. Though their views were totally incompatible, there was truth on both sides.

The King was worried about the Government's plans and wrote to the Prince of Wales on March 2: 'After all the blood & treasure we have expended it would [be] terrible indeed if the country were handed over to the Boer.'[38]

There was now some discussion in the Cabinet about whether to continue to employ the existing governors in South Africa, all of whom had been appointed by the Conservatives. The Governor of Natal was an out-and-out Milnerite and Selborne himself had been Chamberlain's colleague, had joined him in attacking C.B. and had been a strong supporter of Milner. C.B. was himself, not unreasonably, inclined to make a change. He took this line in Cabinet, but this led Elgin to protest.[39] Selborne was retained. But C.B. himself continued to have misgivings about him, and in June wrote to Robertson: 'It is difficult for the Imperial Authorities to manage the Empire when all our agents abroad are either openly, or at least really, hostile to them – and at the best unsympathetic.'[40]

The Commission were three months in South Africa. While they were there they came into conflict with Selborne, who was reproved by the Cabinet, but pressure to remove him was resisted. The Committee were back by the middle of July. Their report was never published because of the emphasis they laid on the need for British predominance. They wrote, for example: 'We regard British supremacy as vital and essential, and we have also looked upon a British majority at the coming General Election as a desirable outward and visible sign of that supremacy....'[41]

When the Committee reported, C.B. was himself once again desperately worried about Charlotte. She had been seriously ill since December, and dangerously so throughout May and June. As always, he put her interests first. So he sent for Winston Churchill and asked him to introduce the South African legislation in the House. He was giving up, in his wife's interest, what should by rights have been his finest hour in Parliament. Lady Violet Bonham Carter described how many years later Churchill told her

... how astonished and overjoyed he had been when he was sent for by the Prime Minister and asked, quite unexpectedly and at a fortnight's notice, to undertake it. He had taken it for granted that Sir Henry Campbell-Bannerman would take charge of the measure himself, and that his own duty would be confined to standing by as a bottle-washer to deal with details when required. He leapt at the opportunity....[42]

Before the battle was joined in the House Balfour spoke at the Albert Hall on July 27, saying that the Government were on the eve of one of the most momentous decisions ever taken by a British Ministry. The issues at stake were those for which the country had fought in the late war, and if the proposals to be made were unwise and were adopted, the Government would have dealt a great blow to the Empire of which they were only the 'temporary guardians'.[43] The same day Kipling had a poem in the *Standard* which exactly reflected Milner's views, asserting:

> At a great price you loosed the yoke
> 'Neath which our brethren lay
> (Your dead that perished ere 'twas broke
> Are scarcely dust to-day).
> Think you ye freed them at that price?
> Wake, or your toil is vain!
> Our rulers jugglingly devise
> To sell them back again. . . .[44]

On July 31 Churchill opened the debate and announced the Government's proposals. He rose magnificently to the occasion. Even the *Morning Post* said that he 'played admirably before crowded benches the part assigned to him' and that he 'spoke as if he were moved by deep conviction'.[45]

In his speech, Churchill dealt with a problem which was still only a small cloud on the horizon, but which held the seeds of menace for the future. In doing so he relied on the Treaty which the Unionist Government had concluded: 'I come to the question of the natives. Under the Treaty of Vereeniging we undertook that no franchise should be extended to natives before the grant of self-government . . . the Boers would regard it as a breach of that treaty if the franchise were . . . extended to any persons who are not white men. . . . We may regret that decision. . . . But we are bound by this treaty.' He added that the Government were reserving to the Secretary of State the right to disallow any legislation which imposed disabilities on natives not imposed on Europeans.

At the end of this speech the House listened for the first time to one of those Churchill perorations which were to enrich its proceedings many times in the next fifty years. He appealed to the Opposition leaders:

> They are the accepted guides of a party which, though in a minority in this House, nevertheless embodies nearly half the nation. I will ask them seriously . . . if they cannot join with us to invest the grant of a free Constitution to the Transvaal with something of a national sanction. With all our majority we can only make the gift of a party; they can make it the gift of England.[46]

Here spoke the man who was to offer joint citizenship to the defeated French in 1940, and who was to appeal to De Valera, after Pearl Harbour, in 1941 – 'Now is your chance. Now or never! A nation once again!' In every case the romantic appeal was rejected, and failed as sadly and inevitably as one of Don Quixote's adventures. On this occasion the response was altogether inadequate. The *Morning Post* said bluntly:

> Yesterday's debate in the House of Commons opened disastrously for the Unionist Party. . . . In a rapidly emptying House Mr. LYTTELTON replied for the Opposition. . . . Mr. LYTTELTON was the lawyer groping about for precedents, incapable of initiative himself, and unable to appreciate initiative in others. The truth is that the Liberals have seized an opportunity which the Unionists missed. . . .[47]

But the Unionists would not admit that they were wrong. Balfour, winding up for the Opposition, spoke darkly about the native problem – 'we have to face facts; it is not true, men are not born equal, the white and black races are not born with equal capacities . . . they will be as eight to one. . . .' He went on to talk about the proposal of self-government:

> No human being ever thought of such an experiment before – that of giving to a population equal to, and far more homogeneous than our own, absolute control of everything, civil and military. There is nothing to prevent the country making every preparation . . . for a new war. . . . I refuse to accept the invitation . . . that we on this side should make ourselves responsible with the Government for what I regard as the most reckless experiment ever tried in the development of a great colonial policy.[48]

This speech revealed Balfour at his worst. His detached, cynical view of life made him incapable of imagining the effect which a generous settlement would have on men like Botha and Smuts. He followed Milner's lead and assumed that they must be irreconcilables, of whom nothing could be expected. Sir Robert Ensor describes his remarks as 'some of the least foreseeing words that have ever fallen from the lips of an English party leader'.[49] Balfour was at home in dealing with hostile extremists like Fenians in Ireland, but was at sea when confronted by men who were quite genuinely prepared to change course in response to an act of faith. To C.B., however, this represented the fulfilment of his whole political philosophy.

The debate had to end, under the rules of the House, at 10 p.m. Balfour began speaking at 9.30 and his thin, repetitious speech took 29 minutes. C.B. was left with exactly one minute to wind up for the Government. Glancing at the clock, he began: 'In the one minute left to me I will only say one thing, that never in the course of my Parliamentary career have I listened to a more unworthy. . . .'[50] The rest of what he had to say was drowned by yells of 'Shame' and 'Withdraw', and only afterwards were reporters told that he had added the adjectives 'provocative and mischievous'. In this ugly pandemonium had ended Churchill's suggestion of a joint move to invest the grant of self-government with 'something of a national sanction'. Margot Asquith, who thought her friend Balfour's speech 'quite wicked – a disgrace', wrote: 'I wish C.B. had had a little more time & cd. have crushed him by moderation instead of anger tho' every word he said was true.'[51] The Government had a majority in the division of 238. One Unionist, Churchill's friend F. E. Smith, voted with the Government.

Milner's idea had been to delay the grant of self-government while trying to build up a British majority by promoting immigration and land settlement. C.B. set his face against this. 'Economically, sentimentally, and politically alike, Ireland is at hand to show us what the result of a "plantation" policy may be.'[52]

He was able to carry through his policy by Order-in-Council, which meant that it did not need to be submitted to the House of Lords. The instrument was the same as that used, so many years before, by Gladstone and Cardwell to put through the abolition of purchase. But what he could do for the Transvaal as a colony he could not do for Ireland, which was still part of the United Kingdom.

Within weeks of the announcement of the Government's decision the atmosphere in South Africa changed. But the greatest change of all was in Botha who, after the elections, became Prime Minister of the Transvaal, and in Smuts. Botha's wife had wandered for months on the veld, after having been driven from her home, while Smuts's wife had been put in a concentration camp, where her firstborn child had died. But the two men were above bitterness.

The grant of self-government to the Transvaal, and directly after to the Orange River Colony, cleared the way for the Union of South Africa in 1910. And its critics were soon silent. In March 1907,

Churchill wrote to C.B. from Biarritz: '. . . I see a great deal of HM here. . . . He is quite reconciled to our African policy, & undoubtedly impressed by its increasing & evident success. Having been in disfavour for a long time I am now apparently entirely forgiven!'[53]

In 1907 Botha came to London to attend the Colonial Conference. Churchill said next year that the invitation to him, 'which . . . struck everybody's imagination, which made us all feel the magnitude of the work which had been accomplished – that action came directly from Sir Henry Campbell-Bannerman's personal suggestion'.[54] Botha was given a great reception wherever he went and was the star of the conference. At a dinner at the Holborn Restaurant C.B. told him that this was the place where he had made the speech about 'methods of barbarism'. It must have given him pleasure to hear Botha say on this visit: 'Today, although a South African, I stand here as a British subject, a son and a brother of our great British Empire. . . . I am a soldier, and I did my duty then as a soldier; but I am ready to do that same duty today on behalf of the British Empire.'[55] Before he left England Botha breakfasted with C.B. at No. 10. These two were kindred spirits.

The Liberals in fact had more difficulty with Natal than ever they had with the Transvaal. Churchill in July 1907 was talking of intervention 'to bring this wretched Colony – the hooligan of the British Empire – to its senses', and he denounced their 'disgusting butchery of natives'.[56] C.B. shared these views and had earlier written to Elgin: 'Those Natal people of yours are tiresome to the last degree. I hope federation will soon squelch them.'[57] He was far more sympathetic to the long-suffering Zulus, and to Elgin again referred to 'the estimable Dinizulu, who seems to have taken it all with quiet dignity'.[58]

From the first there was a fairly general realization that the Transvaal settlement was C.B.'s crowning accomplishment. As time went on this view increasingly prevailed. Joseph Chamberlain had been too ill to attend the House of Commons debate, but his son Austen did and later on, on November 17, 1921, made a remarkable admission at the time when Southern Ireland was eventually given self-government.

> I have been in Parliament for nearly thirty years; I have given goodness knows how many votes; . . . There are only one or two I would undo, and I will tell you one. . . . There came a change of Government, and with a new Government a new policy. And by

a great act of daring faith they conferred upon our recent enemies in the Transvaal and the Orange Free State on the morrow of our victory full self-government. I voted against it. I thought it a rash, a wicked, thing to do. If I could have seen further into the future . . . I should have known that that great act of faith was not, as I thought it, the destruction of our policy, but its completion and its fulfilment.[59]

The one permanently dissenting voice was, predictably, that of Milner, who said in August 1907: 'People here – not only Liberals – seem delighted, and to think themselves wonderfully fine fellows for having given South Africa back to the Boers. I think it all sheer lunacy.'[60] But to turn bitter enemies into firm friends was not lunacy.

When Botha, in London in 1909, invited the Cabinet to dine with him, there were only two toasts, first that of the King, then Botha rose and said simply: 'To the memory of Sir Henry Campbell-Bannerman.'[61]

Writing to Churchill on September 9, 1907, to send him 'a special line of congratulation and recognition of the large part you have had' in bringing about the South African settlement, C.B. said: 'It is not only the greatest achievement of this Government (which is a comparatively small matter) but it is the finest & noblest work of the British power in modern times . . . a large part of the credit of it must be always attributed to you. . . .'[62]

Churchill was touched, and replied:

Bareno 15 Sept. 1907

My dear Sir Henry,

Your letter has given me the keenest pleasure and I shall always keep it and value it. Since my first speech in Parliament your kindness to me has been unvarying. I was proud to join your Administration & I am delighted that you should feel able to say that I have in some degree contributed to its great & growing success. I have done my best to defend and sustain the South African policy of the government; and with my heartfelt agreement. But of course it has been *your* policy throughout & in decisive moments has been controlled always by your personal intervention.

Once more thanking you, I remain,

Your sincere friend

Winston S. Churchill.[63]

Smuts said: 'They gave us back our country in everything but name. After four years. Has such a miracle of trust and magnanimity ever happened before? Only people like the English could do it. They may make mistakes, but they are a big people.'[64] He maintained also that:

> . . . if England had not given the Boers responsible government in 1906, Boer would not have stopped Boer from fighting England and supporting Germany in 1914. And not only would there have been a new war in South Africa, but the Germans would have had their submarine bases in German East and German West and the history of the war and the world might have been different.[65]

And on March 26, 1919, when he wrote to Lloyd George at the conclusion of a greater war, Smuts said: 'Your and Campbell-Bannerman's great record still remains not only the noblest but also *the most successful* page in recent British statesmanship.'[66]

Two years earlier, in 1917, C. P. Scott of the *Manchester Guardian* lunched at the Savoy with Smuts and noticed that he 'identified himself completely and naturally with Britain and British interests, always speaking of "us" in connection with any issue of war or policy. . . .'[67] That a man who had been our bitter enemy, in arms against us, in 1902, should by 1917 have talked thus, and become a member of the War Cabinet controlling the destinies of the British Empire while it was struggling for its existence, was the supreme justification of C.B.'s policy. Botha and Smuts brought South Africa into the First World War, put down a rebellion of pro-German Boers, defeated the Germans in South-West Africa and took on the burden of hunting them down in East Africa. Smuts brought South Africa into a world war a second time on Britain's side in 1939. All this flowed from C.B.'s actions in 1906.

C.B. was not a man of great intellect, but his instinct was sound, and in this instance it had led him to raise the question above that of cautious checks and balances to the level of a great act of generosity. All his life had led up to this. G. M. Trevelyan wrote of him: 'In history he will live chiefly for one thing, the reconciliation of the white races in South Africa after the Boer War . . . it is . . . more than doubtful whether Great Britain could have survived the two world wars if South Africa had not been previously reconciled.'[68]

South Africa today is no longer the South Africa of Smuts and

Botha. Smuts's increasing preoccupation with international affairs and his gradual loss of influence among the Platteland Boers, leading to the victory of the Nationalist Party in 1948, the withdrawal of South Africa from the Commonwealth, and the rigorous imposition of apartheid and separate development, are not part of this account. But it is reasonable to ask whether, in the light of what has since happened in South Africa, C.B.'s government can fairly be criticized for making a settlement which was eventually to lead to a state of affairs so much in conflict with Liberal ideals.

It is hard to see how the Liberal Government could have acted differently so as to secure better treatment for the non-white peoples of South Africa. It has fairly been said that their eyes were open but their hands were tied.[69] The terms of the Treaty prevented them giving any political rights to non-whites before self-government, and for the Treaty of Vereeniging they were not responsible. Had they attempted to retain control the Boers would have become embittered and might well have joined the Germans in 1914, as indeed some of them tried to do. Moreover in 1906 few people realized the difficulty and intractability of the colour question in South Africa. What was then called the 'racial' question was that of the relationship between Boer and Briton.

In any case it is not possible in this world to deal with more than one great problem at a time. In 1906, the problem that needed to be dealt with was a settlement with the Boers. There was never any possibility of Britain retaining control over the whole of South Africa. If the Boer War proved nothing else, it proved that the Boer people, the Afrikaners, were a small people of outstanding courage, determination and tenacity. No lasting settlement in South Africa could have been made without their consent. What was done in 1906 was right, and the reward was South Africa's support, freely given, in 1914 and 1939. C.B. and his colleagues cannot reasonably be blamed for what happened after 1948, forty years after C.B. himself was dead.

CHAPTER 32

The First Year at No. 10

THE new House of Commons, which met for the first time, with C.B. as its leader, on February 13, 1906, was very different from its predecessor. 318 out its 670 members took their seats for the first time. Among them were 157 Nonconformists, the largest number in any Parliament since Cromwell. Many familiar faces were gone, and in their place was a great Liberal host. All sorts of people were sitting on the Liberal benches – businessmen like Sir Hudson Kearley and Alfred Mond, lawyers like Rufus Isaacs and John Simon, John Bright's son, Hilaire Belloc, A. E. W. Mason and Horatio Bottomley. It was a time of heady enthusiasm. As Sir Robert Ensor wrote:

> Radicalism and socialism alike, released from the supressions of two decades, were radiant with sudden hopes of a new heaven and a new earth. No leader not alive to that morning glory could have carried the house with him; and that was where Campbell-Bannerman in his kindly and generous old age gave the parliament an incomparably better start than the efficient but earth-bound Asquith could have done.[1]

Speaker Lowther was re-elected, and the young Philip Snowden noted that C.B., who 'looked the part of a Prime Minister', nevertheless 'betrayed a nervousness which was painful to see'.[2] C.B. made a graceful gesture towards Rosebery by asking his son Lord Dalmeny, who had been returned for Midlothian, to second the address. It is sad to relate that this approach was rebuffed, Dalmeny being compelled to decline, on the ostensible ground of his 'youth and inexperience', because his father did not wish to see him honoured by C.B.[3]

Among Liberals there was a feeling of excitement and hope. The voters had made it clear that they were against any abandonment of Free Trade, against the continuance of the Balfour style of government, against the use of Chinese labour in the Transvaal. As so often, it was less obvious what they were for. But committed Liberals, apart from wanting a new deal in South Africa, hoped to see something done about Ireland, to reverse the favour shown to the established Church by Balfour's Education Act of 1902, and to bring in a broad programme of social reform, which would involve a cut in naval and military expenditure. C.B. was now in a position to carry out this programme. South Africa he dealt with at once, Ireland he had agreed with his colleagues to leave over for a later Parliament. Social reform he was free to tackle, but he faced the road block Gladstone and Rosebery had encountered – the determined opposition of a House of Lords, not yet shorn of its powers, in which the Unionist Party had an overwhelming majority.

Now that he was Prime Minister, C.B., who had endured for so long the execration of so much of the press and of society, suddenly found himself basking in the sunshine of public favour. One journalist wrote: '. . . the Premier is daily strengthening his position, growing in favour with M.P.'s and commoner mortals. The latest proof of his popularity is a proposal, started yesterday in the Reform Club, to have his portrait painted. . . . *Ave Caesar!*'[4] This project had an unhappy ending, for C.B. thought poorly of the painting – he called it 'Bring me another bottle' – and Vaughan Nash had to insist that it should not be exhibited outside the club.[5]

About this time C.B. encountered a senior civil servant, recently retired, and asked him frankly what was being said about the new Government.

'Well,' said C.B.'s friend, 'it is generally admitted that it is good individually, collectively above the average strength. But they say –' and here he hesitated.

'What do they say?' enquired C.B.

'They say the tail wags the head.'

'They are quite right,' C.B. replied, 'and I am the tail.'[6]

On February 18, on the eve of the session, C.B. gave a dinner to his principal supporters in the House of Commons and afterwards he and Charlotte gave a celebration party at Downing Street. The crush was terrific and Whitehall was a chaos of carriages, motor cars and hansom cabs. Lord Spencer was one of those who were unable to make their way through the crowd on the stairs. Many people were in uniform, including John Burns 'in gold braid and lace' and Winston Churchill who, according to the *Daily News*, 'seemed very slight and very pale, and whose chest is hardly broad enough for his decorations'.[7] There was a Conservative party at Lansdowne House the same night, at which, it was observed, there was a larger number of the unemployed in evidence.[8]

Soon after taking office C.B. asked all his colleagues for details of the directorships they held, and in most cases asked them to relinquish them, saying that he did not want the Front Bench to become a 'sty for guinea-pigs'.[9]

On February 22 the House spent a day discussing Chinese labour. The Opposition, conscious of the damage that the charges about Chinese 'slavery', made by Lloyd George and others, had done them at the election, sought to prove that this word was grossly misleading. C.B. said that he adhered to his description of the ordinances as being practically slavery in the popular and generally accepted sense, if not in the technical sense. 'The British people', he added, 'have always been guided by sentiment and morality, and it is that fact largely which gives them their power and standing.'[10] But he had been persuaded by Asquith that it was impracticable to stop the embarkation of coolies for whom licences had already been issued. Militant radicals would have liked a much stronger line. Hilaire Belloc, for example, called for the deportation of all Chinese from South Africa, with the whole cost falling on the mine-owners, a suggestion that *The Times* called 'dangerous rant'.

The 12th of March was a memorable day in the life of the new Parliament. On that day Balfour returned to the House as one of the members for the City of London. He at once took the opportunity to speak on a Free Trade motion. But in the very different atmosphere of the new House the old Parliamentary master could not find the right note, and the impression he made was disastrous. Edward Clarke described it bluntly as a 'pitiful performance'. 'As he went on refining, and distinguishing, and inquiring,' wrote Clarke, 'the cheers on his own side gradually grew fainter, and when he sat down no Minister rose to reply.'[11]

Balfour's speech was dialectical and discursive, and Massingham said next day that 'his style grew increasingly loose, cogitating and

Balfour and C.B. Cartoon by F. C. Gould

The House of Commons after the Liberal victory of 1906

unhappy' and that 'a roar of ironical laughter greeted his complaint that the Government was raising "unnecessary controversies".'[12] When C.B. made no reply, he jeered: 'So the Government do not know their own mind.' 'Is the Right Honourable gentleman serious?' asked C.B. 'Is he ever serious?' cried his supporters.[13] Undeterred, Balfour put more questions to the Government, continuing to pretend that they could answer them at once, and Chamberlain also pressed for a reply. C.B. took no notice. At last he rose. One observer said that his face was 'alight with passionate anger',[14] another that he looked like a 'mouton enragé'.[15] He turned to Balfour:

The right hon. gentleman is like the Bourbons. He has learned nothing. He comes back to this new House of Commons with the same airy graces – the same subtle dialectics – and the same light and frivolous way of dealing with great questions. He little knows the temper of the new House of Commons if he thinks those methods will prevail here. The right hon. gentleman has . . . asked certain questions which he seemed to think were posers. . . . I have no direct answer to give to them. They are utterly futile, nonsensical and misleading. They are invented by the right hon. gentleman for the purpose of occupying time in this debate. I say, enough of this foolery. . . . Move your amendments – he declared, with a final blow at the box, pointing at Balfour who sat flushing uneasily under this rebuke – move your amendments and let us get to business.[16]

The Liberals punctuated every sentence with a roar of applause. C. F. G. Masterman described the final cheer as the greatest he had ever heard in the House.[17]

Philip Snowden wrote: 'This telling speech lasted only four minutes, but it was one of the most effective I ever heard in the House of Commons. It aroused the House to a frenzy of enthusiasm.'[18] Balfour's own sister-in-law was in the gallery, and wrote later:

. . . the flash of angry lightning was met by a roar of thunderous applause which rose and swelled, and seemed as if it would never die down. In it, Chamberlain's Propaganda went down for ever. . . . I always put it as the greatest Parliamentary triumph that I had ever witnessed.[19]

Next day the debate was much discussed. There had been Lloyd George's first speech as a Minister, and a maiden speech by F. E. Smith which was to become celebrated as a *tour de force*. But the great topic was Balfour's failure and C.B.'s devastating reply.

Old Parliamentarians rubbed their eyes. The peerless 'Prince Arthur', who, they remembered, had so often wiped the floor with his opponents in general and with C.B. in particular, had failed hopelessly, while the plodding C.B., whom they had so often dismissed and derided as the best asset the Unionists had, and whom, only three months before, Grey and Haldane had sought to relegate to the Lords because of his Parliamentary incompetence, had, suddenly and astonishingly, emerged as a champion who could floor his opponent in four minutes. At once C.B. became the hero of the Liberals, and established a commanding position in the House which he held to his death.

He told one of his private secretaries, Higgs: 'When you try to unravel these spider-webs you only get your fingers into a sticky mess. The best thing to do is to take the housemaid's broom and sweep them away – ouf!'[20] At last he had found the answer to Balfour's Parliamentary technique. Balfour never baited him again.

C.B. had for years had to make his way in the House against the tide – to struggle against bitter and patronizing opponents in Balfour and Chamberlain, and against fellow Liberals in the House who were contemptuous or frankly hostile. He did not flourish in such a chilling climate. Few men would have done so, and he was more easily put off his stroke than most. Now at last he was addressing a friendly House, with an admiring, united and enthusiastic host behind him. He became a different man. A Conservative member wrote of him:

In Opposition he had been a despised and unpopular leader; many people, including some of his own followers, doubted if he would survive for more than a few weeks as Prime Minister. But from the first days of his Premiership he . . . displayed powers of character, tact and resource which had been latent in him; in a few months he was a very popular Leader of the House.[21]

What the new Liberal members thought of Balfour was recorded by Masterman:

For the first time in the new Session the House understood what it was that England had repudiated. For the first time also the House was really angry. Mr. Balfour has spoken every day last week. The sentiment is one of deepening bewilderment and repugnance. . . . Two remarks one hears repeated everywhere: The first, 'How did this man manage to retain the leadership of the House for ten years?' The second, 'Now, for the first time, the history of the past ten years becomes explicable.'[22]

Massingham wrote of Balfour on March 13:

> . . . the new members . . . thought his speech drivel. . . . Yet I have heard him make just such a speech as he delivered last night – as empty and wandering – and the House has resounded with applause at his cleverness. And now not only does the whole Liberal and Labour Party endorse 'C-B's' rough but perfectly suitable description of his performance as 'foolery', but if I am not much mistaken a good half of his nominal following has the same view.[23]

Massingham's acute eye had noticed the uneasiness on the Unionist benches. C.B.'s attack had damaged Balfour, and that day accelerated the process of his decline, which was to culminate in the 'Balfour Must Go' movement and his replacement by Bonar Law.

The Times could only complain that C.B. had been 'positively rude'.[24] The King, clearly influenced by this view, wrote to the Prince of Wales on March 19: 'The accounts of the debates in H. of C. are not dignified. The P.M. having so large a majority does not care what he says or does and the rudeness of his language is deplorable. As for Mr. Churchill he is *almost more* of [a] cad in office than he was in opposition.'[25] Perhaps C.B. had been rude. He had suffered a great deal at Balfour's hands over the years, he had never cared for him, and now his impatience, his resentment and his contempt had lent wings to his words. 'Enough of this foolery' was a phrase that would be remembered.

On the following evening C.B. told the Reform Club that the first thing Liberals had to do with their majority was to get fair play for it. The country was sick of dilly-dallying with politics. He said that he was in favour of a drastic reform of the rules of the House.[26]

C.B.'s government was now getting into its swing. Views on the Cabinet differed. Haldane found it

> . . . a congested body of about twenty, in which the powerful orator secured too much attention. The Prime Minister knew too

little of the details of what had to be got through to be able to apportion the time required for discussion. Consequently, instead of ruling the Cabinet and regulating the length of the discussions, he left things much to themselves. We had no Secretary, no agenda, and no minutes. . . .[27]

Morley, however, writing to Minto in India at the end of 1906, said: 'The Cabinet is the most harmonious that ever was, and the Prime Minister exercises in a singularly quiet and easy way an extraordinary ascendancy over both the Cabinet and the House of Commons.'[28]

As head of a Cabinet, Morley said, C.B. was

. . . cool, acute, straight, candid, attentive to affairs, considerate. He always knew his mind, and we were all aware that he knew it. . . . He had no turn for overstraining his proper authority and influence, nor for grasping power that did not belong to his office; he had none of the small weaknesses of jealousy and suspicion, from which even strong and honest men have not always been free. He had no spark of the pettish. Such words as crisis, emergency, unprecedented, unparalleled, and other superlatives of political excitement, were not much in his vocabulary. On the other hand, he had nothing in common with the foolish and provoking people who try to make a policy out of euphemisms, the fear of facing hard facts and giving things their right names. Stout-hearted Sir Robert Walpole, though of heavier build, would have understood him, and so, although of lighter weight, would Lord Melbourne.[29]

Haldane told Gosse that the Government 'was if anything, too conservative . . . with that dear old Tory, C.B., at the head of it, determined to do as little as a fiery majority will allow him'.[30]

One would imagine that C.B. was an easy-going chairman, and it is surprising to find that in 1909, after his death, Sir Almeric Fitzroy wrote: 'It is the opinion of those best qualified to judge that Asquith's control of the Cabinet is less than Sir H. Campbell-Bannerman used to exercise.'[31] C.B. was in fact more successful than Asquith at controlling his colleagues and preventing their differences getting out of hand. But the Cabinet suffered, like most modern Cabinets, from its size. As Morley wrote: 'Pitt had first six, then seven colleagues, Peel twelve, and Gladstone fourteen. To-day we are a score.'[32]

Balfour had rested his hopes on Liberal dissensions, and in a letter to Chamberlain on November 2, 1905, had mentioned 'personal differences and jealousies, which will make the next Cabinet an eminently unfriendly collection of friends'.[33] These expectations proved to be vain. That this was so was due very largely to the way C.B. formed and conducted his government. Even Lloyd George, under his leadership, behaved himself, more or less, and did no more than circulate disparaging accounts of his colleagues, saying of Loreburn, for example, that in Cabinet 'he grumbles the first half of the time and sulks the second half'.[34]

To the Liberal Imps C.B. in office was a revelation. Grey wrote later of him:

> From the moment his Cabinet was formed he made no distinction in personal relations, in intimacy and sympathy between those who had helped him and those who had made difficulties for him. . . . Haldane was now at the War Office. Campbell-Bannerman's previous experience and knowledge enabled him to give special help to anyone who held that very difficult post, and he gave it unsparingly and whole-heartedly to Haldane. In return, he expected equal loyalty from everyone, and he received it. . . . For the two years of his Premiership the Cabinet was peculiarly and happily free from personal differences and restlessness.[35]

Goldwin Smith told Merriman in June:

> Campbell-Bannerman is the right man to hold a motley Government together. But a very motley Government it is: Home Rulers and anti-Home Rulers; Imperialists and anti-Imperialists; Capitalists and Labour men; Feminists and anti-Feminists; moderate Liberals and extreme Radicals, looking with anything but favour on each other.[36]

C.B., as always, did not drive himself or others. He was well suited to those leisurely days. Even so, Ministers were not then surrounded, as they are now, by large personal staffs looking after their every need. Among C.B.'s papers is to be found, for example, a telegram about Chinese labour, in his own handwriting on Downing Street paper, with all the cipher numbers written down alongside, indicating that he must have had to decipher it himself.[37]

In March a resolution was moved that Members should be paid

£300 a year. C.B. said that the Government were in complete accord with the principle of the resolution but that, as in 1893 and 1895, there were no funds to carry it out.

The King was getting to know his new Ministers, but it took time and it was not until 1907 that Esher was able to write: 'The King saw his Chancellor for the first time *en intimité* and liked him, as he was sure to do, for no better fellow lives. John Burns, in knee breeches, was a revelation.'[38] John Burns, for his part, said of the King: 'Me and 'im get on first-rate together.'[39]

In the Lords Lord Ripon carried the main burden for the Government. He was described by Gosse:

> Lord Ripon gets furiously angry. He is an extraordinary little man, very tubby and strutting like a turkey-cock. His fine square head is adorned with a mass of grey hair and a great broad beard. He hits the small of his back with his fist, flings about papers, stamps with his foot, and makes the table rattle again with blows of his emphatic hand. Tonight, when he sat down ... his chest was heaving and one could hear his breath, sucked in and puffed out with the tremendous effort and energy, like a little steam-engine, and he is seventy-eight.[40]

Gosse also described him as having the air of an 'indignant elderly robin'.

It was in the Lords that trouble developed. For now, once again, there was a row about Milner. In his maiden speech in the Lords on February 26, he had bitterly attacked the Government's South African policy. Gosse said that he flung the word 'pro-Boer' at the Government Front Bench 'as if he were aspurging them with vitriol', and that 'during Lord Elgin's reply, Milner sat on the cross-benches, with his face lifted to the roof, and his nostrils dilated with scorn, a vivid but not an amiable figure, supported, however, with evident approval, by Lord Rosebery on one side and Lord Roberts on the other'. Gosse thought Elgin's speech 'prudent and sensible', but noted that 'Winston Churchill, who stood beside me at the bar, made no scruple of disapproving, and thought his Chief ought to have shown more spirit'.[41]

On March 21, a resolution was introduced in the House of Commons by a Liberal back-bencher censuring Milner for allowing the flogging of Chinese. The Government moved an amendment preserving the substance of the condemnation but expressing the House's desire to 'refrain from passing censure on individuals'. Churchill introduced this amendment in words for which he was never forgiven by Milner's admirers:

> Lord Milner has gone from South Africa, probably for ever. The public service knows him no more. Having exercised great authority he now exercises no authority. . . . Having disposed of events which have shaped the course of history, he is now unable to deflect in the smallest degree the policy of the day. . . . Lord Milner has ceased to be a factor in public life.[42]

It was carried by 355 votes to 135.

Margot Asquith was depressed by the whole affair. Though she admired Milner's intellect and character, she wondered 'what it was that had produced the violence of his mind'. But she thought Churchill's speech 'ungenerous, patronising and tactless', and concluded gloomily: 'I do not see Henry's chance in this House of Commons under Campbell-Bannerman in spite of our huge majority. The fluctuating mind and uninspiring personality of our Prime Minister cannot impress others and is not easily impressed.'[43]

The Unionist peers decided to hit back. On March 26 Esher wrote to his son:

> C.B., with whom I had a gossip this morning, has been corresponding with Lansdowne about the motion expressing confidence in Milner. They both think it is a mistake to bring the two Houses into collision upon a question of that kind. . . .
> The only person who can effectively intervene would be Milner himself. . . . I should, were I in his place, and should ask Halifax not to move the resolution.[44]

Milner, however, urged that the Halifax resolution should be supported. He was never a man to compromise. Even Grey was, late in the day, forming doubts, and was to write of Milner in 1908: 'He always says such rasping things, and he cannot keep attacks upon the Government's South African policy out of his speeches – a policy which he says the people of England should have "spat out of their mouths".'[45]

The Times and the *Morning Post* were in full cry in Milner's support, and his friends were outraged that he should have been criticized, even by implication, by the Government. James Rendel told him: 'What a sneaking pitiful hypocritical set of damned humbugs and impostors from C.B. down to the mean hound Portsmouth, they are.'[46] A certain Canon Knox-Little of Worcester expressed to Milner his sympathy at his treatment at the hands of 'our unworthy servants in the House of Commons – "the Westminster Menagerie" – and above all at the insolence of that Mountebank Churchill'. He added: 'We have fallen low indeed in England – to have such a Prime Minister, such an Under Secretary for the Colonies – and such a House of Commons.'[47]

In his Cabinet letter to the King of March 26, C.B. said that he and his colleagues were against reviving the old controversy about Milner. C.B. said that harm had been done 'by Lord Milner's intemperate speech in the House of Lords a short time ago', and that, if the Lords made violent partisan speeches, a 'mischievous, and unseemly, and wholly unnecessary, conflict between the Houses would thus arise'.[48] The King minuted on this: 'I cannot consider Ld Milner's speech in H of Lds was "intemperate". If it was what were Mr. W. S. Churchill's speeches in H of Commons.'[49]

The Lords persisted with their resolution, and passed it by 170 votes to 35. Milner was presented with a testimonial signed by 370,000 members of the public. *The Times* declared that the Lords had exercised their 'peculiar privilege – a privilege denied to the House of Commons by the very nature of its composition – of giving expression to the abiding wishes of the country, as distinguished from the passing waves of party feeling'.[50] The affair played its part in intensifying the conflict between Lords and Commons.

Winston Churchill declined to take *The Times*'s view of 'the abiding wishes of the country'. In June he told a London audience that it was in South Africa 'that Imperialism had been carried to the wildest excesses; it was there every crack-brained experiment had been played out to the bitter or the bloody end'. Ian Hamilton, the soldier, told Spender next year: 'Milner began . . . with all the enthusiasm any man could start with . . . By the time he had taken his leave to England . . . there was the greatest difficulty experienced in dragging a certain small number of Johannesburgers of either race to the Station to receive him, so unpopular had he made his administration. . . .'[51]

There now occurred an episode which made it clear that C.B. was in no sense the prisoner of more forceful colleagues. The Cabinet had decided to introduce a Trades Disputes Bill to allow trade unions to operate freely within the law, a right that had been endangered by the Taff Vale judgement of 1900, which laid down that a trade union had the same liabilities under the law as a private individual.

C.B., Burns and a minority of the Cabinet wanted a straightforward provision that trade unions should not be actionable for damages. But the majority, led by the legal members of the Cabinet, and in particular by Asquith, thought that this would give trade unions too privileged a position, and held that it would be enough to restrict the law of agency in its application to trade unions.[52] The lawyers had their way. But when the Bill was introduced by the Solicitor-General, Robson, on March 28, it became apparent that in political terms C.B.'s instinct had been right. Many radical members could not make head or tail of its involved wording, and the trade union members decided to bring in their own Bill, on the lines C.B. had argued for. This was done by Mr. W. Hudson, his Bill being strongly opposed by the Attorney-General, Lawson Walton, who tore it to pieces in his best forensic style. The debate had not progressed very far when C.B. rose. 'I have never been,' he said, 'and I do not profess to be now, very intimately acquainted with the technicalities of the question, or with the legal points involved in it. The great object then was, and still is, to place the two rival powers of capital and labour on an equality so that the fight between them, so far as fight is necessary, should be at least a fair one. . . .' He then went on to advise the House to pass the second reading of Mr. Hudson's Bill, adding: 'I always vote on the second reading of a Bill with the understood reservation of details, which are to be considered afterwards. That is the universal practice. Shall I repeat that vote today? [Cries of "Yes".] I do not see any reason under the sun why I should not.'[53]

Without warning, C.B. had thrown over the Bill his own Ministers had introduced and voted for the Labour alternative, which was much closer to his own idea of what was wanted. This was certainly an unusual step. Wyndham said that he had heard the conclusion of the Prime Minister's speech with blank amazement. It was incredible that he should on Friday ask the House to vote for a Bill which his Attorney-General had solemnly denounced on Wednesday. C.B. probably did not mind too much about the rebuff to the Law Officers. He was not close to Walton, and Robson he had described to his friend Robertson in 1901 as 'a hot Lib. Imp. and a conceited crank to boot'.[54]

Asquith and the Government lawyers were put out. The argument went on inside the Government. But when the matter was finally settled in Committee in August, it was C.B.'s alternative which was adopted. So the trade unions acquired a privileged legal position which they were to retain for sixty-five years.

This affair raised C.B.'s stock among the Labour members. He had always been sympathetic to their aims. As early as January, 1891, he had replied to a complaint from Elgin that he had supported the workers in a railway strike in a speech at Coatbridge by saying: 'it was nonsense for the Companies to refuse to recognize the Union'.[55] Keir Hardie had described Asquith and Haldane as 'cold-blooded reactionaries of the most dangerous type',[56] and had hitherto been only a little less critical of C.B. Now he became positively favourable. In June he wrote in *The Labour Leader*: 'Mr. Winston Churchill is no longer pert and chippy; Mr. Lloyd George, the erstwhile fiery Rupert of debate, is flat and stale as the Minister for War; . . . the one man who faces the situation with head erect is the Prime Minister.'[57]

C.B. was no Socialist, but he got on well with Labour leaders and understood them. In his Government he had John Burns, continually talking about 'taking a 'ill-top view'. And, though Keir Hardie was critical of Burns, C.B. found no difficulty in hitting it off with both of them. Some of his colleagues were less successful. In August the Master of Elibank, a government Whip, talked in a speech of the need for a Liberal crusade against socialism. Keir Hardie retaliated by declaring that 'Liberalism has ever been a devotee of Mammon'.[58]

Like his predecessors, C.B. had to write a letter to the King in his own hand after each Cabinet meeting describing what took place. His private letters were cogent and entertaining, and peppered with characteristic turns of phrase, but he never acquired the art of rendering these Cabinet letters interesting and amusing. He clearly regarded the writing of them as a tiresome chore, and his were stodgy and uninformative.[59] The King often wrote irritable minutes on them – 'The information as usual is meagre', 'What valuable information!', 'A very brief account!', 'I should have hardly thought it worth P.M.'s while to send me enclosed account of C. Council which virtually gives none at all'.[60] These complaints were justified. When C.B. said in one letter that an enquiry was to be put in hand the King minuted: 'The Govt. or rather Cabinet seem always to shirk coming to any conclusion & always shelter themselves behind a R. Commission!'[61] In November 1907 Knollys complained to Esher that the accounts of Cabinet proceedings C.B. gave were 'really making an absolute fool of the King', and that 'there is no use in Ministers *liking* the King if he is treated like a puppet'.[62] Esher replied that 'no one can make a silk purse out of a sow's ear', and that C.B. was 'too old not to be incurable'.[63] In his journal he wrote of C.B.: 'The indolence of age is upon him. I don't for a moment believe that he wishes to keep the King in the dark, but he cannot bring himself to write. It thoroughly bores him. . . . The result is sad. . . .'64

The King also complained to Esher, who replied:

Your Majesty has noticed that the communications from the Prime Minister are few and somewhat trivial. From what he has seen of the way the Government business is managed, Viscount Esher believes the reason of this to be that the Prime Minister has aged a good deal lately, and finds it even more difficult than hitherto to fix his attention upon details.

Never a laborious man, his disinclination to master troublesome subjects has now given place to impossibility, and Viscount Esher believes that the main reason why he writes so meagrely to Your Majesty is that he has very little to tell.

The work of the Government, even on large questions of policy like the Education Bill, is carried on in the various Departments, practically without reference to the Prime Minister. . . . Viscount Esher feels sure that the present régime will not last very long, and that the P.M.'s health will not stand even the modest strain which he places upon it. . . .65

When C.B. resigned office in 1908 the Russian Ambassador, Count Benckendorff, reported that the King 'a trouvé toujours C.B. "terriblement léger" '.66

After the first shock of C.B.'s counter-attack on Balfour, the Unionists began to recover their spirit. When Easter came, nevertheless, the Government's position was generally satisfactory, though a storm was brewing on the Education Bill, and a powerful agitation against it began during the recess. C.B.'s administration had made a start with its reforming legislation, introducing Bills to deal with trade disputes, merchant shipping, workmen's compensation, plural voting and education.

Knollys told C.B. next month that the King hoped the Trades Disputes Bill 'will not include a clause allowing, what he thinks is rather absurdly described, "peaceful picketting", as if it could be ensured that any form of "picketting" could be free from occasional acts of violence, and at any rate of constant intimidation'.67

The most important and difficult of these measures was the Education

Bill. It was designed to rectify the clerical bias of Balfour's Act of 1902, to place all schools paid for out of rates and taxes under the control of local authorities, who would appoint the teaching staff, and to abolish religious tests. It was strongly supported by the Nonconformists and furiously opposed by the Church of England and by Roman Catholics, since it withdrew from paretns the right to secure specific religious teaching for their children in maintained schools.

Lord Wolverhampton, as H. H. Fowler had become, asserted that C.B. was weak in allowing so much legislation to be promised. This may be a valid charge, but in 1906 it would have been difficult to go too slowly in the light of the pent-up enthusiasm of a party which had been out of power for ten years. C.B. was criticized later for making little use of what one writer described as 'almost unlimited political power'[68] when it was put within his grasp. It is perhaps true that, apart from South Africa, his solid achievements as Prime Minister were few, but it is not true that he had unlimited political power. What he could do was severely circumscribed by an active and hostile House of Lords. As President Kennedy was to discover many years later, popular enthusiasm cannot necessarily prevail over legislative hostility when it comes down to trying to put through concrete new measures.

In the House C.B. relied a great deal on Asquith, whose debating power was unequalled. 'Send for the sledgehammer' was his first thought when things grew difficult in the chamber. He had no difficulties now with Asquith. The only Liberal Imp who gave him any trouble was Haldane. When a Vice-Chamberlainship became vacant Haldane went to Whiteley, the Chief Whip, and gave him the name of the man he said was the Liberal League's candidate for the place. When Whiteley showed surprise Haldane told him that the League did not intend to be ignored in such matters and would 'flutter the dovecotes' unless properly consulted. Whiteley told C.B., who briskly instructed him to tell Haldane that the very fact that his man had been put forward as a Liberal League candidate had ruled him out of court and that any claim by the League to separate recognition would mean a reconstitution of the Government. He had no further trouble.[69]

In June C.B. received an honorary degree from Oxford, along with Prince Arthur of Connaught, Grey, Kipling, Rodin, Mark Twain and General Booth of the Salvation Army. On this occasion one observer noted that he was 'much changed, all his bright look had gone, he appeared stolid & wooden'.[70]

In Downing Street he lived among his private secretaries, doing a good deal of official entertaining, and occasionally showing flashes of his old, gay self, as when an argument was going on at the far end of the table and he called out to Ponsonby: 'I can't hear what you are saying but I agree with every word.' Sometimes after dinner he asked to see any abusive letters that had come in. Ponsonby would give him a packet, and he would read them out with great solemnity until everyone was helpless with laughter.[71]

C.B. presided easily over the administration. Churchill said in 1912:

> Premiers have to give so many important decisions and are so pressed for so many concessions, that they have to protect themselves by some sort of shield. Campbell-Bannerman's was a kindly manner which caused the applicant to go away feeling that his request would if possible be granted, and that if it was refused the Premier would regret the refusal more than anyone else.[72]

C.B. took trouble over the lesser lights in the party, telling the new members stories about the days of Dizzy and Mr. Gladstone. Once when he paused by the Speaker's chair to listen to an obscure back-bencher making a good speech on armaments, he went to his room and wrote him a little note saying how much he had liked his speech. The member had the note framed. Another day, in May 1906, Higgs saw him after a Cabinet meeting:

> We had [said C.B.] a very all round discussion – the Morocco question, the Near East, the Armenian question, and constant talk about places not marked on the map. But James Bryce was always ready. He knew every place, how to get there, how long it took you to get to the railhead and how long to cross the desert by camel: and the rest of it. Just as we were rising, Herbert Gladstone told us about a Miss Cass who had been arrested in Regent Street on a charge of loitering and soliciting. Bryce cleared his throat and began, 'When I leave the House at night I often walk home by Regent Street and –' Here I put my hand on his shoulder and said 'My dear Bryce, you must allow us to know something about Regent Street.'[73]

C.B. benefited from what the *Nation*, after his death, called 'the attraction which plain men felt for a 'russet-coated captain'.[74] His position in the House was extraordinary. He looked so comfortable and uninspired, yet his influence, and his influence alone, could control the ranks behind him. It was said of him, that when he got up 'the discontented became reconciled; the rancorous were transformed into geniality; the rebels came back to the fold'.[75]

1906 was the year that the suffragettes began to be active in their struggle to obtain votes for women. Their demonstration at the Albert Hall speech the previous December was one of their first appearances. C.B. was philosophic about them, writing to Lady Aberdeen: 'I am not sure that the two or three foolish ladies at the Albert Hall did not do something to enliven the meeting! But they ought to realise that no cause can be benefited by what is nothing more than a composition of vanity and bad manners.'[76]

As a good Parliamentarian he believed that violence, when used against the phlegmatic English people, does not pay. The suffragettes were only one of the many groups who were to prove him wrong. After the Albert Hall meeting they had constantly interrupted his speeches during the general election. The agitation continued and increased. On May 19, 1906, he saw a deputation of three hundred, led by Emily Davies, the founder of Girton. He personally sympathized, though without enthusiasm, with the aims of the movement. Over thirty years before he had told his constituents that he did not think women would be much better off with votes than they were without them,[77] and he did not vote when a private member's bill was brought in in 1892 and opposed by a majority which included Asquith, Chamberlain, Randolph Churchill, Curzon, Harcourt and Labouchere.

He knew that his own party were divided on the question and that some of the Cabinet, notably Asquith, were strongly opposed. In 1904 he told Robertson: 'I am friendly enough to that cause, but it would never have done for us to vote, as it would have been at once elevated into a new pledge for the Party, and this is not the moment for new and rash pledges.'[78]

He took the same view now. He decided that nothing could be done for the present, but that he would make his own personal view clear. He told the deputation, therefore, that 'in his opinion, they had made out before the country a conclusive and irrefutable case,' but said that when he came to speak to them 'not as expressing his own individual convictions, but as speaking for others, he had only one thing to preach to them, and that was the virtue of patience. "Go on pestering" was his advice to them.'[79]

Some of the moderates were pleased. 'C.B. as Prime Minister', wrote Lady Frances Balfour, 'did not disappoint. He breathed hope into our serried ranks.'[80] But the militants were enraged. 'Sir,' cried Annie Kenney, jumping on to a chair, 'we are not satisfied!'[81] Indeed C.B.'s impotent sympathy was, to them, more irritating than frank hostility. The growing violence of the movement received a substantial boost. It had not perhaps been handled in C.B.'s happier manner.

In 1907 the women marched again on Parliament and were dispersed by mounted police. A number of them went to prison. A Women's Enfranchisement Bill was introduced on March 8, the proposer referring to the gallantry of the Boer women and the British nurses who had risked their lives on the battlefield. C.B. said that the Government would leave the decision to the House, but, speaking personally, he added:

> I am in favour of the general principle of the inclusion of women in the franchise . . . a woman pays taxes. She has to obey the laws . . . in shaping which she has no share. I think the stage is long past when it can be urged that woman by her position in society is sheltered in some mysterious way from the rough and tumble of life, and is precluded from exercising a share in public affairs.

He said that he would vote for the Bill as a declaration 'that the exclusion of women from the franchise is neither expedient, justifiable, nor politically right'.[82] But its opponents, who included a number of Liberals, succeeded in having it talked out.

The King wrote to the Prince of Wales: 'Thank heaven those dreadful women have not yet been enfranchised. It would have been far more dignified if the P.M. had not spoken on the Bill – or backed it up. But he appears to wish to stand well with everyone!'[83] This comment did less than justice to C.B.'s motives. To C.B. himself the King wrote on March 29: 'The conduct of those so called "suffragettes" has really been so outrageous & done that cause such harm – (for which I have no sympathy) – that I cannot understand how the Prime Minister could speak in their favour.'[84]

In fact four hundred M.P.s were pledged to support votes for women, but both parties were worried about the effect that any particular measure would have on their electoral fortunes, the Liberals fearing that only a limited number of predominantly Conservative women would get the vote, while the Conservatives feared that the enfranchisement of a large number of women would strengthen the Liberals.

The suffragettes secured another interview with the Prime Minister by pure chance. In April 1907, when C.B. was travelling to Cannes, he went to the restaurant car of the train. Two suffragettes, Annie Kenney and Mary Gawthorpe, were having tea at the next table. The opportunity was too good to miss and they introduced themselves. C.B. told them that he could hold out no immediate hope, but he admitted that the Liberal Government were embarrassed by the agitation. The two women, for their part, made it clear that the agitation would go on until women received the vote.[85]

And go on it did. In 1908 the same cycle was repeated. When a Cabinet meeting was held at 10 Downing Street in January, about a dozen women tried to surround C.B. They were kept off by police but some, shouting 'Votes for Women!', chained themselves to the area railings and two got into the house.

The agitation was to outlive C.B. In 1912, when Asquith and his daughter were driving to Stirling to unveil C.B.'s statue, they were held up at Bannockburn by a band of furious women, who sprinkled them with red pepper and attacked them with a dog whip. But women did not get the vote until 1918.

In July 1906 C.B.'s friend T. P. O'Connor wrote a piece on him, in which he said:

> Never has there been a leader of the House who has a position of greater dominance. It is a difficult House to lead. . . . And yet there are no difficulties for Sir Henry Campbell-Bannerman. He can manage the House almost as if it were a school-room. The most vehement Radical, the most impatient Irishman, even the advanced Labour man bows to his wishes. . . .
>
> A few weeks before there was an almost angry protest . . . against the refusal of Mr. Haldane, the Secretary for War, to promise an immediate reduction of the Army. . . . The Radicals below the gangway were apparently united against the War Minister. The Irish were very restive and almost certain to support the Radicals . . . it was possible that there might be such a vote as would have rendered the position of the Government, and especially of the War Secretary, impossible. Towards the end of the debate Sir Henry Campbell-Bannerman got up, made a brief speech, and in a trice the whole situation was transformed.
>
> The same thing has happened over and over again with regard

to the question of Chinese labour. . . . Mr. Winston Churchill . . . has had on many times to get up and plead for delay. The plea would have been disregarded, and the Government would have been left in a minority on several occasions, if it had not been for the trust and faith in Sir Henry Campbell-Bannerman. When things get very hot a deputation is sent to Sir Henry Campbell-Bannerman. He listens calmly to what is said. He then makes a little speech; the situation remains exactly what it was before.

What is the secret of this extraordinary influence exercised by one man? It is not that Sir Henry Campbell-Bannerman has one of those arrogant and dominating personalities that terrorise people into submission. He is one of the gentlest and most conciliatory of men. It is not that he can deliver one of those tremendous orations which Gladstone used to deliver, that have the power of making the right and the wrong reverse places. Nor, on the other hand, is it that Sir Henry Campbell-Bannerman is a play-actor who has the power of simulating feelings he does not hold or pretending to be anything different from what he is. . . . There is no 'cannier' man in the House than Sir Henry Campbell-Bannerman. . . . But at bottom the man is sincere, frank, and thorough. And it is this that accounts for his power over his followers. . . .[86]

In a later account O'Connor revealed that on the War Office vote the Irish had responded to a personal appeal made privately by C.B. – the only man, he said, who could have made such an appeal successfully. He also commented: 'There was something comic in Mr. Haldane having to rely for Parliamentary rescue on a man whom he had opposed for so many years, but politics is full of these comic ironies.'[87]

C.B. seldom interfered with his colleagues. It was said of him that he did not think every subject worth worrying much about. He got on well with all of them and was amused by their foibles. Burns especially he liked, and he was one of the few men whom C.B. addressed in letters by his Christian name. He used to find some of Burns's speeches 'rather too rich', especially when the entire speech consisted of a single sentence. Burns said later that C.B. used to talk to him 'as an employer would speak to his chief foreman'.[88] C.B. resisted efforts by the King in February 1907 to get him to take Burns to task for a speech made twenty years before.[89]

Morley was prickly and sensitive. When C.B. saw a leading Indian without telling Morley first this produced two indignant letters from the Indian Secretary, whose nose was easily put out of joint. But the Lord Chancellor, Loreburn, was a man after his own heart. A. G. Gardiner described him as a 'plain, unvarnished man, large of frame and soft of voice, stiff in opinion, honest and unimaginative . . . the relentless enemy of the Liberal League', and added, 'his love of the plain man was the secret of his devotion to Sir Henry Campbell-Bannerman, as it was of Sir Henry's attachment to him – an attachment not blind to his little defects'.[90]

The summer holidays came, and with them a heat wave, the temperature reaching 93° in Norfolk. In August Margot Asquith wrote to J. A. Spender, saying: 'Personally as long as C.B. leads & Whiteley is whip my interest in party politics is diminished tho' I am not crabbing C.B. for I agree he has done *far* better in a very hard position than his greatest friends predicted.'[91] In another letter, however, she maintained that C.B. 'is not dignified & doesn't rebuke his own men enough'.[92]

For C.B. himself, however, the time was clouded by private anxiety and distress.

CHAPTER 33

The Death of Charlotte

I N January 1906, a Parliamentary correspondent had been shocked
by Charlotte's appearance. He later wrote:

> I remember few sights so sad as seeing her at the last great
> reception she gave at 10 Downing Street. It was the last, and also
> the first. The party was in the highest of spirits, and the Prime
> Minister himself could not but be pleased as he looked round on
> the victors of that great campaign. For some hours Lady Campbell-
> Bannerman stood shaking hands with the guests as they came in.
> Then a sudden fatigue seemed to come over her, and she asked for
> a chair. Her husband still stood shaking hands with the guests, and
> she sat by him, with lowered head, half crushed with fatigue. There
> was already death on her face.[1]

From Easter on it had been apparent that, despite his public success,
C.B. was suffering from a deep private sorrow. For weeks on end he
was seldom seen in the House. Even when a motion he had himself put
down was discussed, he made a brief speech at the beginning and then
was seen no more. During the hours when the Education Bill was
being discussed, his place was usually empty, despite the importance of
the measure. In July he was described as looking worn and pale, and as
receiving the sympathy of all parts of the House.

Charlotte had become seriously ill. C.B. was deeply anxious about
her, spent every moment he could by her bedside, and suffered broken
nights, as he had to keep getting up to look after her.

She had been ill for many years, and pain and sleeplessness had
been her lot. She had had a paralytic stroke in 1902 and, as she slowly

grew worse, she became more and more dependent on her husband. He put her interests before everything else, including his political responsibilities. Five years before she had been in a sad state, suffering sharp pain and getting very little sleep. C.B.'s doctor, Maclagan, told him in July 1901 that she had no real organic disease, but that her nervous system had been weakened by long continuance of sugar in the blood, a condition that made her very susceptible to all depressing and disturbing agencies, cold, fatigue, worry, anxiety. He went on:

> She is not fit for London life. She is not fit to face the fatigue and bothers involved in managing a household. The best thing for her would be to spend the winter in a warmer climate. . . . I have no hesitation in saying that she ought not to be in London during the winter and spring. . . .[2]

Maclagan made it clear that he was advising solely from the point of view of Charlotte's own health. His prescription, made at a time when medical science had no answer to Charlotte's problem, would have meant the end of C.B.'s political life. This Charlotte herself would not have wanted. So they carried on.

But she was seldom better for long and from 1902 on suffered constantly from what C.B. described as 'an excruciating pain in the sciatic nerve which, when in a recumbent position, simply tortured her and made sleep impossible, except for snatches sitting up'.[3] He grew sceptical of the London diagnosis of 'neuritis' which he described as an 'English doctor's disease', and told Sinclair: 'Nothing seems to do it good, and yet if it is not cured life is not worth having. . . . It is, in fact, the complete nervous breakdown which Maclagan always predicted. . . . She can hardly walk at all, and is so weakened in nerve and through want of sleep that she can hardly rise from her chair without help.'[4] The only slight improvement came when in 1902 they found a Swedish masseuse, Miss Thorbjörn, recommended by a doctor in Baden-Baden. Her ministrations gave Charlotte some relief.

Sir Thomas Barlow was called in but said that 'patience and time must be the remedy, as no active remedy is possible'. As Hilaire Belloc wrote of Henry King:

> Physicians of the Utmost Fame
> Were called at once; but when they came
> They answered, as they took their Fees,
> 'There is no cure for this Disease.'

In fact, at that time, there was not. Charlotte almost certainly had diabetes, which could not be treated before insulin was isolated in 1921. Her pains may well have been diabetic neuritis.[5]

C.B. put Charlotte before his political duties, writing about her to the Chief Whip: 'She is helpless, & though she has two nurses & is well attended to, I *cannot* leave her. . . . I am ready for any consultn *in this house*. But I cannot go from under the roof where she is.'[6]

There were times when he was near the end of his tether, and in August 1903 he wrote to Lefevre: '. . . it is almost impossible for me to go on if my wife does not further improve, & so far from being desirous of any conspicuous position or high responsibility I have no humour for anything of the sort. But I feel that in some sort I hold the pass, and I will do what I can to save it.'[7]

One result of Charlotte's condition was that she became enormously fat. She disliked No. 10 Downing Street, and only moved reluctantly to it from Belgrave Square. She was entirely wrapped up in her husband and shared his interests, but, being childless, and subject to the restrictions which affected all women at that time, she lived a lonely life. When she went to Downing Street she rather pathetically begged Lady Mersey to come and see her and to bring some young people and children.[8]

C.B. was fiercely devoted to her. He was greatly touched when Morley said in a letter of 1906: 'I wish I could have said more of the valiant lady who is with you. We owe her much.'[9] The year before, in thanking Morley for a speech he had made, he said that Morley's words not only gave encouragement to his own 'often embarrassed soul – they say *sursum corda* to one under this roof, long tried and distressed, for whose contentment I care more than for all the parties, politics, aye, and principles, on earth. Thanks with all my heart.'[10]

In the spring of 1906 Charlotte became suddenly much worse. C.B. was obliged to try to double being a full-time nurse with being Prime Minister, and when she needed oxygen it was he who gave it to her. The strain on him was enormous. Esher wrote to his son on May 24: 'C.B. is very much broken. He gets no sleep, and is up 3 or 4 times every night. He won't allow anyone but himself to nurse Lady C.B. It cannot possibly go on.'[11] Ponsonby told his wife: 'All household business is all over the shop from Lady C.B. never being able to cope with it and it is impossible to expect C.B. to interview scullery maids in the intervals of the Cabinet & H. of Commons.'[12]

When C.B. met a friend and spoke of Charlotte, tears would come to his eyes. He said of her that she had a gay nature. But she had now to endure what he called 'months of pain, feebleness, and distress'.[13]

It was remarkable that he managed to keep going. Sir George Clarke wrote: 'I had sometimes to see him during Lady Campbell-Bannerman's illness, after sleepless nights, and no signs of impatience or irritation were ever visible.'[14]

But C.B. was worried about the public aspect of this state of affairs, and in July he wrote in a letter to Knollys:

> I have deeply felt for some time the neglect of duty implied in my absence day after day. My wife however is so weak and ill that I cannot leave her for long, and my colleagues and the House generally have been most forbearing and indulgent. I fear I must continue on the same footing till the adjournment, but I am profoundly sensible that it is not right.[15]

A press correspondent wrote:

> Walking through Hyde Park on a spring day in 1906, I noticed a lonely figure sitting on one of those garden seats which keepers let to you at a price. It was at the time of Lady Campbell-Bannerman's illness, and I was thinking at that moment of the sadness of that tragedy. As I came level with the seated figure I suddenly saw that it was the Prime Minister. For a short hour he had left the sick-room and was sitting there to get some air. For a short hour – and then to return to that sick-room. For it was not the least pitiful and touching incident of that illness that Lady Campbell-Bannerman would take no food except from her husband's hand.[16]

On August 13 C.B. took the dying Charlotte to Marienbad, the place she loved above all others, where she had spent so many happy autumns with him. But she continued to go downhill. On August 27 Ponsonby wrote to his wife: 'Things are looking very bad. Lady C.B. has had no food for 3 days & she is inclined to give up the struggle. He also thinks it is hopeless. Dr. Ott comes in constantly and of course she has this marvellous power of recovering that it is impossible to say what may happen.'[17]

Ponsonby did all he could to take C.B.'s mind off things by showing him the more interesting official papers. He got on very well with him but it was a wretched time. 'Poor man,' Ponsonby wrote, 'he looks very grey and worried today.'[18] C.B. was not, however, to be left alone with his sorrow. The King arrived on the 16th and C.B. had to join the convivial round, though, as he told his doctor: 'We shall be riding on a single slip-anchor now and I do better to stay at home.'[19]

C.B. and Ponsonby had their meals in the sitting room with the door left open to Charlotte's bedroom, and every few minutes C.B. would go through in response to Charlotte's call. Dr. Burnet came out from London but there was nothing that he or Ott could do.

The end came on August 30. Ponsonby was in the sitting room when C.B. was called in for the last time. Ponsonby wrote: 'It was a blazing summer afternoon, the street outside was silent except for the clicking of the horses' hoofs in the carriages standing outside. The only other sound was the gradually slackening breath of the dying woman. . . . She died about 5 o'clock.'[20]

The partnership of nearly fifty years was over. In his tiny engagement book C.B. wrote the single word 'Eheu'. Ponsonby went round to tell the King and then to arrange the funeral service with an Austrian pastor and the English chaplain, which the King attended.

Next month, in a letter to the wife of the Chief Whip, C.B. wrote:

> Among other things I am thankful that my poor brave wife 'never said die'; . . . it was only on the last morning that she ceased, from mere exhaustion, to be fully conscious; and she passed quietly away without a murmur . . . in her favourite room, in her favourite place, with . . . friends and her trusted . . . doctor about her. God be thanked.[21]

So C.B. and Ponsonby set out with Charlotte's body on what Ponsonby called 'a long, hot, wearisome journey home', with an uncomplaining C.B. who, for the greater part of the journey, 'just sat idly thinking'.[22] On their way through Frankfurt they dined with the Consul-General, Francis Oppenheimer. C.B. talked about his first visit to Germany, in 1851, when, as a boy, he had seen some of Frederick the Great's veterans at the unveiling of the monument to the Emperor in the Unter den Linden.[23] In the continuing heat-wave they journeyed by way of No. 10 to Belmont. C.B., said Ponsonby, 'told me it was all over for him in the little service in the chapel at Marienbad'. The second funeral at Meigle seemed to him an anti-climax.[24]

John Morley wrote to Minto on September 2:

I am starting in a few hours for a very melancholy expedition to Scotland, to the funeral of poor Lady C-Bannerman. . . . What a curious change in the Prime Minister's public position has been seen in the last few months! He has become generally popular; his ascendency over the H. of C. has never been surpassed; in the Cabinet he is felt to be the one indispensable man among all of us. His wife has been his inseparable companion for 46 years, and her influence over him was boundless. She had an extremely strong will, any amount of courage, and, as he said to me yesterday, an extraordinarily good political *flair*.

She kept well away from political cliques and sets, and seemed to read both the character of men and the significance of events by a sort of intuition. It will be lonely for him, but he will stick to the ship. He has sold his private house in Belgrave Square, so I suppose he intends to spend the rest of his days in Downing Street![25]

On the 5th Charlotte was buried in the churchyard at Meigle, C.B. looking wretched with, as one reporter wrote, 'nervous lips and twitching fingers'. A gentle Scottish rain fell as he watched his beloved 'Poo Ole' being lowered into the grave. A reporter wrote, in the expansive style of the period:

On the lawn was gathered a strange assemblage of mourners about the coffin of a Premier's wife. The hard-cut Scottish faces, bronzed and toil-worn, of the people of the country, mingled with the ascetic faces of Mr. Asquith and Mr. Morley; the wide-flung form of Lord Reay, the business shapes of Lord Tweedmouth and Lord Portsmouth, towered above Lord Advocate Shaw and the Premier himself. . . . The company straggled informally . . . down the drooping country road, under oaks and ashes and sycamores, to where the village cottages, bowered in clematis and China tea-roses, looked their best. . . . On the kirk knoll stood the villagers, bare-headed. . . . No organ played, no choir sang, no bell knelled. . . . In silence the coffin was lowered . . . lightened with wreaths of heliotrope which gave out Sir Henry's last message, which had been his first to her who had gone, 'Je t'aime.'[26]

For C.B., the loss of Charlotte was a blow from which he never fully recovered. The life of this plain, unglamorous woman had been rendered a burden by illness and pain. Two years later Lord Tweedmouth, whose brain was going at the time, referred to her in a speech in the House of Lords as 'a lady of sterling value but of no personal charm'. The Hansard editors of 1908 were too discreet to report these words.[27] She had been childless and lonely, and had made many demands on her husband. But her life had been irradiated by her devotion to C.B. and by his love for her. For nearly half a century they had shared the same interests, the same tastes, the same jokes. Every stroke of adversity had seemed as nothing in the face of so intimate a partnership. Now Charlotte was gone, and C.B. could truthfully say, in the words of Emily Brontë:

> No other Sun has lightened up my heaven;
> No other Star has ever shone for me:
> All my life's bliss from thy dear life was given –
> All my life's bliss is in the grave with thee.

CHAPTER 34

The Seeds of War

I T has often been asserted that C.B. took little interest in foreign affairs but this is not true. He did not, like some Prime Ministers, try to be his own Foreign Secretary and take matters into his own hands whenever a problem became of the first importance or politically sensitive, but he was very much concerned with major questions of foreign policy.

A weakness in his administration was that he had acquired, in Grey, a Foreign Secretary who was neither personally nor politically close to him and had indeed, in the very recent past, been strongly opposed to him on the main overseas issue of the day. Grey admitted in due course that he had been wrong about C.B., but there never grew up any close relationship between the two men, and they saw comparatively little of each other except at Cabinets. Ponsonby, who was critical of Grey as a Roseberyite and Liberal Imp, went so far as to say: 'C.-B.'s relations with Sir Edward Grey were strained. He did not trust him politically and the estrangement prevented him from interfering in the Foreign Office, with which his transactions were cold and correct. They never met intimately.'[1]

Ponsonby saw a great deal of C.B. in his last two years, but this statement seems to reflect his own prejudices rather than the actual relationship, which, as far as can be judged from the evidence which survives, was quite harmonious. But Grey's relatively distant relations with C.B. did not make it easy for the new Government to follow a consistent foreign policy reflecting the political convictions of the Cabinet as a whole.

When the new Government took office in December 1905, the main cause for anxiety was the expansionist policy of Germany, which had been pursued in an increasingly unscrupulous and aggressive way since Bismarck began the search for colonies and maritime power in 1884. Germany had unleashed a forward drive in the Near East, the *Drang nach Osten*, and had pushed her way into South West Africa, the Cameroons and East Africa. There had been the Kaiser's strongly worded telegram to Kruger after the Jameson Raid and the German Navy Bill of 1900, under which Admiral Tirpitz was able to set about the creation of a German High Seas Fleet, 'of such strength that, even for the mightiest Naval Power' (which could only be England), a war with Germany 'would involve such risks as to jeopardise its own supremacy'.[2] The *éminence grise* of the Wilhelmstrasse, Baron von Holstein, who always carried a loaded revolver and was described by Bismarck as 'the man with the hyena eyes',[3] increasingly threatened France, and in 1905 he and the German Chancellor, Prince Bülow, challenged the French position in Morocco. The Kaiser landed at Tangier and made a bellicose speech. By December war had become a serious possibility, though it was agreed that the Moroccan problem should be discussed at a conference at Algeciras. The French sacrificed their Foreign Minister, Delcassé, in June, in a vain effort to appease the militant Germans, and were greatly alarmed.

They now had, however, the *entente cordiale* with Great Britain, negotiated by Lansdowne and Delcassé in 1904, and the composition of the new government seemed to them encouraging. Their Ambassador in London, Paul Cambon, had reported of it: 'Son chef est un ami de la France; il manie bien notre langue, il a pour notre littérature un goût très vif, fréquente volontiers notre pays. . . .'[4] The French felt entitled to put British friendship to the test. On December 20 the French military attaché, Major Huguet, met General Grierson, the Director of Military Operations at the War Office, in Rotten Row. Grierson told Huguet that if war came he did not think Britain would stand aside, and he claimed that over a hundred thousand British troops were available. He repeated this when the two men met next day.[5] Eight days later, on December 29, the military correspondent of *The Times*, Colonel Repington, wrote to the Foreign Secretary:

I had a confidential talk with the French military attaché last night, lasting some five hours. . . .

Major Huguet confessed that his Embassy felt anxious upon the question of the attitude of the new Government in England. His people, he said, had nothing to complain of, since the speeches of

Sir Henry Campbell-Bannerman, as well as yours, had produced an excellent effect. It was not a question of sympathies but rather of acts, of what the British government were prepared to do. . . . There is another matter, he continued. M. Cambon cannot speak a word of English: he has tried to learn, but says he is too old.* Sir Edward Grey is believed not to be so perfect in French as Lord Lansdowne and M. Cambon feels he will have a difficulty in seizing all the nuances of a conversation on such a delicate matter. . . .'[7]

Ministers were soon immersed in the election campaign, but in London Repington was in touch with Esher, Sir George Clarke, the secretary of the Committee of Imperial Defence, and Fisher at the Admiralty. On January 2 Fisher told the French naval attaché of his ideas for a naval war against Germany. Esher and Clarke went further, and sent Repington to see the French military attaché with a detailed list of questions for the French General Staff. Some of these were far-reaching, for example:

> What is the French opinion concerning landings on the German coasts? If we could send 100,000 men for such operation and assisted France with transports, could she supply another 100,000 men, and in what time and from what ports? . . . Would it be possible for France to capture Togoland and the Cameroons, if we captured German E. and S.W. Africa and German possessions in the Pacific?[8]

Huguet left for Paris on January 7. He went first to the Deuxième Bureau of the French General Staff, and told Repington that he had found them 'deeply engaged upon the elaboration of an academic plan for the invasion of England'. They were 'transfixed with surprise' when told that the English were planning to come to their help.[9]

All this was done without any authority from the new Government. But on January 9 Clarke saw Grey and told him of the contact with Huguet. Clarke wrote the same day to Esher saying that he had explained to Grey that he had 'said nothing to C.-B. and he seemed to think it was better not to do so at this stage. Of course if Grierson will play up loyally and intelligently there is no need in involving the P.M. just now.'[10] Grey apparently agreed to keep the Prime Minister in the dark about the military contacts for the time being, and when he wrote

---

* Esher believed that Cambon's professed inability to speak or understand any English was a pose.[6]

to C.B. at Belmont on January 9, he said merely that he had promised the French diplomatic support but no more, and had told the German Ambassador that if France got into trouble as a result of the entente feeling in England might oblige the Government to go to her help. He added: 'Indications keep trickling in that Germany is preparing for war in the Spring; France is very apprehensive. I do not think there will be war. . . . But the War Office ought, it seems to me, to be ready to answer the question, what could they do, if we had to take part against Germany, if for instance the neutrality of Belgium was violated?'[11]

The French Ambassador now returned from Paris, where he had gone to consult Rouvier, the Foreign Minister, and at once went to see the Foreign Secretary. Next day, the 10th, Grey wrote again to C.B.:

> I wrote in innocence last night: this afternoon Cambon put the question to me directly and formally. I enclose the record: Sanderson* was present at the whole conversation.
>
> I assume you will have a Cabinet directly the elections are over to decide what I am to say. Before that happens I shall be glad of the opportunity to talk it over. . . .
>
> I have kept a copy of this Conversation: I am leaving it to you to decide to whom it should be circulated & when.[12]

The enclosure which, like the letter, was in Grey's own hand, told the Prime Minister that:

> The French Ambassador asked me today whether in the event of an attack (une agression brutale) by Germany upon France arising out of the Morocco difficulty, France could rely upon the armed support of England.
>
> I said I could not answer this question: I could not even consult the Prime Minister or the Cabinet during the elections. I was sure that there would be a strong sentiment and sympathy on the part of the English public; more than that I could not say and all I could promise was diplomatic support now. . . .
>
> M. Cambon said he would again ask me after the Elections were over.[13]

It has been pointed out that the record of this meeting which Grey sent to C.B. left out a key point which was included in the despatch

* Sir Thomas Sanderson, Permanent Under-Secretary at the Foreign Office.

sent to Sir Francis Bertie, the Ambassador in Paris, and it has been asserted that Grey gave instructions that the despatch was not to be printed and circulated to his colleagues.[14] The passage which was included in the despatch, but not in the letter, represented Grey as learning from Cambon that:

> he thought it advisable that unofficial communications between our Admiralty and War Office and the French Naval and Military Attachés should take place as to what action might advantageously be taken in case the two countries found themselves in alliance in such a war. Some communications had, he believed, already passed, and might, he thought, be continued. They did not pledge either Government. I did not dissent from this view.[15]

It seems unlikely that Grey was still attempting to keep C.B. in the dark after January 10. The original file in the Public Record Office shows Grey's red ink minute on the draft of the despatch: 'Not for print at present', but indicates also that copies went to the King, the Prime Minister and Lord Ripon.[16] So C.B. did presumably get a copy, though there seems to be no evidence to support J. A. Spender's assertion that 'Sir Edward submitted the draft of this despatch to the Prime Minister', nor is it established that the King and C.B. only received abbreviated copies.[17]

Sanderson was concerned lest the soldiers should have gone further with the French than they should have done.[18] He had some reason to be. Next day, the 11th, the French military attaché returned from Paris, bearing the detailed replies of the French General Staff to the questions put by Clarke and Esher through Repington. On the same day Louis Mallet, Grey's private secretary at the Foreign Office and the most extreme of the anti-German 'hawks', wrote to the Ambassador in Paris:

> Cambon . . . put the crucial question. . . . There is of course only one possible answer & that is that if the aggression arises out of the Entente . . . we shall take our share of the fighting. There is however no certainty that the Govt. will give such an answer. Sir E. Grey is, between you and me, much upset at being asked the question & is writing to the Prime Minister, who alone of the Ministers is at present to know of the conversation, he gives no opinion at all himself.

In speaking to me he seemed very nervous, & said it was a great step to take without Parlt. . . .

I am writing because I want you if you agree to write a very strong personal letter to Grey. . . . It will go to the King, Campbell-Bannerman & Ld. Ripon. Will you also prime C. Harding [*sic*]. He must, supposing he agrees, do everything he can to buck up these miserable creatures. . . .[19]

Charles Hardinge, who had been Ambassador in St. Petersburg, was in Paris on his way home. At the age of forty-seven, already a G.C.M.G. and a Privy Councillor, he had been appointed Permanent Under-Secretary at the Foreign Office.

On the 11th also Fitzmaurice wrote to C.B. enclosing a letter from Ripon. Ripon pointed out that we were bound to nothing beyond full diplomatic support, but he saw that the French were expecting more if serious trouble with Germany arose. He commented:

If that occurs and we decline, as I think we ought to decline, to go farther than diplomacy will reach, I cannot but fear a cry of 'perfide Albion' and a destruction of the present friendship between the two nations. The situation requires great wariness, but we may trust to Grey for that. . . .[20]

C.B. replied to Fitzmaurice: 'We have happily a little time for deliberation, as the French Ambassador cannot expect an answer during the elections, and things appear to be looking a little more favourable & ∴ there is less urgency. I keep Ripon's letter meantime & will write to him when I can find a moment.'[21]

Meanwhile Grey returned to Northumberland, and saw Haldane, now Secretary of State for War, at Berwick. They discussed the military conversations and Haldane agreed to seek C.B.'s authority for them.

Haldane claimed that he saw C.B. in London very shortly afterwards – according to Repington during the weekend of Sunday, January 14.[22] In his book, *Before the War*, Haldane wrote:

I saw Sir Henry Campbell-Bannerman at his house in London in January, 1906. He at once saw the point, and he gave me authority for directing the Staff at the War Office to take the necessary steps. He naturally laid down that the study proposed was to be carefully guarded, so far as any possible claim of commitment was concerned, that it was not to go beyond the limits of purely General Staff work, and further that it should not be talked about.[23]

Repington wrote that C.B., in talking to Haldane, 'was very firm and clear on the point that we should be prepared for all emergencies, and that conversations between the two Staffs, without any binding agreement between the Governments, were permissible measures of prudence'.[24] Repington also wrote: 'It was arranged that a paper should be signed by Grierson and Huguet stipulating that the conversations should not commit either Government, and this was done. C.-B. was a fine old Tory in Army matters. He was also a warm friend of the French, and quickly realised the whole position.'[25]

These accounts are clear enough, but the fact is that C.B. was not in London, or anywhere near it, over the weekend of January 14. He was in Scotland taking part in the election campaign. He spoke at Meigle on Friday the 13th and at Glasgow on Monday the 15th. Over the weekend he was at Belmont, and on Sunday the 14th he wrote a letter to Fitzmaurice, in which he said, 'I expect to be up in town, perhaps about the 25th'.[26] It has been pointed out, too, that Haldane's daily letters to his mother make no mention of any London meeting with C.B.[27] So it seems clear that, despite what Repington wrote, C.B. was not informed or consulted about the military talks before they were put in hand.

The talks, however, now had Haldane's and Grey's approval, and on January 16 British staff officers began discussing officially with the French, without commitment, plans for war with Germany, and, before January was out, the British representatives had told the French of their intention, if authorized, to send a hundred thousand men to France within a fortnight of the outbreak of war.[28] Such was the origin of the concept of the British Expeditionary Force and the 'first hundred thousand' who were to go to their deaths in 1914.

When a despatch came in from Bertie, recommending support for the French, Grey minuted: 'Nothing is to go to the Cabinet, till I have seen the Prime Minister, which I hope to do next week. This despatch . . . should go to Lord Ripon (who is in London & whom I hope to see on Monday) as well as to the Prime Minister. . . .They should of course be added to the papers . . . to be prepared & considered as a whole by the Cabinet eventually.'[29] That 'eventually' never came.

C.B. wrote to Grey on the 21st, saying: 'When would you like to have a Cabinet? Would 30th, 31st, or 1st do? Would you like the

C.B. arrives at Windsor Station for the Kaiser's State Visit, November, 1907

No. 10 Downing Street in C.B.'s time:
he called it 'this rotten old barrack of a house'.
It was the house in which he died

answer for the French to be confirmed by a Cabinet before it is given.'[30] Grey answered that the date for a Cabinet had better not be fixed till he had talked the matter over with C.B.[31]

C.B. was uneasy about the way the assumption was being made that we should without question support the French if it came to war. On the 25th he wrote again to Grey:

> Do you see an outrageous interview with Genl. Sir F. Maurice in a French paper, describing all that wd. happen if Germany & France went to war; how we should of course join France; how we would operate from Denmark, not from Schleswig Holstein, & so on.
>
> I have written to Haldane to the effect that in my opinion Genl. Maurice should be severely reprimanded (if he is still in the service) – and if possible that his whole view should be publicly repudiated.
>
> For a man to speak in such terms at this moment is little short of criminal.[32]

On the night of the 26th C.B. travelled south to London. He saw Grey, Haldane and Sir George Clarke, who at last told him about the staff contacts and informed Esher that the Prime Minister 'was not at all inclined to be alarmed at what I told him we had done'.[33] On the 27th C.B. went to stay the weekend with the King at Windsor, where Grey joined him. On the 31st he presided over the fourth meeting of his new Cabinet, but neither he nor Grey mentioned the staff talks. C.B.'s Cabinet letter to the King said merely that 'Sir E. Grey informed the Cabinet as to the progress of affairs at Algeciras and the little difficulty with Turkey at the head of the Red Sea'.[34] On the same day Grey gave his answer to Cambon. He told him that he had consulted the Prime Minister, that England gave France unreserved diplomatic support, but could give no solemn undertaking without the Cabinet's authority. A defensive alliance could not be kept secret from Parliament. If Germany were to force war upon France to break up the Anglo-French *entente*, public opinion would undoubtedly be very strong on the side of France. But Grey warned Cambon that England would be reluctant to find herself engaged in a great war.[35]

The despatch recording this was copied to C.B., as was Cambon's note on the conversation, but again there is nothing to support Spender's assertion that the draft was cleared with him.[36]

Immediately following this, on February 1, Dorothy Grey was

thrown from her dog-cart in Northumberland and was carried in unconscious. Grey had to go north again. C.B. told Ripon on February 2: 'Cambon appears satisfied. But I do not like the stress laid upon joint preparations. It comes very close to an honourable undertaking: and it will be known on both sides of the Rhine. But let us hope for the best.'[37]

Dorothy Grey died on the 4th. Grey offered to resign or move to a less important office, but C.B. encouraged him to go on.[38]

All this activity had taken place in the context of the immediate crisis over Morocco. When the Algeciras Conference met, however, the Germans gave way and the threat of war receded. Ministers in London ceased to be preoccupied with the problem. But the staff talks, with their implied moral commitment to the French, continued.

A great deal has been written about the fact that the Cabinet were never consulted about these staff talks, and that some of its members remained ignorant of them until 1911. Both Grey and C.B. have been censured for this. Ensor wrote that the omission was difficult to reconcile with the practice of constitutional government.[39]

Dorothy Grey's accident and the passing of the immediate crisis may have played a part in this. Almost certainly, however, C.B. decided not to put the matter before the full Cabinet because there was no binding commitment and he did not want to put at risk the unity of his administration. The only Ministers who knew were C.B., Grey, Haldane, Ripon, Fitzmaurice and Asquith. Cambon reported to Paris on March 31 that he had confidential information about the conversations the King had had with C.B. and Grey when they had been at Windsor. They had, he said, recognized the identity of interest between England and France in the event of a German attack but had agreed that an extension of Anglo-French agreements would lead to a discussion in the Cabinet which, at that moment, 'aurait des inconvénients', since some Ministers would be taken aback at the opening of talks between the military staffs of the two countries. They had concluded, Cambon wrote, that it would be best to say nothing and continue discreet planning, so as to put the two Governments in a position to act rapidly together if the need arose.[40]

C.B. knew his colleagues intimately, and he must have known that the staff talks would have been fiercely opposed by men like Loreburn, Morley and Bryce, the men whom Hardinge described as the 'peace at any price section of the Cabinet headed by the Lord Chancellor'.[41] Loreburn himself was a convinced isolationist, who held that 'our policy for generations had been not to take a hand in the quarrels of the continent', and that that policy was right.[42] That C.B. himself had misgivings, his letter to Ripon of February 2 makes clear. But he must have been even more worried about the possibility of a veto on the talks by the radicals. Grey's subsequent claim that if the matter had been discussed in Cabinet 'we should doubtless have had criticism but not, I should say, opposition'[43] is difficult to accept. C.B. had been, for several years past, receiving warnings about the warlike spirit in Germany and in early January had seen a private warning from Mr. Albert Vickers of Vickers Maxim, reporting that Germany was secretly preparing for war.[44] His love for France was deep and strong, and to have a breach with the French at the outset of his administration would have been an unhappy prospect for him. The sagacious Ripon, whose opinion he valued more than that of any other of his colleagues, was with him. He distrusted Morley's judgement to the extent that he had been determined under no circumstances to give him the Foreign Office. So he decided to keep the radicals in the dark. He was not the first or the last Prime Minister to take such a course.

Prime Ministers have to judge when unpalatable proposals are best put to colleagues who are known to have strong views, and it is not unknown for members of a Cabinet not immediately concerned with foreign policy to be kept in the dark for long or short periods by the Prime Minister – Gladstone's complaint against Rosebery was that as Foreign Secretary he kept both the Cabinet *and* the Prime Minister in the dark.[45] In this instance, however, some of the radicals were outraged when they eventually found out. Loreburn claimed that he was told nothing, which does not square with Fitzmaurice's statement to Sinclair in 1919 that 'if nobody else told Loreburn of the conversations with Cambon, I did'.[46] One historian has written: 'Grey's omission to keep the Cabinet informed on such an important matter is consistent with the deviousness he had displayed in obtaining Campbell-Bannerman's consent. The episode as a whole exhibits a lack of candour on his part and the introduction of a new conception of the relations between the Cabinet and Foreign Secretary.'[47] A man like Ponsonby who, though the Prime Minister's principal private secretary, knew nothing about the staff talks, would have agreed heartily with this view. He later wrote:

> I am fully persuaded that C.-B. never apprehended the significance of the conversations with France, nor did he see how we were being gradually committed. As a matter of fact I doubt if

Grey did either. Cambon with consummate skill was enmeshing Grey, pretending to him all the while that he was free, but knowing that when the moment came he had bound him with chains of iron ... that Morley and Loreburn should have known nothing ... proves to my mind beyond doubt that C.-B., while he may have been technically and officially informed, was himself completely in the dark.[48]

Loreburn, too, wrote that 'some of those who knew Sir Henry Campbell-Bannerman, and were in close confidential communication with him in December 1905 and January 1906 will not believe that he understood the scope and significance of what was in fact done unless some evidence of it is given'.[49] Ponsonby and Loreburn, strong partisans of the anti-Grey school, undoubtedly believed this sincerely, and Ponsonby was at No. 10 all through the crisis, but the weight of evidence seems to be against them.

As it was, the unity of the Liberal Government on foreign affairs did not come under strain till July 1914, when Morley wrote: 'For the very first time something of the old cleavage between the Liberal League and the faithful Campbell-Bannerman, Harcourt and myself began to be very sensibly felt. Hitherto not a whisper of the old schism of the Boer war.'[50]

Trevelyan's biography stresses that Grey regarded the staff talks as 'a technical affair of soldiers not concerning the statesmen of the Cabinet'.[51] As Harold Nicolson wrote of Grey in his life of his father, the Germans

... did not understand that this perfected type of British parliamentarian did not attribute any but a purely technical and conditional importance to such conversations as soldiers or sailors might hold. These conversations, to his mind, were mere matters of routine which could be reversed with a stroke of the pen. They possessed, to his mind, no more importance than discussions between the London Fire Brigade and the Westminster Water Works. It cannot be expected that anyone not deeply imbued with the doctrines of British parliamentary liberalism will understand this point of view.[52]

C.B., of course, *was* deeply imbued with these doctrines. The view he and Grey took of the talks was not that held by the French or by the

British soldiers who took part in them. He had apparently forgotten what he had written in his minority report for the Hartington Commission, when he had dismissed the need for 'planning possible operations in possible wars against' our neighbours. Planning of this sort was just what we were now starting to do with the French, while the Germans were evolving the Schlieffen Plan for an assault on Belgium and France.

Grey, in his book *Twenty-Five Years*, mentioned C.B.'s apprehension lest the military talks should lead to an obligation or at least an 'honourable understanding', and added:

> With more experience I might have shared that apprehension at the time. But the honourable understanding between myself and M. Cambon was very clear, and it was that nothing that passed between the French and British military authorities was to entail or imply any obligation whatever on either Government. It was an understanding that was honourably kept, even in the week of anxiety and distress before the outbreak of the war in 1914. . . . The appeal was made to our interest; it was never suggested that our honour or good faith was involved.[53]

There is no evidence to suggest that C.B. gave way on this question to pressure from the Liberal Imps. Had he felt strongly, he had only to rally the radicals in the Cabinet against Grey, and this he never did. It seems certain that he felt that on balance the course which Grey took was right, provided that it was pursued prudently and warily and with a full understanding on both sides of the absence of any political commitment. General Ewart, who took over from General Grierson as D.M.O. in October 1906, was certainly cautious. Very different, however, was the attitude of Sir Henry Wilson, who succeeded Ewart in 1910. It is a curious fact that British public servants, who are supposed to be so phlegmatic and unemotional, tend often to become caught up with the policies they are engaged in carrying out, sometimes to the point of displaying a burning, fanatical enthusiasm. Of such a nature was Henry Wilson's devotion to France. In 1911, on the field of Mars-la-Tour, he solemnly laid at the feet of a statue symbolic of France a piece of map showing the areas of concentration planned for the British Expeditionary Force in France.[54] It is perhaps fortunate that C.B. did not live to see the staff talks he had approved fall into the hands of one whose attitude was so far from being cool and prudent.

The episode put Grey at odds with Rosebery, who was deeply suspicious of the French and preferred the Germans, and Trevelyan wrote of Grey that it 'was one of the things that led to a more "genial epoch" as between himself and that loving friend of France, Campbell-Bannerman'.[55]

C.B. supported the *entente* but later told Knollys: 'there is some danger of the "entente cordiale" being worn threadbare if . . . demonstrations are overdone'.[56] Knollys replied that the King 'agrees . . . still more so, *if possible*, with your remarks. . . .'[57]

Foreign and defence policies necessarily go hand in hand. If the Government were proceeding on the assumption that a war with Germany was not to be excluded, this called into question the amount that needed to be spent on the Army and the Fleet. Any increase in defence expenditure, however, cut across the new administration's wish to make real progress in the field of social reform, and many Liberals were strongly opposed to increased spending on armaments.

The question of the Naval Estimates first came up at Easter. The previous government had built four large warships in 1905 and had made plans for four more each year. At first the new Government accepted this, but they soon had second thoughts. C.B. came under pressure from Liberal M.P.s to reduce the programme. Though three capital ships were to be laid down in 1906, C.B., Asquith and Grey thought that a cut-back in the naval programme would help the prospects for the Hague Conference, planned for 1907, and persuaded Fisher and the Admiralty to be content with only two ships for the 1907–8 estimates, with a third to be added if the disarmament proposals came to nothing at The Hague. C.B. thought privately that the 'two-power standard', a rule of thumb under which the Royal Navy had to be strong enough to take on and defeat a combination of any two other powers, was 'a sort of fetish'.[58] From 1906 on the Navy had only, in practice, to consider the threat from Germany, and he thought it more realistic to plan with that, and that only, in mind. But the King was not happy, and minuted on C.B.'s Cabinet letter of July 10: 'Evidently the "cheese paring" policy of the Govt. is also to be extended to the Navy.'[59]

In the meantime a crisis had arisen in the Near East, where Cromer reported that the Turks were trying to seize the Sinai peninsula. Grey kept in close touch with C.B., who wrote him four long letters on the problem from Dover and who took a firm line from the start against the pretensions of 'Abdul the Damned'.

On April 28 he told Grey: 'The political importance of keeping these fellows out of the peninsula is immense.'[60] When C.B. felt that his country was in the right, he was not in the least disposed to be chicken-hearted. In this case firmness paid. The Turks, faced with a determined attitude by the British Government, gave way. The Cabinet had safeguarded British interests without becoming involved in a war.

In May a party of German burgomasters visited England. C.B. made them a speech of welcome, as did John Burns, Winston Churchill and Haldane, who eulogized the Kaiser as a 'true child of the time-spirit'.[61]

On July 23 the fourteenth Inter-Parliamentary Union Conference opened in the Royal Gallery of the Palace of Westminster. C.B. had been asked to welcome the delegates, who included a party from the Russian Duma. He decided to speak in French, the language which would be understood by most of the delegates. Just before he was to speak, news came through of the dissolution of the Duma by the Czar, after only ten weeks of existence. C.B. took a sheet of Downing Street paper and wrote out a paragraph to add to the official draft. It ran:

> Je ne fais pas de commentaire sur les nouvelles qui ont éclaté ce matin: ce n'en est ni le lieu ni le moment. Nous n'avons pas une assez grande connaissance des faits pour pouvoir blâmer ou louer.
>
> Mais ceci du moins nous pouvons dire, nous qui fondons notre confiance et nos espoirs sur le régime parlementaire.
>
> Les nouvelles institutions ont souvent une jeunesse accidentée sinon orageuse. La Douma revivra d'une forme ou d'autre.
>
> Nous pouvons dire avec toute sincérité – 'La Douma est morte – Vive la Douma.'[62]

Having finished writing his paragraph, C.B. gave it to Ponsonby, who had just come in, saying he wanted to add it to his speech, and adding, 'Rather too late, I think, to send it over to the F.O.'[63] This was the man whom Rosebery had scorned to make Foreign Secretary. Yet what other Prime Minister since Palmerston could himself draft, unaided, in correct and harmonious French? To another of his private secretaries, Henry Higgs, C.B. said: 'There are some things you can say in French which you cannot say so well or even say at all in English. French admits not only of finer shades but of a higher emotional pitch than is consistent with our insular ideas of self-restraint.'[64] Not for nothing had C.B. spent all those autumn months with Charlotte on the continent.

The speech was delivered the same day to an audience of five hundred from twenty-two parliaments. C.B. was looking his best, wearing his frock coat and a white waistcoat, his French accent was excellent, and in Ponsonby's opinion he 'delivered the speech far better than any English speech I ever heard from him'.[65] His improvised peroration was received with immense enthusiasm. The speech was undoubtedly a complete success. The *Manchester Guardian* described it as one of his finest.[66] Massingham wrote:

> The Prime Minister's speech is the sensation of the hour. Nothing else is spoken of . . . everyone feels that it will ring round Europe. . . . It has awakened a most enthusiastic feeling in the Party here, and has advanced to a still higher point the Prime Minister's remarkable personal ascendance and complete control of its destinies. . . . I do not think that any public man of great responsibility has ever gone so far in denouncing war and all its works.[67]

The American William Jennings Bryan, who sat beside the Prime Minister, told reporters that he thought the speech splendid.[68]

C.B. had taken care to word his reference to the Duma with discretion. The Czar was mentioned, with the Duma, as a prime promoter of European peace (the name of Nicholas being received with one or two hisses). But the Foreign Office and the Russian Ambassador were apprehensive. Hardinge wrote to Knollys on July 24: 'C.B.'s remarks were most injudicious. Benckendorff spoke to me about them this afternoon. All I was able to say was that his final remark must not be taken too seriously or tragically.'[69] Two days later he wrote: 'You may like to know that C.B. met Benckendorff last night at Marlborough House and expressed his regret at having used terms in his speech which were liable to misrepresentation. . . . The latter is, I hear, perfectly satisfied.'[70]

The Ambassador reported to St. Petersburg, tactfully, that the dissolution of the Duma just as the Conference opened 'a été au-dessus de l'équilibre de Campbell-Bannerman'.[71] Nevertheless the Czar was much irritated. When the Russian Ambassador told Grey that he thought the phrase might give offence in St. Petersburg, Grey blandly told him that since the Czar had said he intended to summon a new Duma, the phrase was merely the equivalent of 'Le Roi est mort; vive le Roi'. This explanation was accepted by Izvolsky, the Foreign Minister, who, however, had a hard time soothing the Czar.[72]

C.B. had spoken out as a lifelong believer in parliamentary democracy faced with a Russia where, a few months after the revolutionary outbreaks of 1905, a foolish Czar had fallen back on repression and the maintenance of autocracy.

On July 27 Robertson, the Secretary to the Admiralty, announced the reduced naval building programme in the House of Commons. Existing plans were to be reduced by one *Dreadnought*, three ocean-going destroyers and four submarines, thereby saving about £2½ million. Robertson stressed that the Board of Admiralty were satisfied that these reductions would not impair British naval supremacy, but there were howls of protest from the Unionists, the Navy League, and the same press lobby that C.B. had encountered in the eighties, whom Fisher described as the 'blue funk school'. Fisher was full of his new ship, the first *Dreadnought*, which was to put to sea in three months' time. C.B. answered the critics and said that no pressure had been put on the Sea Lords, who had advised and recommended the amended programme. When the two-power standard was talked about, who were these powers? He asked if France and Germany were likely to be allied against us. He pointed out that until 1909 we should be the only power with a *Dreadnought*; in 1909 we should have four, and other nations would still be building. As for disarmament, we could set an example more easily than other powers, and it was specially incumbent on us to do so.[73]

In August the King and C.B. were at Marienbad. Efforts were made to assure the Germans that England wished them nothing but well and that the *entente* with France was in no sense a challenge to them. The King went with Hardinge to Cronberg to see the Kaiser and Haldane paid a visit to Berlin. C.B. encouraged these moves. He was an incurable optimist and saw no reason why we should not have good relations with Germany. But he had few illusions about the Kaiser. He told Knollys on December 28:

> There are many signs of a desire in that quarter to be civil to this country. I do not wish to be unduly suspicious, but there is an ugly Italian proverb that often comes to my mind. It runs thus –
>
> > Chi ti carezza più che non suole
> > O t'ingannato ha, o inganno vuole.

This sent the Palace to their dictionaries, and in the margin they put the translation of the proverb: 'He who is kinder to you than he is wont has either injured you or wishes to do so.'[74]

Esher took a more sombre view of the situation. On September 4 he wrote to his son:

> There is no doubt that within measurable distance there looms a titanic struggle between Germany and Europe for mastery. The years 1793–1815 will be repeated, only Germany, not France, will be trying for European domination. She has 70,000,000 of people and is determined to have commercial pre-eminence. To do this England has got to be crippled and the Low Countries added to the German Empire. France contains 40,000,000 of people. England about the same. So even combined, the struggle is by no means a certainty.[75]

This prescient view seemed to point the way to an expansion of naval building, but this was not Fisher's opinion. He told the Prince of Wales in October: 'Pure party feeling solely dictates the present *"Press"* agitation. . . . *Reduced Navy Estimates are no sign of reduced naval efficiency.*'[76]

1906 had been a critical year in foreign affairs. 1907 was to be almost equally important. On January 1 Eyre Crowe, head of the Western Department of the Foreign Office, submitted a memorandum on the state of British relations with France and Germany. This celebrated paper described the history of twenty years of German expansion and of futile British attempts to buy it off by conciliation, and argued that there could be two explanations of German policy – either that Germany was 'definitely aiming at a general political hegemony and maritime ascendancy, threatening the independence of her neighbours and ultimately the existence of England', or was spreading her influence without any precise clear-cut aim, waiting for a suitable opportunity to grab what she could. He pointed out that our relations with France had actually improved when we had at last stood firm at Fashoda in 1898. Now therefore Germany should meet '. . . on England's part with unvarying courtesy and consideration in all matters of common concern, but also with a prompt and firm refusal to enter into any one-sided bargains or arrangements, and the most unbending determination to uphold British rights and interests in every part of the globe'.[77]

Grey accepted the conclusions of this paper and passed it to C.B. But if Ministers were to stand up to Germany they needed the means to do so. Already the Cabinet were locked in another struggle about the Naval Estimates. At the time Britain was spending over £32 million a year on her Navy; Germany just over £14 million. But Germany had launched fourteen battleships in the five years following the naval law of 1900, and her ship construction and gunnery were outstandingly good.[78] On New Year's Day 1907 Nash wrote from Belmont to Ponsonby: 'There are ructions between Asquith & the Admiralty over Estimates. . . . C.B. will have to play up for all he is worth. He foresees resignations all round at the Admiralty.'[79]

C.B. did not believe that any urgent increase was needed. He was at one with Asquith on this and wrote to him on January 4 saying:

> I entirely share your dislike and suspicion of the Navy prospects. . . . We are equally at sea about the Army. We have left the W.O. an absolutely free hand, but after all it is for the Cabinet to decide Military policy. . . . I am in the last degree uneasy about the whole case of these 'spending Departments.' 5 Jany. This mornings post brings me a blast from Fisher – which I enclose. . . . Evidently the whole thing is honey-combed with personal jealousies. . . .[80]

Fisher's letter to C.B. ran to six vivid pages. C.B. must have smiled to read a denunciation of press agitation by the man who had been at the heart of the 'Truth about the Navy' scare in 1884. Nevertheless arguments for economy from his principal naval expert were helpful to him. With great difficulty a compromise was hammered out and in March Robertson announced a reduction of £450,000 in the Naval Estimates, to £31½ million.

On March 2 a new Liberal weekly, the *Nation*, edited by Massingham and backed by Joseph Rowntree of York, appeared for the first time, and in it was an article by C.B. on 'The Hague Conference and the Limitation of Armaments'. It had been cleared with the Foreign Office and was the sort of anodyne piece appropriate to the pen of a Prime Minister in office. It said that 'the sea power of this country implies no challenge to any single State . . . that power is recognized as non-aggressive, and innocent of designs against the independence, the commercial freedom, and the legitimate development of other States. . . .'

But this innocuous production caused an immense hubbub in France and Germany. The French suspected that they were being betrayed. The Germans saw the plea for disarmament as a sinister attempt to ensure the perpetuity of British naval supremacy. The agitation in the German press culminated in a declaration by Bülow, on April 30, that Germany would refuse to discuss disarmament at The Hague. So poor C.B.'s single foray into public diplomacy had been a total failure. The King wrote testily to Hardinge: 'I wonder if the Prime Minister realizes how he has angered the French and German Press by his most injudicious article in *The Nation*? Ministers nowadays seem to forget the responsibilities of their office and ventilate their opinions as if they were private individuals.'[81]

Hardinge does not record whether he admitted to the King that the article had been seen and agreed to by Grey and the Foreign Office. The King was feeling dissatisfied with C.B., and minuted on his Cabinet letter of March 12: '. . . I am disgusted at his article in "The Nation" & backing up the Women's Franchise Bill – Both so unnecessary & latter so undignified. I suppose he will support the Channel Tunnel Bill next!'[82]

Admiral Tirpitz, when told in January that the British Government was sincere in advocating disarmament, said: 'I myself realise the Puritan form of thought such as is possessed by Sir Henry Campbell-Bannerman, and that he is perfectly honest and feels it a religious duty; but . . . from the point of view of the public it is laughable and Machiavellian, and we shall never agree to anything of the sort. . . .'[83]

C.B. believed, as he had always done, in peace and goodwill, and for him these were no empty words. But, sadly, the world cannot be remoulded nearer to our heart's desire. In dealing with foreign powers, at all periods, one encounters a great deal of original sin. His own trustful, generous temperament was just what was needed for dealing with Botha and Smuts and, given more time and better circumstances, might even have been effective in dealing with Ireland, but it was no use with the leaders of Imperial Germany. In the dark field of foreign affairs, where 'the crimes, follies and misfortunes of mankind', which Gibbon thought was what history largely consisted of, still make up, for the most part, the pattern of each year's events, a weary scepticism, coupled with persistence and a willingness to look facts in the face, is, sadly, a more reliable guide than faith and hope.

In April 1907 there occurred an episode which made it clear that there was still a considerable gulf between C.B.'s view of how we stood with the French and the French Government's view of British responsibilities. On the 7th C.B. went over to Paris. On the 9th he saw the French Prime Minister, Clemenceau, privately at the Embassy. Clemenceau naturally wanted to take this first opportunity of a direct talk with the British Prime Minister to discuss Britain's position in the light of what had been said to Cambon fifteen months before and of the military staff talks which had been continuing ever since. The forthcoming attitude of British diplomatists and British soldiers had encouraged him to think that Britain now regarded herself as virtually committed to come to the help of France if she became involved in war with Germany. He assumed that C.B. took a similar view. But he received a rude shock. For C.B. made it clear that he did not regard Britain as in any way committed. C.B. had never shared the belief of men like Louis Mallet that we were bound to take part in any continental war on the side of France, and he may not even have been aware that the staff talks he had authorized in January 1906, in the context of the Morocco crisis, were still continuing. So what he said came as a douche of extremely cold water to Clemenceau, who was seriously worried.

Next day Clemenceau saw his old friend Admiral Maxse's daughter, Lady Edward Cecil. She, her husband, and her future husband Lord Milner were all on holiday in Paris at the time. Among the Milner papers is a note in Violet Cecil's hand which throws an interesting light on Clemenceau's meeting with C.B.:

April 10th 1907.

Imperial Hotel
Paris

I am just back from a play with Monsieur Clemenceau . . . we dined together at the Café Anglais. I saw that he was preoccupied and he soon told me the reason . . . he had yesterday met Sir Henry Campbell-Bannerman at the British Embassy in great secrecy. . . . Bertie was not present. Clemenceau was . . . very much . . . perturbed because Bannerman then and there took back all the guarantees of the Entente Cordiale – 'Quel père imbécile, quel idiot' he said. . . . Bannerman thoroughly understood the German menace, knew the ambitions of the German government and relied for his defence on 'the English people being against war' . . . Clemenceau said . . . 'I am totally opposed to you – we both recognise a great danger and you are . . . reducing your army and weakening your navy.' 'Ah' said Bannerman 'but *that* is for economy!' 'Pardon' said Clemenceau 'je pourrais économiser le prix de mes chaussettes sortir, et attraper une fluxion de poitrine, mais ce ne serait pas une économie.' 'Yes but' said Bannerman 'You see we have really made the army more efficient.' 'Vous n'allez pas dire cela à *moi*' said C. 'parce que ce n'est pas la peine. Je ne suis pas un de vos électeurs. Je sais qu'on ne rend pas une armée forte en la réduisant de 40,000 hommes.' He then said that he thought the English ought to have some kind of military service, at which Bannerman nearly fainted and said that the English would rely upon the volunteers. . . .

'It comes to this' said Clemenceau 'in the event of your supporting us against Germany are you ready to abide by the plans agreed upon between our War Offices and to land 110,000 men on the coast while Italy marches with us in the ranks?' Then came the crowning touch of the interview. 'The sentiments of the English people would be totally averse to *any* troops being landed by England on the continent under any circumstances.' Clemenceau looks upon this as undoing the whole result of the entente cordiale and says that if that represents the final mind of the British Government, he has done with us. . . . Clemenceau . . . is knocked over by the combination of waste and imbecility. 'That's the Liberal Party' I observed. . . .[84]

No doubt Clemenceau's account of this talk was a vivid but *ex parte* one, and it was noted down by a strong Conservative, but it described a clash between two fundamentally different philosophies. C.B. may also have been put out to learn how far the War Office had carried their contingency planning.

Next day Clemenceau hastened to put his anxieties to the Ambassador, and Bertie wrote to the Foreign Secretary:

. . . Clemenceau this morning . . . said that he must speak to me very frankly but seriously with regard to one subject referred to during his conversation with Sir Henry Campbell Bannerman here on Tuesday . . . he . . . had been quite taken aback by the Prime Minister having said (lui ayant jeté à la figure) that he did not think that English public opinion would allow of British Troops being employed on the Continent of Europe. Clemenceau thought that the Prime Minister could not be aware of the communications which had passed between the General Staff French and the General Staff British during the acute stages of the Morocco crisis. . . . Was there now to be a change of attitude on the part of England? . . .

he hoped that the Prime Minister had spoken without full consideration of the effect of what he said. . . .[85]

C.B., when he saw this, scribbled a note to Grey: 'I do not accept Clemenceau's version as accurate, and if my words had so startling an effect on him as he implies, there was no sign of it in his demeanour. I will tell you my version – I meant to report the whole conversation, but yesterday we had other fish to fry.'[86]

Grey replied to the Ambassador, clearing the text of his letter with C.B.: 'The Prime Minister tells me that he dwelt upon the reluctance of the British people to undertake obligations, which would commit them to a Continental war, but that he made no statement to the effect that under no circumstances should we allow British troops to be employed on the Continent of Europe. . . .' After reminding Bertie of the arrangements made, with C.B.'s knowledge, at the time of the Algeciras conference, Grey continued: 'The whole thing is really in a sentence: public opinion here would be very reluctant to go to war, but it would not place limits upon the use of our forces, if we were engaged in war. . . . It is not a matter to be made the subject of any written communication, but you should take any opportunity of correcting M. Clemenceau's impression. . . .'[87] On the file copy Grey minuted: 'Sent to the Prime Minister, who returned it to me at the Cabinet saying it was all right. E.G.'[88]

Louis Mallet added in a letter of his own to Bertie the same day:

> . . . I trust that Sir Edward's explanation will smooth Clemenceau down. It is very stupid of him to raise this question again now à propos of nothing and with C.B. of all people.
>
> H.M.G. will never give a categorical assurance of assistance but they went very far last year and if Germany made an unprovoked attack on France I feel confident that we should intervene.
>
> The French are evidently in a very jumpy condition.[89]

The reference to 'C.B. of all people' showed that the hawks were still afraid of his influence.

To this Bertie replied two days later:

> I suspect that Clemenceau put the case too straight and that C-B in order to avoid giving a distinct answer or make any definite statement shied at it and ran into the ditch on the opposite side of

the road by laying too much stress on the unwillingness of the British Public to land men on the Continent.[90]

On the 17th Bertie saw Clemenceau and reassured him. In his report he said:

> What Sir Henry Campbell Bannerman said to Clemenceau was I suppose intended as a douche to cool any martial ardour that he might feel in reliance on military support from us. The French Government are however anything but bellicose. They are terribly afraid lest Germany should place France in a position in which war would become unavoidable. As Pichon told me this evening that Clemenceau had been pleased with your explanations and assurances I think that the latter must be more satisfied than he chose to admit to me. . . .[91]

Cambon described the whole affair serenely as 'un petit malentendu'.[92]

It is an odd episode and clearly C.B. would have done better to have Bertie with him at the talk. It seems likely that he had not really grasped how far the Foreign Office and the War Office had slid down the slippery slope of moral commitment to France, that his instinct was still very much against becoming involved in a continental war if there was any possible way of avoiding it, and that, with his usual honesty, he made his position clear to Clemenceau, who was taken aback and perhaps took C.B.'s attitude to be more categorical than it was. Such misunderstandings grew out of the secretiveness of Grey and the War Office, their determination not to say too much to the Prime Minister about the continuing staff talks to avoid the danger of having them stopped, and from the lack of really close relations between C.B. and Grey.

Meanwhile Germany was in a neurotic state. Sir Frank Lascelles reported from Berlin on April 19 that 'the day before yesterday, Berlin went stark staring raving mad', and said that there was 'great suspicion of England generally and of the King in particular. The demand that the question of the limitation of expenditure on armaments shall be discussed at the Hague Conference is looked upon as a deep laid plot to put Germany in a false position. . . .' Lascelles said that the Germans were in a state of great exictement and fear, and seemed to think that war was imminent.[93] Six weeks later, on June 1, J. A. Spender had an interview with Prince Bülow, who protested, mendaciously, that no one from the Kaiser down to the man in the street had the faintest idea of attacking England or wished mischief to her, and went on to ask Spender about C.B. – 'Was it not very unusual that a man should develop such talent and come to such a remarkable position so late in life? I said that Sir Henry was still comparatively young for English politics. . . .'[94]

The Hague Conference was held from June till October. C.B.'s disarmament proposals had been wrecked by Bülow's refusal to cooperate. Other lesser plans he put forward, such as an effort to secure the abandonment of automatic mines in naval warfare, were no more successful. The Germans looked on them all as mere devices by Britain to retain permanent naval supremacy.

After this there could be no doubt about the German naval challenge. But Fisher continued to believe in quality rather than quantity. Nevertheless the turning point had now been reached. C.B.'s government had, the year before, reduced the Navy Estimates from £36 million to £31. From now on they began to rise steadily as the German menace became ever more real. In November the Germans announced a 25 per cent increase in the rate of battleship construction, plans clearly designed to break Britain's command of the seas.

Since June 1906, Grey, the Foreign Office and Nicolson in St. Petersburg had been busy negotiating an agreement with Russia. In this they had C.B.'s full support. Many doctrinaire Liberals disliked the thought of any dealings with the Czarist autocracy. They had been cheered by C.B.'s Duma speech, and encouraged when the brutal suppression of uprisings in Russia had led to the cancellation of a goodwill visit by the British fleet. But C.B. believed that continued British Liberal attacks on the Czar's despotic rule only defeated their own purpose by making the Czar more rigid and determined. On October 8, 1906, he had written to Grey about

> the folly of the deputation to Russia. It is bad taste and ill timed and may be mischievous. I also was consulted by the same Donald Smeaton, M.P. who wrote to Nicolson, and I told him to have nothing to do with it, on two main grounds (1) That the visit might offend the Russians, even the progressives, as an illbred interference; and thus (and as giving a flavour of foreign origin generally) set back the tide of reform and liberty. (2) That it enabled the Russian

Government to say if this is the sort of friends you are going to be, we prefer the Kaiser. And where should we be then?[95]

He thoroughly approved of the new agreement, which diminished the likelihood of an alliance between Russia and Germany and secured India's northern frontier by laying down spheres of influence in Persia. In his view it removed, for a time at least, the danger of 'an Asiatic avalanche'.[96]

Morley was sceptical, and later came to regard this agreement as the beginning of all evil. But the danger had been a real one. The Germans had been wooing the Russians. On March 3, 1908, Bülow was still trying, and wrote to the German Ambassador at St. Petersburg:

> Your Excellency might say to Mr. Stolypin: 'Look at . . . the Western powers: of these France is a republic reeking with Radicalism and with Socialists. It is inconceivable that these elements should *bona fide* desire the maintenance of the Czardom. England is in very much the same position with her outspoken Liberalism.' Stolypin will remember the illuminating phrase of Campbell-Bannerman 'La Douma est morte; vive la Douma!' An alliance of Russia with these two powers can only result in undermining and endangering the Czardom.[97]

In the Liberal Party there was still great anxiety about the level of naval expenditure. Sir John Brunner, M.P., and 150 other members of the House of Commons, most of them warm supporters of C.B., sent him a memorial which Fisher, now bemused by his own theories, described to the King on October 4 as 'one of the best papers I have read, convincingly showing that we don't want to lay down any new ships at all – *we are so strong*. It is quite true!'[98]

Fisher's enemy, Lord Charles Beresford, was pressing for an enquiry into Admiralty policy, and threatening to resign from the service. C.B. promised Fisher that there would be no such enquiry, and Fisher noted joyfully, 'I think the Prime Minister fancied him a bit off his head.'[99]

By this time C.B. was seriously ill. What the Foreign Office thought by now of this Prime Minister who was supposed to take no interest in foreign affairs was made clear in a letter which the Permanent Under-Secretary sent to Bryce in Washington: 'There are sinister rumours about C.B.'s health. . . . If anything happened to him it would be a bad day for this Office, as he is the best Prime Minister that this Office has ever had to deal with – Yrs very sincerely, Charles Hardinge.'[100]

Hardinge was by no means telling Bryce simply what he would like to hear. He wrote in very similar terms to Villiers, the Minister at Lisbon, on January 7, 1908, saying: 'It would be a great misfortune to us if anything were to happen to C.B., as he is the best Prime Minister there has ever been from the F.O. point of view and supports us in everything....'[101]

In January C.B. was in Paris again and once more saw Clemenceau. This time there were no misunderstandings.

Next month there was another Cabinet row on the Navy Estimates, the worst so far. Lloyd George, Churchill, Harcourt, Morley and Burns made a tremendous effort to get naval expenditure cut back. Some of them were prepared to back Beresford for First Sea Lord if Fisher resigned. Haldane wrote to his mother on February 5: 'There is a crisis impending. On naval & military expenditure. The H. of C. may turn us out . . . our party is hopelessly divided. . . .'[102]

Soon after he wrote again:

I have been having much the same time as a man who is walking on a volcano in an active state. . . . The naval estimates cannot be much reduced so Lloyd George and his friends have turned on me but I have met them with fixed bayonets, and the wonderful old P.M. & H.H.A. have ranged themselves on my side. We may be beaten on Murray Macdonald's motion. . . . A split will come sooner or later. . . . Lloyd George calls me 'The Minister of Slaughter'. . . .[103]

Haldane, who had in the days of opposition poured so much scorn on C.B. and intrigued so hard and persistently to remove him, was now singing a very different tune. In the end C.B. decided that the Navy Estimates must stand, but he made Haldane cut £300,000 from the Army Estimates and the increase in the Navy Estimates was reduced to £900,000.

This was not the end of the matter. Esher wrote a letter to the Imperial Maritime League which ended by saying: 'There is not a man in Germany, from the Emperor downwards, who would not welcome the fall of Sir John Fisher.' Thereupon the Kaiser wrote a nine-page letter in his own hand to the First Lord, Lord Tweedmouth, claiming that 'it is absolutely *nonsensical* and *untrue* that the German Naval Bill is to provide a Navy meant as a "challenge to British Naval Supremacy" ' and remarking of Esher: 'I am at a loss to tell whether the supervision of the foundations and drains of the Royal Palaces is apt to qualify somebody for the judgement of Naval Affairs in general.' Tweedmouth's mind was beginning to fail and he was childishly flattered. A new and even larger row developed, but by then C.B. had passed from the scene, and arguments about Naval Estimates could trouble him no more.

CHAPTER 35

The Confrontation with the Lords

T HE problem of the House of Lords, with its substantial powers and vast Unionist majority, had to be faced by every Liberal Prime Minister. In the early years of Queen Victoria, when Chartism was at its height and the French Revolution was by no means a distant memory, the Lords, under the leadership of men like the Duke of Wellington and Lord Aberdeen, acted with great prudence, and took care to avoid a direct clash with the Commons. But, as stability returned and the spectre of social unrest receded, they grew bolder. Over twenty years before he became Prime Minister, in 1884, C.B. told his constituents: 'It is absurd that the Second Chamber should be worked . . . as a mere part of the machinery of the Tory Party.'[1] On another occasion he said that this unsatisfactory relationship between the two Houses had existed 'ever since the end of those happy and halcyon days in which the same class which now dominates the House of Lords dominated the House of Commons'.[2]

The problem became more acute in the nineties. The Lords killed Mr. Gladstone's second Home Rule Bill in 1893. Thereafter they were ready to take an unashamedly party stand in blocking radical legislation.

In October 1894, even so conservative a man as Rosebery said in a speech at Bradford that the next election would have to be fought on the issue of the House of Lords, which was 'a great national danger'. He declared that the House of Commons would move a challenging resolution to end an intolerable situation. On that occasion he was repudiated by his colleagues, whom he had omitted to consult. But Liberal frustration was great. C.B. wrote to his cousin in February of that year: 'the Lords . . . have raised a wind which will not go down until their wings are well clipped in one way or other'.[3] In October, he said at Stirling that the House of Lords had ceased to be a Senate, and had become a body of violent and reckless partisans.

Early in November 1894, C.B. was staying at Balmoral as Minister in Attendance. The Queen had been alarmed by Rosebery's Bradford speech, so much so that she had taken the extraordinary step of writing to the leading Opposition statesman, Lord Salisbury, on October 25, denouncing what Rosebery had said as 'mischievous in the highest degree and she must add disloyal', and asking bluntly: 'Is the Unionist Party fit for a Dissolution *now*?'[4] Salisbury's reply made it clear that it was not.

C.B.'s presence at Balmoral now provided an obvious opportunity for her to discuss the problem with a senior member of the Liberal Government. But, as Hamilton noted: 'Her surroundings are almost wholly Tory and she knows nothing but Tory gossip and Tory vicars. Moreover she won't discuss a disagreeable matter with anybody who is not likely to be in accord with her.'[5]

C.B.'s letters to Charlotte from Balmoral described what happened:[6]

Saturday 3 Nov.: the Princess [Beatrice] & I discussed the H of Lords! She is much more open minded than you wd. think on the subject, but told me that the Q is *terribly* exercised, & hurt by Archie's speech! . . .

Monday Nov 5: I went to the Princess L. [Louise] who speaks quite openly: wished the Q would speak to me about the H. of L; knows I could not originate it, but hoped she would; had asked her to do it; had told her all that I had said to the Princess the night before. Then herself discussed it most reasonably – she favours Home Rule all round . . . condemns the action of the Lords, etc. . . . Really it is quite marvellous, and I think her influence will have the best effect.

Carrington says Archie's speech fell like a bombshell among them: all the Alec Yorkes & others were loudmouthed in denouncing it; treason, revolution etc. etc. The ignorant set, not to know that it was sure to come! Then he says all this has such an effect on the Q to whom it is conveyed – 'everyone thinks so & so' 'all the gentlemen at lunch were saying so & so'. – 'the gentlemen'! what is their opinion worth?

Tuesday 6 Nov. 11.30 a.m. Bigge . . . announced that she will see me today to discuss the H of L. . . . It is very ticklish & indeed critical, & I hope I shall come well out of it. She dreads an argument, & I will take care not to be too contradictious while putting the whole case before her. She quite understands that I shall speak only for myself & not for Archie or colleagues. . . . I am a little bit nervous!

It is the Princess L. who is the divine influence here. Bigge is I presume a Tory. . . . I . . . appealed to the . . . commonsense of the thing apart from prejudice, & I am certain he sees it all in a light he never saw it before. . . .

After talking to C.B., Bigge wrote to the Queen, reporting that C.B. was 'rather despairing as to mending the H. of L.', advising her to see him and adding reassuringly: 'He would only tell Your Majesty his opinions and not, of course, enter into argument.'[7]

With this letter Bigge enclosed a memorandum entitled: 'Mr. Campbell-Bannerman and the House of Lords'. The main points in this note of C.B.'s opinions were:

> The present state of things has become indefensible.
>
> The extension of the Franchise has given a democratic basis to Parliament which does not admit of a House . . . in its spirit antagonistic to the democratic tendency of things.
>
> . . . The huge (intemperate) majorities in the House of Lords against recent measures are not representative of the opinion of the country and do harm. . . . he has foreseen for the last ten years that the two Houses could not continue without things coming to a deadlock.
>
> He thinks reform is also much needed in the H. of Commons.
>
> He alludes to the view held by many that there should be Parliaments (single chambers) for England, Scotland, Ireland and even Wales – and one Chamber like the Reichstag – for *Imperial* purposes – but of course this would have to be a *representative* chamber.

C.B.'s letter to Charlotte continued:

7 p.m.: . . . Bigge wrote to her this morning a précis of our conversa^n last night, and before starting she wrote him a note of a very uncompromising kind though civil towards me. He read it to me: and he & the Princess*es* have been busy over it . . . certainly her opinions as expressed in the note are irreconcilable in the last degree! I could not have believed it: and Bigge says you must remember what the Q is, how apart she is, how little she knows of what goes on, and above all who her grandfather was.

C.B. made the following notes of the Queen's letter to Bigge:

... Mr. C.B. forgets the danger of increasing the power of the H. of C. and having no force to resist the subversive measures of the so-called Liberals but better called destructives. Could never agree to taking from the Lo. their power to alter or reject measures – this might be obtained from a President, not from her. Thinks it cruel that after her long reign at her age, with her many cares, she shd. be obliged to refuse her assent to proposals of her ministers where it would be her greatest pleasure to support them.[8]

It was certainly distinctly unpromising.

Wednesday 7 Nov. 12 o'c.: The Q has fixed seven o'clock tonight to see me. Bigge ... says she has *never* done such a thing before. ...

So at last C.B. saw the Queen. He made a note of the conversation immediately afterwards. What the Queen said he noted under 'Q', and what he said under 'S.S.W.' (Secretary of State for War.) The Queen's reaction to the points he made he noted underneath in footnotes. His record ran:

7 Nov. 94 Balmoral Castle.
    Q. wished to talk to me about this terrible question: so anxious there should be no agitation and no public meetings. ...
    Quite admitted that the H. of L. might require reform: Lord S. thought it did. But we must have a check against the H. of Commons which too strong & had been ever since Ld. Beaconsfield's most unfortunate Act. Feared there were some shocking people in the H. of Commons, mentioning the Irish Members & Mr. Conybeare: men who would sweep every thing away.
    Admitted that it was not wise to oppose a barrier to public opinion, better to guide it & moderate it. ...
    Made a point of the alarm of all the better classes – the Budget being the latest instance – and pointed out that all the Liberal Peers turned against us. ... It was this alarm that caused the antagonism between the two Houses, so that it was our fault.

S.S.W. ... it was not we who raised the question but peers who brought it on by their contemptuous treatment of the opinions represented in H. of C.[a] believed there was no violent feeling in the country but a strong steady conviction that present position was neither solid nor safe: ridiculous to have this elaborate repres[ve] system, and maintain a House to check its result: check only applied to legislation not to whole sphere of administration[b] result as to legislation frequently that more violent Bills of Tories are passed when moderate Liberal Bills are refused[c]: no check in fact at all while Tories in power . . . better to trust those who have been given the power[d]: reasonable and sensible feeling throughout the masses[e]: House of Commons also not so bad as she thought: even Irishmen good sort of fellows: Conybeares also among peers.[f] No agitation necessary: cannot prevent discussion at public meetings: no necessity for violent language, case being so strong.

    a. admitted that the numbers by which recent Bills rejected were unfortunate.

    b. this appeared to impress & to be new

    c. admitted

    d. admitted as general principle

    e. admitted

    f. admitted.[9]

The Queen's own record in her journal (at any rate as transcribed and edited by Princess Beatrice) was briefer: 'Nov. 7th 1894. Saw Mr. C. Bannerman after tea & had some conversation with him on the vexed question of the House of Lords.'[10] Ten days later Bigge wrote to the Prince of Wales telling him of the Queen's talk with C.B., and saying: 'Mr. C. Bannerman told me almost half the Cabinet are in favour of a single Chamber.'[11]

That the Queen was actually prepared to consider forcing a general election on the issue of Lord Rosebery's attack on the House of Lords showed how seriously she took this question, which she looked on as a challenge to the hereditary principle. In her old age, too, she had become extremely conservative and inflexible. But C.B.'s talk with her helped a good deal to lower the temperature.

In his 1895 election address C.B. declared that the obstacle of the resistance of the House of Lords 'can only be overcome by taking from the irresponsible Chamber the power of overruling the judgement of the representatives of the people'.[12] In 1899, he said that he wanted to see the Lords' veto abolished, but that he wished to leave them some of their ancient constitutional powers.[13]

Now, as Prime Minister, he was face to face with the problem, like a general at the head of an army who saw before him the line of the enemy holding a steep ridge, an enemy, moreover, who had, he knew, repulsed earlier attacks without much difficulty.

The issue on which battle was joined was that of the Education Bill. This measure, designed to redress the grievances of the Nonconformists, outraged the more militant Anglicans and Catholics and aroused furious controversy. But the Liberals had a clear mandate for it and Morant, the official who had been mainly responsible for Balfour's Act of 1902, was still at the Board of Education and took care that it left untouched the educational machinery then established. Moreover some moderate Anglicans, like Canon Hensley Henson and the Bishop of Ripon, Dr. Boyd Carpenter, were not opposed to it.

The Archbishop of Canterbury, Randall Davidson, saw C.B. and other Ministers in March in a vain effort to get the proposals modified. The Bill was introduced by Birrell on April 9, 1906. The Archbishop wrote to the King, who was cruising in the Mediterranean, explaining why the Church objected to it. The King minuted on this letter of the Archbishop's:

> he has not been well treated by the Govt. Who has by this Bill? . . .
> The P.M. professes to like the Archbishop & values his opinion –
> at least he told me so – But I certainly do not believe in him – and
> the way he forces these violent measures with such haste on H of
> Commons does not augur well for the future! . . .[14]

The King took a rather *simpliste* view of the problem, and Sir Philip Magnus records that he wrote to Esher on April 14, saying: 'I look with considerable alarm to the way the Prime Minister is going on. . . .'[15]

The passage of the Bill through the House of Commons took three months. C.B., preoccupied with Charlotte's illness, left the conduct of it largely to Birrell, though Balfour, who knew the question thoroughly, attacked it fiercely and now regained something of his old Parliamentary verve. 'Never', wrote Birrell, 'have I drawn my breath in so irreligious and ignorant an atmosphere as that of the House of Commons when debating religion. It often shocked me.'[16]

The third reading was carried, by a majority considerably larger than the first, on July 30. But Balfour said blandly: 'I think most of us have begun to feel that the real discussion . . . must be elsewhere.'[17] The Bill duly went to the Lords, where on August 3 it was read a second time without a division after a three-day debate.

In September, just after Charlotte's funeral, the Archbishop stayed the night with C.B. at Belmont, afterwards going on to see Balfour. His biographer says that he was disappointed with both, and was 'amazed' by C.B.'s 'real ignorance of the question'.[18] The education quarrel itself was not indeed one about which C.B. cared very much, or about which he was at all deeply informed. In January 1901, he had told Vaughan Nash: 'Education is I confess to me much what the French call a "terrain vague" – weeds, broken bottles, no fence, "rubbish shot here", are suggested by its aspect. And I have a notion it is the same to everybody. One must cover its vagueness by an excess of platitudinous zeal.'[19]

In October and November, the Lords were engaged in so amending the Bill, at Balfour's instigation, that it was turned inside out. It was clear that things were rapidly approaching an impasse. The Liberal Bill had been passed by the House of Commons by a majority of some two hundred. The House of Lords was turning it into a Tory measure. Unless a compromise could be found there was bound to be a clash between the two Houses. The Lords, who had made no difficulty about Balfour's far-reaching Bill of 1902, introduced by an ailing administration, saw nothing incongruous in mutilating the first big measure introduced by a Liberal government, fresh from a massive victory at the polls.

The King constantly objected to what Lloyd George said in public about the Lords. C.B. admonished Lloyd George, and told Knollys:

> As a matter of fact it is wretchedly bad tactics, from the point of view of the Government, to challenge and provoke a quarrel with the Lords. . . . Lloyd George is essentially a fighting man, and he has not yet learned that once he gets inside an office his sword and spear should only be used on extreme occasions, and with the consent of his colleagues. In all business connected with his department and in House of Commons work, he is most conciliatory, but the combative spirit seems to get the better of him when he is talking about other subjects. I greatly regret his outburst, and hope it will not be repeated.[20]

It was, and soon. On November 1 Knollys, who had conceded to C.B. on October 16 that 'your view of Mr. Lloyd George appears to be a fair & good one', wrote to the Prime Minister:

> . . . H.M. desires me to say that notwithstanding your remonstrance, he sees that Mr. Lloyd George has made another indecent attack on the House of Lords. Mr. Lloyd George is very anxious that the King & Queen should go to Cardiff next summer to open some new Docks there, and they have given a half consent that they would do so, but the King says that nothing will induce him to visit Cardiff unless Mr. Lloyd George learns how to behave with propriety as a Cabinet Minister holding an important office. . . .[21]

Next month there was trouble again. Lloyd George concluded a speech about the House of Lords at Oxford by asking 'whether the country was to be governed by the King and the Peers or by the King and his people'. This produced an excited reaction at the Palace, the King objecting to Lloyd George introducing 'the Sovereign's name into these violent tirades of his'.[22] C.B. had to concoct, with Lloyd George's help, a long, soothing reply, which nevertheless pointed out that, if the Lords took an extreme line, 'I fear that we must be prepared for forcible language being employed generally, and even by Ministers'.[23] This only partially mollified the King, as did C.B.'s ingenious suggestion that 'some of these speeches are made in Welsh and are not very accurately translated'.[24]

Over the weekend of November 17 to 19 both C.B. and the Archbishop were at Windsor staying with the King. C.B. wrote to Robertson on the 18th saying: 'The Archbishop is here . . . and I am at it hammer and tongs with him.'[25] The Archbishop wrote of C.B.: 'He began by saying: "This is a very bad business . . . I should not be able, even if I tried, to restrain my people at all from making sharp work of what you have been doing." ' The Archbishop thought that C.B. was depressed and unhappy, and wrote: 'I left him with the impression on my mind that he is terribly in the hands of the more popular force among his followers and that he greatly underrates its anti-Church character.'[26]

C.B. himself made no record of his talks with the Archbishop, but Ponsonby, writing from No. 10 to his wife on November 19, said: 'C.B. enjoyed himself at Windsor, he had a long talk with the Archbishop & warned the King of the flare up with the Lords until the K was quite alarmed.'[27]

In the meantime the Cabinet had a stormy meeting on the 21st. Many of its members were in favour of drastic action. Others argued that the great mass of English people were not particularly interested in the Education argument, so that it was not a good issue on which to fight a major battle against the Lords. This was indeed the Liberals' dilemma. They could only successfully challenge the Lords on something on which they were certain that the majority of ordinary people were strongly with them. It was no good doing it on an issue like Home Rule, on which most English and Scots people were against them, or like Education, which appealed only to a particular group – in this case the Nonconformists – and in which C.B. himself, the leader of the party, was not greatly interested.

At the request of the King, C.B. saw the Archbishop at Lambeth, but the Archbishop found him scarcely 'more familiar with the Bill than he was when I talked to him at Windsor', adding, 'In some respects he had forgotten what I then tried to teach him.' The Archbishop was irritated because C.B. simply took the line that his supporters must be satisfied, saying, 'These are points on which my people are very hot.'[28] C.B. was not going to repeat Mr. Gladstone's mistake of 1874 in flouting Nonconformist opinion.

In fact, as C.B. explained to the King, the meeting did nothing to bridge the gulf. On the main issue no accommodation was possible. The Nonconformists thought it totally unacceptable that the Church, at whose hands many of them had suffered so much, should expect the state to pay all the costs of their schools while it retained the right to appoint teachers who would teach its own doctrines. To the Church it seemed equally intolerable that teachers should be forbidden to teach what they believed.

The Bill, duly turned inside out, now came back from the Lords. The Cabinet's decision was soon taken. It was that there should be no compromise. On December 8 C.B. told the King that the Government had decided to reject the Lords' amendments *en bloc*.

On December 12 the House of Commons debated the issue. Many Conservatives, seeing clearly the threat to the future of the House of Lords which would follow a decision to bring the two Houses into direct conflict on a matter of such importance, were uneasy about the line Balfour was taking, against the instincts of men like Lansdowne and the Duke of Devonshire. Almeric Fitzroy noted that Balfour spoke 'in the most defiant tones. . . . His own party were evidently taken by surprise, and, though they responded . . . by some perfunctory cheers, I am told that never, even in the failing days of his Ministry, did he encounter so much latent antagonism in the House of Commons.'[29]

The Commons voted by 416 to 107 to reject the Lords' amendments, a majority of 309. Even the Irish Catholics voted with the Government. Efforts still continued to try to save the Bill. Knollys wrote to C.B. on the 14th saying, 'one or two of the Leaders of the Opposition are in my humble opinion very shortsighted in their actions'.[30] Many of the leading Conservatives pressed for concessions, but Lord St. Aldwyn told the Archbishop: 'Our real difficulty lies in the fact that the leader of the Party does not want a peaceable solution.'[31] Esher wrote to his son on December 18: 'If the Bill is destroyed, then the Ministers declare that the Commons will refuse to vote supplies until the H. of L agrees to reform itself. No doubt this screw *could* be put upon them, but it is revolution.'[32]

Fitzroy described the scene in the House of Lords on December 19, which followed final efforts to reach a compromise in a meeting at Crewe House:

> After forty-eight hours spent in negotiation, the curtain rose on a policy of no surrender. The passions of political wreckers were unchained. . . .
> There is no doubt . . . what was the obstacle to an arrangement. . . . The Tories are persuaded that the issue will not be the House of Lords *v.* the People, but Church *v.* Chapel, and on that basis they believe it possible to reconstruct the Opposition as an effective force.
> The subordination of Lord Lansdowne's riper judgement to these speculations was seen . . . when . . . with a harassed air and dejected manner, he delivered his message in terms which gave the impression of a mind harnessed by order to a weary and distasteful task. He . . . must have realised that the power which should be reserved for a supreme crisis of State was being risked in a party wrangle.[33]

Balfour was far more responsible than Lansdowne for carrying matters to extremes. Sir Robert Ensor, however, makes no distinction between them in the analysis he makes of their motives in taking this course:

The Constitution was to be exploited with no scruples regarding fair play – a course bound eventually to cause fatal collision with the fair-play instincts of common Englishmen . . . no student can avoid asking, how practical men like Balfour and Lansdowne . . . could be so short-sighted. The psychology of it was that both were aristocrats born in the purple. Passionately devoted to the greatness of England, these men were convinced that she owed it to patrician rule. In their view her nineteenth-century parliamentarism had worked successfully, because the personnel of parliaments and cabinets was still (with a few much-resented exceptions like Bright) upper-class, and the function of the lower orders was limited to giving the system a popular *imprimatur* by helping to choose which of two aristocratic parties should hold office . . . from their standpoint the house of commons elected in 1906 was far worse than that of 1880. . . . To persons born like Lansdowne and Balfour (and only a little less to Rosebery) it appeared out of the question that a house of commons so composed and led should effectively rule the nation; and . . . they felt justified in using any resource . . . to crush the challenge. . . .[34]

The Lords voted on the 19th by 132 to 52 to insist on their amendments. C.B. received the support of one Church leader, the radical Bishop of Hereford, Dr. Percival. Significantly, the Duke of Devonshire, who had refused to lend his authority to Balfour's tactics, voted against the resolution. The Bill was dead, but the House of Lords had put itself in a position of extreme danger. C.B. asked the House of Commons on December 20: 'Who can doubt that a sense of weariness, and nausea, and a dislike of clerical and sectarian squabbles have spread from one end of the country to the other?'
Of Balfour he went on to say:

One member unfortunately raised a jarring note, and his sentence, at least – as on a memorable occasion in poetry – was for open war. I do not know whether it was dictated by any part of the spirit that seems to have lost for him the paradise of the Treasury Bench; but I am sure of this, that it is not by the exhibition of that spirit that paradise will be regained.

He put in a nutshell what the Government wanted: 'Our aim is . . . to secure a national and not a denominational system, public and not sectarian, on the general basis of a common Christianity instead of sectional Christianity. . . .'

He concluded by asking:

> Is the General Election and its result to go for nothing? . . . the resources of the British Constitution are not wholly exhausted . . . and I say with conviction that a way must be found, a way will be found, by which the will of the people, expressed through their elected representatives, will be made to prevail.[35]

The argument of the speech was exactly that he had put to Queen Victoria in 1894. When he sat down there was a tremendous outburst of cheering.

The Lords had also killed the Plural Voting Bill, introduced by Loulou Harcourt to correct what C.B. called 'a monstrous and intolerable electoral anomaly and privilege',[36] and severely mangled two other Bills. The Liberal Party was incensed. The Government now had to decide whether or not to dissolve and go to the country on the issue of the obstruction of the House of Lords. The bolder spirits were for a fight. Two years later Winston Churchill told Massingham: 'Both Lloyd George and I were willing to fight . . . but the Cabinet and C.B. took another view. . . .'[37]

C.B. and a large majority of his colleagues did indeed decide that the time for a showdown was not yet. Most historians consider that he was right. Sir Ivor Jennings has written:

> the Conservative peers were correct in their belief that they could with impunity destroy or mutilate legislation desired by Nonconformists, but that it would be unwise for the Conservative party to be associated with the rejection of proposals designed to improve the conditions of the workers. The Liberal Party could not, and did not, dissolve Parliament over Church schools or liquor licensing because most of the Liberal electors did not care a brass farthing about either.[38]

This is perhaps putting it too strongly, but at all events the Liberal leaders opted for the cautious line. They decided on the policy of sending up legislation to see how far the Lords would go – what was called 'filling the cup'. Bryce later wrote to Ponsonby: 'Looking back on 1906, our mistake seems to have been in tabling a Bill too complicated for the mass of the people to follow, so that when the Lords killed it, our people didn't quite know what had been killed.'[39] Incomprehension is a poor basis for a fight to a finish. But C.B. used to wonder afterwards if he had been right, and whether an immediate appeal to the country would not have been the best course after all.

Balfour had got his way, but many Conservatives thought that a profound mistake had been made. The King said irritably: 'I hope the Prime Minister will not abolish the House before I return. . . .'[40] Knollys told Esher: 'Between ourselves, I don't think the King will ever like "C.B." politically. I do not believe that the latter understands him any more than Mr. G. understood the Queen.'[41]

C.B. himself made clear in all his speeches, in and out of the House, his determination to bring matters to a conclusion. At Manchester in May, for example, after saying that 'no Liberal Government in my memory has ever been credited by its opponents with sincerity unless that suggestion was coupled with a broad and kindly suggestion of insanity', he declared: 'The present House of Commons was not elected to pass only such Bills as commend themselves to the House of Lords. . . . We do not intend to be a Government on sufferance, or to act as caretakers in the House of a party which the country has rejected. . . .'[42]

A month later, at Plymouth, he said:

these successive blows at the authority of the House of Commons . . . are part of the general scheme for discrediting – not this Government, that is a small affair – but discrediting any Liberal Government, and impressing the country with the view that a Liberal Ministry, be it ever so powerful, ever so united, is impotent to carry its measures . . . but there is one thing I have learned in my Parliamentary experience . . . it is not cleverness that pays in the long run. The people of this country are a straightforward people. They like honesty and straightforwardness of purpose. They may laugh at it and they may be amused by it and they may in a sense admire it, but they do not like cleverness. You may be too clever by half. . . .[43]

In discussing with his colleagues what should actually be done about the Lords, C.B. set his face against any attempt to tamper with the composition of the House and to establish some form of senate in place of the hereditary peers. He was clear that what needed to be changed were the powers of the upper House. A Cabinet Committee was set up under Loreburn to consider the problem and produced a plan, fathered by Ripon, for differences to be resolved at joint sittings between a delegation of a hundred peers and the entire House of Commons. C.B. thought this a bad plan – 'too artificial and complicated' – and one that involved dangers for any future Liberal government with a small majority. He shot it to pieces in a trenchant memorandum circulated to his colleagues on May 31. In this he argued that 'a scheme which is to obtain general assent should be easily intelligible to the plain man', that an assembly of 770 would be 'a multitude, a mob', and that unless the Government could count on a working majority of about 70 in the Commons the scheme would break down.

> The most serious objection [he added] is that it practically abolishes the legislative power of the House of Lords. . . . The House of Commons has only to say the same thing twice and it becomes law, just as a Mahommedan husband, by pronouncing the words of divorce three times, can get rid of his wife. But may not this objection be mitigated, if not removed, by securing intervals and opportunities for reflection, deliberation, and negotiation before the final decisive word is spoken?

He suggested an alternative – a version of the suspensory veto – and concluded:

> What is necessary is to avoid the risk of hasty or arbitrary action. . . . What is essential is, that the power of overriding the Lords should be available as a last resort. If such a power existed the Lords would, except when dealing with a shaky Government or towards the close of a Parliament, practically always give way at an earlier stage.[44]

After much discussion, he had his way, and persuaded his colleagues to agree to the proposal for the suspensory veto, first suggested by James Mill in 1836.

Although T. P. O'Connor, who met C.B. in Parliament Street a few days before, was struck by the good healthy colour of his cheeks and 'his general air of excellent spirits and tranquillity of soul',[45] the fact was that his strength was failing. Ponsonby managed to get him off staying the weekend at Windsor, so as to give him time to prepare his speech for the House of Commons, but on the Saturday he had to go to to a Royal garden party for the King of Siam, at which he caught a chill, and he had another heart attack on the Sunday. He determined, however, to carry on, and spoke in the House on the Monday, with Ponsonby standing by to go to the rescue if things went wrong.[46] So, on June 24, 1907, he moved –

> That, in order to give effect to the will of the people as expressed by their elected representatives, it is necessary that the power of the other House to alter or reject Bills passed by this House should be so restricted by law as to secure that within the limits of a single Parliament the final decision of the Commons shall prevail.

He declared that he must say 'a frank word' about his old enemy Balfour, 'the right hon. gentleman at the winding of whose horn the portcullis over the way comes rattling down'. He did so in these terms:

> The situation, as the House knows, has been aggravated by the part taken by the right hon. gentleman opposite. . . . I cannot conceive of Sir Robert Peel or Mr. Disraeli treating the House of Commons as the right hon. gentleman has treated it. Nor do I think there is any instance in which as leaders of the Opposition they committed what I can only call the treachery of openly calling in the other House to override this House. These great statesmen were House of Commons men. . . . The right hon. gentleman's course has, however, had one indisputable effect. It has left no room for doubt, if it had ever existed before, that the second Chamber is being utilised as a mere *annexe* of the Unionist party. . . . One begins to doubt, in fact – I certainly doubt – whether he or his party have ever fully accepted representative institutions.

He set out the procedure he had in mind, on the lines of his Cabinet memorandum, adding:

> unless you are going to fall back upon some foreign method, such as the *referendum* or the mandate or the *plebiscite*, or some other way of getting behind the backs of the elected to the electors themselves, such as was advised by both the first and third Napoleon . . . there

is no course open but to recognise ungrudgingly the authority which resides in this House. . . .

On this, he quoted Edmund Burke's saying that – 'The virtue, the spirit, the essence of the House of Commons consists in its being the express image of the nation.'[47]
O'Connor wrote of this occasion:

> C.B. says of himself that he has not the gift of the gab, which in a sense is true, and in a sense is false. He speaks somewhat stumblingly, has none of that easy and almost overwhelming flow of language for which Gladstone was distinguished, none of the easy delivery for which Chamberlain in his best days was famous. But when he does get the word he is seeking, it is always the right word. I know no man in the House of Commons who can make a speech more lucid, more choice and terser in diction than C.B. But he is not very ready. He never speaks without a considerable bundle of notes. The notes are not anything approaching, I believe, a verbatim copy of what he is going to say. . . . With several sheets of ordinary note-paper C.B. rises. He has a curious little mannerism, which is to use the bundle of notes as a fan. . . . Without these notes he would be lost. . . .
> The speech was one of the very best – if not the best – that the Prime Minister has delivered. . . . It was full of fire, of fight and of eloquence from its first word almost to its last. And in some passages it was unusually vehement, not to say merciless, in personal attack. C.B. is a gentle and kindly man, but he has his antipathies, and I am inclined to believe that Mr. Balfour is one of these antipathies. . . . C.B. used to Mr. Balfour language of unusual severity and of a directness of attack which showed a certain underlying bitterness. . . .
> Mr. Balfour . . . tucked down his head and seemed abashed. . . . And I thought there came an angry and confused flush on his face when C.B. applied to his action the ugly word 'treachery' to the House of Commons. . . . Whatever may be the future of this struggle, it is certain that it started out on a fiercer war-note than has been usual with C.B. during his Parliamentary struggles. The speech, above all, showed a mastery and a self-confidence which seemed to enable the Prime Minister to speak with a rapidity, an ease, and a command of the rapt attention of the House that mark

out the occasion from almost any other in the many addresses he has made since he has had the splendid dignity he now enjoys.[48]

Loulou Harcourt wrote saying that he also thought it one of the best C.B. had ever made in the House, while 'poor A.J.B. was wretched in reply'. 'I appreciated much', said Loulou, 'the passages intended for H.M.'s consumption.'[49] It was an extraordinary achievement for a man who had had a heart attack the day before.

The debate which followed was a famous one. Two future Prime Ministers, Winston Churchill and Lloyd George, delivered tremendous philippics against the House of Lords. Churchill, in what F. E. Smith later called a 'brilliant and rancorous speech', said that 'the general election of 1906 was the most vehement expression of public opinion which this generation had any knowledge of; and that expression of public force was countered . . . by the most arbitrary and uncompromising assertion of aristocratic privilege'. The upper House, he declared, was 'one-sided, hereditary, unpurged, irresponsible, absentee.' 'Had the House of Lords', he asked, 'ever been right?' and he gave a long catalogue of their follies. No one who heard the speech would have imagined that the speaker would one day be a Conservative Prime Minister. Lloyd George, pointing out that there was no substantial representation of the Nonconformists in the Lords, arraigned them for their treatment of those outside the established Church. 'The only Nonconformist Bill that was allowed to get through the first time,' he declared, 'was the Burials Bill.' The House of Lords, he added, was no mastiff, 'it is the right hon. gentleman's poodle; it fetches and carries for him, barks at and bites anybody he sets it on to. . . .' He ended by saying:

The Prime Minister has had a longer experience of Parliamentary life than any man in the House; I deliberately ask the House of Commons, and through the House of Commons the people of the country, to accept counsel given at the end of a great career by a statesman who stands today not merely in the British Empire, but throughout the world, as the man who embodies the noblest, the most exalted traditions of British statesmanship.[50]

C.B.'s motion was carried by a majority of 285. Despite his failing health the whole debate had been a triumph for him.

Ilbert, the Clerk of the House, told Bryce:

C.B. showed me a rough draft of what he proposed to say and I made one or two criticisms and suggestions. I was responsible for the 'tag' from Burke, which was hackneyed, but went down, and, partly, for the strong language about Balfour – though the phrase I suggested was not 'treachery', which was too strong, I think, but 'treason' – and for the contrast with Peel and Disraeli. Balfour was deeply stung, and I think cowed for a time, but the charge was deserved.[51]

C.B. was not to live to see the final issue, which came in the Parliament Act of 1911, after a long and bitter struggle. But he had set the course for his party and the solution he proposed was that which was finally adopted. Most of his colleagues were convinced that he was right.

Three years later, in Edinburgh, Lloyd George listed the great Liberal leaders, including 'another great Scotsman – the greatest Liberal statesman of his day, Sir Henry Campbell-Bannerman, the truest, tenderest, wisest man I have ever met in politics almost', and declared that – 'all these men spent the strength of their years trying to get Liberal and progressive legislation through, always checked, always thwarted. By what? By this institution that has stood there in the citadel . . . but which is crumbling to dust now.'[52]

Grey, rather surprisingly, was more militant than C.B. on this issue, and was for replacing the House of Lords by an elected second chamber. 'If we fail,' he wrote, 'a seat in the House of Commons will cease to be worth having for any Liberal.'[53] But, looking back, Winston Churchill, in a letter to King George V written in February, 1911, said: 'The deep sagacity of Sir Henry Campbell-Bannerman in not interfering with the composition of the Lords but dealing only with relations does not become less apparent as the days pass by.'[54]

CHAPTER 36

Back in Harness

A<small>FTER</small> Charlotte's death, C.B. sat down in the great lonely rooms of Belmont to answer his letters of condolence. He was exceedingly conscientious, and he did it all himself, but he found it hard to keep track of all the letters. He sent Lord Crewe two replies, rather than overlook him.

To Sir Ralph Knox C.B. wrote of Charlotte:

> She has been sacrificed to my public life. We both wished and strove to get out of it, but could not. London always sapped her strength, and we both longed for a quiet life with each other, but, latterly especially, circumstances were too strong for us, and of course, for the last two or three years, her longing to escape was mingled with a keen desire to see me vindicated; as she said, to see me 'get my reward.' The only pleasure I had in it was that it pleased her. . . .
>
> Now I am alone in the world. But, with God's help, I will go on, until such forces as without her I can muster fail altogether. I must 'dree my weird' alone. . . .[1]

He told Ripon:

> I have many consolatory facts for which I am grateful to God . . . the fact that she is now at rest after her long years of suffering; the fact that I can now look back . . . and recall her as she was in the brighter days; the extraordinary demonstration of sorrow and sympathy . . . most remarkable of all in Marienbad, where one may say the whole place was in tears. . . .[2]

Nash noted that at Belmont meals did not take half as long as in the old days. He, the Sinclairs and Charlotte's Swedish masseuse, Miss Thorbjörn, were with C.B. But nothing could ever be the same again. Later on Lord Rendel found him 'terribly bereaved at heart', and C.B. told him that life was dreary to him. Charlotte, he said, had been part and parcel of himself.[3]

On her grave he put two texts; a line from Tasso:

La cara moglie
Che di conforme cor mi ha data il cielo

('his dear wife who with heart at one with his had made heaven for him') – in which he had, with unfailing tact, substituted 'cara' for the original 'antica' – and *My trust is in the tender mercy of God for ever and ever.*

The shock of Charlotte's death had been profound, and he seemed to have little will to survive her. Less than a month after the Scottish funeral he had a heart attack. W. S. Blunt noted in his diary: 'Dillon says that Bannerman is much broken since his wife's death, and will probably go to the Lords with Fowler.'[4] C.B., however, recovered from his attack, pulled himself together, and began to take up the reins again. He wrote to Ripon on October 9: 'I quite agree with you that our Whips have been too frisky and too noisy.'[5] A few days before, in another letter to Ripon, who had warned him that the Government were being criticized for not taking a firm enough line with Keir Hardie and the Independent Labour Party, he wrote: 'Why should we not go straight on, and never mind the silly things which Mr. Hardie's vanity, or his malice, may prompt him to do.'[6] He invited Ponsonby to 'camp out with him' at Downing Street,[7] Donaldson at Belmont was instructed to 'pick up a good £5 dog', and life began again.

Down in Wales, Lloyd George was telling his countrymen:

the Prime Minister . . . states very clearly . . . that Welsh Disestablishment is still an integral part of the Liberal programme. . . . There is one thing to be said about the Prime Minister; no man has ever been so severely criticised and had such scorn poured upon him from time to time, but his worst opponent will admit that he is a man of his word.

There is another fact, if you want an additional pledge of the Prime Minister's sincerity; he is the first Prime Minister since the days of Oliver Cromwell who has had a genuine belief in the emancipation of religion from State control.[8]

This, in fact, was true enough. C.B. had been in favour of disestablishment in the three kingdoms ever since he had first entered politics. In one election address he had said: 'I am in favour of the principle of a "free church in a free state"; and I would apply this principle at the earliest opportunity in Scotland and in Wales.'[9]

The party conflict revived. Churchill at Glasgow referred to Milner as 'the disconsolate Proconsul'. C.B. had been impressed by the work Lloyd George and Winston Churchill had done in Parliament in 1906 and he sent for them to say so.[10] On November 15 Ponsonby wrote to his wife about an adjournment debate: 'It is a tight corner and Winston is not the man to inspire them with confidence but C.B. will wind up. He had a Cabinet all this morning so unfortunately he is very tired but I hope he will get through all right.'[11]

Mrs. Morton Campbell, the wife of C.B.'s nephew Hugh, arrived at 10 Downing Street to act as his official hostess. Ponsonby found her nervous and 'not particularly light in hand', and, as a hostess, 'impossible altogether'. She and her son seemed to him 'silly and tiresome'.[12] But if C.B. noticed he said nothing.

In September Grey had decided to replace the Ambassador in Washington. In mid-November the King and C.B. discussed the problem at Windsor. President Roosevelt, so C.B. later told Esher, had asked for a real 'man'.[13] On the 20th the King wrote in his own hand to C.B. suggesting that the post be given to Hardinge with a peerage.[14] This was not the first time the King had pushed him. It was he who had got him sent to St. Petersburg in 1903.[15] C.B. and Grey were, however, reluctant to move Hardinge who was himself reluctant to go. Hardinge also spoke to Knollys, who said that if he didn't want to go, 'pray bring forward some eligible man . . . I cannot believe that Rosebery would accept it. He is however the greatest living man for surprises.'[16]

The King wrote another far from legible letter to C.B. on the 23rd, still urging that Hardinge should be appointed, and adding: 'German influence and indeed intrigue, has been so paramount at Washington, that it wants the ability and Diplomatic tact and knowledge possessed by Sir Charles to counteract the first, which is important for the maintenance of our good relations with the United States Government and the peace of the world.'[17] The minutes of the Prime Minister and the Foreign Secretary on this were brief: 'Ecce iterum. H.C.B.' 'I am sure we can't spare Hardinge & it would not be fair to him to move him. E.G.'[18]

C.B. sent for Hardinge, and sensibly suggested that he should explain his objections personally to the King. This Hardinge did at Sandringham, and was asked to propose somebody else. As he described it:

> I racked my brain that night . . . and in the small hours of the morning a brainwave reached me and I thought of Bryce. . . . I realised that he would be greatly appreciated in America as knowing far more of the history and Constitution of America than most Americans. He also had the quality of liking to make long and rather dull speeches on commonplace subjects which I knew to be a trait that would be popular with the American masses. He had also a charming and agreeable wife. I felt therefore on safe ground in putting forward his name to the King. . . .[19]

But in the meantime, possibly at the King's suggestion and possibly at Hamilton's, Grey had decided to offer the post to his old leader. He had never been happy to see him left out in the cold. On November 30 Hardinge wrote to Knollys:

> Rosebery saw Grey this morning. He emphasised the difficulties and the disagreeable side of the post at Washington and half said 'no' but added that he would write in a day or two . . . How extraordinary it is that Rosebery cannot make up his mind. . . . I hear privately that C.B. is not enthusiastic about the idea of Rosebery being appointed as he is of opinion that if R. did very well at Washington it would improve Rosebery's position too much with the Liberal party! Such are party politics![20]

It seems a little doubtful whether at this stage C.B. really worried very much about the threat from a Rosebery rejuvenated by a sojourn in America. He knew him too well.

Rosebery told Hamilton that 'the thing is for a thousand reasons impossible', and that 'the amb^r who goes to Washington without a wife would be mad'.[21] The King did his best to induce him to accept but Rosebery was adamant, saying that 'the want of a hostess was so insuperable an obstacle that it was unnecessary to go further into the business'.[22] Loulou Harcourt was proposed, but C.B. said that he had been such a success in Parliament that he could not be spared.[23] So Hardinge's suggestion was taken up – the King deciding to put it forward as his own – and the post was offered to Bryce. Bryce accepted, decided not to take a peerage, and duly went to Washington, where he was a notable success. So one of C.B.'s closest political associates found a job more agreeable and more suited to his talents than dealing with the Irish. This is, perhaps, the only occasion on which a Foreign Office official has refused the Embassy in Washington and recommended a member of the Cabinet as the second best choice.

Bryce's appointment created a vacancy at the Irish Office and in the Cabinet. But before he could deal with this C.B. had trouble with Morley. Morley's temperament was one of the crosses he had to bear. Morley was a prima donna, and was constantly threatening to resign, or actually sending in his resignation, for one reason or another. He now wrote a friendly letter asking C.B. to think over the hint he had earlier dropped, 'in a shambling sort of way', that he might depart, since at sixty-eight 'I must be thinking of my latter end'.[24]

C.B. knew Morley too well to suppose that there was not something behind this. He saw him and managed to talk him out of it, but Morley remained ever ready to take up his hat and depart, usually on the ground of real or imagined slights. On December 29, Esher went to see him at his house at Wimbledon, called, appropriately enough, Flowermead, which Esher described as 'a rather commonplace villa'. He was, however, impressed by Morley's fine library of over 11,000 volumes, but said in a letter to the King next day:

> Mr. Morley, as Your Majesty knows, is extremely sensitive . . . he was not consulted by the Prime Minister about Mr. Bryce's appointment. It was certainly only an oversight, but it left a little soreness. . . . The Prime Minister, as Your Majesty is aware, is not a voluble correspondent, and Mr. Morley feels that he cannot get into complete touch upon these matters, which he considers of first-rate importance, with his Chief – hence a little 'feeling'.[25]

Knollys replied: '. . . Of course C.B. ought to take him into his confidence especially about Irish matters, but then in whom does he confide! In anybody?'[26]

The King was still complaining about the sparseness of C.B.'s accounts of Cabinet proceedings. Knollys passed on the complaint and C.B. wrote, characteristically, on November 24:

I am much concerned to hear that His Majesty thought my account of last Cabinet somewhat meagre. . . . As a matter of fact . . . my report could hardly have been more full. There was a vague, disjointed conversation as to various Bills. . . . The consideration given to the Education Bill did not amount to much. . . . I would ask you to assure The King that I have every desire that he should at once be made aware of every decision of importance: but I shrink from troubling Him with any detailed account of a general conversation on Business. . . .[27]

C.B. himself seems to have found the Cabinet discussion tedious and discursive, and he could not manage to manufacture a lucid but specious account for the King.

When the Workmen's Compensation Bill came to be debated, it was practically the story of the Trades Disputes Bill over again. The Cabinet Committee which worked out the Bill decided to exclude domestic servants, and in the House efforts to get them included were resisted by the Home Secretary, Herbert Gladstone, and by the Law Officers. The Bill was being discussed on December 5 when C.B. came in, sat down on the front bench, and listened to some speeches from Lord Robert Cecil, Donald Maclean and Keir Hardie urging the servants' inclusion. He knew very little about the Bill, but was impressed by what he heard, so there and then he stood up, without having consulted any of his colleagues, and said that he would accept the amendment which brought them in.[28] His stock with Labour rose still higher, and his colleagues recognized once again that his instinct was right. This at any rate was one occasion when speeches made in the House of Commons directly influenced the chief of the executive.

So ended 1906, a year of personal tragedy for C.B. but one in which he and his administration had made a convincing start. His own authority and popularity had grown enormously. The great achievement of the year had been the Transvaal settlement. It had been a good year.

CHAPTER 37

Bishoprics and Peerages

O NE of the duties of a British Prime Minister is to appoint bishops and deans in the Church of England. For a Presbyterian and a lifelong advocate of disestablishment, C.B. took a remarkable interest in these matters. As soon as he had taken office he had had a friendly letter from the Archbishop of Canterbury, Randall Davidson, offering his help on any ecclesiastical matters, personal or general, but saying that he would perfectly understand it if C.B. preferred 'to rely wholly upon others for such information'.[1] C.B. replied that he would value the Archbishop's help and advice.[2]

But Mr. Henry Higgs of the Treasury, as patronage secretary, was his principal adviser on ecclesiastical appointments. He kept dossiers of all likely candidates, noting, for example, about a certain Dr. Turner that he was 'of evident but not obtrusive goodness'.[3] C.B., however, took trouble himself, and if necessary made his own choices. He said at the outset that he wanted to give the Evangelical Churchmen 'a turn', since, in his opinion, they had been neglected for a long time. Higgs wrote later:

> I soon discovered that he had no objection to a Broad Church-man, but had little liking for the type of High Churchman who sails as near as possible to Roman Catholicism. 'What I dislike intensely,' he said 'is the idea of a mediating priesthood, standing between the individual and his Creator, claiming to reserve sacra-ments, and to have a right of introducing the laity to the Deity as if they were a privileged caste.'[4]

He was asked by C.B. to go to a service taken by an Evangelical rector who had been said by his Bishop to be lacking in culture. According to Higgs:

He was not a product of one of our older Universities, and had a provincial burr in his speech. My report and advices were very favourable and C.B. said 'Note him for consideration.' Then turning to the Bishop's view he added warmly 'I have no patience with professors of a religion founded by fishermen who think that the higher posts in the Church must be preserved for the highly born and the highly educated. I have little doubt that St. Peter dropped his h's and that Our Saviour's Sermon on the Mount was uttered in the broadest Galilean dialect.'[5]

Higgs also wrote:

When I attended a Kirk service with him in Scotland he asked me what I thought of it. The time was approaching when the Minister's term would expire and the question of renewing it was under discussion. 'I think' he said, 'we manage these things better in Scotland. The members of the congregation choose the Minister themselves, and after a limited period they can reconsider their choice. In England a patron puts in his nominee, who may hold office for life to the great dissatisfaction of the parishioners.'[6]

'I am a Presbyterian,' C.B. used to say, 'and I do not know even what is a Rural Dean. But Higgs knows all about these matters. He is a member of the Church of England and keeper of my Ecclesiastical conscience.'[7]

C.B. and the Archbishop became good friends. C.B. referred to him as 'my countryman Randall'. But the Archbishop used to say that no one more constantly sought his advice and more seldom took it.[8] Matters were not, of course, helped by the clash between the Liberals and the clergy over the Education Bill. Birrell wrote to C.B. on January 12, 1907: 'I do hope that when any thing really good turns up our few *Liberal* Clergy may be rewarded. . . . I am still smarting under the Bishops' rods.'[9] In his reply C.B. said: 'I am greatly disposed to make Liberalism & Broad views the test for all promotions.'[10]

He consulted those he felt would give him good, dispassionate advice, regardless of whether or not they had themselves any connection with the Church of England. He also received a good deal of unsolicited advice about Church appointments. In August 1907, he had a letter from Princess Louise:

I hear . . . that Mr. Burnaby of East Cowes I of Wight is in hopes of being a candidate for St Peters Vere Street. I can safely say he is a good & original preacher. A man who has read & studied. He is rather wasted in the quiet little parish at East Cowes – Mr. Burnaby having asked us not to forget him if ever he had a chance of getting moved to another living & the Duke & myself having known him for many years write to ask you to kindly consider his name. . . .[11]

C.B. had a soft spot for Princess Louise and Burnaby duly went to St. Peter's. But when Lord Althorp wrote suggesting a candidate for the Deanery of Manchester, C.B. replied:

> I doubt if Dr. Wood would suit this particular case: he would be better fitted for a more quiet and academic chapter. The man for Manchester should be a man of energy, accustomed to work among the poor, etc. Also, as it is my first big appointment, he must be (to say the least) a non-Ritualist. That quarrel runs very high on the spot.[12]

Next year he wrote to Lord Aberdeen about a Dr. Wright:

> . . . his age and his bookish life do not fit him for every post.
> At Canterbury . . . the Chapter is handicapped (or perhaps hamstrung) by having in it the Head of a College at Cambridge & the Head of a College at Oxford. It is true that the latter is I am told the most learned commentator on Dante in Europe, but the poor people of Canterbury & the railway men of Ashford are not much the better for that.[13]

One person he consulted was the Newcastle Liberal Dr. Spence Watson who was, in fact, a Quaker. To him he wrote on June 10, 1907:

> Who would be a good Bishop of Newcastle? . . . One has not to choose the man most of one's own kidney however much one may like it, but must consider prejudices, circumstances, balances of opinion, fairness of distribution among parties, political interests and social. So please don't be annoyed if your advice is not taken![14]

Having chosen his man he wrote again on July 13:

> About Bishops!
> I take infinite pains in the matter, and my object . . . is . . .

1. to strengthen the Episcopal Bench and upper dignitaries with broad-minded men
2. to encourage hard working spiritually minded men in humble positions by shewing them that their views are not boycotted.

It seemed to me most desirable after the prolonged dose of High Churchmen to which the Church has been subjected, to mark a more catholic (with a small c) spirit. Therefore I have appointed at Truro a broad and liberal Bishop, at Newcastle an avowed Evangelical; at Manchester a Low Church Dean, at Ely an Academical Scholarly Right Centre Dean, each suited to his locality.

As to secular politics . . . I am to appoint Liberals but to avoid extreme Ritualists – that is what I am told. But all the new school of Church Liberals are Sacerdotolists; while all the Evangelicals of mark are pronounced Tories. What is a poor devil to do?

I thought it fair to make a decided Evangelical appointment and Newcastle seemed a most fitting place. The new Bishop is a great out-of-door preacher and Evangeliser, suitable to communities of pitmen. . . .

I must peg away on my own lines but we cannot find each quality in each new man.[15]

The appointment of Dr. Stratton to the Bishopric of Newcastle was suggested by Lady Wimborne. C.B. was struck by some pictures of the large crowds to whom the Bishop preached in the open air in the island. He knew that Stratton's appointment to Newcastle would cause something of a stir, that it would be said he had gone out of his way to select a narrow-minded Conservative in politics, and a narrow-minded Evangelical in religion, and that Stratton had no claim to academic distinction either as a scholar or a theologian. But his mind was made up to 'strike a note' in his first choice.[16] There was some grumbling from Liberals.

But it was Chichester which gave him the most trouble. The Bishopric was worth, in those days, £4,200 a year, with, besides, first-fruits of £80, and was described as a 'small, compact and easy diocese'. The Palace, C.B. was advised, 'formerly a death trap, is now perfectly healthy,' the chief problem being 'a plague-spot of Mariolatry at Brighton'. He found it 'an exceedingly difficult place to fill'.[17] He wrote from Balmoral to Sinclair on September 29:

. . . Chichester vacancy. I met your friend Gardiner at a Paddock-hurst week-end, and liked him. Randall recommended him for St. Peter's, Vere Street – but I doubted if he was preacher enough; it is nothing but preaching there, and hardly his sort. (I do not find either Randall or Him of Hereford very sound or decided in their judgement of men.) As to Gardiner's pets I would not touch Lang with a barge pole. Say what you like he is in with the real sacerdotal lot, and if it can be told of him that he refuses to go into his father's church, that is enough for me. Then Glyn of Peterborough has not much brain and must have less since his accident. The diocese is in a frightful state and wants a strong man, but not a fighting Evangelical which the Protestant Societies are shouting or agitating for. Such a man wd. play old Boots in the place, but a manly sensible conciliatory but firm man. Where is he to be found! I am going to write to Randy, he is little to be [hoped] to. Stephen G. is archisacerdotal – I will none of them. . . . 17 Vicars or curates have gone over bodily to Rome in Brighton, Worthing etc.! That is enough![18]

On November 5 he was still searching and told the Archbishop:

I am afraid you will think me very finnicky and fastidious: but I have not yet found my man for Chichester. . . . I am using much freedom with you, in always bothering you, and, as you once said, never acting on your advice. But you will be lenient to my doubts and perplexities.[19]

When the Archbishop started to send in suggestions and criticisms about Church appointments, Higgs grew alarmed for the principles of the Reformation, especially when the King joined the Archbishop as an ally. When C.B. proposed a candidate for Chichester, Knollys said that the King regarded him as 'not suitable'. Knollys added:

The King is always very reluctant to disagree with any recommendation of yours, but he has his own views as to the qualifications required for the higher appointments in the church, & he is afraid he must ask you to be so good as to submit the name of some other Clergyman for the Bishopric of Chichester.[20]

Knollys went on to say, however, that the King would give way if the Archbishop of Canterbury agreed with C.B.

This provoked from Higgs a manifesto to C.B. on the point of principle:

> The letter ... is a sinister document ... the selection of a Bishop is an Act-of-State which the Reformation cut off from the Church and handed over to the Head of the Nation. Our horror of being priest-ridden appears in our lay patrons ... and State patronage of all Deaneries and Bishoprics, and in the control of Parliament over the services of the Church. .... Responsible as you are, your advice ought not to need the concurrence of the Primate. The constitution of the Church gives him no voice. ... It is bad enough that he should cripple your legislation without blocking your executive action.
>
> Still more unpleasant is the reticent remark about 'having his own views as to these appointments.' I feel pretty sure that these views are something like this – 'Above all things get a gentleman!' ... This ... Early-Victorian view ... will keep the poor Bishop of Hereford, 'like a sparrow that sitteth alone upon the housetops,' solitary upon the Bench without a fellow-Bishop to join him in the lobby, for all time. Such an argument almost always assumes that a normal 'gentleman' is a Tory. ...[21]

In the end Ridgeway, the Dean of Carlisle, was appointed to Chichester early in 1908.

*　　　*　　　*

Another question that took up a good deal of C.B.'s time, as it does that of all Prime Ministers, was that of honours. In C.B.'s case the problem was aggravated by the fact that the Liberal Party had been for so long in the wilderness. Now that they had reached the promised land the faithful looked for their reward.

C.B. was sometimes criticized for the number of peerages he recommended, but, considering the ten years the party had spent in opposition, and the fact that the House of Lords was overwhelmingly Conservative, the number he put forward was relatively modest – a total of twenty-one peers in two years, or ten a year. There have been times when they have been created more rapidly. Pitt, for example, bestowed eighty-three peerages in seven years – some twelve a year – and Rosebery wrote that 'as for his baronets, their name was legion, and his knights were as the sands of the sea'.[22] Salisbury made an average of seven a year, and Balfour six. It was only after C.B.'s time that the system was seriously abused. Asquith maintained his rate of recommendations without the excuse of the ten years in the wilderness. And with Lloyd George matters got out of hand – there were thirty peerages in 1916 – and after the war the arrangements broke down altogether for a time in scandal and abuse.

The fastidious had winced at some of the honours bestowed in the past by both parties. Now C.B. was in charge of this difficult business. King Edward was unhappy both about the number of his recommendations and about some of those proposed for peerages. In June 1906 C.B. had a letter from the King's Private Secretary, recording the King's doubts about an honour for the head of Harland and Wolff in Belfast, Mr. Pirrie,[23] and in October the King raised difficulties about some other recommendations, in one case because he looked on a radical M.P. as 'a rather violent and mischievous man',[24] and in another because he wondered whether the son and heir was reputable.[25]

On the whole, however, C.B. got his way, even with Pirrie. Some proposals created no difficulties. No one quarrelled with an O.M. for Lord Cromer, on Hardinge's recommendation, a G.C.B. for Edward Hamilton, or a knighthood for W. S. Gilbert. C.B. also showed that he bore no rancour towards a colleague who had voted against him on the cordite vote in 1895, writing in June 1906 to Leonard Courtney to offer him a peerage and saying: 'It will save you for active public life, and will so far maintain its standard. It will gratify men of right views throughout the country – and let me add, to be the instrument of your receiving this recognition & this opportunity, will be a pride & a delight to me.'[26] Peerages for people like Shaw-Lefevre, Lord Edmond Fitzmaurice and Philip Stanhope were either arrangements for Government representation in the Lords (as with Fitzmaurice) or consolation prizes for those left out of the administration.

C.B. recommended Florence Nightingale for the Order of Merit. No woman had received it, but no one could have a higher claim. Though at first nothing was done, because the King was opposed to women being given the Order,[27] it went through in November, 1907.[28] Sadly, she was by then beyond knowing what was being done.

A number of people proposed themselves for honours. One man asked for a baronetcy, citing the numerous elections fought by his family, his wish 'to bring my sons into the arena', his influence as a large landowner and the numerous industries he ran, and complaining that his rivals had been greatly favoured.[29]

Not every case was straightforward, and in his first year at No. 10 C.B. heard suggestions that the Chief Whip was trying to extort money for the party from those proposed for honours. He wrote to Ripon, who had proposed for a peerage a distinguished Yorkshireman married to a daughter of the Earl of Portsmouth, on October 27, 1906: 'Please see enclosed from Mr. Milnes Gaskell qui nolit baronificari. It wd. involve a step down for his wife & also for his dau.-in-law – which may have some influence in the refusal. But Whiteley may have been trying to wring money out of him. I shall know about this on Monday. . . .'[30] This suspicion did not prevent Whiteley himself from being made a Privy Councillor next year.

In July 1907, there was a public row about honours. C.B. was asked in the House whether the new peerages were to be hereditary and there was laughter when he replied: 'They are of the usual sort.'[31] Mr. James Smith of Stirling had been made a knight, and C.B. was asked by Mr. Lea on July 11 whether Mr. Smith had been knighted as a supporter of C.B. and chairman of his election committee, or as a director of the Ayrshire Foundry Company, or as subscribing to Liberal Party funds. The Speaker intervened, saying that the Prime Minister was not responsible to the House for his advice to the Sovereign on honours. The background to this was that the Ayrshire Foundry Company, of which Smith was a director, had supplied a defective rudder for the battleship *King Edward VII*, the defect having been hidden by electric welding, executed by trusted employees in secret on a Sunday, but subsequently revealed by a discharged worker. It was not a particularly pretty story, but it was held that the directors did not know of the fraud.[32]

Mr. Lea wrote to *The Times*, asserting that 'honours are bought and sold, the proceeds going principally to the war chest of the party in office at the time these so-called honours are conferred. The party funds are presided over by the Chief Whip.'[33] Lord Robert Cecil thereupon raised the matter in the House, quoting a letter in the *Daily News* from G. K. Chesterton, which said that the crucial evil of English politics was the secret party fund: 'So long as that mass of money remains unaudited, that mass of money is omnipotent. Rich men pay into it and are made peers. Poor men are paid out of it and are made slaves.'[34] C.B. said in the House that both his Chief Whip, Whiteley, and his former Chief Whip, Gladstone, 'give a most explicit denial to any assertion that they have brought influence to bear on this ground of pecuniary assistance'.[35] Balfour gave a similar assurance on the part of the Conservatives.

What C.B. said was, no doubt, strictly true, but criticism, directed against both party machines, continued. One M.P. cited the impeachment of the Duke of Buckingham for selling a peerage for £10,000. The *Saturday Review* asserted that

> 'the fountain of honour' has become . . . a dirty spray of dishonour. . . . Two Sterns and a Harmsworth are a severe strain upon the patience and respect of the British nation. . . . Is it true or false that the peerages of Michelham and Northcliffe were sold for so much cash down? And did the cash go into the war-chest of the Conservative party? . . . that these peerages were conferred from a sincere belief in the public merits of the recipients or from any other mercenary considerations is plainly incredible.[36]

C.B. was responsible for none of these creations. One was Rosebery's and two, including Northcliffe, Balfour's. The Attorney-General said that the article was not to be treated seriously.

C.B. had himself told William Robertson as long before as September 1901 that 'The money affairs of Party funds are *entirely* in the hands of the Chief Whip – the P. Minister himself knows (generally) nothing of them, unless in some particular case facts come out.'[37] That was the well-established tradition for many years.

What really happened was well described by J. A. Spender in his book *The Public Life*:

> the work thrown on political parties . . . entails the expenditure of very large sums of money which must be found from somewhere. . . . The older British parties have generally obtained this money from wealthy supporters and rewarded them with 'honours'. . . . The chief drawback to this method was that it could not be openly acknowledged . . . the fiction had to be maintained that the honour was the reward of some public service. . . . The endower of a hospital . . . might be raised to the peerage amid general applause, but the announcement that a man had been made a peer for contributing £50,000 to the funds of his party would probably have been hailed with laughter and shocked surprise . . . the . . . party fund . . . was a secret fund . . . of the existence of which the Prime Minister

or Leader of the Opposition was officially unaware . . . there was in fact no more rigid etiquette among Chief Whips of the old school than that the Prime Minister should 'know nothing' about these things.[38]

Gladstone recorded later that, as Chief Whip, he raised £275,000. The election of 1906, he said, cost the party £100,000. He went on:

> In no single case did I hint directly or indirectly at an honour. I kept the whole business in my hands.
> I submitted the names of four men to C.B. and Asquith who I thought ought to receive peerages. All four had done great service to the Liberal party for 30 or 40 years. All of them were in the first rank of famous business men. The names were approved and ultimately the peerages were given on C.B.'s recommendation. They were given absolutely free from any condition. As a matter of fact two of them gave nothing to my fund, I may candidly add, to my great disappointment.[39]

Gladstone admitted that he had obtained C.B.'s agreement to an honour in one case where a secondary honour was expected to lead to a contribution of £10,000 to the party funds, but he claimed that the honour was justifiable on other grounds, since the man was a sound supporter of C.B., of unblemished character and munificent.[40]

One proposal which was to lead, after the war, to the most notorious of all honours cases concerned the South African mining magnate, J. B. Robinson. The origin of this was a letter from Winston Churchill to C.B., written on May 19, 1906. In this, with the problem of Chinese labour in mind, Churchill urged that Robinson should be asked to give a man called Creswell a mine in South Africa to try out a scheme of white contract labour. He said that he had put this idea to Robinson, who had agreed to give it a trial and to give Creswell a mine for the purposes of the experiment. Churchill continued:

> In return, he asked me if he did all this, whether the Government would be grateful to him, and whether they would give him an honour (baronetcy I presume). I replied of course that I did not know, but that I was sure you would watch the white labour experiment with great interest & sympathy, that he would be rendering an

important public service, & that I should bring the matter to your notice. I own he rather surprised me by his request. . . .

He added that he had subscribed to the Liberal party funds at the last election & that he had never been on good terms with the Tories since the Jameson Raid. . . .

I do trust that you will give most favourable consideration to this. . . .[41]

Churchill wrote again about this from Blenheim on May 24, saying:

Even at risk of being insistent, I venture to express a hope that the Robinson business will not fall through.

I never intended of course to suggest that any actual promise would be required on your part. Such an undertaking would be I am well aware wholly incorrect. But might it not be worth while for you to see Robinson & use a few suave phrases about services to the public, 'valuable & interesting experiments' etc? . . .[42]

Presumably C.B. did see Robinson, for, over a year later, on November 15, 1907, when C.B. was seriously ill, Sir Francis Hopwood at the Colonial Office wrote to Churchill:

J. B. Robinson has been to see me in really a furious passion, because he did not receive a baronetcy. He says that he spent enormous sums of money, to a great extent at the bidding of the Government, and that he understood from the Prime Minister, and also I gather from you, that it would be alright.

I am taking steps to let the Prime Minister know Robinson's very strong feeling on the subject. . . . I really think it a pity to give this serious ground for complaint for what is after all a trifling matter. . . .[43]

On Asquith's recommendation, Robinson was given a baronetcy in 1908. But when, in 1922, Robinson was recommended for a peerage by Lloyd George, the outcry was so great, on account of his subsequent financial activities in South Africa, that he was compelled to withdraw his name. In the debate in the Lords then, startling details were given of the way in which, under Lloyd George, touts sold honours, with a regular tariff. The then Lord Chancellor, Lord Birkenhead, said on that occasion:

Sir Henry Campbell-Bannerman was advised by General Botha to confer a baronetcy upon Sir Joseph Robinson. . . . General Botha at least knew South Africa. . . .

In the year 1907 Sir Henry Campbell-Bannerman – I do not know for what reason, but I understand that these recommendations are sometimes slow in obtaining fruition – did not grant this recognition, but in 1908 the recommendation, as I am informed, was repeated, and more insistently repeated, by General Botha. . . .[44]

No letter to C.B. from General Botha appears to survive. But the fact remains that C.B. himself gave no honour to Robinson.

Ponsonby wrote of C.B.: 'Making up the honours list was a source of great amusement to him. His comments on the applicants or more often their wives were very funny.' After this in his note is a sentence which was crossed out, but which read: 'But he became alarmed when he found that Whiteley the Chief Whip was sometimes extracting very large sums of money from them. This had to be severely restrained.'[45] But not, apparently, stopped altogether.

There were, however, pleasanter aspects. Churchill wrote recommending a peerage for Jack Poynder, adding: '& let it not be forgotten – his charming wife & beautiful home are in every respect suited to maintain the proper dignity of a Barony'.[46] C.B. wrote to Ripon on August 7, 1906: 'The pleasing task of giving a Garter has now come on the scene: I should be glad of a hint $? \begin{cases} \text{Carrington} \\ \text{Northampton} \\ \text{Aberdeen.'} \end{cases}$[47]

Ripon recommended Northampton, saying, 'I think that it is wiser not to give these honours to members of the Cabinet', though 'Truth obliges me to say that I was made a K.G. when I was in the Cabinet and did not protest.'[48] But it was the amiable Lord Carrington who received it and who wrote the nicest possible thank-you letter.[49]

The last honour C.B. recommended was the Garter for Crewe at the end of March, 1908, when he had no longer the strength to write in his own hand.

But by far and away the most troublesome honours case he had to deal with was that of Lord Curzon.

Curzon, as Viceroy of India, had been the ultimate loser in a desperate struggle for supremacy with the Commander-in-Chief, Lord Kitchener. He had, fundamentally, been in the right in asserting the primacy of civilian control, but he had done it so clumsily, and Kitchener had intrigued against him so cunningly, that in the end he had had to go, and he had finished up in total and bitter conflict with his Unionist colleagues in the Balfour Government. With Brodrick, the Secretary of State for India, he was not on speaking or writing terms. C.B. thought the whole affair deplorable, and wrote to Ripon in September 1905: 'The subsequent squalid quarrel is not only discreditable, but, as you point out, dangerous to the prestige of the Indian Government.'[50] Curzon was back in England at the beginning of December. Neither Balfour nor any other Minister met him. Curzon had made up his mind to refuse the normal earldom if it was offered to him by Balfour. He still thought of returning to the House of Commons, to which his Irish peerage was no bar. But he was unable to find a seat, so he changed his mind about taking a United Kingdom peerage.

The King had pressed Balfour twice to give Curzon an earldom, 'and at once'.[51] But Balfour told Knollys that, though Curzon deserved an honour, 'it would never do so to time this public recognition of his services as to suggest that it was in the remotest degree connected with his action in the Curzon-Kitchener dispute. In that dispute he was (as I think) in the wrong. It would be absurd to take a step which would be universally interpreted as meaning that I believed him to be in the right.'[52] He argued that a decision should be put off until January or February. So indeed it was, but by then Balfour had resigned and C.B. was Prime Minister.

The King remained anxious for Curzon to get an earldom, and Esher asked C.B. to give Knollys 'your "raisonnement" on this most tiresome question'.[53] C.B. wrote accordingly:

I have carefully considered the question of a British peerage for Lord Curzon . . . and it is with much personal regret that I find it out of my power to be the medium of submitting it. . . .

The mere fact of his being a prominent and while at home an active political opponent is not in itself sufficient to make such a recognition impossible. . . . But this is not an ordinary case.

Lord Curzon resigned while his friends were still in power and resigned without receiving any sign of favour or approbation which was frankly – I would almost say ostentatiously withheld. On leaving office they submitted & published a great list of honours but his name was not included. How could I explain my action if many weeks afterwards, I advised the King to take a view of his career which Ld. Curzon's friends had refused to take? And this consideration gathers force from the fact that my political friends have not always viewed with sympathy the methods & actions of Lord Curzon although we all respect his devotion to the public service and the industry & ability he has exhibited. I wish I could have received the idea in a more agreeable way. . . .[54]

It was C.B.'s normal practice to refer to political colleagues as 'friends', but on this occasion the description of Balfour and Brodrick as Lord Curzon's 'friends' could hardly have been intended to be free from irony.

Knollys replied: 'H.M. desires me to say that though he is sorry you do not feel yourself at liberty to recommend Ld. Curzon for that dignity, he is able to enter into your arguments and to recognise your position. . . .'[55]

Curzon was outraged by the arguments advanced in the letters both C.B. and Morley had sent to Knollys, which he described as 'preposterous and disingenuous',[56] and appealed to the King. The King tried again with C.B., who was not inclined to budge. He agreed to see Curzon, however, but the interview cannot have been a very amiable one, and after it C.B. sent Curzon a pretty categoric letter, saying bluntly, 'I do not expect to find it my duty, in the circumstances, to advise His Majesty to raise you to the British peerage in recognition of your services in India. I fully appreciate the necessity you were under of ascertaining from me what the decision was.'[57]

This was still not the end of the story. Over a year later Morley wrote two letters raising the question again.[58] C.B., who must by now have become both bored and irritated with this undignified agitation for a coronet, would have none of it.[59] Curzon never forgave C.B., and his decision to stand against him in the 1908 election for the Rectorship of Glasgow University appears to have been taken out of pure spite.[60] Here again he was to be frustrated, for C.B. died before the election.

CHAPTER 38

The Final Year in Downing Street

A<small>T</small> the beginning of 1907 C.B. was riding high. He was described by T. P. O'Connor as 'personally, as well as officially, the great outstanding personality of the . . . Ministry, dwarfing and submerging all the others'.[1] The Conservatives were in disarray. Leo Maxse, a militant right-winger, editor of the *National Review*, wrote to Bonar Law about Balfour, 'who has fallen into complete disrepute outside the House of Commons', saying that he 'is utterly discredited – that is the A.B.C. and the X.Y.Z. of the political situation'.[2]

C.B. spent January at Belmont. Old friends like the Sinclairs and the Buchanans came to stay, shot his pheasants, and played billiards. Asquith came to lunch and dine on the 12th and John Burns for two nights. On the 25th C.B. was given the freedom of the City of Glasgow. He was greatly touched by this tribute from his native city. In his speech of thanks he said:

> I occupy, it is true, the most conspicuous and, it may be, the most powerful office under the Crown, but I am profoundly conscious that I owe this exalted position not to any merits or qualifications of mine, but, in the first place, to the grace of the Sovereign; in the second place to the uniform confidence towards me of the House of Commons, in which I have passed the greater part of my life – and last, but not least – do not let me forget it – to the fidelity and favour of my political friends throughout the country.

He went on to say something about the problems of life in the great cities:

the concentration of human beings in towns . . . is contrary to
nature, and . . . this abnormal existence is bound to issue in suffering,
deterioration, and gradual destruction to the mass of the population
. . . countless thousands of our fellow-men, and a still larger
number of children . . . are starved of air and space and sunshine.
. . . This view of city life, which is gradually coming home to the
heart and the understanding and the conscience of our people, is so
terrible that it cannot be put away. What is all our wealth and
learning and the fine flower of our civilisation and our Constitution and our political theories – what are all these but dust and
ashes, if the men and women, on whose labour the whole social
fabric is maintained, are doomed to live and die in darkness and
misery in the recesses of our great cities? We may undertake
expeditions on behalf of oppressed tribes and races, we may conduct
foreign missions, we may sympathise with the cause of unfortunate
nationalities; but it is our own people, surely, who have the first
claim upon us . . . the air must be purified . . . the sunshine must be
allowed to stream in, the water and the food must be kept pure and
unadulterated, the streets light and clean . . . the measure of your
success in bringing these things to pass will be the measure of the
arresting of the terrible powers of race degeneration which is going
on in the countless sunless streets. . . .[3]

Here in his birthplace, C.B., in his old age, had sounded a warning
about those problems of man and nature, of the environment around
us, which were so greatly to exercise succeeding generations.
Vaughan Nash wrote to Ponsonby on January 27:

Glasgow was a tremendous success & it has freshened the P.M.
up and brought him up to his best Downing Street form which he
had fallen away from pretty badly before. . . . The stay at the
Lord Provost's was most successful – nice, simple, warm-hearted
people who did it to perfection. . . .[4]

During the last days of December and the greater part of January,
while he was at Belmont, C.B.'s main preoccupation had been the
Cabinet reshuffle. Now that Bryce had been chosen for Washington,
someone had to be found for Ireland and, though Morley had been
persuaded to stay, there was a vacancy in the Cabinet, for which the
strongest contenders were McKenna, Churchill and Loulou Harcourt.

There was also an Under-Secretaryship vacant at the India Office, as J. E. Ellis had resigned because of ill-health.

C.B.'s first thought was to send Loulou to Ireland, but Loulou showed no enthusiasm for this. C.B. then offered the post to Birrell, judging no doubt that he might welcome a change now that his Education Bill was dead. Birrell had guessed that this might happen. He later described how the offer was made, mentioning a colleague who was clearly Shaw, the Lord Advocate for Scotland, a close friend of C.B.'s, but one to whose faults he was alive, and probably the colleague whom he described to Asquith as being, too often, 'Maximus in minimis, minimus in maximis':[5]

> C.B., always the frankest of men, at once confirmed my suspicions by telling me that he wanted me to go to Ireland. I instantly demurred to the proposal and indicated that it was not at all to my mind. 'Of course it is not,' said C.B., 'but tell me, if it is not you, who is it to be?'
>
> I had my answer ready, and named a colleague who I had reason to believe would not be unacceptable to our Irish friends, and of whose energy and ability there could be no question. 'Good gracious,' replied C.B., 'why "Tommy" is a great friend of mine.' I answered this with as much hauteur as I ever have been able to command in the crises of life. 'I hoped I was also one of your friends.' C.B. laughed heartily, and assured me that he meant no more but that 'Tommy', being a particular friend of his, he knew that as a lawyer his ambitions lay in the direction of his own profession.
>
> I confess, when I heard this, I thought somewhat ruefully of the years between 1873 and 1906 spent by me in daily attendance at No 3 New Square, Lincoln's Inn, studying and practising, both in stuff and silk, the mysteries of an Equitable Jurisprudence. Was I not a lawyer? Had I no right to be mildly ambitous in the direction of my profession? However, I had the good sense to perceive that this was not an occasion to enlighten the ignorance of my chief or to try to excite his interest in my biography, so after a few further protestations I accepted the office. . . .[6]

Here then was one post settled, and the Education Office was vacant. For this C.B. thought of either Churchill or McKenna. He put the pros and cons of each in a letter to Birrell on Christmas Day:

McK. would be safe & sober, hard-working, conciliatory, having a strong claim from years of useful work in Opposition, having proved himself (George Murray says) the best of all recent holders of his present place. . . . But he has small personal prestige and has no standing in the public eye.

W's promotion would be what the public might expect, and what the Press is already booming; he has done brilliantly where he is, and is full of go and ebullient ambition. But he is only a Liberal of yesterday, his tomorrow being a little doubtful, – and, after all, I can *with a stretch* allow the excuse made for giving full pay to an eleventh hour workman, on the other hand I do not imagine that the husbandman ever thought of giving the part of foreman to one of those who had been sowing tares among his wheat. Also, wholly ignorant of and indifferent to the subject. . . . Further, anxious at all hazards to make a splash. . . .[7]

Morley wanted Buchanan, C.B.'s friend, to be moved from the War Office to help him at the India Office. Mindful now of Morley's sensitivities, C.B. wrote to him at the end of December setting out the possibilities. By this time he was inclined to have doubts about Churchill for Education. Nash wrote to Ponsonby on New Year's Day, 1907, saying: 'I don't think Winston is any longer in the running for Education.'[8] Churchill's prospects receded even further when C.B. received Morley's reply, in which he said:

January 1. 1907   India Office
Secretissimus   Whitehall
My dear C.B.,

. . . I should say that the Bd. of Edn. is literally the only post in the Govmt. (save the Woolsack) for which C. is essentially unfit and even unthinkable. Your summary of the *pros* and *cons* is really conclusive, and (with a little discreet pruning) might be made to appear so even to C. himself. . . . The idea of him as umpire between Church and Chapel, and haggling over Syllabuses with the Abp. and Dr. Clifford, would be both ridiculous and a *scandal*.

Of McK. I don't know much. . . . His ally, friend, and inspirer in general politics, is Spender. . . Is it out of the question to send Loulou to Edn.? He is the only man I know of, on whom you could count in cabinet. There are a good many flaws in his character, but he would undoubtedly be 'Voster homo' in every sense; and he would do something to soften the sourness of the Edn. row, if it can be softened. Pray, don't make your cabinet larger, whatever else you do.... Ever Yr. J.M.[9]

Two days later Morley wrote again:

... *Winston* sent in word to see me.... He ... said ... that he would cheerfully acquiesce in being left where he was if you thought it best.... I said, 'Do you authorise me to talk to the P.M. so?' He replied: 'I not only authorise but I should be extremely obliged. The tension is rather severe....' I told him frankly that *I* thought that he was not fit for Edn. Rather ruefully, he thought I might be right.

He mentioned that 2 *under* places would be vacated, whatever happened, and hinted that the appointment to one of them of *Jack Seely*, would be to himself, Winston, a considerable consolation ....[10]

Jack Seely had crossed the floor with Churchill. He had been in the South African War, where he had shown great courage and was described as going 'into a blue passion if you talk to him about farm burning'. He had in fact refused point-blank to burn down a farm when ordered to do so. In his absence he was elected M.P. for the Isle of Wight, 'owing', as it was said, 'to the address of his beautiful young wife who simply asked the electors to understand how anxious she was for the election of her husband who was absent at the war'.[11]

Meanwhile C.B. had made another offer to Loulou, this time of the Education Office: Loulou replied:

I have never studied nor understood the Education question at all: I never comprehended the Bill of last year or even listened to the debates and I do not understand at all the local school questions ... and I detest all the distinctions of creeds.... What I value most of all is your desire to have me in the Cabinet ... But I am not 'a young man in a hurry'....[12]

Since Loulou had cried off, and C.B. believed that Churchill's appointment 'would cause great disappointment among the real stalwarts',[13] he decided on McKenna, telling Asquith that he had 'nearly all the qualities – in fact all save notoriety, and that is better absent'.[14]

On the 24th one Goddard wrote out of the blue to C.B. asking for the post of Financial Secretary to the Treasury and adding that he was 'very willing to serve'.[15]

Esher, as always, had heard all about these moves before they were announced, and told his son on January 9: 'The P.M. won't hear of Winston being in the Cabinet at present. He is, like Mr. G., old fashioned and disapproves of young men in a hurry.'[16]

On January 22 C.B. wrote to the young man in question asking him to stay on at the Colonial Office,[17] and Churchill made no difficulties.

Next day there was another effort by Morley to kick over the traces. This time he was sulking because C.B. had decided not to move Buchanan from the War Office but to give him Mr. Charles Hobhouse as Under-Secretary. C.B.'s reasons had been explained in a letter to George Whiteley: 'Buchanan is almost alone in resisting re-action, extravagance & folly in the W.O. Administration, and is much more useful there than in the I.O.'[18]

C.B. added a postscript to the letter he was writing to Sinclair on the 27th, saying: 'J.M. has just tendered to me his resignation!!!'[19] Three days later he again wrote to Sinclair, saying:

> J.M. is bent on retiring. Cannot face labour of Indian problems which are in near future without Buchanan.
>
> I fear partly petulance at not getting the man he wanted, partly consciousness of the big things he has to settle.
>
> Can we afford to let him go out of the Cabinet? Whiteley says he is no use in H. of C. or on platform. But his name is an asset, and he is sound in the Cabinet. . . . I am writing to ask him would it ease matters if he went to the Lords. . . .[20]

Once again it all blew over. Morley remained a member of the Government until he resigned in 1914, and did not go to the Lords until after C.B.'s death. He finally got Buchanan as his Under-Secretary after C.B.'s death in April 1908, and wrote of him to Minto: 'He has been an intimate of C.B.'s and is of the same type in some ways – only more educated: Balliol, First Class, Fellow of All Souls: unselfish, loyal, plain, assiduous.'[21]

So, with a reconstituted administration, C.B. was able to return to the routine of government business. Goldwin Smith, who had grown conservative in his old age, wrote on February 18 to Merriman in South Africa:

Campbell-Bannerman . . . is personally popular and shows great tact in keeping up the ostensible union of his motley host, but he is far from being a ruler of men or capable of grappling with a desperately difficult situation. He is evidently going to concede prospective Home Rule, which means dismemberment, besides a set of socialistic measures, and what you agree with me in abhorring, Woman Suffrage. This will amount to a revolution.[22]

The question of the Channel Tunnel came up again. Knollys had written to C.B. in January, saying that the King hoped 'that you are not now in favour of the Channel Tunnel scheme'.[23] C.B. replied, saying:

For myself I have never thought much of the so-called military objections or seen actual danger in the proposed tunnel; but undoubtedly it would cause great uneasiness and might lead to panics, and that is quite reason enough for hesitating to sanction it. Besides, I doubt its commercial advantages to this country.[24]

The Cabinet endorsed this view. C.B. made a statement on March 21 saying that the Government were against the tunnel as it seemed to offer few advantages and 'there would be a constant feeling of insecurity leading to constant demands for increased military and naval expenditure'. It would be better to consider alternatives 'such as a ferry'.[25]

A row blew up in the House about the New Hebrides Labour Ordinance, which the Conservatives claimed was on the same footing as Chinese labour. C.B., never a man for mastery of detail, admitted that he had not read the blue book on the New Hebrides, which was honest, if it was nothing else. His colleagues did not give him much help. Austen Chamberlain wrote in his diary: 'Winston was flippant and thin: Grey was grave but very weak; and C.B. was pitiable.'[26]

In March Loulou was brought into the Cabinet, keeping his job at the Office of Works as he wished. He wrote to C.B. expressing his deep gratitude, adding: 'there is nothing left for me to desire. I wish my dear father could have *seen* it – as I have not the least doubt that he *knows* it.'[27]

Once again Churchill was passed over.

In March, too, a new and harsh voice was heard from the Conservative benches in the House. In a combative speech, Bonar Law warned the Government that they would not be allowed to forget

Chinese labour and accused them of gerrymandering the Transvaal Constitution to bribe the Boers. C.B. indignantly repudiated this charge.[28]

C.B. still held a commanding position in the House, and no one now talked of his going to join Rosebery in the Lords. Rosebery, now entering the long, sad twilight of his life, addressed this month what was left of the Liberal League, said that he owed the Government 'neither allegiance nor confidence – perhaps not even the common courtesies of life', commended the work of those members of it who were vice-presidents of the League, expressed alarm that the Liberal Party might be connected with hostility to property, and then, typically, described his own intervention as 'the croaking of a retired raven on a withered branch'.[29] A journalist at the time remarked on Rosebery's obvious personal antipathy for the Prime Minister, and reflected how odd it was that C.B., genial, courteous and entertaining, seemed to have the capacity of arousing a feeling of animosity in political opponents – 'Rosebery has this one link in common with the Leader of the Opposition. He can't abear "C.-B." '[30]

As Prime Minister, C.B. had to adjudicate in a row between Fisher, who was resolved to scrap the obsolete ships showing the flag in many parts of the world and to concentrate on the fighting fleet at home, and the Foreign and Colonial Offices, which wanted to retain them. C.B. ruled in favour of Fisher.[31]

One night the Courtneys had him to dinner with J. A. Hobson and Bertrand Russell. Kate Courtney recorded that it 'went well & would have gone better if the P.M. had not had to come in his Court dress & absurdly tight it was so that he could hardly sit down or turn his head....'[32]

At Easter he went for a few days to stay with Lord Rendel at Cannes, gossiping in the sun and driving over one day to see his old stricken friend Spencer. When he got back, Ponsonby told Bryce: 'The P.M. is never improved by a holiday but ... as soon as he gets to work again he will be as active & alert as ever. He deludes one sometimes by apparently letting things slide & then at the last moment when the drifting looks dangerous he gives a lurch which sends the boat on the course which he always intended it to take.'[33]

In April the Colonial Prime Ministers arrived in London for a Colonial Conference. There were then only eight self-governing countries in the Empire – Great Britain, Australia, Canada, New Zealand, Cape Colony, Natal, the Transvaal and Newfoundland – compared with more than thirty at latter-day Commonwealth Conferences. Besides Botha, Dr. Jameson turned up again, this time as Prime Minister of Cape Colony. C.B. opened the conference with an address of welcome. The King commented to the Prince of Wales: 'I quite agree with you that the P. Minister's speech . . . was a very good one and the allusion to Chamberlain was a happy thought.'[34]

Ponsonby wrote to his wife a few days later: 'We had Andrew Carnegie at luncheon. Such a funny little manny, wildly keen and enthusiastic, waving his napkin over his head, tremendously but amusingly flattering to C.B. Full of curious rather elementary & childish international ideas. . . .'[35]

London society liked to sneer at the Prime Minister of an administration it detested. On April 17 the Prince of Wales gave a dinner for the Prime Ministers at Marlborough House. Austen Chamberlain told his wife a story which was going the rounds about Lady Derby when she attended this dinner.

'Who', she asked of Sir Wilfred Laurier, the Canadian Prime Minister, 'is the pleasant-looking gentleman next Lady Laurier, who is enjoying his dinner so much?'

'That,' replied Sir Wilfred, 'is *your* Prime Minister.'[36]

On April 12 C.B. was back in Parliament after the Easter recess. But he was getting to be an old man now. One member wrote of 'his voice thick and muffled, his speech halting and unready, and the copious notes of his admirably constructed sentences . . . held by a tremulous hand almost within smelling distance of his nose'.[37]

He introduced a proposed new standing order on procedure. It was all very cosy and good-tempered. Balfour appealed 'to the Prime Minister, sitting in discreet immobility, like Aaron, between two supporters'. C.B. intervened to say that Balfour must mean Solomon, as Aaron was 'not the man in the centre on that occasion'. He chided the House for having spent three days over seven lines of an amendment.[38]

But the main issue in domestic politics, now that the Education Bill had been killed, was land reform. In November 1905, C.B. had talked of the need to set about 'colonising our own country'.[39] His Government introduced four land Bills in 1907 for England, Scotland and Ireland. He wanted to do something for the agricultural labourers and small tenants. Carrington, the Minister of Agriculture, believed strongly in land reform and had divided up his own estate into small holdings.[40] On April 20 C.B. spoke at a great luncheon, attended by ninety-nine M.P.s, in response to the toast 'Land Reform'. He said that he and his colleagues were not extreme revolutionaries, though they did not shrink from formidable changes. The depopulation of the country-side must be arrested. The number of farm workers had decreased by 30 per cent in twenty years. He urged that the strong demand for small holdings throughout the country should be met. If it were, 'the young men and the best men in the villages, instead of setting their faces in despair towards the town, would be glad to remain at home'. Compulsory powers would be necessary, but the Government did not mean to steal anyone's property.[41]

Later, in the House, he said that our land system was unique. He was not blind to its merits, but for the tillers of the soil it was not a success, and the young and vigorous were leaving the land. He hoped that the Government's legislation would re-create self-reliance and enterprise.[42]

He was right about the problem, but the solution he proposed was not, unfortunately, realistic. He had in mind the yeoman or Scottish crofter, and he would have liked to see that admirable type spread through the country. But economics were against him. The trend was, inexorably, towards larger farms and a smaller population in the countryside. There was a strong social side to his argument. He wanted to extend the independence of the smallholder, as opposed to the agricultural labourer dependent on a landlord, whose interests might be more in shooting and hunting than in farming. But the landlord was equally on the way out. On this issue C.B. was like Canute, trying vainly to push back an economic tide that was creeping up the beach.

On May 9 he was in Manchester, and spoke for an hour at a Liberal banquet, wearing the red sash of the Bath. He was described by the press as alert, vivacious and robust.[43] He denounced the efforts Balfour had made to turn the Colonial Conference into a manifesto for tariff reform, affirmed his faith in Free Trade, spoke with pride of the settlement in South Africa and attacked the House of Lords. The *Manchester Guardian* used the occasion to applaud the wisdom of generosity in politics, in words which got to the heart of C.B.'s philosophy. Having spoken of the Transvaal settlement, the paper said:

> Even if the Liberal Government did nothing else, it would be remembered for having thus triumphantly re-delivered English politics from the obsession of cynical materialism, that 'ancient

blasphemy', as the Premier said last night, of exclusive belief in the uses of force. . . .

It is no part, however, of the Government's intention to limit to the Transvaal the renewed application of the principle by which our colonial Empire has grown and gained health. Why, as the Premier asked last night, leave Ireland untouched by the spell that has transformed the Transvaal into a united community? And why not make the corresponding appeal to the undeveloped powers of our own landless labourers on the land? Everywhere the cynic's answer . . . is that it is not safe. . . . Well, some millions of English people have of late seen and heard General Botha. . . . And what do they think of it all? Do they think General Botha receiving the freedom of Manchester or a little crowd of Irish villagers having their heads broken by armed policemen is the pleasanter spectacle. . . . The one result is as natural as the other. Hate and fear and distrust people, and they will earn your fear and ill-will; trust them, and they will earn your trust too. It will always stand to Sir Henry Campbell-Bannerman's credit that in days of extraordinary difficulty and at the cost of violent though passing obloquy to himself he brought this central princple of the English art of government out of eclipse into the light again.[44]

A Prime Minister deals with a rapid succession of problems, some of great importance, some trivial. C.B. returned from Manchester to find a letter from Lady Aberdeen at Vice-Regal Lodge in Dublin, saying: 'We are in despair here at the proposal that Their Majesties should come *here* for one night & stay on their yacht the second. . . . I know full well the King cannot abide me, although he tolerates A.'[45]

At this stage things were not going quite so well for the Government. Their Irish legislation, which has been described in an earlier chapter, had run into the sand, and cattle-driving and outrages were spreading widely in Ireland. The Colonial Conference had given a shot in the arm to the tariff reformers, the suffragettes were a continuing irritant, and at a by-election in Wimbledon Henry Chaplin, that pillar of English conservatism and of the legendary 'Merrie England' of farming and hunting the fox, defeated a young Liberal supporter of votes for women, Mr. Bertrand Russell.

June came and once more brought complaints from Morley, this time because he imagined that a recommendation he had made for a K.C.B. had been ignored. Ponsonby wrote to him saying that C.B.

had at once added the name to the list and added: '. . . after seeing you I cannot help most deeply deploring your entire misconception of the Prime Minister's attitude towards you which I know from close intimacy with him to be one of gratitude and affection.'[46]

This was just the balm which the prickly Morley needed and he replied at once:

> I owe you a real debt for what you have told me about the feelings of your Chief towards a certain person. It clears altogether away some hazy clouds or vapours that occasionally interpose themselves in my mind – when I'm in a humour to have the black dog on my back. The said black dog shall never again emerge from his kennel in respect of the P.M. So you have played a downright good part, and I thank you de tout mon cœur. . . .[47]

C.B. kept only a general overseeing eye on the administration. Occasionally he administered a reproof, for example: 'We look to the Board of Education for a high example in graceful and intelligible language. How elegant are these: "Non provided Schools", "facilities instruction". H. C.-B.'[48]

On June 22 Lady Monkswell saw him at a garden party at Windsor 'looking very old & sad & solemn'.[49] Ponsonby wrote to his wife: 'Rather crucial Cabinet over Ireland. People losing their head except C.B. who is as calm & cool and sane as he can be.'[50]

Philip Snowden left a picture of C.B. as he saw him in the House from the Labour benches:

> I always thought that 'C.-B.' was the very type of what one would expect the Prime Minister to be. In personal appearance he was the sort of man one would like to have for a grandfather or an uncle. He had the faculty of commanding personal affection. He was not brilliant in debate, but he was always effective. He often succeeded in extricating the Government from a difficult situation by simple tact, common sense and humour where a mere genius would have utterly failed. His own personal sentiments were, I believe, very democratic; but he recognised that he was the leader of a very heterogeneous collection of political atoms. He would have gone further if he could have been sure of carrying his Government with him. His sympathy with and his encouraging attitude to the Woman Suffrage question is one

instance of how he was, through the restrictions of his position, prevented from following his own inclinations. The Labour Party in Parliament had every reason to be grateful to him. . . .[51]

There were the usual crop of minor difficulties. Lord Portsmouth, an Under-Secretary in the Government, had trouble with his tenants. Ponsonby told C.B. and had to help sort it out, telling his wife: 'of course Ld P is a regular tory landlord a privileged capitalist at heart & a buffoon and a poop to deal with besides being a grotesque clown to look at . . .'[52] Then there was a row because performances of *The Mikado* were stopped during the visit of a Japanese prince.

In June Morley had been thinking yet again of running out. In a postscript to a letter to C.B. on the 10th he wrote: 'N.B. My contract time is up, and I am practising a beautiful psalm of "Nunc Dimittis" for, say, August 12.'[53] Once more C.B. talked him out of it, but perhaps in doing so he displayed symptoms of irritation, for ten days later Morley was writing sulkily: 'There is no chance of my being ready to speak. You sent me to the Ganges and Brahmaputra, and I stick to the business of my department. I am sorry, as I told you the other night, to be so little use to you, but so it is.'[54]

It was not only John Morley who was inclined to be restive. In Wales there was some impatience because nothing had yet been done about the disestablishment of the Church. Lloyd George went down to Pontypridd to rally support for C.B. once more, as only he could:

As a Welshman, I appeal to Welshmen to give him a chance ['clywch, clywch', and loud applause]. If he fails, very well, try another. But I tell you frankly, and I have had seventeen years of very intimate acquaintance with public life . . . that I cannot see another man who can serve the people as Sir Henry Campbell-Bannerman can [loud applause].[55]

On July 20 C.B. and McKenna received a deputation of Bishops, Peers and others on the Education Bill, led by the Archbishop. The report of this suggests that C.B. was becoming a little weary of this acrimonious dispute: 'The Prime Minister wound up the interview by declaring that these complicated questions could be settled by the reciprocal application of a little common sense.'[56]

In August, Rosebery, giving freer and freer rein to his essentially conservative instincts, delivered a slashing attack on the Government's Scottish Small Holdings Bill. Almeric Fitzroy noted that the 'contemptuous tone of his references to the Secretary for Scotland indicated the measure of his esteem for that amiable henchman of the Prime Minister'.[57] C.B. reacted calmly and wrote to Robertson: 'We think we are doing very well here. We shall pass a lot of good Bills. The Scotch Land Bill is a great stumbling block and rock of offence to the Tories, and even more to the Lib. Imps., who still rear their head now and then!'[58]

The Roseberyites had a final fling on this Bill. Haldane claimed that Sinclair had disregarded the whole body of non-political and expert opinion in Scotland, and told Fitzroy that he 'attributed a great deal of the mischief to a Prime Minister who persistently cuts himself off from contact with the forces it is his business to guide and control'.[59] Next day C.B. in the House asked who was to control legislation for Scotland – the Scottish representatives, or the Peers and a small section of the Commons? The issue raised was the control of Scottish affairs and on that the Government had no doubt of their course. Haldane, however, claimed that half the Cabinet were against the measure and that only Sinclair and C.B. himself were wholeheartedly for it. A few days later Fitzroy heard from McKenna that the Cabinet had accepted the Bill without enquiry, 'on the strength of Sinclair's assurance that all Scotland wanted it'. He commented:

> This, taken in connection with Haldane's statement last week, clearly discloses the parentage of the measure, for the assurances of a young and inexperienced Minister like Sinclair would not have been so readily accepted had they not received all the backing which the Prime Minister could give, while his disinclination to tackle any problem thoroughly reduces his authority on such a point to the level of Sinclair's.[60]

The Bill sought only to extend the established crofter system to the Lowlands, and was the type of measure which C.B. very much approved, but he had perhaps underestimated the opposition of Scottish landowners to a measure which sought to give compulsory powers to 'agricultural commissioners' and provided for judicial 'fair rents' on the Irish pattern. There was powerful opposition to this attempt to increase the number of small independent farmers by the use of coercive powers and the legislation was destroyed by the Lords.

C.B. must perhaps have wondered if he would not have done best to stick to his original idea of making Sinclair Chief Whip rather than Scottish Secretary. Nevertheless at the end of the Session the Government's position was still strong, the Opposition still in disarray, and C.B.'s own position stronger than ever. Morley, now restored to equanimity, wrote to Minto in Delhi:

> Our majority has stood firm as a rock. . . . We have rather broken our knees over the Irish Council Bill and the Scottish Land Bill, but the fracture does not seem to be particularly painful. The H. of L. has done us the service of giving us something to swear at and swear by. . . . There is no chance of a general election for a couple of years, as I think, for the only thing that could precipitate one earlier would be the withdrawal of the Prime Minister, and I am glad to say that he is in better condition every day.[61]

C.B. was given a private dinner at the Reform Club by some Peers and M.P.s. Asquith made an impromptu speech testifying to the absolute unanimity of the Cabinet, and their unqualified trust in, and personal affection for, their leader.[62] Henry Lucy noted this month that there was no doubt that C.B. was 'in fact as well as in name the head of the Cabinet . . . master of the varying situation . . . his predominance based upon esteem and affection rather than any principle of discipline'.[63]

In August C.B. was in touch with Knollys and with his colleagues about the decision of the Transvaal Government, under Botha, to present the Cullinan diamond to the King. There was a great to-do about whether it ought to be accepted, in view of the fact that the English Progressive Party in South Africa had voted against the gift, and that a large British loan to the Transvaal was pending. The Cabinet took rather a feeble line. C.B. told Knollys on August 21:

> This question of the big diamond is an extremely awkward one. The Boers are a touchy and imaginative people. They have made the offer in token of real honest goodwill and loyalty, and they may be sorely offended by refusal.
>
> At the same time the idea is not *at all* liked here, especially at a moment when they are requiring a loan. . . .
>
> The Cabinet . . . concluded that it was only H.M.'s well known tact, & right & prudent instincts, that could find a way out.[64]

Responsibility was being ducked. Selborne strongly advised acceptance, arguing that he believed it to 'be intended by General Botha as an unmistakeable sign . . . that he and his friends have accepted incorporation into Your Majesty's dominions and the British Flag once and for ever', and that refusal would be 'nothing less than a calamity'.[65] His advice was accepted, Churchill commenting to C.B.: 'It is remarkable that Selborne should agree with Botha & not with his old friends the Progressives.'[66]

Now that he was alone, C.B. had no wish to go any more to Marienbad, but went up to Belmont on August 29. Next day, the anniversary of Charlotte's death, he noted simply in his diary: 'Dies illa Lacrymabilis'.[67] He never got over her loss. One day, after he had been cheerfully discussing political problems with his Belmont neighbours, Ponsonby took him some letters, after they had gone and he was alone in his study, and found him with his head bent down on his desk, sobbing.[68] He was at Belmont throughout August, and at the end of the month stayed for a few days at Balmoral. On October 6, George Wyndham wrote to Gladstone's daughter, Mary Drew, that all shades of opinion 'seem equally disgusted with things in general, except C.B. He "sits on a stile & continues to smile".'[69]

In October C.B. began the autumn campaign with a major speech at Edinburgh on the 5th and another at Dunfermline on the 22nd. Rosebery wrote to the Duke of Devonshire, saying: 'My impression is that the P.M.'s Edinburgh speech (which I have not heard) has fallen very flat. . . .'[70] On November 2 C.B. was back at Downing Street. He approved the idea of an official secrets bill, drafted by Esher, but this was later dropped owing to representations from the press.[71]

Early in November Lloyd George, by the exercise of his gifts of persuasion, had managed to settle a serious railway dispute which had looked certain to lead to a long and bitter strike. C.B. sent the King a memorandum by Lloyd George on the settlement, adding himself: 'the country is largely indebted for so blessed a conclusion of a time of great anxiety and danger to the knowledge, skill, astuteness and tact of the President of the Board of Trade and those around him in his Department'.[72] The King was constantly complaining about Lloyd George's attacks on the House of Lords. Here was an opportunity to put to the King the other side of the coin, and C.B. took it at once. He told Lord Rendel that Lloyd George was admirable in his management of his Department and his Bills, a first-rate negotiator, with a very clear head and persuasive and conciliatory ways, but that he made too many speeches in which he used unguarded expressions.[73]

On Saturday, November 9, C.B. spoke at the Lord Mayor's Banquet at the Guildhall. He was preceded by his friend Fisher, who took the opportunity to pour scorn on the critics of naval policy, saying that the fleet was *nulli secundus* and that he could say to his countrymen, 'Sleep quiet in your beds'; and by General the Hon. Sir Neville Lyttelton, who, *The Times* said, was 'indistinctly heard'.[74]

C.B. himself began by saying that 'we are entitled to congratulate ourselves . . . on our escape from the national catastrophe of a railway strike . . . the loss to the public at any rate would have been without any compensation, while a blow might have been dealt at the trade of this country under which it would have reeled for years'. It seems a far-distant time when a Prime Minister of Great Britain could talk in these terms of a strike threat. He paid a tribute to Lloyd George, who had brought 'to bear on the situation, which indeed at one time appeared to be almost intractable, his great gifts of unconquerable hopefulness, of unfailing courage, and of alert diplomacy'.

He then turned to the traditional review of foreign affairs which a Prime Minister has to make at the Lord Mayor's Banquet, speaking of the Hague Conference, the Anglo-Russian Treaty, India, the Congo and the forthcoming visit of the Kaiser. Typically, as he ploughed through his Foreign Office brief, he apologized to his audience 'for taking up one after another matters so dry and tedious'.[75]

Esher noted a detail about this speech in his journal a week later:

. . . Morley told me that in the passage of C-B's speech at the Guild Hall which referred to India, and which Morley drafted, he had used the word 'stern', qualifying attitude or language. C-B altered no word in the draft except that one, for which he substituted 'firm'. When asked by J.M. for reasons, he said 'Firm is a word of principle. Stern is a word of passion.' This discrimination and the literary neatness are strange coming from C-B.[76]

Four days later, on November 13, C.B. was at Bristol, speaking at the Colston banquet. This was essentially a party speech. It was on the eve of a Unionist Convention at Birmingham, and he painted an entertaining picture of Balfour travelling to a Midland Canossa to make his submission to Chamberlain before emerging 'as an honest protectionist – positive, settled, full-blooded and aggressive'. He again attacked the House of Lords, saying:

> Do not take my word for it. I will give you the words of another. This is what has been said: – 'The House of Lords for over 100 years has never contributed one iota to popular liberties or popular freedom, or done anything to advance the common weal; and during that time it has protected every abuse and sheltered every privilege.'

He pleased his audience by telling them that these were the words of Joseph Chamberlain: 'They may be an extreme way of putting the matter [a voice, "He was in his right mind then"] with which I should not care to identify myself, but they roughly represent the truth.'

Finally he had a word to say about the 'Socialist dragon':

> I should have thought that if there was one country in the world where property was more secure than another, it was this country . . . because it is a country in which men's hearts have neither been wholly spoilt by social wrong nor wholly hardened by wealth out of all responsiveness to social obligations. Therefore, it is a country with the will and capacity to move quietly and steadily forward along the path of social reform towards a fairer and more enlightened common life, free from the disgrace of the existence of unnecessary and unmerited misery and poverty.[77]

He had to contend with interruptions from the suffragettes, and at the end of the evening he looked pale and tired. But little did anyone who heard his closing words imagine that they were listening to C.B.'s last platform speech, or that the speaker would be dead in five months.

Part 9

The Break-up

CHAPTER 39

The Last Illness

C.B.'s Bristol speech followed a period of intense activity. He had spoken at the Guildhall on the 9th, the Kaiser arrived for a state visit on the 11th, and for the next three days C.B. had to go up and down to Windsor for the ceremonies of his reception. On the 12th there was a Cabinet, an audience with the King, and a state banquet, followed by a reception, for which he had to wear uniform. On the 13th there was a luncheon for the Kaiser at Guildhall, and C.B. had then to dash off to Bristol, with another major speech to make. It would have been a strenuous programme for a young, fit man. For an ailing man of seventy-one it was too much. Nemesis came on the night of the 13th. Next day Nash wrote to Ponsonby:

> It was the very devil last night – the old story but very much more stubborn. Happily the attack came on before we had all gone to sleep & the sound of his bell soon brought him help such as it was ... it seemed an age before the doctor came. They sent a motor for him. He was rather unnerved . . . but . . . his remedies – ether & hypodermic injections of strychnine brought him round the turning point. But it was touch & go. . . . He will . . . I hope refuse ever to take any more big meetings. He must be content with dinner audiences. . . .[1]

C.B. had never been as robust as he looked. He was constantly confined to bed or to his house by colds, chills and influenza. In 1889 he had trouble with a lung and described himself ruefully as in 'a pretty condition for a Gladstonian separatist in these days of active warfare!'[2] When, after becoming Prime Minister, he visited Dunfermline, someone remarked that he looked just like his father. 'Ah,' said

C.B., 'I know it. One of my sayings when I do not feel well is, "I have seen my father in the looking glass this morning." ' And then he added in a subdued voice: 'I really do not feel very well.'[3]

1906 was a grim year, with constant vigils during Charlotte's last illness, and C.B. had a heart attack at Belmont early in October. The doctor from Alyth thought then that his attack had been brought on by the emotional strain of Charlotte's death.[4] In a day or two C.B. was better and he made a rapid recovery, despite the ministrations of Mrs. Campbell who, according to Nash, 'does rattle & shriek rather more than is good for the P.M.'.[5]

Just under nine months later, in June 1907, C.B. had another attack and his regular London doctor, Robert Burnet, wrote to Ponsonby, saying: 'His social engagements must be limited.'[6] This very necessary advice was not taken. After the Windsor reception for the Kaiser C.B. told his secretary, as he unbuckled his sword-belt and collapsed into a chair: 'I have been standing for two hours. I must have rest.' On November 23 J. A. Spender wrote to Winston Churchill:

> The PM was sharply ill at Bristol – the result of a life disordered by speeches, dinners and Royal junketings, quite unfit for an old gentleman to lead. I am told that the King and the Emperor kept him standing for two hours and a half on end the day before his seizure. Poor old Ripon was so exhausted that he reclined on a table and got Mrs. Sydney Buxton to spread her skirts in front of him . . .[7]

Rest was prescribed, and on November 27, C.B. left for Paris with Ponsonby. They stayed at the Hotel Palais d'Orsay, but here C.B. had yet another heart attack in the early hours. He pulled round rapidly, but it is bizarre that his staff thought it adequate to send the Prime Minister, in his then state of health, to stay in a foreign hotel without his own doctor. On December 1 Ponsonby wrote to his wife:

> It passed off pretty quickly but it showed this time that indigestion had nothing to do with it – it has made him despondent and depressed. If these attacks are going to recur frequently they will wear him out. . . . His head is very clear and he wrote an excellent letter to Knollys about Bishops . . . directly he feels at all better he makes light of everything and jokes. . . .[8]

After five days in Paris, C.B. and his party, now including Dr. Burnet, travelled on to Biarritz.

Meanwhile at home there was speculation about his future. Winston Churchill wrote to his mother from the shores of Lake Victoria: 'I am concerned to read of CB's illness. Such attacks however overcome are vy serious at 72. His removal from the scene would lead to many changes; & I should be sorry to lose a good friend who has always shown me kindness. . . .'[9]

Biarritz in December was not particularly pleasant, and Ponsonby, though agreeable, was no substitute for Charlotte. Even less so were Mrs. Morton Campbell and her son Hugh, who had now joined him. C.B. relaxed, though in those far-off, formal days he and Ponsonby wore top hats when they went out to the cliffs. But, despite visits to Bayonne and San Sebastian and some social activity, boredom overcame him. But he soon began to pick up, and Burnet went back to London on December 6. When, one day, the subject of death duties came up, C.B. remarked: 'People seem to think I am a rich man. I am afraid they will find themselves disappointed. I have tried in my time to do some small service to the State, but it will not be posthumously continued in the shape of excessive death duties.'[10]

Ponsonby had had to go back to London on the 20th and Nash took his place. C.B. was now much better and could give some thought to other people's problems. Just before Christmas he had a letter from Lord Rendel[11] suggesting that something might be done to help Lloyd George financially, and he replied:

> Your generous and kindly thought of some recognition of L. George's merits & services, by provision being made for his children, deserves and will receive the best consideration. It would be necessary to make some enquiries of a delicate kind before making any appeal however confidential: and as Arthur Ponsonby has had to return to London I have entrusted him with this. . . .[12]

Next day Asquith wrote to C.B. saying that Lloyd George had urged a change for the better in the status (and salaries) of the Board of Trade, with more for himself as President. Asquith added that John Burns had got to hear of the request and demanded equal treatment.[13]

At the end of the year Ponsonby wrote a long, frank letter to Knollys about C.B., in which he said:

> He has lost ground considerably during the last two years. The whole year before Lady Campbell-Bannerman died his strength . . .

was overstrained to a degree which was never suspected at the time. It led to an inevitable reaction. . . . Six weeks of complete rest may work wonders as apart from this he is very tough and strong constitutionally . . . the position Sir Henry has made for himself as practically the only man who can keep together our rather unwieldy party, makes even the bare possibility of his relinquishing his post a question of the highest national importance. . . . I sincerely hope that he will have the strength anyhow to see this Parliament out but a man in the position of Prime Minister cannot be effectually safeguarded against moments of strain & excitement. I am glad to say his niece Mrs. Morton Campbell (wife of the Right Hon. J. A. Campbell's son) who now lives with him is a most devoted and watchful companion. . . . I mention this detail as so little is known of Sir Henry's private life and I have had much trouble (unknown to him) during the last eight or ten months in preventing the most absurd and scandalous rumours, invented I suppose by malicious & thoughtless political enemies and without even a vestige of foundation, from appearing in the Press. I expect these rumours must have reached you but I have no doubt they were treated in your entourage with the contempt they deserved.[14]

Knollys replied:

The King . . . learns with the greatest possible regret, both on personal & public grounds, the indifferent account which you give of the state of the Prime Minister's health. . . . H.M. considers that the loss of Sir Henry's services as Prime Minister would be a most serious one, alike to the Crown & to the Country, for, as you say he enjoys a popularity & an influence with his Party to which neither Grey nor Asquith could pretend. . . .

With respect to the reports to which you allude, I heard them frequently during the summer, but I need hardly tell you that I felt certain there was not one word of truth in them & I therefore took it upon myself invariably to contradict them. It was cruel & cowardly to set about these stories so soon after his wife's death to whom everybody knew he was deeply attached. I need hardly say that the King never attached the slightest credence to them. . . .[15]

The rumours to which Ponsonby referred had been circulating in London among those who enjoyed scandalous gossip. People who did not care for C.B. suggested that Mrs. Morton Campbell, his nephew's wife, an Australian, who had come to Belmont after Charlotte's death to act (with indifferent success) as his official hostess, was in reality his mistress. It is not unknown for a twentieth-century Prime Minister to have an illicit liaison. Recent books have described Balfour's relationship with Lady Elcho and Lloyd George's with Frances Stevenson. But in this case the suggestion was wildly improbable. C.B.'s devotion to Charlotte was unqualified. He was sixty-nine when she died and he had a heart attack immediately after she was buried. There is abundant testimony that he never really got over her loss. He was an old man, deprived of his life's companion, in failing health, living in the goldfish bowl of No. 10 and Belmont, surrounded by private secretaries, colleagues and friends. To suggest that in all these circumstances he took his nephew's wife as a mistress is so fanciful as to be absurd.

Another rumour, equally absurd, was that he lived with Miss Thorbjörn, Charlotte's Swedish masseuse, who was at Belmont at the time of her funeral. The gossip reached Miss Thorbjörn herself, who was deeply distressed and, after talking to Nash, wrote to Ponsonby, saying how shocked she had been by the talk.[16]

In fact C.B. had heard the gossip. In a letter Ponsonby wrote to his wife in May 1907, he said: 'It appears that C.B. was very much cut up on Saturday about the Thorbjörn business, but the whole thing will disappear now.'[17]

Nash arrived at Biarritz on December 30, and wrote to Ponsonby: 'there is a wonderful change & his face has almost lost its careworn look'.[18] From Blenheim Lady Randolph Churchill wrote to her son: 'I hear old CB is at Biarritz eating & drinking far too much. I am told that HG will be shunted & that you will be in the Cabinet. I hope so. . . .'[19]

Now that he was feeling better, C.B. had to attend to political problems. This year of 1907, Hilaire Belloc had published his poem about Lord Lundy, whose lamentable political career had compelled his grandfather to declare, as the last of all resorts: 'Go out and govern New South Wales!' C.B. now had in very truth to find a Governor for New South Wales. No doubt he had read the poem. At any rate he suggested to Elgin some of their colleagues who, like Lord Lundy, had been disappointments, among them Lords Burghclere and Portsmouth.[20]

Sinclair complained bitterly to him because Tweedmouth had

attacked the Scottish Land Bill. C.B. replied on New Year's Day:

> I thought your letter to T. about his strange speeches quite excellent. It was pointed, effective, unanswerable, and yet conveyed no offence. . . . I should have thought he had quite troubles enough in Whitehall without boiling any other water. . . . The only politicians in the place are Mr. Gilbert Parker and Mr. Geoffrey Drage . . . they have long conversations with each other which I am glad to say I entirely escape.[21]

Next day Nash wrote to Ponsonby: 'His working powers . . . are improving. . . . We have been bombarded with telegrams about Curzon & Cabinet changes but have taken no notice of any of them.'[22]

C.B. was now in the hands of a Dr. Malpas, who gave him carbolic baths. He took things easily and didn't make an appearance until noon. For the first time he was dictating his correspondence, instead of writing it all in his own firm, round hand. But by January 7 he was feeling better than ever, laughing at the doctors and deciding to stay two days longer in Paris. Nash wrote that day: 'He is quite astonishing & shows no trace whatever of his breakdown.'[23]

On the 9th C.B. had a letter from Grey, written from Fallodon on the last day of 1907:

> I am so glad that you have recovered. My thoughts have often gone back to the days when this Govt. was being formed & I have felt from the early days of this Parliament that all my forecast before the Elections was wrong & that your presence in the House of Commons has been not only desirable but essential to manage this party & keep it together, & so it continues to be . . .[24]

Nash told Ponsonby about this expression of penitence, adding: 'I did what I could to praise Grey for it & I think he appreciates it. I am very glad it has happened.'[25]

C.B. was favourably impressed by a clergyman named Fish, who was doing temporary duty at the British Church, and described him to Ponsonby later as 'un véritable merle blanc'.[26] He asked Higgs a few days before he died not to forget Fish.

Now, however, he began to think about Paris, and, to the consternation of Nash and Mrs. Campbell, appeared to look forward with relish to having talks with large numbers of leading Frenchmen. He consulted Grey and then the Ambassador. Nowadays all this would have been done by private secretaries, but in Edwardian days even Prime Ministers disdained to communicate through intermediaries, and C.B. wrote to the Ambassador himself; saying that he had been invited to a meal, to meet some leading Frenchmen, by Sir Thomas Barclay. He suspected that this might be intended 'ad majorem gloriam Barclayi'.[27] Bertie discouraged the idea, holding that he ought to give any luncheon or dinner at the Embassy, and C.B. replied with disarming but characteristic modesty, abandoning the plan and saying: 'I am really sorry that there should have been so much fuss and so much trouble to you connected with my little passage through Paris, which it would have been my wish to make as innocuous and unobserved as possible.'[28]

The visit to Paris went well enough. He was there for four days, staying at the Hotel Metropolitan, and dining on the 18th with the Gaston de Breteuils. Bertie saw him on the 19th and told Hardinge that C.B. was quite satisfied with his conversations with Pichon and Clemenceau. But he noted that he had a slight sore throat.

C.B. was back in London on the 20th. Two days later he went to his last dinner party, with his old friend Madame Novikoff. But on the 24th he was in bed again with a cold and had to cry off a visit to Windsor. Nevertheless between January 21 and February 12 he took eight meetings of the Cabinet, when the main problems discussed were measures for the new session, Ireland, the Transvaal and the Indian problem, the Naval Estimates, a row between the Governor of Jamaica and an American admiral, a punitive expedition against the Pathans and the sending up of Scottish Bills to the House of Lords. When the meetings began, C.B. was fairly brisk, but after the first hour his attention began to relax and a colleague observed that there came over his face the grey look that indicates extreme fatigue.[29]

In the meantime the announcement had been made of Ponsonby's resignation as private secretary because of his wife's health and his replacement by Vaughan Nash, with a Mr. Montgomery of the Foreign Office as assistant. One newspaper, lamenting Ponsonby's departure, wrote loftily: 'He came of the right stock for the work, for he is the son of Sir Henry Ponsonby. . . . His successor, Mr. Vaughan Nash, represents a different class and training. A few years ago he was a working journalist. . . .'[30]

C.B. missed the opening of Parliament on the 29th. Haldane wrote to his sister: 'The session opens in a doubtful fashion . . . C.B. is the only person who can hold this motley crew together & he is not there.'[31]

On the 30th Ilbert told Bryce that he had learned from C.B. that it was the French doctor who had diagnosed 'asthma cardiaque', and that, though Biarritz had done him a great deal of good, the London fog had got into his throat on his return and set up troublesome coughing fits.[32] Rosebery wrote to the Duke of Devonshire on February 1:

> C. Bannerman is I suspect in a very declining state of health, but his cohesive properties are so invincible that they would keep him if he were bedridden. I doubt his going to the House of Lords, whence his influence could only reach the H. of Commons in a very diluted form.[33]

Esher noted on February 4: 'Francis Knollys told me that the King found C.-B. very languid and feeble. He could not bring his mind to bear upon any large question of policy.'[34]

On that day C.B. was back in the House of Commons, and moved that an Address should be presented to the King expressing the indignation of the House at the murder of the King of Portugal and his son. This was the sort of thing that he did very well. His statement was a model of its kind – an unqualified denunciation of 'this mad, revolting crime', a brief but vivid picture of 'the main street of a great city . . . filled on a quiet afternoon with the usual crowd of peaceable and busy citizens', broken by the sudden horror of the crime, praise of an intelligent king and his affable and accessible family, a tribute to the Portuguese Queen and a word about the traditional friendship between England and Portugal.[35] Hardinge wrote:

> C.B. made a very impressive speech in the H. of Commons in proposing his resolution and fortunately no Socialist or Labour Member got up to make indecent remarks. This was much feared and it is thought that this would have happened if anybody else had proposed it other than C.B.[36]

Nash told Ponsonby on February 7: 'C.B. got down to the House on Tuesday & had a very good reception . . . his voice was quite strong & clear . . . every day now he is making way & getting back jauntiness & spirits. His brother after being quite given up has rallied & may go on for some time.'[37]

The reference was to C.B.'s elder brother James, who was seriously ill at Stracathro. Nash recorded that C.B. was telling Montgomery his old stories and that he was playing billiards after dinner.

On February 12, C.B. presided over his final Cabinet, and on the same day he made his last speech in the House of Commons, a short business statement on the timetable for the Scottish Land Bills. Just before he left the House he had a conversation with Redmond about the Irish motion fixed to come on the following Monday. For forty years the House of Commons had been part of his life. He had experience of it going back longer than any other member. Now he left it for ever.

Next day his heart gave way yet again, and his own doctor called in the King's physician. Nash wrote to Ponsonby:

this morning there was a . . . much longer attack. Burnet was alarmed . . . & sent for Barlow. . . . Barlow seemed to think that he might get to the House on Monday & even speak on a Home Rule motion of Redmond's. I doubt it myself &, at the moment, I almost doubt if he will be able to stick to it. . . .[38]

On the 16th Nash wrote: 'yesterday morning Burnet announced that he had influenza. . . . it's the greatest relief to him to know that what he has now is nothing worse. It's a question how much longer things can go on in this sort of fashion. . . . It was a touch & go business on Thursday. . . .[39]

Two days later he reported:

. . . he feels increasingly the uncertainty of his holding on but I don't think he will look at the Lords. We had a talk about it yesterday & he agreed that it would involve more speaking & bother besides being quite uncongenial & he doesn't like it as a winding up of his career. 'Humiliating' is the word he selected. . . .[40]

On the 20th Hardinge wrote to Villiers, the Minister in Lisbon:

. . . C.B. is, I am sorry to say, down with influenza, & from the weakness of his heart the accounts one hears of him inspire one with anxiety. The party has already broken up into such a lot of groups that he is the only person who can hold them together. I hear that it

is practically settled that Asquith will take his place before very
long, but he is so personally disliked in the House that I doubt if
he will be able to hold the party together for very long. Altogether,
I am not very happy about the state of affairs, as although I am not
a radical, I am very anxious from a F.O. point of view to see the
present régime go on. . . .[41]

C.B. asked Nash to ask T. P. O'Connor to recommend some
books, saying only that they should be distinctly non-educative and
should not be too sad. But on the 19th things took a turn for the
worse. Next day Nash wrote: 'The P.M. had a bad day yesterday. . . .
Last night a nurse was established. . . . He is wonderfully patient and
sweet. He sees nobody but reads his 'Times' & looks at a few papers.
I don't see myself how the question of resignation can be long postponed...'[42]

Most people assumed that Asquith was the inevitable successor.
Most Liberals were content that it should be so. But one notable
Liberal was far from happy at the prospect of exchanging C.B. for
Asquith. C. P. Scott of the *Manchester Guardian* distrusted Asquith as
a Liberal Imp who had been wrong about the war and had not, like
C.B., been sound in the true faith in the dark days. An article in *The
Times* on February 17 brought a reaction from the *Manchester Guardian*
two days later:

On Monday the 'Times', with a somewhat suspiciously marked
abstention from incivility to the PREMIER, pressed him to lighten
his work by going into the House of Lords, and so short are
politicians' memories that even in some Liberal quarters we have
seen the suggestion treated as an expression of guileless good-will . . .
at the time when the present Cabinet was being formed . . . it . . .
came out with remarkable clearness that in the view of the most
astute Opposition leaders the evil of a Liberal and Free Trade
House of Commons would be very much abated if it were not
led by Sir HENRY CAMPBELL-BANNERMAN. And we give them
credit for their insight. For at that time the PREMIER's full
power of directing the House of Commons wisely and usefully was
not fully known among Liberals generally. His extraordinary hold
on the respect and affection of the new House came as a gradual
revelation, and to many an amazing one. . . . It is no wonder that
at the first fancied opportunity they resume their importunities to

a uniquely formidable opponent to retire from the only serious arena of modern English politics. . . .[43]

The article went on to point out that the 'enemy' were now selecting Asquith as C.B.'s successor. They were right to praise him. But he was not the only other man on the Government front bench: two other Ministers (no doubt the *Manchester Guardian* had Lloyd George and Winston Churchill in mind) had shown 'rare gifts of personal influence oratorical power, and political or administrative initiative'. C. P. Scott hoped that C.B. could stay long enough to allow someone else – presumably Lloyd George – to challenge Asquith for the succession. Scott later wrote to Goldwin Smith on March 15:

> Campbell-Bannerman will I fear never be able to take up the heavy burden of the Premiership again. Asquith . . . is a sort of natural successor, and his claim is reinforced by his readiness and force as a leader in the daily Parliamentary scrimmage, but his political record is bad, and the present Cabinet with Asquith simply substituted for Campbell-Bannerman could not command confidence in the country, and will, I hope, never be accepted by the genuine Liberals in the Cabinet.[44]

Scott was not the only person to have doubts about Asquith. Stead wrote: 'No one could imagine Mr. Asquith standing like C.-B. four-square to all the winds that blow in defence of an unpopular cause.'[45] Others had doubts about Asquith from another point of view. On January 4 Austen Chamberlain wrote to his stepmother:

> I called on Lord Knollys this morning. . . . He . . . said he was told by Liberals that if anything happened to C.B. the Party would go to smash in six months. I became communicative, and was rewarded by Knollys's observation that of course Grey was the best man to succeed him, that the choice lay with the King, and that of course he might send for Grey, and overrule Grey's personal objections. 'Personally', he added, 'I like Asquith, and I like Mrs. Asquith, though some people don't; but I don't think he is quite the right stamp of man for Prime Minister.'[46]

Ponsonby wrote of the two: 'They were extraordinarily different – Asquith outwardly strong, C-B outwardly easy-going; Asquith inwardly pliable, C-B firm and resolute.'[47]

On February 19 Morley wrote to Minto, the Viceroy of India, about C.B.:

> King Edward once sagaciously warned one of his ministers that what broke men down was not the work of their offices, but big dinners, late hours, and casual speechifying after the office work of the day was over – about as sensible a doctrine as King or commoner could propound. We can hardly look for his recovery of full strength.[48]

News came to C.B. that a Free Trade group was trying to acquire *The Times*, and that if they were successful J. A. Spender was to edit it. He sent Spender a message saying that he hoped the deal would go through. C.B. had had a raw deal from *The Times*. For over ten years it had denounced him, sneered at him and belittled him. He must have reflected that it would be agreeable if, even at this late hour, it could be converted to what he regarded as the true faith. But it was not to be. For Mr. Moberly Bell, the backer of the Jameson Raid, was secretly engaged in delivering the paper into the hands of the future Lord Northcliffe, who won the battle for control on March 16.[49]

Now the Leader of the Opposition was sounded by the Palace. On the 24th Arthur Balfour wrote to Knollys: 'I gather . . . that you would like to have – informally and unofficially – my views. . . . As regards the conduct of public business during C.B.'s illness – it is no doubt very inconvenient to have no working Prime Minister: but I should venture to suggest that it would be quite constitutional for H.M. to treat Asquith as *de facto* head of the Government.'[50]

On February 26 Esher wrote:

> I called on Arthur Balfour this morning. He was in bed, a small brass bed. . . . He generally remains there till about mid-day. . . .
>
> He does not think C–B can hold out much longer. A mummified Prime Minister, in these days, he thinks an impossibility. The view was corroborated by Morley, with whom I lunched.
>
> He feels sure that before Whitsuntide C–B will have retired. For a month now he has not seen a colleague or a paper. Asquith he looks upon as inevitable.[51]

But C.B. was not finished yet. He rallied a little, and on February 27 Knollys wrote to Nash: 'The King rejoices to hear the good news about the Prime Minister today. . . . He much wishes that Sir Lauder Brunton or a very rising Dr. Dawson, of whose cleverness everybody speaks highly, were called in.'[52] The King's advice was followed, but there was nothing that these physicians could do for the Prime Minister.

On the 28th Nash reported: 'Today he is much brighter & inclined to crack jokes. Sufficient unto the day.'[53] But C.B.'s enemy was still 'looking round the corner 'at him, and soon caught up with him. On March 1 Nash wrote:

> There was another bad turn last night. . . . They *may* contrive to patch him up but I don't think so. He has got into a sadly nervous state about the breathing . . . if the heart can't stand the strain it's no good pretending to hope. . . . He is very patient & brave. He doesn't know how bad he is & there is nothing to be gained & something to be risked by telling him, as he has got to be encouraged.[54]

It is sad to know that in these last weeks of his life C.B.'s advisers thought it better not to tell him the truth. Grave illness unfortunately encourages untruthfulness in everyone around the patient. But at the Palace there were no illusions. Esher wrote on March 3: 'This afternoon I was sent for by the King. . . . He told me of his arrangements with Asquith, and although he respects the P.M. designate, I think he doubts whether his relation with him will be as pleasant as with C-B – for whom he has quite a warm feeling.'[55]

Next day C.B. dictated a letter to Asquith. The phraseology of his letter, as Asquith realized, was unmistakably his own:

> 10 Downing Street
> Whitehall S.W.
> . . . I cannot let slip so good a time without sending you a word of acknowledgement of all that you & my colleagues have done for me while I have been laid up . . . influenza is not content with the benefits that it spreads itself but it routs about for any recent skeletons that it can find in any cupboard in the human frame. . . . I have . . . been wholely disqualified from being of any use to my colleagues or to the party – I can only assure them that my inability to do anything for them has been one prolonged regret & impatience.

Fortunately, however, most of our Bills and other work had

been pretty well thought out. . . . And as on all these points my views were generally known I flatter myself that I wasn't much missed.

This, however, doesn't detract from my deep obligation for the kindness, loyalty & great consideration shown to me & I would ask you to convey to all members of the Cabinet, but above all to accept for yourself, my most profound gratitude for this indulgence.

Nothing could be more satisfactory . . . than the progress made with the Licensing Bill & the Education Bill and the question of military expenditure. They all stand clearly before the country in what gentlemen on the other side would no doubt call their naked deformity. . . .

I can get nothing whatever out of the doctors. . . .[56]

The acting Prime Minister replied from the Cabinet room on the ground floor:

> 10 Downing Street
> Whitehall S.W.
> 4 March 1908

My dear Prime Minister

I read your letter to the Cabinet and in their name I have to congratulate you on the clear evidence it affords of your mental vigour and of your close and continuous interest in all our affairs.

The Cabinet . . . hope that the time may be short, but there is nothing which they would deprecate more than that you or your advisers should feel that there is any need for hurry.

We all value, & no one more than I, your kind expressions, which go far beyond what we any of us feel that we deserve.

> Yours always,
> H. H. Asquith.[57]

On March 3, in fact, the King had seen Asquith, who told his wife:

He said he had quite made up his mind to send for me at once in the event of anything happening to C.-B., or of his sending in his resignation. He thought it a pity C.-B. would not go to the Lords, and said there was no inconsistency in his doing so with his House of Lords policy. I told him I was sure C.-B. would never do it. He said he thought C.-B. very useful so long as he was equal to the job, as making things smooth and keeping people together. But it was evident that he was breaking up, and we must provide for the future. . . .[58]

The same day Knollys wrote to Nash:

> When I came back from Downing Street this afternoon, the King asked me whether it would be possible for him to see the Prime Minister for a minute (merely to take him by the hand) tomorrow – H.M. goes abroad on Thursday morning. I said I was afraid from what you told me he was far too ill. . . .[59]

The King really did wish to say goodbye to his Prime Minister, but he also did not want to have to cut short his holiday at Biarritz, so he wanted to discourage C.B. from resigning before early May. For the same reason he had got Asquith to agree to come out to Biarritz to kiss hands if the need arose. In fact he did call at No. 10 and see C.B. for the last time the following day. Nash told Ponsonby: 'The King appeared on Wednesday. . . . He stopped about twenty minutes & Sir H. was none the worse for it . . . but I was glad when the old place fell back into its proper gloom & quietude.'[60] C.B. had taken his last leave of his Sovereign. The King urged the Prime Minister not to resign for the time being. A card came from Queen Alexandra saying: 'A few violets I brought back from Windsor in the hopes that they may cheer the poor patient. With heartfelt wishes for a speedy recovery.'[61]

Meanwhile a journalist recorded that 'the House of Commons is getting along as well as could be expected in the absence of its Leader . . . the Chancellor of the Exchequer's manner is a little grim. Members on both sides think wistfully of C-B's canny ways, his contagious smile, his little jokes, and his success in imperceptibly getting his own way in difficult circumstances.'[62]

Nash wrote on March 6: 'We have got nearly through another week . . . it begins to look as if lung troubles are going to set in. He has morphia every night to make him sleep. . . .' But he concluded: 'He has not in the least degree given up hope & courage.'[63]

The political stream flowed on. On the 12th Rosebery, now almost a ghost from the past, again addressed a resurrected Liberal League, denouncing the Scottish Land Bill, calling for a reformed Second Chamber and declaring: 'Socialism is the end of all things – Empire, religious faith, freedom, property',[64] – strong words for one on whom the Webbs had pinned their hopes. But C.B. was now past caring about these things.

Morley wrote to Minto on the same day:

> Preoccupations about our brave Prime Minister float mistily all day among one's departmental business. . . . Apart from the sore regret of every one of us at the disappearance of so gallant, honest, and experienced a Chief of our party, with his extraordinary command of the majority in the H. of C., more than one question of a rather delicate kind will fail to be settled . . . the disappearance of the Prime Minister shifts the centre of gravity. As a Cabinet, we have been the most absolutely harmonious and amicable that ever was known. . . .[65]

The same day Ilbert wrote to Bryce:

> No one has or can have anything like the same hold on the present House as C.B. One feels the difference of atmosphere when he is away, but his influence is very great even in his absence. Asquith is less unpopular than he was, has been steadily gaining ground . . . and is the only possible successor. But one of the sources of C-B's strength was his complete independence of social influences, and the man below the gangway will always find it difficult to place implicit confidence in the husband of a society woman.[66]

By mid-March it was clear in Downing Street that there could only be one end. Nash wrote on the 13th:

> It is very sad here & one can only just stand it at times. Sir H. is . . . not up to signing his name or feeding himself. . . . the sinking away of his strength & vitality is going on fast. He still thinks its the flu & we keep it up as much as we can. Burnet & I have agreed that he is to know the truth only when its clear that it would ease his mind to know it . . . if it is to be a long business it wouldn't do for his own reputation's sake or from the public point of view for him to stay. . . . But Burnet doesn't think it will be very long. . . . His sweetness & patience are what you would expect. . . . He has oxygen occasionally when the breathing is very bad & morphia every night . . . when it gets very bad Burnet will see that he doesn't suffer. I had a talk with Asquith & Harcourt on Wednesday. . . . A. agreed that it was entirely a matter for the doctors as to whether

he should come to any decision about resigning & be told the facts
but that there was no urgent reason why he should . . . Lloyd
George will try to be the Ch. of the Exer.: Whiteley is pushing
Winston. The suspense is very trying to the party & makes them
restless & uncomfortable. . . . We entertain Zulie amongst us down
here in the afternoon as he romps & snorts about the bedroom &
jumps on the bed. . . .[67]

Away at Biarritz, the King was still worried that C.B. might resign
at an early and inconvenient moment. A letter came to Nash from
Sir Arthur Davidson: 'The King wishes you to impress on Sir Henry
. . . his earnest hope that he will not think of resigning before Easter.
Apart from any political considerations, the King feels sure that it
would react injuriously on Sir Henry's health & might retard his
recovery. . . .[68]'

Nash wrote to Knollys on the 18th, saying: 'Yesterday Sir Henry
mentioned the question of his position and I told him that his colleagues
felt that there was no public purpose to be gained by his coming to
any decision at present. . . . I felt justified in telling him of the King's
wish. . . . I think this helped to quiet his mind. . . .'[69]

C.B.'s condition was becoming known. On March 19 Almeric
Fitzroy wrote: 'The Prime Minister's health continues a matter of
grave concern; Mrs. Buxton told me his weakness was such that the
effort of washing his face and hands in the morning left him in a state
of prostration all the forenoon.'[70] Still, however, the King worried
about the possibility of resignation. On March 20 Davidson wrote again
to Nash encouraging C.B. to stay on.[71]

The political heir apparent was, however, becoming restive. On
March 22 Asquith wrote to Knollys:

> It is, I think, clear . . . that the status quo cannot go on. There
> is absolutely no hope of a return to public life, and the prolongation
> of the present uncertain [sic] is having very demoralising results.
> The House of Commons has become a gossip shop . . . it has
> become my opinion, which is shared by all my leading colleagues,
> that whatever reconstruction has to be done should be done at
> once, & once for all. . . .[72]

Knollys sent this letter on to the King.
Nash wrote to Ponsonby on March 22: 'The uncertainty of the

length of the illness is due more than anything else to his courage. He means to fight through if he can. I do hope he may live to see you again.'[73]

From Buckingham Palace came a message on rather different lines from the communications from Biarritz – 'That God may give you recovered health & strength is the earnest prayer of Yours Very Sincerely Alexandra.'[74] On the 24th, far away at Cannes, another old colleague of C.B.'s, the Duke of Devonshire, the Hartington of his early days in the Government, died of pneumonia. It seemed as if they were hurrying to the shades together.

Ilbert wrote to Bryce on the 26th:

When I looked in at Downing Street this morning Vaughan Nash had just left him, and was much upset for C.B. had evidently been saying something in the nature of farewell words to him. Until quite recently he had kept up his courage and his hopes, but he is now very weak . . . and is beginning to long that it should be over. . . . It is very melancholy to think of him gradually fading away in that dismal house without anyone to look after him except that poor little niece. . . .[75]

Margot Asquith wrote in her diary:

On the 27th of March, Henry . . . told me that Sir Henry Campbell-Bannerman had sent for him that day to tell him that he was dying. They had talked for over an hour, and Henry's voice shook as he repeated their conversation to me.

C.B. began by telling him the text he had chosen out of the Psalms to put on his grave. . . . He was resigned and even cheerful, but after a little while . . . he turned the subject deliberately on to material things, flimsy matters – such as patronage, titles and bishops etc. . . .

Henry was deeply moved when he went on to tell me that Campbell-Bannerman had thanked him for being a wonderful colleague.

'So loyal, so disinterested and so able!'[76]

C.B. himself now raised the question of his resignation and, according to Nash, returned to it persistently. The Archbishop, a brother

Scot, came to see him and read to him from Ecclesiasticus. He was surprised at the frankness with which C.B. discussed his colleagues, whose weaknesses he knew so well.[77]

On March 30 C.B.'s old friend Tom Buchanan went to see him for ten minutes. He found him 'sitting in a chair, all white, with a white shawl, looking like a Pope', but calm and cheerful and still with a twinkle in his eye. C.B. told him:

> I have not been able to get anything definite out of them, but I feel the struggle is perhaps going against me. I am a very weak man and God is very strong and I must just trust in Him. . . . Four or five times I have been given up by the doctors and I expected to die and see all doctrines in a new light. But I got better and remained on earth. You know, Tom, I was (or we were) brought up on 'O God of Bethel' and that religion and that is what we have to trust to.[78]

Though the King was himself largely responsible, Knollys wrote to Crewe, saying: 'I do not believe there has ever been such a political situation before; Lord Chatham's case when he was Prime Minister 150 years ago is the nearest approach to it.'[79] This was something of an exaggeration, but Knollys took the same line in writing to the King, saying that 'the appointment of Prime Minister has for the last 4 or 5 weeks been in complete abeyance', and adding: 'The only member of the Cabinet whom Sir Henry has seen is Mr. John Morley . . . Sir Henry, for the first 5 or 6 minutes, talked sensibly enough, but at the end of that time he began to ramble & to be incoherent.'[80] In fact C.B. had been slightly better and had been able to see Loreburn, Ripon and Asquith as well as Morley.

But by now he realized that he could not go on. He dictated a last message to his friends at Stirling and Dunfermline which was kept by Nash and sent to Robertson next month. It ended: 'What do I not owe you all for loyalty, energy, courage and kindness. God bless you all.'[81] A telegram came from the King at Biarritz yet once more urging postponement of any decision to resign. This brought matters to a head. C.B. had been speaking more and more frequently of resignation, and, with Dr. Burnet's agreement, Nash now told him that some of his principal colleagues had been saying that the situation in the immediate future would be difficult if no decision were taken. C.B. needed no further hint. In the presence of Dr. Burnet, on All Fools'

Day, he dictated, with difficulty, a letter to the King, asking permission to resign.[82] To make clear to the King that matters could not continue, Nash telegraphed to Davidson on the 2nd: 'Dr. Dawson saw him last night & . . . laid great stress absolute necessity for his giving up public work in every form and "lightening the ship" with as little delay as possible.'[83]

The King telegraphed on April 3 saying that under the circumstances he had no alternative but to accept C.B.'s resignation. On that day Nash wrote out, at C.B.'s dictation, the words: 'Sir Henry Campbell-Bannerman with his humble duty to Your Majesty submits his resignation of the appointments of Prime Minister and First Lord of the Treasury.'[84] With an effort C.B. signed his name under it, firm, clear and legible. After he had done so, he said to Nash: 'There's the last kick. My dear fellow, I don't mind. I've been Prime Minister for longer than I deserve.'[85]

On the 3rd also the King wrote to him saying how sorry he was, 'as it has always been a great pleasure and satisfaction to me to do business with you. . . .'[86]

Parliament reassembled on April 6, and the departure of the Prime Minister overshadowed everything else in members' minds. Asquith said that for the moment he could not trust himself to do more than say that in the annals of our country there was no man who, after long years spent in the thick of public contention, ever laid down the highest office under the Crown more universally or more deservedly beloved. There was not a single member in any quarter of the House who did not feel himself to be under the shadow, not merely of a political, but also of a personal loss. Balfour followed, with a few graceful words, and then Redmond for the Irish members, saying that Ireland had suffered a loss second only to that which she suffered when Gladstone retired.[87]

His closest political friend, Jack Sinclair, wrote: 'The sad news has come upon us all. I shudder to think of it. But I have no doubts, for you had none. . . .'[88]

Nash wrote to Ponsonby: 'You will see that the resignation business is all over. He doesn't take much notice of the fuss in the papers but he is relieved to have it off his mind.'[89]

C.B.'s course was run. All accounts were settled. Some of the warmest letters he received were from his chief critics of December 1905, the Relugas conspirators. There is no doubt that they were wholly sincere:

I have long ago recognized that the difficulties I made when the Government was formed were short-sighted and ill judged and we all feel now that troubles, which your presence at the head of the Government, kept in abeyance, will have to be faced.

I hope you realize how widespread and sincere is the regard and goodwill, which is felt for you. . . . I wish the time had come when I could retire as honourably and with as good fame as you are doing.

Yours very sincerely,
Edward Grey.[90]

My dear Chief,

It was with very real sadness that your announcement of last night came to me personally. None among your Cabinet has more real cause to be grateful to you. In a task of great magnitude and difficulty you trusted and helped through, as few men would have taken the risk of doing . . . with your name the Completion of the building which Gladstone and Cardwell commenced will be inseparably associated. Without your strong hand and guidance and complete sympathy my effort for you had been a hopeless one. I am grateful. . . .

Yours has been a great and notable administration & there is no member of your Cabinet who has realised more what he has learned and gained from you than myself.

Always yours with affectionate regards,
R. B. Haldane.[91]

Henry Higgs came in to say goodbye. He was told by his chief that he would get 'a C.B. from C.B.' – 'I hope it will serve to remind you of me and of the interesting and often amusing years we have spent together.' He told Higgs that he would like to leave something for his constituents to remember him by but thought it would be a bad example. It would make it harder for poor men to get into Parliament. He went on: 'If people should say of me that I tried always to go straight there is perhaps no credit to me in that. It may have been mere indolence. The straight road always seemed to me to be the easiest.'[92]

There were still problems to be sorted out, including the succession in his constituency. Ponsonby was looking for a seat and the Whips thought of Stirling, though Nash told him in a letter on the 7th that

'C.B. is very keen on Robertson, or some local man. . . . He talked a good deal about it yesterday . . . & told me to tell J. B. Smith, who was in turn to write to Robertson & others urging a local candidate. . . .'[93] But Ponsonby settled his candidature when he sat next to the Provost of Dunfermline at Belmont after C.B.'s funeral, and he it was who succeeded C.B. as the member for the Stirling Burghs.[94]

Now, however, the attention of the world was on Asquith, hurrying to Biarritz to receive the King's command, and, in Downing Street, C.B. could only wait for death. Nash wrote to Fritz Ponsonby at the Palace on April 8, saying that C.B. was so weak that he was finding it an effort to hold up a newspaper and that his condition was one of 'unalleviated weariness and misery', so much so that 'he cannot stand having his old dog, who was Lady Campbell-Bannerman's constant companion during her illness, in the same room with him'.[95] But, in his room at No. 10, C.B. talked to Charlotte in French as he had done long ago when they had been young.

London was waiting for the Cabinet changes Asquith would make. Esher heard about them from Morley and wrote on the 10th: 'Lloyd George "put a pistol" to Asquith's head, and *asked* for the Ch. of the Ex. with a threat of resignation. . . . He . . . spoke deprecatingly of Asquith. His final summing up of him was: "He is a man of no initiative, and requires to be briefed." '[96]

Now that C.B. had gone, the seeds of future difficulties were being sown.

On the 10th, too, Asquith got back from Biarritz. He and Margot drove to Downing Street, where Asquith went in to enquire about C.B. Margot, who waited outside, wrote:

> The street was empty, and but for the footfall of a few policemen there was not a sound to be heard.
>
> I looked at the dingy exterior of No. 10 and wondered how long we should live in it.
>
> Leaning back I watched the evening sky reflected in the diamond panes of the Foreign Office windows, and caught a glimpse of green trees. The door opened and the Archbishop came out.
>
> The final scene in a drama of Life was being performed in that quiet by-street. The doctor going in and the priest coming out; and as I reflected on the dying Prime Minister I could only hope that no sound had reached him of the crowd that had cheered his successor.[97]

Asquith formed his new Cabinet. Churchill was brought in, Morley went to the House of Lords, Lloyd George duly became Chancellor of the Exchequer, McKenna replaced Tweedmouth at the Admiralty (who got a two-line note, with no attempt at explanation) and Elgin was dropped. Asquith lacked C.B.'s graceful style in doing these things, and Elgin was hurt at the manner of his dismissal, a curt letter, with the offer 'How about a marquessate?' flung in a way that was almost insulting. 'I venture to think', he wrote, 'that even a prime minister may have some regard for the usages common among gentlemen.'[98] Nash, who in due course became Asquith's private secretary, as he had been C.B.'s, was tidying up at No. 10, and wrote to Ponsonby on the 13th: 'Everything is arranged now down to Tommy Lough's departure with a P.C. and Portsmouth's with nothing, although old Fowler still hangs on & J.B. hasn't been got rid of. . . . Asquith is A1 to have dealings with. . . . Mrs. A. I find an effort. . . .'[99]

On the 17th Knollys told Nash: 'It must be very distressing for those who are around Sir Henry to see him linger on in this sad way.'[100] There was not long to go. On the 19th Nash reported that there had been

> a lot of mental confusion . . . he fancies we are engaged in some conspiracy against him. It is partly morphia but more the bad state of the blood owing to the lungs being so loaded.
>
> The monarch came without a word of warning and sat in your old chair, nearly knocking the bottom out of it . . . and I talked to to him as fearlessly as I could, remembering your maxim. He was extremely jolly though I had to fend him off from going upstairs to see Sir H. . . .[101]

For the next two days C.B. was only intermittently aware of what was going on, and he was unconscious throughout the night of the 21st. At 9 o'clock on the morning of Wednesday, April 22, he had another heart attack. He remained unconscious and at 9.15 his heart stopped. His last battle was over.

As soon as the news of his death was known, tributes and messages of sympathy poured in. In Manchester two future Prime Ministers in his administration spoke of their lost chief:

> I have never met [said Lloyd George] a great public figure . . . who so completely won the attachment and affection of the men

who came into contact with him. He was not merely admired and respected, he was absolutely loved by us all. . . . The masses of the people of this country, especially the more unfortunate of them, have lost the best friend they ever had in the high places of the land. . . . He was truly a great man. A great head and a great heart. He was absolutely the bravest man I ever met in politics. . . .[102]

Winston Churchill commented in his different style on 'the sad intelligence conveyed to us this morning', adding:

I should like to say, as one of the younger men of the Liberal party . . . how generous and indulgent he always was . . . how ready to trust us even with work and political expositions of great responsibility, and yet at the same time how ready he always was to look kindly and with a friendly eye on any little mistake. . . . It is generally known what a large part Sir Henry Campbell-Bannerman played in the South African settlement. To begin with, the fact that he was there made for peace, alone made the Dutch race in South Africa ready and anxious to come forward and take from the hands of the British Government what they might have looked at with distrust if it had come from any other quarter. But, knowing as I do in detail the whole history of the policy which has created free self-governing States . . . in South Africa, I say that almost every important movement in that policy was taken on the personal initiative of the late Prime Minister. . . . It was only at the end of his life that he emerged into the sunshine – the sunset it was – of popularity, of public affection, to the trust of the House of Commons, and to great political power. . . .[103]

On the morning of April 27, a girl arrived at No. 10, carrying a small bunch of lilies, with a card saying 'From a working girl'. She asked if she might see C.B. whom, she said, she had never been able to see in his lifetime. It was too late, but her flowers were put with the more magnificent wreaths. None would have given greater comfort to the dead man.[104]

At noon the first part of the funeral service was conducted with pomp and circumstance at Westminster Abbey. Rain began to fall as the open hearse was drawn through the streets by four black horses, but the drivers of the cabs and buses drawn up by the side of the road removed their caps, and London's flags were at half-mast. In the Abbey a great congregation included the Prince of Wales and Clemenceau as the representative of France. Ponsonby told his wife: 'I heard cackling & pushing behind us & there were the inevitable advertisers Winston & Lloyd George who had come late on purpose so as to attract attention. I . . . told them to stand back.'[105]

Outside, the crowds stood silently in the rain as the procession slowly wound its way through London. Ponsonby wrote: 'What bowled me over was the expression on the faces of the endless crowd to Euston – intense reverence & sympathy.'[106] The train north, which C.B. had taken so many times, carried him to Alyth for the last time, as he went home to lie beside Charlotte in Meigle churchyard, the old housekeeper biting her lip as he was lowered into the ground. Ilbert wrote to Bryce, saying: 'The poor man seems never to have really recovered from the shock of his wife's death –

> . . . "a while he tried
> To live without her, liked it not, and died." '[107]

On the afternoon of the funeral, Asquith, now Prime Minister, had to say a few words about his predecessor in the House. Asquith had been regarded as undeniably competent but not very agreeable and not altogether human. The general view of him was described in a letter his own wife, Margot, sent to Leo Maxse – 'a cold hard unsympathetic man, loved by none, admired by a few'.[108] He was called 'metallic'. But now, when he came to speak about his lost leader, he revealed that he had a heart after all. His tribute to C.B. increased his own hold on the House. In it he said:

> It is within a few months of forty years since Sir Henry Campbell-Bannerman took his seat in this Chamber. . . . Among the newcomers there were probably few . . . who seemed less obviously destined than Mr. Campbell, as he then was, to fill the position he ultimately reached. . . . Our late Prime Minister belonged to that . . . class whose fitness for such a place, until they had attained and held it, was never adequately understood. . . .
> What was the secret of the hold, which in these later days he unquestionably had, on the admiration and affection of men of all parties and men of all creeds? . . . he was . . . always disposed to despise victories won in any sphere by mere brute force; an almost

passionate lover of peace; and yet we have not seen in our time a man of greater courage – courage not of a defiant and aggressive type, but calm, patient, persistent, indomitable. . . .

He was not ashamed, even on the verge of old age, to see visions and to dream dreams. He had no misgivings as to the future of democracy . . . none the less, in . . . the choice of this man or that for some particular task, he showed not only that practical shrewdness which came to him from his Scottish ancestors, but a touch of the discernment and insight of a cultured citizen of the world. . . . He never put himself forward, yet no one had greater tenacity of purpose; he was the least cynical of mankind, but no one had a keener eye for the humours and ironies of the political situation. He was a . . . strong party man, but he harboured no resentment. He was generous to a fault in appreciation of the work of others, whether friends or foes. He met both good and evil fortune with the same unclouded brow, the same unruffled temper, the same unshakeable confidence in the justice and righteousness of his cause . . . to-day in this House, of which he was the senior and the most honoured member, we may call a truce in the strife of parties, while we together remember our common loss. . . .

> How happy is he born or taught,
>   That serveth not another's will;
> Whose armour is his honest thought,
>   And simple truth his utmost skill!
>
> This man is freed from servile bands
>   Of hope to rise, or fear to fall;
> Lord of himself, though not of lands;
>   And, having nothing, yet hath all.[109]

Strangely enough these lines of Sir Henry Wotton's had been quoted to C.B. on his last visit to Belmont by Henry Higgs, as they were walking with Sinclair in the grounds. C.B. was greatly struck with them and asked Higgs to repeat them.[110]

So C.B. passed from the scene, and the House of Commons knew him no more. There were no children to carry on his line. In November the contents of his will were made known. Apart from his three estates, his property amounted to just under £55,000 gross or £38,000 net, much less than most people had imagined. He left Belmont, his pictures, plate and horses to Mrs. Campbell, with reversion to her son Hugh, his papers to Jack Sinclair, £1,000 to Vaughan Nash, a year's wages to all servants who had worked for him for over ten years and six months' to those with less service, and articles worth £50 to Arthur Ponsonby.

After that C.B. became only a memory.

CHAPTER 40

The Balance Sheet

WRITING of C.B.'s successor, A. G. Gardiner said:

Mr. Asquith has not . . . the fundamental conviction of his predecessor: his roots are less deep in the democratic soil. Campbell-Bannerman was

'True as a dial to the sun
Although it be not shin'd upon',

but Mr. Asquith has not that instinctive certitude in great crises. He trusts his intellect where Campbell-Bannerman trusted his faith. His inferiority is spiritual, and when he fails, as in the case of the South African War, he fails . . . because . . . he bases himself upon the calculations of the material factors and the motives of expediency and is deaf to the promptings of the primal instincts of man.[1]

That passage is as illuminating about C.B. as it is about Asquith.

In some ways C.B. might be called the last of the Victorians. The modern world came in with Asquith. Ahead lay a falling off in the standards of political life. The next few years were to see the Prime Minister the worse for wear for drink in the House,[2] the Marconi scandal and, under Lloyd George, the sorry tale of Maundy Gregory and the widespread sale of honours.

C.B. looked back to Cobden, to whose ideas he was invariably faithful, and to Gladstone, whose minister and follower he had been. It was in the spirit of the Cobdenite and Gladstonian tradition that he gave self-government to the Transvaal and the Orange Free State.

Had he lived longer he would undoubtedly have tried the much more difficult task of giving self-government to Ireland. But he also looked forward to a time when Labour would be a major political force in the land. For him, Labour members held no terrors. He welcomed them in the House. He was no socialist, had no sympathy with Marxism and little time for the Webbs and their ideas, but for all that he was essentially a man of the left. Lord Winterton wrote of him: 'Had his great chance come earlier in life, before the inevitable misfortunes of old age overtook him, he might have altered the course of political history; he might, indeed, have preserved the Liberal Party. . . .'³ Had he lived longer, he might have helped to forge a close union between Liberals and Labour, and the left-wing, progressive party in Britain might have evolved on different lines.

His greatest achievement was the South African settlement, and the conversion of Botha and Smuts into lifelong friends and allies of this country. This was his doing, as Churchill said, and as Botha and Smuts themselves always realized, and the reward came in 1914 and in 1939. In a wider sense, too, it undid the harm done to British standing in the world by the Jameson Raid and by the aggressive policy of Chamberlain and Milner. In its place C.B. won for his country a reputation for generosity, magnanimity and fair-dealing.

His second major achievement was the welding together of a political coalition of the left, the greatest ever constructed in this country. He laid the foundation of this as Leader of the Opposition after 1899, when he held the Liberal Party together in the dark days of the Boer War, though it seemed then almost inevitable that it must break apart. When the fight was joined for the defence of Free Trade in 1903, he broadened the front on the right by bringing in some of the 'Free Fooders' from the Unionist benches, the most distinguished of them being Winston Churchill. In the year same he widened it on the left, by encouraging his Chief Whip to make an electoral pact with Ramsay MacDonald. In the end he had constructed a political alliance which stretched from Edward Grey to Philip Snowden. The result was the signal triumph of 1906.

He beat off the challenge of Imperial Preference, made by Chamberlain in 1903, and secured a longer life – another twenty-five years – for the policy of Free Trade, on which the wealth and greatness of England had been established. On this issue he had no doubts. He believed in the benefits of unrestricted trade, and had no time for the moats and curtain walls of small, protected trading systems.

These are great and solid achievements. But, as the years roll by, the achievements of the past become less important to us and less relevant to our own problems. The statesmen of past years live for us primarily as personalities. It is as persons, not as the architects of particular policies, that Fox and Disraeli are interesting. What then was C.B. like as a person?

After years of respectable obscurity, he had become, by a series of accidents, the leader of his party. He suffered first neglect, and then obloquy, before emerging into the sunshine of his short period as Prime Minister, when it was written of him, as Leader of the House of Commons, that 'now, in an assembly where he wields undisputed power, he is the most popular statesman of our generation'.[4]

He never inspired awe, as did Gladstone, or Queen Victoria, or Winston Churchill in old age. He was a much less exalted person, his reputation that of a worldly, easy-going and domesticated man, original and canny, devoted to the quiet life.

As an administrator – as a junior Minister, as Chief Secretary for Ireland and as Secretary of State for War – he was competent but no more. For many years he was content to play a modest part. He was too relaxed and too diffident to want to bend the course of events, or to shape and mould them to his own greater glory. He shared not at all the desire of so many politicians to be able to say: 'I am the man who . . .'. But he had his good points as a Minister. He left people alone and never engaged in futile and time-wasting activity for activity's sake. T. P. O'Connor wrote of him: 'Fuss, worry, loquacious zeal – all these things to him were a torment and a bore.'[5] If he had had his own way he would have ended his career as Speaker, presiding urbanely over the House of Commons. The activists thought he was useless. Dilke, for example, claimed that all his work was done for him by his subordinates and that 'he had only to read novels, prepare jokes, look inscrutable and fatherly'.[6] But between Dilke and C.B. there was never any love lost. And there was another side. Even *The Times*, a paper which was consistently hostile to C.B., wrote that at the War Office, 'he showed a proper and courteous regard for the opinion of his military advisers; he got through his paper work quickly, showing a great gift for getting at the heart of a memorandum without wasting time; and his own notes and instructions' were 'always short, adequate and to the point'.[7] The *Daily Telegraph* described him as a 'highly popular administrator – partly, probably, because he was entirely free from any wild eagerness for change'.[8] He was shrewd about people, and he worked very well with soldiers and officials. He was at his best when dealing with a problem requiring great reserves of tact, patience and guile, such as the long negotiation to induce the Duke of Cambridge to retire.

But it must be admitted that there was a residuum of truth in what Dilke said. C.B. was an idle man; as time went on he was increasingly reluctant to master detail. He was too apt to write a two-line minute and leave it at that. Arthur Ponsonby, however, wrote:

> His easy-goingness had a curious side to it. Just as one imagined that he was inattentive and indifferent, ready to take the line of least resistance, or do nothing, or yield suddenly, one came up against a rock, an obstinate determination, a perfectly clear and set conviction which in time upset everyone's calculations.[9]

And Margot Asquith's view was that:

> No one can become Prime Minister of this country without having exceptional qualities; and in spite of being easy-going to the point of laziness, Sir Henry had neither lethargy nor indifference. He recoiled from what was not straight and had a swift and unerring insight into his fellow men.[10]

As a politician, in Parliament and in the country, C.B. was more impressive, but as a speaker he seldom emerged from the second rank. He did not often make his audiences' hearts beat faster, or set them alight with a glowing and magical phrase. He was not an orator. He was, nevertheless, effective on the platform, where he drew encouragement from the great audiences of those days, and his big, set-piece speeches, which often read well, were praised by such different but knowledgeable critics as Lord Rosebery and Sir William Harcourt. He was, perhaps, too cautious in sticking to his little sheaf of carefully prepared notes, and had better have relied more on his native wit. While his major speeches in the House tended to lack sparkle, his answers to supplementary questions were often admirable, and allowed his natural sense of humour and his shrewdness to appear. When, as Prime Minister, he did throw aside his notes and speak off the cuff it was a great success. Many of his Conservative opponents, and notably Balfour, made the mistake of writing him off as a dull mediocrity.

But Chamberlain never did. When he was over seventy he told Spring-Rice that C.B. was a clever man and a brave man and that he thought Balfour's attacks on him were a mistake.[11] Above all C.B., as a politician, had an inexhaustible fund of quiet determination. He was seldom flabby or wobbly, and never on issues of real importance.

As Leader of the Opposition, he had an almost impossible task. He was elected because Rosebery, Harcourt and Morley had all eliminated themselves, and he was regarded as a mere warming pan for Rosebery's return. He led a party which was hopelessly divided, and he was given less than the minimum loyalty and support by his chief colleagues. He was even left to sit by himself on the front bench. In the Boer War he refused to join the extremists on either wing of the party, but he never wavered in saying that the war was wrong and unnecessary and he defied the whole stream of patriotic emotion to speak out against 'methods of barbarism'. With real guts and determination he hung on, and stuck like a terrier to his principles and to the truth as he saw it, enormous though the pressure was to give way. He was denounced with unparalleled fury, but in the end moderate people came to see that he had been, to a large extent, right, and he had his reward, for English people warm to a man who keeps on saying what he believes to be right at whatever cost in temporary unpopularity. That he managed to hold his party together and lead it to the triumph of 1906 was an extraordinary feat.

C.B. was lacking in panache as a party leader; he was often criticized for not boldly giving a lead. But he was wiser than his critics. At great personal cost, he avoided precipitating a crisis or forcing any section out of the party. A man like C. P. Scott of the *Manchester Guardian*, who watched him all through the Boer War period, wrote of him in 1919: 'A great man if ever there was one by force of conviction and character. How we have missed him.'[12] It was as a result of his leadership of the Opposition that Lloyd George said of him in after years: 'He was a big figure and got bigger as he advanced.'[13]

By the end of his time as Leader of the Opposition, it was plain for all to see what manner of man he was. As Prime Minister, he came into his own and enjoyed what T. P. O'Connor called the splendid sunset of his career. His two years at No. 10 brought about something of an apotheosis. It was he who held the party together. His authority was immense. Herbert Samuel wrote that 'his premiership was common sense enthroned'.[14] In the Cabinet, under his chairmanship, differences melted away. Lord Crewe, who was one of his Ministers, wrote of him:

I cannot conceive a more capable or equable chairman of an executive committee than Sir Henry at the Cabinet. He encouraged general expression of opinion, but never allowed time to be wasted, showing patience without slackness. Starting as the subject of some prejudice and with only a few ardent followers, he finished with unchallenged authority and in an atmosphere of convivial affection.[15]

In the House of Commons his ascendancy was a marvel to all observers. Edward Grey admitted to Esher in 1908 that in 1905 he 'did not see that the H. of C. would be grasped by the heart, and not by the head (which was too small) – and that C.-B. only could do this'.[16]

On occasion, C.B. could take his own line when he judged it right, even against his chief colleagues, as he did over the Trades Disputes Bill and the Workmen's Compensation Bill. He helped the first generation of working-class M.P.s to find a place in the existing political framework. Lloyd George, who called his 'one of the kindest hearts and one of the wisest heads that ever filled the high position of chief counsellor to his Sovereign', said that 'he was a man of deep, tender sympathies, a true friend of the people, a man who, whenever he was in doubt, always dropped on the side of the people'.[17] His position in his own party was unique. Lord Fisher wrote: 'I don't believe any Prime Minister was ever so loved by his followers as was Campbell-Bannerman.'[18]

This is a remarkable record for a man who had only two years as Prime Minister, the first darkened by his wife's illness and death, which exhausted him emotionally and physically, and the second marked by his own failing health and strength.

Morley wrote of him:

Campbell-Bannerman had none of the shining and indisputable qualities that had marked the last five holders of his exalted office. Among his colleagues were men superior to him in power of speech; in talent for grasping great masses of administrative difficulty; and up to a certain time, but not after his worth was fully measured, even in striking or interesting the popular imagination. And yet he was indispensable, the only man possible . . . he always thought more of his policy, and making it prevail, than he thought of himself. . . .

639

As soon as ever Parliament met, it was evident that the new leader, with his bonhomie, humour, plain and lively common-sense . . . not without occasional points of pleasant malice . . . was exactly fitted for the new assembly. . . . More and more they liked him and respected him, and felt that he was thoroughly at home in his business and their own. . . .

He did not think too well of human nature. He had one or two active dislikes, and was capable of extremely shrewd criticism even on friendly colleagues and their infirmities. But nobody ever appreciated service more generously. People of good temper are not always kind people. Campbell-Bannerman was a spontaneously kind-hearted and helpful man.[19]

Ponsonby said:

I do not think it would be possible to find a man more charming or more easy to get on with. He had a great sense of humour and a very telling wit, but the characteristic which might be looked for in vain in almost any other prominent public man was his entire absence of pose. He was always himself. He never played the part of a leader, a Prime Minister, a celebrity. In fact he was continually forgetting that he *was* Prime Minister. He would ask why people crowded round when he went off shopping alone – a very favourite occupation of his. . . .

He loathed prigs and pretentious people; eager intellectual specialists bored him . . . Vanity he always declared was the root trouble with most men. . . .[20]

It was said of C.B. that his motto was 'Solvitur ambulando' – or, as Mr. Goschen rendered it, 'We'll settle it as we toddle along.'[21] A writer in *Le Figaro* in April 1908 described him as 'après le soleil de Gladstone, une lune gladstonienne'.[22] Yet it was easy to exaggerate his defects. The writer in the *Saturday Review* of 1908, who said that 'not since the first reformed Parliament has there been a Prime Minister of England who had rendered slighter services to the nation as the head of a Department, or who had more slender claims to intellectual distinction',[23] was mistaken. Esher underestimated him, summing him up as 'an amiable man; possibly below the calibre of his predecessors, with the exception of Perceval, Addington, Goderich and Liverpool'.[24]

But C.B. would have laughed at the idea that he should be considered to be on a par with the great Prime Ministers – with Gladstone and Disraeli, Peel, Pitt and Walpole. He belongs with solid, sagacious men like Eisenhower, Truman and Attlee.

Nevertheless he had some fine qualities. A man of 'transparent honesty' was how he was described by T. P. O'Connor. He was clear and unshakeable on his fundamental principles, which he was prepared to defend at whatever cost. It was truly said of his most notorious pronouncement that 'that forthright, unimpassioned, unequivocal and unexplained and unapologised-for denunciation of "the methods of barbarism" was one of the bravest rebukes ever given to a nation that had lost its sense of right and its measure of things'.[25] He became a wise old bird, and he never lost his sense of fun. A remarkably urbane man, a good linguist, excellent company, a good letter writer, he contributed to making political life in his period a civilized undertaking.

But above all this he showed, when dealing with the never-ending problem of the relationships between different peoples – between Briton and Boer and between the British and the Irish – a sure touch and a fine vision. He was, however, without any similar vision of the British Empire. He saw only the rant and the bullying and the boasts, and did not see the ideal that inspired men like Rhodes and Milner, or the patient, unsung devotion of countless colonial administrators all over the world.

At home he was a moderate on social reform. He wanted more equality and a better deal for the poor and the workers but, like Gladstone, was opposed to too much state interference.

He had easy relationships with Queen Victoria and King Edward VII. Everyone who came into close contact with him liked him. And at the end he was looked on with affection by great masses of his countrymen. When a statue was put up to him at Stirling, shillings and half-crowns came in from all manner of humble people. He thought of himself, not altogether justifiably, as an average man, and this gave him a great sympathy with the ordinary person, and made him suspicious of those who were intellectually arrogant or superior or pretentious.

Asquith wrote that

> His was by no means the simple personality which many people supposed: it had its complexities and apparent incongruities, and, even to those who were most intimate with him, sometimes its baffling features. But of all the men with whom I have been

associated in public life, I put him as high as any . . . in both moral and intellectual courage.[26]

Margot Asquith, who had been touched by C.B.'s final tribute to her husband, said that she '*loved* C.B. for his generosity', and that he 'was less of a fool than any one but no doubt he had no wings and was a cynic au fond without *any kind* of illusion but a *wonderful* judge of character'.[27] C.B. was, above all else, a thoroughly nice man, a thoroughly decent man, relaxed, temperate, balanced and wise.

He was not in any sense a brilliant man, but on this a true word was said by H. W. Massingham:

> Is it possible that the world is over-intellectualized; and how has it profited its lost soul to be so tremendously clever? Well, 'C.B.' was not 'clever'. He was a singularly unshowy figure . . . with the half-learned, half-traditional wisdom, applied to politics, that the good shepherd directs to the tending of beasts and the watching of weather. And yet he was the only British statesman since Gladstone who visibly added to his country's power, in the act of raising her in the sphere where conscience sits and holds her all but unregarded reign.[28]

Modern political parties do not, on the whole, look for men like this to lead them. The Liberal Party did not do so in 1899. They only took C.B. when no one else was available. But perhaps there is something to be said for the plainer, more homespun qualities, and for putting first the desirability of common sense at No. 10.

Bibliography

I am grateful to the authors or estates and publishers of the books marked with an asterisk for permission to quote from them.

OFFICIAL PUBLICATIONS

1st and 2nd Report from the Select Committee on Navy Estimates, Hansard 1888.

Report from the Select Committee on British South Africa 1896 (Jameson Raid report) and *Second Report* July 13 1897 311 & *Minutes of Evidence*.

*British Documents on the Origins of the War 1898–1914. Vols IV–VI. Edited by Gooch & Temperley. H.M. Stationery Office.

Documents Diplomatiques Fràncais (1871–1914) 2ᵉ Série (1901–11). Paris. Imprimerie Nationale, 1946.

OTHER WORKS

*ADAM SMITH, JANET. *John Buchan*. Rupert Hart-Davis, 1965.

ADYE, GENERAL SIR JOHN. *Recollections of a Military Life*. Smith Elder, 1895.

*ALEXANDER, GILCHRIST. *The Temple of the Nineties*. William Hodge & Co., 1938.

AMERY, JULIAN. *Life of Joseph Chamberlain*. See Garvin.

*AMERY, RT. HON. L. S. *My Political Life*. Hutchinson, 1953.

The Annual Register 1868–1908 inclusive.

ARTHUR, SIR GEORGE. *The Letters of Lord and Lady Wolseley 1870–1911*. Heinemann, 1922.

ASQUITH, H. H. *Studies and Sketches*. Hutchinson, 1924.

— *Occasional Addresses* 1893–1916. Macmillan, 1918 (see also Oxford and Asquith, Lord).

*ASQUITH, MARGOT. *Autobiography*. Thornton Butterworth, 1920. Vol. II Thornton Butterworth, 1922 (see also Oxford, Margot).

ATHERLEY-JONES, L. A. *Looking Back*. H. F. & G. Witherby, 1925.

*ATLAY, J. B. *Lord Haliburton*. Smith Elder & Co., 1909.

BACON, ADMIRAL SIR R. H. *The Life of Lord Fisher of Kilverstone*. Hodder & Stoughton, 1929.

BAGEHOT, WALTER. *The English Constitution.* 2nd ed. Kegan Paul, Trench, Trubner & Co., 1920.

BALFOUR, ARTHUR JAMES, First Earl of. *Chapters of Autobiography.* Cassell & Co., 1930.

*BALFOUR, LADY FRANCES. *Ne Obliviscaris.* 2 vols. Hodder & Stoughton, 1930.

BEALY, FRANK and PELLING, HENRY. *Labour and Politics 1900–1906.* Macmillan, 1958.

*BEERBOHM, MAX. *Mainly on the Air.* William Heinemann, 1946.

*BELL, BISHOP G. K. A. *Randall Davidson.* Oxford University Press, 1935.

*BELOFF, MAX. *Imperial Sunset.* Methuen, 1969.

BIDDULPH, GEN. SIR ROBERT. *Lord Cardwell at the War Office.* John Murray, 1904.

BIRRELL, AUGUSTINE. *Things Past Redress.* Faber & Faber, 1937.

BLAKE, ROBERT. *Disraeli.* Eyre & Spottiswoode, 1966.

*BLUNT, WILFRID SCAWEN. *My Diaries.* Martin Secker, 1919, 1920.

*BONHAM-CARTER, VIOLET. *Winston Churchill as I Knew Him.* Eyre and Spottiswoode and Collins, 1965.

*BOWLE, JOHN. *Viscount Samuel.* Gollancz, 1957.

BRIGHT, JOHN. *Diaries.* Cassell & Co., 1930.

BROWN, JOHN. 'Scottish and English Land Legislation, 1905–1911'. *Scottish Historical Review* XLVII 1 No. 143, April, 1968.

BRYCE, JAMES. *Studies in Contemporary Biography.* Macmillan, 1903.

*BUCHAN, JOHN. *Memory Hold-the-Door.* Hodder & Stoughton, 1941.

*BUTLER, JEFFREY. *The Liberal Party & the Jameson Raid.* Clarendon Press, Oxford, 1968.

CAMBON, PAUL. *Correspondance 1870–1924.* II. Editions Bernard Grasset, Paris, 1940.

CAMPBELL-BANNERMAN, THE RT. HON. SIR HENRY. *Speeches by, 1899–1908.* Selected and reprinted from *The Times.*

CECIL, LADY GWENDOLEN. *Biographical Studies of the Life and Political Correspondence of Robert, Third Marquis of Salisbury* (n.d., printed for private circulation).

CHAMBERLAIN, RT. HON. SIR AUSTEN. *Down the Years.* Cassell, 1935.

*— *Politics from the Inside.* Cassell, 1936.

CHANNING, FRANCIS ALLSTON. *Memories of Midland Politics 1885–1910.* Constable, 1918.

*CHESTERTON, G. K. *Autobiography.* Hutchinson, 1936.

CHILDERS, LT. COL. SPENCER. *The Life and Correspondence of the Rt. Hon. Hugh C. E. Childers.* 2 vols. John Murray, 1901.

*CHILSTON, ERIC ALEXANDER 2ND VISCOUNT. *Chief Whip.* Routledge & Kegan Paul, 1961.

*CHURCHILL, RANDOLPH S. *Winston S. Churchill*: Vol. II *Young Statesman* and Companion Vol. II parts I–III. Heinemann, 1967.

*CHURCHILL, WINSTON S. *Great Contemporaries*. Thornton Butterworth, 1937.

CLARKE, RT. HON. SIR EDWARD, K.C. *The Story of My Life*. John Murray, 1918.

*COLLIER, HON. E. C. F. *A Victorian Diarist. Extracts from the Journals of Mary Lady Monkswell 1873–1895. John Murray*, 1944.

*—ibid., *Later Extracts, 1895–1909*. John Murray, 1946.

CORDER, PERCY. *The Life of Robert Spence Watson*. Headley Bros., 1914.

CRATON, MICHAEL & MCCREADY, H. W. *The Great Liberal Revival 1903–6*. Hansard Society, 1966.

CREWE, LORD. *Lord Rosebery*. 2 vols. John Murray, 1931.

*CURTIS, LIONEL. *With Milner in South Africa*. Basil Blackwell, 1957.

*DOUGLAS, ROY. *The History of the Liberal Party 1895–1970* (foreword by the Rt. Hon. Jeremy Thorpe, M.P.). Sidgwick & Jackson, 1971.

DRUS, ETHEL. 'A Report on the Papers of Joseph Chamberlain Relating to the Jameson Raid and the Inquiry': *Bulletin of the Institute of Historical Research* XXV 1952; and

— *The Question of Imperial Complicity in the Jameson Raid*. 1953.

*DUGDALE, BLANCHE. *Arthur James Balfour*. 2 vols. Nat. Book Association. Hutchinson, 1939.

*DUNLOP, COL. JOHN K. *The Development of the British Army 1899–1914*. Methuen, 1938.

DU PARCQ, HERBERT. *Life of David Lloyd George*. 4 vols. Caxton Publishing Co., 1912.

ENGELENBURG, DR. F. V. *General Louis Botha*. George G. Harrap, 1929.

*ENSOR, SIR ROBERT. *England 1870–1914*. Clarendon Press, Oxford, 1936.

ESHER, REGINALD VISCOUNT. *Journals and Letters*. 4 vols. Ivor Nicholson & Watson, 1934.

— *The Influence of King Edward and Essays on Other Subjects*. John Murray, 1915.

— *Cloud Capp'd Towers*. John Murray, 1927.

FARQUHARSON, RT. HON. ROBERT. *In and Out of Parliament*. Williams & Norgate, 1911.

— *The House of Commons from Within*. 1912.

*FISHER, ADMIRAL OF THE FLEET LORD. *Records*. Hodder & Stoughton, 1929.

*— *Memories*. Hodder & Stoughton, 1919.

*FISHER, H. A. L. *James Bryce*. 2 vols. Macmillan, 1927.

*FITZROY, SIR ALMERIC. *Memoirs*. 2 vols. Hutchinson, 1925.

*FORTESCUE, THE HON. J. W. *A History of the British Army*. Vol. XIII. Macmillan, 1930.

FROUDE, J. A. *Lord Beaconsfield.* Sampson Low, Marston, Searle & Rivington, 1886.

FRY, A. RUTH. *Emily Hobhouse.* Jonathan Cape, 1929.

*FYFE, HAMILTON. *T. P. O'Connor.* George Allen & Unwin, 1934.

*GARDINER, A. G. *The Life of Sir William Harcourt.* 2 vols. Constable, 1923.

*— *Pillars of Society.* James Nisbet, 1913.

*— *Prophets, Priests and Kings.* Alston Rivers, 1908.

— *Life of George Cadbury.* Cassell, 1923.

*GARVIN, J. A. and AMERY, JULIAN. *Life of Joseph Chamberlain.* 6 vols. Macmillan, 1935–69.

GEORGE, DAVID LLOYD. *War Memoirs* I. Ivor Nicholson & Watson, 1933.

GILBERT, BENTLEY B. 'The Grant of Responsible Government to the Transvaal. More notes on a Myth'. *Historical Journal* X 4, 1907, 457–9.

GLADSTONE, W. E. *Special Aspects of the Irish Question.* John Murray, 1892.

Glasgow High School Magazine, June 1948.

*GOLLIN, A. M. *Proconsul in Politics.* Anthony Blond, 1964.

— *The Observer and J. L. Garvin.* Oxford University Press, 1960.

*GOOCH, G. P. *Life of Lord Courtney.* Macmillan, 1920.

*— *Under Six Reigns.* Longmans Green, 1958.

*— *Studies in Modern History.* Longmans Green, 1931.

GORDON WALKER, PATRICK. *The Cabinet.* Revised edition. Cape, 1972.

*GOWER, SIR GEORGE LEVESON. *Years of Endeavour 1886–1907.* John Murray, 1942.

*GRENFELL, FIELD MARSHAL LORD. *Memoirs.* Hodder & Stoughton, 1925.

GREY, VISCOUNT of FALLODON. *Twenty-Five Years.* Hodder & Stoughton, 1925.

GRIFFITH-BOSCAWEN, RT. HON. SIR ARTHUR. *Fourteen Years in Parliament.* John Murray, 1907.

*GWYNN, DENIS. *The Life of John Redmond.* George G. Harrap, 1932.

GWYNN, STEPHEN. *The Letters and Friendships of Sir Cecil Spring-Rice.* 2 vols. Constable, 1930.

— *John Redmond's Last Years.* Edward Arnold, 1919.

— and TUCKWELL, GERTRUDE N. *The Life of the Rt. Hon. Sir Charles Dilke M.P.* 2 vols. John Murray, 1917.

*HALDANE, RICHARD BURDON, VISCOUNT. *Autobiography.* Hodder & Stoughton, 1929.

— *Before the War.* Cassell, 1920.

HALIBURTON, LORD. ('Constitutionalist'.) *Army Administration in Three Centuries.* Edward Stanford, 1901.

HAMER, D. A. 'The Irish Question and Liberal Politics, 1886–1894'. *Historical Journal* XII, 3 (1969) 511–32.

— *John Morley, Liberal Intellectual in Politics.* Clarendon Press, Oxford, 1968.

HAMER, W. S. *The British Army, Civil-Military Relations 1885–1905*. Clarendon Press, Oxford, 1970.

HAMILTON, LORD GEORGE. *Parliamentary Reminiscences and Reflections*. John Murray, 1922.

*HAMMOND. J. L. *Gladstone and the Irish Nation*. Longmans Green, 1938.

*HANCOCK, SIR KEITH. *Smuts*. 2 vols. Cambridge, 1962 and 1968.

*— and VAN DER POEL. *Selections from the Smuts Papers* II. Cambridge University Press, 1966.

*HANKEY, LORD. *Diplomacy by Conference*. Ernest Benn, 1946.

*HARDINGE OF PENSHURST, LORD. *Old Diplomacy*. John Murray, 1947.

HARRIS, JOSE F. and HAZELHURST, CAMERON. 'Campbell-Bannerman as Prime Minister' in *History*, Oct. 1970, 360–83.

HAULTAIN, ARNOLD A. *A Selection from Goldwin Smith's Correspondence 1846–1910*. T. Werner Laurie (n.d.).

*HEADLAM, CECIL, ed. *The Milner Papers*. 2 vols. Cassell, 1931, 1933.

HEALY, T. M. *Letters and Leaders of My Day*. 2 vols. Thornton Butterworth, 1928.

HEUSTON, R. F. V. *Lives of the Lord Chancellors. 1885–1940*. (Lives of Lords Herschell, Loreburn & Haldane.) Clarendon Press, Oxford, 1964.

HIRST, FRANCIS W., MURRAY, GILBERT, and HAMMOND, J. L. *Liberalism and the Empire*. R. Brimley Johnson, 1900.

*HIRST, FRANCIS W. *In the Golden Days*. Frederick Muller, 1947.

— *The Six Panics and Other Essays*. Methuen, 1913.

HOLLAND, BERNARD. *The Life of Spencer Compton, 8th Duke of Devonshire*. Longmans, 1911.

HOPE, JAMES F. *A History of the 1900 Parliament*. I. 1908.

HOUGH, RICHARD. *First Sea Lord* (Admiral Lord Fisher). George Allen & Unwin, 1969.

*HYAM, RONALD. *Elgin and Churchill at the Colonial Office 1905–1908*. Macmillan, 1968.

IZVOLSKY, ALEKSANDR. *Au Service de la Russie* (correspondance diplomatique) Paris. Les éditions Internationales. 2 vols. 1937 and 1939.

— *Mémoires*. Paris, 1923.

*JAMES, DAVID. *Lord Roberts*. Hollis & Carter, 1954.

JAMES, ROBERT RHODES. *Rosebery*. Weidenfeld & Nicolson, 1963.

JENKINS, ROY. *Asquith*. Collins, 1964.

— *Sir Charles Dilke*. Collins, 1958 (revised ed. 1965).

— *Mr. Balfour's Poodle*. William Heinemann, 1954.

*JENNINGS, SIR IVOR. *Party Politics*. 2 vols. Cambridge, 1960, 1961.

— *Cabinet Government*. Cambridge University Press, 1951.

JOHNSON, FRANKLYN ARTHUR. *Defence by Committee. The British Committee of Imperial Defence 1885–1939*. Oxford University Press, 1960.

JONES, R. B. 'Anglo-French Negotiations 1907: a memorandum by Sir Alfred Milner.' *Bulletin of the Institute for Historical Research*, 31 (1958).

JONES, THOMAS. *Lloyd George*. Oxford University Press, 1957.

*KENNEDY, MAJOR GENERAL SIR JOHN. *The Business of War* (edited by Bernard Fergusson). Hutchinson, 1957.

KENT, WILLIAM. *Labour's Lost Leader: John Burns*. Williams & Norgate, 1950.

Kilvert's Diary. 3 vols. edited by William Plomer. Jonathan Cape, 1938.

KOSS, STEPHEN E. *Lord Haldane, Scapegoat for Liberalism*. Columbia University Press, 1969.

LAURENCE, SIR PERCEVAL. *The Life of John Xavier Merriman*. Constable, 1931.

LEHMANN, JOSEPH H. *All Sir Garnet. A Life of Field Marshal Lord Wolseley*. Jonathan Cape, 1964.

*LE MAY, G. H. L. *British Supremacy in South Africa 1899–1907*. Clarendon Press, Oxford, 1965.

*LEE, SIR SIDNEY. *King Edward VII*. 2 vols. Macmillan, 1925–7.

LEWSON, PHYLLIS. *Selections from the Correspondence of John X Merriman 1895–1905*. 3 vols. Van Riebeeck Society, Cape Town, 1966.

The Liberal Magazine. Liberal Publication Department, 1893–1908.

*LONDONDERRY, MARCHIONESS OF. *Henry Chaplin, A Memoir*. Macmillan, 1926.

LONG, B. K. *In Smuts's Camp*. Oxford University Press, 1945.

LOREBURN, EARL. *How the War Came*. Methuen, 1919.

LUCY, SIR HENRY. *Sixty Years in the Wilderness*. 3 vols. Smith Elder & Co., 1909, 1912, 1916.

*— *The Diary of a Journalist*. 3 vols. John Murray, 1920, 1922, 1923.

— *Peeps at Parliament*. George Newnes, 1903.

— *Later Peeps at Parliament*. George Newnes, 1905.

— *A Diary of the Salisbury Parliament 1886–1892*. Cassell & Co. 1892.

— *A Diary of the Unionist Parliament 1895–1900*. Bristol, J. W. Arrowsmith, 1901.

*— *The Balfourian Parliament 1900–1905*. Hodder & Stoughton, 1906.

— *A Diary of Two Parliaments*:
    The Disraeli Parliament 1874–80. Cassell, 1885.
    The Gladstone Parliament 1880–85. Cassell, 1886.

— *A Diary of the Home Rule Parliament 1892–1895*. Cassell, 1896.

*LYONS, F. S. L. *John Dillon*. Routledge & Kegan Paul, 1968.

MACCALLUM, R. B. *The Liberal Party from Earl Grey to Asquith*. Victor Gollancz, 1963.

MACCARTHY, DESMOND. *Portraits*. MacGibbon & Kee, 1949.

MCCOURT, EDWARD. *Remember Butler*. Routledge & Kegan Paul, 1967.

MCCREADY, H. W. 'Sir Alfred Milner, the Liberal Party and the Boer War.' *Canadian Journal of History*, March 1967.

MACKIE, J. B. *The Model Member. Sir Henry Campbell-Bannerman, Fifty Years Representative of the Stirling Boroughs.* Dunfermline, 1914.

MACMILLAN, GERALD. *Honours for Sale.* Richards Press, 1954.

MAGNUS, PHILIP. *King Edward VII.* John Murray, 1964.

*— *Gladstone.* John Murray, 1954.

*MALLET, SIR CHARLES. *Herbert Gladstone. A Memoir.* Hutchinson, 1932.

*MALLET, VICTOR (edited). *Life with Queen Victoria. Marie Mallet's Letters from Court 1887–1901.* John Murray, 1968.

*MARDER, ARTHUR J. *From the Dreadnought to Scapa Flow: The Royal Navy in the Fisher Era.* Vol. I. Oxford University Press, 1961.

— *British Naval Policy 1880–1905.* Putnam, 1946.

— *Fear God and Dread Nought. Correspondence of Admiral of the Fleet Lord Fisher of Kilverstone.* 3 vols. Jonathan Cape, 1952.

*MANSERGH, NICHOLAS. *South Africa 1906–1961. The Price of Magnanimity.* George Allen & Unwin, 1962.

*— Article on John Redmond in *The Shaping of Modern Ireland*, edited by Conor Cruise O'Brien. Routledge & Kegan Paul, 1960.

MASSINGHAM, H. J. *H. W. M. A Selection from the Writings of H. W. Massingham.* Jonathan Cape, 1925.

MASTERMAN, LUCY. *C. F. G. Masterman.* Nicholson & Watson, 1939.

*MAURICE, MAJ. GEN. SIR FREDERICK. *Haldane 1856–1915.* 2 vols. Faber & Faber, 1937.

— and ARTHUR, SIR GEORGE. *The Life of Lord Wolseley.* Heinemann, 1924.

MAUROIS, ANDRÉ. *Edouard VII et Son Temps.* Paris, Les éditions de France, 1934.

MELVILLE, COL. C. H. *Life of Gen. the Rt. Hon. Sir Redvers Buller.* Edward Arnold, 1923.

MENZIES, SIR ROBERT. *The Measure of the Years.* Cassell, 1970.

*MERSEY, VISCOUNT. *A Picture of Life.* John Murray, 1941.

*MIDLETON, THE EARL OF. *Records and Reactions. 1856–1939.* John Murray, 1939.

*MILLIN, SARAH GERTRUDE. *General Smuts.* 2 vols. Faber & Faber, 1936.

*MILLS, J. SAXON. *Sir Edward Cook, K.B.E.* Constable, 1921.

MOLTENO, SIR JAMES TENNANT. *Further South African Recollections.* Methuen, 1926.

— *The Dominion of Afrikanderdom.* Methuen, 1923.

*MONGER, GEORGE. *The End of Isolation. British Foreign Policy, 1900–1907.* Thomas Nelson & Sons, 1963.

MORGAN, BRIG. JOHN H. *John Viscount Morley.* John Murray, 1924.

*MORLEY, JOHN, VISCOUNT. *Recollections.* 2 vols. Macmillan, 1917.

*— *Memorandum on Resignation, August 1914.* Macmillan, 1928.

— Life of Gladstone, 2 vol. edition. Macmillan, 1906.

— Notes on Politics and History. Macmillan, 1913.

MOSLEY, LEONARD. *Curzon.* Longmans, 1960.

MUGGERIDGE, KITTY and ADAM, RUTH. *Beatrice Webb.* Secker & Warburg, 1967.

MUNZ, SIGMUND. *King Edward VII and Marienbad.* Hutchinson, 1934.

Murray's Handbook for Travellers in France. 1856.

The Navy Annual 1900. Portsmouth. J. Griffin & Co.

NEVINSON, HENRY W. *Changes and Chances.* Nisbet, 1923.

NEWTON, LORD. *Retrospection.* John Murray, 1941.

*NICOLSON, HAROLD, *Sir Arthur Nicolson, Bart., First Lord Carnock.* Constable, 1930.

O'BRIEN, R. B. *The Life of Charles Stewart Parnell.* Smith Elder, 1898.

*O'CONNOR, T. P. *Sir Henry Campbell-Bannerman.* Hodder & Stoughton, 1908.

— Memoirs of an Old Parliamentarian. 2 vols. Ernest Benn, 1929.

*OMOND, LT. COL. J. S. *Parliament and the Army 1642–1904.* Cambridge, 1933.

OPPENHEIMER, SIR FRANCIS. *Stranger Within.* Faber & Faber, 1960.

OWEN, FRANK. *Tempestuous Journey. Lloyd George, His Life and Times.* Hutchinson, 1932.

*OXFORD AND ASQUITH, EARL OF. *Fifty Years of Parliament.* 2 vols. Cassell & Co., 1926.

— Memories and Reflections. 2 vols. Cassell & Co., 1928.

*OXFORD, MARGOT. *More Memories.* Cassell & Co., 1933. (See also Asquith, Margot.)

PAGET, WALPURGA, LADY. *In My Tower.* 2 vols. Hutchinson, 1926.

PAKENHAM, ELIZABETH. *Jameson's Raid.* Weidenfeld & Nicolson, 1960.

PEARSON, HESKETH. *Labby. The Life and Character of Henry Labouchere.* Hamish Hamilton, 1936.

PEASE, SIR ALFRED E. *Elections and Recollections.* John Murray, 1932.

PENTLAND, LORD (chosen by). *Early Letters of Sir Henry Campbell-Bannerman to his sister Louisa, 1850–51.* T. Fisher Unwin, 1925.

PENTLAND, LADY. *Memoir of Lord Pentland.* Methuen, 1928.

PETRIE, SIR CHARLES, BT. *The Life and Letters of the Rt. Hon. Sir Austen Chamberlain.* 2 vols. Cassell, 1939 and 1940.

*POIRIER, P. P. *The Advent of the Labour Party.* George Allen & Unwin, 1958.

*PONSONBY, ARTHUR (LORD PONSONBY OF SHULBREDE). *Henry Ponsonby.* Macmillan, 1943.

*PONSONBY, SIR FREDERICK. *Memories of Three Reigns.* Eyre & Spottiswoode, 1953.

*POPE-HENNESSY, JAMES. *Lord Crewe.* Constable, 1955.

*PYRAH, G. G. *Imperial Policy and South Africa 1902–10.* Oxford, 1955.

Bibliography

RAMM, AGATHA. *The Political Correspondence of Mr. Gladstone and Lord Granville*. 2 vols. Oxford, 1962.

RAYMOND, E. T. *Portraits of the New Century*. T. Fisher Unwin, 1928.

— *The Man of Promise: Lord Rosebery*. T. Fisher Unwin, 1923.

*RENDEL, LORD. *The Personal Papers of*. Ernest Benn, 1937.

*REPINGTON, LT. COL. À COURT. *The First World War 1914–18*. Constable, 1920.

— *Vestigia*, Constable, 1919.

*RIDDELL, LORD. *Intimate Diary of the Peace Conference and After 1918–1933*. Victor Gollancz, 1933.

*— *More Pages from My Diary*. Country Life, 1934.

*ROBBINS, (DR.) KEITH. *Sir Edward Grey*. Cassell, 1971.

ROBERTSON, F. M. SIR WILLIAM. *From Private to Field-Marshal*. Constable, 1921.

*ROBINSON, RONALD and GALLAGHER, JOHN (with DENNY, ALICE). *Africa and the Victorians*. Macmillan, 1961.

*ROSE, KENNETH. *Superior Person*. Weidenfeld & Nicolson, 1969.

ROSEBERY, LORD. *Lord Randolph Churchill*. Arthur L. Humphreys, 1906.

*ROWLAND, PETER. *The Last Liberal Governments*. Barrie & Rockliff, The Cresset Press, 1968.

ROWNTREE, B. SEEBOHM. *Poverty: A Study in Town Life*. 4th ed. Macmillan, 1902.

*RUSSELL, GEORGE W. E. *Prime Ministers and Some Others*. T. Fisher Unwin, 1918.

*— *Malcolm MacColl. Memoirs and Correspondence*. Smith Elder, 1914.

*— *Sir Wilfrid Lawson. A Memoir*. Smith Elder, 1909.

*ST. AUBYN, GILES. *The Royal George. Life of HRH Prince George, Duke of Cambridge*. Constable, 1963.

*SAMUEL, VISCOUNT. *Memoirs*. The Cresset Press, 1945.

C. P. *Scott, 1846–1932. The Making of the 'Manchester Guardian'*. Frederick Muller, 1946.

SHAW OF DUNFERMLINE, LORD (LORD CRAIGMYLE). *Letters to Isabel*. Cassell & Co., 1921 (and 1936).

SHEPPARD, EDGAR. *George, Duke of Cambridge*. 2 vols. Longmans Green, 1907.

*SIMON, RT. HON. VISCOUNT. *Retrospect*. Hutchinson, 1952.

SIMPSON, PATRICK CARNEGIE. *The Life of Principal Rainy*. 2 vols. Hodder & Stoughton, 1909.

*SMUTS, J. C. *Jan Christian Smuts*. Cassell & Co., 1952.

SNOWDEN, PHILIP VISCOUNT. *An Autobiography*. 2 vols. Ivor Nicholson & Watson, 1934.

*SOMMER, DUDLEY. *Haldane of Cloan*. George Allen & Unwin, 1960.

*SPENDER, J. A. *Life of the Right Hon. Sir Henry Campbell-Bannerman, G. C. B.* Hodder & Stoughton. 2 vols. 1923. (World rights held by Kraus Reprint Corporation.)

— *Men and Things.* Cassell, 1937.

★— Life, Journalism and Politics. 2 vols. Cassell, 1927.

★— The Public Life. 2 vols. Cassell, 1925.

SPENDER, J. A. *Sir Robert Hudson.* Cassell, 1930.

— and ASQUITH, CYRIL. *Life of Herbert Henry Asquith, Lord Oxford and Asquith.* Hutchinson, 1932.

STANMORE, LORD. *Sidney Herbert.* John Murray, 1906.

STANSKY, PETER. *Ambitions and Strategies. The Struggle for the Leadership of the Liberal Party in the 1890's.* Clarendon Press, Oxford, 1964.

STEAD, W. T. Pamphlets: *Are We in the Right? Jan. 9, 1900; Joseph Chamberlain, Conspirator or Statesman.* Jan. 15, 1900; *The Scandal of the South African Committee.* Oct. 25, 1899; *Our New Rulers. The Liberal Ministry of 1906.* Jan. 1906; *Methods of Barbarism.* July 1901. And *The M.P. for Russia. Reminiscences and Correspondence of Madam Olga Novikoff.* 2 vols. Andrew Melrose, 1905.

STEINER, ZARA S. *The Foreign Office and Foreign Policy.* Cambridge University Press, 1969.

— 'Grey, Hardinge and the Foreign Office' in *Historical Journal,* X (1967), 415–37 and 'The Last Years of the Old Foreign Office 1898–1905', *Historical Journal,* VI (1963), 59–90.

STEWART, WILLIAM. *J. Keir Hardie.* I.L.P. edition issued for the Keir Hardie Memorial Committee, 1921.

★STRACHEY, RAY. *The Cause.* G. Bell & Sons, 1928.

SUTRO, SIGISMUND. *Lectures on the German Mineral Waters.* Longmans Green, 1865.

SYDENHAM, COL. LORD (OF COMBE) (SIR GEORGE CLARKE). *My Working Life.* John Murray, 1927.

SYMONS, JULIAN. *Buller's Campaigns.* The Cresset Press, 1963.

★TAYLOR, A. J. P. *The Troublemakers. Dissent over Foreign Policy 1792–1935.* (Ford Lectures, Oxford, 1956). Hamish Hamilton, 1957.

TEMPLE, SIR RICHARD. *Life in Parliament.* John Murray, 1893.

— *Letters and Character Sketches from the House of Commons.* John Murray, 1912.

THOMPSON, L. M. *The Unification of South Africa 1902–1910.* Oxford University Press, 1960.

THOROLD, ALGAR L. *The Life of Henry Labouchere.* Constable, 1913.

★*The Times, The History of,* III (1884–1912). *The Times,* 1947.

★TREVELYAN, G. M. *Grey of Fallodon.* Longmans Green, 1937.

TROLLOPE, ANTHONY. *An Autobiography.* 1883. (1950 edition, edited by Geoffrey Cumberledge. Oxford University Press.)

TYLER, J. E. 'Campbell-Bannerman and the Liberal Imperialists' (1906–1908) in *History.* Dec. 1938. Vol. 23, 254–62.

Bibliography

— *The British Army and the Continent 1904–1914*. Edward Arnold, 1938.

*VAN DER POEL, JEAN. *The Jameson Raid*. Oxford University Press, 1957.
*VANSITTART, LORD. *The Mist Procession*. Hutchinson, 1958.
VERNER, COL. WILLOUGHBY. *The Military Life of H.R.H. George Duke of Cambridge*. 2 vols. John Murray, 1905.
*VICTORIA, QUEEN, *The Letters of:* Second Series 2 vols. edited by George Earle Buckle. John Murray, 1926. Third Series 3 vols. John Murray, 1931.

WALKER, ERIC A. *A History of Southern Africa*. Longmans Green & Co., 3rd edition, 1957.
— 'The Jameson Raid'. *Cambridge Historical Journal*, VI, 3, 1940.
WATSON, ROBERT SPENCE. *The National Liberal Federation*. T. Fisher Unwin, 1917.
*WEBB, BEATRICE. *My Apprenticeship*. Longmans, 1926.
*— *Our Partnership*, edited by Barbara Drake and Margaret I. Cole. Longmans Green, 1948.
WEST. *The Private Diaries of the Rt. Hon. Sir Algernon, G.C.B.,* ed. by Horace G. Hutchinson. John Murray, 1922.
WHEELER, CAPT. OWEN. *The War Office Past and Present*. Methuen & Co., 1914.
WHYTE, FREDERICK. *The Life of W. T. Stead*. 2 vols. Jonathan Cape. 1925.
*WILKINSON, H. SPENSER. *Thirty Five Years. 1874–1909*. Constable, 1933.
*WILLIAMSON, SAMUEL H. JR. *The Politics of Grand Strategy*. Harvard University Press, 1969.
WILSON, SIR GUY FLEETWOOD. *Letters to Somebody*. Cassell, 1922.
*WILSON, TREVOR. (ed) *The Political Diaries of C. P. Scott, 1911–1928*. Collins, 1970.
*WINTERTON, EARL. *Pre-War*. Macmillan, 1932.
WOLF, LUCIEN. *Life of 1st Marquess of Ripon*. John Murray, 1921.
WOODHOUSE, C. M. 'The Missing Telegrams and the Jameson Raid.' *History Today*, June and July 1962.

*YOUNG, KENNETH. *Arthur James Balfour*. G. Bell & Sons, 1963.

*ZETLAND, MARQUESS OF. *Lord Cromer*. Hodder & Stoughton, 1932.

Notes and References

ABBREVIATIONS

MANUSCRIPT SOURCES

The British Museum
Campbell-Bannerman papers **CB**
Ripon papers **Rip**
W. E. Gladstone papers **WEG**
Herbert Gladstone papers **HG**
Balfour papers **Bal**
Edward Hamilton papers (including the diary) **EHP**
J. A. Spender papers **Spend**
Dilke papers **Dil**

The Bodleian Library
Bryce papers **Bry**
Asquith papers **Asq**

The Royal Archives
Letters and papers **RA**
Duke of Cambridge papers **Ra Cam.**
Queen Victoria's journal **RAQVJ**

National Library of Scotland
Rosebery papers **Ros**
Haldane papers **Hal**

Public Record Office
Buller papers **Bul**
Copies of Cabinet letters **Cab**

Cambridge University Library
Hardinge papers **Har**
Crewe papers **Crewe**

Public Library, Hove
Wolseley papers **Wol**

Beaverbrook Library
Lloyd George papers **Ll.G**

New College, Oxford
Milner papers **Mil**

Shulbrede
Ponsonby papers **Pon**

University of Liverpool
Birrell papers **Birr (Liv.)**

University of Edinburgh
Birrell papers **Birr (Edin.)**

Churchill College, Cambridge
Esher papers **Esh**

Chatsworth
Devonshire papers **Dev**

Stanton Harcourt
Harcourt papers **Har**
Diary of Lewis (Loulou) Harcourt **DLH**

Haddo House
Haddo House Mss. (Aberdeen papers) **HH**

Althorp
Spencer papers **Spenc**

Hopton Hall
Philip Lyttelton Gell papers **Gell**

Newtimber House
Buxton papers **Bux**

Rhodes House
Rhodes papers **Rhod**

PUBLISHED SOURCES

J. A. Spender. *The Life of the Rt. Hon. Sir Henry Campbell-Bannerman G.C.B.*
(1923) **Spender Life**
T. P. O'Connor. *Sir Henry Campbell-Bannerman* (1908) **O'Connor C.B.**
Esher, Reginald Viscount. *Journals and Letters* **Esh J&L**

The Letters of Queen Victoria. 2nd Series **LQV 2**
The Letters of Queen Victoria. 3rd Series **LQV 3**
Origines de la Guerre. Documents Diplomatiques Français. **D.D.F.**
British Documents on the Origins of the War 1898–1914. **Brit.Docs.**

PREFACE
1. Westminster Abbey muniment 59274 G May 20, 1908.
2. muniment 59274 A May 1, 1908.
3. muniment 59274 A (minute on reverse).

PART 1: GO SOUTH YOUNG MAN

CHAPTER 1: 1868
1. Esh *J&L* IV 256.
2. *Elections and Recollections* 45.
3. *London Revisited:* broadcast of 29 Dec., 1935 from *Mainly on the Air.*
4. *The Young Lady's Pleasure Book* Ward Lock & Co. (n.d.).
5. *The Diaries of John Bright* 61.
6. Ibid. p. 140. Bright was told by Dr. Gray of the Museum on April 13, 1853. The panic measures were taken in April 1848.
7. *Illustrated London News* July 18, 1868.
8. *Gladstone* Introduction.
9. *Kilvert's Diary* II 356.
10. *Illustrated London News* Oct. 17, 1868.
11. *LQV* 2 I 518.
12. Ibid. I 549–50.
13. J. A. Froude *Lord Beaconsfield* I.

14. *LQV* 2 I 564.
15. Morgan *John Viscount Morley* 94.
16. *LQV* 2 I 538.

CHAPTER 2: A BOY FROM GLASGOW
1. CB 41242. Selections published 1925 as *Early Letters of Sir Henry Campbell-Bannerman* (see Bibliography under Pentland, Lord).
2. CB 41248.
3. Spender *Life* I 19.
4. J. G. Kohl *Reisen in Schottland* Dresden 1844, quoted in Campbell-Bannerman centenary number of *Glasgow High School Magazine* June 1948.
5. *Things Past Redress* 242.
6. CB 41212.
7. CB 41212 f. 11.
8. CB 41212 f. 19.
9. CB 41212 f. 93.
10. CB 41250A f. 43.
11. CB 41248B.
12. CB 41248B ff. 72 and 75.
13. CB 41248B.
14. CB 41248B f. 64.
15. CB 41248D ff. 25–6.
16. Ibid f. 34.
17. CB 41250A f. 63.

CHAPTER 3 PARLIAMENT:
1. CB 41212 f. 153.
2. *Diaries* 304.

3. by Mr. Thomas Shaw
4. Quoted in *Western Mail* April 23, 1908.
5. J. B. Mackie *The Model Member* 22–3.
6. Bry uncatalogued Jan. 26, 1913.
7. *The English Constitution* Introduction to Second Edition.
8. referred to in his speech introducing the National Education (Ireland) Bill March 24, 1885.
9. CB 41252. Memorandum by Henry Higgs.
10. Mackie *op. cit.* 36.
11. Nov. 14, 1871.
12. Spender *Life* I 62.

CHAPTER 4: CARDWELL AND THE WAR OFFICE

1. Lord Stanmore *Sidney Herbert* II 369, quoting letter from her Nov. 18, 1859.
2. April 23, 1908.
3. Maurice and Arthur *Life of Lord Wolseley* 56.
4. Verner *Military Life of Duke of Cambridge* II 1–5.
5. Evidence before the Finance Committee, quoted in *Verner, op. cit.* II 5.
6. Ibid. II 5.
7. Bernal Osborne in debate on Army Regulation Bill 1871. C.B.'s own account of the abolition of purchase, in a letter to a constituent in July 1889, is at CB 41233 ff. 42–5.
8. A. M. Gollin *Proconsul in Politics* 188–91.

9. St Aubyn *The Royal George* 71–2.
10 Verner *op. cit.* I 109.
11. Monypenny & Buckle *Disraeli* VI 473–4, quoted in Omond *Parliament and the Army* 133.
12. *The English Constitution* Ch. VI 206.
13. Spender *Life* I 41–2.
14. Esh *J&L* II 196.

CHAPTER 5: THE JUNIOR MINISTER

1. *Annual Register* 1871 17–18.
2. Mackie *op. cit.* 41.
3. CB 41244.
4. Henry Lucy *A Diary of Two Parliaments (The Disraeli Parliament)* 22–3.
5. *Times* March 16 (and Feb. 23 for report of an earlier speech).
6. RA A48/32 March 17, 1875, quoted in Magnus *Gladstone* 236.
7. Mackie *op. cit.* 51.
8. Gwynn & Tuckwell *Life of Dilke* I 233 Appendix.
9. Dev. 340. 747.
10. O'Connor *C.B.* 38–9.
11. Mackie *op. cit.* 50–1.
12. *Life of Childers* I 245.
13. Oxford & Asquith. *Fifty years of Parliament* I 207–8.
14. *Chapters of Autobiography* 141.
15. biography of William Pitt written for the *Encyclopaedia Britannica*.
16. *Diaries* 297.
17. Mackie *op. cit.* 57–8.
18. *Fifty Years of Parliament* I 136.
19. J. S. Omond *Parliament and the Army* 128.
20. Childers to Gladstone Oct 1,

1844, quoted in *Life of Childers* II 166.

21. CB 41232 f. 22. from Cairo Sept. 1888.
22. CB 41229 f. 323 to C. Robert Spencer (Lord Althorp) May 18 (copy).
23. CB 41252 f. 226.
24. WEG 44131 ff. 178–80.
25. Spender *Life* I 57.
26. EHP 48638 ff. 11–12 and 34.
27. CB 41232 ff. 105–6.
28. CB 41226 f. 100.

PART 2: IRELAND

CHAPTER 6: THE CHIEF SECRETARY

1. Sampson *Anatomy of Britain* 1st ed. 325 & Macmillan 60–1.
2. Introducing, as Colonial Secretary, Irish Free State Bill in House of Commons, 1922.
3. Gladstone's denunciation of the way in which the Union was carried is elaborated in his *Special Aspects of the Irish Question* (1892).
4. Quoted, most recently, in Blake *Disraeli* 178–9.
5. *Diaries* 102.
6. *Diaries* 103.
7. Esh *J&L* I 76.
8. EHP 48637 f. 119.
9. O'Connor *Memoirs of an Old Parliamentarian* I 31 and 220.
10. *Fifty Years of Parliament* I 186.
11. *Great Contemporaries*. Essay on Charles Stewart Parnell.
12. Gardiner *Sir William Harcourt* I 422.

13. H. A. L. Fisher *James Bryce* I 205–6.
14. Gardiner, *op. cit.* I, 451–2.
15. Mackie, *op. cit.*
16. F. S. L. Lyons *John Dillon* III.
17. Oxford and Asquith *Fifty Years of Parliament* I 121–2.
18. Gwynn and Tuckwell *Life of Sir Charles W. Dilke* I 440.
19. Collier *A Victorian Diarist Later Extracts* 204.
20. Margot Oxford *More Memories* 79 and 85.
21. EHP 48637 ff. 15 and 30.
22. WEG 44311 f. 197.
23. EHP 48637 f. 124.
24. DLH.
25. Spender *Life* I 58–9.
26. Ibid. 59.
27. WEG 44311 f. 209.
28. Birr (Liv.) MS. 10.2.8 (6) 25 Dec. 1906.
29. EHP 48638 ff. 2, 9, 11. WEG 44311 f. 214.
Ramm, *Political Correspondence of Mr. Gladstone and Lord Granville.* II 279.
30. Ros Oct. 27, 1884.
31. *Life of Childers* II 190.
32. CB 41221 f. 221.
33. Mackie *op. cit.* 65.
34. *Fifty Years of Parliament* II 28.
35. O'Connor *C.B.* 23.
36. *Spectator* Feb. 17, 1894 223.
37. O'Connor *C.B.* 24–6.
38. CB 41228 ff. 39 and 50.
39. CB 41228 f. 140 (copy).
40. Wol Autograph collection, Bannerman I.
41. CB 41251 B.
42. WEG 44117 f. 13.
43. Spenc. CB letters I 55.

44. Ibid. I 27.
45. Committee of Ways and Means March 20, 1885 *Hansard* col. 190.
46. Spenc CB letters I 36.
47. G. W. E. Russell *Prime Ministers and Some Others* 71.
48. Spenc CB letters I 68.
49. Spender *Life* I 70.
50. Ibid.
51. Spenc CB letters II March 27, 1885.
52. Spenc CB letters II March 27, 1885. No. 177.
53. WEG 44312 f. 69 March 26, 1885.
54. March 12, 1885. *Hansard*, cols. 923–8.
55. Spenc CB letters II 166.
56. Spender *Life* I 73.
57. CB 41251 B f. 26.
58. CB 41207 f. 3.
59. Spenc CB letters II 118 Feb. 13, 1885.
60. CB 41228 f. 148 Feb. 28 (copy).
61. CB 41215 ff. 7 and 8 and Ibid f. 281 (copy).
62. Ibid f. 230 (copy).
63. CB 41228 f. 260 (copy).
64. Garvin *Life of Chamberlain* I 604.
65. Spenc CB letters II June 17, 1885.

CHAPTER 7: HOME RULE AND THE LIBERAL SPLIT
1. *Annual Register* 1871 105–6. Speech at Aberdeen.
2. CB 41228 f. 296.
3. *Daily News* Dec. 23, 1885 (see CB 41228 f. 301).
4. Arthur Ponsonby *Henry Ponsonby* 202.
5. Spender *Life* I 90–1.
6. Ibid. I 91–2.
7. Ibid. I 92–5.
8. Ibid. I 95–7, to Spencer.
9. RA T9/59.
10. Esh *J&L* I 126.
11. *Times* May 14, 1886.
12. *Hansard* Third Ser. cccv 932–48.
13. Pease *Elections and Recollections* 132
14. *Times* May 14, 1886.
15. Temple *Letters and Character Sketches from the House of Commons* 71, 162-4.
16. quoted in *Liberal Magazine* II 338.
17. CB 41232 ff. 218, 220 & 227.
18. CB 41232 f. 231.
19. CB 41232 f. 253.
20. CB 41232 ff. 300-3 July 21.
21. Wol Autograph collection, Bannerman 3.

CHAPTER 8: IRELAND: THE LAST TWENTY YEARS.
1. *Fifty Years of Parliament.*
2. Margot Asquith *Autobiography*, 137–8.
3. CB 41215 ff. 27–9 Dec. 10.
4. Gardiner *Sir William Harcourt* I 34.
5. CB 41246 f. 8.
6. In the *United Irishman* June 19, 1886, quoted in F. S. L. Lyons *John Dillon* 79.
7. Temple *Letters and Character Sketches from the House of Commons* 289.
8. *Times* July 12, 1887 and *Annual Register* 1887, p. 117.
9. July 14, 1887.

10. July 12, 1887.
11. CB 41242 f. 20 Feb. 27, 1889.
12. March 27, 1890, quoted in Hammond *Gladstone and the Irish Nation* 730.
13. *Fifty Years of Parliament* I 181.
14. CB 41228 ff. 20–1. O'Shea to Dilke Oct. 26, 1884 endorsed 'Chamberlain – if you agree will you send this confidentially to Campbell-Bannerman C.V.D.'
15. Quoted in Hammond *op. cit.* 645.
16. Spender *Life* I 121–2.
17. Hammond *op. cit.* 632.
18. Nov. 22, 1890, quoted in Gardiner *op. cit.* II 83.
19. Ibid. 87.
20. Healy *Letters and Leaders of My Day* I 339.
21. *Annual Register* 1890 263.
22. EHP 48658 f. 6. diary May 24, 1892.
23. Lyons *op. cit.* 156.
24. *Hansard* vol. 58, cols. 130–2. Quoted in Lyons *op. cit.*
25. DLH.
26. *The Private Diaries of Sir Algernon West* 80–1 (see also DLH Nov. 18).
27. Margot Asquith *Autobiography* 126 (Dec. 27, 1892).
28. Quoted in Verner *Military Life of the Duke of Cambridge.* II 379–81.
29. CB 41230 ff. 231–5. Note by C.B. on position of the Army in Ireland under Home Rule. May 1, 1893. *Annual Register* 1893.
30. CB 41252 f. 45.
31. *Annual Register* 1899.
32. Ibid.
33. Lucy *The Balfourian Parliament* 140, Feb., 1902.
34. H. W. McCready *Home Rule and the Liberal Party* 1899. 1906 (*Irish Historical Studies* XIII 1962–3).
35. Crewe. Copy Crewe to CB Nov. 19, 1905 and CB to Crewe Nov. 3, 1905.
36. HG 45988 f. 201
37. HG 45989 f. 131.
38. HG 45988 f. 196 (from Vienna).
39. Redmond papers, Dublin. Memo by J. E. Redmond Nov. 14, 1905.
40. *Times* Nov. 24, 1905.
41. Lyons *op. cit.* 280–1.
42. Copy in Redmond papers.
43. Goldwin Smith papers. Cornell University.
44. Kenneth Young, *Arthur James Balfour* 319.
45. RA R 28/3. C.B. to Knollys.
46. CB 41211 f. 344.
47. Ibid. f. 353.
48. Pon. Letter to his wife May 7, 1907.
49. *Prophets, Priests and Kings* 303.
50. Speech at Manchester, May 10, 1907.
51. Fyfe *T. P. O'Connor* 217.
52. Pon May 28, 1907.
53. CB 41223 f. 247.
54. Bryce to Goldwin Smith May 31, 1907, quoted in H. A. L. Fisher. *James Bryce* I 355.
55. CB 52512.
56. Asq 10 ff. 224–5 Sept. 5.
57. Cabinet letter. Copy at CB 52513. Original does not

appear to be in RA.
58. quoted in Gwynn *Life of John Redmond* 153.
59. Ibid. 154.
60. CB 41240 ff. 173–4.
61. *Times* Jan. 7, 1970.
62. His essay on John Redmond in *The Shaping of Modern Ireland* 42. The suggestion that Redmond aspired to fill the rôle of an Irish Botha is made in Mansergh *South Africa 1906–1961: The Price of Magnanimity* 96.

PART 3: C.B.'s WAY OF LIFE

CHAPTER 9: A VANISHED WORLD

1. F. W. Hirst *In the Golden Days* 256–7. Notes by Arthur Ponsonby.
2. O'Connor *C.B.* 8–9.
3. CB 41246 f. 140.
4. CB 41218 f. 361.
5. *The Scottish Review* April 30, 1908.
6. *L'Evénement*, Paris, April 23, 1908.
7. Viscount Mersey *A Picture of Life* 192.
8. CB 41214 f. 145.
9. Lady Pentland *Memoir of Lord Pentland* 77.
10. Pon.
11. CB 41246 f. 283.
12. CB 41215 ff. 37–8.
13. CB 41251 A.
14. Collier *A Victorian Diarist* 265 and Ibid. *Later Extracts* 57.
15. Lucy *Sixty Years in the Wilderness* III 145.
16. Pon. Aug. 21, 1906.
17. Collier *op. cit. Later Extracts* 57.
18. EHP 48641 ff. 34 and 36.
19. *The Personal Papers of Lord Rendel*, 167.
20. Hirst. *op. cit.* 261. Notes by Ponsonby.
21. I 147.
22. *Times* Jan. 3, 1903.
23. *Things Past Redress* 243.
24. *The Scottish Review* April 30, 1908. 'C.B. at Home' by Sarah A. Tooley in the *Daily Chronicle* April 23, 1908. CB 41252 f. 218. The pictures and some of the furniture are now in the possession of Mrs. Hugh Campbell.
25. CB 41252 f. 218.
26. CB 41252 f. 232 Blanche de Hoeltzke to Lord Pentland, and f. 146 memo by Henry Higgs.
27. Information from the late Marjorie, Lady Pentland.
28. Spender *Life* II 48.
29. Margot Asquith *Autobiography* 164.
30. O'Connor *C.B.* 119.
31. Ibid.
32. All in CB 52520 IX.
33. All in CB 41206 f. 80.

CHAPTER 10: MARIENBAD

1. Sir Frederick Ponsonby, *Memories of Three Reigns* 229.
2. *Lectures on the German Mineral Waters* 1865.
3. *Records* 30–1.
4. CB 41246 f. 71.
5. Fisher *Memories* 157
6. CB 41206 ff. 304, 307, 308 and 310.

7. Wol LW/P 15/17.
8. Wol Sept. 4, 1890. LW/P 16/22.
9. HG 45987 f. 14 Aug. 27, 1899.
10. CB 41246 f. 71.
11. CB 41221 f. 268 Aug. 13, 1900.
12. CB 41230 f. 39.
13. Sigmund Munz *King Edward VII at Marienbad* 24, 147.
14. CB 52517.
15. Bry uncatalogued Aug. 26.
16. Aug. 30, 1905. CB 52518 (copy).
17. CB 41217 f. 25.
18. CB 41252 f. 70.
19. Quoted in Mallet *Herbert Gladstone* 190.
20. *Memories of Three Reigns* 234.
21. CB 41252 f. 146 memo by H. Higgs.
22. CB 41249 x.
23. Pon to his wife Aug. 15, 1906.
24. Edinburgh University Library. CB to Mrs. Langenbach March 12, 19??

CHAPTER 11: THE MEMBER FOR STIRLING

1. HH 1/5 'Letters from P.M.'s' C.B. to Lady Aberdeen Nov. 6, 1904.
2. *Daily Chronicle* April 23, 1908.
3. CB 41246 f. 55 to James Campbell.
4. *Review of Reviews* Jan. 1906. *Character Sketch: The New Cabinet* 18.
5. Marchioness of Londonderry *Henry Chaplin*.
6. CB 41246 f. 37: to James Campbell May 11, 1891.
7. Article in *The Nation and the Athenaeum* May 21, 1921 281 note.

8. *Autobiography* 146.
9. In The *Reader* March 9, 1907.
10. *The Review of Reviews* Jan. 1906. *Character Sketch: The New Cabinet.*
11. CB 41221 ff. 272–6.
12. CB 41221 ff. 234–8.
13. Notes by Arthur Ponsonby quoted in Hirst *In the Golden Days* 261
14. CB 41252 f. 218. Notes by Sir Gordon Voules.
15. CB 41221 f. 218 and 41246 f. 39.
16. CB 41231 f. 214. Sept. 11, 1906.
17. CB 41219 ff. 74–5 and 76–9. Letters of Dec. 31, 1894 and Jan. 8, 1895.
18. Spender *Life* I 180.
19. Har Mar. 6, 1895.
20. Ibid.
21. CB 41212 f. 202.
22. Ibid. f. 207.
23. CB 41246 f. 24.
24. Ibid. f. 26.
25. CB 41232 f. 143.
26. RA Cam. July 7, 1886.
27. CB 41237 f. 105.
28. CB 41246 f. 12. Oct. 15, 1887.
29. CB 41246 f. 24.
30. Dec. 6, 1908.
31. CB 41214 f. 145.
32. CB 41233 f. 46.
33. Shaw *Letters to Isabel.*
34. Bry uncatalogued Oct. 30, 1904.
35. CB 41246 f. 30. to James Campbell.
36. CB 41246 f. 33 (1890).
37. Bry uncatalogued Jan. 17.
38. WEG 44117 f. 59 July 9, 1886.
39. CB 41236 f. 214.

PART 4: THE SECRETARY OF STATE

CHAPTER 12: THE WAR OFFICE AGAIN
1. p. 189.
2. EHP 48641 f. 132.
3. RA T 9/59 Jan. 31.
4. RA T 9/61 Feb. 1.
5. LQV 3 I 42 Feb. 3.
6. RA QVJ. Feb. 3.
7. RA C37/285.
8. Feb. 4.
9. CB 41215 f. 9. Gladstone to CB Feb. 4.
10. Feb. 10. Spender *Life* I 101.
11. CB 41252 f. 146.
12. CB 41215 f. 9.
13. DLH Feb. 15, 1886.
14. Har Feb. 26, minute to Lord Ripon, 'for Campbell-Bannerman'.
15. Ibid.
16. Dil 43938 ff. 18–19.
17. Esh *J&L* I 269.
18. CB 41206 f. 1 Feb. 17.
19. RA Cam. CB to Duke of Cambridge April 5, 1886.
20. CB 41216 f. 48.
21. RA B 37/62 May 11.
22. WEG 44117 f. 50.
23. WEG 44117 f. 82.
24. *Hansard* Third Ser. cccxxxiii col. 1478.
25. Rip 43517 f. 7 Nov. 12, 1888.
26. Dev 340–2213.
27. Rip 43517 f. 3.
28. C. 5979 *Preliminary and Further Reports of the Royal Commissioners appointed to enquire into the Civil and Professional Administration of the Naval and Military Departments and the Relation of those Departments to each other and to the Treasury 1890.*
29. Dev 340–2225 Jan. 12, 1890.
30. C. 5979 pp. XXIX to XXXI.
31. *Hansard*. 3rd ser. cccxlvi cols. 876 and 878.
32. Arthur Ponsonby. *Henry Ponsonby* 217.
33. St. Aubyn. *Royal George* 301.
34. CB 41246 f. 39.
35. Ponsonby *op. cit.* 217.
36. Quoted in Viscount Grey, *Lord Haldane* in *Public Administration* Oct. 1928.
37. DLH August 1.
38. RA Cam. letter of Aug. 15, 1892.
39. 1928 memo quoted in Young, *Arthur James Balfour* 111.
40. RA Cam. letter of Nov. 10, 1892.
41. CB 41230 f. 303 Oct. 6, 1894.
42. Wol Autograph collection, Bannerman 4 Nov. 25, 1892.
43. Maurice and Arthur. *Life of Lord Wolseley* 264.
44. CB 41233 ff. 182–5.
45. RA QVJ.
46. copy at CB 41206 f. 82.
47. WEG 44117 f. 99 Nov. 1.
48. CB 41206 f. 85 Nov 1.
49. Ibid. f. 91.
50. Ibid. f. 92 Nov. 26.
51. Ibid. f. 96 Dec. 5.
52. Ibid. f. 103.
53. CB 41226 f. 133.
54. CB 41226 f. 135. Dec. 29.
55. Har Sept. 27.
56. Sir Guy Fleetwood Wilson *Letters to Somebody* 131–2.
57. *Memoirs of F. M. Lord Grenfell*, 116.

58. Earl of Midleton *Records and Reactions* 83–4.
59. CB 41252 f. 203.
60. Quoted in the *Western Mail* April 23, 1908. Other references make clear that this was Stead.
61. March 7, 1892. *Hansard* 4th ser. II c. 202.
62. *Memories and Reflections* I 90–2.
63. Ibid. II 161.
64. *Letters and Character Sketches from the House of Commons,* 164.
65. CB 41242 f. 50.
66. WEG 44314 f. 70.
67. *Hansard* 4th ser. IX cols. 1800–2.
68. *Hansard* 4th ser. IX 1529–30.
69. Ibid. col. 1544.
70. Ibid. col. 1545.
71. *Annual Register* 1893 86 and 89.
72. *Hansard* 4th ser. XXXI 1132.
73. Ibid. col. 1714.
74. Har Nov. 23, 1892.
75. Har Jan. 4, 1893 (copy).
76. Spenc 1893 Box A–D.
77. CB 41219 ff. 64–5. Jan. 19, 1894.
78. WEG 44117 ff. 119–21. June 29, 1893.
79. *LQV* 3 II 308 Sept. 2, 1893.
80. CB 41209 f. 85.
81. Ibid. f. 89.
82. CB 41206 f. 138.
83. Quoted by Mr. Dalziel in House of Commons debate *Times* Sept. 12, 1893.
84. CB 41206 f. 163.
85. Sept. 21. *LQV* 3 II 308.
86. *Times* Sept. 12, 1893.

87. CB 41206 f. 164.
88. *LQV* 3 I 627 and 629–31.
89. Feb. 17, 1894.
90. Wol Autograph collection, Bannerman 8.
91. CB 41233 ff. 153–7.
92. Wol. Autograph collection, Bannerman 9.
93. CB 41226 f. 217.
94. CB 41206 f. 119.
95. Fleetwood Wilson. *op. cit.* 73–4.
96. CB 52517.
97. Rip 43517 f. 80.
98. CB 41226 f. 160 Jan 15, 1894.
99. CB 41206 ff. 176 and 196.
100. WEG 44117 f. 108. See also CB 41233 ff. 176–7.
101. Nov. 1, 1893 '*To Your Tents O Israel*' by the Fabian Society. Beatrice Webb points out in *Our Partnership* that it was written by Shaw.
102. Jan. 3, 1895. Collier *A Victorian Diarist* 262.
103. *Records* 51–3.
104. *Hansard* 4th ser. XXII c. 167 March 13, 1894.
105. Ibid. XXXI col. 1158.
106. Ibid. col. 1184.
107. Spenc Box 1895 A–H Feb. 1.
108. Omond *Parliament and the Army* 140–1.
109. *Hansard* 4th Ser. XXXIV 1677–8.

CHAPTER 13: THE DISLODGING OF
THE DUKE

1. EHP 48665 f. 99.
2. Ros.
3. *LQV* 3 II 500–1 and Verner *Military Life of the Duke of Cambridge* II 395.

4. RA E41/8.
5. RA E41/11.
6. Ibid.
7. Ibid.
8. *LQV* 3 II 502.
9. Ibid. 503.
10. Ibid. 504.
11. Ibid. 506.
12. Ros May 14.
13. RA E 41/47.
14. RA QVJ May 15 (also quoted in *LQV* 3 II 507).
15. Ros May 15.
16. *LQV* 3 II 508.
17. Ros May 16.
18. RA QVJ May 16. Quoted in *LQV* 3 II 509.
19. Ibid. May 17.
20. *LQV* 3 II 510.
21. Ros.
22. Ros.
23. CB 41226 f. 211.
24. CB 41209 f. 204.
25. Ros May 19.
26. Ros May 19.
27. CB 41206 f. 257.
28. *LQV* 3 II 512–13 and Verner, *op. cit.* II 395.
29. Verner *op. cit.* II 241.
30. *LQV* 3 II 513.
31. CB 41206 f. 263.
32. *LQV* 3 II 514.
33. Ibid. 516–7.
34. Ibid. 517 June 11.
35. CB 41206 f. 269.
36. Ibid. f. 267.
37. RA E 41/87 (quoted in *LQV* 3 II 517–8).
38. CB 41209 f. 209.
39. *LQV* 3 II 518–19.
40. Ibid. 519.
41. CB 41209 f. 209.
42. *LQV* 3 II 520.
43. Ibid. 519.
44. to Bigge. Ros.
45. RA E 41/109.
46. *Fifty Years of Parliament* I 231.
47. *Hansard* 4th ser. XXXIV c. 1673–5.
48. *LQV* 3 II 522. Memo by Queen Victoria June 22, 1895 on talk with Rosebery.
49. CB 41226 ff. 222–3 P.P.S. and 41209 f. 221 June 22.
50. CB 41209 f. 222 (copy).

CHAPTER 14: THE CORDITE VOTE
AND AFTER

1. Jan. 21, 1924 was the last time a government (that of Baldwin) resigned because of a defeat in the House on an issue of confidence, but this was not caused by the defection of Conservatives but because the election of 1923 had failed to produce a decisive result. In May 1940 Neville Chamberlain resigned although he still had a majority, since he had lost the confidence of a large section of the House. Over 30 Conservatives voted against him and about 60 abstained. This was the last occasion on which a government was brought down by a vote in the House. (Information from Research Division, Library, House of Commons.)
2. Earl of Midleton *Records and Reactions* 87–90.
3. *Hansard* 4th ser. XXXIV cols. 1687–1713.

4. Griffith-Boscawen *Fourteen Years in Parliament*.
5. *Letters to Somebody* 131.
6. J. B. Atlay *Lord Haliburton* 130.
7. G. W. E. Russell *Sir Wilfrid Lawson* 224.
8. *Manchester Guardian* June 22, 1895.
9. *Fifty Years of Parliament* 231.
10. *Memories and Reflections* I 137–8.
11. RA QVJ June 21 (quoted in *LQV* 3 II 521).
12. Har June 21 7.30 p.m.
13. CB 41233 f. 224.
14. CB 41226 f. 218 (copy).
15. EHP 48667 f. 35.
16. RA QVJ June 22.
17. DLH June 23.
18. RA QVJ June 22.
19. *Life of Gladstone*, 1906 2 vol. edition II 416–17.
20. *Things Past Redress* 143
21. CB 41233 ff. 225–6.
22. *Times* June 22.
23. June 24.
24. CB 41246 f. 57.
25. CB 52517.
26. CB 41226 f. 229.
27. CB 41226 ff. 219–20 June 24.
28. CB 41246 f. 63 July 1.
29. CB 52520 Memo by Mrs. Mayne, Oct. 1921.
30. CB 41233 f. 250.
31. Collier *A Victorian Diarist* 272.
32. Midleton *Records & Reactions* 88.
33. Quoted in appreciation of Wolseley by Lonsdale Hale. *Journal of the Royal United Service Institution* LVII No. 422, April 1913.
34. CB 41212 f. 227.
35. RA Cam. June 1, 1896.
36. Wol. W/P 24/91/7.
37. DLH June 29.
38. *The Times*.
39. RA C40/86.
40. *Times* April 23, 1908.
41. DLH July 2.
42. *Hansard* 4th ser. XXXV cols. 100–15.
43. CB 41218 ff. 335–6. C.B. to Haliburton Aug. 15, 1895.
44. *Annual Register* 1901.
45. *Memoirs of Field-Marshal Lord Grenfell* 120.
46. In the *Manchester Guardian* Dec. 6, 1905.
47. Atlay *Lord Haliburton* 117.
48. Har.
49. *LQV* 3 II 556.
50. Atlay *op. cit.* 211.
51. Ibid.
52. CB 41218 ff. 338–40 Jan. 12, 1898.
53. Atlay *op. cit.* 216.
54. P.R.O. Bul WO 132/5 June 29, 1899.
55. Wol W/P 27/27 June 22, 1898.
56. Feb. 16. *Annual Register* 1900 and Dunlop *Development of the British Army*.
57. Jan. 26. CB 41235 f. 193.
58. *Annual Register* 1900 and 1901.
59. Har Nov. 21, 1901.
60. Bry uncatalogued Jan. 26.
61. Young *Arthur James Balfour* 229–30.
62. Gardiner *Life of Harcourt* II 448.
63. Spenc. Box 1903 A–H.
64. HH 1/11 Bundle 1 Sept. 13, 1903.
65. Spenc. quoted in Robbins *Sir Edward Grey* 133–4.

66. Esh *J&L* II 50.
67. CB 41226 f. 60 June 17.
68. House of Commons March 29, 1904, quoted in Spender *Life* II 150.
69. CB 41212 f. 282.
70. CB 41218 ff. 356–7.
71. Rip 43518 f. 31. Feb. 25, 1905.
72. Young, *op. cit.* 232–3.
73. CB 41218 ff. 360–1 Feb. 27, 1906.
74. Esh *J&L* II 153.
75. *History of the British Army* XIII 570.
76. p. 162.
77. CB 41210 f. 289.
78. CB 41218 ff. 177–84.
79. March 10. Quoted in Koss *Lord Haldane* 46
80. Hankey *Diplomacy by Conference.*
81. Gosse diary 73.
82. Ibid.
83. Spend 46390 f. 152.
84. *Hansard* 4th ser. CXVIII 1588.
85. HH 1/11 Bundle 1 March 12, 1903.
86. Esh *J&L* II 127.
87. Hankey *op. cit.* 54.
88. RA W 39/127.
89. Esh *J&L* II 208 and 224.
90. CB 41240.
91. CB 41252 f. 131 to Lord Pentland, Sept. 17, 1919.
92. Esh *J&L* II 267.
93. Koss *op. cit.* 44.
94. Asq 10 f. 196 Jan. 5, 1906.
95. CB 41210 f. 258 Jan 7.
96. Pon.
97. CB 41230 f. 172.
98. CB 41213 f. 358 Oct. 10.

99. *Hansard* 4th ser. CLXII 1397–8.
100. Viscount Mersey *A Picture of Life* 220.
101. CB 41213 f. 326.
102. CB 41213 ff. 294–7.
103. Sydenham *My Working Life* 213.
104. Maurice *Haldane* I 225.

PART 5: C.B.'s ACCESSION TO THE LEADERSHIP

CHAPTER 15: NEARING THE SUMMIT

1. Feb. 17, 1894 223–4
2. EHP 48641 f. 3.
3. EHP 48644 f. 15 diary May 31, 1886.
4. CB 41223 f. 3 Nov. 1.
5. Quoted in Beatrice Webb *My Apprenticeship* 185 and in turn by Lord Oxford and Asquith in *Memories and Reflections* I 41, and Magnus *Gladstone* 323.
6. Magnus *Gladstone* 405.
7. *Grey of Fallodon* 170.
8. Essay on C. P. Scott *Liberal and Humanist* in *C. P. Scott 1846–1932: The Making of the Manchester Guardian* 84.
9. *Autobiography.*
10. Quoted in *The Liberal Magazine* for Jan. 1898, 530.
11. *Memories and Reflections* I 135.
12. CB 41246 f. 42.
13. CB 41246 f. 44 to James Campbell Nov. 20, 1893.
14. CB 41246 f. 39 Aug. 15, 1892.
15. EHP 48658 f. 103 diary for Aug. 1892.

16. WEG 44791 f. 42 *Recorded Errors.*
17. Gardiner *Life of Sir William Harcourt* II 182–3.
18. DLH.
19. *Private Diaries of the Rt. Hon. Sir Algernon West*, entries for May 3 and June 20. Letters from Knollys of Aug 6 (p. 187) and Aug. 7 (p. 186).
20. Speech at Royal Colonial Institute March 1893.
21. Margot Asquith *Autobiography* 122.
22. Esh *J&L* II 239 and I 170–1.
23. R. R. James *Rosebery* 84 note.
24. Desmond MacCarthy *Portraits* 127. Essay on Sir William Harcourt.
25. Esh *J&L* II 84.
26. E. T. Cook's diary for March 18, 1893, quoted in J. Saxon Mills *Sir Edward Cook* 146.
27. 1st edition 75.
28. Wol Autograph collection, Bannerman 1, Jan. 10.
29. *Private Diaries of Sir Algernon West* 190–1.
30. Har.
31. WEG 44117 f. 98.
32. Robinson, Gallagher & Denny *Africa and the Victorians* 319.
33. *Private Diaries of Sir Algernon West* 123.
34. Zetland *Lord Cromer* 203.
35. CB 41246 f. 45 Nov. 20.
36. Collier *A Victorian Diarist* 241.
37. WEG 44791 f. 42 *Recorded Errors.*
38. WEG 44117 ff. 129–30 June 30, 1897.
39. CB 41215 ff. 56–7 July 5.
40. Collier *op. cit.* 241–2.
41. *Things Past Redress* 137.
42. *Fifty Years of Parliament* I 221–2 and 224.
43. *Rosebery* II 440.
44. DLH.
45. quoted in Crewe *Rosebery* II 441.
46. EHP 48663 f. 7.
47. EHP 48662 f. 85 diary Jan. 30, 1894.
48. DLH.
49. EHP 48663 f. 105 May 10.
50. EHP 48665 ff. 36–7 diary Nov. 3.
51. March 12.
52. CB 41211 f. 5 (copy).
53. March 5, 1894. *History Today* Jan. 1952, 22.
54. Har March 7.
55. Har March 7.
56. Har.
57. DLH April 6.
58. DLH.
59. EHP 48664.
60. EHP 48664 f. 97 diary Aug. 26, 1894.
61. Ibid. f. 95 Aug. 24.
62. CB 41246 f. 52 Feb. 1895.
63. 1891 p. 24.
64. *The Personal Papers of Lord Rendel* 164.
65. *Fifty Years of Parliament* I 224.
66. CB 41210 f. 159.
67. Beatrice Webb, *Our Partnership* 121 quoting diary for Jan. 20, 1895.
68. Feb. 26, 1897 quoted in Crewe. *Rosebery* II 536–7.
69. Har.
70. Esh *J&L* I 181.
71. CB 41246 f. 52.

CHAPTER 16: THE SPEAKER'S CHAIR

1. Lucy *A Diary of the Home Rule Parliament* 472.
2. DLH.
3. EHP 48666 f. 42.
4. DLH.
5. *Things Past Redress* 139.
6. Farquharson *In and Out of Parliament* 294 and Lucy *Later Peeps at Parliament* 118–19.
7. Gardiner *Harcourt* II 354.
8. Ros March 9, 1895.
9. DLH March 11.
10. Spender *Life* I 174–5.
11. CB 41226 ff. 196–7.
12. DLH March 12.
13. DLH.
14. *Diary of a Journalist* 198.
15. CB 41233 f. 212 March 16.
16. To Mr. D. Gorrie of Dunfermline March 19. Spender *Life* I 176.
17. DLH.
18. DLH March 15.
19. DLH.
20. EHP 48666 f. 57.
21. Ros March 17 (copy).
22. WEG 44290 f. 256.
23. DLH.
24. Gardiner *Harcourt* II 355–6.
25. RA A 71/28 B.
26. EHP 48666 ff. 70–1.
27. *Personal Papers of Lord Rendel* 128.
28. RA T10/44.
29. EHP 48611 f. 3.
30. EHP 48666 f. 76. March 28.
31. *Personal Papers of Lord Rendel* 128.

CHAPTER 17: ROSEBERY DEPARTS

1. CB 41246 f. 66 July 30.

2. Bell *Randall Davidson* 244.
3. CB 52517.
4. CB 41226 f. 222.
5. Ros.
6. Gardiner *Harcourt* II 418.
7. EHP 48638 f. 47 Nov. 12, 1884.
8. Spender and Asquith *Life of Lord Oxford and Asquith* I 115.
9. Ibid. 117 Oct. 9, 1896.
10. HH 1/5 Nov. 21, 1900.
11. CB 41221 f. 237.
12. Sheffield Nov. 23. *Annual Register* 1896.
13. *Diary of the Unionist Parliament* 106.

CHAPTER 18: THE JAMESON RAID

1. H. A. L. Fisher *James Bryce* I 216.
2. Quoted in article on Morley by Bodley *Times* Dec. 31, 1923.
3. May 22, 1908.
4. For Stead's account see his pamphlet *Joseph Chamberlain: Conspirator or Statesman*, 1899. He saw Rhodes on Feb. 5.
5. Mil 6 pages 20–5 June 2, 1897.
6. *Hansard* LXXVII c. 125 Oct. 17, 1899.
7. *History of The Times* III ch. IX.
8. J. Van der Poel. *The Jameson Raid* (Oxford 1951): Ethel Drus. *The Question of Imperial Complicity in the Jameson Raid* 1953.
9. Quoted in Van der Poel *op. cit.* 62.
10. Memo early 1896 quoted in Drus 'A Report on the Papers of Joseph Chamberlain

Relating to the Jameson Raid and the Inquiry.' *Bulletin of the Institute of Historical Research* XXV 1952.

11. Har (copy).
12. EHP 48666 ff. 48–9 diary Nov. 10, 1895.
13. Esh *J&L* I 201.
14. *Second Report from the Select Committee on British South Africa.* July 13, 1897 311. Minutes of Evidence. Qs 3368 and 3392. For subsequent exchanges quoted see Qs 4601–2, 5002, 5015, 5054, 8904, 9764, 9766, 9767, 9769 (hereafter referred to as 'Second Report').
15. CB 41221 f. 251.
16. W. T. Stead memo on interview with C.B. on Oct 26, 1899 (Courtesy Prof. Joseph O. Baylen, Stead's biographer) p. 10 (hereafter described as 'Stead memo').
17. Vol. III Ch. IX.
18. *Hansard* 4th ser. LI c. 1159 July 26, 1897.
19. Stead memo 5.
20. Ibid. 4.
21. *Second Report* Tel. no. 1556. To 'Telamones' London from C. J. Rhodes.
22. Spender *Life, Journalism and Politics* I 81–2.
23. *Hansard* 4th ser. LXXIX cols. 626–7.
24. W. S. Blunt *My Diaries* Oct. 1, 1904.
25. Stead memo 4.
26. Spend. 46393 f. 93 Bowen to J. A. Spender June 25, 1903.
27. Ibid.
28. July 27, 1897.
29. July 27.
30. See Butler *The Liberal Party and the Jameson Raid.*
31. Crewe *Rosebery* II 540.
32. Quoted in Butler *op. cit.* 207.
33. Ibid. 207.
34. Ibid. 208.
35. Ibid. July 16.
36. CB 41235 f. 88 Oct. 20, 1899.
37. Bry uncatalogued 'A' Box All Jan. 20, 1900.
38. CB 41214 f. 63.
39. *Hansard* 4th ser. LXXXVII 184 and 259.
40. Har.
41. *Times* Feb. 21, 1900, and *Hansard* 4th ser. LXXIX 599–699.
42. *Spectator* Aug. 3, 10 and 17 and Oct. 12, 1901. Copy Rhodes to Schnadhorst sent to Rosebery May 2, 1895, in Rhodes papers MSS. Afr. I 5 ff. 497–8 dated Feb. 23, 1891. Arnold Morley's letter is in Har. Letter to Robertson is at CB 41226 ff. 14–16.
43. Har Oct. 16, 1901.
44. Ibid. Tel. and letter of Oct. 19 and letter of Oct. 22, 1901.
45. Robertson. Sept. 19, 1901. CB 52517.
46. *Hansard* 4th ser. CXXIX 492 Feb. 5, 1904.

CHAPTER 19: THE CHOICE OF LEADER
1. *The Milner Papers* I 181
2. *Times* Dec. 21, 1897.
3. CB 41246 f. 68. Oct. 6, 1898.
4. CB 41211 f. 7.
5. Texts in *The Liberal Magazine* VI 554–7.

6. Spender *Life* I 213–14 Dec. 12 and 13, 1898.
7. Har. Harcourt to Morley, Dec. 14, 1898.
8. Gardiner *Sir William Harcourt* II 478.
9. *Annual Register* 1898 p. 184 and *Times* Nov. 25, 1898.
10. Dec. 14.
11. *Manchester Guardian* Dec. 17, 1898.
12. CB 41211 f. 11.
13. Bry uncatalogued R/18.
14. Mills *Sir Edward Cook* 177.
15. *In the Golden Days*, quoting a letter by himself.
16. Jeffrey Butler in *The Liberal Party and the Jameson Raid.*
17. Esh *J&L* II 263 Nov. 28, 1907.
18. *Review of Reviews* Jan. 1906: *Character Sketches: The New Cabinet.*
19. Spender and Asquith *Life of Lord Oxford and Asquith* I 120–1. Memo of Dec. 1898.
20. Ibid. 122.
21. Ensor *England 1870–1914* p. 239 note.
22. CB 41210 f. 155 Dec. 19, 1898.
23. Asq 9 ff. 139–41.
24. Har Dec. 17.
25. Dil 43895 f. 206.
26. Asq 9 f. 143.
27. CB 41214 f. 219.
28. Asq 9 ff. 147–52.
29. Bux.
30. Petrie *Life and Letters of Austen Chamberlain* I 314.
31. CB 41231 f. 47.
32. Young *Arthur James Balfour* 169–70.
33. CB 41218 ff. 141–3.
34. Asq 9 ff. 153–5.
35. Hal.
36. CB 41210 f. 157.
37. Asq 9 ff. 157–8.
38. Bry P. 1.
39. CB 41246 f. 69.
40. *Times* Jan. 6, 1899.
41. CB 41226 f. 242.
42. CB 41234 f. 45.
43. CB 41211 f. 15.
44. CB 41211 f. 17.
45. Asq 9 ff. 167–8.
46. CB 41210 f. 162 and CB 41214 f. 228.
47. Har.
48. *Memoirs of an Old Parliamentarian* I 295.
49. Spender *Life, Journalism and Politics* I 70.
50. CB 41218 f. 2.
51. CB 41214 f. 58.
52. CB 41241 ff. 166–7 Feb. 2, 1899.
53. *Fifty Years of Parliament* I 265.
54. CB 41234 f. 107.
55. Ibid. f. 143.
56. Ibid. f. 171.
57. CB 41234 f. 96.
58. *Times* Feb. 7, 1899.
59. *Fifty Years of Parliament* I 265.
60. *Times* Feb. 7, 1899.
61. *Fifty Years of Parliament* I 265.
62. *Recollections* II 84.
63. Crewe *Rosebery* II 558.
64. CB 41226 f. 244.
65. G. W. E. Russell *Sir Wilfrid Lawson* 240.
66. A writer in the *Nation* April 25, 1908, and Spenc Box 1899 A–R.
67. Pope-Hennessy *Lord Crewe* 59.
68. *Nation* April 25, 1908.

PART 6: THE LEADER OF
THE OPPOSITION

CHAPTER 20: THE BOER WAR

1. Lord Milner's 'Credo',
published in *The Times*
July 27, 1925 quoted in
Gollin *Proconsul in Politics*
128–9.
2. Mil. 6(a) pp. 164–70 Nov. 18,
1897 (copy).
3. *Memory Hold-the-Door* 102.
4. Essay on Milner in *The Post
Victorians* (1933).
5. *The Milner Papers* I 222.
6. *Pillars of Society* 326 (essay
on Milner).
7. Massingham *The Next
Government* in the *Anglo-
Saxon Review* 1901.
8. Mil. letter to Selborne May
17, 1899: passage suppressed
by Headlam in published
edition of *The Milner Papers*.
9. Dec. 6, 1905.
10. *Hansard* 4th ser. LXXVIII
378 Feb. 1, 1900.
11. *The Measure of the Years* 15.
12. EHP 48674 f. 60 diary Feb. 11,
1899.
13. RA B 50/82 Feb. 7.
14. Har Feb. 8.
15. CB 41229 f. 56.
16. Dec. 6, 1905.
17. Har Feb. 14.
18. Lucy *A Diary of the Unionist
Parliament* 266.
19. Har Feb. 24.
20. Har Feb. 25.
21. Ros.
22. Ros Box 2.
23. CB 41226 f. 245.
24. CB 41223 ff. 62–3.

25. Har.
26. Har April 5, 1899.
27. Har letters to Harcourt of
March 9 and 14, 1899.
28. *Times* March 9, 1899.
29. EHP 48611 f. 60 March 25
and Ros RY Box 15 March
14.
30. *Times* June 6, 1899.
31. Asq 9 ff. 177–8 and 179–80
and CB 41210 ff. 163 and 167.
32. *Times* June 19, 1899.
33. *Times* June 22 report from
Johannesburg correspondent,
and leading article June 23.
34. CB 41241 ff. 190, 191, 195
and 197 and *Times* Feb. 6,
1904.
35. *Times* Feb. 6, 1904, report of
debate on the address – War
Commission report.
36. CB 41241 f. 191.
37. RA P2/75.
38. CB 41213 f. 118.
39. Ibid. ff. 122–5.
40. Esh *J&L* I 247 July 11,
1899.
41. *Life of Joseph Chamberlain*
III 141.
42. *Annual Register* 1899 158.
43. Lord Sydenham *My Working
Life* 138.
44. CB 41226 f. 247.
45. Lucy *A Diary of the Unionist
Parliament* 307–8.
46. Har.
47. CB 41230 f. 19 (copy).
48. CB 41230 f. 16.
49. CB 41246 f. 72.
50. To Allard Sept. 23, University
of Birmingham Library L
Add 15.
51. HG 45987 f. 16.

52. CB 41230 f. 18.
53. HG 45987 f. 16.
54. CB 41230 f. 18.
55. HG 45989 f. 24.
56. CB 41211 f. 28 (copy).
57. HG 45987 f. 20
58. Har.
59. *Times* Oct. 7, 1899.
60. Gardiner *Sir William Harcourt* II 503. Harcourt to C.B. Oct. 8.
61. Ibid. II 504. Oct. 10. Also in Spender *Life* I 246–7.
62. HG 45987 f. 25.
63. Har Oct. 13, 1899.
64. Spenc Box 1899 A–R.
65. *Times* Oct. 12, 1899 p. 10.
66. Oct. 17.
67. RA B 51/24 published in *LQV* 3 III 407.
68. RA QVJ Oct. 17, 1899.
69. Oct. 19, 1899 *Hansard* 4th ser. LXXVII 300.
70. CB 41246 f. 73.
71. Webb *Our Partnership* 188.
72. CB 41214 f. 62.
73. Rip 43517 f. 140 and CB 41224 f. 106.
74. CB 41211 f. 61.
75. *The Milner Papers* II 23.
76. *Times* Nov. 16, 1899.
77. CB 41215 f. 140 letter from Theodore Gregory to H. Gladstone.
78. Nov. 16, 1899.
79. Har Nov. 16.
80. Har.
81. Spenc Box 1899 A–R.
82. Spenc Box 1899 A–R Nov. 19.
83. HG 45987 ff. 41–2 and CB 41215 ff. 141–3.
84. *Times* Nov. 25, 1899.

85. Chamberlain's speech was May 8, 1896. CB 41243A ff. 3 and 4 'notes for speeches'. e.g. C.B.'s speech at Edinburgh Oct. 29, 1901.
86. CB 41246 f. 75.
87. HG 45987 f. 55 Dec. 9, 1899.
88. *Prophets, Priests and Kings* 33.
89. Bry 13 f. 118 Dec. 25, 1905.
90. Spend 46388 f. 31.
91. Mil 17 f. 627A.
92. *Life of Sir William Harcourt* II 495.
93. Har. Harcourt to Morley Nov. 27, 1899.
94. Har. Morley to Harcourt Nov. 28, 1899.
95. Spenc Box 1899 A–R.
96. Mil 17 f. 632.
97. HG 45987 f. 48.
98. HG 45987 f. 52.
99. CB 41215 ff. 169–70. Dec. 12, 1899.
100. Esh *J&L* I 251.
101. To Spenser Wilkinson March 8, 1900, quoted in Wilkinson's *Thirty Five Years* 248.
102. *Times* Dec. 20, 1899.
103. CB 41235 f. 166.
104. CB 41210 f. 179.
105. CB 41211 f. 78.
106. CB 41211 f. 83.

CHAPTER 21 : THE STRUGGLE AGAINST
THE LIBERAL IMPS

1. Birr (Edin) MS. 10.2.7/5.
2. Repington *Vestigia* 207.
3. Spenc Box 1900 A–H.
4. HG 45987 f. 66 Jan. 5.
5. Spender *Life* I 270.
6. CB 41215 f. 217.
7. HG 45987 f. 80.
8. Ibid. f. 82.

9. CB 41218 f. 6.
10. CB 41215 f. 216.
11. Mil 29 ff. 355–6.
12. Gell March 23, 1900.
13. Nicolson *Lord Carnock* 143.
14. RA B 51/36.
15. CB 41246 f. 77.
16. Spenc Box 1900 A–H.
17. Mil. 29 ff. 84–5 Jan. 12, 1900.
18. Mil 29 f. 408.
19. *Annual Register*, 1900, 83.
20. Quoted in *The Scotsman* April 23, 1908.
21. HG 45987 ff. 101–2.
22. CB 41224 ff. 116–17 June 1, 1900.
23. *Times* June 8, 1900.
24. *Times* May 30, 1900.
25. CB 41218 f. 154 June 9, 1900.
26. Gell April 4, 1900.
27. *LQV* 3 III 568 June 29, 1900.
28. *The Nation and the Athenaeum* May 21, 1921, p. 281.
29. Viscount Samuel *Memoirs* 41.
30. *Autobiography* II 70.
31. *My Political Life* II 7.
32. *Life, Journalism and Politics* I, 128.
33. *The Globe* April 22, 1908.
34. Labouchere in *Truth* April 29, 1908.
35. *Annual Register* 1900 165.
36. Har. Morley to W. V. Harcourt July 26 describing talk with Herbert Gladstone.
37. Har.
38. Ros.
39. Mil 29 f. 369.
40. Mrs. Dilke's diary. Feb. 7, 1887.
41. CB 41211 f. 105.
42. Har.
43. Mil 29 ff. 3–9.
44. *Annual Register* 1900.
45. To Marie Mallet at Osborne Aug. 7. *Life with Queen Victoria.*
46. In the House of Lords Dec. 6, 1900. *Hansard* 4th ser. LXXXVIII c. 36.
47. HG 46020 ff. 48–9.
48. Ibid. f. 52.
49. Ibid. f. 59.
50. HG 45989 f. 36.
51. CB 41211 ff. 119 and 124. Letters of Oct. 1 and 27.
52. HG 45987 f. 119.
53. CB 41211 f. 118.
54. HG 45987 f. 89.
55. HH 1/11 Bundle 1.
56. Webb *Our Partnership* 201.
57. *Liberal Magazine* Vol. 8 Nov. 1900 Supplement vi.
58. HG 45989 f. 42.
59. CB 41221 f. 276 (copy).
60. CB 41224 f. 124. Oct. 26, 1900.
61. CB 41214 f. 85.
62. Spenc Box 1900 A–H Nov. 6, 1900.
63. Rip 43517 f. 157.
64. Trevelyan *Grey of Fallodon* 79.
65. Oct. 19 *Annual Register* 1900 211.
66. Gardiner *Sir William Harcourt* II 524.
67. *Dundee Advertiser* Oct. 23, 1900.
68. HG 45987 f. 125.
69. Spender *Life* I 297 Oct. 21, 1900
70. Memo quoted by Hirst *In the Golden Days* 254–5.
71. Rip 43517 f. 154.
72. CB 41214 f. 91.
73. HG 45987 f. 146 Nov. 15.

74. *Times* Nov. 16, 1900.
75. Har. Harcourt to Morley Nov. 23, 1900.
76. CB 41218 ff. 8–12.
77. Ibid. ff. 17–19 (copy).
78. Ibid. f. 24.
79. CB 52517 draft letter to Kimberley Nov. 22, 1900.
80. Bux.
81. HG 45989 f. 46.
82. CB 41216 ff. 57–8.

CHAPTER 22: METHODS OF BARBARISM
1. Rip 43517 f. 176.
2. Har.
3. Har Jan 12, 1901.
4. CB 41212 f. 278.
5. Bry uncatalogued.
6. Bry 16 ff. 152–3.
7. Bry uncatalogued Feb. 9, 1901.
8. Rip 43517 f. 182 Feb. 9.
9. Bry uncatalogued Feb. 9.
10. Rip 43517 f. 190 Feb. 26.
11. CB 41236 f. 94.
12. Rip 43517 f. 189 Feb. 16.
13. *Annual Register* 1901.
14. Eric A. Walker *History of Southern Africa* 498.
15. Curtis *With Milner in South Africa* 143–5.
16. Gell Feb. 19, 1901.
17. Gell Mar. 14.
18. Sir George Arthur *Life of Lord Kitchener* II 26.
19. *Liberal Magazine* IX 66
20. Gardiner *Life of Harcourt* II 529.
21. RA X 37/28.
22. EHP 48606 f. 92.
23. *Times* May 16, 1901 p. 10.
24. Ll.G A/10/1/14. *Bradford Observer* May 16, 1901.
25. EHP 48678 f. 54.

26. *Annual Register* 1901.
27. Berwick May 30.
28. Montrose June 14.
29. Beatrice Webb *Our Partnership* 217–218 and Poirier *The Advent of the Labour Party* 110 quoting Beatrice Webb's diary for Dec. 15, 1900.
30. Fry *Emily Hobhouse.*
31. CB 41252 f. 244.
32. *Times* May 25, 1901.
33. *Times* June 15, 1901.
34. Parliamentary correspondent in the *Manchester Guardian* April 23, 1908.
35. Quoted in letter from CB to J. B. Smith June 24, 1901. Spend 46388 ff. 40–1.
36. June 18.
37. *Times* June 18, 1901.
38. Crewe *Lord Rosebery* II 569.
39. Le May *British Supremacy in South Africa* 90.
40. Salisbury papers: Christ Church, Oxford. Minute by S. McDonnell July 8, 1901 and letter from Knollys July 9: and R. R. James *Rosebery* 425.
41. *Times* June 24 and 28.
42. *Hansard* 4th ser. XCV c. 599.
43. April 22, 1908.
44. CB 41236 f. 117.
45. *The Troublemakers* (Panther edition) p. 100.
46. Spend 46387 ff. 45–6.
47. Rip 43517 f. 197.
48. CB 41236 f. 143: to Charles McLaren July 6.
49. HG 45989 f. 49 June 27.
50. *The Balfourian Parliament* 85–6.
51. Mallet *Herbert Gladstone* 182.

52. Ibid. and CB 41216 ff. 122–3.
53. Quoted in the *Daily Mirror* April 23, 1908.
54. EHP 48678 f. 72.
55. Du Parcq *David Lloyd George* II 258.
56. HG 45989 f. 5.
57. Lucy ('Toby M.P.') *The Balfourian Parliament* 90–2.
58. *Times* July 11, 1901.
59. *Annual Register* 1901 162–3 and *Times* July 10, 1901.
60. CB 41226 ff. 12–13.
61. Spend 46388 ff. 42–3.
62. July 15. Hal. Box 1899–1901 quoted in McCready *Sir Alfred Milner, the Liberal Party and the Boer War.*

CHAPTER 23: THE WIDENING
            BREACH WITH ROSEBERY

1. *Times* July 17, 1901.
2. Ibid. July 20.
3. Beatrice Webb *Our Partnership* 219.
4. July 20.
5. Ll.G A/10/1/21. *Pontypridd Chronicle* July 20, 1901.
6. CB 41213 f. 62.
7. Spender *Life* II 3.
8. Amery *Life of Chamberlain* IV 16.
9. David James *Lord Roberts* 360.
10. Spender *Life* I 351.
11. Ibid.
12. Bry uncatalogued: copy at CB 41211 ff. 167–8.
13. HG 45987 f. 191.
14. In an article entitled *Lord Rosebery's Escape from Houndsditch.*
15. HG 45987 f. 191.
16. Har.

17. Har.
18. Har Oct. 3.
19. *Our Partnership* 232 quoting diary for March 19, 1902.
20. October, *Annual Register* 1901.
21. Nicolson *Carnock* p. 128.
22. Mil 36 ff. 79–86.
23. *Spectator* June 22, 1901. Adam Smith *John Buchan.*
24. Adam Smith *op. cit.*
25. Har.
26. Har Oct. 21, 1901.
27. Har.
28. *Times* Oct. 26, 1901.
29. Har to Morley Oct. 27.
30. Har to Harcourt Oct. 29.
31. Rip 43517 f. 209.
32. Har Nov. 8.
33. Har.
34. *Times* Nov. 20, 1901, p. 6.
35. Har Nov. 21.
36. Har Nov. 25, 1901.
37. Har Nov. 26.
38. Rip 43517 f. 215.
39. HG 45987 f. 202.
40. *Times* Nov. 29.
41. Gardiner *Sir William Harcourt* II 536.
42. Har Dec. 11.
43. Mallet *Herbert Gladstone* 183 copy in HG 45986 ff. 44–5 in his own hand.

CHAPTER 24: CHESTERFIELD AND
            BERKELEY SQUARE

1. Bry Dec. 13, 1901.
2. CB 41211 f. 175.
3. CB 52517.
4. Crewe *Rosebery* II 571.
5. *Times* Dec. 17, 1901 10–11.
6. CB 41213 f. 66.
7. CB 41236 f. 248 enclosure.

8. Lady Pentland *Memoir of Lord Pentland* 63.
9. Spend 46391 f. 95 Dec. 17.
10. CB 41216 ff. 171–2.
11. HG 45987 f. 211. 'Sydney' misspelt thus by C.B.
12. Spenc Box 1901 A–C.
13. Bux Dec. 18.
14. Spend 46389 ff. 1–5.
15. Wolf *Life of Lord Ripon* II, 267.
16. Mil 39 ff. 164–5 (earlier part quoted in *The Milner Papers* II 287).
17. Har.
18. Gardiner *Life of Harcourt* II, 537.
19. HH 1/11 Bundle 1 Dec. 31.
20. CB 41236 ff. 257–8 copy in C.B.'s hand.
21. CB 41216 ff. 181–3 (copy).
22. CB 41216 ff. 179–80 Dec. 28.
23. HG 45987 f. 217 Dec. 31, 1901.
24. Bry Jan 2. CB 41224 f. 208.
25. CB 41211 f. 190.
26. HG 45988 ff. 1–2.
27. Spend 46388 f. 9.
28. CB 41236 f. 279.
29. HG 45995 f. 30.
30. Ibid. f. 34.
31. Har.
32. Har Dec. 27 and 29.
33. CB 41218 ff. 33–5 Jan. 2, 1902.
34. HG 45988 f. 3.
35. *Grey of Fallodon* 76.
36. *Pall Mall Gazette* Jan 3, 1902. 'A Talk with Mr. Lloyd George.'
37. HG 45988 ff. 5–6.
38. HG 45989 ff. 57–60.
39. Asq 10 f. 52: reply at CB 41210 f. 215.
40. HG 45988 ff. 5–6 postscript and f. 9.
41. HG 45986 f. 47, CB 41226 ff. 256–7 and f. 258 (draft).

CHAPTER 25: COURAGE REWARDED

1. A. G. Gardiner *Prophets, Priests and Kings* 281.
2. Quoted in Gardiner *Pillars of Society* 221.
3. Chesterton *Autobiography* 207.
4. Bry 16 f. 172.
5. *Annual Register* 1902 p. 2.
6. Quoted in Pyrah *Imperial Policy and South Africa* 68.
7. CB 41210 ff. 219–21.
8. *Times* Jan. 22, 1902.
9. Ibid. leading article.
10. Rip 43518 f. 5.
11. *Liverpool Daily Post*.
12. Ll.G A/10/7/6 *Carnarvon Herald* Jan. 24, 1902.
13. Mil 40 ff. 121–3 Jan. 26, 1902.
14. To Canon MacColl. Jan. 26. Quoted in Russell *Malcolm MacColl* 386–7.
15. *Times* Feb. 20 1902.
16. *The Nation* April 25, 1908 (clearly H. W. Massingham).
17. CB 41223 ff. 93–4 Feb. 20.
18. *Times* Feb. 21, 1902.
19. Interview with *North Wales Observer* Feb. 28, 1902. Ll.G H/10/2/10.
20. CB 41237 f. 17 letter from S. Compston Feb. 22, 1902.
21. Leveson Gower *Years of Endeavour* 230.
22. Spend 46388 f. 46.
23. Quoted in Buchan *Memory Hold-the-Door* 63.

24. Dinner of the National Liberal Club.
25. Randolph S. Churchill *Winston S. Churchill* Companion Vol. II Pt. I 117–18.
26. CB 41220 ff. 58–9.
27. Spend 46391 ff. 99–103 Feb. 25.
28. To Mrs. Montefiore Feb. 21, 1902. Mil 85 f. 75 a–6.
29. CB 41216 ff. 205–6 and HG 45988 f. 12.
30. Spenc Box 1902 A–D.
31. HG 45988 f. 18.
32. Ibid. f. 10.
33. *Correspondence of Goldwin Smith* 382, to John Ogilvy of Dundee Liberal Association.
34. CB 41237 f. 37.
35. CB 41242 f. 204.
36. Ibid. Article in the *New York Evening Post* sent to C.B. by Joseph H. Choate.
37. CB 41236 f. 239.
38. Quoted in Spender *Life* II 68: also in Amery's *Life of Joseph Chamberlain* V 17.
39. Bry uncatalogued Sept. 23, 1902 from Baden-Baden.
40. CB 41236 f. 106 June 3, 1901.
41. Mil 49 ff. 154–7 Aug. 27, 1902.
42. Spend 46388 ff. 47–9. Sept. 1 to J. B. Smith.
43. Ibid.
44. Har (from Paris).
45. CB 41230 f. 60.
46. B. Webb *Our Partnership* 248.
47. Webb *op. cit.* 249 (quoting diary for Nov. 15, 1902) 232, 231.
48. Spenc Box 1902 A–D.
49. From the Montrose Burghs.

50. *Times* Jan. 3, 1903.
51. Bry uncatalogued.
52. Har April 29, 1903.
53. Mil 85 ff. 46–8.
54. Har.
55. Har.
56. Har June 24.
57. Bal 49692 ff. 72, 74 and 76.
58. Foreword to Roy Douglas's *The History of the Liberal Party 1895–1970* (1971).
59. *The Clarion* May 22, 1903.
60. Crewe *Rosebery* II 585–7.
61. Ibid.
62. HG 45988 f. 59 Nov. 9, 1903.
63. CB 41230 ff. 70–1. CB to Sinclair Nov. 20, 1903.
64. Ll.G A/11/2/46. *South Wales Argus* Dec. 1, 1903.
65. Har.
66. CB 41237 ff. 212–13.
67. HG 45989 f. 90.
68. Bry uncatalogued.
69. Bry uncatalogued.
70. Spenc 1904 Box A–B April 5.
71. Mil 41 f. 54.
72. *Times* March 22, 1904.
73. *The Milner Papers* II 476–7 and A. M. Gollin 'Asquith: A New View' in *A Century of Conflict, Essays for A. J. P. Taylor 1966.*
74. Trevelyan *Grey of Fallodon* 86.
75. Gollin *Proconsul in Politics* 65.
76. A. T. Bassett *Life of John Edward Ellis* 207.
77. Mil 41 ff. 41–2.
78. CB 41226 ff. 58–9.
79. *Annual Register* 1904.
80. Mil 20 f. 125. Sir Henry Bale to Milner.
81. Mil 35 ff. 179–80 March 27, 1904.

81. Mil 44 ff. 127–8. Milner to Miss Bertha Synge May 23, 1904
82. *Winston S. Churchill, Companion* Vol. 11 Pt. 1 321.
83. *The Nineteenth Century* Oct. 1904. *The Next Liberal Ministry* 679–85.
84. *The Balfourian Parliament* 334–5.
85. Quoted in Le May *British Supremacy in South Africa* 167.
86. Har (copy).
87. CB 41220 f. 169.
88. Speech at Norwich Oct. 26, 1904.
89. *Prophets, Priests and Kings* 121.
90. Hirst *In the Golden Days* 256.
91. *The Personal Papers of Lord Rendel* 168.
92. Gosse diary 10.
93. Ros Oct. 4, 1904.
94. HG 45988 f. 132.
95. Ibid. f. 134 Dec. 23, 1904.
96. CB 41212 f. 284.
97. Bux Jan. 24, 1905.
98. *Times* March 21, 1905.
99. CB 41223 f. 148 March 22.
100. HG 45988 f. 54 and CB 41226 f. 63 April 1, 1905.
101. CB 41246 f. 285.
102. Hal.
103. March 3, 1905, quoted in Chilston *Chief Whip* 323.
104. Sir Sidney Lee *King Edward VII* 442 and CB 41212 f. 286.
105. *Annual Register* 1905.
106. Dev 340 3149 Aug. 14.
107. *Grey of Fallodon* 84.
108. CB 52518 and HG 45988 f. 204.

CHAPTER 26: THE DEFENCE OF FREE TRADE

1. *Autobiography* II 53.
2. Spender *Life* II 96–7.
3. Ibid. 97.
4. Bal 49759 f. 33.
5. CB 41210 f. 233.
6. CB 41237 f. 155. Aug. 29, 1903.
7. *Annual Register* 1903.
8. *Winston S. Churchill Companion* Vol. II Pt. I 188 May 29, 1903.
9. Ibid. May 30.
10. Ibid. pp. 188–201.
11. *Times* June 6, 1903.
12. On June 17. *Times* June 18.
13. Rip 43518 f. 16.
14. Bry (uncatalogued).
15. Har.
16. Mil 41 ff. 18–20.
17. Spender *Life* II 108 June 17.
18. Ibid. 111.
19. *Life of Chamberlain* V 255.
20. Spend 46388 ff. 51–2.
21. HG 45988 f. 54.
22. Spenc Box 1903 A–BE.
23. CB 41237 f. 169.
24. Gosse diary 2.
25. Quoted in Spender *Life* II 114.
26. Letter to organizing secretary of Cobden Club conferences of cooperators and trade unionists, published in *The Times* Oct. 6, 1903.
27. *Times* Oct. 16, 1903.
28. CB 41214 f. 131 Nov. 10.
29. Rip 43518 f. 23 Oct. 19, 1903.
30. Amery *Life of Chamberlain* VI 474.
31. CB 41226 f. 50 Oct. 17.
32. Quoted in Spender *Life* II 123.
33. Bry uncatalogued.

34. *Times* Dec. 21, 1903.
35. Amery *op. cit.* VI 549.
36. Asq 10 f. 122–3.
37. CB 41210 f. 227.
38. CB 41214 f. 258.
39. Speech at Norwich.
40. Gardiner *Sir William Harcourt* II 563.
41. Spend 46388 ff. 54–5.
42. *Winston S. Churchill Companion.* Vol. II Pt. 1 313 note 2.
43. Ibid. 313.
44. *Daily Chronicle* June 6, 1904.
45. Ibid. and *Manchester Guardian* June 6.
46. Lucy *The Balfourian Parliament* 321.
47. EHP 48684 f. 4.
48. CB 41214 f. 143 Jan. 2, 1905.
49. *Autobiography* 164.
50. March 22 House of Commons. *Hansard* 4th ser. CXLIII c. 899.
51. Gosse diary 48.
52. CB 41226 f. 74 Oct. 27, 1905.
53. Bal 49759 f. 124.
54. Ibid. f. 126 July 14.
55. *Annual Register* 1905.
56. *Fifty Years of Parliament* II 36.

PART 7: THE PLOT THAT
FAILED

CHAPTER 27: THE RELUGAS
CONSPIRACY

1. Gosse diary 32.
2. Ibid. 38.
3. EHP 48683 f. 20 Feb. 18, 1905.
4. Gosse diary 40.
5. Ibid.

6. *Recollections* II 131–2.
7. EHP 48683 f. 8.
8. Oct. 7, 1903 quoted in Robbins *Sir Edward Grey* 109.
9. Esh *J&L* II 56.
10. Fitzroy *Memoirs* I 220.
11. Asq 10 ff. 98–98A. Herbert Gladstone to Asquith Oct. 29, 1903.
12. Gosse diary 30–1.
13. Haldane *Autobiography* 157.
14. Hirst *In the Golden Days* 264.
15. CB 52518.
16. *Grey of Fallodon* 97.
17. Spend 46394 f. 26 copy Spender to G. M. Trevelyan ca. 1936.
18. CB 41226 ff. 66 and 70. C. B. to William Robertson Aug. 31 and Sept. 10.
19. HG 45988 ff. 185–6 and CB 52518 (copy C.B. to Sinclair Aug. 30 1905).
20. In fact on 22 and 29 Aug. and 1, 2, 3, 6 and 7 Sept.
21. CB 41226 f. 70 (copy).
22. Haldane *op. cit.* 158–9.
23. Ibid. 159.
24. Maurice *Haldane* I 147.
25. Ibid. 151.
26. Sommer *Haldane of Cloan* 148.
27. CB 41238 ff. 64–5 Oct. 1, 1905.
28. Asq 10 ff. 153–6.
29. Haldane *op. cit.* 161.
30. Esh *J&L* II 115.
31. Rip 43518 f. 46 Nov. 7.
32. *Winston S. Churchill Companion* Vol. II 473.
33. Gosse diary 60.
34. CB 41223 f. 158 Nov. 3.
35. *Autobiography* II 66–8.
36. Spend 46388 f. 161 Mar. 26, 1921.

CHAPTER 28: GREY AND HALDANE

1. CB 52520.
2. Rip 43518 f. 50.
3. Bry uncatalogued.
4. HG 45989 f. 135.
5. CB 41210 ff. 247.
6. Cf. Grey to Asquith Nov. 24 quoted in Heuston *Lives of the Lord Chancellors* 142–3.
7. CB 52520.
8. CB 52518
9. Spend 46388 ff. 59–75.
10. CB 52518.
11. HG 45988 f. 209.
12. Esh *J&L* II 121.
13. CB 52518.
14. CB 41223 ff. 170–1 and 172–3.
15. CB 52520.
16. Spender *Life, Journalism and Politics* I 125 and 132.
17. CB 41234 f. 23.
18. CB 41238 f. 112–13.
19. CB 52520.
20. Hal.
21. Esh *J&L* II 1222.
22. Asq 10 ff. 180–1.
23. Spend 46394 f. 26 Spender to G. M. Trevelyan ca. 1936.
24. Spender *op. cit.* I 126–7.
25. *Manchester Guardian* Dec. 6, 1905.
26. CB 41206 f. 6.
27. Spender *op. cit.* I 129.
28. Trevelyan *Grey of Fallodon* 99–100.
29. *Times* Dec. 5, 1905.
30. Asq 10 ff. 186–7.
31. CB 52518.
32. *Autobiography* II 71–3.
33. Gosse diary 47.
34. RA AA 24/30.
35. HG 45992 ff. 112–13. Memo by Gladstone on interview with Grey Dec. 5.
36. Spend. 46388 f. 62.
37. Esh *J&L* II 123.
38. Trevelyan *op. cit.* 100.
39. CB 41238 ff. 134–7.
40. CB 52520.
41. *Times* Dec. 6, 1905.
42. Ibid.
43. *Autobiography* II 73–4.
44. Trevelyan *op. cit.* 100.
45. CB 41238 f. 137.
46. CB 52518.
47. Zetland *Lord Cromer* 16 quoting Cromer's biographical notes.
48. Quoted in Hyam *Elgin and Churchill at the Colonial Office* 237.
49. *Westminster Gazette* Dec. 6, 1905 and Spend 46388 f. 62.
50. Spend 46388 f. 62.
51. Note by Gardiner in the *Athenaeum* June 4, 1921 (courtesy of Stephen Koss).
52. *Recollections* II 142.
53. CB 41223 ff. 262–3 to C.B. Sept. 5, 1907.
54. *Times* Dec. 7, 1905.
55. *Autobiography* II 74–5.
56. CB 52520.
57. Trevelyan *op. cit.* 101.
58. CB 41210 f. 253.
59. CB 41237 f. 154 Aug. 29, 1903.
60. Spend 46388 f. 62.
61. Haldane *Autobiography* 169–70.
62. Spender and Asquith *Life of Lord Oxford and Asquith* 174–5.
63. CB 41220 f. 194.
64. CB 41218 ff. 44–7 and Esh *J&L* II 125.

65. CB 52518.
66. Haldane *op. cit.* 171–81.
67. CB 52518 Acland to C.B. Dec. 17, 1905.
68. Spend 46388 f. 62.
69. CB 52518 Acland to C.B. Dec. 17.
70. CB 41217 ff. 283–4.
71. Haldane *op. cit.* 180.
72. Ibid. 180.
73. CB 52518 Acland to C.B. Dec. 17. See also Spend 46391 f. 119 Acland to Spender Dec. 7, 1905.
74. *Memoirs* I 271.
75. CB 52518 Acland to C.B. Dec. 17.
76. CB 41218 ff. 161–2.
77. CB 52520.
78. *Autobiography* II 76.
79. Ibid.
80. Shaw *Letters to Isabel* 261–5.
81. Alexander *The Temple of the Nineties* 264.
82. Margot Asquith *More Memories* 131.
83. Hal.
84. Esh *J&L* II 126.
85. *The Mist Procession* 79–80.
86. Spend 46393 f. 150. Esher to Spender Jan. 29, 1928.
87. *Records* 31–2.
88. *The Personal Papers of Lord Rendel* 171.
89. Gooch *Life of Lord Courtney* 505 quoting Courtney's journal.
90. G. W. E. Russell *Prime Ministers and Some Others* 75.

CHAPTER 29: FILLING THE POSTS
1. *Times* Dec. 9, 1905.
2. *Winston S. Churchill* Companion Vol. II Pt. 1, 411 and 416. CB 41238 f. 150. *Times* Dec. 15, 1905.
3. CB 41238 ff. 152–4 (inaccurately transcribed in Spender *Life*).
4. RA Add VIC ADDL MSS A/17/1033.
5. *Our New Rulers: The Liberal Ministry of 1906* pamphlet Jan., 1906.
6. *Annual Register,* 1905 238.
7. CB 41238 f. 125.
8. Gosse diary 62 Dec. 19.
9. CB 41214 f. 195.
10. Ibid. f. 197.
11. Ibid. f. 199.
12. Ibid. f. 203 and Jenkins *Sir Charles Dilke* 411.
13. CB 52518 Dec. 12.
14. Ibid. Dec. 13.
15. CB 41225 f. 76.
16. Fisher *James Bryce* I 339.
17. Gosse diary 65.
18. Dil 43882 f. 140.
19. Dil 43895 f. 259.
20. *Personal Papers of Lord Rendel* 164.
21. Lord Riddell quoting talk with McKenna in *More Pages from my Diary* 177.
22. Bowle *Viscount Samuel* and HG 45988 f. 31.
23. CB 41212 f. 290
24. CB 52518 Acland to C.B. Dec. 17, 1905. See also HG 45995 Sinclair to H. Gladstone Dec. 31, 1905, Spend 46391 f. 190 C.B. to Acland April 9, 1906 and ff. 171–4 Gladstone to Acland Dec. 28, 1905.
25. Gosse diary 71.

26. CB 41225 ff. 184 and 186.
27. *The Mist Procession* 77.
28. D.D.F. 2nd ser. VIII No. 219.
29. Margot Asquith *Autobiography* II 76.
30. *Our Partnership* 325–6.
31. Margot Asquith *op. cit.* II 78.
32. *Review of Reviews* Jan. 1906 *Character Sketch: The New Cabinet*, later expanded and published as a pamphlet *Our New Rulers: The Liberal Ministry of 1906.*
33. Jan. 1906. *The Pattern Englishman and His Record* by 'Scrutator'.
34. In *The Nation and the Athenaeum* May 21, 1921, 281.

PART 8: THE PRIME MINISTER

CHAPTER 30: THE ELECTION OF 1906
1. Pon. Notes by Arthur Ponsonby
2. Nuffield College Library. Mottistone MS 1 f. 100. C.B. to Seely Dec. 25, 1905.
3. CB 41207 f. 11 Knollys to C.B. Dec. 21.
4. Hyam. *Elgin and Churchill at the Colonial Office* Dec. 26.
5. HG 45988 ff. 139–40 Jan. 2, 1905.
6. *Morning Post* Oct. 23, 1923.
7. Lord Riddell *More Pages from My Diary* 133.
8. *Times* Dec. 22, 1905.
9. *Times* April 23, 1908.
10. D.D.F. 2nd ser. VIII No. 264.
11. CB 41246 f. 299 Dec. 21.
12. *Prophets, Priests and Kings*

essay on Mrs. Pankhurst (1908).
13. Rowland *The Last Liberal Governments* 24.
14. RA R 27/14.
15. Hyam *op. cit.* 66.
16. Asq 10 f. 192.
17. W. E. Gladstone in *Lessons of Irish History in the Eighteenth Century* (1887) in *Aspects of the Irish Question.*
18. Margot Asquith *Autobiography* II 78.
19. CB 41226 f. 81.
20. Spender *Life* II 220.
21. Pon.
22. Lady Pentland *Memoir of Lord Pentland* 80.
23. *Retrospection* 146.
24. *Sunday Times* Nov. 4, 1923. Reprinted in *Studies and Sketches* (205).
25. Dugdale *Arthur James Balfour* I 329.

CHAPTER 31: SOUTH AFRICA
1. See p. 327.
2. Quoted in Beloff *Imperial Sunset* 123 note.
3. See Hyam *Elgin and Churchill at the Colonial Office* 46–7 and Haldane to Milner March 3, 1901, *The Milner Papers* II, 187.
4. *The Nation and the Athenaeum* May 21, 1921, 282.
5. Millin *General Smuts* I 193–4.
6. Hyam *op. cit.* 108.
7. Ibid. 110.
8. Ibid. 111.
9. Ibid. 112.
10. Robbins *Sir Edward Grey* 167–8.

11. In his maiden speech Feb. 1901.
12. PRO CO 879 African (South) No. 804.
13. Ibid. No. 823.
14. Hyam *op. cit.* 125.
15. PRO CO 879 No. 837.
16. Graham, Assistant Under-Secretary, quoted in Mansergh *South Africa: The Price of Magnanimity.*
17. Hancock and Van der Poel *Selections from the Smuts Papers* II 279.
18. At a luncheon Nov. 1943. Kennedy *The Business of War* 316.
19. *Glasgow High School Magazine.*
20. Hancock *Smuts* I 215.
21. Le May *British Supremacy in South Africa* 185.
22. PRO CAB 41/30/39.
23. See Patrick Gordon Walker *The Cabinet* 57–60.
24. Feb. 8 Hyam *op. cit.* 128.
25. Rip 43552 ff. 28–9.
26. Millin *op. cit.* I 213–14.
27. *More Pages from My Diary* 144–5.
28. Ensor *England 1870–1914* 390 note 2.
29. Spend 46388 f. 96.
30. Bentley B. Gilbert *Historical Journal* X 4 (1967) 457–9.
31. CB 41213 f. 310.
32. CB 41238 f. 36.
33. Lady Pentland *Memoir of Lord Pentland* 82.
34. Pon. Memo *Campbell-Bannerman* (undated).
35. Trevelyan *Grey of Fallodon* 88.
36. *Glasgow Herald* April 23, 1908, reporting Churchill speaking at Manchester Corn Exchange.
37. *Times* Feb. 27, 1906.
38. RA AA/24/42.
39. CB 52515 March 8.
40. CB 41226 f. 85.
41. Hyam *op. cit.* quoting African (S) 853.
42. *Winston Churchill as I Knew Him* Ch. XIV.
43. *Annual Register* 1906.
44. *The Standard* July 27, 1906.
45. *Morning Post* Aug. 1, 1906.
46. *Hansard* 4th ser. CLXII 729–804 and *Times* Aug. 1, 1906.
47. Aug. 1.
48. *Hansard* CLII 707–21. *Times* Aug. 1.
49. Ensor *op. cit.* 389.
50. *Times* Aug. 1.
51. Spend 46388 f. 147 to J. A. Spender Aug. 8, 1906.
52. Hyam *op. cit.* 165.
53. CB 52516 March 28.
54. *Glasgow Herald* April 23, 1908 reporting Churchill speaking at Manchester Corn Exchange.
55. *Times* April 27, 1907 Dinner at National Liberal Club. The earlier dinner was given by the Eighty Club.
56. *Hyam.* op. cit. 251.
57. Ibid. 283 Jan. 2, 1907.
58. Ibid. 283.
59. quoted in J. A. S. Simon *Retrospect* 78.
60. *The Milner Papers* II 534.
61. Morley *Recollections* II 145.
62. *Winston S. Churchill* Companion Vol. II Pt. 1 667.

63. CB 52516.
64. J. C. Smuts *Jan Christian Smuts* 99.
65. Millin *op. cit.* 209–11.
66. Millin *op. cit.* II 211.
67. C. P. Scott's diary May 2, 1917. *The Political Diaries of C. P. Scott 1911–1928.*
68. *Campbell-Bannerman* by George M. Trevelyan O.M. *Glasgow High School Magazine* June 1948.
69. By Nicholas Mansergh in *South Africa 1906–1961: The Price of Magnanimity* 71.

CHAPTER 32: THE FIRST YEAR AT NO. 10

1. Ensor *England 1870–1914* 391.
2. Snowden *Autobiography* I 122.
3. Asq 19 f. 82 Feb. 1.
4. Lucy *The Diary of a Journalist* 250.
5. Pon. Letters from Nash and notes by Ponsonby.
6. Lucy *op. cit.* 63.
7. *Daily News* Feb. 19, 1906.
8. *Memoirs of Sir Almeric Fitzroy* I 282.
9. Farquharson *The House of Commons from Within* 75.
10. *Times* Feb. 23 and Mar. 22, 1906.
11. Sir Edward Clarke *The Story of My Life.*
12. *Daily News* March 13.
13. Ibid. and *Times* Nov. 13.
14. Lady Frances Balfour *Ne Obliviscaris* II 419.
15. Earl Winterton *Pre-War* 30.
16. *Times* Mar. 13.
17. Lucy Masterman *C. F. G. Masterman.*
18. Snowden *op. cit.* I 139.
19. Balfour *op. cit.* II 419.
20. CB 41252 f. 146.
21. Winterton *op. cit.* 85–6.
22. Masterman *op. cit.* 72.
23. 'Pictures in Parliament' *Daily News* March 13, 1906.
24. *Times* March 13, 1906.
25. RA GV AA 24/45.
26. *Annual Register* 1906.
27. Haldane *Autobiography* 216–17.
28. India Office Library Morley papers MSS EM D 573/1.
29. Morley *Recollections* II 143–4.
30. Gosse diary 73.
31. *Memoirs* note of Sept. 1, 1909.
32. Morley *Politics and History* (1913).
33. Young. *Arthur James Balfour* 253.
34. Atherley-Jones *Looking Back.*
35. Grey *Twenty Five Years* I 65–7.
36. June 5 *Correspondence of Goldwin Smith.*
37. CB 52518.
38. Esh. *J&L* II 223.
39. Ponsonby's notes. Hirst *In the Golden Days* 263.
40. Gosse diary 36 (March 13) and 81.
41. Ibid. 76.
42. *Times* March 22, 1906.
43. *Autobiography* II 86–7.
44. Esh. *J&L* II 153.
45. Trevelyan *Grey of Fallodon* 79. To Lady Helen Munro-Ferguson March, 1908.
46. Mil 45 f. 160 Mar. 20, 1906.
47. Mil 45 f. 117 Mar. 27.
48. PRO CAB 41/30/51.
49. RA R 27/42.
50. *Times* March 30, 1906.

51. *Times* June 22, 1906 and Spend 46391 ff. 223–4 Ian Hamilton to Spender Nov. 21, 1907.
52. PRO CAB 41/30/52, CB 41239 f. 74, Burns papers British Museum 46282 f. 30.
53. *Times* March 31, 1906.
54. CB 41226 f. 20 (copy).
55. CB 41214 f. 6.
56. Steward *J. Keir Hardie* 222.
57. June 22. Signed article entitled: *Courage, Brithers!*
58. *Annual Register* 1906.
59. In RA: copies in PRO (CAB 41) and in CB 52512 and 52513.
60. RA R 27/36, 48 and 70, R 28/71 and W 64/102.
61. RA R 27/61.
62. Esh 10/49 Nov. 29, 1907.
63. Magnus *King Edward VII* 282.
64. Esh *J&L* 265.
65. Ibid. II 160–1.
66. To Izvolsky 2–15 April, 1908 quoted in Izvolsky *Au Service de la Russie* II 154.
67. Feb. 13 CB 41207 f. 48.
68. *Memoirs of Almeric Fitzroy* note of Dec. 8, 1908. *Daily Express* April 23, 1908.
69. *The Personal Papers of Lord Rendel* 170–1.
70. Collier *A Victorian Diarist: Later Entries* 197.
71. Pon. Notes by Arthur Ponsonby.
72. Riddell *More Pages from my Diary* 109 Dec., 1912.
73. Pon. Notes by Ponsonby and CB 41252 f. 146.
74. *Nation* April 25, 1908 (anonymous, but clearly by A. G. Gardiner).
75. O'Connor *C.B.* 96.
76. HH 1/5 'Letters from P.M.'s' Jan. 6, 1906.
77. Mackie *The Model Member* account of meeting in 1872.
78. CB 41226 f. 58 (copy).
79. *Times* May 20, 1906.
80. Balfour *op. cit.* II 140.
81. Strachey *The Cause* 297–301. *The Standard* March 3, 1906.
82. *Daily News* March 9, 1907.
83. RA. G.V. AA 25/7 March 12.
84. CB 52513.
85. Pon. Letter from Mary Gawthorpe April 5, 1907.
86. *P.T.O.* July 14, 1906 *At the Bar of the House* by T.P.
87. O'Connor *C.B.* 97–8.
88. Kent. *John Burns* 362 and *Times* Nov. 3, 1913 report of Burns's speech at unveiling of C.B.'s statue in Stirling.
89. Pon. Knollys to A. Ponsonby Feb. 14, 1907 and draft of reply.
90. Corr. with Morley CB 41223 ff. 199–200 and 197–8. Loreburn: Gardiner *Prophets, Priests & Kings* 197.
91. Spend 46388 f. 147 Aug. 8, 1906.
92. Ibid. f. 149 Aug. 29.

CHAPTER 33 : THE DEATH OF
CHARLOTTE

1. *The Primitive Methodist World* April 23, 1908.
2. CB 41246 ff. 127–30.
3. Bry Sept. 23, 1902.
4. CB 41230 f. 43.
5. I am indebted for this diagnosis to Dr. Oliver Plowright.

6. HG 45988 f. 36.
7. HH 1/11 Bundle 1 Sept. 13, 1903.
8. Lord Pentland's commonplace book Feb. 27, 1921.
9. CB 41223 f. 194 April 15.
10. Morley *Recollections* II 143.
11. Esh *J&L* II 164.
12. Pon. undated fragment.
13. Spender *Life*. II 365.
14. Sydenham *My Working Life* 213.
15. RA R 27/79 July 19.
16. *The Primitive Methodist World* April 23, 1908.
17. Pon.
18. Ibid.
19. CB 41246 f. 168 to R. W. Burnet.
20. Spender *Life* II 293. Arthur Ponsonby's diary.
21. CB 41231 f. 215 to Mrs. Whiteley Sept. 11, 1906.
22. Spender *Life* II 293. Arthur Ponsonby's diary.
23. Oppenheimer *Stranger Within*.
24. Pon. Notes by Arthur Ponsonby.
25. Morley *Recollections* II 183.
26. Newspaper report Sept. 6, 1906.
27. Lord Hardinge of Penshurst *Old Diplomacy* 151.

CHAPTER 34: THE SEEDS OF WAR
1. Notes by Arthur Ponsonby quoted in Hirst *In the Golden Days* 262.
2. *The Navy Annual* 1900 432.
3. G. P. Gooch *Baron von Holstein* in *Studies in Modern History*.

4. D.D.F. 2nd ser. VIII No. 219.
5. Ibid. No. 256.
6. Esh *J&L* III 213.
7. P.R.O. FO 800/110 ff. 276-9.
8. Repington *The First World War* I 8.
9. Ibid. 10.
10. Esh quoted in Williamson *The Politics of Grand Strategy* 72.
11. CB 41218 f. 49.
12. Ibid. ff. 51-2.
13. Ibid. ff. 53-4.
14. Monger *The End of Isolation* 250 and Robbins *Sir Edward Grey* 146.
15. P.R.O. FO 371. File 1447.
16. Ibid.
17. Spender *Life* II 241 and Williamson *op. cit.* 74.
18. *Brit. Docs.* III 171-2.
19. P.R.O. FO 800/164 f. 78.
20. CB 52518. Ripon's letter is also Jan. 11.
21. CB 41214 f. 212.
22. Repington *op. cit.* I 12.
23. pp. 162-3.
24. Repington *op. cit.* I 13.
25. Ibid.
26. CB 41214 f. 212.
27. Williamson *op. cit.* 76.
28. Monger *op. cit.* 251.
29. P.R.O. FO 371 No. 2207.
30. P.R.O. FO 800/100 f. 15.
31. CB 52514.
32. P.R.O. FO 800/100 f. 17.
33. Esh Clarke letters Jan 27.
34. P.R.O. CAB 41/30/38.
35. P.R.O. FO 371 No. 4059 despatch to Sir F. Bertie.
36. Spender *Life* II 256.
37. Rip 43518 f. 70.

38. CB 41207 f. 44.
39. Ensor *England 1870–1914* 401.
40. D.D.F. 2nd ser. IX No. 106.
41. Monger *op. cit.* 255 quoting Lascelles MSS.
42. Loreburn *How the War Came* 11.
43. Gooch. *Under Six Reigns* 228.
44. CB 41231 f. 109 and ff. 112–13.
45. WEG 44791 f. 43 *Record of Special Errors.*
46. CB 52520.
47. Monger *op. cit.* 256.
48. Quoted in Hirst *In the Golden Days* 264.
49. Loreburn *op. cit.* 105.
50. Morley *Memorandum on Resignation* 7.
51. Trevelyan *Grey of Fallodon* 144.
52. Harold Nicolson *Lord Carnock* 177–8.
53. I 85.
54. Tyler *The British Army and the Continent 1904–14* 97 quoting Callwell *Sir Henry Wilson* I 105.
55. Trevelyan *op. cit.* 83.
56. RA R 27/75 July 13, 1906.
57. July 14 CB 41207 f. 108.
58. CB 41231 f. 134.
59. RA 27/24.
60. P.R.O. FO 800/100 ff. 36–7.
61. *Annual Register* 1906 137.
62. Spender *Life* II 262–3.
63. Pon.
64. CB 41252 f. 146.
65. Pon.
66. July 24.
67. *Daily News. Pictures in Parliament* by H.W.M. July 24, 1906 7.
68. Ibid.
69. RA W 49/80.
70. RA W 49/81.
71. Count Benckendorff to Izvolsky 12–25 July. Izvolsky *Au Service de la Russie* I 336.
72. Izvolsky *Mémoires* 201.
73. *Hansard* 4th ser. CLXII 114–19.
74. RA R 27/130.
75. Esh *J&L* II 180.
76. Marder *Fear God and Dread Nought* II 105 note.
77. *Brit. Docs.* III pages 397–420.
78. Marder *British Naval Policy 1880–1905* 460.
79. Pon.
80. Asq 10 ff. 220–2 (Fisher letter is at CB 41210 f. 281).
81. Hardinge *Old Diplomacy* 140–1.
82. RA R 28/77.
83. Marder *From the Dreadnought to Scapa Flow* I 131.
84. Mil 45 ff. 36–8. R. B. Jones's article 'Anglo-French Negotiations 1907: a memorandum by Sir Alfred Milner'. *Bulletin of the Institute for Historical Research* 31 (1958) asserted that Milner wrote his note in his own handwriting. This seems to be wrong. It is not in Milner's hand but appears to be in that of Violet Cecil. There is a signed pencil note on it that she re-read it in 1931. Milner and the Cecils were holidaying separately in Paris at the time (Milner 270, diary for 1907) but Milner made no comment on this memo.

85. P.R.O. FO 800/50 ff. 62–3.
86. P.R.O. FO 800/100 f. 88.
87. P.R.O. FO 800/164 ff. 138–9 also at FO 800/50 ff. 66–8.
88. *Brit. Docs.* VI 24.
89. P.R.O. FO 800/164 f. 140 April 13.
90. Ibid. 141 April 15.
91. P.R.O. FO 800/50 ff. 72–5.
92. D.D.F. 2nd ser. X No. 472.
93. *Brit. Docs.* VI No. 15.
94. Spender *Life, Journalism and Politics* I 209.
95. Quoted in Trevelyan *op. cit.* 190.
96. Ibid. 189.
97. *Letters of Prince von Bülow* to Count von Pourtales.
98. Marder *Fear God and Dread Nought* II 141.
99. Ibid. II 151.
100. Bry MSS Bryce USA 27 ff. 197–200 Dec. 19, 1907.
101. P.R.O. FO 800/24 f. 31.
102. Hal.
103. Hal.

CHAPTER 35: THE CONFRONTATION
WITH THE LORDS

1. Mackie *The Model Member.*
2. Ibid.
3. CB 41246 f. 48.
4. RA A 70/70 copy. Q. Vict. to Salisbury Oct. 25, 1894.
5. EHP 48665 diary Nov. 8, 1894.
6. All in CB 52520.
7. RA B 47/93 and 93a.
8. CB 41206 f. 216.
9. Ibid. f. 219.
10. RA QVJ Nov. 7, 1894.
11. RA A71/4a.
12. CB 41244 f. 59.
13. *Annual Register* 1899 25.
14. RA W 64/99.
15. Magnus *King Edward VII* 353.
16. Birrell *Things Beyond Redress* 188.
17. July 30. *Hansard* 4th ser. CLXII c. 545.
18. Bell *Randall Davidson* 522.
19. CB 41236 f. 87.
20. RA 27/90 and 91.
21. CB 52513.
22. RA 27/114.
23. CB to Knollys Dec. 4, 1906. RA R R27/116.
24. CB 41252 f. 70.
25. CB. 41226 f. 85.
26. Bell *op. cit.* 523.
27. Pon.
28. Bell *op. cit.* 525.
29. Fitzroy *Memoirs* I 308.
30. CB 41207 f. 164.
31. Bell *op. cit.* 528.
32. Esh *J&L* II 207.
33. Fitzroy *op. cit.* I 310–11.
34. *England 1870–1914* 387–8.
35. *Times* Dec. 21, 1906.
36. In speech to National Liberal Federation at Plymouth June 7, 1907.
37. *Winston S. Churchill* Companion Vol. II pt. 2 873.
38. *Party Politics* II 223.
39. Pon from New Hampshire Sept. 16, 1907.
40. Esh. 10/49 Knollys to Esher March 21, 1907.
41. Ibid.
42. *Times* May 10, 1907.
43. *Times* June 8, 1907.
44. CB 41242 f. 231.
45. *At the Bar of the House* by T.P. in *T.P.O.* III No. 56 July 6, 1907.

46. Pon.
47. *Times* June 25, 1907.
48. Article cited (No. 45).
49. CB 41220 f. 218.
50. *Times* June 26 and 27, 1907.
51. Bry 13 ff. 124–7 July 22, 1907.
52. Ll.G *Scotsman* report of meeting in Edinburgh Nov. 26, 1910.
53. Trevelyan *Grey of Fallodon* 171 to Asquith Feb. 1910.
54. *Winston S. Churchill* Companion Vol. II pt. 2. 1052.

CHAPTER 36: BACK INTO HARNESS
1. CB 41221 f. 292 (copy).
2. Rip 43518 f. 104.
3. *The Personal Papers of Lord Rendel* 169.
4. W. S. Blunt *My Diaries* Nov. 25, 1906.
5. Rip 43518 f. 121.
6. Rip 43518 f. 111 Oct. 1, 1906.
7. Pon.
8. Ll.G Report in *South Wales Daily News* of speech to national convention of Welsh Liberal Council Oct. 11, 1906.
9. That of 1895. CB 41244 f. 59.
10. Pon. Notes by A. Ponsonby.
11. Pon. Arthur Ponsonby to his wife Nov. 15, 1906.
12. Pon. Ibid. Nov. 13.
13. Esh *J&L* III 208.
14. CB 52513.
15. Steiner 'The Last Years of the Old Foreign Office'. *Historical Journal* VI 1 (1963) 59 and 90 quoting Hardinge papers.
16. Hardinge papers Nov. 24, 1906.

17. CB 52513.
18. CB 41207 f. 148.
19. Hardinge *Old Diplomacy* 131–2.
20. RA W 50/86.
21. EHP 48606 f. 149.
22. RA W 65/37. Rosebery to King Edward VII Dec. 6, 1906.
23. RA W 50/105. Hardinge to Knollys Dec. 6, 1906.
24. CB 41223 ff. 202–3.
25. Esh *J&L* II 211–12.
26. Esh 10/49 Dec. 31, 1906.
27. RA R 27/107.
28. Spender *Life* II 280. *Annual Register* 1906.

CHAPTER 37: BISHOPRICS AND PEERAGES
1. CB 41238 f. 163.
2. Bell *Randall Davidson* 502–3.
3. CB 52519 Higgs to C.B. Nov. 29, 1907.
4. CB 41252 f. 146 Memo by Henry Higgs Dec. 1919 (hereafter 'Higgs memo').
5. Ibid.
6. Ibid.
7. Ibid.
8. Bell *op. cit.* 1239.
9. CB 41239 ff. 196–7.
10. Birr (Edin.) Jan. 14, 1907.
11. CB 52519.
12. CB 41229 f. 334 May 11, 1906.
13. HH 1/5. 'Letters from P.M.'s' March 8, 1907.
14. CB 41242 f. 253.
15. Ibid. f. 254.
16. Higgs memo.
17. CB 52519 minute by Higgs Sept. 20, 1907.

18. CB 41230 f. 195.
19. Bell *op. cit.* 1239.
20. CB 52513 Nov. 23, 1907.
21. CB 52519 Higgs to C.B.
    Nov. 26, 1907.
22. Rosebery *Pitt* 275 and 277.
23. CB 52513 Knollys to C.B.
    June 17.
24. Ibid. Oct. 31.
25. CB 52513 Knollys to CB
    Oct. 28, 1907.
26. CB 41239 f. 90.
27. CB 41208 f. 49 June 12, 1907.
28. Ibid. f. 119.
29. CB 52517.
30. Rip 43518.
31. July 2, 1907.
32. *Annual Register* 1907 189.
33. *Times* July 12, 1907.
34. *Daily News* July 15.
35. *Hansard* 4th ser. CLXXVIII
    c. 354.
36. *Saturday Review* July 20.
37. CB 41226 ff. 14–16.
38. II 86–8.
39. HG 46118 f. 69 Draft of
    Autobiography.
40. Ibid.
41. CB 52516.
42. Ibid.
43. *Winston S. Churchill*
    Companion Vol. II Pt. 2 699.
44. June 29. *Times* June 30, 1922.
45. Pon. Notes by Arthur
    Ponsonby.
46. CB 52516 Oct. 15, 1907 from
    H.M.S. *Venus* Gulf of Suez.
47. Rip 43518 f. 102.
48. CB 41225 f. 133 Aug. 9, 1906.
49. CB 41212 f. 333.
50. Rip 43518 f. 42.
51. Young *Arthur James Balfour*
    242–3.

52. Ibid.
53. CB 41207 f. 63.
54. CB 41207 f. 65 (copy).
55. Ibid. f. 67. March 2, 1906.
56. Rose *Superior Person* 367–70.
57. CB 41239 f. 89.
58. CB 41223 f. 257 Aug. 12,
    1907 and ff. 264–5 Sept. 23.
59. Ibid. ff. 278–9.
60. Mosley *Curzon*.

CHAPTER 38: THE FINAL YEAR IN
DOWNING STREET

1. O'Connor *C.B.* 87.
2. Bonar Law Papers
   Beaverbrook Library. Leo
   Maxse to Bonar Law Jan.
   2, 1907 (wrongly dated 1906).
3. *Glasgow Herald* Jan. 26, 1907.
4. Pon.
5. Lord Oxford and Asquith
   Memories and Reflections I 250.
6. Birrell *Things Past Redress* 195.
7. Birr (Liv.).
8. Pon.
9. CB 41223 ff. 207–8.
10. Ibid. ff. 209–12.
11. Curtis *With Milner in South
    Africa* 205.
12. CB 41220 ff. 201–7 Jan. 3.
13. Pon. Note by C.B.
    underneath pencil note by
    Ponsonby.
14. Asq 20 ff. 222–3 C.B. to
    Asquith Jan. 5, 1907.
15. CB 52519.
16. Esh *J&L* II 215–16.
17. *Winston S. Churchill*
    Companion Vol. II Pt. 1 624.
18. Extract recorded in Lord
    Pentland's commonplace
    book. The letter was dated
    Jan. 18, 1907.

19. CB 41223 f. 232 and 41230 ff. 170 and 171.
20. CB 41230 ff. 170–1 Jan. 30.
21. Morley *Recollections* II 252.
22. Goldwin Smith papers. James M. Olin Research Library Cornell University.
23. CB 41208 f. 1 Jan. 15, 1907.
24. RA R 28/3.
25. *Annual Register* 1907.
26. Austen Chamberlain *Politics from the Inside* 57.
27. CB 41220 ff. 216–17 March 23, 1907.
28. *Annual Register* 1907 54–5.
29. Ibid. 75.
30. Lucy *The Diary of a Journalist* 258–9.
31. Marder *From the Dreadnought to Scapa Flow* I 54.
32. Kate Courtney's diary (London School of Economics) March 9, 1907 (Vol. 33).
33. Bry Box 13 Ponsonby to Bryce May 24, 1907.
34. *Times* April 17, 1907. RA AA 25/13 April 21.
35. Pon. Ponsonby to his wife May 28, 1907.
36. Chamberlain *op. cit.* 75.
37. Farquharson *In and Out of Parliament* 285.
38. *Times* April 12, 1907.
39. At Partick. CB 41238 f. 114.
40. John Brown *Scottish and English Land Legislation 1905–11. Scottish Historical Review* XLVII I No. 143 April, 1968.
41. *Times*, April 22, 1907. *Annual Register* 1907 101.
42. Ibid.
43. *Manchester Guardian* May 10, 1907.
44. Ibid.
45. CB 41210 f. 106.
46. Pon (draft).
47. Ibid. June 23, 1907.
48. Pon undated.
49. Collier *A Victorian Diarist: Later Extracts* 185.
50. Pon undated.
51. Snowden *Autobiography* I 176–7.
52. Pon. Ponsonby to his wife April 29, 1907.
53. CB 41223 f. 250.
54. Ibid f. 252.
55. Ll.G B/5/1/19 Report in *South Wales Daily News* of meeting in Pontypridd Town Hall July 20, 1907.
56. *Annual Register* 1907.
57. Fitzroy *Memoirs* I 329.
58. CB 41226 f. 89 Aug. 14, 1907.
59. Fitzroy *op. cit.* I 329.
60. Ibid. 330.
61. Morley *op. cit.* II 226–7.
62. Lucy *The Diary of a Journalist* 279.
63. Ibid.
64. RA X 16/23. See also CB 41208 ff. 76, 78, 79, 83 and 90. Knollys was against acceptance.
65. CB 41208 f. 90 Selborne to the King and CB 52516 Selborne to Elgin Aug. 28.
66. CB 52516 Aug. 22.
67. CB 41249 entry for Aug. 30, 1907.
68. Pon. Notes by Ponsonby.
69. British Museum. Mary Gladstone papers 46241 f. 102.
70. Dev. 340–3294. Oct. 20, 1907.

71. Esh *J&L* II 257.
72. RA R 28/94. Knollys's reply is at CB 41208 f. 105.
73. *The Personal Papers of Lord Rendel* 173.
74. *Times* Nov. 11, 1907.
75. Ibid.
76. Esh *J&L* II 259.
77. *Times* Nov. 14, 1907.

PART 9: THE BREAK-UP

CHAPTER 39: THE LAST ILLNESS
1. Pon.
2. CB 41246 f. 23.
3. Mackie *The Model Member* 130.
4. Pon.
5. Ibid.
6. Ibid.
7. *The Western Mail* April 23, 1908 and *Winston S. Churchill* Companion Vol. II Pt. 2 708.
8. Pon. Ponsonby to his wife.
9. Churchill *op. cit.* 706 Nov. 23, 1907.
10. Lucy *The Diary of a Journalist* 238.
11. CB 52519 Dec. 18.
12. Rendel papers III National Library of Wales, Aberystwyth.
13. CB 52519 Dec. 23.
14. RA R 28/97 draft in Pon.
15. Pon Jan. 1, 1908.
16. Pon.
17. Pon May 29.
18. Pon.
19. Churchill *op. cit.* 734.
20. Belloc *Cautionary Tales for Children* 1907.

CB 5216 Elgin to CB Dec. 28, 1907 and Feb. 21, 1908. In the event Sir Frederick Thesiger, later 1st Viscount Chelmsford, Viceroy of India and Warden of All Souls, was appointed.
21. CB 41230 f. 208.
22. Pon.
23. Pon.
24. CB 41218 f. 126.
25. Pon Jan. 9.
26. CB 41252 f. 146.
27. P.R.O. FO. 800/165 f. 4 Jan. 7.
28. Ibid. f. 7.
29. O'Connor *C.B.* 154.
30. *Sunday Review* Jan. 16, 1908.
31. Hal Feb. 1, 1908.
32. Bry 13 f. 132.
33. Dev 340 3318.
34. Esh *J&L* II 280.
35. *Times* Feb. 5, 1908.
36. To Villiers Feb. 6. P.R.O. FO 800/24 ff. 41–2.
37. Pon.
38. Pon.
39. Pon.
40. Pon.
41. P.R.O. FO 800/24 ff. 54 (v).
42. Pon.
43. See *The Political Diaries of C.P. Scott 1911–1928*, introduction 28–31 and *Manchester Guardian* Feb. 19, 1908.
44. Goldwin Smith papers James M. Olin Research Library, Cornell University.
45. *Review of Reviews* Jan. 1906 *Character Sketch: The New Cabinet.*
46. Petrie *Life and Letters of Austen Chamberlain* I 213.

47. Hirst *In the Golden Days* 262 quoting notes by Arthur Ponsonby.
48. Quoted in Morley *Recollections* II 247.
49. Spender *Life* II 381. *History of the Times* III Chap. XVII.
50. RA W 71/24a.
51. Esh *J&L* II 289–90.
52. CB 41208 f. 142.
53. Pon.
54. Pon.
55. Esh *J&L* II 290.
56. Asq 11 ff. 7–9.
57. CB 41210 f. 314.
58. Spender and Asquith *Life of Lord Oxford and Asquith* I 195 Letter of March 4, 1908.
59. CB 41208 f. 143.
60. Pon.
61. CB 41208 f. 181.
62. Lucy *The Diary of a Journalist* II 192.
63. Pon.
64. *Annual Register* 1908.
65. Morley *op. cit.* II 248.
66. Bry 13 f. 136.
67. Pon.
68. CB 41208 f. 150.
69. RA R28/124.
70. Fitzroy *Memoirs* I 343.
71. CB 41208 f. 157.
72. RA R 28/126.
73. Pon.
74. CB 41208 f. 184.
75. Bry 13. f. 140.
76. Margot Asquith *Autobiography* II 89–90.
77. Bell *Randall Davidson* 579.
78. CB 52520 Notes from Buchanan's diary.
79. Pope-Hennessy *Lord Crewe* 63.
80. RA X 34/382 March 31.
81. CB 41226 f. 99.
82. RA W71/25. Only a copy, in Frederick Ponsonby's hand, appears to survive.
83. RA R 28/130.
84. RA W 71/31.
85. Spender *Life* II 388–9.
86. CB 41208 f. 164.
87. *Times* April 7, 1908.
88. CB 41230 f. 214.
89. Pon.
90. CB 41218 ff. 134–5 April 7.
91. Ibid. ff. 200–1, April 6.
92. CB 41252 f. 146. Memo by Higgs.
93. Pon.
94. Pon. Ponsonby to his wife from Belmont April 29, 1908.
95. RA X 34/392.
96. Esh *J&L* II 303.
97. Margot Asquith *op. cit.* II 98.
98. Fitzroy *op. cit.* I 348 and Hyam *Elgin and Churchill at the Colonial Office* 511.
99. Pon.
100. Pon.
101. Pon.
102. *Glasgow Herald* April 23, 1908.
103. Ibid.
104. *Times* April 28, 1908.
105. Pon. Ponsonby to his wife April 28, 1908.
106. Ibid.
107. Bry 13 ff. 150–5 May 7.
108. April 24. Maxse papers, quoted in Koss *Lord Haldane* 54.
109. *Times* April 28, 1908.
110. CB 41252 f. 159.

CHAPTER 40: THE BALANCE SHEET

1. Gardiner *Pillars of Society* 118.

2. See Randolph Churchill *Winston S. Churchill* Companion Vol. II Pt. 2 1069 – 'On Thursday night the PM was very bad: & I squirmed with embarrassment. He could hardly speak: & many people noticed his condition . . .' This was Asquith.

3. Winterton *Pre-War* 86.

4. *The Reader* March 9, 1907 article *The Prime Minister* by H. W. Massingham.

5. O'Connor *C.B.* 28.

6. Gwynn & Tuckwell *Life of Sir Charles Dilke* II 552.

7. *Times* April 23, 1908.

8. *Daily Telegraph* April 23, 1908.

9. Quoted in Hirst *In the Golden Days* 261.

10. Margot Asquith *Autobiography* II 70.

11. Feb. 1908. Amery *Life of Chamberlain* VI 927.

12. CB 41252 f. 164 letter to Lord Pentland.

13. Lord Riddell *Intimate Diary of the Peace Conference and After* 51.

14. Samuel *Memoirs* 56.

15. *Manchester Guardian* Aug. 29, 1942. *Memories of British Prime Ministers* (1) '*C.B.*' by the Marquess of Crewe.

16. Esh. *J&L* II 346.

17. Ll.G C/33/1/5. *Manchester Guardian* report of speech by Lloyd George at by-election in Manchester April 22, 1908.

18. Fisher *Records* 32.

19. Morley *Recollections* II 140–4.

20. Hirst *op. cit.* 259.

21. *Morning Post* Oct. 23, 1923.

22. Eugene Lautier April 23, 1908.

23. *Saturday Review* April 23, 1908.

24. Esh *J&L* II 301.

25. *The Freeman's Journal*, Dublin. April 23, 1908.

26. *Sunday Times* Nov. 4, 1923 review of Spender *Life*.

27. Spend 46388 f. 161 Margot Asquith to J. A. Spender March 26, 1921.

28. *The Nation and the Athenæum* May 21, 1921 282.

Index

Index

Index